American Literature

D0217959

This comprehensive history of American Literature traces its development from the earliest colonial writings of the late 1500s through to the present day. This lively, engaging and highly accessible guide:

- offers lucid discussions of all major influences and movements such as Puritanism, Transcendentalism, Realism, Naturalism, Modernism and Postmodernism
- draws on the historical, cultural and political contexts of key literary texts and authors
- covers a range of American literature: prose, poetry, theater and experimental literature
- includes substantial sections on native and ethnic American literatures
- explains and contextualizes major events, terms and figures in American history.

This book is essential reading for anyone seeking to situate their reading of American Literature in the appropriate religious, cultural, and political contexts.

Hans Bertens is Distinguished Professor of the Humanities at Utrecht University, the Netherlands.

Theo D'haen is Professor of English and Comparative Literature at the University of Leuven, Belgium.

American Literature

A history

Hans Bertens and Theo D'haen

Routledge
Taylor & Francis Group

LONDON AND NEW YORK

First published 2014
by Routledge
2 Park Square, Milton Park, Abingdon, Oxon OX14 4RN

and by Routledge
711 Third Avenue, New York, NY 10017

Routledge is an imprint of the Taylor & Francis Group, an informa business

© 2014 Hans Bertens and Theo D'haen

British Library Cataloguing in Publication Data
A catalogue record for this book is available from the British Library

Library of Congress Cataloging in Publication Data
Bertens, Johannes Willem.
American literature : a history / Hans Bertens and Theo D'haen.
pages cm
Includes bibliographical references and index.
1. American literature--History and criticism. I. D'haen, Theo. II. Title.
PS121.B517 2014
810.9--dc23
2013018669

ISBN: 978-0-415-56997-2 (hbk)
ISBN: 978-0-415-56998-9 (pbk)
ISBN: 978-0-203-79843-0 (ebk)

Typeset in Garamond
by Taylor and Francis Books

Contents

Foreword

American Literature: A History is a thoroughly revised (and somewhat shortened) version of our Dutch-language *Amerikaanse literatuur: een geschiedenis*, published by ACCO in Leuven, Belgium, in 2008. We are grateful to ACCO for its gracious permission to recycle that book's material for the current volume. As in the ACCO book, Hans Bertens covered the periods 1585–1810 and 1810–61 (Chapters 1 and 2), and 1945–80 (Chapter 5), while Theo D'haen is responsible for the periods 1861–1945 (Chapters 3 and 4) and 1980–2010 (Chapter 6). Spelling and punctuation of the older quotations follow modern American usage, except in a few cases where it seemed more appropriate to remain faithful to the original text.

Part I

A superpower in the making: beginnings to World War I

1   Beginnings to 1810

Introduction

The literature of the United States is more commonly called American literature, a term that seems self-explanatory and simple enough. But in literary histories – in all histories, for that matter – nothing is simple. What, after all, is 'American'? When did the descendants of the mostly English citizens who had survived a dangerous Atlantic crossing become 'Americans'? When did the later immigrants who joined them become Americans? '*He* is an American', the Franco-American essayist St. John de Crèvecoeur claimed in his *Letters from an American Farmer* (1782), 'who, leaving behind him all his ancient prejudices and manners, receives new ones from the new mode of life he has embraced, the new government he obeys, and the new rank he holds'. For Crèvecoeur, still warmed by revolutionary fire, to be an 'American' is a matter of mentality, of a radical personal reorientation made possible by the new Republic's freedom and democracy. But by Crèvecoeur's time the question of who was an 'American' could also, and far more easily, be settled by way of citizenship: all the inhabitants of the thirteen English colonies who had decided to stay during the Revolution were now citizens of the United States of America, no longer subjects of the United Kingdom. But how American were the inhabitants of, say, Boston, around 1700, when the word 'American' makes its first appearances? Their writings tell us that they still see themselves as English subjects – even if they begin to feel increasingly unhappy with what far-off London decides for them – but also show that they were acutely conscious of the fact that they are both English and in a subtle way less English than their grandparents, who almost without exception had been born in England.

And what is 'literature' – another term that seems self-evident? For early historians of American literature like Charles Richardson, who published his *American Literature (1607–1885)* in 1886–88, and Barrett Wendell, whose *Literary History of America* appeared in 1900, the history of American literature did not really begin until the early nineteenth century. Practically nothing published in the first two hundred years after 1607 – the year the first permanent settlement was founded in Jamestown, Virginia – was worth discussion. For Richardson and Wendell the only literature really worth considering was that imaginative literature that met the aesthetic criteria of their own time, the late nineteenth century.

Things would change, but slowly. In 1955, in his *The Cycle of American Literature*, the influential literary historian Robert E. Spiller was still pretty negative about early American writing: 'Except for a few sturdy volumes like William Bradford's *Of Plimoth Plantation* [...] much of the writing left by these early explorers and settlers makes rather dreary reading today [...]. Writers sought mainly to justify their own enterprises, to take possession of the new lands, riches, and peoples for the monarchs who had sponsored their undertakings, and to describe geographic and economic conditions in order to help those who were to follow them. The temptation to belittle the hardships and to overstate the possibilities of the future was great'. However, recognizing that the origins of American culture must be sought in the first two hundred years of settlement, Spiller singles out three eighteenth-century 'architects of culture' for special attention: the theologian and poet Jonathan Edwards (1703–58), the businessman, inventor, politician and all-purpose writer Benjamin Franklin (1706–90), and the plantation owner, politician and essayist Thomas Jefferson (1743–1826), who all three of them still feature prominently in every American literary history.

Published twenty-four years after Spiller's *Cycle of American Literature*, the first edition of the *Norton Anthology of American Literature* (1979), one of the massive anthologies that are produced for the academic undergraduate market, has a completely different view of the early stages of the history of American literature. The section called 'Early American Literature 1620–1820' takes up no less than 572 pages. With as their starting point the radically expanded view of literature that had by then been widely accepted, its editors include personal and collective histories, theological discussions, private journals, essays, autobiography, political writings, and other texts that for Richardson and Wendell would not have qualified as literature. Obviously, the aesthetic criteria applied by Richardson and Wendell, or, for that matter, other aesthetic criteria, no longer are decisive. 'Literature' may not quite equate with 'texts', but clearly all texts that throw a light on the development of what one might call Early American – or Colonial – Culture come in for literary scrutiny.

In the 1979 edition of the *Norton Anthology of American Literature*, American literature begins with the writings of the Puritans, the English Calvinists who in the early seventeenth century left England to seek religious freedom and whose small vanguard in 1620 more or less by accident founded Plymouth, Massachusetts. In fact, for the editors, seventeenth-century American literature is the exclusive domain of Puritan writing. Their first non-Puritan text – Ebenezer Cook(e)'s long satirical poem 'The Sot-Weed Factor' – dates from 1708. But literature, and more particularly any national literature, is a moving target. The seventh edition of the *Norton Anthology* of 2007 no longer features 'Early American Literature 1620–1820'. Instead we have 'Beginnings to 1700' and 'American Literature 1700–1820', together taking up over 900 pages (and with a layout that accommodates considerably more words per page than the 1979 edition). There seems no end to the expansion of early American literature. In some ways, this expansion is not only understandable, but quite welcome. In the past decades, due to the efforts of scholars of early American literature, more and more texts that had completely disappeared have again come to light and have enriched its history. Moreover, the whole idea of 'American literature' has once again become more inclusive. Like its competitors on the anthologies market, the *Norton Anthology* now pays a good deal of attention to Native American literature. We read Native Creation stories, trickster tales, and speeches by great Native leaders like Pontiac, Logan and Red Jacket. In other words, American literature has come to include the oral literature of the original inhabitants of the territory that is now the United States of America. But it has come to include a lot more. In 1979, the Puritan writers included in the *Norton*'s first edition, although mostly born in England, had all lived and died in the New World. But in the last three or four decades American literature has incorporated texts of those English writers who spent some time in the New World, or played a significant role in one of the English settlements, but never made the New World their permanent home. The most famous of these is the adventurer Captain John Smith, who wrote extensively about his exploits in the New World, but there were many others who left a record of their transatlantic experience after their return to Europe.

Potentially more controversial than this redefinition of American literature, which seems reasonable enough, is another expansion in a different direction. The seventh edition of the

Norton Anthology prints sections of letters by the Genoese sailor Christoforo Colombo – Christopher Columbus, in the English-speaking world – and extracts of historical narratives written by the Spanish friar Bartolomé de las Casas and the Spanish explorer Álvar Núñez Cabeza de Vaca. The inclusion of the latter, who in 1542 published an account of his harrowing adventures in what is now Florida, Texas and Northern Mexico – an epic trek that even brought him to the Gulf of California – is, again, not unreasonable. Cabeza de Vaca writes with an anthropologist's interest and with growing sympathy about the various Native peoples he encounters and is an important source of information about their first contact with the European invaders. Although Cabeza writes in Spanish, and firmly belongs to Spanish literature – he died in Seville in 1558 – the inclusion of his personal narrative in an anthology of American literature is understandable if we accept that writings pertaining to what is now U.S. territory have a rightful place in a history of American literature. This does raise the question why the Dutch-language texts that came out of the Dutch colony that centered on New Amsterdam (later New York) – such as Adriaen van der Donck's *Vertoogh van Nieu-Nederland* (1650) – and the writings of, for instance, the great French explorer Samuel de Champlain – *Voyages* (1613), *Les Voyages de la Nouvelle France* (1632) – who had been one of the first to sail down the coast of New England, anticipating even Captain John Smith, should not be considered American literature, but maybe we should not expect rigid consistency in literary histories or anthologies.

But with Columbus and de las Casas the connection with American literature becomes extremely tenuous and strains our credulity. Do the editors seriously believe that Columbus and de las Casas stand at the very beginning of what would eventually become American literature? Not very likely. Still, their decision to go back to Columbus is not at all unique in recent anthologies of American literature. In *The English Literatures of America, 1500–1800*, an anthology that also covers the English presence in the Caribbean and was published in 1997, the editors, Myra Jehlen and Michael Warner, go even farther back. They begin with a brief extract from a book published around 1298 by the Venetian merchant Marco Polo, who had traveled to China and had lived there for a number of years, and then present an excerpt from Sir John Mandeville's rather fantastic *Travels* (1356). The point here is that Columbus (who also is anthologized), Amerigo Vespucci (who follows him), and other early witnesses of the momentous meeting of the Old and New World, were part of a European culture in which descriptions of, and fantasies about, unknown territories and strange peoples who spoke incomprehensible languages already had a long history (Columbus actually took a copy of Marco Polo's *Travels* with him on his first voyage and knew Mandeville's book). We may assume that their expectations of and reactions to the New World were to some extent influenced by such earlier texts and we can sometimes actually point to descriptive elements that seem to have been borrowed directly from them.

The same must have been true for the Englishmen who began to explore and settle North America a hundred years after the Spanish had shown the way. By that time, the European 'discovery' of the Caribbean, Central America and much of South America had already generated an extensive literature that circulated widely in the Old World and no Englishman who was interested in the New World was wholly unaware of it. Those writings, with on the one hand their emphasis on hardship and mysterious dangers, but on the other their suggestion of future riches and easy, if not utopian living, shaped the expectations with which the English approached the New World. Soon after Columbus had returned to Spain in the spring of 1493, one of his letters describing what he had seen already appeared in print. After singing the praise of the natural harbors of that part of the Caribbean that he had explored – an important feature for a sailor, especially in a region often visited by severe storms – he goes on to describe the eternal spring he has found: 'All [mountains] are most beautiful, of a thousand shapes, and all are accessible and filled with trees of a thousand kinds and tall, and they seem to touch the sky. And I am told they never lose their foliage, as I can understand, for I saw them as green and lovely as they are in Spain in May'. De las Casas, who traveled with Columbus on that first voyage, in describing the very first encounter between the Spanish and Native Americans, attributes to the latter an almost Edenic quality. The Indians, he tells us, 'walked among them and drew close, with such nonchalance and ease, with all their shameful parts uncovered, as though the state of innocence was restored or had never been lost'. Later, he and his compatriots are impressed by 'their natural kindness, their innocence, humility, tameness, peacefulness, and virtuous inclinations' – these inclinations even including a willingness to be converted to de las Casas' Catholicism. In spite of imprisonment and even enslavement at the hands of Native Americans, Cabeza de Vaca offers a similar sense of wonderment at their humaneness in his *Relación*. The Malhado, who live on the Gulf Coast, near present-day Galveston, 'love their offspring more than any in the world and treat them very mildly', he tells us, and the Avavares, who live further inland, 'always treated us well'. Such descriptions picture the New World as paradisiacal and the Native American as a noble child of nature. Other descriptions, equally in debt to earlier narratives of encounters with unknown worlds, offer a completely different picture, calling attention to cannibalism, human sacrifice, and violent warfare.

Marco Polo, Sir John Mandeville, Christopher Columbus and Bartolomé de las Casas can of course not be called American writers, and the fact that the word 'America' makes its first appearance in an English text in the 1509 translation of Sebastian Brant's satire *Das Narrenschiff* (*The Ship of Fools*, 1494) likewise has nothing to do with the beginnings of American literature. However, all literatures and all myths and fantasies are indebted to other literatures, myths, and fantasies and the earlier European narratives describing wondrous travels to the Far East made themselves felt in the way the Spanish saw and described the New World, and it is not surprising that the English, in their turn, were tempted to see the New World in terms suggested by the narratives of those Europeans who had preceded them, a world of great danger and enormous promise.

But to return to the question that was posed at the beginning of this introduction: what is 'American' – or 'United States' – literature? For the purposes of this book it is the oral and the written literature created in that part of the North American continent that is now the United States of America, with the proviso that those literatures – like the Dutch-language writings of New Netherland and the French travel literature of Champlain and others – that played no role in the development of American culture and America's self-image will not be considered. For the colonial period and the period right after the American Revolution, literature will be defined very broadly in order to grasp as fully as possible the development of the diverse cultural threads that come together in the making of American culture. From the 1820s onwards literature will be defined more narrowly as imaginative literature – with some major exceptions – so that the focus of this book will gradually shift towards the aesthetically more successful fiction, poetry, and drama that American writers have produced. There are American literary historians who would rather not speak of 'American' literature and are generally reluctant to use the word 'American'. That demonstrates a praiseworthy sensitivity to the fact that, in a sense, all inhabitants of the Americas are Americans and that to call the literature of the United States of America and the earlier colonies 'American literature' may raise eyebrows outside the United States. However, to call the United States 'America' or to refer to its literature as 'American' is not necessarily an act of arrogation. Practically the whole world uses 'America' and 'American' and, more importantly, the citizens of the U.S.A.'s closest neighbors would hotly dispute being 'American'. This book, then, uses 'America' and 'American' for purely practical reasons and without a hidden imperialist agenda.

Beginnings

The enormous excitement generated in Europe by the discovery of the New World, soon led to an English expedition, headed by the Venetian citizen Giovanni Caboto (anglicized as John Cabot), that explored and named Newfoundland in 1497. Although Cabot's voyage was officially backed by the English crown (even if financed by Bristol merchants), it did not lead to serious exploration, let alone colonization, of the North American coast. It took the English almost a hundred years to follow the Spanish and Portuguese example and to establish colonies on the American mainland and then the first two attempts, financed by the dashing courtier Sir Walter Ralegh, ended in failure. Roanoke Colony, in what is now North Carolina, was founded in 1585, but abandoned the next year, when all its inhabitants, threatened by starvation and by a Native population that had been provoked into enmity, returned to England, and a second attempt, in 1587, to establish a settlement at the same place, ended mysteriously. When after three years the colony's leader, who had sailed back to England for supplies, finally returned, he found that all 120 colonists, including his young granddaughter, the first English child to have been born in America, had vanished without a trace.

We have a fascinating account of the first Roanoke settlement by Thomas Hariot (1560–1621), who was in Ralegh's employment and accompanied Ralegh's colonists to the New World in 1585. Two years after his return, in 1588, he published his *A briefe and true report of the new found land of Virginia* – a bit of an exaggeration, even though he had traveled as far as the Chesapeake Bay, given the fact that at the time 'Virginia' covered everything from the mouth of the Hudson to Spanish Florida. Hariot's *Report* gives us detailed descriptions of the local flora and fauna and is quite informative about the Native Americans in this particular area since he had managed to learn their language – a circumstance that also substantially contributed to his knowledge of the region. Much of the *Report* clearly aims at prospective settlers. Hariot pays a good deal of attention to what he calls 'merchantable commodities' – in sections entitled 'Of Roots', 'Of Fruits', 'Of Fowle', 'Of Fish', and so on – and emphasizes Virginia's natural advantages: 'For English corne nevertheless, whether to use or not to use it […]. Of the growth you need not doubt: for Barley, Oats, and Peaze, we have seene proofe of, not being purposely sowen, but fallen casually in the worst sort of ground, and yet to be as faire as any we have ever seen here in England'. More generally, 'the aire here is so temperate and holsome, the soyle so fertile, and yielding such commodities', that settling such a wonderful world becomes the natural thing to do. In a section devoted to the Native population Hariot's Indians, as far as their religious beliefs are concerned, turn out to be remarkably like the English: 'They believe also the immortalitie of the soule, that after this life as soone as the soule is departed from the body, according to the workes that it hath done, it is either carried to heaven the habitacle of gods, there to enjoy perpetuall blisse and happinesse, or else to a great pitte or hole, which they thinke to be in the furthest part of the world toward the Sunne set, there to burne continually'. Perhaps this is a faithful account of what Roanoke's Indians believed, perhaps Hariot shaped what he heard to fit his Christian framework. We have no way of knowing. What we certainly do know is that his account of the terrible toll the English presence takes on the Indians must be true. In every Native village the English visit, they bring diseases against which the Indians have no immunity and which everywhere begin to carry off large numbers. This terrible mortality rate among Native Americans as a result of contact with the European invaders is a recurrent element in all early accounts. Bernal Diaz del Castillo, a Spanish soldier who took part in the conquest of the Aztec capital Tenochtitlán in 1519, and who recounted his experiences (and those of others) in his *Historia verdadera de la conquista de la Nueva España* (*The True History of the Conquest of New Spain*), first published in 1632, tells us about Tenochtitlán: 'We could not walk without treading on the bodies and heads of dead Indians [...] the dry land the lagoon and the stockades were piled high with the bodies of the dead'. Many of these dead had become the victim of the incredible ferocity of the superiorly armed Spanish, but many more had died from the smallpox that the Spanish soldiers had brought with them. In the decades following first contact perhaps up to ninety percent of the Native population succumbed to smallpox, measles, and other diseases that in Europe were rarely fatal, but that in the Americas were absolutely disastrous. Neither party knew what caused these epidemics, but for Hariot's Indians the fact that the English were hardly affected by whatever killed the Indians themselves in such terrible numbers made them even more awe-inspiring.

Although Roanoke was a failure, its model proved very influential. Obviously the sparsely populated coast of North America, with a Native population that in comparison with the Aztecs and other Central American peoples lived in very primitive circumstances, could not yield the sort of riches in silver and gold that the conquest of New Spain had brought to the Spanish. If there were profits to be made, they would not be made by robbing a Native population of their natural resources or by plundering the treasure-chests of their rulers. Profit would require long-term investment by financial backers and a population equally willing to invest in its own future. But first of all that population had to be convinced to try its luck in the New World. Prospective colonists had to be offered a good and substantial reason for undertaking a risky and arduous voyage to a wholly unknown place at the absolute edge of the world. And so, in order to recruit interested parties, each Roanoke settler was promised a substantial tract of land, larger by far than anything they might ever hope to acquire in England. This settlement model, called 'planting', would in the course of the seventeenth century lead to a large English presence along the coast of North America and in the Caribbean.

On the North American mainland that presence becomes permanent with the founding of Jamestown, near what is now Williamsburg, Virginia, in 1607. Jamestown, too, staggered on the verge of failure, but was saved by renewed support from its backers, the Virginia Company, and the efforts of Captain John Smith, who provided the necessary effective leadership. Whereas Roanoke had in fact been the initiative of one single investor, the Jamestown enterprise had a more promising corporate base, a joint stock company, but even so the colony's future would in the decades of its existence regularly hang in the balance. In any case, five years after its founding, the newly arrived John Rolfe cultivated Jamestown's first tobacco crop and shipped it to England, the beginning of a trade that in the long run would prove to be enormously profitable. Thanks to Hariot and others, tobacco had already acquired a reputation as a medicinal miracle – a cure for various diseases and an aphrodisiac to boot – so that demand had soared in spite of such prominent early tobacco-haters as the English king James I, who in his 'Counter-Blaste to Tobacco' of 1604 presciently calls smoking 'A custome lothsome to the eye, hatefull to the Nose, harmefull to the braine, dangerous to the Lungs', and compares 'the blacke stinking fume thereof' to the smoke that presumably is produced in hell. The European demand for tobacco and other agricultural products suggested that 'planting' was a viable and even quite profitable form of colonialization and drew new 'planters' to Virginia, so that before long the colony was faced with a shortage of labor, leading to the importation of indentured servants from England and, in 1619, the arrival of a first shipload of some twenty African slaves, who were set to work on the Jamestown plantations. Eventually, with the growth and spread of settlements, slavery would largely replace the indenture system, because many indentured servants disappeared before they had fulfilled their contract to seek a better and free life elsewhere in the colonies. Since tobacco is a crop that after seven years has exhausted the soil, its cultivation also led to a permanent shortage of land and necessitated continuous expansion, a process that was bound to lead to ever new and serious conflicts with the Native population.

What Thomas Hariot did for Roanoke, Captain John Smith (1580–1631) did for Jamestown, with a report called *A True Relation of Such Occurrences and Accidents of Note, as Hath Hapned in Virginia*, that was published without his knowledge in London in 1608, and in the much more detailed, and co-authored – because Smith never visited Virginia after 1609 – *The Generall Historie of Virginia, New England, and the Summer Isles* of 1624. Smith is one of the most colorful characters of the period of first exploration and settlement. A farmer's son both gifted with and hampered by a fiery temper, a hankering for adventure, a propensity for violence, and a well-developed self-confidence, he left England at age sixteen to fight with the Dutch in their war with Spain, was involved in privateering in the Mediterranean, served in the Austrian army – hence his captaincy – and was taken prisoner in one of their battles with the Turks and sold into slavery. Murdering his master, Smith managed to escape and made his way back to England via Russia and Poland. At twenty-four Smith had seen much of Europe, had proved his mettle in the most desperate circumstances and shown a very useful instinct for survival. Even if we take his exploits with a grain of salt – Smith himself is after all our only source for most of them – he must have had an impressive record when he sailed with the first contingent of settlers to Jamestown. Not surprisingly, given his temperament, he found himself in serious trouble with the expedition's leadership – and under arrest – before they were halfway, but when after their arrival in Virginia the Company's sealed directions were opened, Smith turned out to have a seat on the settlement's ruling council and was later that year elected as president of the council, Jamestown's highest position of authority.

Smith's writings must be approached with caution. His 'I thank God I never undertook anything yet [for which] any could tax me of carelessness or dishonesty' (*The Generall Historie*) does not really inspire the confidence that he may have had in mind. He also tends to give different versions of one and the same event in different publications. But he is a lively and observant writer with a strong interest in the more adventurous side of things. His most famous adventure, his 'rescue' by the Native girl Pocahontas, has even become an American myth, retold again and again, fairly recently in the 1995 Disney movie *Pocahontas*.

In the *Generall Historie*, fifteen years after the event – which he strangely enough does not mention in his report of 1608 – Smith tells us how he and two other Englishmen are ambushed by a party of Indians while exploring Jamestown's environment. His two companions are killed and Smith – he very effectively writes about himself in the third person – is made a prisoner and taken to a local Chief, Powhatan. Although Smith, whose knowledge of Algonquin, his captors' language, is absolutely elementary, has no clear idea what is going on, he does at a certain point realize that things must be taking a turn for the worse. But then Pocahontas intervenes: 'two great stones were brought before *Powhatan*: then as many as could layd hands on him, dragged him to them, and thereon laid his head, and being ready with their clubs, to beate out his braines. *Pocahontas* the Kings dearest daughter, when no intreaty could prevaile, got his head in her armes, and laid her owne upon him to save him from death'. Was Smith really in deadly danger? Did he misinterpret what in reality was some sort of Native initiation ceremony? We have no way of knowing. What we do know is that Pocahontas, who in her turn was captured by the English in 1613, converted to Christianity and stayed with them, marrying the already mentioned John Rolfe. Accompanying him to London where he sought new investors in the Virginia enterprise, she tragically died far from her native shore in 1617.

Smith, who as leader of his small group was held responsible for the death of his two companions, left Jamestown under a cloud in 1609. In 1614 he returned to North America, again in the service of the Virginia Company, to explore the coast of Maine and Massachusetts. Naming the area New England, and giving English names to salient geographical features, he published an influential account of his journey in his *A Description of New England* (1616). Smith informs us about New England's coasts, its forests, climate, vegetation, crops, and does not hesitate to display its abundance of natural resources. 'He is a very bad fisher', he tells us, 'who cannot kill in one day with his hook and line, one, two, or three hundred Cods: which dressed and dryed, if they be sold there for ten shillings the hundred, though in England they will give more than twenty'. In short, 'Here nature and liberty afford us that freely, which in England we want, or it costs us dearly'. And there is a simple way to relieve English parishes of burdensome duties towards the poor and to simultaneously settle this wonderful land: 'But that each parish, or village, in Citie, or Countrey, that will apparel their fatherless children, of thirteen or fourteen years of age, or young married people, that have small wealth to live on; here by their labour may live exceeding well'. But we should not put too cynical an interpretation on this last suggestion, even if the promotion of settlement is never far from Smith's mind. For Smith the exploration and settling of North America has a genuinely heroical dimension. New England – and, by implication, Virginia – presents a unique occasion for great deeds, for acquiring new knowledge, for spreading Christianity and civilization, and, not least, for contributing to the glory of England: 'What so truly suits with honour and honesty as the discovering things unknown: erecting towns, peopling countries, informing the ignorant, reforming things unjust, teaching virtue; and gain to our mother country a kingdom to attend her'. For Smith and for many of his compatriots who would follow him to North America settling the New World was much more than a way to escape the limitations, financial and otherwise, of life in England. It was a great and unprecedented challenge, an opportunity to show character and courage, to create one's own destiny in the face of adversity and danger. For even if Hariot, Smith, and others like Richard Hakluyt (*c.* 1552–1616) who had never even set foot in America and had drawn on others in his *Voyages and Discoveries* (1589–1600), had highlighted the New World's paradisiacal aspects and played down its darker side, their accounts do not altogether hide that colonization was a highly uncertain and very risky enterprise that did not come with any guarantees.

Native Americans

With Hariot and Smith, Native Americans enter English colonial literature. We do not know how many Native Americans lived in what is now the U.S. when the first English colonists arrived in Roanoke. Estimates range from not more than a couple of million to eighteen million and more and are invariably contested. What we do know is that North America was home to an extraordinary diversity of languages, cultures, and religious beliefs. Compared with North America, Europe, overwhelmingly Christian and with languages that with only a few exceptions belonged to the Western branches of the Indo-European language family, was a miracle of homogeneity. All these Native American peoples had their own creation stories – narratives that explained the origins of the Earth, the Sun and other celestial bodies, and of mankind itself (as often as not equating mankind with the people in question, putting them and their culture at the center of creation). These stories explicitly or implicitly provide a moral framework, condemning certain acts and praising others, and so offer guidelines for acceptable and responsible living. All these peoples entertained religious beliefs – we get a glimpse of one culture's beliefs in Hariot's *Briefe and true report* – and all of them knew tales that were handed down from generation to generation.

Since the Native peoples of North America did not use writing, we do not know these stories, beliefs, and tales in their authentic form – or, rather, authentic forms, since these forms were not generically fixed in genres or subgenres, as in European literature of the time, but endlessly flexible. When in the second half of the nineteenth century anthropologists started recording them, often in very literal translations which could not possibly do justice to the oral, interactive, and dynamic nature of especially the tales and ceremonial chants, all Native peoples had been exposed to Western culture. We cannot know to what extent these nineteenth-century tales and stories were influenced by the European presence. Still, when in so-called trickster tales greedy and treacherous whites get their just deserts through a smart trick that Coyote or another trickster hero plays on them, we may well be dealing with an authentic, pre-conquest tale in which only the original victim of the trickster's manipulations has made place for a new enemy. But perhaps we should simply shelve the question of authenticity. The world that we encounter in Native American stories and tales is so radically different from the Judeo-Christian world of western culture that it is not very relevant that it may have differed even more.

Creation stories are of all times and all places, and have since time immemorial served to explain the world and our existence, if not the special status that the Creator has accorded us (and not our enemies across the mountains). And so in the Navajo story the Navajo are guided to their promised land by 'Changing Woman', with the help of 'Spider Woman' and a heroic pair of twins. But there is an endless variety in the way the Creators of these stories actually go about creating us. In the highly elaborate story of the Pima people – also from the Southwest – creation goes through a number of false starts, with a dissatisfied creator destroying his first efforts by allowing the sky to fall on his handiworks. The often entertaining inventiveness of many of these stories and the more than occasional presence among their cast of characters of the trickster discussed below suggest that their audience is not quite expected to view them as Christian fundamentalists see the Biblical creation story. Some stories show signs of having been adapted or even created in response to historical events. In an Iroquois story that is admittedly more about foundation than about creation – and that is mentioned here because the nineteenth-century poet Longfellow used it for a famous narrative poem and because Walt Disney borrowed its hero's name – the godlike Hiawatha, a historical Iroquois chief, returns to Earth to unite the various Iroquois nations before returning to the sky in a white canoe.

Trickster tales, too, are an important element in many cultures. Their heroes revel in insubordination and in defying and undermining authority. Self-important and pompous authority is the preferred target, but any authority will do. In medieval Europe the fox Reynard and Til Eulenspiegel delighted audiences with the impudent tricks they played on their so-called superiors (and on unsuspecting rivals), and in Afro-American culture Brer Rabbit did the same. But Native American trickster tales tend to be both more ferocious and, paradoxically, to be more in tune with natural forces. The Native American trickster, quite often Coyote, but also appearing as Rabbit, Spider or in other guises, is a creature of amazing contradictions. He is courageous but not above fleeing like a coward, is smart but may act foolishly, is ruthless and selfish but on occasion noble and humane. Gifted with magical powers, the trickster can disguise himself, assume practically any form, at times even change sex at will – whatever serves his devious purposes. The trickster is invariably ready for not always innocent mischief or to gratify his not particularly modest sexual appetite. But he may also feature in tales that are less earthy and that are most of all brilliantly inventive and entertaining. Whatever he is, he is a masterful survivor, able to keep one step ahead of chaos with a resourcefulness that delights the audience, even if that chaos has been unleashed by his own less prudent actions.

Trickster tales obviously entertain an audience, but they also have a social function. They may explain taboos – or, since taboos are not always explicable, at least clarify them – and they serve to illustrate desirable or undesirable behavior. Certain actions will be punished and others will be rewarded so that the audience is left in no doubt as to its culture's norms and values. And if the trickster gets away with actions that are morally dubious, it is only because these actions have exposed a larger wrong that otherwise would have gone unpunished, perhaps even unnoticed.

What distinguishes Native trickster tales from European equivalents is the trickster's radical shape-shifting, which makes virtually anything possible and gives great scope to a narrator's powers of invention, and the way they are interwoven with Native religion. The world of the trickster tales is a world in which everything, animate and inanimate, is gifted with a spiritual nature and in which everything is interrelated and exists on more or less the same plane. There is no obvious hierarchy that places us above the animals. Humans may change into animals and animals may turn human, and sexual relations and even intermarriage belong to the natural order. Likewise, the sacred and the profane, the bawdy and the spiritual coexist in what is perceived as a natural balance. Universal coexistence is central to these tales, even if they do not shy away from violence and death. The trickster's individual and selfish actions may seem to contradict their message, but trickster tales teach their audience that such individualism and selfishness, even if they may serve to expose greed or other vices, lead to chaos and are ultimately destructive. Each and every one of us has a role to play in a community and that community is part of a larger world to which we owe respect.

The first Puritans

Whatever the attitude of Native American peoples towards their Creation stories, the English Calvinists who landed in New England in 1620 as the vanguard of a mass migration of Calvinists to North America took their story very seriously indeed. For these fundamentalist Christians, followers of the French Reformer Jehan Cauvin (1509–64; anglicized as John Calvin), every word of their Protestant Bible – which does not include the so-called deuterocanonical books of the Catholic Bible – was literally true. The Bible, the Word of God, had absolute authority. These Puritans, as they were derogatorily called in England, were deeply unhappy with the Anglican Church, which admittedly had broken with Rome, but had retained the Catholic Church's hierarchical structure and much of its ceremonial trappings. It was, moreover, corrupt and theologically unsound. However, the Anglican Church was the national state church and the lives of so-called Dissenters were at the very least made uncomfortable. When in 1603 Queen Elisabeth I died and was succeeded by James I who started out by taking repressive measures against Dissenters, both Catholic and Protestant, many Puritans began to feel actively persecuted and those who had set up their own secret congregations outside the Anglican Church, which was of course against the law, had good reason to fear the authorities. And so, in 1608, a small group of these so-called Separatists from Scrooby, a village in Northern England, decided to leave the Anglican Church and England altogether and to settle in the Dutch Republic, where they hoped to find religious freedom. They did, but found that the Republic's tolerance not only extended to other religions than Calvinism, but also to ways of life that they considered sinful and a serious threat to their children's salvation. This, coupled with difficult economic circumstances and a sense that they would never really feel at home in the Netherlands, persuaded them to take the very drastic step of moving to North America. In 1620, having obtained a charter under the title of the Plymouth Company and after various setbacks they set sail for Virginia in the *Mayflower*. Although the Separatists constituted a minority on board – this was, after all, a commercial venture backed by investors who weren't much interested in the motives of the emigrants whose enterprise they were funding – the *Mayflower* and the so-called Pilgrim Fathers, a term used to describe the (male) Calvinists that it carried to America, would much later acquire legendary status. This piece of myth-making was helped by the fact that the *Mayflower* was blown off course and was by adverse circumstances more or less forced to land in what is now Massachusetts, west of Cape Cod. Naming the place where they had landed Plymouth, they decided to stay even though their charter was for Virginia, much to the south. Realizing that they had settled without a proper legal basis, they drew up their own charter, the famous Mayflower Compact, which on the one hand took care to recognize the English king as their sovereign, but on the other hand established a Calvinist community that, exceptionally in those times, was governed by (male) majority rule and because of that came later to be seen as exhibiting a proto-democratic American spirit.

Plymouth Plantation, with its not exactly affluent settlers, never became a booming colony. But its existence on the Massachusetts coast became important when other, middle class and even upper middle class English Calvinists began to think about emigration. The large majority of those Calvinists had no desire to leave the Anglican Church, even if they rejected both the Anglican hierarchy and its teachings. But when after the death of James I in 1625 his son Charles I began to seek what seemed a rapprochement between the Anglican and Roman Catholic Churches, they, too, felt that Anglicanism and Calvinism were irreconcilable. Settling in North America offered a solution to their dilemma, since it allowed them to stay nominally with the Anglican Church, and thus within the law – important for people with property and other monetary interests – while de facto they were free to organize their own Calvinist congregations, a loose network of religious communities (local churches) that guarantees each congregation its independence since there is no overarching and hierarchical organization. Whereas the Roman Catholic Church is centrally organized and its dignitaries are appointed by a hierarchical organization, with the Pope at its very summit, Calvinist congregations elect and appoint their own ministers and church functionaries (and occasionally send them packing, in cases of serious misconduct or fundamental theological differences). And so non-Separatist Calvinists began to think of leaving England for the New World. The arrival in 1630 of a fleet of eleven ships, with over 700 emigrants, under the leadership of John Winthrop, established a bridgehead at Boston and in the next ten years more than 20,000 English Calvinists crossed the Atlantic to find religious freedom in the properly chartered Massachusetts Bay Colony. And so, with immigration continuing at a steady pace, in the late seventeenth century New England had a fairly homogeneous population, united by a vision of individual, congregational, responsibility and religious freedom – freedom for themselves, that is. As we will see, the Massachusetts Bay colonists had little patience with what from their point of view were dissenting views.

They did of course have virtually everything in common with their Separatist co-religionists at not too far-off Plymouth Plantation, with whom they almost immediately established friendly relations. The Puritan minister and historian Cotton Mather gives us in his *Magnalia Christi Americana* of 1702 a fascinating glimpse of that earliest period:

> In the year 1632, the governor [Winthrop], with his pastor, Mr. Wilson, and some other gentlemen, to settle a good understanding between the two colonies, traveled as far as Plymouth, more than forty miles, through an howling wilderness […]. The difficulty of the walk was abundantly compensated by the honorable, first reception, and then dismission, which they found from the rulers of Plymouth, and by the good correspondence thus established between the colonies.

Eventually, in 1691, Plymouth Plantation and the Massachusetts Bay Colony would merge.

By then, coastal New England south of Maine was densely populated compared to the rest of North America, was relatively well-educated because of the Protestant insistence on literacy, and was home to a distinctive culture of lively, often intense religious and political debate, dominated by its ministers. Although historians disagree about how influential New England culture has been in shaping the future United States, there is no doubt that its sense of itself as representing a holy vanguard – 'a Colony of Chosen People', as Cotton Mather put it – as giving shape to God's will in founding a Calvinist theocracy in the New World, and as making a new beginning for mankind after the obfuscations and corruption of the Roman Catholic Church and its Anglican successor, has contributed significantly to the widely accepted idea that the United States of America has an exceptional status among nations and still has a historical mission. That idea is, in any case, part of the standard rhetoric of recent American presidents. In his autobiography Ronald Reagan tells us that 'America is a country whose people have always believed we had a special responsibility to try to bring peace and democracy to others in the world'. His successor George Bush spoke of 'the strength that has made America the beacon of freedom in a searching world' and George W. Bush, echoing his father, in his first speech after the attacks of 11 September 2001 called the United States the 'brightest beacon of freedom [...] in this world'.

Early Puritan history

We know a good deal about the early histories of both colonies because their long-time leaders, William Bradford in the case of Plymouth Plantation and John Winthrop in the case of Massachusetts Bay, left detailed accounts of those early years. Bradford (1590–1657) was elected governor of Plymouth in 1621 upon the death of the colony's first governor and served in that function for over thirty years. In 1630 he began writing *Of Plimoth Plantation*, which he completed in 1650, but which would not be published until 1856 as *History of Plymouth Plantation*. Bradford's history is an extraordinarily vivid account in what in his manuscript he calls 'the plain style'. This plainness is not so much the result of Bradford's lack of formal education, but a deliberate choice. The Puritans strongly believed in directness and simplicity and distrusted ornamental flourishes and non-functional decoration, not only in the churches they built and in the way they dressed, but also in the language they used. They avoided ornate, figurative language except when it was used for religious purposes and absolutely opposed the theater with its deliberate role-playing and other ambiguities.

Bradford's story is essentially that of a chosen people led out of bondage – 'that grosse darkness of popery which had covered and overspred the Christian world' – to the promised land. He is fully aware of the dangers and hardships that will await them in the New World, of 'the continual danger of the savage people, who are cruel, barbarous, and most treacherous, being furious in their rage', but convinced that they must obey their destiny. Ironically, it is one of these 'savages', the Native American Squanto, who practically saves them the first winter that they spend in Plymouth – even if in spite of his help half the company dies – and characteristically Bradford does not hesitate to see the hand of God in Squanto's generosity: 'Squanto [...] was a special instrument sent of God for their good beyond their expectation'. This is a recurring feature of Puritan writing which attributes every single event, no matter how trivial, to the workings of either God or His great antagonist, the Devil. One of the sailors on board the *Mayflower* takes great pleasure in ridiculing and insulting the Puritan passengers, expressing the hope that he will have the additional pleasure of throwing their dead bodies overboard. But God comes to their rescue: 'But it pleased God before they came half seas over, to smite this young man with a grievous disease, of which he died in a desperate manner, and so he was himself the first that was thrown overboard. Thus his curses lighted on his own head; and it was an astonishment to all his fellows, for they noted it to be the just hand of God upon him'.

From the Puritan perspective, there is no such thing as chance. God is omnipotent and that omnipotence, even if contested by the Devil, leaves no room for chance. As a consequence of this conviction, Puritans are forever busy attributing supernatural significance to whatever befalls them or their communities. The desire to 'read' God's will through His actions is in fact an important driving force behind the amazing number of histories, memoirs, and diaries that they have left us. Bradford's *Of Plimoth Plantation* is not only a detailed record of his company's history but also, and especially in its first part, an attempt to understand God's plans with regard to this vanguard of His troops. As *Of Plimoth Plantation* illustrates, God's will is not easily readable – Bradford's history ends on a somber note. The Devil's activities, however, are an open book to the faithful. When in 1627 a certain Thomas Morton (*c.* 1579–1647), who had established a settlement near Plymouth, had the temerity of erecting a Maypole and then proceeded, with his company, and joined by Native American men and maidens, to indulge in dance, drink, and no doubt other sorts of licentiousness, Bradford had him arrested and deported to England, only to repeat the whole procedure after Morton had returned to Massachusetts. For the Puritans, Morton, whose *The New English Canaan* (1637) offers his own view of the events, was an evil force. His Anglicanism and pride in his classical education – a bit too obvious from the poor poetry he rather boastfully prints in *Canaan* – were in itself enough to disqualify him, but he also sold guns to the Native Americans and taught them how to use them. Morton is not only informative about those Native Americans, whom he vastly prefers to the Puritans, whose notion that they are modern-day Israelites is ridiculed in his title, but is on occasion also rather funny at the expense of the 'precise separatists', as he calls them. Having escaped from the Puritans' prison he tells us, with a reference to their refusal to wear their hair long – which they considered worldly vanity – that they were so disappointed by his disappearance that they 'were eager to have torn their hair from their heads, but it was so short that it would give them no hold'.

As the Separatists' unease with Morton's no doubt very modest arms deal shows, relations with the Native Americans living near their settlement had deteriorated since Squanto had so generously come their rescue. With the explosive growth of nearby Massachusetts Bay beginning in 1630 and a new colony in Connecticut tension increased and in 1637 culminated in open warfare between the allied Puritans – who would in 1643 formalize their military cooperation in the New England Federation – and the Pequot nation. After the Pequot had attacked a settlement and killed a number of colonists, the Puritan revenge was terrible. We have an eyewitness report in the Massachusetts commander John Underhill's *Newes from America* (1638) in which even the Puritans' Native American allies are deeply upset by their violence: 'The manner of *English* men's fight is too furious, and slays too many men'. And we also have William Bradford, who does not whitewash the violence, but situates it within the familiar framework of the chosen people's struggle, with God's help, against the devil's forces:

> Those that escaped were slain with the sword; some hewed to pieces, others run throw with their rapiers, so as they were quickly dispatcht, and very few escaped.
>
> It was conceived they thus destroyed about 400 at this time. It was a fearfull sight to see them thus frying in the fire, and the streams of blood quenching the same [...] but the victory seemed a sweet sacrifice, and they gave the praise thereof to God, who had wrought so wonderfully for them, thus to inclose their enemies in their hands.

This massacre of some seven hundred men, women, and children brought, at least temporarily, the desired peace. But it soon appeared that there were greater evils than even the Native Americans. Writing in 1650, at the end of his history Bradford must sadly conclude that the Separatists' dream of founding a new Jerusalem, a community that will find nothing but favor in the eyes of the Lord, has failed. With ever greater prosperity, corruption and sin have come to Plymouth Plantation, 'especially drunkenness and uncleanness; not only incontinencie between persons unmarried, for which many both men and women have been punished sharply enough, but some married persons also. But that which is worse, even sodomie and bugerie [...]'. Bradford's history then turns into an early jeremiad, a typically Puritan genre in which in the manner of the Old Testament prophet Jeremiah a spiritual leader laments current backsliding and calls on his followers to return to the old days and old ways when the Lord still had reason to be pleased with his chosen people. Although mostly used in sermons the jeremiad format became widely popular in the second half of the seventeenth century and led to a variety of impassioned writings, always meant to reinvigorate the Puritan enterprise of founding a perfect theocracy in the New World.

The power of that ideal is wonderfully expressed by John Winthrop, governor of the Massachusetts Bay Colony from their arrival in 1630 until his death in 1649, in a famous lay sermon called 'A Modell of Christian Charity', addressed to his company either just prior to their setting sail for North America, or on board of the *Arbella*, the ship that would take him there. Majestically disregarding the fact that the world was completely unaware of their enterprise and could not have cared less if it had known, he tells his audience: 'wee must Consider that wee shall be as a City upon a Hill, the eies of all people are upon us; soe that if wee shall deal falsely with our god in this worke wee have undertaken and soe cause him to withdraw his present help from us, wee shall be made a story and by-word through the world'. Nothing could better illustrate the megalomaniacal dimension of the Puritan enterprise, but there's also nothing that could better illustrate the extraordinary drive at the heart of it. These Calvinists were, for better or worse, deeply convinced that they were involved in an epoch-making undertaking that like nothing else before would contribute to God's reign on earth. They had, as Winthrop told them, 'entered into a covenant with Him for this work'.

On board of the *Arbella*, Winthrop began a journal that he would keep until his death and that would not be fully published, as *The History of New England from 1630 to 1649*, until 1825–26. Winthrop's journal is more personal and less of a consciously conceived history than Bradford's account of Plymouth Plantation. Gradually, however, Winthrop's observations and reflections – involving some self-justification concerning his decisions as governor of the colony – grow longer and more penetrating, so that the journal begins to double as an informal chronicle of the colony's history. Like Bradford, Winthrop sees the hand of either God or Satan in everything that happens: 'The Indians near Aquiday being pawwawing in this tempest, the devil came and fetched away five of them'. And like Bradford, he records the vicissitudes of the early years in the firm belief that the colony is acting out the will of God and will therefore succeed in its 'errand into the wilderness', as the Puritan minister Samuel Danforth would put it in 1670 in his sermon – and prototypical jeremiad – *A Brief Recognition of New England's Errand into the Wilderness*. As in Plymouth, the greatest danger would come from within. With its relatively affluent colonists, Massachusetts Bay prospered almost right from the start and prosperity began to threaten the Puritan ideal. 'The end is to improve our lives to do more service to the Lord', Winthrop had said in his 'Modell of Christian Charity', but inevitably improving their lives led to improved economic circumstances and led away from the more or less equitable distribution of income that had been part of the ideal. Winthrop relates in 1639 how, responding to a court case in which a merchant was charged with overpricing, the famous minister John Cotton (1585–1652) preaches a sermon warning against such practices: 'These things gave occasion to Mr. Cotton, in his public exercise the next lecture day, to lay open the error of such false principles, and to give some rules of direction in the case. Some false principles were these – 1. That a man might sell as dear as he can, and buy as cheap as he can. […]. 4. That, as a man may take advantage of his own skill or ability, so he may of another's ignorance or necessity'. With prohibitions like these our capitalist economy would go into a nosedive, but they perfectly illustrate the Puritans' idea of what sort of society would find favor in God's eyes. Like Plymouth, Massachusetts Bay appeared not to have conquered all sinful instincts, in spite of such drastic measures as hanging for adultery (1644) and for witchcraft (1648).

And soon other problems begun to manifest itself. Seventeenth-century Calvinism was nothing if not rigid – Calvin's *Institutes of the Christian Religion* (1536) had laid down the law and dissent was not appreciated. When the prominent citizen Richard Saltonstall in a letter to the Boston church cautiously sought to plead for freedom of conscience, his plea was immediately rejected. 'Truely, friends', he wrote in 1652, 'this your practice of compelling any in matters of worship to doe that whereof they are not fully persuaded, is to make them sin, for soe the apostle (Rom. 14 and 23) tells us, and they are made hypocrites thereby, conforming in their outward man for feare of punishment'. His minister, John Cotton, wrote back, likewise, and in typical Puritan fashion, with reference to a Bible text, pointing out his error: 'Josiah compelled all Israel, or (which is all one) made to serve the Lord their God, 2 Chron. 34.33. yet his act herein was not blamed but recorded amongst his virtuous actions'.

Calvinism

Calvinism's starting point is our utter depravity. Because of Adam and Eve's fall in the Garden of Eden we are conceived and born in sin and destined for eternal damnation. But not all of us will end up in that place where there is everlasting 'weeping and gnashing of teeth', to quote Matthew's gospel. Because Jesus Christ has sacrificed himself for us on the cross some of us will be saved. We are powerless, however, to influence our destiny. Calvinism rejected Arminianism, named after the Dutch theologian Jacob Arminius who taught that through Christ's sacrifice salvation is offered to all of us and that we are free to accept it through repentance and faith or to refuse the offer and choose damnation – a position eventually embraced by almost all Protestants. For the Puritans, we have no such choice. Election is only possible through God's grace which we can neither earn – through faith, good works, or by other means – nor resist. At the beginning of time God has inscrutably decided to whom He extends His grace, and thus eternal life, and to whom He denies it. This doctrine, called predestination, places a heavy burden on its followers. Powerless to work towards their own salvation, Puritans still could not very well embrace the fatalism that predestination invites and give themselves over to licentiousness even if, theoretically, licentiousness would not prevent salvation. And so they developed the idea of preparationism. Arguing that everyone should in any case be *prepared* for grace, they thereby tacitly created the illusion – which as a doctrine they would have vehemently rejected – that such preparation served a purpose.

For those who were convinced that God had extended His grace to them, life, in spite of its troubles and pain, was a joyful curtain-raiser before eternal life began. The great Puritan poet Edward Taylor (1642–1729), who will be discussed later, could write with lyrical exuberance about the smallest aspects of God's Creation. But for those who were less sure of their salvation, and for those who were aware that such certainty might be a trap laid by the Devil, the question of their eventual salvation was and remained a central issue. It is no wonder that that question led to intense introspection and self-examination and to the mass production of histories, journals, diaries, autobiographies, and other texts from whose cumulative events and incidents God's intentions concerning either the community or the individual might be inferred. Much of this was for private use, but many texts circulated in manuscript, while a substantial number were printed and published after the first printing press in the colonies was established in Boston in 1638 (and had its first bestseller in the immensely popular *Bay Psalm Book* of 1640). If we add these secular writings to the astonishing number of sermons, theological tracts, meditations, elegies and other religious texts that were published we get a picture of an intense and vigorous culture with great respect for literacy and learning – Harvard College, now Harvard University, in Cambridge, near Boston, dates from 1636. It was, of course, also a one-dimensional culture in which the borders of Calvinist theology were strictly patrolled and transgression was immediately exposed and from which the transgressor, admittedly after due process, was expelled.

This happened to Anne Hutchinson (1591–1643), who had come over in 1634 with her minister John Cotton, and who soon after her arrival began to organize religious meetings in her own home during which she was critical of several Boston ministers, suggesting that they leant too much towards Arminianism, replacing Calvin's 'covenant of grace' with a 'covenant of works'. Winthrop, who in his journal gives an account of Hutchinson's trial and conviction, calls her 'a woman of ready wit and bold spirit', but sides with her accusers, claiming that she has succumbed to 'two dangerous errors'. The worst of these was antinomianism – the idea that, since God's grace is the only truly necessary condition for salvation, human law and human institutions (like churches and church-going) are at best of minor importance. Hutchinson was a match for her accusers, as the trial records show, but made a slip, claiming she had had a private divine revelation, that allowed them to question the orthodoxy of her beliefs. She was banished in 1637 and found a tragic end when, with almost all her family, she was murdered in a Native raid in 1643.

The most famous dissenter was Roger Williams (1603–1683) who had taken holy orders in the Church of England but had then turned towards Calvinism and who came to Boston in 1631. Williams was a true radical. He refused a minister's position in Boston because the Boston Calvinists were nominally loyal to the Church of England, questioned the right of the English Crown to hand over Native land to English settlers (thus undermining Massachusetts Bay itself), proposed a strict separation of church and state (which strikes at the heart of a theocracy), and advocated freedom of conscience, and therefore of religion. Williams's ideas find expression in *The Bloody Tenent of Persecution, for Cause of Conscience, Discussed* (1644), a reply to a public accusation by the Boston minister John Cotton, and *The Bloody Tenent Yet More Bloody* (1652), another reply to Cotton who had renewed his accusations in a typically Puritan exchange of religious hostilities.

By that time Williams had long left Massachusetts Bay. After he had just escaped arrest for incitement, early in 1636, by fleeing to what is now Rhode Island (Dutch for 'red island') where he was welcomed by the Narragansett Indians from whom he bought land, he managed to obtain a charter for Providence Plantation where freedom of conscience was a fundamental right and was even written into the renewed charter of 1663 – a first in the English-speaking world. Williams's most important legacy is probably *A Key into the Language of America* (published in London in 1643), which perfectly illustrates his open-mindedness (even if theologically, as in the matter of Separatism, he was often quite dogmatic) and his perhaps patronizing but deeply human attitude towards Native Americans. With some exceptions, the Puritans did not show much interest in Native American languages, customs, or ways of life and in spite of their rhetoric felt a less than pressing interest in converting them. One such an exception was William Wood, who in his 1634 *New England's Prospect* offers detailed descriptions of Native American life and customs, sometimes critically, sometimes with wonderment, as upon seeing their 'houses, whose frames are covered with close-wrought mats of their own weaving which deny entrance to any drop of rain, though it come both fierce and long [...]. They be warmer than our English houses'. Another was the missionary John Eliot (1604–1690), the 'apostle to the Indians', who in 1663 translated the Bible into the Algonquin language. Williams, however, seems interested in the Native population for their own sake and his *Key* offers a wealth of information on the Algonquin language, on Native history, beliefs, culture, and social organization, and does not hesitate to hold their world up to that of the English: 'although they have not so much to restraine them (both in respect of God and Lawes of men) as the *English* have, yet a man shall never heare of such crimes amongst them [as] robberies, murthers, adulteries, &c. as amongst the *English*'. His admiration for their sense of morality also expresses itself in stanzas such as the following in which a Native American speaker, addressing the colonists, effectively inverts the usual order:

> We weare no Cloths, have many Gods,
> And yet our sinnes are less:
> You are Barbarians, Pagans wild
> Your land's the Wilderness.

Puritan verse

Like Williams, many other Puritan chroniclers, diarists, biographers, and autobiographers used verse to emphasize certain points. All that occasional verse has not much to recommend it. The same goes for the first collection of more lasting verse – more lasting from the Puritan perspective – that was published in New England. In the seventeenth century Protestant congregations enlivened their Sunday services with the singing of psalms, a practice that made of every churchgoer an active participant. These psalms were translations from the Hebrew, put to music, of the 150 religious poems collected in the Bible's *Book of Psalms*. An English translation had been completed in 1562, but the Puritans disliked its flowery language and in the 1630s decided to produce a new translation. The result, *The Whole Book of Psalms Faithfully Translated into English Meter* (soon known as *The Bay Psalm Book*) was published in 1640 and inevitably became a bestseller. But the literalness of it translations, the Puritan distrust of art, the choice of the homely – but familiar – ballad form, and perhaps the modest skills of the translators led to verses that, as John Cotton somewhat defensively put it in his preface, 'are not always so smooth and elegant as some may desire or expect', adding that those who felt that way should 'consider that God's Altar needs not our polishings'. But some polishing was soon felt to be necessary and in 1651 a revised edition was published, illustrating that 'a little bit more of Art' – as another influential minister, Cotton's grandson Cotton Mather, was to put it later – was no longer thought blasphemous. A similar ballad form, which helps memorization, was used in New England's all-time bestseller, the *New-England Primer* (1689?). The *Primer*, which taught children the alphabet with verses while offering religious instruction (the Z for instance with 'Zaccheus he / Did climb a tree / His Lord to see'), sold over five million copies in 150 years and was known by heart by countless American children, and not just in New England.

As the revision of the *Bay Psalm Book* suggests, around the middle of the seventeenth century Puritan vigilance with regard to 'Art' gradually relaxed, although in 1726, in his old age, the just-mentioned Cotton Mather would still warn aspiring ministers that 'the powers of darkness have a library among us, whereof the poets have been the most numerous as well as the most venomous authors. Most of the modern plays, as well as the romances, and novels and fictions, which are a sort of poem, do belong to the catalogue of this cursed library'. Fortunately, not all Puritans felt that their poetic efforts would bolster the powers of darkness. In 1650 a London printer published *The Tenth Muse, Lately Sprung Up in America*, a collection of poems by Anne Bradstreet (1612–1672), who had come to Massachusetts Bay with John Winthrop. Bradstreet's poems, which had circulated among family and friends, were taken to England by a brother-in-law who without letting her know arranged for their publication and so not only made her the first published American poet but also the first female poet to publish a book of poetry in English.

The Tenth Muse is rather derivative, once again going over the classical themes that had earlier exercised the minds and skills of English and French poets. But in a second volume, *Several Poems* (1678), published posthumously, which reprints her earlier work but adds a whole new collection of poems that directly address her own life in New England, Bradstreet finds a far more personal voice and makes us share her hopes and hardships. Her independent mind had already shown itself clearly in her first book. 'I am obnoxious to each carping tongue / Who says my hand a needle better fits', she complains in that book's 'Prologue', continuing, 'For such despite they cast on female wits: / If what I do prove well, it won't advance, / They'll say it's stolen, or else it was by chance'. But she really comes into her own in the new poems of her second collection, where we find love poems dedicated to her husband – 'If ever two were one, then surely we / If ever man were loved by wife, then thee' ('To My Dear and Loving Husband') – elegies on the deaths of grandchildren, a meditation on the burning of her house, and other poems concerned with private joy and sorrow. Still, in her poetry – now meant for publication – Bradstreet never wavers in her acceptance of God's will. The death of a grandchild can thus turn into a reason for rejoicing:

> Farewell dear child, thou ne'er shall come to me,
> But yet a while, and I shall go to thee;
> Meantime my throbbing heart's cheered up with this:
> Thou with thy Savior art in endless bliss.
> ('In Memory of My Dear Grandchild Anne Bradstreet, Who Deceased June 20, 1669,
> Being Three Years and Seven Months Old')

And when she must watch her house and all her possessions go up in fire she ends with a similar acceptance: 'And when I could no longer look, / I blest His name that gave and took'. Though movingly frank about private grief and sorrow, these poems always seem to come to the same very Calvinist resolution, avoiding the complexity the events described would normally invite. But we should perhaps not so easily come to that conclusion. In her 'To My Dear Children', a letter written late in life, Bradstreet indeed attests to her deep faith in her Savior. But she is also remarkably honest about the doubts that have plagued her from time to time: 'Many times hath Satan troubled me concerning the verity of the Scriptures, many times by atheism how could I know whether there was a God; I never saw any miracles to confirm me, and those which I read of, how did I know but they were feigned?' Anne Bradstreet exemplifies the best traits of the Puritans: their piety, their honest self-appraisal, and their fearlessness.

The other major early Puritan poet, the Malden, Massachusetts, minister Michael Wigglesworth (1631–1705) was, at least in his verse, far less adventurous than Bradstreet. The diary Wigglesworth kept as a young man (published in 1965) shows him tormented by doubt and tempted by sins that are not specified. He lives in constant fear that he is destined for eternal damnation. But while damnation plays a central role in his verse, his personal struggles are kept out of sight. In 1662 he published *The Day of Doom*, 224 stanzas of each eight lines and with insistent internal rhymes that in a pounding ballad meter describe the terrors of God's Judgment Day. Like his Christ, Wigglesworth shows little pity with the damned:

> They wring their hands, their caitiff hands
> And gnash their teeth for terror;
> They cry, they roar for anguish sore,
> And gnaw their tongues for horror.
> But get away without delay,
> Christ pities not your cry:
> Depart to hell, there you may yell,
> And roar eternally.

In spite of such lurid scenes *The Day of Doom* became a bestseller, presumably because its cataloguing of sins and sinners and its insistence on God's omnipotence served as religious instruction, and Wigglesworth found himself celebrated as the great poet of Puritanism. *The Day of Doom* was followed by the unpublished *God's Controversy with New England* (1662), a jeremiad in verse form, describing all the ways in which New England failed to live up to the founders' covenant with God, and by the curiously titled *Meat Out of the Eater* (1670). This second and again bestselling long poem, the title of which was taken from the story of Samson in the *Book of Judges*, strikes a much gentler tone – 'out of the strong came forth sweetness', as the verse in question tells us – and comforts its audience with the assurance that after life's pain and suffering God's blessing awaits them.

Bradstreet and Wigglesworth were famous in their lifetime, but Edward Taylor (1642?–1729), with Bradstreet the most accomplished of the Puritan poets, wrote almost exclusively for himself – although some of his poems had circulated in Boston he forbade his heirs to publish his poetry – and his very substantial body of work remained virtually unknown until 1937. Like Bradstreet and Wigglesworth born in England, he came to New England in 1668 and from 1671 until his death served as pastor in Westfield, Massachusetts. This is relevant information because many of Taylor's poems are directly connected to his religious duties. From 1682 to 1725 he wrote 217 *Preparatory Meditations*, poems that served to prepare him spiritually for the Lord's Supper, the monthly communion, and the sermon he had to deliver on that occasion. But the long earlier poem *God's Determinations Touching His Elect*, his reworking of the psalms, and the dense and massive *Metrical History of Christianity*, which would have seriously discouraged even the most dedicated Puritan, also bear the stamp of his ministry. And if his poetry is not directly related to his calling it still concerns itself with the soul's struggle and God's grace. Taylor's work suggests a more than passing familiarity with that of the English Metaphysical poets – John Donne, George Herbert and others. Since he did not leave England until his mid-twenties we may assume that in the course of his education he had read their poetry and come to admire their wit, their complex and extended metaphors, and their knotty, emotion-suffused intellectualism. Those qualities, in any case, characterize his own verse, exemplified by for instance the famous 'Huswifery', in which the everyday spinning wheel becomes an ever more elaborate metaphor for his soul's desire to submit to God's will:

> Make me, O Lord, Thy Spinning Wheel complete.
> Thy Holy Word my Distaff make for me.
> Make mine Affections Thy Swift Flyers neat
> And make my Soul Thy holy Spool to be.

> My conversation make to be Thy Reel
> And reel the yarn thereon spun of Thy Wheel.

As this stanza also illustrates, Taylor's poetry takes grammatical liberties for the sake of rhyme and his meter may stumble into awkward lapses. But his best poetry is immensely powerful, as in 'Meditation 22' (from the first of the two series of *Preparatory Meditations*):

> One glimpse, my Lord, of Thy bright Judgment Day,
> And Glory piercing through, like fiery Darts,
> All Devils, doth me make for Grace to pray,
> For filling Grace had I ten thousand Hearts.
> I'd through ten Hells to see Thy Judgment Day
> Wouldst Thou but Gild my Soul with Thy bright Ray.

Although always concerned with man's depravity and the immense wonder of God's grace, Taylor has the true poet's impulse to experiment with form, as in 'Upon a Spider Catching a Fly', with its staccato meter and the very effective lengthening of the stanza's third line which (in this particular stanza) repeats the rhyme. Observing the way spiders deal with the wasps and flies they find caught in their web, Taylor concludes that the Devil – 'Hell's Spider' – weaves a similar web for us and that only God's grace can free us, 'break the cord':

> But mighty, Gracious Lord,
> Communicate
> Thy Grace to breake the Cord; afford
> Us Glorys State.

Taylor's deeply emotional relationship with his Creator leads him far away from the 'plain' language advocated by earlier generations of Calvinist ministers. Although God's glory or grace can never be expressed in language, his exuberant rhetoric sometimes seems to attempt just that. If mysticism was not so alien to the Calvinist spirit we might be tempted to believe that such rhetoric serves to evoke mystical visions of redemption through God's grace.

Typology

Very much in line with that Calvinist spirit, however, is Taylor's extensive use of typology. For Christian theologians, typology meant finding parallels between the Old and the New Testament – a famous example is the three days that Jonah spent in the whale and that Jesus later spent in the tomb – and interpreting an Old Testament event as a prefiguration of its New Testament echo. Calvinists, and especially the New England Puritans, cast their typological net much wider and applied the typological method to contemporary and worldly events in order to assign to these events their true and fundamental meaning. For these Puritans, their exodus to the New World (the contemporary 'antitype') was foreshadowed in Israel's forty-year trek from Egypt to the Promised Land (the Old Testament 'type'). And so we find Cotton Mather in his 'The Life of John Winthrop' (in *Magnalia Christi Americana* of 1702) referring to Boston as 'our American Jerusalem'. Once you start looking for 'types' that point forward to contemporary 'antitypes' in a long and complex text like the Old Testament, you will find them everywhere, but even so Taylor's poetry is more than averagely alert to Biblical history repeating itself in contemporary guise. This Puritan tendency to see events in terms of other, earlier events would cast a long shadow. Although strictly speaking not allegorical, it comes close enough to allegory to have made an allegorical – and, by extension, symbolic – mode of writing dominant in New England well into the nineteenth century. The writings of Ralph Waldo Emerson, Nathaniel Hawthorne, Herman Melville and others still bear witness to that typically Puritan habit of mind.

Naturally, typology, in its wider sense, also keeps recurring in Puritan historiography. We find it in Bradford and Winthrop and in histories that were published during their authors' lifetime, such as *The Wonder-Working Providence of Sions Saviour in New England* (1654), also known as *The History of New-England*, by Edward Johnson (1598–1672) or *New England's Memorial* (1669), by Nathaniel Morton (1613–85). Both histories, together with similar efforts by other early historians, suffer in comparison with Bradford and Winthrop, who were better placed to write comprehensive histories, even if Morton served as Bradford's secretary for a number of years and, as keeper of Plymouth Plantation's records, had direct access to whatever had been preserved on paper. In that last capacity, he offers interesting details that Bradford omits. In Johnson's history typology plays a major role. Active, enthusiastic, but not very reflective, Johnson – like many more sophisticated Puritans – saw the establishment of a theocracy in New England as the first and necessary step in a process that would establish a new Zion on American soil and would lead to Christ's soon to be expected Second Coming.

Theocracy in trouble

If Johnson had lived longer, his optimism would have suffered a severe blow. With the increase of New England's population, two intractable problems had become ever more pressing. The first problem was theological, with important social repercussions because official church members enjoyed certain civil privileges. True to their nickname, the Puritans sought to keep their own congregations free from impure elements. Ideally, every single member of a congregation had experienced a personal conversion. From the mid-1630s on, afraid to harbor members of doubtful credentials, congregations demanded ever stricter proof of conversion, including a public 'confession' of faith, as often as not with a description of the actual conversion experience. So what to do with those who were regular churchgoers but had not yet experienced a conversion, or were too afraid to claim it, fearing that in their zeal they had deceived themselves? And what to do with the children of those who had not made a public 'confession' and who were therefore considered not converted? According to the rules, such children could not even be baptized. For many church members, the specter of allowing infants, possibly their own grandchildren, to enter this wicked world without the benefit of baptism was unthinkable. And so, in 1662, after much acrimony and polemical exchange, the Boston Synod relaxed the original rules, leading to what by its opponents was called the Half-Way Covenant. From now on 'persons' who had themselves been baptized but who had 'not receive[d] faith' could be full members and could have their children baptized (if, of course, their way of life did not provoke objections). One of the most prominent opponents was the young Increase Mather (1639–1723), who had just married a daughter of John Cotton, and would the next year become the father of the already mentioned Cotton Mather. This Cotton Mather, by the way, would in 1724 publish a biography of his father, just as the young Increase would write a biography of his father Richard (1670), who had supported the Half-Way Covenant. From a distance of three hundred years, this dynasty of honorable – and powerful – ministers writing with great gravity about each other still has an element of the awe-inspiring even if that awe is mixed with incredulity.

The Half-Way Covenant averted a serious theological crisis, although it left the more orthodox church members dissatisfied. But the expanding population soon triggered a new one. Although the artisan and merchant class kept growing – and would eventually come to dominate New England's economy – more and more land was needed for agricultural purposes and its acquisition often left Native Americans with serious grievances. Feeling victimized by injustice after injustice, the Wampanoag, joined by other tribes, and under the leadership of their war chief Metacom or Metacomet, went to war in June 1675, wreaking havoc all over New England. The war, called King Philip's War after the name Metacom had used in earlier negotiations with the Plymouth colony, was virtually won when Metacom was killed the next summer, even if it lingered on until the Spring of 1678. By then twelve towns had been destroyed and over 600 New Englanders had been killed or wounded. The war brought enormous economic damage, but it signaled the end of a substantial Native presence in New England and, having revived the New England confederacy, also served to strengthen New England's sense of identity. Inevitably, an event of such magnitude and importance had to be scrutinized for the workings of God's hidden hand, and so Increase Mather almost immediately (1676) produced his *A Brief History of the Warr with the Indians in New-England* (expanded in the following year). Later in 1676, Mather would use the occasion for a jeremiad with the self-explanatory title *An Earnest Exhortation to the Inhabitants of New-England.*

The captivity narrative

This is exactly how one of the victims of King Philip's War, Mary Rowlandson, sees the war – as God's message to New England. 'I can but admire to see the wonderful providence of God in preserving the heathen for further affliction to our poor country. […] how to admiration did the Lord preserve them for His holy ends, and the destruction of many still among the English', she writes in what has become known as *A Narrative of the Captivity and Restoration of Mrs. Mary Rowlandson* of 1682. Early in 1676, Mary Rowlandson (1636?–1711), wife of the minister of Lancaster, was with three of her children and twenty other settlers captured in a raid that destroyed much of Lancaster and left many of its inhabitants dead or wounded. Pursued by the colonial militia, her captors take her into the wilderness, and in a period of eleven weeks take her from one provisional encampment to another, in a total of twenty 'removes', before she is finally ransomed and allowed to rejoin her family. It is estimated that in colonial New England, beginning with King Philip's War, some 1,600 men, women, and children were taken captive and eventually released. A number of these captives told their story in so-called captivity narratives that emphasize the captive's ordeal and picture the captors as the Devil's henchmen, but place their captivity – as Rowlandson in the above quotation – within a redemptive framework: God has not only sent this affliction to chasten His children but He will eventually also show His mercy. The format resembles that of the jeremiad, but goes beyond that in its resolution: repentance is followed by mercy. Of these captivity narratives Mary Rowlandson's has proved the most enduring because of the liveliness of its writing, its suspense, and its honesty.

Inevitably, the Native attackers are seen as devils. This was of course the standard Puritan view. Early in his *Journal* Winthrop expresses the belief that the smallpox epidemic that had decimated the Native population around Boston was sent by God in order to make room for His Chosen People, a belief that often was reiterated. But Rowlandson also had good reasons for her negative emotions. She had barely survived a massacre, her youngest child, an infant, dies – in a very moving passage – in her arms and she is separated from the other children. In spite of this, she still sees in every bit of luck the hand of her Creator: 'before us there was a great brook with ice on it; some waded through it, up to the knees and higher, but others went till they came to a beaver dam, and I amongst them, where through the good providence of God, I did not wet my foot'. The most wonderful example of this good providence is that, astonishingly, a Bible comes her way: 'I cannot but take notice of the wonderful mercy of God to me in those afflictions, in sending me a Bible. One of the Indians that came from Medfield fight, had brought some plunder, came to me, and asked me, if I would have a Bible, he had got one in his basket'.

As this last incident shows, the Indians do not lack empathy. And they treat her well and behave quite civilly: 'not one of them offered the least imaginable miscarriage to me'. When she suffers a rare mistreatment she probably without realizing it breaks a code or a taboo. Rowlandson's genuine grief and suffering, her self-scrutiny, and her seemingly realistic portrait of her captors give her narrative a persuasiveness that is still gripping, in spite of its traditional Puritan framework in which the Indians, as the unwitting instruments of God, have confronted both Rowlandson herself and all of Puritan New England with their sinfulness and have made them repent. For Rowlandson, her captivity thus serves to reaffirm her faith (and has, at a more mundane level, the positive side effect of breaking her habit of smoking a pipe – 'a bait the devil lays to make men lose their precious time'). For the Puritans, captivity narratives confirmed their view of Native Americans, as was especially the case with the often retold story of Hannah Dustin who was taken prisoner in 1697 and escaped with two other captives after killing ten Indians – mostly children – and taking their scalps, for which they received a reward of £50, an enormous sum.

Diaries

Hannah Dustin was captured in Haverhill, Massachusetts, on the New Hampshire border, and immediately taken up north where Native Americans still were a considerable presence. Further south, such raids had by 1700 largely become memory. When in 1704 Sarah Kemble Knight (1666–1727) travels on horseback from Boston to New Haven and then on to New York, to return in the Spring of 1705, there are far more real dangers than being taken into captivity, such as that of crossing rivers in far from stable crafts: 'The canoe was very small and shallow, so that when we were in, she seemed ready to take in water, which greatly terrified me, and caused me to be very circumspect, sitting with my hands fastened on each side, my eyes steady, not daring to so much as lodge my tongue a hair's breadth more on one side of my mouth than t'other'. This is a passage from the *Journal* (first published in 1825), in which Knight gives an account of her trip, and a good example of her entertaining, mildly self-deprecating but supremely confident style. Knight's *Journal* is a unique document, brimming over with humorous asides, astute general commentary, and all sorts of social observations – on the 'good, sociable' people of Connecticut, on 'most savage' Native Americans, on the 'French muchets' worn by New York's 'Dutch' women, and so on. A formidable woman, who clearly was not at all deterred by the dangers facing a woman traveling alone (although, in the absence of sign-posts, she is usually accompanied by a guide), she is not reticent about the shortcomings of the less educated, the economically underprivileged, or the Native Americans that happen to cross her path. Although certainly religious, she is, unlike her Boston contemporaries, not overly concerned with her Creator, who is simply referred to as 'my great Benefactor'. We are much closer here to contemporaries elsewhere in the colonies, such as Robert Beverley or William Byrd II, both of Virginia, who will be discussed later, than the great Puritan diarist Samuel Sewall. For Sewall, as for other Puritans, the diary is a powerful instrument for self-observation and self-analysis. The diarist produces a record of his or her life that allows later reviewing and interpretation – hence the inclusion of at first sight trivial details and events – and may thus lead to better understanding, perhaps even of God's ways.

Sewall (1652–1730), who was born fourteen years before Sarah Knight but outlived her, is one of the greatest diarists of this period, the other being the influential minister Cotton Mather, who produced *The Diary of Cotton Mather for the Years 1681–1708*, published in 1911–12 and *The Diary of Cotton Mather, D.D., F.R.S. for the Year 1712* (1971). Although also concerned with worldly matters, Mather's diaries tell us much about his spiritual life. Again and again his faith must reassert itself in the face of disaster: his first two wives and several children die, one son is lost at sea and his third wife succumbs to mental illness. Stubbornly, Mather hangs on to his conviction that such adversity can only be a preparation for God's grace. Sewall's *Diary*, which he started in December 1673 and only abandoned in December 1728, is more lively in the variety of its interests and is a goldmine for anyone interested in the social and cultural history of New England. Sewall, born in England but educated at Harvard, where Edward Taylor became a life-long friend, was a prominent Boston merchant and in 1692 was appointed as justice to the Superior Court. Earlier in 1692 he had served on a special court, judging a case that would come to haunt him and that would become a personal trauma.

Sewall's detailed record of his own and of New England life reveals a deeply pious, very conscientious Puritan who over the years adopts a more liberal outlook, even if his faith in Calvin's teachings never wavers. An entry for 1695 that describes a fierce hailstorm and features Cotton Mather neatly illustrates the old Puritan habit of scrutinizing worldly events for signs of the divine will: 'Mr. Cotton Mather dined with us [...]; He had just been mentioning that more Minister Houses than others proportionally had been smitten with Lightening; enquiring what the meaning of God should be in it'. And in an entry for 1707 that shows that even Puritan Boston was not crime-free we find the by now familiar but still paradoxical Puritan habit of giving thanks for misfortune: 'My House was broken open in two places, and about Twenty pounds worth of Plate stolen away, and some Linen; My Spoon, and Knife, and Neckcloth was taken: I said, Is not this an Answer to Prayer? Jane came up, and gave us the Alarm betime in the morn. I was helped to submit to Christ's stroke, and say, Welcome CHRIST!' The most anthologized parts of the diary concern Sewall's rather amusing courtship of a very independent Boston widow after his wife's death. Commentators have noted how meticulously he records the price of each separate gift, perhaps indicative of a sensibility too much preoccupied with worldly matters. But when he finds that the object of his amorous attentions is not at home and decides to wait for her, he reads the New Testament Epistles to the Galatians and Ephesians (in Latin) and Psalm 103. In Sewall, the old Puritan spirit coexists with a businessman's preoccupations.

The Salem witch trials

Sewall's journal was not published until the middle of the nineteenth century, but he was already famous in his own lifetime. In 1692 he had published a sixty-page text that argued that New England was the new Zion, typologically linking it up with the *Book of Revelation*. Of far more importance, however, was his membership of the already mentioned special court, the Court of Oyer and Terminer ('to hear and determine') in Salem, in that same year. Early in 1692 in several towns north of Boston people were accused of witchcraft. Such accusations were nothing new in the Christian world and since the late fifteenth century tens of thousands of witches, overwhelmingly female, had been convicted and executed for witchcraft, usually at the stake or by hanging. In New England during an earlier outbreak of accusations fifteen witches had been executed between 1645 and 1663. But the witch-hunt of 1692 was historically late.

And the Salem witch-hunt, as it has come to be called, had an extraordinary scale: all in all twenty people were executed. The collective hysteria that led to these executions is hard to explain, especially since accusations of witchcraft had for thirty years not been taken very seriously by the clergy. Now, however, Cotton Mather and his father Increase were amongst those who actually claimed to have seen an 'Imp', a sort of junior Devil.

The trials and executions had a sobering and humbling effect on many Puritans. In 1697, Sewall, burdened by his conscience, stood up in church and confessed his guilt in sending innocent fellow-citizens to their death and begged for forgiveness. His magnanimous example was not generally followed but Sewall's public confession sealed the reversal of public feeling about the trials. Three years later he again created commotion by publishing *The Selling of Joseph*, a pamphlet that condemns slavery as an ungodly practice, as violating God's designs with humankind. Still, Sewall's plea for equal rights does not mean that he sees African Americans as equals and rejects the stereotypes and prejudices of his time.

Puritanism and Enlightenment

The same can be said of Cotton Mather, who published his own repudiation of slavery, *The Negro Christianized*, in 1706, although Mather comes closer to full acceptance than Sewall, for instance in inviting the African Americans who attended his church to his home for further religious instruction. On the other hand, when his congregation presented him with a slave, he did not turn the present down. Mather is an intriguing figure, given to self-punishment over what we would consider imaginary sins, suffering bereavement after bereavement, and still working and writing with enormous energy. His history of New England – the 800-page *Magnalia Christ Americana* (1702) – tries once again to vindicate the Puritan view of New England as the new Zion to which Christ would in the foreseeable future return. It also urges New England to resume its missionary activities, for which he himself learned the Iroquois language. While a staunch believer in witchcraft – as evidenced in his *The Wonders of the Invisible World* (1693) – he was also deeply involved in the study of the flora and fauna of New England, sending his descriptions to the still young Royal Society, of which he would eventually become an elected member. Even more impressive is his passionate recommendation of inoculation, of which he had read, during the small-pox epidemic of 1721. Ridiculed by the very young Benjamin Franklin – who would later change his mind – and many others, he persisted and inoculation was eventually introduced. Still, like Sewall, Mather never really became a child of the eighteenth century, a century that in America would practically be embodied by the just mentioned Franklin, born in 1706. Although they were clearly touched by the new spirit of frank curiosity and unprejudiced reappraisal of existing structures and institutions that would come to dominate the new century, they were both still imprisoned within the traditional Puritan framework with its millenarian expectations. In his *The Christian Philosopher* of 1721 (philosopher in the sense of scientist) Mather is still more interested in how things fit into God's design than in the empirical question of how they work.

Jonathan Edwards

But by the time Mather published *The Christian Philosopher*, orthodox, hard-core Puritanism was gradually giving way to more enlightened views. Not, however, without producing a last brilliant star on the firmament of early American writing. Jonathan Edwards (1703–58) was educated at the then recently founded Collegiate School, soon to be renamed Yale College, one of whose purposes was to defend and keep alive the religious orthodoxy that Harvard

College was in the process of abandoning. In 1729 he succeeded his grandfather as minister of Northampton where he served as pastor for twenty-one years until in 1750, in a rare but perfectly legal maneuver within Puritan congregations, an overwhelmingly large majority of his flock voted him out of office. Edwards refused ministries that were offered to him and more or less went into exile, becoming pastor in a tiny community and preaching as a missionary in isolated Western Massachusetts, before seven years later, on the basis of his powerful writings, he was invited to become president of the College of New Jersey, later to become Princeton University. Like Cotton Mather a strong advocate of small-pox inoculation, he had himself inoculated when a new epidemic was on the horizon, and died of the infection soon after moving to New Jersey.

Like Mather, Edwards combined a strong and lively interest in the new discoveries and the philosophical debates of his time with orthodox Calvinism. Familiarity with John Locke's empiricism and Locke's ideas on how our subjectivity is shaped – which would inspire much of his writing – did not prevent him from a strict adherence to traditional Puritanism (which would eventually bring him on a collision course with his Northampton congregation). And when Locke and Puritanism contradicted each other, Puritan doctrine naturally won out. Locke's notion of the mind as a *tabula rasa*, as initially 'empty', cannot be right, for 'There is laid in the very nature of carnal men a foundation for the torments of hell', as Edwards puts it in his famous fire-and-brimstone sermon 'Sinners in the Hands of an Angry God' of 1741.

But orthodoxy did not come easy to Edwards. In the autobiographical 'Personal Narrative', written some time after 1739 but published posthumously in *The Life and Character of the Late Reverend Mr. Jonathan Edwards* (1765), he recounts in classically Puritan fashion his soul's struggles, in this case how he wrestled with the concept of predestination, which seemed until then 'a horrible doctrine'. Later, after he has come to see the 'doctrine of God's sovereignty' as 'an exceeding pleasant, bright and sweet doctrine', he has an extraordinary and deeply emotional experience:

> Once, as I rid out into the wood for my health, *anno* 1737; and having lit from my horse in a retired place [...] I had a view [...] of the glory of the Son of God; as mediator between God and man; and his wonderful, great, full, pure and sweet grace and love, and meek and gentle condescension. This grace, that appeared to me so calm and sweet, appeared great above the heavens. The person of Christ appeared ineffably excellent, with an excellency great enough to swallow up all thought and conception. Which continued, as near as I can judge, about an hour; which kept me, the bigger part of the time, in a flood of tears, and weeping aloud.

We may assume that it was such experiences – the following year he again 'br[oke] forth into a loud weeping, which held me some time' – that led Edwards to his advocacy of a Puritanism that was as emotional as it was cerebral, as deeply felt as it was based on rational acceptance. For Edwards the grace of God makes itself felt in those who are saved and illuminates their lives, so that the saved, in their turn, illuminate the world. As he puts it in one of his key publications, *A Treatise Concerning Religious Affections* (1746), the soul of the saved 'receives light from the Sun of Righteousness in such a manner that its nature is changed, and it becomes properly a luminous thing: not only does the sun shine in the saints, but they also become little suns'. The saved, therefore, celebrate the wonders and beauty of God's Creation, as did Edwards himself, taking aesthetic pleasure in the earthly manifestations of His omnipotence. And they see things in a much clearer light than those who have not yet received God's grace and must until then see everything as if in 'twilight'.

Edwards did not hesitate to use his considerable rhetorical powers to literally put the fear of God into his congregation. In the already mentioned *Sinners in the Hands of an Angry God* he tells them that '[t]he God that holds you over the pit of hell, much as one holds a spider or some loathsome insect over the fire, abhors you, and is dreadfully provoked: His wrath towards you burns like a fire', adding for good measure that before the year would be over members of his audience would burn in hell. But the force of Edwards' rhetoric was equally capable of stirring positive emotion, of whipping up an enthusiasm for conversion and salvation that Puritanism had never seen. Unleashing this rhetoric on his Northampton congregation, he became one of the central figures in the so-called Great Awakening of the 1730s and 1740s, the first of several revivalist movements that would sweep through the colonies and the young Republic in the eighteenth and nineteenth centuries. Noting in a letter of 1735 that 'Satan seems to be in a great rage, at this extraordinary breaking forth of the work of God', he maintained his support for the revivalist movement, even when its emotional excesses led to disapproval among his fellow ministers. During his wilderness years after his dismissal in Northampton Edwards tirelessly wrote treatises such as *Freedom of Will* (1754), defending classical Puritanism and its old ways. Not, however, without attempting to create a synthesis between Puritan dogma and the new ideas generated by the European Enlightenment. These dense and learned theological–philosophical writings, for the most part published after his death, are widely seen as the intellectual high-water mark of Puritanism. In support of this it may be worth mentioning that several of Edwards' treatises appeared in the decades after his death in translation in the Dutch Republic, where the large contingent of Calvinist ministers knew how to appreciate a bold and original fellow-theologian.

Enlightenment in Virginia: Robert Beverley and William Byrd

Although it would cast a long shadow, Puritanism was definitely a waning force when Edwards died in 1758. Rather than by Edwards, the spiritual future of New England would be defined by leaders such as the very influential Boston minister Charles Chauncy (1705–87), who came to reject predestination and to believe that God offered salvation to us all. Chauncy's so-called Universalism pointed forward to the Deism of Benjamin Franklin, Thomas Jefferson, and many others involved in the American Revolution and prepared the way for such typically New England products as the Unitarianism and Transcendentalism of the early nineteenth century. Chauncy's writings, produced in the course of a long life, illustrate how the scientific discoveries of Isaac Newton (1642–1727), the philosophy of John Locke, Scottish so-called Common Sense philosophy, and other Enlightenment developments gradually came to dominate intellectual life in the colonies. In the second half of the eighteenth century the truths of natural science came to rival those of revealed religion.

This was in particular the case south of New England where, with some local exceptions, Puritanism had never been a real force. The absence of the fierce spiritual drive of New England Calvinism with its narrow doctrinal basis had its advantages. On the other hand, probably because of that absence the Atlantic seaboard south of New England was slow and far less active in leaving written records, let alone imaginative writing. Its best-known writers of the early period are the poet Ebenezer Cooke (or Cook), and the chroniclers and diarists Robert Beverley and William Byrd II. Cooke (1665?–1732?), of whose life we know very little, but who probably divided his time between his birthplace London and Maryland, wrote *The Sotweed-Factor, or A Voyage to Maryland, A Satyr* (1708) in which the hapless tobacco agent of the title bewails his adventures among the primitive, querulous and dishonest colonials he encounters, finally cursing Maryland's hostile shores: 'May Wrath Divine then lay those Regions wast / Where no

Man's Faithful, nor a Woman Chast'. Cooke obviously was aware of the English taste for satire at this time and may have felt that ridiculing backward colonials, while simultaneously questioning their visitor's stamina and courage, would cater to a refined English public's sensibility.

Like Cooke, Beverley and especially Byrd were much better acquainted with contemporary English fashion and sensibility than the Puritans up north. Robert Beverley (1673?–1722), a Virginia planter, dissatisfied with what until then had been written on the history of Virginia, in 1705 published *The History and Present State of Virginia*, which he enlarged and brought forward to 1710 in 1722. The book is not only a history, but offers a good deal of information on 'the natural productions and conveniences of the country' (it was published in London and no doubt had a promotional function), on the region's Native Americans, and on the current 'polity of the government'. Beverley writes with wit, with an eye for lively detail, and is remarkably open-minded. Looking back upon the earliest period of colonization, he reflects on how different things might have been: 'Intermarriage had indeed been the Method proposed very often by the *Indians* in the Beginning, urging it frequently as a certain Rule, that the *English* were not their Friends, if they refused it. And I can't but think it would have been very happy for that Country, had they embraced this Proposal'. However, the famous union of John Rolfe and Pocahontas had been a rare exception and Beverley blames much of the violence that would ensue – 347 colonists killed on 22 March 1622 – on the Indians' sense of having been grievously rejected. Far from assuming that they are the Devil's instruments, Beverley tries to understand their motives. Tellingly, he is not always as understanding in his often entertainingly satirical remarks about his compatriots, both the well-to-do planters (and their families) and 'Persons of low Circumstances'. Yet Beverley believes in reason and in progress, in looking forward where an enlightened future beckons.

William Byrd II (1674–1744) was at the age of seven sent to England by his wealthy planter father to be educated there and more or less divided his life between England and Virginia. He expanded his father's land holdings into a vast estate on which in 1737 he founded the city of Richmond, named by him, and lived in the life style of the English landed gentry in Westover, his great (and still-standing) mansion, accumulating the largest library in the colonies. An influential colonial politician, Byrd was in 1728 asked to be chief representative of Virginia in a surveying expedition that was to establish once and for all the disputed boundary line between Virginia and North Carolina. The diary he kept during the expedition would become the basis for his *The History of the Dividing Line Betwixt Virginia and North Carolina*, which circulated among his Virginia and London friends, but was not published until 1841, and for a shorter version, 'The Secret History', which Byrd apparently wrote for his personal pleasure and which probably antedates *The History*. The histories cover more or less the same ground – literally, because essentially they are travel accounts – and present an urbane, ironical, (usually mildly) satirical narrator who in particular in the secret version has a sharp eye for the follies of the other members of the surveying party and of the people they meet, who are not invariably pleased with the results of the party's activities: 'The Line cut two or three Plantations, leaving Part of them in Virginia, and part of them in Carolina. This was a Case that happen'd frequently, to the great Inconvenience of the Owners, who were therefore oblig'd to take out two Patents and Pay for a new Survey in each Government'. Byrd, as much belonging to the fashionable world of early eighteenth-century London, in which wit and light-hearted satire were much appreciated, as to the colonies, finds in his role as gentleman-observer obliging targets in uncouth Carolinians and other country bumpkins. In the expanded *History* he also offers a good deal of information on Virginian history, echoing Beverley's enlightened sentiments regarding intermarriage, and on Virginia itself, on occasion coming close to propaganda. In its descriptions of the varied landscapes the surveyors travel through, Byrd's *History* illustrates his lively interest in natural history. He was a member of the Royal Society and corresponded for thirty-five years with the famous English naturalist Sir Hans Sloane and like his fellow-member Cotton Mather sent over plants, seeds, and even live birds and animals.

Byrd also wrote two other accounts of frontier expeditions, including the significantly titled 'Journey to the Land of Eden', but his greatest fame rests on his diaries, written in a private shorthand, and discovered, deciphered and published in the middle of the twentieth century. These diaries, covering the periods 1709–12, 1717–21, and 1739–42, reveal Byrd as a highly educated man who is also not averse to more physical pleasures. His London diary – 1717–21, composed after his first wife had died – records numerous amorous encounters both with ladies of his own class and with prostitutes: 'then went to Mother Smith's where I supped with Betty G-r-n-r and then we went to bed and I rogered her two times very powerfully'. The diaries contain a wealth of information on plantation life in the early eighteenth century, including the often cruel treatment of Byrd's many slaves, and of life in London, where Byrd habitually met prominent figures in the city's social and cultural life. But they are also disappointing because Byrd was not much given to introspection. We read about the vicious quarrels with his first wife but he never wonders what makes their relationship so acrimonious. He meets the famous of the period, but we never hear what he thinks of them or of their work. In London Byrd enjoys the pleasures offered by the metropolis, in Virginia those of the colonial countryside, including the planning of improvements and developments which will realize the colony's potential. But wherever he is, the reflection, let alone the soul-searching, that characterizes Puritan diaries seems alien to his temperament.

In the writings of Chauncy, Beverley, Byrd, and others the Enlightenment definitely took hold in the colonies. In the first half of the eighteenth century most educated Americans would come to accept that the universe is governed by physical laws that we can discover and understand and that our first duty is not to sing God's praise and work towards His greater glory, as the Puritans believed, but to our fellow human beings, with whom we share an innate moral sense, and not merely depravity, as again the Puritans had taught. God, the Supreme, and supremely reasonable Being, had also provided us, his most noble creatures, with reason, a faculty that allowed us to comprehend the world and, more importantly, allowed us to be free agents and to create our own destiny.

The Enlightenment personified: Benjamin Franklin

This profound change in eighteenth-century America was practically personified by the already mentioned Benjamin Franklin. Franklin (1706–90) was an astonishing figure who from the proverbial humble origins rose to become a successful businessman, an equally successful inventor and scientist, an influential politician, and one of the leaders of the colonies' movement towards independence. One of the most publicly minded citizens of the American eighteenth century, he also found time to be a prolific writer who earned lasting fame with his *Autobiography of Benjamin Franklin* (1791 and 1868), which looks back to the Puritan autobiography in its public confession of 'errata' – bad decisions, immoral behavior – but belongs firmly to the eighteenth century in its emphasis on self-determination and self-creation.

Born in Puritan Boston, Franklin was put to work at the age of ten and was two years later apprenticed to a half-brother, a printer. When he was sixteen he started to write contributions to his brother's paper, under the name of Silence Dogood. The next year (1723) he broke his contract and ran off to Philadelphia, where he found work in a printing shop, leaving no word for his family. After a lengthy visit to England he set up his own press and started publishing

The Pennsylvania Gazette (1726–29). In 1733 he published the first issue of his *Poor Richard's Almanack*, which offered practical advice, folk wisdom, maxims, and social commentary. Supposedly the work of one Richard Saunders, and modeled after *Poor Robin's*, an English almanac, the *Almanack* was an immediate success, appearing annually until 1758 and selling over 10,000 copies a year. By that time, Franklin's name was known throughout the colonies, in England, and on the European continent. He wrote tirelessly – on education, on politics, on the future of the colonies, on Native Americans, on everything that caught his eye. He produced ideas and proposals – for a city police, a circulating library, for lighting the streets of Philadelphia (and for sweeping them) – and tinkered and experimented with the most diverse objects and phenomena, ranging from stoves to lightning. It was Franklin who in a famous experiment – flying a kite during a thunderstorm – proved that lightning was an electrical phenomenon, a feat that he published in *Experiments and Observations of Electricity* (1751–54) and that earned him international admiration plus the membership of the Royal Society.

We find an amusing example of Franklin's intensely curious mind in his autobiography when, listening to the famous English evangelist George Whitefield, who is preaching on the steps of Philadelphia's Court House, he starts wondering how large an audience Whitefield, one of the founders of Methodism, could possibly address:

> Being among the hindmost in Market Street, I had the Curiosity to learn how far he could be heard, by retiring backwards down the Street towards the River, and I found his Voice distinct till I came near Front Street, when some Noise in that Street, obscur'd it. Imagining then a Semi-circle, of which my Distance should be the Radius, and that it were fill'd with Auditors, to each of whom I allow'd two square feet, I computed that he might well be heard by more than Thirty Thousand. This reconcil'd me to the Newspaper Accounts of his having preach'd to 25,000 people in the Fields, and to the ancient Histories of Generals haranguing whole Armies, of which I had sometimes doubted.

The passage illustrates Franklin's ever-inquisitive turn of mind, but also his mild skepticism, his rational practicality, and his lucid and supple style. This prose style, practiced in his younger days with the example of London's Joseph Addison – of *Spectator* fame – firmly in mind, but obviously influenced by the 'plain' style of his Boston background, was equally well suited to the home-spun advice and simple wisdoms of the *Almanack* as to the sarcasm of for instance 'Rules by Which a Great Empire May Be Reduced to a Small One' of 1773, which already hints at revolution: 'that the possibility of this separation may always exist, take special care the provinces are never incorporated with the mother country; that they do not enjoy the same common rights, the same privileges in commerce; and that they are governed by *severer* laws, all of *your enacting*, without allowing them any share in the choice of their legislators'. His supple style allowed Franklin to create a range of voices, such as that of Polly Baker, a Connecticut woman of somewhat loose morals, who in 'The Speech of Polly Baker' (1747) appears in court for having given birth to a fifth 'Bastard Child' and defends herself with verve: 'Can it be a Crime (in the Nature of Things I mean) to add to the Number of the King's Subjects, in a new Country that really wants People?'

The no doubt useful but rather uninspiring wisdom of the *Almanack* – '*lost time is never found again*'; '*little strokes fell great oaks*' – might leave the impression that Franklin was a worthy but cheerless citizen. There is, however, a good deal of mischief in Franklin, as Polly's speech suggests, and it is this and his wit that make him still so eminently readable. That wit occasionally even slips into Poor Richard's voice. 'I have sometimes quoted myself with great gravity', Richard Saunders tells the reader in the twenty-fifth issue of the *Almanac*, in which he brings together twenty-five years of folk wisdom in an often reprinted essay usually referred to as 'The Way to Wealth' (1757). The title epitomizes one side of Franklin: the self-made man who has indeed found the way to wealth through hard work, stubborn practicality, common sense and self-discipline, and who stands for the material opportunities that America offers to all of those willing to make the effort.

But Franklin was much more than a self-made man in this narrow material sense. In *The Autobiography of Benjamin Franklin*, written between 1771 and 1788, and initially intended as a letter of advice to his son, we meet a man who with a good deal of frankness – and a good deal of well-dosed reticence – gives an account of his life, taking it to the year 1757, when he was 51. Franklin presents himself as a character who with great determination takes his life into his own hands. Still in Boston, he develops schemes for moral self-improvement based on Cotton Mather's *Bonifacius, or Essays to Do Good* (1710), which, as he notes, 'perhaps gave me a Turn of Thinking that had an influence on some of the principal future Events of my Life'. Moral self-improvement played no role in one of his most important acts of self-determination, running away without notifying his family or anybody else for the next seven months, but in general Franklin emerges from his autobiography as a consummately responsible citizen, fully aware of his civic duty. Having left Calvinism both literally and figuratively behind he becomes a 'thorough Deist' who is convinced 'that the most acceptable Service of God [is] the doing of Good to Man'. Franklin believes firmly in moral and social progress, based on reason and moderation. There is much of Puritan New England in Franklin's autobiography – the self-scrutiny, the insistence on self-discipline, the sense of civic duty – but piety has given way to reason and morality, predestination to self-fashioning, and hard work and ingenuity may without self-recrimination lead to wealth. In Franklin's lifetime, America adopts a modern outlook, even if the influence of orthodox religion remains strong, as we see in for instance the *Journal* (1774) of the Quaker preacher John Woolman (1720–72) or the earlier *Journal* – published by Jonathan Edwards in 1749 – of the Puritan missionary David Brainerd (1718–47). With Franklin modern man, the man who trusts empirical evidence rather than preconceived ideas – 'This is the Age of Experiments', he declared – and whose life is a successful project rather than a ride on a predetermined track, enters the world of American letters. And with *The Autobiography* American literature enters the modern world. Franklin's retrospection results in a book that with its witty, ironic, and lively narrative voice and its exciting story of spiritual growth and worldly success measures up to the English novels of the period.

Revolution

In the last thirty years of Franklin's long life great changes took place, not the least important of which was the decision of the thirteen North American colonies to declare themselves independent from the mother country. It is not a period that produced an abundance of great writers, perhaps because so much intellectual energy was invested in political debate, perhaps because, with some fortunate exceptions, there simply were no major talents, even if in the decades before the Revolution literary clubs, modeled upon English examples, organized themselves in most of the larger cities. Quite probably the literature of the period was not served either by the widespread assumption that it must advance the cause of freedom, function as a figurative call to arms, or, after the Revolution, sing the praises of the new Republic. For such calls or praise, literary-minded Americans almost inevitably turned to poetry, and in particular poetry of the loftier sort. A famous example is 'A Poem: On the Rising Glory of America' (1771) by two young Princeton students, Philip Freneau (1752–1832), who would become an important poet, and Hugh Brackenridge (1748–1816), who would go on to write a rambling picaresque and satirical novel, *Modern Chivalry* (1792–1815). Their 470-line poem, largely attributable to Brackenridge, amounts to a miniature epic of the New World, beginning with Columbus and ending with its last speaker's frequently quoted vision of the future: 'Paradise anew / Shall flourish by no second Adam lost'. Indeed, 'Another Canaan shall excel the old'.

Animated by the success of the Revolution other attempts at epic of the period straight-forwardly place that paradise on what now has truly become American soil. Timothy Dwight (1752–1817), a grandson of Jonathan Edwards, speaks in his *The Conquest of Canäan* (1785), a poem of epic proportions if not of epic quality, of 'blissful Eden' and sees in the biblical Joshua's conquest of Canäan a prefiguration of the events of the 1770s. For Dwight, a religious conservative, political freedom can only thrive within a properly religious context. His *The Triumph of Infidelity* of 1788, a far more modest but still substantial effort, despairs of the fulfillment of this condition and resembles the Puritan jeremiad, expressing its sorrow at humankind's condition in the amazing lines 'In vain thro realms of nonsense – ran / The great Clodhopping oracle of man'. Dwight's friend Joel Barlow (1754–1812) produced a far more secular epic with his *The Vision of Columbus* (1787), modeled upon Augustan examples rather than upon Dwight's Milton. Like many other poets of the period Dwight and Barlow blend in various ways classical elements with Puritan themes and images (such as Dwight's Canäan). Twenty years later, when Barlow had embraced Deism and become a friend of true revolution-aries like Thomas Paine, he revised, expanded and renamed his poem (*The Columbiad*). Dwight is best remembered for his pastoral poem *Greenfield Hill* (1794) and Barlow for his 'The Hasty Pudding' (1796), an unpretentious poem in which he abandons the grand style of his epics and favorably compares the simple, but honest American hasty pudding with whatever France, where he is living, has to offer:

> I sing the sweets I know, the charms I feel,
> My morning incense, and my evening meal,
> The sweets of Hasty Pudding. Come, dear Bowl,
> Glide o'er my palate, and inspire my soul.

A similarly light and satirical tone characterizes John Trumbull's *The Progress of Dullness* (1772–73), which in Hudibrastic lines targets the misdirected educational efforts of American colleges, and his mock epic *M'Fingal: A Modern Epic*, first published in 1776 and expanded in 1782. Trumbull (1750–1831) was like Dwight and Barlow a product of Yale and is usually grouped together with them (and two or three others) as the Connecticut (or Hartford) 'Wits'. Trumbull's iambic tetrameters roll on with great energy and wit. A colonial constable ready to read the Riot-act discovers that his audience is in no mood for British law:

> [He], now advancing tow'rd the ring,
> Began, 'Our Sovereign Lord, the King' –
> When thousand clam'rous tongues he hears,
> And clubs and stones assail his ears.

Revolutionary fervor had begun to run high in the 1760s – 'rather than freedom we part with our tea, / And well as we love the dear draught when a-dry, / As American Patriots our taste we deny' Milcah Martha Moore (1740–1829) rhymed in the *Pennsylvania Chronicle* in 1768, five years before the Boston Tea Party – and lasted until well into the first decades of independence. The desire for freedom and the (future) greatness of America that were the major themes of the poetry of the period also dominated its most important literary genre, the argumentative essay, the most brilliant of which was the 1776 text that has entered history as the American Declaration of Independence. Nominally the product of a committee of five that included Benjamin Franklin and John Adams, but in fact the work of a single member, Thomas Jefferson (1743–1826), who represented Virginia, it presents the case for independence with a stylistic lucidity, moral clarity and rhetorical force that still compels admiration. It is one of the great documents of human history: 'We hold these truths to be self evident: that all men are created equal; that they are endowed by their Creator with certain inalienable rights; that among these are life, liberty, and the pursuit of happiness; that to secure these rights, governments are instituted among men, deriving their just powers from the consent of the governed; that whenever any form of government becomes destructive of these ends, it is the right of the people to alter or to abolish it […] '. From our vantage point in history much of this rings false. After all, the 'inherent and inalienable rights' mentioned in this declaration were exclusively reserved for white (and propertied) males. Moreover, within the context of the period the infringements upon those inherent rights were far less earth-shaking than the Declaration wants us to believe. The colonial elite were ready for complete self-government and self-government was not possible without independence. But in sharp contrast with for instance the French Revolution of the next decade, the American Revolution did not dislodge the elite, but was expertly managed by them, enabling them to quietly fill all positions of authority after the smoke of the battle had cleared. Still, the Declaration is a rightly celebrated and quintessentially American text which one and a half century after John Winthrop's great metaphor of the Massachusetts Bay Colony as a 'cittie upon a hill' gave the idea of America's unique destiny among nations a new, political dimension. For many Americans the Puritan conviction that their New England theocracy meant a new beginning for humankind with the Puritans themselves as God's Elect, entrusted with a historic mission, now, and in a secular version, seemed true of the new Republic, with 'democracy' replacing 'theocracy' and all of the free and democratic United States of America as the new 'cittie upon a hill'.

Thomas Paine

One of the most enthusiastic and eloquent promoters of the Revolution as the herald of a new beginning and of the unique status of the new Republic as the vanguard of democracy, was Thomas Paine (1737–1809), a largely self-taught English radical who at the age of 37 came over to America at the invitation of Benjamin Franklin. 'The cause of America is in a great measure the cause of all mankind', Paine wrote in the introduction to his first-ever publication, the pamphlet 'Common Sense: Addressed to the Inhabitants of America'. 'The sun never shone on a cause of greater worth'. Published in January 1776, the 77-page pamphlet sold 100,000 copies in the first three months after publication – eventually selling almost half a million – and its plea for immediate independence had enormous impact. 'Without the pen of the author of "Common Sense", the sword of Washington would have been raised in vain', the later President John Adams noted. Telling his readers, in a new version of the old Puritan vision, that the Reformation was preceded by the discovery of America 'as if the Almighty had graciously meant to open a sanctuary to the persecuted', Paine urges them to resist the British oppressor. Joining the revolutionary Continental Army, to which he donated the proceeds of 'Common Sense', Paine went on to write sixteen pamphlets all entitled 'The American Crisis', the first of which was read aloud in December 1776 to George Washington's exhausted troops to boost their morale. Given the troops' performance on the day after, verdicts like 'Every Tory is a coward, for a servile, slavish, self-interested fear is the foundation of Toryism' probably served their purpose. They certainly illustrate Paine's rhetoric and his no-prisoners-taken approach with regard to political and intellectual differences. Not surprisingly, given his firebrand temperament, Paine left for France in the early 1790s to participate in the French Revolution and only returned to the U.S. in 1802. By then the radicalism of his *The Age of Reason* (1793–94) and his earlier *The Rights of Man* (1791) had made him a social outcast. Once a hero, his claim that all churches are 'no other than human inventions set up to terrify and enslave mankind' or his expressed conviction that the Nativity story 'is hearsay upon hearsay' for which there is no 'evidence' (both in *Age*), had alienated almost all his earlier admirers, including George Washington. It was only later generations that rehabilitated Paine's contribution to the American cause.

Crèvecoeur

Like Paine, J. Hector St. John de Crèvecoeur (1735–1813), another famous promoter of the American Republic as the new world of the future, was more cosmopolitan than American. Born as Michel-Guillaume de Crèvecoeur in France, he crossed the Atlantic to Canada – then New France – in 1755 and traveled south four years later. Working as a surveyor and in the trade with Native Americans he saw a good deal of the colonies before starting a farm in New York State in 1769. In 1780 he returned to France, coming back to the U.S. as French consul for a couple of years, but staying in France permanently after 1789. Crèvecoeur's *Letters from an American Farmer* (1782), purportedly written by a prosperous farmer, was amazingly successful and equally influential. The most famous of the twelve narrative essays that make up *Letters* (enlarged and rewritten in French in 1784 and again expanded in 1787) is 'Letter III', entitled 'What Is an American?' Americans are 'tillers of the earth', 'cultivators' – like Jefferson, to whom we will return, Crèvecoeur sees America's future in pastoral terms – but most of all

> The American is a new man, who acts upon new principles; he must therefore entertain new ideas, and form new opinions. From involuntary idleness, servile dependence, penury, and useless labor, he has passed to toils of a very different nature, rewarded by ample subsistence. – This is an American.

Irrespective of his country of origin, upon reaching American shores the immigrant is 'regenerate[d]' by 'new laws, a new mode of living, a new social system'. Indeed, here in America, immigrants who were 'as so many useless plants' in Europe 'are become men'. In 'this great asylum' immigrants from all over Europe 'are melted into a new race of men, whose labors and posterity will one day cause great changes in the world'. Here we have the famous image of America as a mythical melting-pot that would for a long time determine immigration discourse. Understandably Crèvecoeur's *Letters* created waves of enthusiasm in a Europe plagued by poverty and malnutrition. But he is by no means blind to the violence and lawlessness of life on the frontier or to the ignominy of slavery: 'There, arranged like horses at a fair, they are branded like cattle, and then driven to toil, to starve, and to languish for a few years on the different plantations of these citizens'. But it is fair to say that the image of the United States as a pastoral utopia and as holding the greatest promise humankind had ever seen dominates the *Letters*.

Thomas Jefferson

Thomas Jefferson has already been linked with that utopian vision which for him was bound up with the direct, decentralized democracy associated with the so-called anti-Federalism of the 1780s. Like most of his co-revolutionaries Jefferson was a man of many talents. The successful owner of a large plantation, he also was an Enlightenment intellectual who founded the University of Virginia and whose enormous library would lay the basis for the Library of Congress. He was an accomplished architect, was deeply interested in natural history, and was for most of his life dedicated to politics: he published his strongly anti-British and widely read *A Summary View of the Rights of British America* when he was thirty-one years old, was one of the founding fathers of the Republic, served as minister to France, and eventually rose to the highest position in the nation. His presidency (1801–9) does not feature in *The Autobiography of Thomas Jefferson, 1743–1790* (1821), which in spite of its eyewitness account of the events leading up to independence and of the formative years of the Republic remains a rather dry report that even his personal opinion on a wide range of issues does not do much to enliven. Jefferson, who saw himself as an agrarian aristocrat, entertained a utopia of an agrarian, pastoral America. 'Those who labor the earth are the chosen people of God if ever He had a chosen people', he writes in his *Notes on the State of Virginia* (1784), adding that '[c]orruption of morals in the mass of cultivators is a phenomenon of which no age nor nation has furnished an example'. For once we see Jefferson, who elsewhere in the *Notes* declares that '[r]eason and free enquiry are the only effectual agents against error', and who is consistently skeptical of unfounded statements, making a fundamental claim unsupported by empirical evidence, a sure sign of his strong belief in an agrarian future for the Republic. The *Notes*, written in response to a list of twenty-two 'queries' submitted to him by a French diplomat stationed in America, discuss in rather exhaustive detail such subjects as 'Its Rivers, Rivulets, and How Far They Are Navigable', 'Mines and Other Subterranean Riches; Its Trees, Plants, Fruits, &c', but also Virginia's population, Native Americans, religion, 'customs and manners', and so on, in their desire for exactness even telling us that according to the 1782 census the state had 567,614 inhabitants. Jefferson uses the opportunity to sing America's praises – 'The *Ohio* is the most beautiful river on earth' – and, incited by the derogatory views of American nature and Native Americans published by leading European naturalists like the French Count de Buffon, takes great pains to convince his correspondent that America is in all respects at the very least equal to Europe, if not actually superior. This equality for once even extends to America's original inhabitants: 'his friendships are strong and faithful to the uttermost extremity […] his sensibility is keen, even the warriors weeping most bitterly on the loss of their children'. Still, although one of the most enlightened minds of his time, Jefferson could not escape its prejudices. In principle an opponent of slavery, he never gave his own slaves their freedom and could never see them as fellow citizens.

African American writing

But even if the fate of African Americans was at this point in American history not yet a central issue, they gradually began to claim a voice in the great American choir. The oldest African American text that has been preserved is the ballad 'Bars Fight' by Lucy Terry (1730?–1821), which commemorates a Native American attack that had taken place near Deerfield, Massachusetts, in 1746. Terry never saw her poem, which was first published in the 1850s, in print. The first African American publication was probably 'An Evening Thought: Salvation by Christ With Penitential Cries', a deeply religious poem by the slave Jupiter Hammon (1711–1800?), published as a broadside in 1761. Then, in 1773, Phyllis Wheatley (1753?–1784), kidnapped by slavers twelve years earlier, when she was seven years old, and brought to Boston where she was bought by the Wheatley family, published *Poems on Various Subjects, Religious and Moral*, a collection of contemplative poems on mostly classical and traditional themes. Invited to come to London after she had caused a minor sensation with her elegiac poem 'On the Death of the Rev.

Mr. George Whitefield' (1770), the evangelist with the formidable voice mentioned by Frank-lin, she was approached by an English publisher who published her first collection when she was twenty years old. She was freed in the same year, but circumstances prevented her from pursuing a literary career and she only published a handful of other poems before her early death, although a number of completed poems may have been lost.

Wheatley's poetry suffers from the mannerisms of her time – 'But see the sons of vegetations rise / And spread their leafy banners to the skies' describes a forest in 'Thoughts on the Works of Providence' – but she was an intelligent and skilful poet, who uses a variety of forms and is more subtle and even subversive than her traditional themes might suggest. Regularly personal emotion asserts itself in poems that otherwise belong first of all to the domain of public discourse. As a good Christian dutifully, and diplomatically, expressing her gratitude that she has come to know her Savior, even if the price was enslavement, she reminds her fellow-Christians that Africans are God's creatures too: 'Remember, *Christians*, *Negros*, black as *Cain*, / May be refin'd, and join th' angelic train' ('On Being Brought from Africa to America'). In another poem she calls attention to the suffering the Christians that have kidnapped her must have caused and rather daringly compares the colonies' experience of tyranny to her own, as a slave:

> What pangs excruciating must molest,
> What sorrows labour in my parent's breast?
> Steeled was that soul and by no misery moved
> That from a father seized his babe beloved:
> Such, such my case. And can I then but pray
> Others may never feel tyrannic sway?
>
> ('To the Right Honorable William, Earl of Dartmouth')

Wheatley's preoccupation with the fate of African Americans expresses itself very forcefully in a letter to Samson Occom (1723–92), a Mohegan who had converted to Christianity and had become a minister who preached to his own people. '[I]n every human Breast', Wheatley writes, 'God has implanted a Principle, which we call Love of Freedom; it is impatient of Oppression, and pants for Deliverance; and [...] the same principle lives in us'. Occom, whose 'A Short Narrative of My Life' (written in 1768 but not published until 1982) is generally regarded as the first Native American contribution to Anglophone American literature, must have agreed and knew very well that as a 'poor Indian' he only nominally had more status than Wheatley in the eyes of most Americans.

After the Revolution other African Americans joined Wheatley in her plea for freedom. Lemuel Haynes (1753–1833), who had actually participated in the Revolution, and would later, like Occom, become a minister – the first black minister to serve a white congregation – asked in his 'Liberty Further Extended: Or Free Thoughts on the Illegality of Slave-Keeping' (1776?): 'Because a man is not of the same couler with his Neighbour, shall he Be Deprived of those things that Distinguisheth him from the Beasts of the Field?' 'Liberty Further Extended' only circulated in manuscript, but *The Nature and Importance of True Republicanism*, in which Haynes presents a forceful argument against slavery and against the racism that had made him leave his first congregation, appeared in print in 1801. By then, Haynes had gained wide respect, receiving an honorary M.A. from Middlebury College three years later, the first ever presented to an African American.

The most important argument for freedom of the period was Olaudah Equiano's *The Inter-esting Narrative of the Life of Olaudah Equiano, or Gustavus Vassa, the African, Written by Himself,* published in London in 1789 and two years later in New York, where it became a bestseller. Equiano (1745?–1797) was taken into slavery in 1756 and via the West Indies brought to Virginia. Some years later he was sold to a Quaker merchant in Philadelphia, who treated him well, allowed him to conduct a little business on the side, and in 1766 accepted the forty pounds that Equiano had been able to lay aside to buy his freedom. Deciding to settle in England, Equiano crossed the Atlantic again, never to return.

There is some doubt about the reliability of the first part of his autobiography, which describes his earliest years in Africa, his enslavement by fellow Africans and the circuitous route to the coast where he is eventually sold to a white slaver, since he may actually have been born in the colonies. If that is indeed the case, he probably relied for that first part on stories told by fellow slaves because his often gruesome account of the crossing of the Atlantic – the so-called 'middle passage' – is consistent with indisputably reliable sources. The larger part of the narrative, however, is corroborated by external evidence (in an amusing passage, we hear how people stood on ladders to see Whitefield preaching in a Philadelphia church). Equiano's auto-biography is a story of hardships and suffering, of inhuman ill-treatment and victimization, but also a story of great determination, courage, and entrepreneurship. Although he must start his journey towards self-fulfillment under circumstances that are incomparably worse than those under which Franklin started, the story of his life is a similar success. The *Narrative* illustrates that remaking oneself is as possible for an African American as it is for a Boston adolescent, in spite of all the differences.

Women writers

Although their lack of freedom cannot seriously be compared to that of African American slaves, we see that women, too, begin to feel uneasy with the restrictions imposed upon them by a male elite which talks of liberty and freedom as inalienable rights. 'Remember all Men would be tyrants if they could', Abigail Adams (1744–1818) playfully writes to her husband John, who represents Massachusetts in the Continental Congress that is meeting in Philadelphia in 1774. And she continues with a sly allusion to the most fundamental American grievance against the British: 'If particular care and attention is not paid to the Ladies we are determined to foment a Rebellion, and will not hold ourselves bound by any Laws in which we have no voice or Representation'. Adams (1735–1826), later the Republic's second president, has no real defense against the implied reproach in one of the eighteenth century's great exchanges of letters in which Abigail's New England skepticism with respect to humankind regularly comes to the surface. 'I am more and more convinced that man is a dangerous creature', she writes in November 1775, 'and that power whether vested in many or a few is ever grasping, and like the grave cries give, give'. The arresting image is just one of many sprinkled over the hundreds of letters that have been preserved and that show us an extraordinarily lively, intelligent, and warm-hearted woman.

But the unequal position of women also led to more public protest. Two years before Mary Wollstonecraft would publish her famous *A Vindication of the Rights of Women* in England, Judith Sargent Murray published her 'On the Equality of the Sexes' in the *Massachusetts Magazine* (1790). 'Is it indeed a fact that [nature] hath yielded to one half of the human species so unquestionably a mental superiority?' Murray, using the pen name of 'Constantia', asks her readers before arguing that all mental differences between the sexes are the result of nurture, of a quasi-educational process of confinement and limitation that leaves young women 'wholly domesticated' by the time their brothers have been introduced to science and other intellectual accomplishments. In her *Poems, Dramatic and Miscellaneous* of the same year, Mercy Otis Warren

(1728–1814) – who would in 1805 publish a three-volume *History of the Rise, Progress and Termination of the American Revolution* – speaks just as clearly of 'The narrow bounds, prescrib'd to female life, / The gentle mistress, and the prudent wife'.

Initially writing for private circulation, then for magazine publication in the larger cities – Boston, Philadelphia, New York – more and more women make themselves heard in the last three decades of the eighteenth century. Some of them, like Annis Boudinot Stockton (1736–1801) or Sarah Wentworth Morton (1759–1846), whose 'The African Chief' of 1824 is an early and passionate literary attack on slavery, achieved only regional fame, but others gained a larger audience. Warren eventually achieved national fame and so did Murray with *The Gleaner* (1798; dedicated to John and Abigail Adams), which collected her previously published work. And women writers turned to what was a wholly new genre in late eighteenth century American literature: the novel. *The Gleaner* includes the story, told in an epistolary exchange, of a Miss Wellwood who imprudently allows herself to be seduced and then talked into prolonged unlawful cohabitation – with the usual result – after which she finds herself abandoned. This leads to much hand-wringing and self-recrimination. Were it not for her (illegitimate) children, Miss Wellwood writes, 'I would seek some turfed pillow, whereon to rest my weary head; and, closing forever these humid lids, I would haste to repose me in that vault, which entombs the remains of my revered parents'. Fortunately, however, all ends well.

That is usually not the case in this kind of story, which owes its seduction theme and epistolary format to the English writer Samuel Richardson (*Pamela*, 1740; *Clarissa Harlowe*, 1747–48). The theme makes its first appearance in what is generally considered the first American novel, *The Power of Sympathy* (1789) by William Hill Brown (1765–93), which openly announces that its aim is 'to expose the fatal CONSEQUENCES OF SEDUCTION'. The promise of sensationalism suggested by those capitals is fully borne out by its story of incestuous seduction and its end in death and suicide. Brown's subtitle, 'Or, The Triumph of Nature', neatly summarizes the standard seduction plot, which pivots around a struggle of reason and self-discipline, represented by the girl, with our lower nature, represented by the man. Since the temptations of the flesh are strong, and the inevitably dashing male is not only perfidious but persuasive, the struggle is an uphill battle, with the girl paying the price – quite often death – and the male at worst tormented by his conscience. We find this pattern in two very early and very popular American novels, *Charlotte Temple* (1794; published in England, in 1791, as *Charlotte, A Tale of Truth*) by Susanna Rowson (1762?–1824) and *The Coquette* (1797) by Hannah Webster Foster (1754–1840). Presumably in order to avoid the charge of titillation, Rowson, like other writers of seduction novels, stresses her high moral purpose, telling the reader in her preface that she will be fully satisfied '[i]f the following tale should save one hapless fair one from the errors which ruined poor Charlotte'. A young and innocent English girl, Charlotte allows herself to be talked into eloping to America (where she will eventually 'sink unnoticed to the grave') by a British officer. The real villain, however, is the officer's friend, who wants Charlotte for himself, and is primarily responsible for her ultimate fate. Describing the perfidy of 'this disgrace to humanity and manhood', Rowson writes with 'the burning blush of indignation and shame' on her cheek.

The young girl of Webster's *The Coquette* is considerably less naive than Charlotte, but far more headstrong. Following the epistolary format, Webster's novel lets us see how Eliza Wharton falls under the spell of Peter Sanford, who in his letters to a friend openly discusses his plans to have her, at whatever cost. Unfortunately, Eliza is not impressed by the warning of an older and wiser friend, who even reminds her of the wiles of the arch-seducer: 'I do not think you seducible; nor was Richardson's Clarissa, till she made herself the victim, by her own indiscretion. Pardon me, Eliza, this is a second Lovelace. I am alarmed by his artful intrusions'.

But Eliza falls for the absolutely shameless Sanford, losing her suitor, the rather stiff Reverend Boyer, who in a farewell letter expresses his grief: 'I gave free scope to the sensibility of my heart; and the effeminate relief of tears materially lightened the load which oppressed me'. This style of heightened and somewhat artificial emotionality is typical of most sentimental novels. Writing to her mother, Eliza tells her that 'my heart and pen turn with ardour and alacrity to a tender and affectionate parent, the faithful guardian and guide of my youth'. Although an imported format, the sentimental novel begins to serve an American purpose in these stories. The seducers invariably have wonderful manners and an entertaining and flattering line of conversation, both of which will have reminded contemporary readers of the widely read *Letters* (1774) that the Earl of Chesterfield had written to his son and that for many Americans, wary of all aristocratic pretensions, did not so much teach good manners as dishonesty and dissimulation.

American self-confidence

We see this theme in one of the first successful American plays, Royall Tyler's *The Contrast* (1787). Just prior to the Revolution Mercy Otis Warren had written plays – *The Adulateur* (1773), *The Group* (1775) – that had attacked political loyalty to the British Crown. Tyler (1757–1826), writing after the Revolution, attacks loyalty to British manners. His hero is a Colonel Manly (!), who has earned his rank in the Revolutionary War, and is regarded with a measure of contempt and pity by the world of upper class New York in which his sister Charlotte moves with a good deal of freedom. But honesty and authenticity prove more durable than falsehood and deception hidden by good manners. Manly does 'neither drink nor game' and the stiffness of his prose makes one almost wish he would: his parents are 'the respectable authors of my existence, – the cherishers and protectors of my helpless infancy'. Still, it is Manly who is genuine and has the right moral instincts, together with his Yankee servant Jonathan, who, in his turn, is looked down upon by the servant of the play's prime villain, an American with British sympathies and manners. Jonathan is the classic country bumpkin, but morally shrewd and not to be intimidated, and a staple character of much nineteenth-century American fiction and drama. 'I'm a true born Yankee American son of liberty', Jonathan declares, implying that the others, although American through citizenship are in a sense not American at all. What was a contrast between authentic, sincere Americans and insincere, dissimulating Englishmen, has become a contrast between Americans of independent judgment and unerring moral insight – Manly, Jonathan – and those under the spell of European fashions. The play's villain Dimple summarizes this neatly, although from the wrong perspective, in his last lines: 'I take my leave, and you will please to observe, in the case of my deportment, the contrast between a gentleman, who has read Chesterfield and received the polish of Europe, and an unpolished, untraveled American'. When Tyler turns to the novel, in *The Algerine Captive* (1797), he has his protagonist, who is from rural New England, go from an early romantic infatuation with England and the European tradition to a mature appreciation of everything America has to offer, even if he does not turn a blind eye to its deficiencies. On the contrary, his years of enslavement in Africa make him more than ever aware of slavery's fundamental immorality.

When in the decades following the Revolution political independence became a thing taken for granted, the attention of American writers began to turn to cultural independence, a notion that earlier had been dismissed by such luminaries as Benjamin Franklin and John Adams who both argued that America's energies would be misspent on the production of literature. The lexicographer, essayist, and politician Noah Webster (1758–1843) even tried to put cultural independence into practice. The first part of his *A Grammatical Institute of the English Language* (1783–85) was revised and published as the *Spelling Book*, which sought to standardize American spelling and distinguish it from English spelling. Webster's *American Dictionary of the English Language* of 1828 is even in its title a declaration of independence but can, in spite of its American spelling and the inclusion of 5,000 new words, of course not hide that the vast majority of the words it includes have an English origin. As Webster must have realized, cultural independence was not easily achieved. In a period in which literature was increasingly supposed to reflect the specific qualities and achievements of a nation, of a people bound together by its traditions, its beliefs, its culture and its language, it was not easy to think of an American literature that would express the unique spirit of the formerly rather diverse colonies, except for a rather narrow literature that would thematize their belief in liberty and democracy – which is indeed what we get in *The Contrast* and many other texts. But another obstacle was the disinterest in literature shown by the large majority of Americans. In his 'To an Author' (1788) a disillusioned Philip Freneau asks of a fellow-poet (or perhaps of himself): 'Tell me, what has the muse to do?' in a place where 'rigid *Reason* reigns alone' and where 'lovely *Fancy* has no sway'. Thirteen years later we find Charles Brockden Brown, America's first important novelist, lament that 'a people much engaged in the labors of agriculture, in a country rude and untouched by the hand of refinement, cannot, with any tolerable facility or success, carry on, at the same time, the operations of the imagination and indulge in the speculations of Raphael, Newton, or Pope'.

Philip Freneau and Charles Brockden Brown

'Nobody will pretend that the Americans are a stupid race; nobody will deny that we justly boast of many able men, and exceedingly useful publications. But has our country produced one original work of genius?' the generally pessimistic Massachusetts politician Fisher Ames (1758–1808) asked in his essay 'American Literature' of 1801. For Ames the answer is that there is no such work and it is hard to disagree with him. Yet, the first decades after independence produced two authors, Freneau and Brown, whose work has withstood the test of time. Freneau (1752–1832), born into an upper-class family, was an ardent supporter of the Revolution and was taken prisoner by the British in the war for independence (in spite of his claim to be a non-combatant). His anger at the way he and other prisoners were treated by the 'brutes' – thousands of American prisoners died during the war – fuels his long poem *The British Prison Ship* (1781):

> Americans, a just resentment show,
> And let your minds, with indignation glow;
> While the warm blood shall swell each glowing vein,
> Let fierce resentment in your bosoms reign;

Such lines explain why he came to be called the 'poet of the American Revolution', but they also show his weakest side. Fierce emotion, effective as it may be, does in Freneau's case not lead to subtle poetry, as in the anti-slavery poem that he eventually titled 'To Sir Toby' (1809): 'In chains, twelve wretches to their labors haste; / Twice twelve I saw, with iron collars graced!' Poetic skills and emotion are in better balance in the poems in which he allows the neoclassical tradition in which he has grown up to be infused by the new Romantic sentiments that have come over from Europe. The transience of flowers ('The Wild Honeysuckle', 1786), the 'retreat' of the Native American ('On the Emigration to America and Peopling the Western Country',

1785), the specter of death ('The Indian Burying Ground', 1788) – everything speaks in measured tones of things irretrievably lost, even if, as in 'On the Emigration', the poem shifts back to a neoclassical mode and in Enlightenment fashion desires to see 'the day, / When man shall man no longer crush, / When Reason shall enforce her sway'. Much more light-hearted and even genuinely amusing are Freneau's satirical poems, such as 'The Drunkard's Apology' (1795) or 'The Indian Convert' (1797), in which the Indian in question is not overly eager to join the Elect:

> The Indian long slighted an offer so fair,
> Preferring to preaching his fishing and fowling;
> A *sermon* to him was a heart full of care,
> And singing but little superior to howling.

Freneau's poetry, especially in its pre-Romantic vein – in which his tendency to sermonize is least apparent – demonstrated that American poetry was catching up with that of England and pointed the way for William Cullen Bryant and other American poets of the next generation.

The novelist Charles Brockden Brown (1771–1810), like Freneau mostly active in Philadelphia, which for a brief period was the new nation's cultural center, was the most accomplished practitioner of what was a wholly new genre for the new Republic and its first professional author. In a burst of frenetic activity he first published *Alcuin: A Dialogue* (1797), a long exchange between Alcuin, a young schoolmaster, and an older widow in which Brown, influenced by English freethinkers like Charles Godwin and Mary Wollstonecraft and by his own Quaker background, defends the equality of women. He then in quick succession wrote *Wieland* (1798), *Arthur Mervyn* (published in two volumes in 1799 and 1800), *Ormond* (1799), and *Edgar Huntley* (1799), four idiosyncratic and wild novels that stand at the origin of one very important lineage in American fiction. Skipping a year, and falling back on more conventional domestic issues and an epistolary format that was more or less outdated, he went on to publish *Clara Howard* and *Jane Talbot* in 1801, after which he turned his energies to political writings and to the editing of several magazines which he also served as a leading contributor.

Brown is the first American novelist to use the sensationalist Gothic mode that was introduced in England by Horace Walpole's *The Castle of Otranto* (1764) and that in the 1790s was at the height of its popularity with the publication of Mrs. Radcliffe's *The Mysteries of Udolpho* (1794), Matthew Lewis's *The Monk* (1796), and other tales of horror and depravity. In his preface to *Edgar Huntly* Brown insists on the specifically American nature of his forays into the field of imaginative literature, telling the reader that 'the field of investigation opened to us by our own country should differ essentially from those which exist in Europe', and that '[i]t is the purpose of this work to [...] exhibit a series of adventures growing out of the condition of our country'. Not all of his four Gothic novels fulfill that ambition in equal measure, although he certainly succeeds in transplanting the Gothic to American settings and in creating gripping narratives. In *Wieland*, significantly subtitled *An American Tale*, an elderly gentleman has a mysterious and deadly encounter with something resembling 'a cloud impregnated with light', we have amazing feats of ventriloquism and a temporarily insane mass murderer; in *Ormond* we have a yellow fever epidemic in Philadelphia; in *Arthur Mervyn* we have more murders and a near escape from being buried alive; and in *Edgar Huntly* we have amazing feats of sleepwalking, a protagonist who is almost killed by friendly fire, and what the novel calls 'incidents of Indian hostility' – a specifically American expansion of the Gothic repertoire, perhaps even more American than Brown realized since the eponymous hero turns out to be far more dangerous than his Indian foes. These terrors are brought to us wrapped in implausible plots while the severe emotional shocks they cause bring female characters 'to the brink of the grave'. And especially these females characters tend to employ the lofty and implausible language that we find in the seduction novels of the time: '"O!" I exclaimed, in a voice broken by sobs, "what a task is mine! Compelled to hearken to charges which I feel to be false, but which I know to be believed by him that utters them; believed too not without evidence, which, though fallacious, is not unplausible"' (*Wieland*'s Clara Wieland, telling her story in long letters to a friend). But in spite of all this, and of an apparently improvisatory way of plotting (most obvious in *Arthur Mervyn*), Brown is an effective novelist, switching tenses for dramatic effect, creating narrative energy with staccato passages – 'No part of the building was on fire. This appearance was astonishing. He approached the temple' (*Wieland*) – or slowing the pace with more leisurely narrated events. More importantly, Brown's exploration of the dark side of sexual desire, of insanity, of fear of the other, of the urge to possess – or to destroy – emphasizes the limitations of Enlightenment characters like Clara Wieland's fiancé Pleyel, who is 'the champion of intellectual liberty, and reject[s] all guidance but that of his reason' and because of that is incapable of seeing the truth. Brown's psychology mostly does not dig deep – there is much absolute blamelessness and much utter depravity – but he also presents characters like the mysterious ventriloquist Carwin in *Wieland* who plays a deeply unsavory role – setting Pleyel against Clara – yet at the end seems to be burdened by genuine remorse. Carwin, like similarly opaque characters in the other novels, defies simple rational explanation and because of that adds to the unsettling effect that Brown's work must have had on contemporary readers. In Brown's novels unsuspecting characters are initiated into a new world where evil and madness wait for them and which forces them to acknowledge their profound ignorance of life: 'How little cognizance have men over the actions and motives of each other!' Edgar Huntly exclaims at the end of his terrible adventures. 'How total is our blindness with regard to our own performances!' It is not surprising that Brown's novels fared better in England – already past the grip of Enlightenment rationality – where they were well received by leading contemporary writers, than in the U.S., where they were not fully appreciated until later writers, like Edgar Allan Poe and Nathaniel Hawthorne, began to follow Brown into the dark territory that he had first explored.

American irony

The seduction novel as practiced by Susanna Rowson and Hannah Webster Foster would remain popular well into the nineteenth century, just like the novel which more directly idealizes – and sentimentalizes – romantic love. But not everybody was beguiled by the promise of romantic love, witness *Female Quixotism* (1801) by Tabitha Tenney (1762–1837). Tenney's novel, which like those of Rowson and Foster easily outsold Brown's fiction, is an energetic story about a not so young woman, Dorcasina Sheldon, who has become infatuated with an impossible ideal of romantic love that she has found in the sentimental novels of the time. She must now either voluntarily return to earth from her orbit in romantic outer space or learn the hard way – although there is nothing really hard in this witty and good-natured novel. Such texts, in which America looks critically at itself, are fairly rare in the decades before and after the Revolution, when virtually everything was treated with high seriousness, and satire and invective – which were certainly around – were directed at the British enemy. Another exception is the rambling satire *Modern Chivalry* by Hugh Henry Brackenridge (1748–1816), which has been mentioned earlier, and which was published over a period of 23 years – the first volume appearing in 1792 and the last, number six, in 1815 – coming to an abrupt end rather than to an ending. The picaresque adventures of its sympathetically irascible but rather naïve hero, Captain John Farrago, and those of his shamelessly ignorant, opportunistic and even unscrupulous servant, offer social and political commentary in which a mildly conservative point of view has the upper hand: 'Though doubtless, in [a fully democratic] government, the lowest citizen may become a chief magistrate; yet it is sufficient to possess the right; not absolutely necessary to exercise it'. Like Tyler's *The Contrast* and like *The Emigrants*, a 1793 novel by Gilbert Imlay (1754–1828), which was not published in the U.S. until 1964 and which situates the true, authentic America far from the Eastern cities in the Ohio Valley, *Modern Chilvalry* has as its hero an officer, a veteran of the American Revolution. The veiled criticism of the young American Republic that we find here implies that it must look toward a leadership of natural aristocrats, with those who are less gifted by nature as their admiring (and obedient) followers. History would soon show itself unimpressed by that vision, even if the next generation of writers – Washington Irving, James Fenimore Cooper, and others – kept on promoting it.

But the satire of Brackenridge, Tenney, and others does not cut deep, just as the novel of seduction, with its naïve young women and its heartless villains, is perfectly predictable and avoids whatever might complicate its simple scheme. Brown at least attempts complexity and, although never as profound as he may have wished to be, he makes great literature a serious possibility. That at least some of his contemporaries were aware of this is illustrated by the biography that the playwright and theater manager William Dunlap (1766–1839), who wrote successful plays such as *The Father; or, American Shandyism* (1789) and *André* (1798), published five years after his death.

The international context

The first two hundred years after the London Company founded Jamestown in May 1607 are far more interesting from a historical and political perspective than from a literary point of view. What began as a series of isolated and, with the exception of Massachusetts Bay, modest settlements in a remote part of the world had become one of the world's largest nations. Its white population had grown from zero to well over six million. But from a literary point of view those years are less impressive. In the early period we have chronicles, diaries, captivity narratives, elegies and jeremiads, didactic poetry, essays, sermons and religious tracts – almost always interesting, sometimes even fascinating, but mostly of cultural historical value. And when in the course of the eighteenth century essayistic writing and imaginative literature establish themselves more firmly, the forms and conventions are neoclassical, still borrowed from a mother country that has already moved on and embraced new ideas and new conventions and is, moreover, not limited by the American themes of liberty and greatness, which lead to much bland writing that sorely lacks the introspection of the Puritan diary. America had produced talented writers. Anne Bradstreet, Edward Taylor, Jonathan Edwards, Phyllis Wheatley, Philip Freneau, Charles Brockden Brown and others had shown the Old World that the colonies and later the Republic were culturally alive, but a brief glance at that Old World illustrates how modest that cultural life was. When Jamestown was settled, William Shakespeare was still alive and writing. Later in the seventeenth century John Milton published *Paradise Lost* (1667), John Bunyan *The Pilgrim's Progress* (Part I, 1678), and Aphra Behn *Oroonoko* (1688). In 1712 Alexander Pope published *The Rape of the Lock*, Daniel Defoe followed with *Robinson Crusoe* in 1719 and Jonathan Swift with *Gulliver's Travels* in 1726. Samuel Richardson's *Clarissa* appeared in 1747–48, Henry Fielding's *Tom Jones* in 1749, and Laurence Sterne's *The Life and Times of Tristram Shandy* from 1760 to 1767. In France Voltaire published *Candide* in 1759, and Jean-Jacques Rousseau published *Julie* in 1761 and *Émile* in 1762. In Germany Johann Wolfgang von Goethe was made famous by his play *Götz von Berlichingen* (1773) and his novel *The Sorrows of Young Werther* (1774), soon followed by Friedrich Schiller with his *The*

Robbers (1781). The list could effortlessly be much expanded, and in all directions – after all, England had its diarists too, with for instance Samuel Pepys and James Woodforde. This is not to belittle the achievement of the writers that have been discussed in this chapter, but to place it in a wider context. The colonies had come a long way and had changed the course of human history with their political institutionalization of a discourse of individual liberty to which they themselves had significantly contributed. Not a mean feat for a motley collection of farmers, lawyers and merchants on the absolute edge of what was then considered the civilized world.

2 Towards cultural independence: 1810 to the Civil War

Introduction

In the first two decades of the nineteenth century American critics, aware that American writing lagged behind, regularly called for a literature that would at the very least catch up with the various European literatures. There were good reasons for such a call. By 1820, the Republic's population had grown to 13 million, almost equaling that of Great Britain (14 million). Its territory had increased explosively with the Louisiana Purchase of 1803, which had added 828,000 square miles to what already was one of the world's largest nations (the mother country could only boast of a puny 89,000 square miles). And American entrepreneurs and politicians, ignoring Thomas Jefferson's vision of an agricultural America of proud independent farmers, had enthusiastically embraced modernization. In 1817 construction of the Erie canal went underway. By the time its 363 miles were completed, in 1825, the canal's importance would soon diminish because of a yet more impressive development, the railway, the first of which – the Baltimore and Ohio – opened in 1830. But even more crucial for American self-confidence was the victory in the War of 1812, a war originating in trade disputes with the former mother country. After some serious setbacks – in 1814 British troops burned the Capitol and the White House – general Andrew Jackson decisively defeated the British in 1815, at New Orleans. In so doing he laid the foundation for his later presidency (1829–37) and for a new, radical interpretation of the idea of democracy that would inspire both strong disdain and eager enthusiasm in the writers of the antebellum period and that was already announced in Maryland's decision of 1801 to abolish property requirements as a condition for voting and holding office. Like other American battles – and even skirmishes – the battle of New Orleans would achieve legendary status and become part of popular culture. (In 1959 the Country and Western singer Johnny Horton's 'The Battle of New Orleans' even reached the Billboard #1 spot: 'In 1814 we took a little trip / Along with Colonel Jackson down the mighty Mississip. / We took a little bacon and we took a little beans / And we caught the bloody British in the town of New Orleans'.) The War of 1812 also produced the lyrics of what in 1931 would become the national American anthem, 'The Star-Spangled Banner', which was inspired by the heroics of the defenders of Fort McHenry in Baltimore.

But while nationalist sentiment was running understandably high America could not yet boast of a national literature. In a review essay called 'A Sketch of American Literature, 1806–7' Charles Brockden Brown had in a somewhat disheartened mood claimed that 'the American states [were], in a literary view, no more than a province of the British empire'. It was not easy for an American writer to make a career out of imaginative writing. The Puritan suspicion of non-religious literature, especially fiction, still lingered and regularly found support in unexpected corners. In an 1818 letter we find Thomas Jefferson complaining that reading fiction might well lead to 'a bloated imagination, sickly judgement, and disgust towards all the real business of life'. Novels rarely sold more than a few thousand copies. Moreover, when after the first decades of the nineteenth century the market especially for novels began to increase dramatically, the absence of international copyright laws became a serious problem. Novels by for instance the immensely popular Walter Scott were published at cut-throat prices while British publishers were free to publish pirated editions of American novels. To protect their work from being pirated American writers could try to publish their work first in Great Britain which also gave them copyright in the United Kingdom, at least until 1849 when English courts declared this maneuver invalid but by then, with 23 million relatively well-educated citizens, the American book market had left the British one behind.

From the 1830s onward there was a fast increasing – and largely male – audience for sensationalist novels that presented a whole range of threats – evil financiers, greedy industrialists, aristocratic foreigners, Catholic conspirators – to the nation's (white and Protestant) future. A bit later this sort of fiction was joined on the bestseller lists by so-called sentimental novels, usually featuring young women who, inspired by their deeply held faith, overcome a variety of circumstances to arrive at their place in life – usually involving a happy marriage. By the early 1850s, with bestsellers often selling well over 100,000 copies, American literature had far outgrown its uncertain beginnings and had become a thriving business. But not in every aspect: what is usually called 'serious' literature had not developed beyond a small niche market. Those writers of the 1840s and 1850s that for later generations would become central to the development of a national American literature – writers such as Edgar Allan Poe, Nathaniel Hawthorne, Herman Melville and Walt Whitman – had great difficulties in securing an audience that would support them as professional writers and predictably had icy things to say about the preferences of the American reading public. Ironically, some of their predecessors of the 1820s, to whom we will now turn, did a whole lot better in a much smaller market. The difference in public appeal between those earlier, equally canonical, writers and the great writers of the 1850s tells us much about the direction that the literature of the young republic would take.

Washington Irving

If Charles Borckden Brown's life had not been cut short by tuberculosis he would have witnessed how in the 1820s American writers, following his own modest success, began to find true international recognition. The first American writer to find a large readership outside his own country was Washington Irving (1783–1859), born and bred in New York City, who in 1802 started writing satirical pieces for his brother Peter's newspaper under a pseudonym, Jonathan Oldstyle, that showed a good deal of self-knowledge. A lifelong bachelor, after the traumatic experience of losing his young fiancée to tuberculosis, Irving tended to withdraw from the realities of his own time and to prefer an idealized past and its legends and traditions to the contemporary world of commerce and polemical politics for which he was temperamentally unsuited, even if he did serve as American ambassador to Spain (1842–46) and was also otherwise occasionally involved in politics.

Irving's literary career took off with his contributions to the *Salmagundi* papers (1807–8), a series of twenty satirical pamphlets that he published in collaboration with his brother William and with James Kirke Paulding (1778–1860) and in which he created the nickname Gotham for New York City. The following year Irving published a mock history of the earliest years of New York City, then called New Amsterdam, purportedly found among the papers of 'the late Diedrich Knickerbocker, an old gentleman, who was very curious in the Dutch history of the province'. *A History of New York from the Beginning of the World to the End of the Dutch*

Dynasty (1809) is not so much a history – Irving even gets most of the Dutch names wrong – as an entertaining series of satirical sketches of a society that in its self-satisfaction has lost touch with reality and that is led by an equally self-satisfied governor, in whom we recognize the then president Thomas Jefferson. Having acquired some fame, Irving traveled to Europe and stayed there, mostly in England, from 1815 to 1832. Europe's traditionality clearly suited him. In 1820 he published the two-volume *The Sketch-book of Geoffrey Crayon, Gent.*, using the pseudonym mentioned in the title.

Irving's pseudonym goes once again to the heart of the matter: *The Sketch-book* mostly presents pastel shade sketches of graceful living in England's Tudor mansions, of venerable traditions, of ancient and imposing monuments, and of other subjects that had caught Irving's nostalgic imagination, which had found encouragement in a meeting with Walter Scott, who had also drawn his attention to the German folktales that in the early nineteenth century had been collected by the brothers Grimm and others. Of the *Sketch-book*'s thirty-three pieces only four deal with America. But we mainly remember *The Sketch-book* because of two tales set in the United States, 'The Legend of Sleepy Hollow' and 'Rip Van Winkle'. Irving borrowed both tales from the German sources that Scott had called his attention to, but he very effectively Americanized them, creating the beginnings of a legendary American past. Both have at their heart the conflict between serene tradition and restless enterprise, between a harmony based on communitarian values and the competitiveness that results from individualism. In 'Legend' the Yankee schoolmaster Ichabod Crane comes to a Dutch-American village in the Hudson valley that contentedly still lives in colonial times. Crane, who has the lanky build and gangling limbs of the stereotypical Yankee, and who 'most firmly and potently' believes in Cotton Mather's *History of New England Witchcraft*, has an eye on a highly appetizing young girl, not least because she is heiress to vast and fertile farmlands. It's not that Crane sees himself as a future farmer: characteristically, he intends to sell off the farm after his future father-in-law's death and to use the proceeds to start a new life, preferably in business, further west. Making use of Crane's superstitious temperament, his local rival for the affections of the heiress concocts a fake apparition and permanently scares him off. The story ends with the suggestion that Crane, restless as ever, has become a lawyer, has then turned to politics and electioneering, and has – no doubt temporarily – ended as a judge.

In 'Rip Van Winkle' the eponymous main character, a notorious idler in a stolidly industrious and tranquil Hudson valley village, goes hunting in the mountains where he presumably falls asleep and dreams of the past, with larger-than-life Dutch colonists gravely playing a game of nine-pins. Waking up, Rip returns to his village, which he hardly recognizes. The 'quiet little Dutch inn of yore' has been replaced by '"The Union Hotel, by Jonathan Doolittle"', there is a whole new population characterized by 'a busy bustling, disputatious tone', there is an unfamiliar flag flying from a tall pole, and there is a new, equally unfamiliar portrait, titled 'General Washington', on the hotel sign. Rip has been asleep for twenty years, missed out on the Revolution, and has awoken to find himself a citizen of the new United States where there is no place for the 'drowsy tranquillity' of the past but where 'a lean, bilious-looking fellow, with his pockets full of handbills, [is] haranguing vehemently about rights of citizens – elections – members of congress – liberty'. Whereas in 'The Legend of Sleepy Hollow' the old order still was capable of resisting the predatory dynamism of the new, Yankee-dominated spirit, in 'Rip Van Winkle' that spirit has taken over, forever changing the character of the former colonies. The essays, sketches, and tales collected in *The Sketch-book* strongly suggest that Irving's sympathies are on the side of tradition and that he watched the direction that an increasingly populist American democracy was taking with the greatest misgivings, and not only because an idealized colonial order was fast disappearing. In 'Traits of Indian Character'

Irving comments on the way Native Americans are treated with the conclusion that '[p]osterity will either turn away with horror or incredulity from the tale, or blush with indignation at the inhumanity of their forefathers'.

Usually, however, Irving's critique of the populism and increasing commercialism of the time took the form of an idealization of those places where the modern spirit had not yet penetrated: the English countryside where the landed gentry carefully preserved its traditions – pictured with his usual elegance and mild ironies in *Bracebridge Hall* (1822) – or other picturesque places where a conservative gentleman could feel at ease (*Tales of a Traveller* [1824]). And then there was of course the past, not yet tainted by contemporary evils. Using original sources in Spanish libraries, Irving wrote *The Life and Voyages of Christopher Columbus* (1828), followed by other histories and by *The Alhambra* (1832), in which he retold Spanish folk stories. His interest in the more glorious moments of history would ultimately lead to a massive biography of George Washington, completed just before his death.

Having returned to the United States after seventeen years in Europe, Irving toured what at the time was the American West. His natural preference for sketches and stories – the short format – perfectly fit his purpose in the book that came out of that experience, *A Tour of the Prairies* (1835), but also in his account of the travels of others: *The Adventures of Captain Bonneville, U.S.A.* (1837). These travel books served to reaffirm his American identity – not uncontested after seventeen years abroad, an honorary degree from Oxford, and an obviously conservative disposition – while they also catered to a fast increasing European interest in all things American. And they find their place in an American tradition of travel writing that had earlier produced the brilliant and baroque *Travels through North and South Carolina, Georgia, East and West Florida* (1791) by the Quaker naturalist William Bartram (1739–1823) – with its famous description of an alligator fight – and the first accounts of the transcontinental expedition led by Meriwether Lewis and William Clark (1804–6), whose own journals would not be published until the twentieth century. Irving's *Tour*, although not very exciting in its genteel picture of the West, also points forward to more realistic books like *The Oregon Trail: Sketches of Prairie and Rocky-Mountain Life* (1847) by the historian Francis Parkman (1823–73) who does not flinch from the more unsavory aspects of Western life, but views them with a patrician disdain that we now feel is especially harsh in its negative judgments of Native American ways of life.

Stimulated by Irving, his brother-in-law and one-time collaborator Paulding wrote his own mock-history of the colonial period, *The Diverting History of John Bull and Brother Jonathan* (1812), but did not follow Irving in his admiration for England. Instead, he sought to present the pioneer as the all-American hero, as in his long poem *The Backwoodsman* (1818) or in his popular humorous play *The Lion of the West* (1830), which not too obliquely mythologized the frontiersman and politician Davy Crockett, who five years later, fighting for the independence of Texas, would add to his legend (and lose his life) in the battle of the Alamo. *The Lion*'s hero, Colonel Nimrod Wildfire, presents himself in the sort of colorful language and with the half-serious, half self-mocking hyperbole that would become a hallmark of frontier – especially southwest frontier – humor: 'My name is Nimrod Wildfire – half horse, half alligator and a touch of the airthquake – that's got the prettiest sister, fastest horse and ugliest dog in the District, and can out-run, out-jump, throw down, drag out and whip any man in all Kaintuck'. Paulding also transplanted Irving's landed gentry to America. In his *Letters from the South* (1817) he presented an agrarian, Jeffersonian South in the same anachronistic, harmonious and golden light with which Irving had pictured England's landowners. This romantic, idealized vision of the South would later, when because of its defense of slavery the South came under increasing pressure, become an important theme in Southern writing, via Irving's friend John Pendleton

Kennedy's *Swallow Barn* (1832), an episodic novel of life on a rather ramshackle but benevolently managed Virginia plantation that again owed much to Irving's sketches. Kennedy (1795–1870) would later, during the Civil War, support the Union, but his harmonious representation of life in the South would become a major theme in Southern writing.

Romantic sentiment

As Irving and especially his English readers well knew, his smooth and elegant prose style drew on that of Joseph Addison and Richard Steele's early eighteenth-century *Spectator* while his sensibility was deeply in tune with the nostalgic strain of European Romanticism. But Irving was only one of many American writers attracted by such an essentially sentimental vision. We find it especially in the poetry of the early decades of the nineteenth century. A good example, although sometimes on the stoical side, is the work of William Cullen Bryant (1794–1867), who succeeded Freneau as America's most prominent poet and would retain that distinction until Henry Wadsworth Longfellow, a poet whose work had a good deal of affinity with Bryant's poetry, would take over that role in the 1840s, when Bryant's poetical powers were clearly on the wane. Bryant's first collection, *Poems* (1821), immediately brought him international fame. When Bryant writes as a nature poet he offers loving descriptions, as in 'To a Fringed Gentian' (1829), of an American nature he intimately knows. His sensibility is vaguely religious and his mood is mostly meditative, hesitating between a stoic Neo-classicism and a melancholy Romanticism in a smoothly rolling blank verse that is very attractive but does not penetrate much beyond the surface, which is in fact what we would expect from a poet who believes that poetry should 'exclud[e] all that disgusts, all that tasks and fatigues the understanding'. His vision of the West's future in 'The Prairies' (1834) illustrates his views:

> From the ground
> Comes up the laugh of children, the soft voice
> Of maidens, and the sweet and solemn hymn
> Of Sabbath worshippers. The low of herds
> Blends with the rustling of the heavy grain
> Over the dark-brown furrows. All at once
> A fresher wind sweeps by, and breaks my dream,
> And I am in the wilderness alone.

Still, among the many poets writing in the sentimentally Romantic vein of the early nineteenth century, Bryant's work stands out for its technical skill and its relative restraint. These qualities are immediately apparent if we look at the work of for instance Lydia Huntley Sigourney (1791–1865), whose enormous and varied output made her one of the most popular antebellum writers and who exemplifies the surrender to sentiment that characterizes most of these poets, male and female. Like other women poets of the period, for instance Francis Sargent Osgood (1811–50), Sigourney dealt with love, faith, and death, as in her famous 'Death of an Infant' (1827). But her conservative and sentimental sensibility was also inspired by figurative deaths, such as the lost cause of the Native American, whose fate she laments with passive nostalgia:

> Ye say they all have passed away,
> That noble race and brave,
> That their light canoes have vanished
> From off the crested wave;

That 'mid the forests where they roamed
There rings no hunter shout,
But their name is on your waters,
Ye may not wash it out.

'Indian Names' (1834)

Very effective in its time, Sigourney's poetry, even if it is wholly in accordance with our own sentiments, as in her anti-slavery poems, strikes us as belabored and sentimental.

James Fenimore Cooper

The writer who most effectively adapted European formats to American circumstances, and in so doing created a truly American literature, was James Fenimore Cooper (1789–1851). Having started writing, according to family history (or myth), because of a bet with his wife, Cooper became a massively prolific author (thirty-two novels, travel books, social and political commentary, a history of the U.S. Navy) and the first American author to be lionized on the European Continent where his work would in the course of the nineteenth century find a number of bestselling imitators (such as the German writer Karl May). After a first feeble imitation of Jane Austen's novel of manners (*Precaution*, 1820), Cooper's second novel, *The Spy* (1821), transplanted to American soil Walter Scott's historical romance, in which imagined ordinary people play important roles in true historical events and mingle not only with their betters but even meet true historical heroes. *The Spy*, which is set during the American Revolution, is the first American novel to make of that revolution its central theme, and is still remarkable for its refusal to endorse everything that takes place in its hallowed name. In fact, some of the fiercest 'revolutionaries' are lawless marauders who exploit the chaotic circumstances, while there are Loyalist opponents of the revolution who are the soul of dignity. This trademark ambivalence returns in many of Cooper's novels. Although he was proud to be an American, Cooper's conservative and patrician leanings and, as the years went by, increasingly cantankerous temperament, made him more and more wary of what he saw as the excesses of American democracy. As the patrician John Effingham remarks, in *Home as Found* (1838), written after a seven-year period in Europe: 'In America, the gross mistake has been made of supposing, that, because the mass rules in a political sense, it has the right to be listened to and obeyed in all other matters – a practical deduction than can only lead, under the most favorable exercise of power, to a very humble mediocrity'.

But in spite of his conservative tendencies Cooper is also touched by the democratic spirit of Romanticism and his most memorable creation is a simple, virtually uneducated frontiersman, a hunter with the unlikely name of Natty Bumppo and the not much less unlikely nickname of Leatherstocking (based on his buckskin clothing). In *Home as Found* the narrator may tell us that 'the end of the affair exhibited human nature in its usual aspects of prevarication, untruth, contradiction, and inconsistency', clearly reflecting Cooper's conservative pessimism, but Bumppo manifests not a single one of these failings. In *The Pioneers* (1823), a historical novel (situated in 1793) which focuses on the pioneer settlement of Templeton – modeled upon Cooperstown in upstate New York which had been founded by Cooper's land-owning father – he is still a minor character who lives with an old Indian friend, Chingachgook, in a cabin in the woods. The novel juggles with land claims – of the dispossessed original Native American inhabitants, of a Loyalist victim of Revolutionary confiscation, of the current land owner, Judge Temple – and offers the mandatory comic element and love interest, but returns again and again to the disruptions and outright destruction wrought by the settlers, the pioneers of the title. Inevitably, Bumppo, who is well beyond middle age in this novel, comes into conflict with both the settlers and their new laws. But even though at one point Judge Temple, who represents the social order that imposes itself upon the wilderness, feels bound to jail him, Bumppo is the novel's conscience, unerringly uncovering the settlement's moral failures, as in the famous scene where the villagers wantonly slaughter thousands of migrating pigeons. Bumppo also stands solidly by his Indian friend, who is mostly a sorry figure even though in one scene he regains an impressive dignity. Three years later, in 1826, Cooper returned to his rather garrulous woodsman and his Indian companion in *The Last of the Mohicans* and now gives them a central role in a story woven around the historical siege, in the summer of 1757, of Fort William Henry – again in upper New York – a siege that presented one stage in the struggle for military supremacy in North America between Britain and France. Here Bumppo, called Hawkeye by his Indian companions, Chingachgook, and the latter's son Uncas, thwart the plans of the Huron Magua to abduct Alice and Cora Munro, the daughters of Fort William Henry's commander, who rather unwisely are on their way to join their father. After a number of gripping adventures the small company safely reaches the fort. However, after the British surrender, in the confusion of the retreat and an attack by the Hurons, Magua once again succeeds in abducting Cora. After more adventures he is finally cornered, with some allies, one of whom kills the hapless Cora. After Magua has killed Uncas, he himself, defiant to the last, is shot by Bumppo.

The Last of the Mohicans is Cooper's most famous novel and warrants a closer look. True to its romance format its characters are either without blemish or wholly given to evil, with the interesting exception of Magua. Cooper's Chingachgook and Uncas exhibit throughout the novel a natural dignity, even nobility, underscored by a total absence of unmanly impatience or curiosity. Although they are not averse to taking life, the moral sense of Cooper's Mohicans is beyond any doubt. As Bumppo puts it, 'nothing short of being a witness will cause me to think [...] that Chingachgook, there, will be condemned at the final day'. But even Magua, the villain of the novel, is not without redeeming features. He, too, has personal dignity and courage and is not wholly beyond good and evil. Cora is, in fact, (relatively) safe in his hands, as Bumppo tells a young British lieutenant: 'he who thinks that even a [Huron] would ill-treat a woman, unless it be to tomahawk her, knows nothing of Indian nature', adding a bit later that '[e]ven the [Huron] adores but the true and living God'. Magua is further exonerated when we learn that Cora's father, foolishly ignoring the offender's sense of dignity, has had Magua flogged for an offense committed under the influence of alcohol. 'Was it the fault of Le Renard that his head was not made of rock?' Magua, referring to himself, asks at one point. 'Who gave him the firewater? Who made him a villain? 'Twas the pale-faces, the people of your own color'. Bumppo can only agree: 'it is not to be denied, that the evil had been mainly done by men with the white skins'.

Yet, in spite of their deep sympathy for the Indians, both Bumppo and his creator cannot bring themselves to cross a certain line, that of racial purity. Throughout the novel Bumppo keeps referring to himself as 'a white man without a cross', that is, without Indian (or black) blood, even though he has learned his craft as a scout and hunter from Indian friends and prefers their company to that of white society. Consequently, he also watches with misgivings how Uncas (like Magua) gradually falls in love with the lovely dark-eyed Cora. In spite of his admiration and deep affection for his Native American friends, Bumppo can only see an alliance between Uncas and Cora in terms of miscegenation. He might have changed his views, however, if he had learned, as we have done earlier, that Cora has black blood. In any case, Uncas' death neatly fits the general tenor of this and other 'Indian' novels of the time, Cooper's later ones included, which is succinctly summarized by the ancient Delaware chief and prophet

Tamenund at the close of *The Last of the Mohicans*: 'The pale-faces are masters of the earth, and the time of the redmen has not yet come again'. Much as Cooper sympathizes with the plight of the Native American, he cannot help himself creating the impression that their forced removal from ancestral lands is simply their irrevocable destiny, a dictate of history that is beyond human intervention and for which, therefore, white expansionism cannot be held responsible.

Having completed *The Last of the Mohicans*, Cooper immediately started another Bumppo novel, *The Prairie* (1827), in which we find the hero, now alone and in his eighties, on the Western prairie. Bumppo, who has once again fled civilization and its constraints, is still perfectly in tune with his natural surroundings, equal to prairie fires and buffalo stampedes, and once again Indian violence is the result of displacement, a response to white aggression. At the end of the novel Bumppo dies, deeply mourned by his Indian friends. But Cooper's imagination could not let go of its own creation. In 1840 Bumppo and Chingachgook returned in *The Pathfinder*, which is set around 1750 and in which Bumppo, realizing that the woman he loves prefers another man, decides to spend the rest of his life in the woods. But Bumppo's vision of domestic bliss in a log cabin deep in the forests – combining the height of individualism with the social demands of marriage – is of course deeply unrealistic from the start. Finally, in 1841, we meet a still younger Bumppo in *The Deerslayer*, the novel which presents his initiation into Indian warfare and in which the first Indian he ever kills before actually dying magnanimously forgives him for being a better shot and also gives him a new name, changing 'Deerslayer', the name given him by the Delaware Indians who have partly raised him, into 'Hawkeye'. The deeply pastoral *The Deerslayer*, set in the 1740s, returns us to Lake Otsego, the scene of *The Pioneers*, but in this later novel still a pristine wilderness.

Cooper's presentation of the Indian as a noble savage owes a good deal to European Romanticism's idealization of the supposedly primitive but authentic 'other', although he also used sources such as the missionary John Heckewelder's *Narrative of the United Brethren among the Delaware and Mohegan Indians* (1820) and in his desire to be historically accurate even interviewed authoritative Native American informants. But his portrayal of the frontiersman as a rugged loner who steers by his own unerring moral compass is probably based upon wholly American sources such as *The Discovery, Settlement, and Present State of Kentucke* (1784) in which John Filson (1747?–1788) had offered a lively record of the exploits and explorations of the legendary scout Daniel Boone. In any case, the mythic status that Cooper's simple hunter acquires in these novels would attract a host of future writers and would even make him part of world literature, while Bumppo's intense reverence for his natural environment adds the idea of the wilderness – for the Puritans still a place of evil – to America's national identity.

In these so-called 'Leatherstocking novels' Cooper brilliantly captures the major tensions characterizing the first decades of the nineteenth century: the conflict between the patrician democracy that Cooper himself championed and the period's increasingly populist tendencies and competitive individualism, and the irony of an undoubtedly genuine admiration for the Native American, whose courage and stoicism are gradually embraced as emblematic for the nation as such, while that same nation simultaneously pursues policies that threaten the Native American's very existence, as in the forced relocation of the Cherokee nation, in 1837, from its homelands in Georgia to Oklahoma, which some 4,000 Cherokees paid for with their lives. But Cooper also creates myth, a powerful legend of doomed heroism that still speaks to us.

This is an astonishing feat for a man who in *Notions of the Americans, Picked Up by a Travelling Bachelor* (1828), which defends the Republic against its British critics, paradoxically remarks about his native country: 'There are no annals for the historian; no follies (beyond the most vulgar and commonplace) for the satirist; no manners for the dramatist; no obscure fictions for the writer of romance; no gross and hardy offences against decorum for the moralist [...]'. Practically all of Cooper's novels fly in the face of such novelistic pessimism. His years at sea led to nautical novels – a genre he invented – with exciting chases, dangerous squalls, and fierce gales (and naturally populated with the characters of romance: '"Honour forbids me to quit a ship that I command, while a plank of her is still afloat"', ringingly declares the 'Red Rover' of the novel of that title [1827]). The Puritan past, complete with gripping scenes of Indian warfare, turned out to be another perfect subject for the historical romance in *The Wept of Wish-Ton-Wish* (1829). In the first of the three so-called Littlepage Manuscripts, *Satanstoe* (1845), which deal with increasing tensions between landowners and renters in Dutch-American upstate New York, we have an astonishing sleigh race against death when the ice on the Hudson River begins to break up and drift. In spite of his stylistic shortcomings, Cooper is an expert story-teller and America, past and present, offers him an abundance of exciting stories.

Even his complaint about the absence of manners is unfounded. In his later work Cooper returns again and again to American manners, broadly defined. His years abroad (1826–33), largely spent in France, proved to be a watershed in his career. While *Notions of the Americans* had still modestly celebrated American democracy, *Home as Found* (1838), whose title speaks for itself, is sharply critical. Returning to the United States Cooper had found a self-declared 'high society' – complete with (pseudo-)literary hangers-on – with absurd pretensions, and a populist democracy that from his patrician perspective had unleashed the common American's worst instincts. Usually these common Americans are New Englanders who have left their native province to harass others with their often sneaky acquisitiveness, hypocrisy, and total disregard for social distinctions. We already have the type in *The Pioneers'* Hiram Doolittle and in *Home as Found* we have the rather vengefully named Aristabulus Bragg. The tension between Cooper's ideal of an admittedly paternalistic social harmony and the new ruthless competitiveness that he saw in a radically democratized America returns in practically all his later novels. 'All principles are swallowed up in the absorbing desire for gain', John Effingham – a descendant of two of the major characters of the still largely optimistic *The Pioneers* – declares in *Home as Found*. 'The desire to grow rich has seized on all classes. Even women and clergymen are infected'.

Cooper found in his personal past and in the past of the nation all those ingredients whose absence he lamented and used them to often great effect. Tellingly, the novels he situated in the European past, such as *The Heidenmauer* (1832), suffer in the comparison although even here Cooper is indirectly concerned with contemporary issues, critiquing the feudalist order and extolling the blessings of the democratic spirit. But Cooper's idea of democracy increasingly was at odds with that of his contemporaries who more and more resented his criticisms of what he saw as their shortcomings. In the end, the American reading public largely deserted him. But by that time Cooper had created an unmistakably national literature with unmistakably American themes.

Frontier women

Even in *The Pioneers*, where Cooper stays close to home, his presentation of the pioneer experience is more concerned with the larger social and moral issues involved in settling the American wilderness than with its domestic aspects, the day-to-day struggle of housekeeping and bringing up children in rough and often adverse circumstances. For such hardships we must turn to *A New Home – Who'll Follow?* (1839) by Caroline Kirkland (1801–64), a satirical look (under the pen name of Mary Clavers) at life in recently settled Michigan, directly based upon the author's personal experiences in a settlement founded by her husband. Although her neighbors were not amused by what she called 'crayon-sketches of life and manners in the remoter parts of Michigan', she continued her sketches of western life in *A Forest Life* (1842) and *Western Clearings* (1845). We find a similar realism, again tempered by a love of pristine nature, in *Life in Prairie Land* (1846) by Eliza Farnham (1815–64), which looks back on the five years she lived in early Illinois. Yet life in the West also allowed Kirkland and Farnham a freedom that in an urban environment, where the lives of middle-class women were dictated by stifling convention, would not have been possible. Paradoxically, in bringing civilization to their new homes, they also helped reintroduce the conventions whose absence they found so refreshing and which they themselves were perfectly able to resist: Kirkland was active in the anti-slavery movement and championed the position of women (even convicted women) and Farnham was likewise active in promoting women's rights. A third female writer, Alice Cary (1820–71), offered in *Clovernook; Or, Recollections of Our Neighborhood in the West* (1851) a more romanticized view of rural life in southwest Ohio, but she, too, has an eye for domestic hardship. Wholly uninterested in mythologizing or glorifying the settling of the land, and temperamentally at odds with the anarchic, macho forces celebrated by the male writers of the Old Southwest that will be discussed below, these female writers of the Old Northwest bring us as near as we can get to the authentic frontier experience.

In Cooper's tracks

Cooper had not been the first to see the fictional possibilities offered by Native Americans. In 1822, for instance, John Neal (1793–1876) had published his *Logan, A Family History*, a baroque and breathlessly romantic – 'this Indian patriarch, this Indian prince' – fictionalization of the life and times of a historic Indian chief, famous for a speech read during negotiations, in 1774, with colonial forces after the murder of part of his family by white settlers ('Who is there to mourn for Logan? Not one'). And in 1824 the very young Lydia Maria Child (1802–80), who would become one of the most influential writers of the antebellum period, had published *Hobomok: A Tale of Early Times*, which daringly presents a marriage between a white woman and a Wampanoag Indian. Predictably, the novel drew sharp criticism – even though the marriage is set in colonial times, and even though it is dissolved after the woman's first husband, presumed dead, turns up again. Child's life-long sympathy for the Native American case and her insight into the psychological mechanisms of displacement show clearly in one of her later *Letters from New York*: 'We who have robbed the Indians of their lands, and worse still, of *themselves*, are very fond of proving their inferiority' (1843).

But it was the immense popularity of *The Last of the Mohicans* that truly pointed the way for other American writers. Only one year after its publication Catherine Maria Sedgwick (1789–1867), having read Cooper's book, published her own 'Indian' novel, *Hope Leslie; or, Early Times in the Massachusetts* (1827), after she had earlier (in *A New-England Tale* [1822] and *Redwood* [1824]) written rather conventional contemporary romances. *Hope Leslie* takes us back to seventeenth-century New England, to the Pequot War of 1637, and makes clever use of Puritan accounts of that war like Bradford's *Of Plymouth Plantation* and William Hubbard's *The Present State of New England, Being a Narrative of the Troubles with the Indians in New-England*, originally published in 1677. In *Hope Leslie*, stripped of its Puritan interpretation, the massacre of the Pequot people, women and children included, appears in all its murderous callousness. Like many of Cooper's hostile Indians, Sedgwick's Indian chief has turned against the colonists because of grievances that are far from imaginary and that include the beheading of his son.

And as in Cooper we have genuine affection crossing racial divides, and not only between the chief's daughter Magawisca and Hope Leslie. But the possibility, offered by the complicated plot, of a marriage between Magawisca and a young Puritan never materializes, even though, in Pocahontas fashion, she physically intervenes when her father threatens to kill him and loses an arm in the process. Here, too, dispossession is ultimately viewed as a historical inevitability, as the fulfillment of destiny, and not as the result of calculated acts of expansionism. Sedgwick differs from Cooper in her presentation of strong, capable, and courageous women and in her emphasis on the role such women have to play in the New World, but like him can only envision a white, protestant American republic.

That is, not surprisingly, the case with all writers who in Cooper's tracks deal with the tensions between the republic's citizens and North America's native population. In *The Yemassee, A Romance of Carolina* (1835) by William Gilmore Simms (1806–70), often called a Southern Cooper, the author obviously sympathizes with the plight of Sanutee, a noble and proud chief of the Yemassee Indians in early eighteenth-century South Carolina, who sees himself forced to resist the never-ending land-grabbing by English colonists. For Simms, whom Edgar Allan Poe in 1845 with some exaggeration called 'immeasurably the greatest writer of fiction in America', that resistance is ultimately futile because it goes against the course of history. It is worth pointing out, in anticipation of things to come, that Simms, a slave-owner, was far less concerned with the fate of African Americans, whose lot was gradually becoming a national issue. *The Yemassee* is also a defense of slavery to the point that the slave Hector refuses his master's offer of freedom after he has saved the latter's life because he cannot envision a life without his master and expects the worst without him. Simms's defense of slavery in both his frontier romances and his more realistic historical novels ultimately alienated his mainly Northern readers – especially after he published *The Sword and the Distaff* (1852; retitled *Woodcraft* in 1854), his 'response' to Harriet Beecher Stowe's *Uncle Tom's Cabin* of 1851–52.

While Simms followed Cooper in his largely sympathetic portrait of Native Americans, Robert Montgomery Bird (1806–54), outraged at what he saw as Cooper's soft treatment of Native Americans, portrayed them as treacherous and bloodthirsty savages. In his most famous novel, *Nick of the Woods; or, The Jibbenainosay* (1837), which is set in Kentucky, Shawnee Indians murder the wife and five children of Nathan Slaughter, a Quaker, and leave Slaughter himself for dead. Abandoning his pacifism after his recovery, the aptly named Slaughter begins a secret second life as the 'Nick' of the title, systematically killing every Indian he meets. Bird's novel was an immense success – like his play *The Gladiator* (1831) which was performed over a thousand times during his own life-time – and strongly influenced the representation of Native Americans in the sensationalist so-called 'dime novels'; one of the very first – Edward Ellis's *Seth Jones; or, The Captives of the Frontier* (1860) – sold over 600,000 copies. In its character Ralph Stackpole, an astonishingly incompetent horse thief, *Nick of the Woods*, too, gives us a glimpse of that frontier hyperbole that especially in the old Southwest developed into a sort of subgenre: '"H'yar, you [...] 'tater-headed paintfaces! [...] you bald-head, smoke-dried, punkin-eating redskins! [...] Git up and show your scalplocks; for 'tarnal death to me, I'm the man to take 'em – cock-a-doodle-doo!' Although not a Southerner – he spent most of his life in Philadelphia – Bird defended slavery, in for instance the curious novel *Sheppard Lee* (1836), whose protagonist dies and then discovers that he has the amazing power to bring to life again and inhabit the bodies of others who have recently died. (Perhaps not accidentally, Edgar Allan Poe, who reviewed the novel, would some years later make the idea of metempsychosis central to his story 'Ligeia'.) Although not blind to slavery's dark side, Bird sees its abolition, like the continued presence of Native Americans, as a threat to the Republic.

Native American voices

Needless to say that Native Americans, as far as they were aware of it, did not relish the way they were treated in novels by Bird and others. But the way they were treated in the actual world was far worse, in spite of the Northwest Ordinance Act of 1787 that had promised that 'The utmost good faith shall always be observed toward the Indians, their lands and property shall never be taken from them without their consent' and other, similar statements, such as Thomas Jefferson's ringing declaration that 'The sacredness of [the Indians'] rights is felt by all thinking persons in America as much as in Europe' (1786). 'I would ask you if you would like to be disenfranchised from all your rights, merely because your skin is white, and for no other crime', William Apess (1798–1839), a Native American from Massachusetts asked his white readers in 'An Indian's Looking-Glass for the White Man' (1833). A Christian himself, Apess argued that the Republic's treatment of the Native American nations mocked the basic principles of Christianity. In the same year the Sauk chief Black Hawk (1767?–1838) complained bitterly in his autobiography that his own and other Indians' ignorance of white ways was criminally exploited: 'What do we know of the manner of the laws and customs of the white people? They might buy our bodies for dissection, and we would touch the goose quill to confirm it, without knowing what we are doing. This was the case with myself […] in touching the goose quill the first time'. But those Native Americans who were perfectly aware of white ways did not fare any better. Like Apess, Elias Boudinot (1804?–39; Native name Gallegina Uwati), a Cherokee from Georgia, was introduced to Christianity at school. Assimilating a good deal of white American culture he went on to become the first editor of the *Cherokee Phoenix*, the first Native American newspaper, printed in English and Cherokee, in which he himself eloquently argued that he and his people – and 'all the Indians' – were 'as capable of improvement in mind as any other people'. But to no avail. President Jackson's Indian Removal Act of 1830 had unleashed forces that even total assimilation would not have stopped and Boudinot ended with what was left of the Cherokee Nation in Oklahoma, where he was killed for his complicity in the tragedy.

Naturally, the literary energy of Native Americans was first of all mobilized to voice their grievances and for political purposes. But they also began to contribute to imaginative literature. Jane Johnston Schoolcraft (1800–41; Native name Woman of the Stars Rushing Through the Sky), of Ojibwe/Irish parentage, had some years earlier started writing poetry in both English and her native language, the first Native American writer to do so. Schoolcraft's poetry largely follows the conventions of her time, as in her poems on the death of her infant son:

> And when May in her bloom
> A soft verdure shall bring
> I shall deck thy loved tomb
> With the flowrets of Spring

'Elegy' (1827?)

But her translations of Indian songs and her renderings of Native tales give us a glimpse of a highly imaginative Native culture. By contrast, John Rollin Ridge (1827–67), like Boudinot a Cherokee (Native name Yellow Bird) and the first Native American novelist, decided to go with mainstream culture and published a novel, *The Life and Adventures of Joaquin Murieta: The Celebrated California Bandit* (1854), that perfectly fits the sensationalist mold that would become popular in the 1830s – the novel is said to have inspired the *Zorro* stories – even if it is critical of the racially motivated disdain with which its white characters look upon their Spanish-speaking fellow-Californians.

Southwest humor

The Native American culture that we find in the writings of Jane Schoolcraft would have been wholly wasted on Ralph Stackpole of *Nick of the Woods* and similar backwoods characters who became increasingly popular in the decades before the Civil War. This popularity starts with newspaper stories about real-life characters, like the Ohio and Mississippi boatman Mike Fink (1770?–1823?) and the frontiersman and Member of Congress Davy Crockett, who probably appealed to the public imagination because of the radically democratic, anti-authoritarian energy they represented. Stories and tall tales about Fink, Crockett, and others, even if they had an ironic edge, seemed to confirm that nothing would curb, let alone stop, American energy and ingenuity. Especially the so-called Old Southwest produced a number of memorable if not exactly loveable imaginary characters. Usually considered humorous, many of the stories in which they appear depend first of all on their rhetorical verve and present callous tricks, aggressive acts, pointless but admittedly colorful boasting, and a generally macho ethos. The first Southwest author to find a national audience was Augustus Baldwin Longstreet (1790–1870), whose *Georgia Scenes, Characters, Incidents, &c. in the First Half Century of the Republic* (1835) is the most civil and the most realistic work of Southwest humor. Even so, its author, a respectable journalist in Augusta, Georgia, preferred to be known as 'A Native Georgian'. *The Adventures of Simon Suggs, Late of the Tallapoosa Volunteers* (1845) by Johnson Jones Hooper (1815–62) is a good deal less attractive. Suggs lies, cheats, and more generally follows his own maxim 'it is good to be shifty in a new country' in a number of chronologically arranged stories. T.B. Thorpe (1815–78), whose 'The Big Bear of Arkansas' (1841) is probably the most famous example of Southwest frontier humor, is milder and far more ironical, with his narrator/hunter, who initially bursts with the usual self-confidence, ultimately admitting a sort of defeat. The last of the Old Southwest humorists was George Washington Harris (1814–69), a former Tennessee River steamboat captain, whose *Sut Lovingood: Yarns Spun by a 'Nat'ral Born Burn'd Fool'* (1867; first story 1843) is told with much energy in almost impenetrable dialect. Like all Old Southwest characters Lovingood has a sound contempt for authority – both worldly and religious – and expends a good deal of ingenuity in harassing or humiliating its representatives. If the intention of these Southwest humorists was to highlight the distinctive characteristics of their own region and its inhabitants – Georgia in Longstreet's case; Alabama in Hooper's; Louisiana and Arkansas in Thorpe's; and Tennessee in Harris's – they cannot be said to have succeeded. What emerges from their work is a fairly uniform picture of an anarchic frontier in which shooting, drinking, and fighting (not to mention bragging) would appear to be the most popular pastimes. However, since its narrators usually possess great verbal ingenuity and even more verbal energy we may deplore their moral shortcomings and still admire their narrative panache – as we may do with Jason Compson in *The Sound and the Fury* (1929) by William Faulkner, who not accidentally is on record expressing his admiration for Harris's Lovingood.

The South

Apart from these humorists and William Gilmore Simms, the American South did not, in the first decades of the nineteenth century, produce many writers that we still remember. To a large extent, this is due to the fact that slavery had become a source of serious political tension – temporarily eased by the so-called Missouri Compromise of 1820, but fanned again by the ever-increasing activity and vociferousness of Northern abolitionists, especially after in 1831 the fierce abolitionist William Lloyd Garrison (1805–79) had started publishing his weekly newspaper *The Liberator*, in which he insistently kept on calling for total and immediate liberation of all slaves, an alarming specter for practically all Southerners since it would destroy the South's economy. As a result, the South increasingly closed its ranks and moderate Southern writers, caught in conflicting loyalties, fell silent. Other writers rallied behind the Southern cause and began to create a vision of a mythic South that was wholly at odds with the essentially egalitarian self-image of Puritan (and post-Puritan) New England. We see how even in the titles of historical romances like *The Cavaliers of Virginia* (1835) and *The Knights of the Golden Horse-Shoe* (1841) by William Alexander Caruthers (1802–46) Southern writers, inspired by the world depicted in Walter Scott's *Waverley* novels, begin to promote the South as a benevolently feudal society. This society is led by natural aristocrats – the 'cavaliers' and 'knights' (the planter class) of Caruthers' titles – and served by a slave-population that is fully aware of its inability to take care of itself and that is therefore most of all grateful to its generous and humane masters. This absurd view of the South was readily embraced by its flattered planter class and so Southern writers sacrificed complexity and depth and sought safety in stereotypes and in rehearsing the same old arguments in favor of slavery. Again and again the issue of slavery enters their romances – as in Kennedy's *Swallow Barn* – in the guise of a discussion between a well-intentioned but ignorant visitor from the North and an enlightened slave owner who is fully prepared to agree that slavery is wrong, in principle, but argues that for practical reasons emancipation is not yet a realistic option. Later, when the tone of the debate over slavery hardened and became ever more radical, Southern writers usually felt compelled to defend the institution of slavery as such, especially after the Fugitive Slave Act of 1850, which made it a criminal offense for Northerners to help escaped slaves.

Edgar Allan Poe

The one Southern writer who kept resolutely aloof from the political debates of the period and followed his own artistic preferences was Edgar Allan Poe (1809–49). For Poe, born in Boston, but raised by his foster parents (the Allans) in Richmond, Virginia – and from 1815 to 1820 in England – regional loyalty was irrelevant. In fact, even national loyalty was a doubtful matter. 'That an American should confine himself to American themes, or even prefer them, is rather a political idea than a literary idea', he wrote in 1845. We can therefore not really classify him as a Southern writer and the recurring themes of his poetry, his short stories and his one short novel – *The Narrative of Arthur Gordon Pym* (1838) – have an at best tenuous link with America and are deeply influenced by European Romanticism and European Gothic themes and motifs. Much of his work is actually set in Europe. But he was most certainly deeply involved in the American literary scene, fiercely defending his own conception of aesthetics, pouring out often acerbic reviews, and working tirelessly, and successfully, to improve both the quality and the circulation of the literary magazines he edited. But his private life was never stable, a situation exacerbated by a serious drinking problem and an abrasiveness which repeatedly caused him to be fired, and in his desperate attempts to keep creditors from his door he turned out a good deal of work that falls short of his own standards, or that at least is open to accusations of mercenary rather than aesthetic intentions – perhaps not a deadly sin for a struggling professional author, but certainly a practice that Poe himself mercilessly attacked.

For Poe, all elements in a poem or story – its theme, mode of narration, locale, narrated events – should work together to achieve a single effect. That effect is more lasting if it leaves the reader with a sense of awe that is not easily dissolved. In his best stories Poe relies on symbolism, pervasive ambiguity and other suggestive strategies to maneuver his readers into the desired frame of mind. In 'William Wilson' (1839), the narrator meets at an English boarding school a double, born on the same day, bearing the same name, who is in all respects his superior. Curiously, the astonishing resemblance between the two boys is only noted by the narrator himself. After school he keeps running into his double, who again and again saves him from serious trouble or interferes on his behalf. Finally, exasperated, the narrator, who has come to hate himself for his evil proclivities, corners his double and kills him. '{T}hou hast murdered thyself', are the double's last words. 'I could have fancied that I myself was speaking', the narrator tells us. In 'The Fall of the House of Usher' (1839) the narrator goes to visit his sick friend Roderick Usher in the latter's lonely and isolated ancestral mansion. Usher's highly nervous behavior is perplexing and goes from bad to worse when his twin sister Madeline dies. During a storm Madeline reappears, apparently not so dead after all, but freeing herself from her tomb has been her last effort: she collapses and dies, and Roderick succumbs with her. Looking over his shoulder when riding off to the civilized world, the narrator sees how the Usher mansion collapses and disappears into the tarn on whose bank it stands. In again another story, 'Ligeia' (1838), which again is situated in Europe, the perfect and much beloved wife of the narrator dies. Having overcome his grief – although Ligeia can never be replaced – he marries the Lady Rowena, who with her fair hair is the opposite of the 'raven-haired' Ligeia. Not long after the marriage, Rowena falls ill and dies – or seems to die, because after a brief spell her body comes to life again. Not as Rowena, however, but as Ligeia, whose ghost may actually have poisoned her.

We never really know how to interpret these and other stories because Poe very skillfully creates the possibility that what we witness may be the internal psychological dramas of their narrators. Poe himself claimed that his terror was not of Germany – that is, Gothic – but of the soul, in other words, psychological. It is certainly the case that he was deeply interested in abnormal states of mind. In such stories as 'The Tell-Tale Heart' (1843), 'The Black Cat' (1843), and 'The Cask of Amontillado' (1846) we have narrators who commit gruesome murders and acts of outright sadism and whom we would now qualify as psychopaths or madmen. But it is hard to say to what extent Poe was here motivated by his aesthetic principles and to what extent he was catering to the American public's increasing taste for violence, horror, and other forms of sensation, stimulated by the cheap press of the period. The same goes for *The Narrative of Arthur Gordon Pym*, a sensational and deeply implausible tale of nautical adventure and 'horrid sufferings'.

It is not surprising, then, that there is very little agreement on the merits and meaning of Poe's work. But there is no denying his professionalism, his craftsmanship, or, for that matter, his inventiveness. Poe may for instance be considered the inventor of the detective story that is based on rational deduction. In such tales as 'The Murders of the Rue Morgue' (1841) and 'The Mystery of Marie Rôget' (1842) he created a format – featuring a detective of astonishing intellect and his more dim-witted friend who narrates the story – that would later be copied by such stellar writers of detective fiction as Arthur Conan Doyle (Sherlock Holmes and Dr Watson) and Agatha Christie (Hercule Poirot and Captain Hastings). For Poe himself poetry, which unfortunately for him was less lucrative than his stories, was the most important literary genre. The unity of effect that for him was the hallmark of true literature – and that required the reader to read a poem or tale in one sitting – was easier to achieve in a genre that allowed the author to stay away from the world's specifics and to manipulate mood and symbol in vaguely suggestive ways. For Poe real poetry 'elevat[ed] the soul', freeing the reader temporarily from mundane concerns. Whereas early in his career poetry was supposed to achieve that goal through 'indefiniteness', later, in 1846, he argues in 'The Philosophy of Composition' that 'the death [...] of a beautiful woman is, unquestionably, the most poetical topic in the world'. Beauty and death had fascinated Poe from the beginning, leading to poems dealing with ruin and romantic decay. His position in 'The Philosophy', however, should perhaps not be taken all that seriously. It appears, after all, in a detailed, and probably not too trustworthy, account of the composition of his most famous poem, 'The Raven' (1845), which indeed deals with the grief occasioned by the death of a 'radiant' woman:

> Ah, distinctly I remember it was in the bleak December,
> And each separate dying ember wrought its ghost upon the floor.
> Eagerly I wished the morrow; – vainly I had tried to borrow
> From my books surcease of sorrow – sorrow for the lost Lenore–
> For the rare and radiant maiden whom the angels name Lenore–
> Nameless here for evermore.

'The Raven' is rather melodramatic – good for reading aloud – but perfectly demonstrates Poe's facility with words (although it contains such tortured lines as 'Much I marveled this ungainly fowl to hear discourse so plainly'). Usually, however, Poe's poetry is less concrete than 'The Raven' and offers images and symbols that, as Poe himself put it, are 'seen only as a shadow or by suggestive glimpses' as in 'The City by the Sea' (1845, first published in 1831):

> There shrines and palaces and towers
> (Time-eaten towers that tremble not!)
> Resemble nothing that is ours.

Poetry should only present an 'under current, however indefinite of meaning'. Its worst sins are didacticism or an '*excess* of the suggested meaning', the sort of excess that 'turns into prose (and that of the flattest kind) the so called poetry of the so called transcendentalists' ('Philosophy'). The most important of these 'transcendentalists', Ralph Waldo Emerson, returned the compliment by calling Poe 'the jingle man', a not wholly inappropriate qualification, given the insistent rhyme and meter of for instance 'The Raven' or 'Annabel Lee' ('For the moon never beams, without bringing me dreams / Of the beautiful ANNABEL LEE; / And the stars never rise, but I feel the bright eyes / Of the beautiful ANNABEL LEE' [1849]). Poe had no affinity with the religio-philosophical movement that Emerson stood for. Shortly before his death, in 1848, he published his own views on the universe and man's relation to the supernatural in the lengthy *Eureka: A Prose Poem*, which not very successfully tries to integrate poetry, philosophy, and the latest scientific discoveries into a unified metaphysical vision.

A controversial and only occasionally appreciated writer in his own time and country, Poe would become a celebrity in Europe. Twenty years after his death, 'The Raven' had been translated into French (by the famous poet Charles Baudelaire), German, Dutch, and other languages. And so Emerson's 'jingle man' became an important forerunner of European Symbolism and, indirectly, of European Modernist poetry.

The Fireside poets

Although Poe's poetry was not without its admirers, the poets that would dominate American anthologies of poetry until the end of the nineteenth century were the so-called 'Fireside' or 'Schoolroom' poets, in the familiar company of William Cullen Bryant, to whom the most prominent Fireside poet, Henry Wadsworth Longfellow – the nick-name was taken from his collection *The Seaside and the Fireside* (1850) – was clearly indebted. Longfellow (1807–82) wrote a travel book (*Outre-Mer*, 1835) and prose romances (*Hyperion*, 1839) but his astonishing popularity rested on his short lyrical poems and more in particular on his long and grandiloquent narrative ones. *Evangeline, A Tale of Acadie* (1847), his first narrative poem, is a tragic love story in unrhymed dactylic hexameters against the background of the forced displacement, between 1755 and 1763, of some 10,000 French-speaking inhabitants of Acadia (now Nova Scotia). The sonorous lines of its prologue roll on, with the stately melancholy that characterizes much of his poetry:

> This is the forest primeval; but where are the hearts that beneath it
> Leaped like the roe, when he hears in the woodland the voice of the huntsman?
> Where is the thatch-roof village, the home of Acadian farmers,–
> Men whose lives glided on like rivers that water the woodlands,
> Darkened by shadows of earth, but reflecting an image of heaven?
> Waste are those pleasant farms, and the farmers forever departed!

Hiawatha (1855), which except for its hero's endorsement of Christianity was very loosely based on Ojibwa myth (as mediated by Henry Rowe Schoolcraft, Jane Schoolcraft's husband), sold 50,000 copies in the two years after publication. *The Courtship of Miles Standish* (1858) was even more successful, selling hugely in England, where Queen Victoria received him in a private audience and where, after his death, his bust was placed in Westminster Abbey's Poet's Corner, an unprecedented honor for a poet who was not a British citizen. But Longfellow's conscious attempts to create American epics were too indebted to European forms and too concerned with things long gone to capture the essence of the nation: its entrepreneurial dynamism and its unbridled optimism.

Longfellow had a cosmopolitan interest in foreign literatures and in the metrical and formal variety that they offered. Thematically, however, there is a good deal of unity in his work, that usually looks wistfully back on the passage of time, ignoring the admonition of his own 'A Psalm of Life' (1838): 'Let us then be up and doing, / With a heart for any fate; / Still achieving, still pursuing, / Learn to labor and to wait'. Far more often we find the poet looking backward: 'We spake of many a vanished scene, / Of what we once thought and said, / Of what had been, and might have been, / And who was changed, and who was dead' ('The Fire of Driftwood'). The same meditative backwards glance informs 'The Jewish Cemetery at Newport' (1854), 'My Lost Youth' (1855), and many other poems. There is more force in the anti-slavery poems of *Poems on Slavery* (1842), a publication that earned Longfellow substantial criticism from his contemporaries, but he never packs the punch of for instance John Greenleaf Whittier (1807–92) in the latter's 'The Hunters of Men' (1835):

> Oh! Goodly and grand is our hunting to see,
> In this 'land of the brave and the home of the free',
> Priest, warrior, and statesman, from Georgia to Maine,
> All mounting the saddle – all grasping the rein –
> Right merrily hunting the black man, whose sin
> Is the curl of his hair and the hue of his skin!

Although he did initially not belong to the debonair, cosmopolitan Fireside group – he was a Quaker from rural Massachusetts and an early and active abolitionist, publishing a large number of fiery abolitionist poems (*Poems*, 1838) – Whittier later in life came closer to Longfellow and the Fireside, as in his long 'Snow-Bound: A Winter Idyl' of 1866 in which he too looks back upon his younger years but with less of Longfellow's resignation:

> What matter how the night behaved?
> What matter how the north-wind raved?
> Blow high, blow low, not all its snow
> Could quench our hearth-fire's ruddy glow.
> O Time and Change! – with hair as gray
> As was my sire's that winter day,
> How strange it seems, with so much gone
> Of love and life, to still live on!

Longfellow and Whittier are the Fireside poets whose work is still anthologized. Their once almost equally famous colleagues James Russell Lowell (1819–91) and Oliver Wendell Holmes (1809–94), like Longfellow members of distinguished New England families, have fared less well. Holmes's accomplished light verse and his equally sanguine sketches and short pieces – collected in *The Autocrat at the Breakfast-Table* (1858) and numerous other publications – confirm his reputation as a witty conversationalist and reflect his rational, ironic, and patrician stance, while his more serious but far less successful fiction – *Elsie Venner* (1861) and other novels – reflects his professorship in Harvard's medical school and his interest in abnormal psychology. Lowell also contributed to the group's name with one of his titles, *Fireside Travels* (1864). He was, like Holmes, at his best in witty, satirical poems, such as the anonymously published book-length *A Fable for Critics* (1848) in which he takes the measure of contemporary American writers. Poe, called 'three-fifths genius [...] and two-fifths sheer fudge', was not amused, and retaliated in a review ('no failure was ever more complete or more pitiable'). *A Fable* is on the whole rather even-handed in its distribution of criticism and praise (with Lowell quite correctly accusing himself of didacticism and moralizing). Lowell's most important contribution to American literature, however, is his *The Biglow Papers* (first series collected in 1848, second in 1867). In these *Papers* Lowell presents letters by the young Yankee farmer Hosea Biglow and his friend Birdofredom Sawin, purportedly edited by Pastor Homer Wilbur. Together, the letters of the first series constitute a fierce attack on the war with Mexico of 1846. Sawin, who serves as a private in the 'Massachusetts Regiment', does so because he has fallen for the propagandists of 'Manifest Destiny', a term probably coined and in any case used in 1845 by the journalist John Louis O'Sullivan to describe the widespread belief of the time that the United States were entrusted with a divinely ordained mission to spread the blessings of democracy to the Pacific coast. But Sawin's eagerness to bring American freedom to what is Mexican and Native American territory is soon dampened by the realities of war: 'Nimepunce a day fer killin' folks comes kind o' low fer murder'. Lowell's contemporary status may be measured by the honorary doctorates he received from the universities of Oxford and Cambridge, but posterity has not shared their enthusiasm for his work.

Sensationalist fiction

For a number of Poe's contemporaries the terror they sought to evoke undoubtedly was first of all Gothic, even if it also served political ends. Beginning in the 1830s and much boosted by the enormous success of the French writer Eugène Sue's *Mystères de Paris* (1842–43), American writers began to produce so-called sensationalist fiction, aiming at the fast growing market for popular reading, a market that kept expanding because of America's ever-growing population, and even more because of the cheaper prices made possible by lower printing costs. The perceived threat to the nation's Protestant character through Catholic conspiracy was sensationalized in such novels as *Six Months in a Convent* (1835) by Rebecca Theresa Reed (1813?– ?), who claimed to describe her own terrible experiences in an Ursuline convent school, and by Maria Monk (1816–49) in her *Awful Disclosures of Maria Monk; or, The Hidden Secrets of a Nun's Life in a Nunnery Explored* (1836). Monk claimed actually to have been a nun and to have suffered sadism, sexual exploitation and other horrors. Amazingly, Monk's wild and obviously spurious tale would sell 300,000 copies in the next twenty-five years.

More serious, although not much less sensational, was *The Quaker City; or, The Monks of Monk Hall* (1844) by George Lippard (1822–54), who dedicated his novel to his fellow Philadelphian Charles Brockden Brown. In *The Quaker City*, too, the American nation is under threat. Not, however, from depraved Catholics, but from its own elite: its bankers, merchants, industrialists, even preachers, who have abandoned the principles of the Founders and given themselves over to greed, corruption, and, of course, unspeakable practices. Sexual violation, always involving innocent girls, is never far away in sensationalist fiction. Fortunately, there is something sinisterly foreign about these miscreants and none of them reflects the true American spirit, which Lippard associates with the country rather than with the corrupted urban environment he depicts in great detail. Lippard continued what he regarded as his exposure of America's morally bankrupt elite in such novels as *Empire City* (1849) and *New York: Its Upper Ten and Lower Million* (1853), in which he dissected New York City. But he was by no means anti-American, as his enthusiastic support for the Mexican War in *Legends of Mexico* (1847) and *Bel of Prairie Eden* (1848) and his historical novels of the Revolution clearly show. He saw his fiction as social commentary, as part of a crusade for social change. So did George Thompson (1823–?) whose *Venus in Boston* of 1849 moved Lippard's attack on the elite to Boston. As Thompson's titles suggest – another one is *The Gay Girls of New York* (1853) – one of his major themes was sexual license and he is, given the period's prudishness, as explicit as circumstances permitted. Other writers of sensationalist fiction were not necessarily committed to social improvement. The most successful of them, the rather unsavory Ned Buntline (1822 or 1823–86; real name Edward Judson), who gave William Cody the nickname Buffalo Bill, had pro-slavery sympathies and made no secret of his main motivation: earning money. *The Mysteries and Miseries of New York* (1848), its sequel *The B'hoys of New York* (1850), and most of his other novels offer a panorama of gambling, theft, murder, and prostitution that in spite of the moralizing asides is first of all presented as titillating entertainment. Rather ironically, because all these writers profess to see urban life as a threat to the nation's moral health, their style reflects the frenetic pace of city life. Because their work was usually serialized before appearing in book form it tends to be episodic and to move from one point of maximum suspense to the next with a cavalier disregard for plausibility.

After the 1850s, with printing again made cheaper by new innovations, the role of the sensationalist novel would be taken over by a new format, the dime novel, which right from the start was enormously successful. The dime novel largely abandoned the theme of urban vice and corruption and revived the heroism of Western exploration, as in *Malaeska: The Indian Wife of the White Hunter* (1860) by Ann Sophia Stephens (1810–86), the first ever dime novel to appear (in the *Beadle's Dime Novels* series) and a reissue of a story she had published in 1839. Stephens had in the 1850s written novels like *Fashion and Famine* (1854) which combined exciting, melodramatic plots with social criticism and was no stranger to sensation. She would remain the only woman writer to contribute to the dime novel – writing *Almo's Plot; or, The Governor's Indian Child* (1863) and five other stories – which is perhaps not surprising given the exaggerated masculinity and the accompanying sense of white supremacy that the format as a whole projects.

Emerson and Transcendentalism

By the time that Poe's work caught the attention of European writers, his *bête noire* Ralph Waldo Emerson (1803–82) had already made a – modest – name for himself in Europe. His essays had been well-received in England, had been translated into German and French (*Essais de philosophie américaine*, 1851) and had been discussed in a leading Dutch periodical, with the reviewer classifying him with the great French essayist Montaigne as an essentially unclassifiable philosopher: 'It is very much the question whether the history of philosophy will ever be able to classify and categorize him […]. Emerson has wholly emancipated himself from the traditions and terminology of [classical] philosophy; he completely abandons that systematic and dogmatic method […]'. This is a pretty accurate assessment. Like his fellow Transcendentalists – originally a mocking nickname – Emerson saw systems and dogmas as constraints that keep us from realizing our full potential as human beings.

After attending Harvard College, Emerson trained for the ministry and was ordained in Boston in 1829. Boston's Calvinism had since long given way to more liberal views, but even the Unitarianism which he was supposed to stand for and which had abandoned such Calvinist fundamentals as original sin and the divine nature of Jesus Christ, soon seemed too formalistic and restrictive. Emerson resigned his pastorate in 1832 and after a lengthy tour through Europe, where he met leading poets and intellectuals, including William Wordsworth, Samuel Taylor Coleridge, and Thomas Carlyle, he began a career of writing and lecturing which would make him the most influential American writer of his age.

We may, with some exaggeration, say that America's cultural independence begins with Emerson. Since he drew for his ideas strongly on important elements of the philosophy of the German philosopher Immanuel Kant, as mediated (and transformed) by British intellectuals, especially Coleridge, there is more than a little irony in this. But one might argue that he gives a specifically American twist to these ideas in using them to call for radical cultural renewal. 'We were socially and intellectually moored to English thought, till Emerson cut the cable and gave us a chance at the dangers and glories of blue water', James Russell Lowell wrote in 1871.

'Our day of dependence, our long apprenticeship to the learning of other lands, draws to a close', Emerson tells his audience in an 1837 lecture that ten years later would be re-titled 'The American Scholar', urging them that they 'have listened too long to the courtly muses of Europe'. The year before, in 'Nature', his first published essay, he had already told his readers that they should break the spell of their own, American past: 'The foregoing generations beheld God and nature face to face; we through their eyes. Why should not we also enjoy an original relation to the universe? […] why should we grope among the dry bones of the past […]?' But to jettison the past, to break with tradition and with received wisdom, is a risky enterprise. If there is no tradition, if there are no established rules to guide us, how do we find our way in what suddenly has become uncharted territory? For Emerson, this question only will come up in pusillanimous souls. In his essay 'Self-Reliance' (1841) he preaches a radical trust in the self and its intuitive convictions. 'To believe your own thought, to believe that what is true for you in your private heart, is true for all men, – that is genius'. This is radical language, but Emerson is still able to surpass it: 'On my saying, What have I to do with the sacredness of traditions, if I live wholly from within? my friend suggested – "But these impulses may be from below, not from above". I replied, "They do not seem to me to be such; but if I am the devil's child, I will live then from the devil"'. Radical self-reliance will not rule out false judgments and mistakes, but these will be retracted and corrected with unshaken confidence: 'A foolish consistency is the hobgoblin of little minds, adored by little statesmen and philosophers and divines'.

How is such fantastic self-confidence possible? On what could it possibly be grounded? This is where Emerson's indebtedness to European philosophy comes into play. Emerson – and the other Transcendentalists – sought to distance themselves from the influential empiricist view, expressed by the English philosopher John Locke, that only our senses could provide us with reliable information about reality. From Locke's empiricist perspective, we could only know what our senses could perceive. Uneasy with such skepticism, the Transcendentalists looked for a more embracing philosophy that would meet the demands of their post-Puritan, and in some ways even post-Christian, but still essentially religious temperament. Such a philosophy was offered by Coleridge's *Aids to Reflection* of 1825, which, drawing heavily on Kant, argued that next to an empirically oriented, rational faculty – Locke's sole instrument for achieving knowledge – we also possess another, superior faculty: an intuition that allows us to transcend empirical reality and to participate directly in the divine and to understand the ways of divinity. For the Transcendentalists, therefore, human nature itself – or at least its essential core – is divine. If we connect with this core, we connect with what we truly are and find that we are one mind, a mind inseparable from the divine mind: 'in going down into the secrets of his own mind, he has descended into the secrets of all minds', Emerson says of his 'Man Thinking' in 'The American Scholar', illustrating 'the doctrine that man is one' – that is, in his authentic state. Too often, however, we fail to achieve this authenticity. In 'Self-Reliance', what keeps us from authenticity is the pressure of our social environment. 'Society everywhere is in conspiracy against the manhood of every one of its members', Emerson declares, adding that 'Whoso would be a man must be a nonconformist'. If we follow tradition merely to please our family or neighbors, if we dissemble for the sake of propriety, we risk losing our true self: 'If a man dissemble, deceive, he deceives himself, and goes out of acquaintance with his own being' ('Nature').

With its combination of the faculty of intuition – which it rather confusingly calls 'Reason' – and the rational-empirical faculty – called 'Understanding' – Transcendentalism tries to have the best of both worlds and confidently thinks to bridge the gap between our minds and the natural world. We may study nature in order to arrive at specific empirical knowledge. But we may also study nature to arrive at an intuitive understanding of all creation, even ourselves. After all, the natural world, too, is a creation of the divine mind. 'Every natural fact is a symbol of some spiritual fact', Emerson tells us. Indeed, at the most fundamental level 'Nature' corresponds with mind.

This sort of mystic vision will not appeal to hard-nosed skeptics and it is not surprising that many contemporaries saw Emerson's essays as the confused musings of a pseudo-philosopher. It must be said that the essays do not work hard to correct such an impression. They glitter with brilliant one-liners but are short on argument, preferring apodictic statement, aphorism, and paradox to methodical analysis, and associative thinking to sequential reasoning. Reading Emerson is a rather maddening experience, not much alleviated by the balm of humor, or even irony. Yet, for all his ellipses and mistiness, there also was a very practical side to Emerson's philosophy, founded on the same desire for authenticity. 'Only so much do I know as I have lived', he wrote in 'The American Scholar', emphasizing the importance, even necessity of a direct, authentic experience of the world. For Emerson the natural world very importantly included what many contemporaries saw as alien to it: 'Readers of poetry see the factory-village, and the railway, and fancy that the poetry of the landscape is broken up by these [...]. Nature adopts them very fast into her vital circles, and the gliding train of cars she loves like her own' ('The Poet' [1844]). In fact, in an important move, all of America, including its log-rolling, stump speeches, fisheries, Indians, trade, plantations, and everything else, noble and low, becomes a poem.

In his second series of essays (1844) we meet a more subdued Emerson. 'I grieve that grief can teach me nothing, nor carry me one step into real nature', he says somewhat disconsolately in 'Experience', no doubt thinking of the death of his five-year-old son Waldo in 1842. And in the much later 'Fate' (1860) he has come to the conclusion that 'Providence has a wild, rough, incalculable road to its end, and it is of no use to try to whitewash its huge, mixed instrumentalities'. But even his earlier exuberance had never blinded Emerson to the realities of his age and he felt compelled to protest the forced removal of the Cherokee nation in a scathing public letter to then President Martin van Buren (1838) and to condemn the Fugitive Slave Act – 'this filthy enactment' – of 1850 in the sharpest terms. That enormously confident optimism of the early years was, however, crucial in bringing about the cultural independence that it called for. Curiously, Emerson's poetry, collected in *Poems* (1846) and *May-Day and Other Pieces* (1867), stuck largely to traditional meter and form. His meditative poetry echoes the essays, but mostly in more conventional terms ('Over me soared the eternal sky, / Full of light and deity; / Again I saw, again I heard, / The rolling river, the morning bird;– / Beauty through my senses stole; / I yielded myself to the perfect whole' ['Each and All', 1830]). He is more impressive in his looser, descriptive poems, as in 'The Snow-Storm' of 1841:

> Come see the north-wind's masonry.
> Out of an unseen quarry evermore
> Furnished with tile, the fierce artificer
> Curves his white bastions with projected roof
> Round every windward stake, or tree, or door.

But we remember Emerson for the gems that are strewn liberally over the essays. And we remember him because we encounter his presence, either as a source of inspiration or as a source of irritation, in practically every important writer of the two decades before the Civil War.

Margaret Fuller

Emerson's American version of European Romantic thought and his call for cultural independence attracted a number of highly talented younger followers. The most important of these were Margaret Fuller (1810–50) and Henry David Thoreau (1817–62), whose *Walden; or, Life in the Woods* of 1854 is for many readers the Transcendentalist classic. But Fuller's *Woman in the Nineteenth Century* (1845), with its passionate defense of women's rights, may also lay claim to classic status.

Although primarily an essayist, reviewer, and journalist, Fuller was one of the nineteenth century's most influential female authors. Privately but thoroughly educated in a period when formal education was severely limited for women, she turned to translation, teaching, and writing and in 1839 began to organize seminars for ladies from the Boston area who sought to improve their minds through intellectual discussion (and were willing to pay for the privilege). The next year she became the editor of *The Dial*, a new quarterly devoted to literature and philosophy that had its origins in the meetings of the so-called 'Transcendental Club', a nickname for the informal meetings at Emerson's home in Concord, Massachusetts – and occasionally elsewhere – devoted to discussion and intellectual inquiry.

It was in *The Dial*, by then edited by Emerson, that she published the essay 'The Great Lawsuit: Man *versus* Men. Woman *versus* Women' (1843) that would be expanded and fine-tuned into *Woman in the Nineteenth Century*. Offering an inspired vision (in rather less inspired prose) she claims for women all basic human rights: 'We would have every arbitrary barrier thrown down. We would have every path laid open to woman as freely as to man'. Male-imposed barriers stand in the way of the self-realization that society encourages in men: 'What woman needs is not as a woman to act or rule, but as a nature to grow, as an intellect to discern, as a soul to live freely, and unimpeded to unfold such powers as were given her'. Reminding her readers of the fate of 'the red man, the black man', she implicitly creates a third – and very large – group to whom the equality promised in the Declaration of Independence is collectively denied. For Fuller, woman participates as much in the Transcendentalist divine as man so that creation itself might be said to demand equality, which should not be confused with sameness, although Fuller argues that 'masculine' traits are not reserved for men, just as 'feminine' traits are not the sole prerogative of women. *Woman in the Nineteenth Century* is the most important statement in a feminist rebellion against the established order that would, for the time being, culminate in the Seneca Falls Convention of 1848, in which some 300 attendees debated the rights of women and produced a 'Declaration of Sentiments' that declared that 'all men and women are equal'.

While revising 'The Great Lawsuit' Fuller had published *Summer on the Lakes, in 1843* (1844), a meditative account of her impressions during a trip to Chicago, then a town with less than 8,000 inhabitants, and two years later she collected a number of reviews in *Papers on Literature and Art*, including 'American Literature. Its Position in the Present Time, and Prospects for the Future'. In that review William Cullen Bryant's 'range is not great, nor his genius fertile', Washington Irving is 'a genial and fair nature', and Charles Brockden Brown is 'as a novelist by far our first point in genius and instruction as to the soul of things' – all judgments which show sharp critical insight. Returning from Italy with her infant son and her Italian partner, she perished, only forty years old, in a shipwreck off Fire Island, New York, where her fellow Transcendentalist Henry David Thoreau vainly walked the beach in search of her body.

Henry David Thoreau

The year before Fuller died, Thoreau had published two of his most important writings, 'Resistance to Civil Government', better known as 'Civil Disobedience', and *A Week on the Concord and Merrimack Rivers*, a book that commemorates a trip he had taken ten years before with his brother John. *A Week* had been written during Thoreau's now famous two-years' stay in a self-built cabin on the shore of Walden Pond, near Concord, that itself would become the subject of his masterpiece *Walden; or, Life in the Woods* (1854). Like *A Week* and later publications, *Walden* was based on his private journal, an undertaking that by the time of his early death had reached massive proportions – almost 2 million words, or close to 5,000 printed pages. Like Emerson, who also mined it for his published work, and like many other New England writers of the period, Thoreau kept the Puritan habit of keeping a diary, as a record of both worldly and spiritual events, very much alive.

Thoreau was a native of Concord, and an early intimate of the Emerson household, where he helped out during Emerson's long lecture tours. He occasionally co-edited *The Dial*, to which he contributed his first major essay, 'The Natural History of Massachusetts' (1842), a celebration of nature in an Emersonian vein, but his fierce independence and an accompanying temperament soon set him on his own course. As Emerson remarked after Thoreau's death, in 1862, 'He was a born protestant', who behaved 'as if he did not feel himself except in opposition'. '"I love Henry"', Emerson quotes one of Thoreau's friends, '"but I cannot like him"'. Perhaps this is an unfair assessment but Thoreau's radical statements give it at least some credibility. 'It is very evident what mean and sneaky lives many of you live', he tells his New England readers, while he generously includes the rest of the world in another provocative statement, 'The mass of men lead lives of quiet desperation'. 'I have lived some thirty years on the planet', he goes on in the same opening pages of *Walden*, 'and I have yet to hear the first syllable of valuable or even earnest advice from my seniors'. 'If there is anything Thoreau repents, it is having lived too much by those seniors' rules: 'What demon possessed me that I behaved so well?'

What makes Thoreau a special case among the Transcendentalists was that he put this radical individualism into actual practice. Preaching the simple life, unencumbered by worldly possessions, he never aspired after even the most modest wealth, never even held a 'steady' job. Preaching self-reliance, he took at the age of twenty-eight the drastic step of building a cabin in the woods and of living there under Spartan conditions for over two years. Convinced that the war against Mexico of 1846 was morally reprehensible, he refused to pay his poll tax and was jailed (although just for a single night), an experience that led to his defense of civil disobedience in the famous essay of that name (if a law 'requires you to be the agent of injustice to another, then, I say, break the law').

A Week on the Concord and Merrimack Rivers is nominally an account of a boat and camping trip from Concord, Massachusetts, to Concord, New Hampshire and back, but Thoreau is not all that much concerned with the actual trip (which in reality took two weeks). As a matter of fact, his much beloved older brother who accompanied him, is only indirectly introduced in 'we two, brothers and natives of Concord', and after that only appears in the narrator's 'we'. Thoreau's focus is on the natural world, sometimes with great effect, as in the introductory chapter on the Concord River, sometimes in tedious detail, as in the catalogue of river fish that takes the brothers 'from Ball's Hill to Carlisle Bridge'. But he is also occupied with less tangible things. In the 'Sunday' chapter we very appropriately find what amounts to an essay on Christianity, in 'Wednesday' a similar discussion of friendship. Thoreau reflects on immortality, on fame, on Goethe, on the utilitarianism that he despises, and supports his descriptions, reflections, and meditations with rather unfortunate poetry. (*A Week* contains almost fifty poems, far too many of them like the first one: 'The respectable folks, – / Where dwell they? / They whisper in the oaks, / And sigh in the hay; / Summer and winter, night and day, / Out on the meadow, there dwell they'.) Thoreau is not yet at his best in *A Week*, and it is not a miracle that the book did not sell. It lacks the waywardness, the sharp paradoxes, and the sardonic humor that make *Walden* still eminently readable. As in *Walden*, Thoreau's goal is spiritual fulfillment, but the immediacy, the unmediated rapport with the natural world that in *Walden* seems relatively easy to achieve, is lacking, possibly because Thoreau does not yet have the language to recreate such an experience.

In *Walden* Thoreau's parallel explorations of the natural world and the world of subjective experience, of consciousness, perfectly complement and deepen each other. His language is precise, razor-sharp, and sculpts almost tangible connections between consciousness and the natural world. Here, too, Thoreau does not offer a literal or even chronological account. He went to live at Walden Pond, not more than a couple of miles from Concord, on Independence Day 1845 and returned to the village in September 1847. But in *Walden* his stay is compressed into one single year and ends with the coming of spring, which 'is like the creation of Cosmos out of Chaos', with a celebration of new life. (For many critics, the coming of spring also signals the rebirth of *Walden*'s author, but there's little evidence that the author's spirit has been in hibernation.) Although *Walden*, then, might be said to be guilty of omission – Thoreau also had much more of a social life than the book suggests – it still stands as the supreme concretization of self-reliance. Thoreau builds his own cabin, clears his own land, sows his own beans, reaps his own harvest, all the while telling us the exact amount of his expenditures and making sure that we know how simple – and frugal – life can be ('by working six weeks in every year, I could meet all the expenses of living'). If this reminds us of Benjamin Franklin and the penny-pinching

Yankees in Cooper's novels, nothing else in *Walden* does. For Thoreau material possessions are a burden ('farms, houses, barns, cattle [...] are more easily acquired than got rid of') and commerce ('trade curses everything it handles') is a corrupting influence, both keeping us from self-realization and ultimate fulfillment.

'I went to the woods', he writes in what is probably *Walden*'s most famous passage, 'because I wished to live deliberately, to front only the essential facts of life, and see if I could not learn what it had to teach, and not, when I came to die, discover that I had not lived'. More threateningly, he wants 'to put to rout all that [is] not life' and 'to drive life into a corner, and to reduce it to its lowest terms', to force it to reveal its essence. Of course, life passes Thoreau's test, although it is a moot point whether he ever meets God in the present moment – he has earlier made the claim that 'God culminates in the present moment' – even if he finds self-fulfillment in moments of immediacy. 'In the midst of a gentle rain [...] I was suddenly sensible of such sweet and beneficent society in Nature, in the very patterning of drops, and in every sound and sight around my house, an infinite and unaccountable friendliness', he tells us in a passage that reminds us of Jonathan Edwards but leaves God out of the picture.

What Thoreau's brilliant rhetoric almost hides from sight is how curiously two-dimensional this confrontation is. It is just Thoreau and the Walden woods – there is nothing else in sight. Love, friendship, sexuality, charity – much of life's social dimension is willfully ignored. Thoreau, who proposes 'to brag as lustily as chanticleer in the morning' if only to wake us up, succeeds in doing so, but once fully awake, and in spite of our admiration for his radical pursuit of self-fulfillment, we may well choose to turn away from his idiosyncratic example and prefer social complexity to solitary simplicity.

Walden was received fairly well and Thoreau began, among other things, to rework the material that had resulted from earlier trips to Cape Cod and that a trip to Maine provided him with. Posthumously collected – *Cape Cod* (1864), *The Maine Woods* (1864) – these and other books do not live up to *Walden*, where the familiar natural environment offers more intimacy than the northern woods or the Cape's empty landscape. When Thoreau died, he was probably most famous for his passionate attack on slavery, 'Slavery in Massachusetts', of 1854, and for his defense of the violent anti-slavery activist John Brown, 'A Plea for Captain John Brown' (1859). We now see Thoreau as one of America's great nineteenth-century writers, even if his simplifications of the complex business of living and his deliberate provocations occasionally make him sound more like a soap-box preacher than like the 'chanticleer' he wanted to be.

Two minor poets

During its heyday Transcendentalism attracted many young and highly educated New Englanders who, like Emerson, no longer found spiritual sustenance in Unitarianism or other forms of New England Protestantism. One of those who briefly associated with the Transcendentalist enterprise was Jones Very (1813–80) from Salem, Massachusetts, whose mysticism is far more profound than that of Emerson or Thoreau. He had ecstatic mystical visions that we now would probably classify as manifestations of religious mania during which, according to Very, poems were directly communicated to him by divine sources. Although Emerson did not take those claims too seriously, publicly wondering why divine sources would have trouble spelling, he thought well enough of the poetry that emerged from Very's mystical experiences to help him publish *Essays and Poems* (1839). Very's intensely religious sonnets are much closer to the poetry of the English metaphysical poet George Herbert or that of the Puritan divine Edward Taylor than to that of the Transcendentalists:

> But soon some answering voice shall reach my ear;
> Then shall the brotherhood of peace begin,
> And the new song be raised that never dies,
> Then shall the soul from death and darkness win,
> And burst the prison where the captive lies;

('I Was Sick And In Prison')

Very is the most interesting of the poets associated with Transcendentalism, but he would have to share that honor with Frederick Tuckerman (1821–73), whose tutor he was at Harvard, if Tuckerman, who also in his younger years was drawn to Transcendentalism, had not turned his back on its optimistic faith in a benevolent Creation. Like Very, Tuckerman lived much of his life as a recluse and during his lifetime published only one collection, *Poems* (1860). Again like Very, he prefers traditional forms, but where Very's verse testifies to his hopes of eternal life, Tuckerman's is brooding, concerned with loss, grief, and anguish:

> An upper chamber in a darkened house,
> Where, ere his footsteps reached ripe manhood's brink,
> Terror and anguish were his cup to drink,–
> I cannot rid the thought, nor hold it close;

('An Upper Chamber')

Largely unappreciated during their life time, they would like other writers of the period not find true recognition until the twentieth century.

Nathaniel Hawthorne

Thoreau's program of self-realization by the work of his own hands as described in *Walden* did not necessarily work for others. Having joined and put a bit of money in the Transcendentalist community Brook Farm in 1841, Nathaniel Hawthorne (1804–64), one of the great antebellum writers, left the utopian experiment that same year. In his novel *The Blythedale Romance* (1852), in which he fictionalizes Brook Farm, his narrator Miles Coverdale is not very positive about the experiment which he, like Hawthorne, abandons after a brief stay: 'the clods of earth, which we constantly belabored and turned over and over, were never etherealized into thought. Our thoughts on the contrary were fast becoming cloddish'. Hawthorne, who in his short story 'The Celestial Rail-road' (1843) had already made fun of a 'Giant Transcendentalist', was far too skeptical to ever become a full-fledged Transcendentalist, even if he had been a member of Emerson's inner circle during his residence in Concord (where Jones Very did his best to befriend him). The young writer Herman Melville might be accused of exaggeration in his review of Hawthorne's short stories, 'Hawthorne and His Mosses', of 1850, but his view of Hawthorne's personality and work was pretty accurate. Speaking of the 'great power of black-ness' in Hawthorne, he tells the reader, 'You may be witched by the sunlight […] but there is the blackness of darkness beyond'. We now see that darkness clearly, and see the work that it inspired as vastly superior to the light sketches of small town life ('A Rill from the Town Pump', 1835) and similar efforts that most of his contemporaries preferred.

Hawthorne, born in Salem, Massachusetts, had left New England Calvinism farther behind than Melville, who himself wrestled with the Dutch Reformed Calvinism of his youth, at the time suspected. In a number of his best stories and in his great novel *The Scarlet Letter* (1850), Puritan New England shows itself a dogmatic and oppressive enemy of moral generosity, of humane understanding and compassion. But Hawthorne was also well aware that one of his direct ancestors, John Hathorne, had been one of the judges in the Salem witch trials of 1692 and self-righteousness and coldness of heart would be among his major themes.

After his graduation, in 1825, from Bowdoin College, Maine, where he was acquainted with Longfellow, Hawthorne returned home, to Salem, and with great dedication spent the next twelve years first writing an adolescently romantic novel, *Fanshawe* (1828), which he later sought to suppress, and then stories that, if he followed his natural inclination, tended to be grim and complex: 'My Kinsman, Major Molineux' (1832), 'Young Goodman Brown' (1835), 'The Minister's Black Veil' (1836), to mention a few early ones. Tellingly, when a friend, without informing Hawthorne himself, arranged for a book publication (*Twice-Told Tales*, 1837), some of the most complex and intriguing stories were omitted – a strategy repeated by Hawthorne himself in the expanded second edition of *Twice-Told Tales* of 1842, no doubt because he was very much aware of his readers' preference for more innocuous tales such as 'Little Annie's Ramble' or 'Sights from a Steeple'. Even so, Edgar Allan Poe, who reviewed the 1842 edition, called him 'one of the few men of indisputable genius to whom our country has as yet given birth'. Perhaps encouraged by such reviews, Hawthorne in *Mosses from an Old Manse* (1846) finally published stories he had earlier left uncollected like 'Roger Malvin's Burial' (1832) and 'Young Goodman Brown', together with such disturbing recent stories as 'The Birth-Mark' (1843) and 'Rappaccini's Daughter' (1844).

The great themes of Hawthorne's major stories and of his novels are the loss of moral innocence, guilt, pride, obsession, and the need for compassion – we must be part of the human chain, or suffer spiritual death. And we can only do so if we first learn to recognize, and live with, our own moral shortcomings. In the early story 'My Kinsman, Major Molineux', young Robin Molineux, a country boy in colonial Massachusetts, travels to Boston to see his kinsman, Major Molineux, an important colonial authority who may help him get a start in life. But when he finally sees his uncle, the Major is tarred and feathered and is being paraded through town on a cart. The victim of a mob uprising against the colonial regime, Major Molineux, frightened and vulnerable, recognizes Robin among the crowd, but Robin can't help himself and joins the others in their malicious merriment: 'Robin's shout was the loudest there'. His innocence gone, Robin will have to live with a diminished sense of self.

In 'Young Goodman Brown', one of Hawthorne's most anthologized stories, the young Puritan Brown, recently married to his young wife Faith, tells her one evening that he must go on an errand, the purpose of which we never learn, that takes him into the wilderness. There he sees, or dreams that he sees, religious leaders of colonial Boston and also his own father making their way into the forest. When Brown thinks he hears his wife's voice he throws all caution to the wind – '"My Faith is gone!"' – rushes on and finds himself at a witches' Sabbath, presided over by the Evil One himself. Dream or not, ever afterwards, Young Goodman Brown is 'a sad, a darkly meditative, a distrustful, if not a desperate man', who even shrinks from his bewildered wife. Has Brown discovered unsuspected evil in himself? In any case, he cannot cope, perhaps because his Puritanism allows no middle way between innocence and evil. A similar enigmatic fate befalls the young Reverend Hooper, who in 'The Minister's Black Veil' one day appears with a black veil over his face and will never again remove it, in spite of the entreaties of his fiancée, who, in the end, like all others, abandons him. Maddening in his refusal to reveal his reasons, Hooper will only say on his deathbed that he sees '[o]n every visage a black veil!' In 'The Birth-Mark' the scientist Aymer cannot live with the small birth-mark on the cheek of his lovely and utterly sweet wife and ultimately kills her in his attempt to remove it, just as in 'Rappaccini's Daughter' young Giovanni Guasconti kills the lovely Beatrice, the victim of her deranged father's experiments, in his effort to purify her from the poison which her father has literally made part of her nature. '"Oh, was there not, from the first, more poison in thy nature than in mine?"' she asks him, just before she dies, and she is right. Hawthorne's obsessed characters obey an inner logic that has its source in narcissism, an excessive self-regard that excludes understanding and compassion.

One of the most memorable of these characters appears in *The Scarlet Letter.* When the novel opens, the beautiful Hester Prynne, who, although there is no husband, has given birth to a baby girl, leaves colonial Boston's prison in order to undergo further public humiliation on the pillory. Sentenced to advertise her transgression by the Boston magistrates, she wears a large letter 'A' on her chest, but has, in tacit defiance, turned it by brilliant embroidery into a work of art. The scene is watched by an older man, the husband that she thought was dead. Calling himself Roger Chillingworth, he extracts the promise that she will keep his true identity a secret and begins an obsessive hunt for the baby's father, whose name she has steadfastly refused to reveal, which will ultimate destroy that father – the Reverend Dimmesdale – but also Chillingworth himself. Dimmesdale is one of those of Hawthorne's characters who are consumed by guilt but finally redeem themselves – making a public confession – just like the innocent, faunlike Donatello in *The Marble Faun* (1860), Hawthorne's last novel, who has murdered a man to save a woman friend (who then in her turn, considering herself responsible, devotes herself to a life of penitence).

Hester Prynne is one of Hawthorne's impressive female characters. Like Zenobia in *The Blythedale Romance* and Miriam in *The Marble Faun* she is strong and self-confident with a barely veiled contempt for the gossips gathered round the pillory. Her natural defiance leads her at a certain point to propose to Dimmesdale to leave the colony and start a new life in England. Claiming that their sexual relation had 'a consecration of its own' she cannot feel the guilt that Puritan Boston has imposed on her. But Hawthorne is no Thoreau, who was perfectly willing to march to his own, radically different drummer. For Hawthorne, she must accept society's moral framework in order to achieve fulfillment. And so Hester, who goes back to England after Dimmesdale's death, later in life, after her daughter has grown up, returns to the colony, takes up a more sober version of the 'A' again, and repays the community that so humiliated her with charity.

In his preface to his second novel, *The House of the Seven Gables*, in which contemporary events are connected to the Puritan past, Hawthorne, calling his book a 'Romance', argues that the romance, which he distinguishes from the novel, has no obligation 'to aim at a very minute fidelity', but may, whatever latitude it permits itself in its creation of a fictional world, not 'swerve aside from the truth of the human heart'. Although often realistic enough, as in his recreation of the Puritan past in *The Scarlet Letter*, or his descriptions of Rome in *The Marble Faun*, the stories and novels do indeed tend towards symbolism and allegory. But Hawthorne's romance has nothing in common with the schematic formats that the term romance – as in 'sentimental romance' or 'domestic romance' – may suggest. He weaves a complex tapestry of innocence and guilt, narcissistic obsession and compassion, and moral dilemmas leading to divided loyalties that makes him one of the nineteenth century's major writers.

Herman Melville

Herman Melville (1819–91), who better than most of his contemporaries saw the 'blackness of darkness' in Hawthorne's stories and novels, was no stranger to that darkness himself, although that is not so apparent in his first novels which are partly based on his own adventurous early years. Born into an affluent family in New York City, Melville's future changed drastically when his father died and left the family in poverty. After he left school at fifteen he had a variety of jobs before he signed on as a cabin boy for a voyage to and from Liverpool in 1839. Apparently attracted by the sea, he went for a far longer voyage on a whaling ship in January 1841, an experience that he would use to great effect in his most famous novel, *Moby-Dick* (1851). In July 1842, after one-and-half-years of the grueling regime on the whaler *Acushnet*, he jumped ship with a friend in Polynesia. There they lived for a number of weeks with a tribe that had had little contact with Western civilization. Although *Typee: A Peep at Polynesian Life* (1846), the novel based on these weeks, suggests a four months' stay, Melville had spent less than a month with the natives when an Australian whaler took him to Tahiti. From there he made his way to Hawaii where in August 1843 he enlisted on an American war ship. In October 1844, almost four years after he had left New Bedford – where *Moby-Dick* begins – he returned to the United States, sailing into Boston harbor.

After his return, Melville began to turn his adventures into literature. In 1846 *Typee* appeared and was an immediate success. He expanded the weeks he spent with the Typee people to four months, depicted himself as a de facto prisoner – although a well-treated one – whose hosts had no intention of letting him go, and fleshed out the story with much ethnographic detail, partly of his own observing, but mostly taken from other sources. *Typee* is an exciting blend of adventure, anthropological information, exotic environments, and at times titillating description – that is, titillating for its early Victorian readers, whose reactions to those passages caused Melville's American publisher to ask him for an expurgated edition. Its plot is provided by its narrator's gentle imprisonment at the hands of the Typee and the plans he makes to escape their too insistent hospitality. It transcends the mere adventure novel, however, in its social commentary. Melville is obviously deeply enamored of the seemingly carefree and uninhibited life of the Typee, even if he is fully aware of the restrictions imposed by incomprehensible taboos, and is sharply critical of the forces that seem bent on destroying island life as it is: evangelical fervour, colonization, and entrepreneurialism. The island is a sort of primitive Eden where the evils of Western society have not yet really made themselves felt.

In *Omoo: A Narrative of Adventures in the South Sea* (1847) Melville further mined his Polynesian adventures, picking things up where *Typee* left them, but, more insistently than in *Typee*, confronting the social and ethical questions that are provoked by what he sees as the destructive results of colonization. In *Mardi: And a Voyage Hither* (1849), he pursues his questioning even further. Seemingly another South Sea novel, *Mardi* pretty soon reveals itself as a voyage through an imaginary archipelago that allows Melville to follow his new philosophical inclinations. But Melville's talents for successfully embedding philosophy within a fictional setting did not yet match his ambition. *Mardi* was a failure with the public and with the critics and so he returned to more straightforward narrative undertakings. *Redburn: His First Voyage* (1849) was based on his first trip to Liverpool (which it turns into a rather hellish, Gothic place) and for *White-Jacket; or. The World in a Man-of-War* (1850) he used his year in the American navy. Melville later called the novels '*jobs* which I have done for money', but he also took their materials quite seriously, calling attention to the brutality of life at sea, especially in the navy, which he depicts in the darkest terms, again borrowing from other sources, such as *Two Years Before the Mast* (1840) by his acquaintance Richard Henry Dana (1815–82). Melville's presentation of the frigate *Neversink*, with its alcoholic captain, brutal ship's surgeon, and constant flogging, may well have contributed to the reforms that followed soon after its publication.

When *White-Jacket* was published Melville was already working on his next novel, for which he went back to the only adventures he had not yet used for his fiction, those on board the whaler *Acushnet*. But what probably started out as another rather conventional reworking of early experience, interspersed with factual information about whales – then a little known and awe-inspiring animal – soon turned into a frightening, epic tale of obsession and disaster. He met Nathaniel Hawthorne, read Hawthorne's tales and discovered not only Hawthorne's darkness, but also, in reading Shakespeare, the Bible, Milton, and other not invariably cheerful sources, his own darkness, which then contributed in no small measure to the greatness of what would become *Moby-Dick* (1850). Not accidentally Melville dedicated his novel to Hawthorne, 'In Token of my admiration for his genius'.

Apart from its narrator Ishmael's musings about his reasons for going to sea, *Moby-Dick*'s opening chapters are genial enough. There is broad humor when Ishmael discovers that his bedmate in a New Bedford inn is a Polynesian harpooner, when the Reverend Mapple, a former sailor, ascends his 'very lofty' pulpit by way of a rope ladder (which he then pulls up), or in Ishmael and his new friend Queequeg's negotiations with Captains Bildad and Peleg, owners of the whaler *Pequod*. But the tone of the novel changes when, several days after the *Pequod* has left Nantucket, its Captain makes his first appearance on deck. Captain Ahab – the name of one of Israel's godless kings – will come to dominate the book. Ahab's face is scarred by a 'livid branch' and he stands upon 'a barbaric white leg' made of ivory because he has lost his own leg in an encounter with a gigantic albino whale, nick-named Moby-Dick. Gradually the crew discover that Ahab's real purpose is not whaling, but to revenge himself on the white whale that has maimed him for life. But even the whale is not the real target of Ahab's crusade. In one of the novel's crucial passages Ahab reveals what most deeply motivates him:

'All visible objects, man, are but as pasteboard masks. But in each event – in the living act, the undoubted deed – there, some unknown but still reasoning thing puts forth the mouldings of its features from behind the unreasoning mask. If man will strike, strike through the mask! How can the prisoner reach outside except by thrusting through the wall? To me, the white whale is that wall, shoved near to me. Sometimes I think there's naught beyond. But 'tis enough. He tasks me; he heaps me; I see in him outrageous strength, with an inscrutable malice sinewing it. That inscrutable thing is chiefly what I hate; and be the white whale agent, or be the white whale principal, I will wreak that hate upon him. Talk not to me of blasphemy, man; I'd strike the sun if it insulted me'.

In such grandiloquent passages Ahab puts the metaphysical questions that obsessed Melville himself. After his last meeting with Melville, in 1856 in Liverpool, Hawthorne noted in his diary: 'Melville, as he always does, began to reason of Providence and futurity, and of everything that lies beyond human ken, and informed me that he had "pretty much made up his mind to be annihilated"; but still he does not seem to rest in that anticipation; and, I think, will never rest until he gets hold of a definite belief. […] He can neither believe, nor be comfortable in his unbelief […]'. Ahab is not the only one on board of the *Pequod* who is concerned with the nature of the universe. For the pious first mate Starbuck there is an obvious answer: '"how can this one small heart beat; this one small brain think thoughts; unless God does that beating, does that thinking, does that living, and not I"'. And Ishmael, who tells us that he is distracted from his duties by 'the problem of the universe revolving in me', also cannot easily reconcile himself with the idea that there is nothing beyond the material world: 'And some certain significance lurks in all things, else all things are little worth, and the round world itself but an empty cipher'. But whereas Ishmael is able to entertain and accept doubt – 'manhood's pondering repose of If' – Ahab cannot do so and must pursue his quest, apparently driven by a rather illogical belief in total determinism: '"This whole act's immutably decreed. 'Twas rehearsed by thee and me a billion years before this ocean rolled"'. In any case, as *Moby-Dick*'s story unfolds, Ahab becomes more and more obsessed with his quest. While in the early stages of the voyage the *Pequod* regularly lowers its boats, allowing Melville the opportunity to give us exciting scenes of whale-hunting and of its aftermath, the almost equally dangerous stripping and processing of the whales, later in the novel Ahab more and more abandons all pretense and sacrifices everything to his monomania, even refusing to help the captain of another whaler find his two sons who are missing in a boat. By then Ahab has ignored omens and warnings from other captains, smashed his sextant, personally re-magnetized the compass, and even forged his own harpoon, which he has 'baptized' in blood donated by the *Pequod*'s three 'pagan' harpooners. And Ishmael's language equally prepares us for an apocalyptic ending: 'the ship groaned and dived, and yet steadfastly shot her red hell further and further into the blackness of the sea and the night'.

Starbuck, the first mate, sensing disaster, considers killing his captain, but cannot bring himself to do so. And so, far, far away from home, the *Pequod* finally catches up with the elusive white whale, an encounter that ends with the death of Ahab and with Ishmael as the *Pequod*'s lone survivor, and with the nature of the universe and the problem of evil unresolved.

There is much to find fault with in *Moby-Dick*. Its characterization is schematic, much of the liberally offered factual information on whales and their literary and pictorial representations makes for tedious reading, its point of view shifts disconcertingly, and we find ourselves without warning in the theater when Melville decides to turn a forecastle scene into a play. But the novel succeeds beyond any expectation in presenting Ahab as the 'grand, ungodly, god-like man' that Captain Peleg sees in him and in also giving him the human dimension that makes Ishmael remember him with an awe tempered by affection: 'But Ahab, my Captain, still moves before me in all his Nantucket grimness and shagginess'. Ahab is one of world literature's great, unforgettable characters and the doomed *Pequod*'s voyage is one of its great tragedies.

Unfortunately, not everybody saw it that way when *Moby-Dick* was published, in 1851. Disillusioned, Melville started a new novel, *Pierre*, 'very much more calculated to popularity'. If this was the case – and its borrowings from the domestic romance format suggest as much – it is a dismal failure. *Pierre* (1852) practically destroyed its author's reputation and in this particular instance one cannot really blame his critics. The novel's young, athletic, strong, and handsome hero Pierre Glendinning – 'the striped tigers of his chestnut eyes leaped in their lashed cages with a fierce delight' – abandons his proud mother, his lovely fiancée Lucy, and his future, when the mysterious dark-haired beauty Isabel tells him that she is his father's illegitimate daughter. Feeling honor-bound to care for her, but unwilling to reveal his father's secret and in so doing deeply hurting everyone who is dear to him, he takes her to Boston where Lucy, who inexplicably remains true to him, will eventually follow him. There is much hand-wringing, there is a good deal of overwrought language – '"Pierre, Pierre, thou hast stabbed me with a poisoned point. I feel my blood chemically changing in me"', his mother tells Pierre's portrait – there are endless pseudo-philosophical digressions, there is a half-hearted attack on the American publishing world, and there is the suggestion of incestuous desire, although we never know for sure that Isabel is indeed Pierre's sister. Amidst all this, Pierre's moral stature rises, falls and rises again until we no longer know how Melville wants us to see him. It is almost a relief that at the end every major character is dead.

After *Pierre*, Melville decided to write short fiction for the magazine market, producing tales and sketches that in 1856 were collected as *The Piazza Tales*. Of these tales, 'Bartleby, the Scrivener' (1853), about a legal clerk who gradually and enigmatically withdraws from life, responding with 'I prefer not to' to every attempt to save him, and the novella-like 'Benito Cereno' (1855), a story based on a historic 1799 mutiny on a slave ship, have become classics. Although 'Benito Cereno' takes no position on slavery itself and ends with the retaking of the ship and the execution of the mutiny's leader, it sharply dissects the racially motivated complacency and blindness of the American captain who happens to come across the mutineers' ship and finally restores its Spanish captain's authority. Returning to novel-length fiction, Melville then published a straightforward and rather uninspired historical romance mostly based upon the real life adventures of a veteran of the Revolutionary War (*Israel Potter: His Fifty Years of Exile* [1855]), which was followed by the last novel published during his life time, *The Confidence-Man: His Masquerade* (1857). Set on the Mississippi river boat *Fidèle* (faithful, loyal, in French) during April Fool's day, the novel is a sly and brilliant exploration of an accomplished confidence man's operations and his victims' credulity and greed, a fierce comedy of masks and unmaskings. It is, however, by no means as accessible as it is brilliant. Apart from the usual philosophical digressions, Melville almost exclusively presents dialogue – most of the time we forget that we are supposed to be on a river boat – and his at times maddening indirectness and pervasive and often self-reflexive irony (chapter XI is titled 'Only a page or so') once again put off potential readers and he gave up writing fiction. He only returned to it late in life, with *Billy Budd, Sailor*, a short novel that was not published until 1924, and in which he once again returns to the problem of evil. Young Billy Budd, one of nature's innocents, is so severely and unjustly provoked by the evil master-at-arms Claggart that he hits him and unintentionally kills him. Condemned to hang by Captain Vere, his last words seem to affirm an order that the reader has come to doubt: '"God bless Captain Vere"'.

Between 1857 and his death in 1891 Melville only published poems, partly because his job as a customs officer in New York City left him little time to write. His *Battle-Pieces and Aspects of the War* (1866) is a collection of poems about the Civil War which does not demonstrate much natural talent:

> When ocean-clouds over inland hills
> Sweep storming in late autumn brown,
> And horror the sodden valley fills,
> And the spire falls crashing in the town,
> I muse upon my country's ills –

'Misgivings' (1860)

The same can be said of his massive narrative poem *Clarel: A Poem and a Pilgrimage* (1876). In *Clarel*'s 18,000 tetrameter lines – which switch to pentameter in the very brief epilogue – Melville once again revisits his old themes ('The running battle of the star and clod / Shall run forever – if there be no God', the epilogue tells us). The narrative set-up, with the young American Clarel and the other discussants, is interesting enough, but he struggles too often with its poetic concretization. Melville was no great poet, and as a thinker never really escaped from the cul-de-sac that Hawthorne described so well, but his greatest fiction has earned him well-deserved world fame.

Sentimental fiction

'America is now wholly given over to a damned mob of scribbling women', Nathaniel Hawthorne wrote to his publisher in January 1855, 'and I should have no chance of success while the public taste is occupied with their trash – and should be ashamed of myself if I did succeed. What is the mystery of these innumerable editions of the "Lamplighter," and other books neither better nor worse [...] when they sell by the 100,000?'

In the 1830s and 1840s the bestseller market, which was then dominated by sensationalist fiction, had been largely in the hands of male writers. In the 1850s, however, female authors, helped by the cult of motherhood and the pious respectability that had increasingly come to characterize middle class America, took over much of that market with sentimental novels which extolled motherhood, family life, and religious experience. This idolization of mother-hood was not exactly new, as we see in Lydia Maria Child's *The Mother's Book* of 1831, which was dedicated to 'American mothers, on whose intelligence and discretion the safety and prosperity of our Republic so much depends' – a quotation that also serves to illustrate the implicit political dimension that was attributed to the efforts of American mothers. And motherhood gained even more status in the decades before the Civil War. The absolute best-seller was Harriet Beecher Stowe's *Uncle Tom's Cabin*, which used sentiment and the politics of motherhood with great effect in its attack on slavery. *The Lamplighter* (1854) by Maria Cummins (1827–66) sold 100,000 copies in its year of publication and in 1850 *Wide, Wide World* by Susan Warner (1819–85; real name Elizabeth Wetherell) had also been a runaway bestseller.

In *Wide, Wide World* we follow young and somewhat wayward Ellen Montgomery after the early death of her mother. Adversity and suffering – at the hands of a bleakly Calvinist guardian-aunt – lead eventually to a deeply felt piety and to happiness as the docile wife of a loving husband. This is a fairly standard pattern in which initial signs of independence give way to a happy submission to God's will and nineteenth-century patriarchy. In *The Lamplighter* it is the young and motherless Gerty Flint who must follow a similar route. The orphan Gerty is 'a child utterly untaught in the ways of virtue'. She is rescued from her abusive guardian by the lamplighter of the title, is adopted by a wealthy woman, and is then doubly rewarded for her spiritual awakening: she is reunited with her long absent father and gets to marry her childhood mate who in the meantime has risen in society through the rational virtues of hard work and self-discipline. Gertie, on the other hand, has found eternal (and worldly) happiness through sentiment: 'cultivate your *heart*' is her advice to other girls who want to be like her – a suggestion that we find again and again in those novels of the 1850s that are first of all inten-ded for an ever increasing female readership. Sentiment is a site of authenticity and because of that of authority. And through the morality that they propagate, sentiment and the domestic sphere become a direct influence on the politics of national life.

An exception to this sanctification of sentiment is the work of E.D.E.N. (Emma) Southworth (1819–99), a prolific author who published more than fifty novels and was the most widely read woman writer of the American nineteenth century. But Southworth belongs perhaps more to the sensationalist tradition of Lippard, Thompson, Buntline, and others. Her most popular novel, *The Hidden Hand* (1859), may serve to illustrate this. Dressed as a boy, its young heroine, Capitola Le Noir (better known as Cap Black) sells newspapers on New York City's streets – in evidence of which she regularly lapses into an innocently sub-genteel vocabulary – and rolls from one adventure into the next, allowing Southworth to bring into her story such unpleasant urban habits as murder, kidnapping, thievery, and of course seduction. Southworth's career, which had started with the serialization of the novel *Retribution* (1849) in an anti-slavery jour-nal, was not limited to urban settings. It did, in fact, take her everywhere, to what then was the West, for instance (*India: The Pearl of Pearl-River* [1853]), but also to the South (in for instance *Broken Pledges: A Story of Noir et Blanc* [1855] in which she, although sympathetic towards the South, exposes the terrible consequences of the sexual abuse that came with slavery).

Sentiment runs rife again in the temperance novels of the period – such as *Ten Nights in a Bar-Room, and What I Saw There* (1854) by T.S. Arthur (1809–85) – that in all probability never reached the alcohol-minded audience for which it was intended, and in its religious fic-tion. Religion is of course a major theme in the sentimental novels of the 1850s, but it has center stage in a number of specifically religious novels. We find Catholic novels, such as *The Governess* (1851) by George Henry Miles (1824–71), in which the Catholic governess of the title is the catalyst that makes the Protestant family she serves embrace the Mother Church. But most of this fiction was Protestant, such as the bestselling *The Prince of the House of David* (1854), which was based on the life of Jesus, by the Reverend Joseph Holt Ingram (1809–60). Rather ironically, Protestant sentimental fiction – and the emphasis on Protestant piety in sentimental fiction itself – substantially helped to neutralize the fear of the 'untruths' of fiction that had pervaded Puritan culture. The (Protestant) American Tract Society, which was instituted in 1825 and which by 1830 already published six million tracts per year and had warned again and again against the dangers of fiction, definitely lost that battle when in the early 1850s sentiment and religion joined forces against its stern injunctions.

But to return to Hawthorne's complaint about his 'scribbling women'. There is no reason to think he changed his mind about their fiction, but he did find a novel by a woman writer that he really admired: *Ruth Hall: A Domestic Tale of the Present Time* (1855), by Fanny Fern (1811–72; real name Sarah Willis Parton). Largely autobiographical, *Ruth Hall* presents an independent young woman who succeeds in making her way in the world through her writing talents in spite of open and less open opposition from the male establishment – in particular her brother, who happens to be the editor of a prominent journal. Fern, who had remarried after the early death of her first husband, had left her second husband and in her early forties had found herself completely on her own, both socially and financially. Undeterred, she turned to writing sketches and very soon became a publishing sensation under her assumed name, selling 100,000 copies of her first collection, *Fern Leaves from Fanny's Port-Folio* (1853). Those sketches are still greatly entertaining, clearly the product of a quick, ironic, and quirkily original mind. 'How did you raise that beard?' she asks after a visit to Barnum's Museum and seeing 'The Bearded Lady from Switzerland'. 'Do you use a Woman's Rights razor? […] How does your baby know you from its father?' Inspired by the morning paper's account of the arrest of a woman for wearing 'man's apparel', she imagines how it must feel to be liberated from the protocol of women's clothes: 'But oh, the delicious freedom of the walk, after we were well started! No skirts to hold up, or to draggle their wet folds against my ankles; no stifling veil flapping in my face, and blinding my eyes; no umbrella to turn inside out, but instead, the cool rain driving slap into my face'. This implicit feminist agenda is not all that common in pre-Civil War literature and Fern's success tells us that American readers could appreciate other things than piety and sentiment.

Walt Whitman

Born in the same year as Herman Melville, but into a working-class family and therefore largely self-educated, Walt Whitman (1819–92) followed an opposite route, moving from the rather dismal fiction of his sentimental temperance novel *Franklin Evans; or, The Inebriate* (1842) to the radically innovative, revolutionary poetry of *Leaves of Grass* (1855) that with its completely free verse would once and forever change the course of American poetry and become a major influence worldwide. Whitman grew up on Long Island and in Brooklyn, where he was trained as a journeyman-printer and wrote his first journalistic pieces. After various teaching jobs on Long Island, he returned to New York in 1840 to become a full-time journalist and editor and, except for a three-month stay in New Orleans in 1848, lived there until 1863, when he moved to Washington, D.C. Having visited a brother who was wounded in a Civil War battle, he decided to stay in Washington to offer care and support to the wounded and sick soldiers in the city's hospitals and took up a part-time post in the Army Paymaster's Office. He had started to write poetry in the late 1840s, had published his first poems in 1850, and had in 1855 published a first collection of twelve poems, introduced by a sort of manifesto and by a long, sensational, untitled poem, which after having been titled 'Poem of Walt Whitman, an American' in 1856, and 'Walt Whitman' in 1860, would in 1881 get its definitive title of 'Song of Myself'. A much recounted anecdote tells us that Whitman sent a copy of *Leaves of Grass* to Emerson, who responded by greeting him 'at the beginning of a great career', which Whitman, without Emerson's authorization, promptly used for the second edition of 1856. More generally, the beginning poet was not indifferent to self-promotion. 'An American bard at last!' said the first edition of *Leaves of Grass*. 'One of the roughs, large, proud, affectionate, eating, drinking, breeding, his costume manly and free, his face sunburnt and bearded, his posture strong and erect'. And feeling that *Leaves* was largely ignored by the press – although one reviewer very perceptively called it an almost perfect combination of 'Yankee transcendentalism and New York rowdyism' – he expediently wrote some positive reviews himself, wisely withholding their author's name.

Whitman's idea to send Emerson a copy of his poetry did not come out of the blue. In 1842, in New York City, he had heard the lecture that Emerson would in 1844 publish as 'The Poet' and *Leaves of Grass* owes an enormous debt to Emerson's statement that 'America is a poem in our eyes' ('The Poet'), with every single aspect of American life, no matter how trivial, how low, a fit subject for American poetry. 'The Americans of all nations at any time upon the earth have probably the fullest poetical nature', Whitman claims in his preface to *Leaves*, outdoing the master himself. 'The United States are essentially the greatest poem'. It is the poet, a not necessarily better person than his neighbors but an Emersonian seer, who is most fully aware of this. But for Whitman, with his urban, working-class background, America, the 'greatest poem', is more all-encompassing than Emerson or the other Transcendentalists could imagine. It encompasses all classes – 'the genius of the United States is [...] always most in the common people' – and, more shockingly, it encompasses the body. Not just the more trivial bodily functions – 'the scent of these armpits aroma finer than prayer', 'Song of Myself' declares – but that in Whitman's time most dreaded of human activities, sex. Reading the Transcendentalists, one gets the impression that living is an exclusively mental activity; reading Whitman one returns to the real world.

In the still untitled 'Song of Myself' and the other eleven poems that make up the first edition of *Leaves of Grass* the body and sexuality are not yet as openly present as in the later poems. 'Song of Myself' is an exuberant celebration of life, to be more precise, of the poet himself and of American life in all its facets. Presenting himself as

> Walt Whitman, a kosmos, of Manhattan the son,
> Turbulent, fleshy, sensual, eating, drinking and breeding,
> No sentimentalist, no stander above men and women or apart from them [...]

Whitman, radically breaking with poetic tradition in his use of a totally free verse which reflects the radical freedom of American democracy, surges into what amounts to a loving and detailed depiction of America's endless variety. 'Song of Myself' lists America's seething activity, its politics, its emotions, and its citizens, all with equal sympathy, again and again working towards an ultimate identification with all of these:

> The peddler sweats with his pack on his back, (the purchaser haggling about the odd cent;)
> The bride unrumples her white dress, the minute-hand of the clock moves slowly;
> The opium-eater reclines with rigid head and just-open'd lips,
> The prostitute drags her shawl, her bonnet bobs on her tipsy and pimpled neck,
> The crowd laugh at her blackguard oaths, the men jeer and wink to each other,
> (Miserable! I do not laugh at your oaths nor jeer you;)

> The President holding a cabinet council is surrounded by the great Secretaries,
> On the piazza walk three matrons stately and friendly with entwined arms [...]
> And these tend inwards to me, and I tend outwards to them,
> And such as it is to be one of these more or less I am,
> And of these one and all I weave the song of myself.

Feeling one with all his fellow Americans, the poet can truthfully say:

> Of every hue I and caste I am, of every rank and religion,
> A farmer, mechanic, artist, gentleman, sailor, quaker,
> Prisoner, fancy-man, rowdy, lawyer, physician, priest.

And so he becomes a spokesman for 'many long dumb voices', for 'the interminable generations of prisoners and slaves'. He becomes the ultimate American democrat for whom democratic equality is a condition for transcendence, for partaking in the divine, and for whom inequality therefore is a turning away from the divine and a diminishment of the self.

At the height of his intense identification with the human and the natural 'other', the poet even 'incorporate[s] gneiss', 'skirt[s] sierras' and 'speed[s] through space'. In the first editions of *Leaves of Grass* – Whitman published a second edition, expanded to thirty-two poems in 1856 and a third edition, with 146 poems, in 1860 – such exuberant, hyperbolic moments of total transcendence are a recurring phenomenon. In the second edition's 'Sun-Down Poem' (in 1860 retitled 'Crossing Brooklyn Ferry') we are told: 'It avails not, time nor place – distance avails not / I am with you, you men and women of a generation, or ever so many generations hence'. And Whitman is with us through his language, the language that makes transcendence possible in the first place and that in, spite of all the exuberance, functions in *Leaves of Grass* as a perfectly tuned instrument of discovery – discovery of the self and, through that, of America at large.

The substantially enlarged *Leaves of Grass* edition of 1860 introduced two sets of poems, the *Children of Adam* poems, and the *Calamus* poems, that celebrated not only spiritual, platonic love but also its down-to-earth, physical counterpart. Although Whitman is explicit enough, the *Children of Adam* poems, which are devoted to heterosexual, 'amative' love, remain strangely impersonal, as in for instance 'A Woman Waits for Me', where the poet might as well be on a government-sponsored mission: 'I pour the stuff to start sons and daughters fit for these States, I press with slow rude muscle / I brace myself effectually, I listen to no entreaties, / I dare not withdraw till I deposit what has so long accumulated within me'. The *Calamus* section, on the other hand, devoted to what Whitman calls 'adhesive' love – that is, love between men – is far more personal and convincing. We have 'the comrade's long-dwelling kiss', but we also have the uncharacteristic anguish of a poem such as the rather enigmatic 'Trickle Drops' ('Glow upon all I have written or shall write, bleeding drops'), which suggests genuine pain over a homosexual love affair. From this third edition onwards, Whitman, who in the first editions celebrated life in all its facets, begins to confront its darker sides, a development no doubt accelerated by the Civil War which broke out the following year and by his experiences in Washington's war hospitals. In the collection *Drum-Taps*, which he published in 1865, and incorporated into the fourth, 1867, edition of *Leaves of Grass*, death is a major theme, as it is in one of his greatest poems, 'When Lilacs Last in the Dooryard Bloom'd', first published in *Sequel to Drum-Taps* of 1865 and incorporated in *Leaves of Grass* in 1881. Inspired by the assassination of Abraham Lincoln in April 1865, 'When Lilacs' is an elegy for the dead president, but even more a reconciliation with death itself, whose devastations are counteracted by a nature that incessantly creates new life and produces the beauty of lilacs and the purity of the hermit thrush's song. Death had from the beginning been a presence in his poetry – 'If you want me again look for me under your boot-soles' he tells us in 'Song of Myself' – but had never been a serious threat to the poet's mystic, life-affirming vision. But the war and the murder of Abraham Lincoln have made death a grimmer presence.

This realization also came to affect the earlier poetry. With every new, and always enlarged, edition of *Leaves of Grass*, Whitman moved poems around and kept revising them. Having realized his ambition to become an 'American bard' – he now quickly gained recognition both in his own country and in Europe – he moved closer to the spirit of the times, to genteel Victorianism, and tended to infuse into his earlier poems a Longfellow-like solemnity that diminishes their exuberance and apparent spontaneity. We find a similar self-conscious solemnity in some of the later poems in which he envisions a world transformed by American democracy, as in 'Passage to India', and in the long essays that he began to publish, such as *Democratic Vistas* (1871). Eventually Whitman's role as America's self-appointed national bard, expecting the honors that he felt came with that position, would lead him far away from the radical egalitarianism of his poetry. But that does not detract from the importance of *Leaves of Grass*, which may be seen as a loosely constructed epic that has as its heroes America's heterogeneous democracy – in particular its urban manifestations – and its singer, the fully democratic poet, and that replaces plot with process, with the ever-developing consciousness of the poet.

The literature of slavery

Although the Missouri Compromise of 1820–21 between the slave-holding states and the 'free' states had for the time being eased the tensions in the political debate on slavery and its future, it had certainly not brought an end to the moral debate. During the 1820s more and more (Northern) newspapers turned against slavery, joined in 1831 by William Lloyd Garrison's *The Liberator*. Anti-slavery societies sprang up everywhere and had well over 100,000 members before the decade was out. Presenting slavery as a moral rather than a political problem, women, who were supposed to stay out of politics, but who, as guardians of the home, were allowed to speak out on questions of morality, could join the debate. Two of the most prominent female spokespersons for abolition were the Grimké sisters, Angelina (1805–79) and Sarah (1792–1873), who had grown up in Charleston, South Carolina, in a slave-holding family, but had joined the Quaker community and moved to Philadelphia. In 1836 Angelina published her *Appeal to the Christian Women of the South* which like many other abolitionist publications argues that slavery is sinful because it reduces human beings to things. Acknowledging that the Southern women she addresses, lacking the right to vote, have no formal, political power, she urges them to use their moral influence as '*the wives and mothers, the sisters and daughters of those who do*'. Grimké's plea provoked a reaction from the influential Catherine Beecher (1800–78), sister of Harriet Beecher Stowe, who in her *An Essay on Slavery and Abolitionism, with Reference to the Duty of American Females* (1837) correctly concluded that Grimké's moral appeal sought to create a role in politics for her female readers and argued that woman's guardianship of morality should not extend beyond the domestic sphere. Grimké immediately connected politics – the issue of 'rights' – and morals in a forceful reply: 'if rights are founded in the nature of our moral being, then the mere circumstance of sex does not give to man higher rights and responsibilities, than to woman' (*Human Rights not Founded on Sex*, 1837). Like Fuller and many other female abolitionists, Grimké, although of course aware of the enormous differences between the plight of slaves and the position of women, sees both groups suffering from the denial of basic human rights. And so does Sarah Grimké in her *Letters on the Equality of the Sexes, and the Condition of Women* (1837–38).

The abolitionist case got a substantial boost by the publication of the *Narrative of the Life of Frederick Douglass, An American Slave, Written by Himself* in 1843. Douglass (1818–95) was born as a slave on the eastern shore of Maryland, the son of a white father and a slave mother, which according to the law – which took the mother's status as decisive – automatically made him a slave. In his *Narrative*, of which he would publish two later, expanded, versions, *My Bondage and My Freedom* (1855) and *The Life and Times of Frederick Douglass* (1881), Douglass first informs us that in Maryland slaves, he himself included, were better fed and treated than further south. True or not, it serves to emphasize the evils of slavery since there is little evidence of humane treatment in his *Narrative*. Douglass gives us a harrowing account of the casual cruelty and sadism he was forced to witness – 'killing a slave, or any colored person, in Talbot county, Maryland, is not treated as a crime, either by the courts or by the community'. He emphasizes the terrible consequences of slavery for the family to expose the Southern myth that the plantation is an extended family in which a benevolent planter-patriarch looks after the welfare of all his children, white *and* black, and he shows us slavery's fundamentally corrupting influence. With a sharp insight in the psychological mechanisms of the master-slave relationship he tells us that an initially kind new mistress who has never before owned a slave soon develops a 'tiger-like fierceness' because of the 'irresponsible power' that her position gives her.

In the *Narrative* Douglass presents himself largely in recognizably American terms, as a man who through will-power and perseverance has created himself and his destiny. As an adolescent he already shows the independence and initiative that will eventually make him an internationally respected leader of the abolitionist movement, for instance in persuading white boys to teach him how to read, or in the famous fight, when he is sixteen years old, with the hated overseer Covey, who is supposed to cure him once and for all of his rebelliousness. Covey almost succeeds, until, 'from whence came the spirit I don't know', Douglass refuses to be whipped once more and attacks his tormentor. 'We were at it for nearly two hours. Covey at length let me go', Douglass tells us, adding that the fight was 'the turning-point in my career as a slave' since it revives the self-confidence he had almost lost. And so in 1838, helped by his later wife, a free black, Douglass escaped slavery, went to live in New England and soon became one of the most eloquent speakers in the Massachusetts Anti-Slavery Society of William Lloyd Garrison, who in 1845 published Douglass's *Narrative* and introduced it with an authenticating preface for its white audience. The book immediately became a bestseller, was translated into all major European languages, and made Douglass a celebrity, allowing him to start his own newspaper, the *North Star*, in the conviction that African Americans should not be content to play a role in an essentially white abolitionist movement, but had to represent themselves as well. In its emphasis on its protagonist's self-made status, the *Narrative* underplays the role of Douglass's grandmother and mother, and that of his later wife. We know that because in *My Bondage and My Freedom* of 1855 Douglass, who now also wants to highlight the importance of family ties in African American culture, gives them their full due, just as in revealing that he was helped by fellow slaves in his battle with Covey he now underlines African American solidarity.

By then Douglass had broken with the monopolizing Garrison and had adopted his own course that asserted African American intellectual independence without refusing close collaboration with white abolitionists. At her request he provided Harriet Beecher Stowe with descriptions of plantation life for the latter's *Uncle Tom's Cabin* of 1850. His own excursion into fiction, the novella 'The Heroic Slave' (1853), is a schematic affair, although based on historical events. Its slave hero, Madison Washington, leads a successful mutiny on a ship that transports slaves from Virginia to Louisiana, taking ship and crew to the Bahamas, where the British authorities grant him and his fellow slaves freedom. A criminal in the eyes of U.S. law, Washington is presented as a revolutionary hero and statesman and not just through his names.

As the white mate of the overpowered ship grudgingly admits: 'It was not that his principles were wrong in the abstract; for they are the principles of 1776'. As this quotation suggests, Douglass strongly believed in what he thought were the principles underlying American democracy. He saw that faith confirmed in Abraham Lincoln's willingness to go to war and it led him to become politically active after the Civil War, although he was increasingly disillusioned by the defeated South's sabotaging of African American emancipation and by the political establishment's continuing refusal to grant women the equal rights for which he also had been an early champion. Douglass's *Narrative*, in which such disillusionment is still far off, has a place of honor in the great tradition of American autobiography that begins with the spiritual autobiographies of the Puritans and gets a more worldly dimension in such books as the autobiography of Benjamin Franklin, which link spiritual and material self-fulfillment to the project of American democracy.

Two years after Douglass had published his *Narrative*, William Wells Brown (1814–84) published his *Narrative of William W. Brown, A Fugitive Slave*, again under the auspices of Garrison. Adding to Douglass's account of slavery, it tells us how slave traders habitually swindle their customers – Brown worked for a while as assistant to a trader – and, more poignantly, that slavery has detrimental moral effects upon its victims (who are then blamed for them). But Brown is more famous for his novel *Clotel; or, The President's Daughter* (1853), which may well be the first African American novel and takes the (very probably correct) rumors that Thomas Jefferson had fathered children upon one of his slaves as its point of departure. A fictionalized slave narrative, the novel, of which Brown would publish three later and substantially revised editions, gives us the story of the slave Clotel, a young woman with 'features as well defined as any of her sex of pure Anglo-Saxon blood' and with 'a complexion as white as most of those who were waiting with a wish to become her purchaser'. Such a description could not fail to move a white female audience, just as the narrator's comment, when Clotel is auctioned off, that we are at a 'Southern auction' and that Clotel's 'chastity and virtue' – in other words, her virginity – add four hundred dollars to her value. Brown emphasizes the constant threat of sexual abuse that slave girls and women are exposed to – 'the real negro, or clear black, does not amount to more than one in every four of the slave population' – and the slave system's total indifference to family life, which of course was very important to his female readers. Clotel's fate – refusing to be recaptured after an escape she jumps off a bridge into the Potomac – likewise could not fail to move a readership that might have been shocked by Brown's audacity in presenting the author of the Declaration of Independence as the villain in a seduction story. One may in fact argue that in this first edition of Clotel – Jefferson was no longer mentioned by name in the novel's later versions – Brown sought to implicate the nation as such, and not simply the South, in slavery's evils.

Brown drew on his own experiences as a slave, but also on other sources, such as Lydia Maria Child's story 'The Octoroon', and a slave narrative in which a female slave had the leading role. Ellen Craft, making perfect use of the fact that she was very light-skinned, had disguised herself as a white man and traveled with her black husband, who posed as her slave, from Georgia to Philadelphia. (One of the most moving passages in William Craft's account of their sensational journey, *Running a Thousand Miles for Freedom: The Escape of William and Ellen Craft from Slavery* [1860], presents their arrival in Philadelphia, where somewhat ironically the traditional role pattern is restored: 'On leaving the station, my master – or rather my wife, as I may say now – who had borne up in a manner that much surprised us both, grasped me by the hand, and said, "Thank God, William, we are safe!" then burst into tears, leant upon me, and wept like a child'.) 'Passing' also plays an important role in *The Bondswoman's Narrative*, a recently discovered slave narrative from the 1850s by 'Hannah Craft, A Fugitive Slave', whose mistress turns out to have African American blood and runs away with her servant. There are doubts, however, regarding both author and story. There is no doubt, however, about what is probably the most poignant of all female slave narrative, *Incidents in the Life of a Slave Girl* by Harriet Jacobs, published in 1861 with a preface by Lydia Maria Child who had also helped Jacobs with her book and found her a publisher. Calling herself Linda Brent, and addressing us directly to authenticate her story – 'Reader, be assured this is no fiction' – Jacobs tells us how as a fifteen-year-old girl she finds herself forced to take an older and well-established white lover by whom she has two children in order to fend off the persistent sexual advances of her brutal owner. Fully aware that this will deeply shock her prudish Victorian readers, she argues that '[i]t seems less degrading to give one's self, than to submit to compulsion'. Confronting her readers with the harsh truth, she goes on to tell them that 'the condition of slavery confuses all principles of morality, and in fact, renders the practice of them impossible'.

To see a girl forced into immorality must have shocked the moral sensibilities of Jacobs's audience, while the subterfuge to which she and her grandmother must have recourse in order to have the children baptized must have offended their Christian principles. But the most profound impact must have been made by the seven years that Jacobs, who hides after her escape in a crawl space in her grandmother's house, can hear her children, can sometimes see them, but can never show herself to them and give them motherly affection. The message is that slavery tears families apart and robs women of what Victorian America saw as their holy duty: to give children unconditional love and to provide them with moral guidance.

In the two decades before the Civil War, African American writing became more than a series of isolated efforts. When a North Carolina slave, George Horton (1797?–1883?) published a collection of poems as *The Hope of Liberty* in 1829, he was practically a lone voice. Horton's poetry, published with the permission of his owner and sponsored by white admirers, could of course not address his own condition and stayed with the safe themes of his time. But Horton was soon joined by others. In 1831 Maria Stewart (1803–79) published *Religion and the Pure Principle of Morality*, while five years later Jarena Lee (1783–1849) followed with *The Religious Experience and Journal of Mrs. Jarena Lee, a Coloured Lady* (enlarged in 1849). Such religious guides and spiritual autobiographies aimed at the African American community rather than a white audience. But in the second half of the 1840s Douglass became a national figure and Brown, too, reached a white audience with his prolific output. Slaves and ex-slaves, male and female, published the stories of their life. Naturally, the overriding theme was slavery and its physical and moral terrors. And the implied message is that African Americans are in all respects equal to their white (former) masters. They do not lack interiority, as the white stereotype has it, and their lives have the same intrinsic value as those of white Americans. And female slave narratives counter the abolitionist notion that female slaves were invariably helpless and ignorant by presenting strong and independent African American women.

But African American authors also started to examine black life north of the Mason-Dixon line. *The Garies and Their Friends* (1857) by Frank J. Webb (1828–94) explores racism in Philadelphia, showing us how easily other ethnic minorities – in this case the immigrant Irish who desperately want to belong to mainstream America – can be incited to racist violence against African Americans. Two years later the New Hampshire-born Harriet Wilson (1808?–1870), in the largely autobiographical *Our Nig*, shows that no matter how morally upright her heroine Frado is, and no matter how pious she becomes with her conversion to Christianity, her color still makes her an object of white abuse and ridicule. In these novels freedom has a bitter ring. Frances Watkins Harper (1825–1911), born free in Baltimore, whose *Poems on Miscellaneous Subjects* (1854) was a national bestseller, would only later, when the Reconstruction of the South had failed, become discouraged by America's lack of progress toward true emancipation. In the lyrical poetry of *Poems* she can still celebrate 'Liberty' in a poem about the successful escape of Eliza Harris – the heroine of Beecher Stowe's *Uncle Tom's Cabin* – across the Ohio River:

> The bloodhounds have miss'd the scent of her way;
> The hunter is rifled and foil'd of his prey;
> Fierce jargon and cursing, with clanking of chains,
> Make sounds of strange discord on Liberty's plains.

'Eliza Harris' (1853)

A similar optimism still marks her famous 'Bury Me in a Free Land' of 1864. But her *Sketches of Southern Life* (1872), a series of linked narrative poems that introduce 'Aunt Chloe', an older woman who offers wise comments in the vernacular, is already touched by disappointment.

It is remarkable how much faith most antebellum African American writers had in American democracy, even when, as in Douglass's 'The Heroic Slave' or in Brown's *Clotel* true freedom is or seems only possible outside American territory. But there were exceptions, such as Martin R. Delany (1812–85), who after an initial collaboration with Douglass became so disillusioned that he publicly encouraged his fellow African Americans to seek new homes outside the United States. Delaney's militancy also inspired his *Blake; or, The Huts of America* (1859, expanded 1861–62) in which his hero actively encourages slaves to rebel against their lot. Most African American writers, however, saw slavery as incompatible with the principles that had given rise to the American Revolution and therefore as fundamentally conflicting with the character of the nation itself, even if, as David Walker (1790?–1830) had already argued in his *David Walker's Appeal, in Four Articles* of 1829, the author of the Declaration of Independence had shown himself a racist in his assertion of white superiority (in his *Notes on the State of Virginia*) and in his personal life. For the militant Walker the use of force in the cause of abolition seemed fully justified. Naturally, abolitionists agreed with the notion that slavery was fundamentally un-American. And so did those white Northern writers who actually addressed the issue. Still, it is rather amazing how marginal slavery, the single most important issue of the period, is in the literature of the antebellum years before the Fugitive Slave Act of 1850 forced writers to see that slavery was a national rather than a regional problem. But of course there were exceptions, as we have seen with Whittier's 'The Hunters of Men'. And there were other voices. Lydia Maria Child had published her *An Appeal in Favor of That Class of Americans Called Africans* as early as 1832 and Longfellow had been equally explicit in his *Poems on Slavery* of 1842. But it took a writer who up to that point had mostly written domestic regional fiction to seek a frontal collision with the 'peculiar institution', as the South euphemistically called slavery.

Harriet Beecher Stowe

By far the most popular and most influential literary engagement with slavery was the novel *Uncle Tom's Cabin; or, Life Among the Lowly* (serialized 1851–52; published as a book in 1852) by Harriet Beecher Stowe (1811–96), daughter of a redoubtable Calvinist minister. While working as a teacher, Beecher began to write stories – her first collection, *The Mayflower; or, Sketches of Scenes and Characters Among the Descendants of the Pilgrims,* was published in 1843 – and took up an interest in abolitionism. But it was the Fugitive Slave Act that inspired her to write the novel that would almost overnight make her world-famous. *Uncle Tom's Cabin* sold over 300,000 copies in its year of publication, was immediately translated into all major European languages, and would become the best selling novel of the American nineteenth century.

Uncle Tom's Cabin tells us how the humane Kentucky slave-holder Shelby sees himself forced to sell his most trusted slave, Tom, and the four- or five-year-old son of Eliza and George Harris to a slave trader who will take them down South. Refusing to be parted from her child Eliza decides to escape by crossing the Ohio River. Directly addressing her female readers, Stowe mobilizes their emotions, making both natural and inevitable what at the time was a criminal offense:

> If it were *your* Harry, mother, or your Willie, that were going to be torn from you by a brutal trader, to-morrow morning, – if you had seen the man, and heard that the papers were signed and delivered, and you had only from twelve o'clock till morning to make good your escape, – how fast could *you* walk? How many miles could you make in those few brief hours, with the darling at your bosom, – the little sleepy head on your shoulder, – the small, soft arms trustingly holding on to your neck?

To bring slavery's brutal disregard of a mother's natural feelings even closer to home, Beecher gives both Eliza and her boy a skin 'so white as not to be known as of colored lineage, without a critical survey'. Finding that floating ice makes it impossible for the ferry to take her across the river to free territory, Eliza, in one the most famous passages in world literature, takes her life and that of her son in her own hands:

> The huge green fragment of ice on which she alighted pitched and creaked as her weight came on it, but she staid there a moment. With wild cries and desperate energy she leaped to another and still another cake; – stumbling – leaping – slipping – springing upwards again! Her shoes are gone – her stockings cut from her feet – while blood marked every step; but she saw nothing, felt nothing, till dimly, she saw the Ohio side, and a man helping her up the bank.

Eliza and her son reach freedom and so does her husband, George, whose independent spirit so galls his owner that he, too, is going to be sold to a trader. But Uncle Tom accepts his fate. On his way to the Deep South he saves the life of a young girl, Eve St. Clare, whose grateful father buys him practically on the spot. But his new master dies, after his young daughter has preceded him in a classically sentimental scene. After the death of St. Clare – fortunately after his daughter had made him see Christ's light – Tom falls into the hands of the thoroughly evil Simon Legree, who in a fit of rage will eventually flog him to death for his refusal to betray two fellow slaves. Tom dies, but not before forgiving him: 'Tom opened his eyes, and looked upon his master. "Ye poor miserable critter!" he said, "there an't no more ye can do! I forgive ye, with all my soul!"' Yet, in spite of Tom's martyr-like death *Uncle Tom's Cabin* ends well, with a number of miraculous discoveries and reunions.

Stowe tries to present a relatively nuanced picture. Shelby and St. Clare, although Southern slave owners, are kind and humane, while the psycho-pathological Legree is a displaced Yankee. It is slavery that is unconditionally evil. It turns human beings into merchandise, denies them every basic right, tears families apart, and gives free rein to sadists, rapists, and other criminals. There is no doubt that Stowe fights the good fight, but even in her own time some prominent readers, Douglass included, questioned her portrayal of African Americans. The novel seems to have a preference for those with lighter skins and tends to present the others as incorrigibly immature and dependent. The impossibly saint-like Tom has 'the soft, impressionable nature of his kind race, ever yearning toward the simple and childlike'. Moreover, Tom's invariably passive acceptance of the vicissitudes of fate, rooted in a deeply felt Christian piety, bordered for many black readers on the offensive. Finally, at the end of the novel Stowe has Eliza and George go to Africa (just like Eva's former playmate, the irrepressible slave girl Topsy, who has embraced Christianity and now wants to spread the Word), a move that by her critics was seen as unsatisfactory and evasive, and that was only possible because the rebellious George had given up his fully justified 'dark, misanthropic, pining, atheistic doubts' for 'the light of a living Gospel'. In *Uncle Tom's Cabin* the African Americans that Stowe approves of prefer passive piety – the attitude of female heroines in the sentimental novels of the time – to active resistance.

After Stowe had published the extensively documented *A Key to Uncle Tom's Cabin* (1853) to defend her novel's truthfulness, which had been fiercely attacked by the Southern press, she offered a less feminized picture of African Americans in *Dred: A Tale of the Great Dismal Swamp* (1856), in which she allows her male protagonist a good deal of license in his attacks on slavery and slave-holders and in planning the sort of heroic radical action – insurrection – that is out of the question in her earlier novel. But Dred – based on the historical slave rebel Nat Turner – dies and the real limelight is for the far less rebellious Aunt Milly, whose resemblance to Uncle Tom is perfectly captured by one of the narrator's comments: 'As far as her own rights were concerned, she would have made a willing surrender of them, remaining patiently in the condition wherein she was called, and bearing injustice and oppression as a means of spiritual improvement'. Aunt Milly may have been based on Sojourner Truth (1797–1883; real name Isabella Baumfree), a former slave and advocate for the rights of black Americans and women, whom Stowe admired. If so, Stowe has certainly toned down the dynamic temper that we find in the story of Truth's life, *The Narrative of Sojourner Truth* (1850, later expanded and republished as *Sojourner Truth: A Bondswoman of Olden Time*). In any case, Stowe's novels, with their brilliantly timed scenes of domestic melodrama and of conversion, were immensely influential and contributed significantly to public anti-slavery sentiment. Although she returned to New England and to far less controversial domestic themes in much of her later work – *The Minister's Wooing* (1859), *The Pearl of Orr's Island* (1862), *Old Town Folks* (1869) – her name was forever connected with the cause of abolition.

Southern outrage at the portrayal of slavery in *Uncle Tom's Cabin* did not remain limited to angry reviews, but also led to literary denials, the first of which was *Aunt Phillis's Cabin* (1852), by Mary Eastman. The most prominent defenses of slavery were published by a respected writer of long standing, Caroline Hentz, who had grown up in the North and in her first novel, *Lovell's Folly* (1833), had already cautioned against a too polemical stance. In *Marcus Warland* (1852) and in her best-known novel, *The Planter's Northern Bride* (1854), she again urges restraint and reconciliation while rejecting Stowe's caricature of plantation life. For Hentz, the typical plantation protects its slaves from the evils of the free market, offering them life-long care in a harmonious environment. 'It is true, they were slaves', *Marcus Warland* tells us and then defends that status with a rather bizarre image: 'but their chains never clanked. Each separate link was kept moist and bright with the oil of kindness'. In *The Planter's Northern Bride* that kindness, based on a humane and stable system of values, is contrasted favorably with Northern industrialism and free market capitalism in general. The bride of the title, the daughter of an abolitionist, is made to see the light by her slave-holding new husband, who easily convinces her that the South's eternal, pastoral values, rooted in the soil itself, offer a more permanent basis for full, worthwhile, living than the restless chase of profit that dominates the North. And the planter's slaves agree, to the point that an escapee returns to the plantation (and is warmly welcomed back). In these and other novels the North exploits its laborers, fires them at will, lets them and their families starve, while the South protects its slaves from the whims of capital. Still, Hentz kept hoping for reconciliation. But North and South had drifted too far apart, as Mary Chesnut, née Miller (1823–86), very sharply saw. In her diary, we find a highly cultivated and well-informed Southern voice – her husband was a personal assistant of Jefferson Davis, the Confederacy's President – that has strong doubts about slavery and is especially sensitive to the position of those Southern wives who must tolerate their husbands' slave mistresses – whom she rather unfeelingly also tends to blame – and illegitimate offspring in their immediate environment. And she has no illusions about reconciliation: 'We separated because of incompatibility of temper. We are divorced, North and South, because we hated each other so'.

Beginning realism

That Southern criticism of Northern industrialism was not wholly unfounded is strongly suggested by the powerful story that Rebecca Harding Davis (1831–1910) published in 1861. 'Life in the Iron Mills' breaks radically with the domestic themes of the sentimental novel and is the first attempt to offer a realistic portrait of America's industrial proletariat – in this case the laborers in an unnamed town's hellish steelworks. '[Smoke] rolls sullenly in slow folds from the great chimneys of the iron-foundries, and settles down in black, slimy pools on the muddy streets. Smoke on the wharves, smoke on the dingy boats, on the yellow river [...]'. Even for those who dimly dream of a better life there is no escape. The story's piling up of misfortunes and injustice may be a bit much, but 'Life in the Iron Mills' broke new ground, as did some of the novels Davis wrote after the enthusiastic reception of her first story (*Margret Howth*, 1862; *Waiting for the Verdict*, 1868). So did *The Morgesons* (1862) by Elizabeth Stoddard (1823–1902) which gives us a picture of New England life that is wholly at odds with its idealized presentation in for instance the fiction of Harriet Beecher Stowe. Stoddard's laconically sarcastic novel has no illusions about the tensions and rivalries that may make family life less perfect than Victorian America made it out to be. And its tough heroine copes with it in ways that in the sentimental novel would have been unthinkable. *The Morgesons* did not fare well with the critics and it did not sell. Like Hawthorne, who encouraged her, and Melville, Stoddard found out the hard way that the American public was not yet ready for a skeptical, questioning view of life.

Emily Dickinson

Of the nearly eighteen hundred poems (and there may have been more) Emily Dickinson (1830–86) wrote in her parental home in Amherst, Massachusetts, only a dozen were published during her life time and their first reliable publication had to wait until 1955. It is true that her poetry was not received enthusiastically by the few editors she approached, but it is equally true that she did not try hard to reach, or create, an audience. 'Publication – is the Auction / Of the Mind of Man' she noted in one of her poems. Much has been written about Dickinson's eccentricity. Leaving home to attend Mount Holyoke Female Seminary, ten miles from Amherst, she returned within a year and spent the rest of her life with her prominent Amherst family – a dutiful daughter who partook in the standard domestic female duties of the time. But gradually she gave up on most other things. First she confined her movements to the grounds of her home, then declined to leave the house itself. And she began to talk with visitors from behind a screen, or even from another room. Having withdrawn from all direct social intercourse – she did keep up an extensive correspondence – she also refused to be published, saying 'I would as soon undress in public, as to give my poems to the world'.

Dickinson is much closer to Hawthorne and Melville than to Emerson, whose essays she was familiar with, or Whitman, of whom she had heard it said 'that he was disgraceful'. Her poetry wrestles with problems of identity, with the enigma of death, with religious faith ('Christ is calling everyone here, all my companions have answered [...] and I am standing alone in rebellion', she wrote in 1850), with the meaning and status of aesthetic experience, and other themes that keep recurring without ever finding resolution. That poetry may, at first sight, appear deceivingly simple. Dickinson prefers a hymn format – four beats followed by three, as in the famous opening lines 'My Life had stood – a loaded Gun – / In Corners – till a Day' or the great lines 'The Lightning showed a yellow Beak / And then a livid Claw' – although she varies it at will and takes similar liberties with its rhyme scheme, often using half rhyme, or even foregoing rhyme altogether. And there are indeed poems that seem easily accessible, as the endearing 'To make a prairie it takes a clover and one bee, – / One clover, and a bee, / And revery. / The revery alone will do / If bees are few'. But such poems are rare in her oeuvre. Dickinson's poetry is compact, dense, often offering only the key words in what is clearly a complex train of thought, further complicated by startling imagery, by its juxtaposition of mutually exclusive views or feelings, and by its idiosyncratic use of dashes instead of a more revealing punctuation. Death is a major theme. Dickinson can 'neither believe, nor be comfortable in [her] unbelief', as Hawthorne said of Melville. Death is either annihilation or immortality, but Dickinson, although dearly desiring certainty, cannot decide: 'I've seen a Dying Eye / Run round and round a Room – / In search of Something – as it seemed – / [...] / Without disclosing what it be / 'Twere blessed to have seen –'. A similar inconclusiveness marks her own imagined death: 'I heard a Fly buzz – when I died – / [...] / I willed my Keepsakes – Signed away / What portion of me be / Assignable – and then it was / There interposed a Fly – / With Blue – uncertain – stumbling Buzz – / Between the light – and – me – / And then the window failed – and then / I could not see to see –'. Dickinson's religious temperament reveals itself in poem after poem, but so does the skeptical side of her nature: 'Apparently with no surprise / To any happy Flower / The Frost beheads it at it's play – / In accidental power – / The blonde Assassin passes on – The Sun proceeds unmoved / To measure off another Day / For an Approving God –'. The world resists interpretation and the ways of God are likewise beyond human understanding – if there is a God, which she sometimes would seem to assume ('This World is not Conclusion'), but at other points seems to deny: 'Those – dying then, / Knew where they went – / They went to God's Right Hand – / That Hand is amputated now / And God cannot be found –'. Dickinson never escaped what either may be seen as a persistent crisis of faith or a stubborn refusal to disbelieve.

In any case, her poetry never leads to an identification with the divine, even if it may express a mystical ecstasy ('Mine – by the Right of the White Election! / Mine – by the Royal Seal!'). It is, more modestly, a mode of finding significance, rather than creating it. But whenever such significance is found, skepticism kicks in and the ground that seemed gained is lost again. True enough, there are moments in Dickinson's poetry when the pendulum stops for a moment and there seems no need to question the world, and there are love poems, although these strongly resist simple readings. All we see is that she projects all the intensity of her emotional life on an unknown object of affection. But poems in which Dickinson's restless and skeptical inquisitiveness is temporarily in abeyance are relatively rare. Nature is not so harmonious when a 'narrow fellow in the grass' – a possibly harmless snake – causes her 'zero at the bone'. Again like Melville, Dickinson defiantly prizes truth and authenticity above everything else. 'I like a look of Agony', she writes,

'Because I know it's true – / Men do not sham Convulsion, / Nor simulate, a Throe –'. Taking nothing for granted, her poetry accepts no restrictions in its explorations of the self, of religion, of cultural conventions – such as gender roles – and of poetry itself. It reflects an intensely lived life, Dickinson's intellectual honesty made her the protagonist in dramas that encompassed the whole universe, and not just her miniature world in Amherst, Massachusetts. By turns hesitant, tormented, exultant, despairing, her unique voice seems astonishingly modern and has nothing in common with the sentimental and nostalgic poetry of most of her contemporaries.

In the first half of the nineteenth century the United States became a major player on the world scene, and its literature followed suit, even if the contemporaries of the writers who mostly contributed to it did not always appreciate their genius. Irving, Cooper, Child, Simms, Hawthorne, and many other writers had created a sense of national history and Emerson and Whitman had turned away from 'the courtly muses of Europe' to embrace a fully democratic muse. It is not accidental that, compared to British and European litera-ture of the period, American literature again and again emphasizes the individual and his, or occasionally her, freedom – the self that finds authenticity outside institutionalized social structures. This is of course a more general Romantic trope, but it also continues the belief of the Puritans that, even though institutions were indispensable to their theocracy, every single one of us is fundamentally alone on the Day of Reckoning. 'We must walk this lonesome valley / We have to walk it by ourselves / O, nobody else can walk it for us', as the hymn has it. Nobody knew it better than Emily Dickinson.

3 Civil War to World War I
1865–1918

Introduction: American society from the Civil War to World War I

In the half century between the Civil War and World War I the United States grew from a nation at the margins of the Western world to one of the leaders of that world. The country underwent tremendous changes in terms of territorial expansion, demographics, and economic and social organization.

In many ways the Civil War, or the War Between the States as it is also known in certain parts of the present-day United States, and particularly the Southern states that made up the old Confederacy, sped up developments that were already well underway before the conflict broke out. The need for both warring parties to manufacture weapons, ammunition, and other army provisions on a very large scale, and to transport all of these on a regular basis and over large distances, had led especially in the already more industrially developed and diversified North to a massive expansion of the industrial base and to the creation of a dense and efficient railroad system. When the conflict ended, with the victory of the Union, which is to say the North, this industrial and transport capacity became available for peace time purposes, and fed both a rapidly expanding consumer society and an equally rapid westward expansion of the Union.

Before 1860 the United States had been a largely agrarian nation predominantly made up of relatively self-providing single household farming families, according to the ideals of Thomas Jefferson. The glaring exception, of course, had been the large slave-holding plantation estates in the South, but these had disappeared with the end of the Civil War. At first it seemed as if also after the Civil War the existing pattern would continue. The 1865 Homestead Act granted one-hundred-and-sixty acres of land to every American that settled in the until then largely unclaimed Middle West and West. This led to a true mass migration, at first to the rich farming areas of Illinois, Iowa and Kansas, and beyond to California and Oregon, and later also to the poorer areas in between. By 1870 the more northern parts of the Great Plains and of the Rocky Mountain region had already been occupied by new settlers, many of them immigrants fresh from Europe. The rapid influx of white farmers sounded the death knell for those Native American tribes that until then had still been holding out against white civilization. Increasingly they were defeated in battle, rounded up, and confined to reservations, invariably located in the poorest parts of their former ancestral lands, or even remote from these. In the South-West the original Spanish-speaking inhabitants, who until almost immediately before the Civil War had been Mexican nationals, but who had become U.S. citizens because of the independence of Texas in 1836 and later its joining the United States in 1845, and because of the ceding to the United States of what eventually became the states of California, Colorado, Utah, Nevada, Arizona, and New Mexico following the Treaty of Guadalupe Hidalgo at the end of the Mexican–American war of 1846–48, became quickly marginalized, and in practice were relegated to second-class citizenship.

In fact, the poorer farming areas of the Great Plains had first been occupied by cattle ranchers, often running very large operations, that replaced the hitherto seemingly inexhaustible herds of buffalo with almost equally gigantic herds of market cattle. This is the brief period – a window of a bare twenty to thirty years – that gave rise to the myth of the cowboy and the western. The inconsiderate and immensely wasteful slaughter of the buffalo also hastened the demise of the Plains Indians, who for their very subsistence depended on these animals. In many places, however, the cattle ranchers soon found themselves besieged by the incoming farmers. The latter wanted to fence off their lands to protect their crops from the grazing cattle. The former wanted open spaces where their cattle could graze freely. All this led to often armed conflicts. It also led to radical changes in the ecology of the American West. Unlike the Jeffersonian-style farmers in the Eastern parts of the U.S., the newcomers to the Mid-West and West most often did not run self-providing household farms but produced market crops for the fast-growing population of the more Eastern parts of the U.S. The resulting mono-cultures of grain and maize (called corn in the U.S.) quickly exhausted the meager soil of the Plains and caused its increasing erosion. Persistent periods of severe drought in the 1880s, contrary to the milder and wetter 1860s and 1870s when most settlers had arrived, only exacerbated the problem. Combined with falling market prices because of over-production, high transport tariffs enforced by monopolist railroad companies, and high debt rates enforced by equally monopolist banks, this resulted in many farmers abandoning or selling out their farms in the 1880s and 1890s.

The lands thus abandoned mostly ended up in the possession of large corporations that concentrated on extensive industrial farming. Unable to compete, Eastern farmers were increasingly also forced to abandon their lands and migrate West or to the cities, where they joined a growing urban proletariat. In the cities the influx of fresh labor benefited the growth of industry, which developed ever faster. Industrial growth was further fostered by the introduction of new methods of production and the use of new sources of energy. Innovation and industrial growth fed upon one another. Railroads opened up the entire territory of the United States. The first railroad between California and the Eastern parts of the United States was completed in 1869, and before the end of the nineteenth century there were four intercontinental rail links. Refrigerator cars made possible the transportation of fresh meat and produce from the West and Mid-West over enormous distances, and turned Chicago into the slaughterhouse of the world, or at least the United States. Because of its geographical position in the middle of the U.S., and its proximity to the cattle territories of the Great Plains, Chicago became the center of the meat processing and packing industry, and thereby also the largest railway hub in the world. Oil and electricity were the new sources of energy, in turn giving rise to whole new industries such as the automotive industry around the turn of the twentieth century. The telephone facilitated and intensified communication and commerce. This contributed to the concentration of industry and commerce in the fast-growing cities. The latter indeed grew phenomenally in this period: between 1850 and 1900 New York grew from five hundred thousand inhabitants to three and a half million, Chicago from twenty-eight thousand in 1850 to one million in 1890.

Living conditions in the cities were poor for the laboring masses, and very much resembled those in the industrial centers of Europe. Low wages, female and child labor, unhealthy working conditions, long hours, insalubrious housing conditions in crowded tenements were the rule rather than the exception. With the exception of some of the older cities on the East Coast such as Boston or New York, or the older plantation areas around Charleston and New Orleans, which both, albeit for different reasons and in different ways, were marked by a relatively stable and long-standing system of social hierarchy, the U.S. had never known any form of specific social stratification. In fact, Jacksonian democracy, named after Andrew Jackson (1767–1845), who was president from 1828 to 1836, and the outcome of the Civil War, had done away, at least theoretically, with such existing hierarchies. Now, however, as was also the case in most of Western Europe, so too in the United States there arose an urban proletariat. And if before the Civil War every American, like Huck Finn in the eponymous 1884 novel by Mark Twain, and at least if white, could still flee any form of social discrimination by moving to the untamed West, the gradual incorporation into states of all of the territory of the continental U.S. effectively did away with such freedom. No wonder that the historian Frederick Jackson Turner in 1893 arrived at the conclusion that the 'frontier', the no-man's land that had served as buffer between encroaching civilization and the untamed wild West, had ceased to exist.

Regardless of all this, social mobility in the U.S. remained far greater than in Europe, and the period between the Civil War and World War I was marked by a mass wave of immigration from Europe, and especially from those parts of the old continent where economic, social and very often also political conditions were unfavorable, such as Ireland, Germany, Scandinavia, and Southern, Central and Eastern Europe. Immigration was aided by lenient immigration laws, designed to relieve industry's need for cheap and plentiful labor, and to quickly settle the West. Although many if not most of these immigrants came with the intention of starting a new life on the land somewhere out West, in practice large numbers never made it beyond the cities, and not infrequently they simply stayed on in New York, their port of entry into the promised land. Most eventually melted into the growing army of factory workers, or were swallowed by the innumerable sweatshops of the garment district. For those however that Fortune smiled upon and that through inventiveness, sheer effort, luck, or lack of scruples succeeded in hewing out for themselves a successful business, the streets were paved with gold in the period after the Civil War. Or perhaps it is more appropriate to speak, with Mark Twain and Charles Dudley Warner in their 1873 book of the same title, not of a golden but rather of a 'Gilded Age', because of the often far from pretty reality beneath the surface. The new hero of America's collective imagination was the savvy and successful self-made businessman. The most successful of these men succeeded in gaining control of entire sectors of industry, by acquiring monopolies, by ruthless competition, and often also by manipulating the law. These are what came to be known as the 'robber barons': J.P. Morgan and J.D. Rockefeller in the oil industry, Cornelius Vanderbilt the railroad tycoon, Andrew Carnegie the steel magnate. The only yardstick these men applied was that of success. Still, while fierce champions of free trade principles and merciless in business, they also liberally funded all kind of philanthropic initiatives.

The changes in the economic sphere paralleled equally dramatic changes in the religious and ethical spheres. In the second half of the nineteenth century American society was rattled by a number of publications that severely questioned its traditionally Biblical foundations. First and foremost among these was Charles Darwin's *Origin of Species* (1859), which explicitly argued that Man represented only a stage in the evolution of life on earth rather than being the Crown of Creation, fashioned in God's image, and that this evolution developed according to its own inherent laws rather than divine decree. Still, as re-interpreted by Herbert Spencer, in his 1864 *Principles of Biology*, in which he coined the famous phrase 'survival of the fittest', Darwinian thought also proved eminently adaptable to the Puritan doctrine of predestination. Indeed, in this tradition material and social success could be looked upon as signs of divine election. Together with the nineteenth-century belief in 'progress' and the instrumental role in this played by industry and entrepreneurism, this led the ethical norms propagated by earlier American thinkers such as Benjamin Franklin, Thomas Paine and Thomas Jefferson to be modulated into a doctrine of social and economic competitiveness.

The burgeoning popular press in the United States enthusiastically upheld the idea that hard work led to success, and to a bright future. The sales figures of dailies, weeklies and monthlies grew exponentially towards the end of the nineteenth century. Concurrently, all kinds of mass-market popular genres, often standardized in form and printed on cheap newsprint, the so-called 'dime novels', sprang up. These included cowboy and detective stories, popular romance, and adventure stories. The most popular author of the period, whose name became almost synonymous with a particular kind of juvenile fiction, was Horatio Alger (1832–99). His countless fictions, with titles such as *Ragged Dick; or, Street life in New York with the Bootblacks* (1868), *Luck and Pluck* (1869), *Tattered Tom* (1871), *Strive and Succeed, or, the Progress of Walter Conrad* (1871), *Abraham Lincoln: the Backwoods Boy; or, How a Young Rail-Splitter Became President* (1883), and *Dan, The Detective* (1884), invariably brought a tale 'from rags to riches', from newspaper boy to millionaire.

Meanwhile, the image that Americans had of themselves changed profoundly. Until the Civil War the idea prevailed that Man, within the limits of God's Will, was master of his own fate. After the Civil War Man, after God, no longer is the center of the universe. The social and economic changes the United States underwent transformed the average American from an independent farmer, tradesman or craftsman into a cog in a giant industrial economic machine. Darwinian evolution denied Man's exceptional position in creation. Instead of the subject of God's attention, as under Puritanism, or the center of a benevolent universe, as conceived of by Transcendentalism, Man now was reduced to an insignificant creature in an incomprehensible world ruled by unfathomable natural and economic forces.

The worsening conditions suffered by those at the bottom of the social and economic ladder in the United States also led to reactions. At the end of the nineteenth century we see the emergence of a trade union movement. This would only become truly significant in the early part of the twentieth century, though. At the same time anarchism also took root on American soil. The growth of trade unionism and anarchist activism culminated in the Haymarket Riots of 1886 in Chicago, in which various people died. Although their guilt was never proved conclusively, four anarchists suffered the death penalty. In 1901 President McKinley, a Republican, was murdered by an anarchist, which opened the way to the presidency for McKinley's Vice-President Theodore 'Teddy' Roosevelt. Roosevelt, who was President from 1901 to 1909, introduced legislation to curb the worst social and economic excesses. Already in 1892 anti-monopolists had joined forces in the Populist Party. This party aimed to defend the interests of the pauperized farmers of the West, Mid-West and South. The Democrats, with William Jennings Bryan as their candidate, ran on a Populist platform in the 1896 elections. Eventually, Bryan ran three times, but he never succeeded in gaining the presidency.

The westward expansion of the United States and the disappearance of the 'frontier' also meant the end of the American Indians, or Native Americans, as an issue in American politics. Between 1865 and 1914 all Native Americans were settled, or re-settled, on Indian Reservations, often after bloody military campaigns and forced relocations. After the closing of their own inner frontier the United States cast their net overseas, annexing or occupying Puerto Rico, Hawaii, and a number of islands in the Caribbean and the Pacific. They intervened militarily in Cuba, the Philippines, China, and Columbia-Panama. The Democrats, under Jennings Bryan, opposed – to no avail – these imperialist developments.

Regionalism and realism

Realism as a literary current or method was first imported into the United States through the works of mid-nineteenth-century English authors. However, even if in general it followed

George Eliot's recipe of striving for 'the faithful representing of commonplace things', on American soil it took on a life of its own, colored by typically American situations and circumstances. The first American practitioners of realism were journalists who catered to their compatriots' desire to get to know better the immensity and variety of their country now that the Civil War was over and the rush toward the West had fully begun. Especially popular became the so-called tall tales, humoristic anecdotes full of exaggeration about larger-than-life characters, often folk heroes, and strange customs in remote parts of the nation, especially the Far West. Often at first circulating in oral form, and honed for stage performance, these stories gradually also made it into local newspapers, and thence into the established press in the Eastern parts of the United States. Eventually they developed into an authentic literary genre as practiced by recognized humorists such as Artemus Ward (Charles Farrar Browne, 1834–67), Petroleum Vesuvius Nasby (David Ross Locke, 1833–88), and Josh Billings (Henry Wheeler Shaw, 1818–85). Assuming the fictitious alter ego of a barely literate know-it-all they cast their contributions to dailies and weeklies in the form of sent-in letters, using quaint dialect and folksy expressions, and routinely employing hyperbole and anti-climax. Ward, Nasby and Billings all gained national fame and were much in demand as stage performers in a tradition that in the nineteenth century was wide-spread and which also for many now more famous authors, such as in England and later also in America Charles Dickens, but also Mark Twain, formed a main source of income. In a certain sense what Ward, Nasby, Billings and others like them did can be considered a folksy equivalent to Sir Walter Scott in the second decade of the nineteenth century describing Scottish Highland customs to his English and Lowlands Scots readers. Just as Scott's descriptions eventually furnished one strain of beginning English realism, so too the humorists' tall tales and their folksy way of telling them filtered into emerging American realism.

Mark Twain

Mark Twain, in whose work American regional realism reached its high point, started out in the tradition of Ward, Nasby and Billings. Twain (Samuel Langhorne Clemens, 1835–1910) was born in Missouri, and spent his youth in Hannibal, a small frontier town on the Mississippi that later served as inspiration for St. Petersburg in *The Adventures of Tom Sawyer* and *Adventures of Huckleberry Finn*. In 1847 Twain's father died. Twain apprenticed himself as a printer. Pretty soon he also started writing short pieces for a newspaper run by his older brother Orion. In 1856 Twain became a river pilot on the Mississippi, a highly respected and well-paid profession. This phase of his life provided him with the material for *Life on the Mississippi* and with the detailed knowledge of the river that speaks from *Adventures of Huckleberry Finn*. The outbreak of the Civil War put an end to shipping on the Mississippi, which until then had served as the major North–South traffic artery in the United States. Twain headed west to join his brother Orion in Nevada. There he took up journalism, eventually becoming a regular reporter on a daily in the booming frontier town of Virginia City in 1862. From that date on he adopted the pen name of Mark Twain, after the marks on a sounding line measuring the depth of the water safe for passage for a Mississippi riverboat, and started providing humorous sketches and stories to various periodicals. Twain humorously chronicled his trek out west, and his experiences there, in *Roughing It* (1872). Fame came in 1865, with the publication of 'The Celebrated Jumping Frog of Calaveras County'. This tall story recounts how the champion jumping frog Dan'l Webster, when his owner, the gambler Jim Smiley, for one moment does not pay sufficient attention, is ladled full of lead shot by a mysterious stranger, and thus loses the jumping contest, and his owner his bet. In many ways this story is typical of the humorous tales then in vogue around the American West: it already circulated in various oral versions before it appeared in print, it is presented as an oral anecdote told to the narrator by an aged folk narrator, it is in dialect, it involves a half-legendary folk character whom the folk narrator apparently uses as a frame device for many of his tall tales, and uses hyperbole and anti-climax, as when the narrator is called away before he can round off his tale.

In 1869 Twain published *The Innocents Abroad*, an anecdotal description of a trip to the Mediterranean and the Holy Land. Twain expressly intended his readers to see these fabled destinations not through the eyes of cultural historians or art lovers rehearsing what their readers *should* see, but rather through the eyes of someone like them. The result is a down-to-earth and even debunking view of what the average European and culture-hungry American was wont to uncritically consider as artistically and historically admirable.

After his marriage to Olivia Langdon, of a wealthy New England family, in 1870, Twain settled in Hartford, Connecticut. It is here, in the comfortable residence he had himself built with the small fortune that *Innocents Abroad* had yielded, that Twain wrote the works he is now most famous for.

One of the first results of Twain's Hartford period was *The Gilded Age* (1873), written in collaboration with Charles Dudley Warner (1829–1900). The subtitle to this novel is 'A Tale of Today', and Twain and Warner indeed sketch a picture of the industrial society rapidly developing in 1860s and 1870s America. Their vivid description of corruption, speculation and financial manipulation ended up giving this turbulent era its name.

Further works to see the light in this period are *A Tramp Abroad* (1880), a sort of sequel to *Innocents Abroad*, as well as the historical phantasies *The Prince and the Pauper* (1882) and *A Connecticut Yankee at King Arthur's Court* (1889). The first of these is set in Tudor England and uses the popular motif of the double. The second book has as its setting the final days of Roman Britain. Both books show a vivid interest in the life and fate of people who have not been favored by society. Although cast as satires, they both nevertheless testify to Twain's growing interest in social and economic issues as they also started to dominate American literature at the time.

In fact, such an interest also spoke from the three major works for which Twain is chiefly remembered: *The Adventures of Tom Sawyer* (1876), *Life on the Mississippi* (1883), and *Adventures of Huckleberry Finn* (1884). For these works Twain drew upon memories of his youth on the Mississippi. Together with its tributaries the Ohio and the Missouri, the Mississippi functioned as America's economic highway during the first half of the nineteenth century. Twain's own youth and the years he spent as a riverboat pilot before the Civil War, preceded by a brief history of the river, form the subject of the first part of *Life on the Mississippi*. The second part, which was only completed some seven years after the first, recounts a voyage Twain made on the Mississippi twenty-one years after he had left off being a riverboat pilot. The writing in this second part is considerably less animated than in the first part, but it is precisely this contrast that underscores the point the book makes. The almost empty river as witnessed by Twain during his voyage as recounted in the second part in nothing compares to the busy waterway of the pre-Civil War years. *Life on the Mississippi* is in the last instance a lament for what has been lost in the changes wrought by the Civil War and its aftermath. The role of the Mississippi as America's major traffic artery has been taken over by the railroads that now cover the entire continent. Moreover, the traditional North–South traffic of before the Civil War, which predominantly went by way of the Mississippi, has been replaced by the ever growing East–West traffic, and this both because of the economic downfall of the South and the explosive growth of the West. The Mississippi as Twain had known it before the Civil War after 1865 definitively belonged to an age gone by.

The nostalgia that speaks from *Life on the Mississippi* also flavors the two books upon which Twain's fame rests beyond the United States. *The Adventures of Tom Sawyer* and *Adventures of Huckleberry Finn* directly hark back to the frontier life of Twain's own youth, and hence to the period before the Civil War. The protagonists of both books are boys in their teens, but whereas *The Adventures of Tom Sawyer* can rightly be seen, and has become famous the world round, as a typical boys' book, *Adventures of Huckleberry Finn* is much more than that, and has equally rightly come to be seen as pivotal to American literature. The unruly Tom Sawyer embodies all-American values such as honesty, fairness, entrepreneurialism (who could forget the famous episode where Tom, having been put to whitewashing a fence by his aunt, tricks his friends into doing the work for him, and into the bargain makes them pay for the privilege!), and a sense of adventure and initiative. In short, he has all that it takes for a man to be a useful and much-appreciated member of a typical nineteenth-century American pioneer community. It is the plot of the book, combining sensational elements, such as the search for a treasure and a murderous Indian, and romantic-sentimental ones, such as Tom and Becky's teenage amours, that warrant calling *The Adventures of Tom Sawyer* juvenile literature. At the same time, though, Twain has succeeded in sketching in great detail life in a small provincial town at the edge of advancing civilization in the first half of the nineteenth century, and in capturing the essence of the American worldview of his time, and some would say ever since. Moreover, there is a deeper meaning to *The Adventures of Tom Sawyer* that however only shines through when one considers it in combination with its successor and sequel *Adventures of Huckleberry Finn*.

In *Adventures of Huckleberry Finn* Twain invests his characters, the adventures they live, and the setting in which they live them, with truly mythical dimensions. Huckleberry – short 'Huck' – Finn is a friend of Tom Sawyer's, and until he came into the little fortune that is his part of the treasure that Tom and he found at the end of *The Adventures of Tom Sawyer*, he went through life as a carefree little orphan vagabond. Now, however, he has been taken in by a St. Petersburg widow, Mrs. Douglas, has to go to school, and in general become civilized. Huck chafes against the rules imposed upon him. Unexpectedly Huck's father, a drunken and mur-derous lout long thought dead, returns to claim Huck's fortune. Huck succeeds in evading his father, and in order to escape further meddling decides to let people in St. Petersburg believe that he has drowned, and to drift down the Mississippi on a raft. He is joined, to the surprise and unease of both, by Jim, a runaway slave hoping to reach the shores of Ohio, a non-slave holding state. In the relationship between these two characters Twain neatly encapsulates the moral dilemma facing nineteenth-century American society. Jim should hand over Huck, a minor, to the authorities, but this would inevitably mean his own recapture. At the same time 'official' America, in the guise of the law but also religion, expects Huck to turn Jim in as a runaway slave, to be returned to his rightful owner, the sister of the widow who had taken in Huck. For most of the book Huck is doing battle with his conscience over this. However, he realizes that in many ways his plight and that of Jim's are similar: they both seek freedom. But whereas it will be Huck's birthright, once of age as a white man, to enjoy his inalienable right to 'life, liberty, and the pursuit of happiness', as famously proclaimed in the *Declaration of Independence*, no such promise holds for Jim. As such, *Adventures of Huckleberry Finn* mercilessly indicts nineteenth-century American society for woefully falling short of that same Declaration's claim that 'all men are created equal'. As in Hawthorne's *The Scarlet Letter*, then, in *Adventures of Huckleberry Finn* too the real battle goes between the laws of men, of society, as laid down in law and in religion, and those of simple human nature, of the human heart. Just as Hawthorne intimated in his novel that the ideals of the Pilgrim Fathers had been corrupted by the insti-tutions their leaders had created, so Twain, without explicitly saying so, in his great novel intimates that the ideals of the Founding Fathers of the Republic have been travestied in the institutions of nineteenth-century America. How the two foundational traditions which this society routinely invoked had been turned against themselves in nineteenth-century American reality most forcefully transpires when Huck, desperate to ease his conscience, sits down to write a letter to Miss Watson denouncing Jim and then starts thinking about how Jim and he have shared life on the Mississippi, and how Jim has always cared for him. Just then, in Huck's words:

> I happened to look around, and see that paper.
>   It was a close place. I took it up, and held it in my hand. I was a trembling, because I'd got to decide, forever, betwixt two things, and I knowed it. I studied a minute, sort of holding my breath, and then says to myself:
>   'All right, then, I'll go to hell' – and tore it up

To choose for the devil here is to choose for charity, for the God of love, and to transgress the law is to obey the dictates of one's human heart. Ironically, it is only via these choices that Huck can return to the original ideals upon which 'America' supposedly was built. Small wonder, then, that Huck at the end of the novel reaches the conclusion that the only chance he has of preserving his innocence, of living according to natural rather than social law, is to head for that part of America not yet settled and incorporated as a state of the Union, with all that would entail in terms of institutional organization. In his own final words in the novel: 'I reckon I got to light out for the Territory ahead of the rest, because Aunt Sally she's going to adopt me and sivilize me and I can't stand it. I been there before'.

Adventures of Huckleberry Finn masterfully evokes American reality as Twain himself had lived it in his early life: the mighty Mississippi, the little frontier towns along its shore, the hustle-and-bustle on the quays and on the river, the colorful doings of a pioneer society. Yet Twain did not only dwell upon the idyllic aspects of this reality. Numerous are the passages in which he mercilessly dissects and satirizes the cruelty and vulgarity of his compatriots. Through it all, though, *Adventures of Huckleberry Finn* is highly entertaining, and downright funny, which undoubtedly has contributed to its success not just in the United States but all around the world, down to our days. Twain achieved this effect primarily through his use of Huck Finn himself as a folksy, extremely down-to-earth and extremely likeable narrator, with whom most Americans could readily identify. As Twain himself explains in a foreword, he took great pains to have each of the characters in the novel use the right dialect. Altogether this means that in *Adventures of Huckleberry Finn* a particular region of the United States comes to life as never before. Ironically, this also made the novel on its first appearance difficult to stomach for some more genteel minds. The book was banned from the library of Concord, the town of Emerson and Thoreau, on the grounds that it was 'rough, coarse, and inelegant' with a hero who is 'the veriest thrash'. Some fifty years later, on the contrary, Ernest Hemingway was of the opinion that 'all modern American literature comes from one book by Mark Twain called *Huckleberry Finn*'.

Another fifty years on it was a wholly different aspect of *Adventures of Huckleberry Finn* that shifted into focus. The influential liberal critic Lionel Trilling in 1948 had enshrined Twain's novel as 'one of the central documents of American culture', and it had quickly become a set piece of the literary canon as taught in American high schools. The African American writer Ralph Ellison could still identify with Huck as an all-American boy, and see the relationship between Huck and Jim, as it develops throughout the novel, as symbolic for the reconciliation between black and white in America. Particularly, he saw the ending of the novel, in which

Jim has been recaptured, but is finally set free after a series of adventure-story interventions of Tom Sawyer, and manumission by Miss Watson, and which by many earlier critics had been seen as a rather weak-kneed return by Twain to the juvenile genre of his earlier success novel, as allegorical for the Civil War, and for the final assumption of responsibility by white society for America's African American population. Ellison's co-African American Julius Lester, though, during the period for the struggle of African American emancipation in the 1960s and 1970s, denounced *Adventures of Huckleberry Finn* as a bad book that hurt African Americans in their self-esteem and confirmed white American males in their feelings of supremacy. In the 1990s, then, the critic Shelley Fishkin Fisher gave yet a further twist to the novel's afterlife by re-interpreting it as the story of a hybrid America, especially in Twain's use of voice, which she saw as heavily influenced by the black American speech Twain had heard in his youth.

The central role *Adventures of Huckleberry Finn* thus has come to occupy in discussions about American identity or identities has for the longest time obscured the fact that with this novel Twain was also conducting a dialogue with European literature. For sure, *Adventures of Huckleberry Finn* from the very beginning has been seen as deliberately distinguishing itself from the European novel as practiced in Twain's lifetime. That the sunken riverboat upon which Huck and Jim in one scene happen is called the 'Walter Scott' then is taken to indicate Twain's aversion to the kind of historical Romanticism he held at least partially responsible for the disaster of the American South. Yet from very early on too critics have pointed out that Twain from the very beginning of his novel invokes the example of Cervantes's *Don Quixote*, and that he regularly, though very obliquely, returns to it. Usually, though, this has been linked to what many critics have seen as the pernicious adventure-and-fairy tale element of the book, which they see coming through at its worst in the much-maligned ending of the book that we alluded to earlier. Still, there is another interpretation. Twain starts off *Adventures of Huckleberry Finn* with Huck warning the reader that he will not 'know' about Huck without having read *The Adventures of Tom Sawyer*. This is true on the level of the characters and the setting. However, it can also be seen to hold on the level of the very meaning of *Adventures of Huckleberry Finn*.

Succinctly put, *The Adventures of Tom Sawyer* and *Adventures of Huckleberry Finn* can be taken as echoing, respectively, parts I and II (1605 and 1615) of the Spanish author Miguel de Cervantes's *Don Quixote*. It has been argued that the *Quixote* part II self-reflexively rewrites the guilt-free buffoonery and economic disinterestedness of part I as almost sadistic cruelty and economic self-interestedness, and that this would reflect Cervantes's negative judgment on Spain's transition from an essentially late-medieval or pre-modern society to an early modern one. Whereas both kinds of society are beguiled by the gap between fact and fiction, with the famous knight serving as the embodiment of the inability, or the refusal, to properly distinguish between the two, Cervantes in the end seems to prefer the more innocent 'folly' of the earlier society, which at least lived by virtues such as chivalry, honor, and charity, virtues that in the *Quixote* part II have definitively had their day, and for the demise of which Cervantes holds responsible the commercialization and commodification occasioned by Spain's colonial expansion. Along similar lines, Twain in *The Adventures of Tom Sawyer* would portray a youthful, buoyant and optimistic America, an America that *Adventures of Huckleberry Finn* can only nostalgically long for, lamenting its passing, and implicitly denouncing the crassness and hypocrisy of Gilded Age America. The famous ending of *Adventures of Huckleberry Finn* might then be read in the light of Don Quixote's equally famous deathbed conversion, when he foreswears all magic, and all books of chivalry which have led him to his madness, and returns to orthodox Catholicism. This can be seen as giving in on Cervantes's part to expectation and religious compulsion, but therefore also as ironical, and hence empty, with no actual hope of salvation for the knight, and in truth madness to be preferred. So too, Huck's announcement of his lighting out for the territory, in a novel written when the frontier, and 'the territory', in practice had already vanished, finally rings hollow. And the same goes for Jim's hope for freedom at a moment when with the end of Reconstruction and the passing of the first Jim Crow laws it was already becoming clear that the promise of emancipation for the U.S.'s black population would not be fulfilled. In both cases, then, instead of a successful escape to freedom, what *Adventures of Huckleberry Finn* holds out to its readers is a grim confirmation of the constraints imposed by 'civilization', where civilization then is also unmasked as travesty of what the word implies. Instead of the untutored native-born genius he has often been taken to be, Whitman's counterpart in prose to Emerson's call for a truly 'American' poet, and a perfect icon for an America that likes to see itself in similar auto-genetic terms, Twain then emerges as a writer intensely dialoguing with European literature, and as much concerned with finding his right niche in world literature as with establishing a native tradition.

As we have just argued, *Adventures of Huckleberry Finn* was already inherently pessimistic, although this was masked by the book's humorous language and the positive outlook on life of its protagonist. After 1890 though Twain's work became increasingly darker. The bankruptcy of the publisher with whom Twain had published since the 1870s, and in which he had invested part of his fortune, did not help in this. Twain succeeded relatively rapidly in regaining his financial footing, but only through a grueling lecture tour around the world. There were also a number of family tragedies. Twain's best novel from this later period is *The Tragedy of Puddn'head Wilson* (1894). As in *The Adventures of Tom Sawyer*, in this novel too the plot revolves at least partially around the solution of a murder. As in *Adventures of Huckleberry Finn* the moral and social implications of slavery are highlighted in the relation between Tom, a white orphan boy, and Chambers, Tom's double and of slave descent. Chambers's mother, who was also wet-nurse to Tom, swapped the boys in their infancy. Chambers is raised as a white man, and Tom as a slave. When Chambers commits a murder everything is brought out by Puddn'head Wilson, the lawyer of the suspected murderer(s). Rightful order is restored, but Twain leaves us in little doubt that the whole thing cannot be undone. Tom will never become a 'truly' white man, and Chambers, who as a slave has now all at once become a precious commodity, escapes punishment and is sold down the river. *The Tragedy of Pudd'nhead Wilson* is a somber book. Unlike for Huck, for Tom the past is clearly not going to go away, and a truly new life is not on the cards.

Twain's pessimism came to a head in 'The Man that Corrupted Hadleyburg' (1900) and the posthumously published *The Mysterious Stranger* (1916). In the first of these long stories a town that prides itself on being the most honest and unselfish town of the country falls victim to temptation in the form of a bag of (supposedly) gold that a stranger left behind. The second story, set in Austria around the year 1600, is a fable about the struggle between Good and Evil, and the roles of God and Satan. How far Twain at the end of his life had strayed from his initial optimism and his uncomplicated folksy humor becomes clear from the final paragraphs of this story, from which speaks an almost solipsistic nihilism. The central position that Twain, with his major works and especially *Adventures of Huckleberry Finn*, during his lifetime had occupied in American literature was recognized, though, by his contemporary William Dean Howells, a major writer in his own right and a good friend of Twain's, when without exaggeration he labeled the latter in 1910, on the occasion of his death, 'The Lincoln of our literature'.

Other regionalists

If Twain was undoubtedly the greatest of regional authors, he certainly was not the only one. In fact, between 1870 and 1900 almost every state in the Union had its own share of regionalist writers. Some of these during their lifetime were quite, or almost quite, as famous as Twain himself. Most of them, however, do not go beyond the folksy humor of Twain's early writings, and they never attain the ultimate seriousness that, for all the fun they may otherwise be, underlies Twain's greatest works.

Bret Harte (1836–1902), a contemporary and a friend of Twain's, like the latter started out writing about the mining camps of California and the American West in the 1860s. Unlike Twain he largely stuck to this setting for the rest of his career. Harte specialized in stories that mixed melodrama, sentimentality and irony, as in the title story of his best-known collection, *The Luck of Roaring Camp and Other Stories* (1870). When the only local whore of a lawless and godforsaken little mining town called Roaring Camp dies giving birth, the inhabitants decide to collectively adopt the newborn child. The little town undergoes a positive metamorphosis. However, a sudden flash flood wipes out the entire town, including the child, baptized 'The Luck', and its guardian, previously the wildest man in town. In 'The Outcasts of Poker Flat', from the same collection, a professional gambler, an unsavory old man, and two whores, one older and one young, are chased from the little mining town of Poker Flat. Winter has set in, yet, against the advice of Oakhurst, the gambler, the party decides to spend the night in a hut in the mountains, instead of continuing on to the next settlement. At nightfall they are joined by Tom and Piney, a young couple who have just eloped. The next morning the old man has gone, taking with him all mounts and most of the provisions. Worse, overnight the party has been snowed in. Tom leaves in order to get help. The others one by one sacrifice themselves for the sake of Piney, who never catches on to the kind of company she in fact is keeping. When help finally arrives everyone has perished, but by their unselfish behavior they have all rehabilitated themselves as human beings. In the United States itself Harte's popularity quickly waned, but he remained popular in England, where he spent the latter part of his life.

Another contemporary of Twain's was Edward Eggleston (1837–1902). In *The Hoosier Schoolmaster: A Story of Backwoods Life in Indiana* (1871) Eggleston drew upon his own experiences to sketch the life of a country school teacher in 'The Hoosier State' Indiana. The novel's plot is rather simplistic and sentimental, its characters flat, and its humor adolescent, but the book also gives a realistic picture of life in a little Midwestern town in the middle of the nineteenth century. Eggleston was a Methodist minister, and he put his work as a teacher in the service of his devout Christian idealism. The success of *The Hoosier Schoolmaster* led Eggleston to write a number of similar works, mostly for a juvenile audience, but he also wrote popular history, and a number of other novels, set in different states, such as for instance *The Graysons: A Story of Illinois* (1888) and *The Faith Doctor: A Story of New York* (1891).

As can be seen from the example of Eggleston, regional fiction quickly became a specific sub-genre in American literature, with its own conventions, including highly detailed local settings, the use of local forms of speech, and usually also a rather moralistic undertone. No state of the Union between the Civil War and World War I escaped becoming the subject of regionalist writing. Like Eggleston in his early writings, so too E.W. (Edgar Watson) Howe (1853–1937) chose the Midwest as subject for his fiction in *The Story of a Country Town* (1883). Joseph Kirkland (1830–94) situated *Zury: The Meanest Man in Spring County* (1887) and *The McVeys* (1888) in the Far West. Mary Noailles Murfree (1850–1922), writing under the penname of Charles Egbert Craddock, published numerous novels and collections of stories about her native state of Tennessee, and especially about the mountainous Appalachian region of the latter. Most famous are the stories from *In the Tennessee Mountains* (1884) and *The Prophet of Great Smoky Mountain* (1885). The neighboring state of Kentucky found its champions in

James Lane Allen (1849–1925), with his most famous novels *A Kentucky Cardinal* (1894) and *The Choir Invisible* (1897), and John Fox Jr. (1862–1919), with *The Kentuckians* (1898) and especially *The Trail of the Lonesome Pine* (1908). *In Ole Virginia: Or, Marse Chan and Other Stories* (1887), by Thomas Nelson Page (1853–1921), glorified the Old South. Grace King (1852–1932) wrote about the women from impoverished genteel backgrounds in New Orleans after the Civil War in *Balcony Stories* (1892).

Most of the regional writers we mentioned in the previous paragraph, and their almost innumerable counterparts writing about every imaginable part of the United States, now have at best an historical significance. Still, as we near the end of the nineteenth century we see that with a number of these regional writers the local interest is increasingly matched by that in social issues, leading to realism, and sometimes already something bordering on naturalism, gaining the upper hand over the folksy humor and often faux-naiveté of earlier work. Two writers whose work parallels that of Twain in addressing race relations in the United States through the medium of regional literature are George Washington Cable (1844–1925) and Joel Chandler Harris (1848–1908).

Cable's earliest sketches, collected in *Creole Days* (1879), breathe the exotic French–Spanish atmosphere of early nineteenth-century New Orleans, which only became a part of the United States with the Louisiana purchase of 1803, when Napoleon sold all remaining French possessions in North America to the U.S. Cable's best novel, *The Grandissimes: A Story of Creole Life* (1880), takes place in New Orleans during the transfer of power to the Americans. Joseph Frowenfeld, an American of German origin, settles in New Orleans, where he becomes involved in a feud between the two most important creole family clans of the city. The plot and its solution are rather melodramatic, with a happy ending in which the families are reconciled while marriage bells are ringing, and the description of the creole milieu of New Orleans is somewhat overdone. Still, Cable's irony compensates for a lot of this, and the novel offers an unmatched insight into the social structure of old New Orleans. What's more, the Mississippi delta and its bayous are realistically and impressively pictured. It is probably no coincidence that these stronger passages figure as part of the story-within-the-story of the untamable slave Bras-Coupé, who seeks refuge in the delta swamps. Frowenfeld is an abolitionist, and the horror of the story of Bras-Coupé, who is captured and beaten to death, leaves no doubt as to whose side Cable was on. Such an attitude, even after the Civil War, did not ingratiate Cable with his fellow-Southerners. Eventually, he had to leave the South. He removed to Massachusetts, and became friends with Twain.

Like many writers of his generation Joel Chandler Harris started out as a printer and journalist before turning to creative writing. He had already gained fame as a local humorist when the first of his Uncle Remus stories appeared in 1876 and made him into a writer of national repute. The first Uncle Remus collection was published in 1881, and was followed by five more such collections. Harris takes his readers to the Georgia of his own youth. Using carefully crafted negro dialect, the old and grizzled Uncle Remus tells a little white boy stories that mix fairy tale, folk tale and animal fable elements. Central to these stories are Brer Rabbit and Brer Fox, who continuously try to trick one another. Both the work of Harris and that of Cable have been cited as feeding into that of William Faulkner, the South's greatest twentieth-century writer. With Harris it is his use of oral structures, the easy trust intimated between the old black man and his little white listener, the faithful and expressive representation of negro dialect, and the positive appreciation of the black man, who is seen as more honest and dependable than his white counterparts, that would have appealed to Faulkner. With Cable it is the depiction of the social relations between the various races.

Women writers and local color literature

If with Cable and Harris the local color elements served to underscore the issue of race in the United States, a number of women writers used these same elements to reflect on the plight of women. Mary E. Wilkins Freeman (1852–1930) grew up in a fiercely Puritan New England household. Her early stories about life in rural Vermont were collected in *A Humble Romance* (1887). In these stories, and in those of *A New England Nun and Other Stories* (1892) Freeman evokes the harsh conditions under which many New England farmers and small-town folk lived, and the narrowness of their existence. In her most frequently anthologized story, 'The Revolt of Mother', Freeman shows how the strict and principled discipline of such a life can unexpectedly lead to spirited resistance, as that of the 'mother' of the story against her husband.

A more tragic resistance informs the work of Kate Chopin (1851–1904). Chopin was born as Katherine O'Flaherty, of mixed Irish and French-Canadian descent, in St. Louis, Missouri, but most of her work is set in the French and Spanish creole societies of New Orleans and Louisiana, where she moved after her marriage to Oscar Chopin in 1870. After being widowed at an early age she returned to St. Louis, where she started writing local color stories that were collected into *Bayou Folk* (1894) and *Night in Acadie* (1897). She is best known, though, for her novel *The Awakening*, of 1899. This novel, which has sometimes been referred to as 'the American *Madame Bovary*', recounts the sexual 'awakening' of a young woman, Edna Pontellier. Unfulfilled in her marriage, she engages upon a passionate extra-marital affair. Still, this affair is only the most immediate form of her rebellion against the limitations her stifling and conventional middle-class environment imposes upon her. As becomes clear from the lives also of various other women in the novel, and foremost that of a woman artist whom Edna comes to regard as a potential role model, the price of freedom is very high for women at the end of the nineteenth century. In the end, Edna will only find the freedom she yearns for by swimming out naked into the ocean, away from the coast, until she drowns. *The Awakening* was very negatively received, and this basically brought Chopin's literary career to an end. Her work fell into oblivion for almost a full century, but it was rediscovered by the feminist movement of the final third of the twentieth century, and now *The Awakening* is recognized as an early call for women's emancipation. These days the novel is frequently anthologized, along with some of Chopin's stories in which she advocates a similar sexual and social freedom. Foremost among these is 'The Storm' (1898). A man and a woman, both happily married to someone else, enjoy a passionate sexual union during a chance encounter when sheltering from a Southern thunderstorm, the violence of the storm evoking the intensity of the encounter. When the storm has passed each goes back to his or her lawful partner, and 'everyone was happy'. Contrary to contemporary moral and religious orthodoxy, no retribution or punishment follows. The detailed attention Chopin brought to Louisiana creole customs and society, and to the local landscape, caused her work for the longest time to be somewhat disparagingly categorized as 'local color' literature, and therefore as of minor importance. In retrospect, however, we can see that with the freedom it manifests towards then established morals and religion it not only heralded women's emancipation, but also the advent of the liberal realism of a Theodore Dreiser in *Sister Carrie* (1900). In the equally detailed way in which Chopin in *The Awakening* enters into the mind of Edna Pontellier, we can at the same time also see her moving towards the psychological novel that would come into its own after the turn of the century, most prominently in England with the work of Virginia Woolf. Another local color author who helped pave the way for this was Sarah Orne Jewett (1849–1909).

In fact, Jewett is often seen as the very embodiment of local color literature. Her work, though, far transcends the limitations of pure local color literature in that it also adds a social dimension that contains a severe judgment on her contemporary America. Already in her teens Jewett started writing sketches and stories set in her native Maine. In 1877 she published *Deephaven*, a collection of stories all set in an eponymous fictional coastal town inspired by any one of the small seaports near her native South Berwick. Here, as in all her further work, which mostly consists of numerous collections of short stories, a few novels, and some juvenile fictions, Jewett perfectly yet unobtrusively catches the speech rhythms and the vocabulary of her remote Northern locale. She used the formula of a collection of loosely intertwined anecdotal stories in what is generally regarded as her masterwork, *The Country of the Pointed Firs* (1896). Mostly centered upon the lives of women, and seen through the eyes of a female visitor-narrator, these stories, in a sparse yet intimate style, unemotionally recount the everyday routines of Dunnet Landing, yet another fictional Maine seaport community, that is slowly dying out, bypassed by more modern urban and commercial forms of life. This is also the theme of Jewett's most frequently anthologized story, 'A White Heron', from the eponymous 1886 collection. One late evening, when a pre-pubescent girl living with her grandmother on a Maine farm is driving her cow home through the woods, she is startled by the sudden appearance of a handsome young man, a visitor from the city. The young man is an ornithologist, hunting for specimens of rare birds, and he has heard that a white heron is nesting in the neighborhood. The grandmother offers the young man a bed for the night, and during dinner he mentions that he is willing to pay ten dollars to whomever can point him to the white heron. Sylvia, the little girl, has seen the heron before, and because she is, although unwittingly, and in her own innocent way, half in love with the young man, but also because of the money, which represents a significant amount for the poor grandmother, she decides to spy out the bird. Early in the morning she sets out for the woods, and at dawn climbs a giant pine tree from where to observe the heron's rising from his nest. Once she has located the nest she returns to her grandmother's, where the young man, and her grandmother, eagerly await her return. However, Sylvia does not reveal the heron's location. Disappointed, the young man leaves, taking with him the excitement of city life, and the prospect of another existence for Sylvia. The story's ending throws into sharp relief Sylvia's choice, and all it has cost her, yet at the same time in its invocation of nature also makes the link with classical European forms of pastoral, just as the story's opening invoked fairy tale conventions:

> Dear loyalty, that suffered a sharp pang as the guest went away disappointed later in the day, that could have served and followed him and loved him as a dog loves! Many a night Sylvia heard the echo of his whistle haunting the pasture path as she came home with the loitering cow. She forgot even her sorrow at the sharp report of his gun and the sight of thrushes and sparrows dropping silent to the ground, their songs hushed and their pretty feathers stained and wet with blood. Were the birds better friends than their hunter might have been, – who can tell? Whatever treasures were lost to her, woodlands and summer-time, remember! Bring your gifts and graces and tell your secrets to this lonely country child!

Jewett obviously here rejects the lure of the modern. Unlike Kate Chopin, though, she does not opt for the affirmation of an absolute freedom for women, even in the teeth of social, moral and religious conventions. On the contrary, she advocates an almost quietist belief in home truths and domestic values, which yet again are not the values of the sentimental domestic fiction in vogue earlier in the nineteenth century, but which instead are grounded in female bonding, and in a stoic acceptance of fate. The latter also brilliantly comes through in one of the last stories Jewett wrote, and which remained uncollected in her lifetime, 'The Foreigner' (1900). Again set in Dunnet Landing, and again using the devise of the visitor-narrator reminiscent of Emily Brontë's Lockwood in *Wuthering Heights*, here relaying a tale as recounted by the native character Mrs. Todd, herself reminiscent of the Nelly Dean of Brontë's novel, this story relates how some forty years earlier a foreign woman came to the town. Reduced to playing and dancing for money through a series of mishaps, the woman, claiming to be French, ends up marrying a local sea captain. After his drowning at sea she stays on in the town, a perpetual stranger. Only Mrs. Todd's mother and Mrs. Todd, then still a young woman, feel any pity towards the foreigner. When the foreign woman lies dying, it is Mrs. Todd that watches over her. Just before her death the woman claims to see her own mother in the room, and Mrs. Todd, recounting the events to the story's narrator so many years later, asserts that she too, 'couldn't tell the shape, but 'twas a woman's dark face lookin' right at us; 'twa'n't but an instant I could see'. The intimation, unspoken yet quite plain, is that the woman, who came not from France but from the French Islands, somewhere in the Caribbean, was actually black, which renders her position as a 'foreigner' and outsider even more tragic. At the same time, this revelation also lifts 'The Foreigner' out of its merely local color environment, and has it participate in the discourses of discrimination, emancipation, and passing unfolding around the turn of the twentieth century, and this not only in 'white' writing in the United States, but also, and obviously primarily, in African American writing.

A special case of a local color writer is Lafcadio Hearn (1850–1904), who was of very mixed European parentage, and actually, being born a British citizen and dying a naturalized Japanese one, never became an 'American', yet, having spent his formative years as a writer, as of the age of nineteen, in the United States, always considered himself an American writer. Hearn started out as a journalist in Cincinnati and New Orleans, and wrote sketches about life in these cities, as he did later about the West Indies, but he now is best known for his stories, mostly retellings of folktales and legends, about Japan, where he had moved in 1890.

Regional poetry

Regionalism was not just a matter of prose, it was also voiced in poetry. Among the more colorful exponents of the latter we mention Joaquin Miller, who himself gave his birth date as 1841, but whom we now know to have been born in 1837 as Cincinnatus Heine (sometimes also spelled Hiner) Miller in Indiana, and who died in 1913. As a boy Miller moved to Oregon and California, and subsequently led a colorful life out west as a newspaper man, judge, and pony express rider. The author of several collections of poetry, he is chiefly remembered for *Songs of the Sierras* (1871), and for an anti-Mormon play, *The Danites* (1878). Like Bret Harte, who encouraged Miller in his vocation as a poet, Miller became especially famous in England, which he visited in 1871. Although he projected the image of the wild westerner also in his clothes and appearance, and in the versions of his past he himself put about, Miller in fact was a much more cultured poet than he let on, who skillfully anchored his poetry in the traditions that paid. In 'Sierras' (1873), written after his successful tour of England, the mention of 'Darien' in line three is a clear echo of John Keats's 'On First Looking into Chapman's Homer', and the stanza in which this reference occurs in the figures of the seamen featured recalls 'stout Cortez' (the Spanish conquistador Hernán Cortés) crossing the isthmus of Panama as envisaged by Keats in his 1816 poem:

> Like fragments of an uncompleted world,
> From icy black Alaska, white with spray,

To where the peaks of Darien lie curled
In clouds, the broken lands loom bold and gray.
The seamen nearing San Francisco Bay,
Forget the compass here; with sturdy hand
They seize the wheel, look up, then bravely lay
The ship to shore by snowy peaks that stand
The stern and proud patrician fathers of the land.

Also born in Indiana, and celebrating his native state in often humorous verse in native dialect, was James Whitcomb Riley (1849–1916). As illustration consider the first stanza of 'When the Frost Is on the Punkin', where 'punkin' is a dialect word for pumpkin:

When the frost is on the punkin and the fodder's in the shock,
And you hear the kyouck and gobble of the struttin' turkey-cock
And the clackin' of the guineys, and the cluckin' of the hens,
And the rooster's hallylooyer as he tiptoes on the fence;
O, it's then's the times a feller is a-feelin' at his best,
With the risin' sun to greet him from a night of peaceful rest,
As he leaves the house, bareheaded, and goes out to feed the stock,
When the frost is on the punkin and the fodder's in the shock.

A wholly different poet was Bayard Taylor (1825–78). Born from a Quaker family in Pennsylvania, Taylor wrote verse about his native state, but also about the many countries he visited as a journalist and diplomat, including Europe, the Near East, Africa, India, and the Far East, and he translated Goethe's *Faust*. Still mostly read today, however, is his travel book *El Dorado; or, Travels in the Path of Empire* (1850), about a trip he took to California and Mexico at the time of the California goldrush.

Celebrating the Old South in verse were Sydney Lanier (1842–81) and Henry Timrod (1828–67). Timrod served in the Confederate army, and gained fame as an ardent patriot, with poems such as 'A Cry to Arms', and 'Carolina', dedicated to his native state on the outbreak of the Civil War, and which ends:

Fling down thy gauntlet to the Huns,
And roar the challenge from thy guns;
Then leave the future to thy sons,
Carolina!

Lanier, a native of Georgia and a musician and English literature professor as well as a poet, also fought for the Confederacy in the Civil War. Early on he wrote a novel, *Tiger-Lilies* (1867), but soon turned to verse, often in the dialect speech of both poor whites and blacks, such as for instance 'Uncle Jim's Baptist Revival Hymn', which includes the following stanza:

Ole Mahster's blowed de mornin' horn,
He's blowed a powerful blas';
O Baptis' come, come hoe de corn,
  You's mightily in de grass, grass,
  You's mightily in de grass.

Usually considered Lanier's best work is a long sequence singing the glory of the salt marshes on the coast of Georgia, and extolling the virtues of a life lived in harmony with nature as contrasted with the duties of modern industrial life, as in the following passage from 'Sunrise', the first of *The Hymns of the Marshes* (1882):

> manifold One,
> I must pass from thy face, I must pass from the face of the Sun:
> Old Want is awake and agog, every wrinkle a-frown;
> The worker must pass to his work in the terrible town:
> But I fear not, nay, and I fear not the thing to be done;
> I am strong with the strength of my lord the Sun:
> How dark, how dark soever the race that must needs be run,
>   I am lit with the Sun.

Overall, though, the regional poets best-known today are Edwin Arlington Robinson (1869–1935) and especially Robert Frost (1874–1963). Both wrote about New England, and both, like Lanier and many local color prose writers, lamented the passing of an older, generally more rural and small town America, and the coming of a commercial and industrial age. Although their lives largely overlap, Frost, because he started publishing only at the outbreak of World War I, lived far into the twentieth century, and lived his greatest moment of public glory when he was invited to read at President J. F. Kennedy's inauguration in 1961, will be dealt with in the chapter on the period between the two world wars.

Gardiner, in Maine, where he grew up, figures as Tilbury Town in E. A. Robinson's early poetry, which is generally considered his best. During his early career as a poet Robinson lived in obscurity and poverty. In 1904 his poems came to the attention of President Theodore Roosevelt, who arranged a civil service job for Robinson. Gradually, his work gained wider recognition, and he became able to live by his pen. In the 1920s Robinson even received three Pulitzer prizes. By then, however, he was writing a very different kind of poetry, mostly long narrative poems based on the Arthurian legends and on the classics, yet re-mastering them, in a rather optimistic vein, for a contemporary readership. Apparently, his own improving circumstances by then had lightened the mood of his poetic vision. In his early poetry, on the contrary, Robinson most often has a narrator observe and reflect on one of his fictional Tilbury Town's ordinary people, laying bare the soul of the character in question, as well as of the town and of the narrator. He did so in traditional verse forms such as sonnets and multi-stanza iambic quatrains in different meters.

What is probably Robinson's most famous, and certainly most anthologized poem, 'Richard Cory' (1896), included in his second collection of verse, *Children of the Night* (1897), consists of four so-called Sicilian quatrains, iambic pentameters rhyming abab, cdcd, etc. Such quatrains are also often called 'heroic' or 'elegiac' quatrains, and this is not without import for the interpretation of 'Richard Cory'. The poem in its first two lines pits the main character against his fellow townspeople, among whom explicitly figures the narrator:

> Whenever Richard Cory went down town,
> We people on the pavement looked at him;

The next twelve lines further elaborate on this opposition, and sketch Richard Cory as the embodiment of all that in the eyes of the town's 'ordinary' people makes him extra-ordinary: he is a 'gentleman from sole to crown', 'imperially slim', he 'fluttered pulses' and 'glittered when he walked', and he 'was rich – yes, richer than a king'. His 'heroic' stature in the eyes of the town is confirmed at the end of the third stanza with:

> In fine, we thought that he was everything
> To make us wish that we were in his place.

The first two lines of the fourth and final stanza by contrast sketch the misery of the ordinary townspeople's lives. Northing, then prepares us, who by dint of the 'we' of the second line of the first stanza have come to identify with the townspeople, for the shock of the final two lines:

> And Richard Cory, one calm summer night,
> Went home and put a bullet through his head.

As we never gain access to the mind of Richard Cory, but only, along with the narrator, observe him from afar, 'we', readers and inhabitants of the town, cannot know what drove him to his suicide. The only thing we know is that the townspeople apparently miscast him as their hero. Was he plagued by the same doubts, the same burdens, as his admirers? Or was it the loneliness his elevated status thrust upon him that caused him to take his life? What is certain is that with the suicide of Richard Cory the townspeople have lost their image of something that transcended the drudgery of their own lives. In this sense the poem is also an 'elegy' not only for a dead hero but also for what he represented. Perhaps it is not even exaggerated to see the poem as a reworking of the traditional New England jeremiad, with Richard Cory standing for a possible better future also for the other townspeople, and his suicide as the denial of such a future. As such, 'Richard Cory' can also be read as a bleak pronouncement on the declining prosperity of New England around the turn of the twentieth century, particularly if one saw such prosperity as vested in the pastoral ideal, long hallowed in American literary tradition, of a Jeffersonian America of agricultural freeholds and small towns.

Gradually, Robinson's tone became lighter, as we can see from two other, next to 'Richard Cory' and 'Luke Havergal', from Robinson's first collection, *The Torrent and the Night* (1896), frequently anthologized pieces, 'Miniver Cheevy', from the 1910 collection *The Town Down the River*, and 'Mr. Flood's Party', from *Avon's Harvest* (1921). Both these poems again feature Tilbury Town characters. Again the verse form plays off against the would-be 'heroic' ambitions of the characters portrayed, both of them drunks. Miniver Cheevy dreams of the glories of the Trojan wars, of Arthurian legend, and of the Middle Ages, but

> Miniver Cheevy, born too late,
> Scratched his head and kept on thinking;
> Miniver coughed, and called it fate,
> And kept on drinking.

In this alternate rhyming ambic tetrameter modified Sapphic quatrain the swiftness of lines one and three, each consisting of three iambs preceded by a trochee, humorously offsets the ponderousness of line two, consisting of four trochees and stopped with a long pause indicated by the semi-colon, while line four, following Sapphic convention consisting of five syllables, creates bathos by its combination of the so-called 'rising' anapest followed by the 'fall' of the final trochee. As a result, the words that stand out in this final line are 'on' and 'drin-king', thus emphasizing the confusion and befuddlement of the protagonist already announced in line two.

'Old Eben Flood', in the poem named after him, on his way home from Tilbury Town with a jug of liquor, is compared to the hero of the medieval *Chanson de Roland*, Charlemagne's nephew and the commander of the latter's rearguard defending the retreating Frankish army (at least so in the poem) from the advancing Moorish armies in the battle of Roncesvalles in 778 C.E. The jug Eben Flood repeatedly raises to his lips takes the place of Roland's horn, which he sounded to summon help. The times in which Eben Flood lives, however, are not heroic, and even though for a brief moment, with the help of his liquor and of the song he sings, he can create the illusion that he is in command of a universe that corresponds to his desires, in the end

> The weary throat gave out,
> The last word wavered, and the song was done.
> He raised the jug again regretfully
> And shook his head, and was again alone.
> There was not much that was ahead of him,
> And there was nothing in the town below—
> Where strangers would have shut the many doors
> That many friends had opened long ago.

Surely it is no coincidence that the song Miniver Cheevy sings is 'For auld lang syne', a celebration of past happiness and togetherness. In 'Mr. Flood's Party' Robinson again uses the heroic of elegiac pentameter quatrain, doubled here in an eight-line stanza. The regularity of the pentameter in this final stanza flatly undercuts the momentousness of the epic references to the *Chanson de Roland* in the earlier stanzas. And as in the final line of 'Richard Cory', the final two lines of 'Mr. Flood's Party' are a bitter comment on the heroic illusions raised in the preceding stanzas, and at the same time a lament for better times past. Still, even though Miniver Cheevy and Eben Flood live definitely unheroic lives, their fate is not as dramatic as that of Richard Cory. But then neither does their fate seem to affect the Tilbury Town community as does that of Cory – indicative in this regard is that in neither of the two later poems the narrator involves himself, or the townspeople, or indeed the reader, via the use of the collective 'we', as in the earlier poem. It seems as if in these later poems Robinson has already acquiesced in the irrevocable pastness of the kind of America, or in this case perhaps more accurately the kind of traditional New England, that Cory, Cheevy and Flood were rooted in. Interestingly, even in these very 'American' poems, he does so by reaching beyond his American frame of reference, inter-textually appealing to European predecessors.

Realism

Parallel to the regionalist writing just discussed, the period after the Civil War also saw the rise of a roughly bourgeois or middle-class realist literature largely along the lines of European realism as practiced by for instance Honoré de Balzac in France or George Eliot in England. Eliot's own definition of realism, as she put it in *Adam Bede* (1859), was 'the faithful representing of commonplace things'. The main representatives of this kind of realism, which basically also upheld the kind of socio-economic liberalism and individualism subscribed to by the ruling classes in the second half of the nineteenth century in the United States, are in first instance William Dean Howells (1837–1920) and Henry James (1843–1916), and of a somewhat later generation Edith Wharton (1862–1937). What is often cited as an early instance of the turn toward realism in the United States after the Civil War, though, is *Miss Ravenel's Conversion from Secession to Loyalty* (1867) by John William De Forest (1826–1906), who for this novel drew upon his own experiences as a captain in the Union army. The protagonist Lillie Ravenel has to decide between two suitors, the New Englander Edward Colburne, an avid abolitionist, and the flamboyant John Carter, who, even though he fights in the Union army, hails from Virginia, and embodies all virtues and vices of the Old South. Initially, Lillie opts for Carter, but soon after their marriage the latter becomes unfaithful to her. Lillie, who in the meantime has born Carter a son, leaves her husband. Carter dies a hero's death in battle, after which Lillie marries Colburne. Lillie's plight clearly parallels the traumatic choice facing the United States in the period leading up to, and through the Civil War. The conclusion to *Miss Ravenel's Conversion* advocates reconciliation between the warring parties. De Forest's plot retains many Romantic elements, especially when it comes to the relations between the characters. With its attention to Southern mores and customs it also inscribed itself in the then growing vogue for regionalism in America. It is especially for its sober and unheroic treatment of the events of the Civil War and its aftermath, though, that *Miss Ravenel's Conversion* is seen as one of the first manifestations of beginning literary realism in the United States. The same qualities also inform later novels of De Forest such as *Kate Beaumont* (1872) and *Honest John* (1875).

William Dean Howells

William Dean Howells was born in Martins Ferry in Ohio, was schooled as a typesetter in his father's printing shop, and eventually turned journalist. He wrote a successful biography of Lincoln in support of the latter's presidential campaign, and was awarded with a consulship in Venice. He gained some early fame with poetry, journalism, and travelogues, but became influential only when, upon his return from Europe, he assumed the editorship (1866–71) and subsequently became editor-in-chief (1871–81) of *The Atlantic Monthly*, one of the leading intellectual periodicals in the United States. During this period Howells not only encouraged Mark Twain and Henry James, two authors who can be argued to take up position on either extreme end of the realist spectrum, while Howells occupies the middle, in their literary endeavors, but effectively helped them in getting their work published.

The Atlantic Monthly was edited and published from Boston, and in general aligned itself with the views of established New England society. Howells thus became the spokesman for a democratic conservatism in most matters, and the defender of a literature that aimed 'to discover principles, not to establish them; to report, not to create', and to do so by describing American reality 'in its more smiling aspects'. For his earliest novels, *Their Wedding Journey* (1872) and *A Chance Acquaintance* (1873) Howells found inspiration in his own travel experiences, and in the first of his novels that is still occasionally read today, *A Foregone Conclusion* (1874), he, like his contemporary Henry James, capitalized on the contrast between Americans and Europeans. Following his own tenets just outlined, in these early novels Howells anxiously avoided anything controversial or likely to offend, in order to reach as wide a readership as possible.

As of the 1880s, though, Howells, in a move parallel to Twain's around the same time, became more interested in drawing the social and moral dilemmas dividing American society. This change first manifested itself in *A Modern Instance* (1882), and then more forcefully in *The Rise of Silas Lapham* (1885). *A Modern Instance* sketches the decay of a marriage under the pressures of unbridled capitalism, and ends with the death of the husband, a journalist and newspaper editor, and the utter loneliness of all other characters involved. *The Rise of Silas Lapham* takes up similar themes, but gives them a completely different resolution. Like the couple from *A Modern Instance*, so too the Laphams have moved from rural New England – Vermont in their case rather than Maine – to Boston. There, Silas Lapham over many years has built himself a thriving paint manufacturing businesss. In spite of his wealth, Lapham has never had any aspirations to gain entry into the better circles of the city. Now, however, spurred on by his wife, who is eager to secure a good match for their two daughters, he decides to have a large new mansion built on Beacon Hill, as proof of his wealth, and as a sign of his family's rising social ambitions.

In the beginning everything goes according to plan. Then, however, disaster strikes. Unexpectedly, Lapham loses the better part of his fortune. Worse, he has lent another part of his capital to Rogers, a former business partner of Lapham's whom the latter wanted to help, accepting as collateral a well-nigh worthless piece of land out west. To compound everything, a couple of younger competitors make their appearance in the paint market. Socially too, things go wrong. Tom Corey, a scion of one of Boston's most highly esteemed families, shows an interest in the Laphams. Everyone is convinced that Tom is in love with the younger Lapham daughter Irene. The Laphams are invited for dinner at the Coreys, where Lapham behaves like a boor and a parvenu. When it then turns out that Tom is in love with the older daughter, Penelope, instead of with Irene, the dismay is complete. Penelope turns Tom down, even though she is in love with him, because she wants to spare Irene's feelings, and also because her Romantic reading fare has inspired her with vague and unrealistic ideas of self-sacrifice.

Suddenly, Lapham is offered the chance to recoup his losses. Rogers puts him in contact with some English speculators who want to buy the piece of land that Lapham is holding as collateral for his loan to Rogers. They then plan to sell this land to unsuspecting investors in Europe. Lapham now is torn between his desire in one go to regain his financial footing and his awareness that it would be morally indefensible to sell what he knows to be a worthless piece of property for an exorbitant price. After a satanic battle with himself and his conscience he refuses to sell. Inexorably now, there follows Silas's downfall. The paint business founders, his capital and credit vanish, the social status of the Laphams hits bottom. As if to seal their fate, and symbolize their downfall, the new house burns down. Lapham retreats to his property in Vermont and resumes the kind of life he also led twenty years earlier: closer to nature, in closer contact with his own roots, and in the bosom of his closest family. Silas Lapham's economic and social downfall has led to his moral rise. And finally, this rise is rewarded. He is able to secure a new partnership with his younger competitors. Irene copes well with her setback. After a period of reflection Penelope, who in the meantime has arrived at a more realistic view of life through her reading of the English realists, even marries Tom. The young couple, however, decide to settle not in Boston, nor in the eastern part of the United States, but out west, where social relations are easier, and where there is more room for initiative and innovation.

The Rise of Silas Lapham paints a realistic portrait of Boston in the third quarter of the nineteenth century, and vividly illustrates the social, economic and intellectual fermentation marking American life during the period concerned. Lapham stands for a whole generation of self-made men that stormed the heights of American society at the time. The relations within and between the families portrayed in the novel reflect the fundamental changes affecting American society. The Coreys, for instance, while still clinging to their social pre-eminence, are slowly being marginalized. Tom Corey realizes this, and therefore opts for a marriage of love, but also with a daughter of the rising entrepreneurial class, and for the greater freedom and the greater possibilities of the West. This is the topical background against which Howells poses the question of the responsibility of the businessman. But this topicality does not abrogate the validity of absolute moral tenets. Silas' dilemma is that of Huckleberry Finn: both have to choose between what is socially required or expected, and what is morally and humanly right.

In his handling of Lapham's dilemma, and especially in its solution, Howells shows himself to have been at heart a didactic moralist. He paints reality as it should be, rather than as it is. For Howells the novel, and the realist novel in particular, was an instrument for the moral elevation of the reader. In this respect it is telling for the power that Howells attributed to literature that Penelope Lapham arrives at a correct and rewarding evaluation of her situation through her reading of the best English realist novels going at the time. Undoubtedly this also had to do with the fact that Howells, and he certainly was not alone in thinking so at the time, felt that the institutions customarily expected to care for the moral well-being of the masses, such as the church, were losing terrain, and that literature had to step in for the relief.

After his resignation as editor-in-chief of *The Atlantic Monthly* Howells collaborated on various other periodicals, such as *The Century* and *Harper's*. In the course of the 1880s he also moved from Boston to New York which, given Howells's prestige and influence, was indicative of the waning importance of Boston, and New England in general, in the intellectual and commercial life of the country. At the same time it confirmed New York's increasingly leading role. Concurrently, Howells's ever growing interest in contemporary social issues resulted in a series of novels that took him far beyond his early realist tenets. He also became more and more personally involved with the changes in American life and society going on all around him. In 1886 Howells condemned the execution of the four anarchists deemed guilty of complicity in the Haymarket Riots in Chicago as 'civic murder'. This event, and his reading of the Russian novelist Leo Tolstoy brought Howells to declare himself a socialist, a deed of considerable courage in the United States even then. His novels of the period deal with specific social issues, and do so from a soberly realist perspective. *Annie Kilburn* (1888) treats the plight of the immigrant poor. The social complexity of New York is at the heart of *A Hazard of New Fortunes* (1890), a novel about the rise of socialism, strikes and strike breakers, and the world of the press.

As of the 1890s Howells occasionally diverged from straight realism. Even then, though, he was driven by the same moral and social impulse that also inspired his earlier realist fiction. *A Traveler from Altruria* (1894) and *Through the Eye of the Needle* (1907) are utopian novels in which Howells contrasts the ugly reality of turn-of-the-twentieth-century America with a vision of a future ideal society founded on egalitarian principles. In these later novels Howells clearly takes a much dimmer view of the United States than he did in *The Rise of Silas Lapham*. Instead of the steadfast self-made businessman following his ingrained sense of moral justice, in these later works we meet ruthless financiers and equally ruthless anarchists.

With the rise of naturalism in the 1890s Howells's kind of realism, even in its later manifestations, fell out of fashion. His reputation as 'Dean of American Letters' remained high, though, and he used all the influence he still had as a critic to foster the fortunes of the naturalists. Soon after his death, however, his work fell almost into oblivion, and his reputation, certainly in comparison with that of his two major contemporaries Twain and James, paled. His best works, *A Modern Instance*, *The Rise of Silas Lapham*, and *A Hazard of New Fortunes*, still are very much worth reading though.

Henry James

Henry James was born into a wealthy and intellectual New York family in 1843. His father, Henry James Sr. (1811–82), was a well-known writer and lecturer on religious and literary topics. Henry's older brother, William James (1842–1910), became one of the most celebrated philosophers and psychologists of his days, professor at Harvard, and author of ground-breaking works such as *Principles of Psychology* (1890), *The Will to Believe* (1897), *The Varieties of Religious*

Experience (1902), *Pragmatism* (1907), and *The Meaning of Truth* (1909). Alice James (1848–92) during the last years of her life, when she was already terminally ill, kept a diary that long after her death was published. Henry James Sr. could afford to give his children an international education, and to this end took them for lengthy periods to Europe, and to various U.S. cities. Henry himself started studying law at Harvard, but in the mid-1860s, encouraged by Howells, he started writing reviews and short stories. His early work shows the influence of Hawthorne, on whom he wrote a brief study in 1879, and of the major European realists of the middle of the nineteenth century. What he borrowed from a number of them, primarily George Eliot, Balzac and Turgenev, next to the realistic treatment, is the mixture of distanced irony and seriousness that characterizes also their best work. As of 1875 James settled in Europe, first in Paris, where he made the acquaintance of Turgenev and Flaubert, then in London, and finally in Rye, a picturesque little town on the southern coast of England.

The majority of James's novels and stories are set in middle- or upper middle-class milieus, and detail the emotional relationships between the various characters. In the early work the plot is determined by a confrontation between European and American culture and society. This so-called 'international theme' is already present in what James preferred to look upon as his first novel, *Roderick Hudson* (1876). In reality, his very first novel, *Watch and Ward*, had already been published in 1871 in serialized form in *The Atlantic Monthly*, but James became so dissatisfied with it that he later disowned it. It is in *The American* (1877), though, that James first fully elaborates his international theme. The American protagonist, Christopher Newman, makes the acquaintance of a rich and attractive young widow in Paris. He wants to marry her, but is thwarted by the woman's family, who look upon Newman as an unworthy *nouveau riche*. The opposition between the refined, but also static and corrupt Europeans, and the kind-hearted, but also naïvely innocent American is starkly drawn in this novel. At the same time *The American* also points us to what James meant when at the beginning of his career he claimed, after Hawthorne, that America in itself did not furnish enough, or sufficiently interesting, material for a novelist. James needed the cultural and social layering of the old continent to bolster his fiction, and especially in his later work he would draw the almost endless complexity of European society in almost endless and endlessly refined detail.

In *The Europeans* (1878) James returns to the international theme, but reverses the situation. Two Europeans of American descent come to stay for a while with relatives they have never met before in the neighborhood of Boston. Eugenia, morganatically married to a German nobleman, hopes to find a wealthy husband in the United States, because she is afraid that her European husband will disown her. Felix, Eugenia's brother, is a painter who is intent on gathering new artistic impressions in America. The contrast between these two refined European minds and their somewhat stilted American relatives gives rise to a number of comical scenes. Gradually, however, Felix comes to appreciate the basic honesty, freshness and innocence of the Americans. Having fallen in love with his American niece precisely because she abundantly exhibits all these characteristics, Felix ends up staying in the U.S. for good. Eugenia, on the contrary, tries to play the subtle social game at which she is such a master in Europe, also in America. While her behavior intrigues the Americans, it also costs her the love of the one American who is really interested in her. Not comprehending what has happened, and where she has gone wrong, she returns to Europe in an effort to save face.

The novella *Daisy Miller* (1879) mirrors the situation of *The Europeans*, but this time set in Europe. The novella's eponymous heroine is a young American woman who, with her mother and little brother, tours Europe as a tourist. Her free American ways, especially with men, and her disregard for social conventions estrange her from those countrymen, and especially women, of hers who have settled in Europe permanently, and for whom the rules of the social game, as they see it, are the more sacred the less they understand them. Winterbourne, the young American whom Daisy falls in love with, and who seems willing to return the feeling, has lived too long in Europe to understand that Daisy is not the promiscuous little vixen his aunt holds her to be. Daisy on the other hand does not see that her free and friendly relationships with European men, by which she thinks to spur Winterbourne into declaring himself to her, only strengthen him in his suspicions. Daisy eventually dies of Roman fever. The Italian with whom she was thought to have compromised herself reveals to Winterbourne that nothing untoward ever happened between him and Daisy, and that she was the most pure and innocent girl he ever met. Winterbourne realizes that he has made a tremendous mistake and has lost his one chance for true happiness, his chance also to find his way back to the innocence and the energy of his native country. Instead, he resumes his empty expatriate existence.

Indisputably a first high point in James's oeuvre is *The Portrait of a Lady* of 1881. The precision with which a range of social milieus are portrayed, and the psychological acumen with which the characters are drawn, make of this novel a masterpiece of realism. The protagonist, Isabel Archer, in many ways resembles Daisy Miller. Isabel is a rich young American woman who travels to Europe in search of fresh impressions and a richer social life. Jealous of her independence she turns down a number of offers of marriage, from an English nobleman, and from a well-to-do American self-made man, Caspar Goodwood, even though she does feel for the latter. Through the offices of Mrs. Merle, an expatriate American, she becomes acquainted with Osmond, yet another American who has settled in Italy. Dazzled by the aura of connoisseurship and refinement Osmond exudes, she marries him. Very rapidly it becomes clear that Osmond, who used to have a relationship with Mrs. Merle, has married Isabel only for her money. Isabel's life turns into a dull and loveless routine. However, accepting that it is her own stubbornness and folly that have brought her so low, Isabel decides to live the consequences of her actions to the full. Even when Goodwood approaches her again, and she realizes that this is true love, she turns him down and returns to Osmond.

Just as in the earlier novels and novellas, so in *The Portrait of a Lady* too the contrast between Europe and America plays a decisive role. Next to this, though, the novel also draws an intriguing portrait of one very specific psyche, rather than sketching a certain type of character. Isabel Archer is an infinitely more complex Daisy Miller. Although she claims to be hankering after new impressions and strong emotions, something in her character also leads her to hold back from true love. Choosing to stay with Osmond, she also opts for self-limitation rather than the self-development she thought she would find in Europe. Quite possibly James in the character of Isabel, and notwithstanding all obvious differences, reflected upon his own feelings with regard to both Europe and America, and Isabel's doubts echo James's.

The 1880s were very productive years for James. In the same year as *The Portrait of a Lady* there also appeared *Washington Square* (1881), a novel about the leading families of old New York (James himself had been born on Washington Square), and in many ways the example from which Edith Wharton would take her cue for much of her fiction. In 1886 there appeared *The Bostonians* and *The Princess Casamissima*. The first of these is a satire aimed at the women's movement in New England at the end of the nineteenth century. The second novel is situated in London, among revolutionaries and anarchists. It is also in this period that James elaborated his theories about the novel, and that he experimented with the genre. His starting point was that a novelist should 'tell' his readers as little as possible but instead should 'show' them everything. The attitudes, feelings and thoughts of the characters should show from their words and their deeds, and should not be recounted or explained by the narrator. To hide as best as possible the intervention of the author James devised the instance of the 'involved narrator'. This is a character that itself is marginally involved in the intrigue, often only as a spectator, but through whose speech and view we witness the words and deeds of the protagonists. An excellent illustration is the short novel *The Aspern Papers* of 1888. James for the rest of his life continued to theorize about the novel, and about literature in general. He also reworked his fictions to bring them in line with his theories. His best-known theoretical statements are to be found in the article 'The Art of Fiction' of 1884, and in the introductions he wrote to the so-called New York (collected) edition of his novels in 1907–9.

Gradually, James also let go of the international theme. *The Bostonians* is wholly set in the U.S., with American characters, and *The Princess Casamissima* highlights the turbulent and teeming London underworld of the late nineteenth century. The last novel from this period, *The Tragic Muse* (1890), a study in the psychology of the artist, is wholly English both as to characters and setting.

During the early 1890s, in search of greater financial rewards, James devoted himself almost exclusively to the theater. None of his plays met with the desired success, though, and towards the end of the century he returned to fiction, with *The Spoils of Poynton* and *What Maisie Knew* (both 1897). In the latter novel we see, through the eyes of a pre-pubescent girl, the corrupt environment in which her parents operate, and their fast-changing love affairs. The girl is not really wanted anywhere, and she is moved about like a pawn on a chessboard. In this hard school of life Maisie soon learns to judge grown-ups at their true value. *The Turn of the Screw* (1898) is a very different kind of story. In this story of the supernatural it is never unequivocally clear whether the spirits that play such an important role in the plot really do exist, or whether they only exist in the imagination of the protagonists. It is the reader herself who has to make up her mind as to what she accepts as truth, what as imagination. Like *What Maisie Knew*, *The Turn of the Screw* too is a study of innocence confronted with a world of complexity and mystery. The same theme again pervades *The Awkward Age* (1899). The novel unflinchingly exposes how in the unscrupulous world of 'society' the most tender emotions of a young girl are made the object of all kinds of plots and interests.

After the short *The Sacred Fount* (1901) James closed his long and fruitful career as a novelist with three works that are now generally, together with *The Portrait of a Lady*, reckoned as his best: *The Wings of the Dove* (1902), *The Ambassadors* (1903) and *The Golden Bowl* (1904). In *The Wings of the Dove* Milly Theale, a young American woman, visits Europe. There she gets to know Kate Croy, a young English woman who is engaged to Merton Densher. Milly knows Densher too, and is secretly in love with him. When Kate learns that Milly is terminally ill she convinces Merton to act as if he is in love with Milly, so that she will marry him and leave him her fortune. Later, Kate and Densher can then get married. Everything goes according to plan, but a disappointed fortune hunter, whom Milly has turned down, brings all into the open. In spite of this Milly leaves her fortune to Densher. Although Kate's original plan can now go through, the marriage between Kate and Densher never happens. Their conscience, and the ghost of Milly Theale forever stand between them.

The Ambassadors, which James himself considered his best novel, is a less tragic affair. The 'ambassadors' in question are a succession of Americans who are sent from Massachusetts to Paris to bring Chad, the son of the rich American widow Mrs. Newsome, back to his native town there to assume the direction of the family business. The prime ambassador is Lambert Strether, Mrs. Newsome's fiancé. Chad, however, is not keen at all to exchange his free and easy Parisian life for the yoke of a Puritan New England existence. More, Strether himself falls under the spell of Europe, and new ambassadors have to be sent, this time also to bring Strether back. Strether will eventually return to America, but Chad remains in Paris. As to theme and plot, *The Ambassadors* is an ironic counterpart to James's earliest novels – notice for instance the parallelism, and the inversion, between the 'Newman' of James first novel and the

Mrs. Newsome (which we may pronounce as 'nuisome') of the later one. The vision of Europe and America that speaks in the later novel is diametrically opposed to that of the earlier one. Although James's long residence in Europe, and the fact that he wanted to support his adoptive home of England against Germany in World War I, undoubtedly also had something to do with it, from a novel such as *The Ambassadors* it becomes clear that James's decision in 1916 to become a naturalized English citizen also reflected the distance he had come to feel from his native country, and his final choice for Europe.

James's last novel, *The Golden Bowl*, starts from a situation that recalls that of *The Wings of the Dove*. The American Maggie Verver and her father Adam Verver are married, respectively, to Prince Amerigo, an impoverished Italian nobleman, and Charlotte Stanton, an American friend of Maggie's. They all live in London. The Prince and Charlotte used to have a relationship, which at a given moment they take up again. Through tact and self-sacrifice Maggie rights the situation. Whereas in *The Wings of the Dove* Milly Theale tragically succumbs and Kate and Densher are marked for life by the experience, *The Golden Bowl*, with a plot that potentially is just as tragic as that of the earlier novel, sketches the moral growth of all characters involved. In the elaboration of the plot an important role is played by a golden bowl which to the eye is perfect, but which has one tiny flaw. It is the smashing of this bowl that sets in motion the process of normalization of the relations between the characters.

James put unusual emphasis upon the responsibility of the writer towards his craft. His own dedication to his art, which showed from a life in the service of authorship, and the intrinsic quality of his work, proved of prime importance for the development of the English-language novel in the first half of the twentieth century. The moral and poetical fervor that characterized his work from the very beginning culminated in his final three novels. James's novels are often full of irony, and in spite of the fact that his style, especially in his later work, can be very complex, and that some of his scenes may come across as long-winded, a lot of these scenes also charm with their well-developed, if subtle (some say too subtle), sense of situational comedy. At the same time his works often exude an underlying sense of tragedy. The fact that the tragedy of his characters is often also that of man in general makes of James the psychological realist par excellence among American novelists. But James's work also marked the 'coming of age' of the American novel on the world scene. While before him American novelists had almost always paid tribute to European examples, with James the American novel became a beacon for European authors, and not just those, such as for instance Joseph Conrad, writing in English, but also beyond. Thus James paved the way for a next generation of American authors – Hemingway, Fitzgerald, Dos Passos, and above all Faulkner – that would change the face of world literature.

Edith Wharton

The influence of Twain and Howells upon their American contemporaries was immediate and clear. That of James initially was more restricted, and made itself felt in Europe rather than the United States, in the work of authors such as the already mentioned Conrad, Ford Madox Ford, E.M. Forster and Virginia Woolf. In the United States James had only one true follower, some even say disciple: Edith Wharton (1862–1937, *née* Jones). Wharton's work is characterized by a similar ambivalence toward American society as that of James. She too makes use of the international theme in *The Custom of the Country* (1913) and in *The Writing of Fiction* (1925) she explicitly invokes James. Wharton finds her subject in the social tensions raised by the fast changes New York underwent in the late nineteenth century, in the demise of the old stable order and the loss of old norms and values. At the same time her predilection for the difficulties of marriage as the crux around which to mold her stories results from her own unhappy marriage to a much older man, which ended in divorce, followed by an unhappy love affair. Wharton's two best novels, *The House of Mirth* (1905) and *The Age of Innocence* (1920), focus upon conflicts between the desires of the individual and the rigors of the established social order. In *The House of Mirth* Lily Bart has to choose between the love of her heart and the need to make a good marriage, and the choice leads her to commit suicide. Far less tragic, but at least as deeply felt, is The *Age of Innocence*, set in patrician New York in the 1870s. Newland Archer, a promising young lawyer of an old New York family, is engaged to May Welland, likewise of solid old New York stock. Enters Ellen Olenska, a remote relative of May's, who has spent her entire life in Europe, where she has married an abusive Polish count from whom she is now separated, and to flee whom she has come to the United States. Ellen is much more lively, witty, and entertaining than any woman Newland has ever met before, and she certainly comes across as much more sensitive than May, who is very staid and conventional. Before long Newland is in love with Ellen, a feeling that is reciprocated, and the rumor of which sets tongues wagging in New York society. True to his word and to social convention, Newland marries May, even while his passion for Ellen continues unabated. Paradoxically, but totally in character, it is her admiration for his sense of duty, and for the firmness of character it stands for, that also forms the bedrock of Ellen's love for Newland. As she tells him in one of the crucial scenes of the book: 'I can't love you unless I give you up'. When shortly after May, unbeknownst to Newland, lets Ellen understand that she is pregnant, the latter hurriedly departs for Europe again. The pregnancy turns out to be a 'mistake', the implication being that May, far from being the guileless *ingénue* that Newland, if not the world, take her for, is in fact fully in command of the situation. The marriage turns out to be a very happy one, even if in a very conventional way. Thirty years later May has died, and Newland, together with Dallas, his grown son and about to be married himself to a woman very much like Ellen at the time, takes a trip to Europe. On her deathbed May has confided to her son that she knew about Newland and Ellen. When Newland and Dallas are in Paris, where Ellen now lives, Dallas goes to see her. She invites him, and his father, to a party at her apartment that night. The son and the father set out for the party, but when they reach Ellen's building Newland tells his son to go up alone. For a while he sits on a bench outside, then he goes back to his hotel, alone, commenting to himself: 'It's more real to me here than if I went up'. By not going up Newland once again vindicates the choice he made thirty years earlier. While acknowledging that modern times, as lived by his son and his generation, call for modern attitudes, Newland, and we feel Wharton with him, cannot help regretting the passing of an older order, with its own beauty and honor, and of which he and May formed the backbone.

The theater

As already mentioned in earlier chapters, the theater in the United States for the longest time lagged far behind the other genres. In the early part of the nineteenth century, next to a few scarce attempts at 'regular' theater, there flourished a popular form of theater that throve primarily on stereotypes. Black Sambo, childish and harmless, was always good for some laughs. The yankee stood for the vitality of the new nation, stubborn, not very civil, but astute and sardonic, and also got the laughers on his side in his frequent confrontations with representatives of the Old World. After the Civil War the figure of the 'backwoodsman', the hardy settler of the Western frontier, became popular, leading to the phenomenal success – also in Europe – of *Davy Crockett* (1872) by Frank Murdoch (1843–72). These stereotypes, which originally only featured in short burlesques, soon developed into the protagonists of full-length plays. It is no exaggeration to say that this popular kind of theater was the real American theater of the nineteenth century. Moreover, it also gave rise to a uniquely American genre. Out of the sketches featuring the stereotypical black American developed the minstrel show, in which a number of blacks (in reality white men with blackened faces), seated in a half moon circle, make jest of the white master of ceremonies. In other scenes they sing songs, and perform variety sketches. The true minstrel show died out at the beginning of the twentieth century, but its colorful variety and spectacle found a home in the musical.

After 1870 things finally started to move in the regular theater in the United States, even though until right up to World War I it would continue to have a markedly melodramatic character. Already before the Civil War New York had become the primary stage for the American theater. Between 1872 and 1890 the American stage was largely dominated by Dion Boucicault (1820–90), an Irish actor, stage manager and author of well over a hundred unabashedly melodramatic but also very successful plays. Upon Boucicault's death his leading role was taken over by David Belasco (1853–1931), who simply continued in Boucicault's vein. Even during Boucicault's reign, though, a movement towards a more realist kind of theater was inaugurated. In the first instance regionalist fiction and poetry inspired a number of playwrights to introduce more realist elements of speech and situation into their own work. Then, and not least encouraged by Howells, who himself wrote some twenty plays, the themes and characters grew more commonly realistic. This development is for instance reflected in the work of James A. Hirne (1839–1901), who on his first plays collaborated with Belasco, but who in 1890 came up with the for its time and place extremely radical-realist *Margaret Fleming*, in which a woman forgives her husband his adultery and adopts the child that sprang from it. Other early, albeit always still rather timid, realists were Bronson Howard (1842–1908) and Clyde Fitch (1865–1909), who was the first American playwright to also gain a reputation in Europe. This beginning realism in the theater reached a first high with *The Great Divide* (1906) by the poet William Vaughn Moody (1869–1910), in which a New England woman has to choose between loyalty to her native background and her love for a Western rancher. In many ways this play takes up themes raised in *The Virginian*, usually considered the first true 'Western', and which had appeared only a few years earlier, to tremendous success – we will return to *The Virginian* further on in this chapter.

However, we should not overrate this American theatrical realism of the period. The ideas and practices of these writers are still very far removed from those of their European counterparts, men such as Ibsen and Strindberg. They still heavily rely on melodrama, and although their characters show some psychological depth, almost never is there any social reflection, and their plays almost invariably have a happy ending. The theater had gained itself a place on the American literary scene, and the acting on the American stage had become much more professional, but the American theater still could not be compared to the European.

Naturalism

As of 1890 naturalism gained a firm footing on American soil. At that moment the literary movement in question had already almost exhausted itself in its country of origin, France, where Emile Zola had been its main practitioner and theoretician. However, it is the period in which naturalism also flourished in most other European literatures – suffice it to mention Thomas Hardy, George Bernard Shaw, Henrik Ibsen, Knut Hamsun, and Gerhart Hauptmann. In the United States the way for naturalism was partly paved by Henry Adams (1838–1918), a scion from an old Boston family that had furnished two of America's first presidents, and himself a distinguished historian. His study of history and politics, coupled with an early interest in the theories of Charles Darwin and Charles Lyell, led him to see the history of man in terms of dynamic evolution ruled by anonymous and impersonal forces. He elaborated these ideas in *Democracy* (1880), a political novel, and *Esther* (1884), a society novel, and in essay format in what are considered his two main works, *Mont Saint-Michel and Chartres* (1904) and *The Education of Henry Adams* (1907).

The idea that impersonal and uncontrollable forces determine the fate of both individuals and nations is what distinguishes naturalism from realism. Huckleberry Finn, Silas Lapham and Isabel Archer were in the last instance responsible for their own deeds and for what they made of their lives. With the naturalists such is no longer the case. Sometimes inspired by Zola's ideas about the 'experimental novel', and Taine's on 'race, milieu, moment', but just as often without recourse to theory of any kind and simply driven by direct observation, the American naturalists regarded man as the plaything of nature and of the economy. With regard to the latter, the naturalists used their work to protest against what they saw as the injustices of con-temporary society. In the final two decades of the nineteenth century the social and moral excesses resulting from an almost unchecked process of relentless industrialization became painfully clear. Small wonder therefore that many naturalist works show an almost documentary bias and tend toward the format of the problem novel, often in support of one or other of the numerous reform movements characteristic of the turn of the twentieth century.

At variance with the realists, who tended to concentrate on the upper middle-classes, the naturalists focus on the lower classes. Along with this new milieu, they also introduced new themes into American literature. In *Maggie: A Girl of the Streets* (1893) Stephen Crane (1871–1900) portrays the life of a working class girl who, hankering after a better life, drifts into prostitution and ultimately commits suicide. In *The Red Badge of Courage* (1895), his best-known work, the protagonist is a common soldier in the Civil War. Other than in most war novels, though, at least until then, Crane does not depict war as heroic and glamorous. Instead, the dull grinding routine of the barracks and the marches, but also the confusion, the noise, the dirt, and the gore of battle are foregrounded. Crane's hero, rather than a courageous warrior is a frightened deserter, who only by chance is re-united with his company, and the 'red badge of courage' for which he is honored is not suffered in battle at all but rather the result of an accident. *The Red Badge of Courage* in some of its descriptions also already borders on impres-sionism. Another writer who around the same time wrote naturalist-realist stories about the Civil War was Ambrose Bierce (1842–1914?). His best-known Civil War story is 'An Occur-rence at Owl Creek Bridge', from his collection *In the Midst of Life: Tales of Soldiers and Civilians* (1891), in which he takes us into the mind of a Southern planter at the very moment he is being hung by Unionists. Bierce however often also wrote horror and mystery stories in the vein of Edgar Allen Poe, as well as a *Devil's Dictionary* (1911), an alphabetical collection of quirky and often contrary definitions Bierce had written over a period of some 25 years for a San Francisco newspaper, and which continues to be popular to this day.

Where we encounter Crane at his most naturalist, though, next to in *Maggie*, is in his story 'The Open Boat' (1898) and in some of his poetry. For 'The Open Boat' Crane found inspiration in his own life when, returning from Cuba as a war correspondent in the Spanish–American war of 1898, he had been shipwrecked. In the story too, the survivors of a shipwreck, the captain, the cook, the oiler, and a war correspondent, find themselves in a rowboat off the coast of Florida. The only one of the four men aboard to be given a name is Billie, the oiler. He is the strongest of the four, does most of the rowing, and keeps the boat on its course. When they near the coast the surf overturns the boat. The captain, the cook and the war correspondent are saved. The oiler drowns. No 'survival of the fittest' here, but sheer blind coincidence.

The same naturalist–nihilist philosophy, if such we can call it, also transpires from the following little poem by Crane, which in its simplicity is devastating:

> A man said to the universe:
> 'Sir, I exist!'
> 'However', replied the universe,
> 'The fact has not created in me
> A sense of obligation'.

(1899)

Nature and the financial markets are the impersonal forces that determine the lives of the poor farmers of the northern parts of the Mid-West in the work of Hamlin Garland (1860–1940). Garland grew up in Wisconsin, Iowa and South Dakota, and had firsthand knowledge of how hard life on the land was for the pioneers who settled the sheer endless plains of the Mid-West. In a spare and grim prose he sketches the back-breaking labor and the spiritual poverty of such lives, subject to the whims of nature and the fluctuations of commodity prices on the stock exchange. In 'Under the Lion's Paw', from his first collection of stories, *Main-Traveled Roads* (1891), a farmer becomes the prey of a ruthless speculator. Garland agitated against the popular romanticizing and idealizing clichés about the West and about life on the great plains that circulated at the time in the eastern United States, not least in the popular press, and that were meant to draw new settlers. Instead, he emphasized the degradation and the hopelessness of the small farmer's existence. In stories such as 'Up the Coulé' and 'A Branch Road' he pictures with outrage, occasionally tempered by nostalgia, how the small farmers are being put out of business by large industrial enterprises, and how German and Scandinavian newcomers buy out the exhausted and impoverished pioneer for a pittance. Weighed down by debts, but also by their own misguided pride, helplessness and ignorance, the farmers are prisoners to their land, while the call of the city grows ever louder. As is clear from 'Up the Coulé', which in thinly disguised form recounts a return visit he himself made to his family's farmstead after he had gone East and set himself up as a writer, and in which he was shocked by the deprivation of his mother's life, Garland pitied especially the women who lived on these remote and primitive farmsteads, devoid of any comfort or ease, with nothing but endless labor as their lot. *Rose of Dutcher's Coolley* (1895) treats a similar theme, and can be seen as Garland's contribution to women's emancipation. Garland coined the term 'veritism' for his own particular brand of naturalism in his collection of essays *Crumbling Idols* (1894), and chronicled his own life in *A Son of the Middle Border* (1917).

California is the setting Frank Norris (1870–1902) chose for his work. In the early 1890s Norris had started out writing Romantic verse in the vein of Sir Walter Scott, but towards the end of the decade he turned to naturalist prose. In *McTeague: A Story of San Francisco* (1899) the eponymous character is a dentist who, through circumstance but mostly through his own weakness and primitive appetites, is reduced to poverty. He kills his wife, who herself is consumed by greed, for her money and because he blames her for his own downfall. Directly influenced by Zola, Norris practices a 'scientific' naturalism (although he himself called it 'Romance' in 'A Plan for Romantic Fiction' [1903]) in which the individual is conceived as a complex of animal reflexes and the victim of uncontrollable forces. In *McTeague* these forces are greed and sexuality. In later work he turned from the psychological naturalism of *McTeague*, and also of *Vandover and the Brute*, his second novel, which however was only published posthumously in 1914, to the social and economic naturalism of his uncompleted Wheat trilogy. In what he called *The Epic of the Wheat* Norris wanted to follow the cycle of the wheat from planting, growing and harvesting in *The Octopus* (1901), through its marketing in *The Pit* (1903, published posthumously), to its consumption in *The Wolf*. Of the latter we only have the title. In *The Octopus* the artist Presley, who is the observant narrator of the volume, reveals the trilogy's intention: looking for a subject he finds it in the daily struggle for existence of the wheat farmers of the San Joaquin valley in California, and especially in their unequal battle against the monopoly of the railroad companies and the banks, upon whom they depend for credit and for the transportation of their harvests. Norris makes it clear that the farmers do not stand a chance against these powers that far outstrip them. At the same time *The Octopus*, next to being a social and economic drama, also has a moral intent. In their fight with the railroad companies and the banks the farmers of the San Joaquin valley also succumb because in order to fight evil they themselves have resorted to the methods of evil.

Of the three naturalists considered hitherto Crane is undoubtedly the most original one. The distance he keeps to his characters permits him to ironically weigh their deeds and ideas, and to puncture general assumptions. Especially in *The Red Badge of Courage* these qualities, along with the impressionistic descriptions of the battle scenes, already announce the advent of modernism. Compared to Crane's, Garland's technique and language are conventional. Norris too is traditional as far as technique is concerned, but his use in *The Octopus* of Presley as narrator and commentator, yet without direct involvement in the events, interestingly swerves from the habitual third-person narrator conventions, and may show the influence of James's theories and practice.

Also a naturalist, but one very much *sui generis*, is Jack London (1876–1916). His enormous literary production falls into two major categories. On the one hand we have the animal stories based on London's own experiences as a gold digger in Alaska. In *The Son of the Wolf* (1900), *The Call of the Wild* (1903) and *White Fang* (1906), London subscribes to an individualistic naturalism rooted in the theories of Darwin, Spencer and Nietzsche. Thematically closely related to this kind of story are those works of London's that take up his experiences as a sailor, such as *The Sea-Wolf* (1904), and his stories about sports, such as *The Game* (1905), about a professional boxer.

The other major part of London's production addresses a collectivistic naturalism, and propagates socialist and anarchist ideas and values. Next to a series of political pamphlets, this side of London also yielded two utopian, or perhaps better dystopian, novels, *The Iron Heel* (1908) and *The Valley of the Moon* (1913). The former has often been seen as an uncanny pre-figuration of the totalitarian regimes, and especially of Nazism, that would come to plague Europe later in the century. *Martin Eden* (1909), finally, is a naturalistic semi-autobiography, replete with all aspects of 'race, milieu, moment', the three categories that according to Zola, after Taine, determine a man's life, and that therefore furnish the decisive elements for the novel as 'experiment'.

With his animal stories London introduced a new genre into American literature. The use of utopian or dystopian novels for the propagation of political and economic ideas however was rather common at the time. Howells produced several examples of the genre, as did Ignatius Donnelly (1831–1901), with *Caesar's Column: A Story of the Twentieth Century* (1891), and Edward Bellamy (1850–98), with *Looking Backward: 2000–1887* (1888). In England too the utopian genre was popular in those days and was practiced by for example Samuel Butler and H.G. Wells.

Finally, mention should also be made here of Harold Frederic (1856–98), a novelist who straddled the borders between regionalism, realism and naturalism. In *The Damnation of Theron Ware* (1896), usually considered his best novel, he detailed the stifling narrowness of life, and especially of the Methodist religion, in upstate rural New York.

Social issues and reform movements

The final decades of the nineteenth century were very turbulent, and calls for social and economic reform were ubiquitous. An author who actively engaged himself in the struggle for social reform to the point of propagating socialism and (unsuccessfully) standing for office in California, where he settled in 1915, was Upton Sinclair (1878–1968). Sinclair published more than one hundred works, under his own name as well as under various pennames, and in a wide variety of genres: novels, stories, essays, political treatises and pamphlets, plays and autobiography. The only work to still be of interest today is his novel *The Jungle* (1906), set in the slaughterhouses and among the immigrant poor of Chicago. The novel was first serialized in a socialist daily, and is usually regarded as the prime example of what at the time was called the 'muckraker movement'. The so-called muckrakers were radical journalists and writers keen on forcing social reform in American society by exposing all kinds of abuses, malpractices and excesses. *The Jungle* targeted the cruel and unhygienic practices of the meat industry as well as the exploitation of the workers, mostly recent immigrants at the mercy of unscrupulous middlemen, in that industry. Other famous – or infamous, depending on where you stood or stand on these matters – muckrakers were Ida Tarbell (1857–1944), who lambasted the oil industry in *The History of the Standard Oil Company* (1904), Lincoln Steffens (1866–1936), who uncovered the unsavory corruption at work in America's larger cities in a series of sensational articles, and David Graham Phillips (1867–1911), who did something similar for the stock exchange and national politics in his novels.

However, the ever louder call for reforms did not stop at politics or the labor market. Especially women's emancipation was a much debated, and much maligned, topic. An authoritative voice in the debate was that of Louisa May Alcott (1832–88), an author we now know almost exclusively for her very successful juvenile fiction, and particularly *Little Women* (1868) and its sequel *Good Wives* (1869). Alcott issued from a very unusual Concord family. Her father, Bronson Alcott (1799–1888), was friends with Emerson and Thoreau and other leading Transcendentalists. Extremely idealistic, he founded the utopian commune Fruitlands (1842–44), as well as a number of experimental schools based on very liberal and progressive precepts which he mostly borrowed from the Swiss educator Pestalozzi. Unfortunately, Bronson Alcott was devoid of all practical genius, and his numerous undertakings invariably ended in failure. As a result, Louisa May Alcott was raised in abject poverty. Determined to escape a similar fate as an adult, and as an aid to her numerous family, she started writing and publishing when she was a bare sixteen years old. She never married and wrote more than three hundred books, working at a relentless rhythm. Some are thrillers, some are gothic tales, yet others are erotic tales – one of the latter, written under a pseudonym, only came to light at the end of the twentieth century. The majority, however, fall under the label of 'sentimental domestic realism' and treat the growth to adulthood of a young girl (occasionally a boy) and how she assumes her proper role in life and in society. This is most prominently the case with *Little Women* and *Good Wives*.

The 'little women' of the first novel are the sisters Meg, Jo, Beth and Amy March. Just like the plot of the novel they are inspired by Alcott's own family and youth. Alcott completed the so-called March family saga with *Little Men* (1871) and *Jo's Boys* (1886). In the character of Jo March she portrayed herself, particularly her involvement with her family but also her road to authorship. This she also does in *Work: A Story of Experience* (1873), an explicit plea for female emancipation through economically remunerative and socially productive work, and particularly art. From this perspective Alcott's work is more militant than that of earlier domestic realists such as Susan Warner, Maria Cummins or E.D.E.N. Southworth. Many of Alcott's contemporaries, though, subscribed to a similar emancipatory program such as she advocated. Some did so in rather covert terms, as was the case with Harriet Spofford (1835–1921) in *The Amber Gods and Other Stories* (1863) and *The Elder's People* (1920). Others were more outspoken, such as for instance Elizabeth Stuart Phelps (1844–1911) in *Hedged* (1870), *The Silent Partner* (1871), *Dr Zay* (1882), about a woman who becomes a successful physician at a time when women were not yet even admitted to university, and *The Story of Avis* (1887). In the latter novel a gifted woman artist, Avis Phelps (note the last name!), finds herself trapped in a marriage that does not leave her room to develop her talents. Phelps in reality was called Mary Gray but wrote under her mother's name, who herself had been a successful juvenile author in the first half of the nineteenth century.

The most outspoken advocate of women's rights, however, was Charlotte Perkins Gilman (1860–1935). Perkins wrote poetry, novels, stories, and essays. Since the feminist wave of the 1960s, though, it is her story 'The Yellow Wallpaper' (1892) that has been a staple ingredient in every anthology of American literature. An upper middle-class woman suffering from 'nerves' is prescribed a cure of complete rest by her husband-physician. She is absolutely forbidden to engage in any strenuous activity, in fact in any activity, and to ensure that she obeys this regime she is effectively imprisoned in the attic room of a villa on a remote southern vacation island. This really drives her crazy. Via some tell-tale references to Charlotte Brontë's *Jane Eyre* it is moreover suggested that in the meantime something is brewing between the husband and the woman's nurse, which also opens up the Pandora's box of nineteenth-century repressed middle-class women's sexuality. 'The Yellow Wallpaper' was partially based on Gilman's own experiences. Suffering from nervous illnesses and depression throughout her life she herself underwent a similar cure, which moreover was not uncommon for women from a certain – elevated – social milieu at the time. Most often, though, the story these days is read as a sharp condemnation of the role forced upon middle-class women in American society at the end of the nineteenth century, and therefore also as a vivid illustration of everything that Gilman, who was very active in the women's emancipation movement, opposed in her innumerable public lectures and publications. Best-known in this regard are *Women and Economics: A Study of the Economic Relation Between Men and Women as a Factor in Social Evolution* (1898), *Concerning Children* (1900), *The Home: Its Work and Influence* (1903), *The Man-Made World; or, Our Androcentric Culture* (1911), and *His Religion and Hers: A Study of the Faith of Our Fathers and the Work of Our Mothers* (1923).

The heroine of Louisa May Alcott's *Work: A Story of Experience* gains her independence by becoming an actress. This is also the road traveled by Carrie Meeber in *Sister Carrie* (1900), by Theodore Dreiser (1871–1945). Carrie, an ambitious young woman from the provinces, comes to seek her fortune in Chicago. On the train she meets Drouet, a flashy drummer or salesman. In Chicago Carrie first rooms with her sister, but she soon moves in with Drouet, whose mistress she becomes. As Carrie is quick-witted and soon vanquishes her initial naiveté she also quickly comes to understand the limitations of Drouet. She leaves him for Hurstwood, a somewhat older man, more intelligent and cultured, better off financially too. However, Hurstwood is also married. Through accident rather than design Hurstwood steals the cash proceeds from the saloon that he manages, and he and Carrie flee first to Canada, and then to New York, where Hurstwood opens his own saloon. His business is not a success, and Hurstwood starts to sink on the social ladder. He becomes embittered and withdrawn. At the same time Carrie's star starts to rise. Having found work as a chorus girl she is picked from the line to replace a leading actress. She proves a success, and quickly becomes a star. When Hurstwood is out of work and out of money it is Carrie who provides for both of them. In the end, she leaves him. Hurstwood finally becomes destitute, enlists as a strike breaker with the Pinkerton agency,

falls to begging, and eventually commits suicide. Carrie in the meantime is lionized everywhere, is given a luxurious suite in one of New York's best hotels as publicity for the business,
and rolls in money. However, although everybody's darling, her heart is empty, and although in
the eyes of the public she is the very embodiment of sex appeal she has no more intimate
relations with men. Ironically, at various times, while sitting in her rocking chair before her
suite's big window giving on to the streets of New York, she witnesses scenes in which
Hurstwood is involved, including the final one when he is found after having committed
suicide, without recognizing or realizing it is him.

From the very beginning Dreiser, and *Sister Carrie* in particular, have been heavily criticized
on stylistic and moral grounds. The novel was supposed to be heavy-handed, uneven in structure, and clumsy of style. Although Hurstwood answers to the naturalist paradigm of decline,
because of his advancing age and his crime, there is nothing in his 'race, milieu, moment' that
predestined him for such a fate. It is mostly the character of Carrie, though, that came in for
criticism. What was found particularly difficult to stomach was that Carrie apparently has no
qualms about trading her virginity to Drouet in exchange for the material comforts he can
offer her, nor about stealing Hurstwood from his wife, nor about leaving both Drouet and
Hurstwood when they have served her purpose and she has no further need of them. Worst of
all, unlike what decorum demanded, Carrie is never punished for any of this but instead thrives.
The only negative note sounded at the end of the novel is that she is alone. In fact, Carrie's
loneliness at the end can be seen as part of the wider picture of big city life that Dreiser paints
in his novel. As an actress, Carrie has become an effigy, an imaginary product in a nascent
consumer society marked precisely by the split between reality and appearance, desire and
fulfillment. In such a society everyone is ineluctably always alone. *Sister Carrie* superbly catches
the raw energy of a big city on the make such as Chicago was at the turn of the twentieth
century. That Dreiser realized apparently more quickly than most of his contemporaries, and his
critics, that this inevitably also implied the loosening of relational ties, and of traditional
morality, can be seen as an asset rather than a shortcoming.

Jenny Gerhardt (1911) definitively established Dreiser's reputation as a novelist. A counterpart
to *Sister Carrie*, in her eponymous novel Jennie sacrifices herself for her lover. The relentless
struggle for material success that drives the plot of *Sister Carrie* also informs Dreiser's later work,
such as the Cowperwood trilogy (*The Financier*, 1912, *The Titan*, 1914, and *The Stoic*, 1947).
Brazen-faced, Dreiser shows that whoever cannot gain success, or who loses it, is doomed. The
price of success, though, is high: loneliness, relinquishing all scruples, foregoing all deeper
emotions, cutting off all truly personal relations. This theme culminates in *An American Tragedy*
(1925). For the characters and plot of this novel Dreiser drew upon a real murder case, but the
novel's true strength lies in its depiction of the social background, and of the motives that led
to the crime. With the story of Clyde Griffiths, who kills his pregnant mistress because she
stands to endanger his rise on the social ladder, Dreiser rendered his harshest verdict on the
American cult of material success.

Dreiser was not the only one to take note of how the fast growing cities of late nineteenth-
century America affected the lives of their citizens. Henry Blake Fuller (1857–1929), like
Dreiser, focused on Chicago. In *The Cliff-Dwellers* (1893) he was the first to fictionally probe
what it was like to live in a skyscraper. Hjalmar H. Boyesen (1848–95) instead explored New
York in *Social Strugglers* (1895). The most searing portrait of New York, however, was painted
not by a novelist but by the sociologist, journalist and photographer Jacob Riis (1849–1914).
Riis, a Danish immigrant himself, extensively roamed the immigrant quarters of New York for
How the Other Half Lives (1890), an impressive record of the squalor, the noise, and the lack of
hygiene ruling the lives of the have-nots of the big city. It is Riis's book that incited Theodore

Roosevelt, during his stint as police commissioner of New York City, to implement sweeping reforms to clean up the city.

'The Color Line'

As we saw in the introduction to Chapter 3, the end of the Civil War and of slavery did not mean the end of racial discrimination and segregation in the United States. Indeed, after the initial euphoria of abolition and Reconstruction, and ever since the end of the latter in the late 1870s, conditions for African Americans had been steadily worsening again, with the imposition, especially as of 1890, of ever stricter so-called Jim Crow laws reinforcing segregation, especially so in the American South. Not surprisingly, then, the relation of African Americans to dominant white majority culture became an overridingly important topic in writing by African Americans. By far the most important contenders, and opponents, in the discursive and essayistic field were Booker T. Washington and W.E.B. Dubois. Like many another of the first and second generations of post-Civil War African American writers and intellectuals, Booker T. Washington (1856–1915) was of mixed black (mother) and white (father, unknown) parentage. Throughout his long career as an educator and writer he advocated the harmonious collaboration and co-habitation of black and white Americans under the 'separate but equal' legal system that as of 1890 had been part of U.S. constitutional law, and that in fact legalized organized racial segregation. Washington first became influential as an educator with his appointment, in 1881, as the first director of Tuskegee Normal and Industrial Institute, a newly founded teacher training college for blacks in Alabama. He would continue as its director until his death in 1915. Instrumental, though, in consolidating Washington's position as the foremost spokesman for black Americans in the difficult 1890s, when especially in the South the civil rights of African Americans were progressively being curtailed, was his 1895 'Atlanta Exposition Address', in which he called upon both African Americans and Southern whites to 'Cast down your bucket where you are'. African Americans he asked to 'Cast [their bucket] down in agriculture, mechanics, in commerce, in domestic service, and in the professions' and to do so in the South. Speaking for Southern blacks he assured Southern whites that 'in our humble way, we shall stand by you with a devotion that no foreigner can approach, ready to lay down our lives, if need be, in defence of yours, interlacing our industrial, commercial, civil, and religious life with yours in a way that shall make the interests of both races one'. And, he further laid Southern white fears, 'in all things that are purely social we can be as separate as the fingers, yet one as the hand in all things essential to mutual progress'. The so-called 'Atlanta Compromise' that resulted from this implied that black Americans would in the first instance content themselves with sticking to the more menial and mechanical sectors of the American economy, and more generally concentrate on economic and social rather than political advancement. Only later, only gradually, and by progressively interiorizing the values and ideals of their more advanced white compatriots, would African Americans emancipate themselves to the same level as that of white America. In return, white America would allow for at least a modicum of education, especially technical and vocational, for African Americans. On the basis of these ideas Washington was able to build an influential network consisting of both white and black business leaders and politicians, including Theodore Roosevelt, Republican president from 1901 to 1909, and Roosevelt's equally Republican successor William Howard Taft, president from 1909 to 1913. The 'Atlanta Exposition Address' eventually became part of Washington's autobiography *Up from Slavery* (1901), which, in the tradition of Benjamin Franklin's *Autobiography,* was at the same time an exposition and an illustration of his tenets, and which continues to be much read even today.

Booker T. Washington's ideas were very influential around the turn of the twentieth century, and most African American authors writing at that time to a greater or lesser degree subscribed to them. The now all but forgotten Otis M. Shackelford (1871–?), for instance, in 1909 published *Seeking the Best*, 'dedicated to the negro youth', which contained a combination of autobiography, verse, and essays. Both this book and his 1915 *Lillian Simmons, or, The Conflict of Sections*, a novel confronting Northern and Southern blacks, yet finally reconciling them, while at the same time integrating them into majority white society, in a collaborative economic venture, read as if they were written according to a Booker T. Washington manual.

Another author to take his cue from Booker T. Washington was Oscar Micheaux (1884–1951). Micheaux (originally Michaux, but he added an 'e' to his name when he started publishing) was born in Illinois, worked as a Pullman porter, and eventually became a homesteader in South Dakota in the early years of the twentieth century. Though he lost his farm in 1915, his experiences in South Dakota inspired his 1913 novel *The Conquest: The Story of a Negro Pioneer* (1913), which bore a dedication to Booker T. Washington. In 1918 Micheaux rewrote *The Conquest* as *The Homesteader*, and made it the basis for a 1919 silent movie with the same title he himself directed. *The Homesteader* was one of the first feature-length movies, and the very first 'race film', made for a black audience by a black director. Micheaux over the next couple of decades went on to direct another thirty or so movies, both silent and talking, almost all of which have now been lost. Although in his casting of characters he himself followed the then common practice of preferring lighter-skinned actors for his heroes and heroines, he undoubtedly contributed to raising the consciousness of African Americans with regard to their position within American society and culture.

Washington's main opponent when it came to envisioning the (then) present and future of African Americans around the turn of the twentieth century was W.E.B. Dubois (1868–1963). Dubois was born in Massachusetts, in a family of freedmen of long standing, and enjoyed an excellent education. He was the first African American to earn a PhD from Harvard, in 1895. Earlier, he had attended Fisk University, a historically black college in the South, Harvard College, where he had studied with the philosopher William James, and the University of Berlin in Germany. Initially, Dubois supported Booker T. Washington, for instance at the time of the latter's 'Atlanta Exposition Address'. Later, however, after he had accepted a professorship at Atlanta university, another historically black institution, in 1897, and influenced by the racial discrimination, including the not infrequent lynching of blacks, he witnessed in the South, Dubois turned more militant, arguing against Washington's acceptance of the 'separate but equal' doctrine, and instead claiming full equal rights for blacks. He outlined his ideas in *The Souls of Black Folk*, a collection of essays that appeared in 1903. In his 'Forethought' he boldly claimed that 'the problem of the twentieth century is that of the color line'. What he had attempted to do in the fourteen essays gathered in his book, Dubois claimed, was to 'sketch, in vague, uncertain outline, the spiritual world in which ten thousand thousand Americans live and strive'. These Americans, being African Americans, Dubois argued, labored under a double consciousness, which made them see themselves as through the eyes of American white majority society. He explicitly rejected Booker T. Washington's Atlanta Compromise, and forcefully upheld the rights of African Americans to enjoy an education, including in the liberal arts, equal to that of any white man. Also in 1903 Dubois published his influential essay 'The Talented Tenth', in which he called for a black elite to lead its people in its struggle for emancipation. In 1909 Dubois was one of the founders of the NAACP, and for the rest of his very long life he would engage himself ever deeper into the black struggle for equality. In his economic and social ideas he moved ever closer to socialism and Marxism, however without ever joining any organized party. In his numerous writings, as editor of *Crisis*, the journal of the NAACP, as essayist and academic, he increasingly also started to highlight the contributions that Africans, including African Americans, had made to culture and civilization, and he urged African Americans to be proud of their African ancestry. Eventually, he came to reject the ideal of the integration of African Americans in white majority society. He also became a proponent of Pan-Africanism, which at the end of his life even led him to leave the United States and settle, in 1961, at the age of 93, in newly independent Ghana, then led by Kwame Nkrumah, a personal friend of Dubois's. In 1963, the year of his death, when the U.S. refused to renew his American citizen's passport, Dubois became a citizen of Ghana. However, all along Dubois also did not hesitate to turn to fiction to propagate his ideas, as in *The Quest of the Silver Fleece* (1911), *Dark Princess* (1928), and the Black Flame trilogy, *The Ordeal of Mansart* (1957), *Mansart Builds a School* (1959), and *Worlds of Color* (1961). *The Quest of the Silver Fleece* follows two African American adolescents in their journey from exploitation, sexual as well as economic, to independence as members of a black commune raising 'the silver fleece' cotton. *Dark Princess* combines many of Dubois's interests in having as its main character an African American student of medicine who because of his race is prevented from finishing his studies, who then becomes a Pullman porter and a politician, and finally forms a union with a beautiful black Indian princess. At times sentimental, at times erotic, and then again almost social realist, Dubois's fiction never had the success his more political and autobiographical writings had. Of the latter special mention should be made of *Dusk of Dawn: An Essay Toward an Autobiography of a Race Concept* (1940).

Other African American authors during the period between the Civil War and World War I entered at least partially into the stereotypes of regional and local color literature to depict the life of African Americans, especially so in the South. Most of these published their best-known works towards the end of the period under discussion. Pauline Elizabeth Hopkins (1859–1930) made use of a number of popular genres, such as the romance novel, but also the mystery story, to highlight the plight of African Americans after the Civil War. Though she had published various works, such as musical dramas, before, the prose works for which she is now primarily known appeared during an extra-ordinarily productive four-year period: 'Talma Gordon' (1900), *Contending Forces: A Romance of Negro Life North and South* (1900), *Hagar's Daughter: A Story of Southern Caste Prejudice* (1901), *Winona, A Tale of Negro Life in the South and Southwest* (1902), and *Of One Blood: Or; The Hidden Self* (1903). The latter three novels, as well as 'Talma Gordon', a story of 'passing' as well as a mystery story, first appeared in *The Colored American Magazine*, a periodical that played an important role in raising the cultural and political consciousness of African Americans during the early years of the twentieth century, and for which Hopkins for a few years acted as one of the editors. As well as under her own name, Hopkins also published stories, essays, and social and political commentary, under the name of her mother, Sarah A. Allen. Her role as editor, as well as the impact her fiction and discursive prose have had, have only properly been recognized since the rise of multiculturalism and the second feminist wave in the 1980s.

Far better known as African American authors until the 1980s were Paul Laurence Dunbar (1872–1906), Charles W. Chesnutt (1858–1932), and James Weldon Johnson (1871–1938). Like Hopkins, who was born in Maine and lived most of her life in Boston, Dunbar, who was born in Ohio from a marriage of ex-slaves, spent most of his life in the North. Still at a very young age he gained popularity with poems written in heavy negro-dialect, and that perpetuated the stereotypical image of the childlike African American familiar from white local color plantation writing. As example the following passage from 'An Antebellum Sermon' may serve:

We is gathahed hyeah, my brothahs,
In dis howlin' wilderness
Fu' to speak some words of comfo't
To each othah in distress.
An' we chooses fu' ouah subjic'
Dis – we'll 'splain it by an' by
'An' the Lawd said, 'Moses, Moses',
An' de man said, 'Hyeah am I'.

Later, Dunbar came to resent dialect writing and turned to a more classical poetics using standard English. His poems were collected in *Oak and Ivy* (1892), *Lyrics from Lowly Life* (1896), *Lyrics of Love and Laughter* (1903), and other collections. A slightly younger set of African American poets that included William Stanley Braithwaite (1878–1962), Georgia Douglas Johnston (1877–1966), and Anne Spencer (1882–1975) followed in Dunbar's footsteps, writing rather conventional lyrical poetry – witness for instance Braithwaite's *Lyrics of Love and Life* (1904) and *House of Falling Leaves* (1908), and avoiding issues of race. Dunbar himself, though, also wrote poems in which he expressed his admiration for African American leaders such as 'Frederick Douglass'.

Despite his soon failing health because of tuberculosis, Dunbar in the course of his short life also produced collections of stories, such as *Folks from Dixie* (1898) and *In Old Plantation Days* (1903), and a number of novels, the last one of which, *The Sport of the Gods* (1902), takes up the issue of prejudice and discrimination. Berry Hamilton after the Civil War has decided not to use his newly-gained freedom to leave the South but instead has continued to serve as loyal butler to the Oakley family, and has built himself a happy family life with his loving wife and two exemplary children. Wrongly accused of theft, though, he is imprisoned. Expelled from their cottage, his wife and children move north to New York, in search of work. There, both the son and daughter soon fall prey to, respectively, alcoholism and the temptations of life as a chorus girl. Berry's wife enters into a relationship with another man, who regularly beats her. The son commits murder and in his turn is imprisoned. When after five years it is discovered that it is actually a member of the Oakley family that committed the theft, and Berry is released, his family has completely disintegrated. The fact that at the end of the novel Berry and his wife are invited by Mrs. Oakley to return to their former life in their Southern cottage does not really do very much to alleviate the bitter hopelessness that speaks from it all, as the final sentence of the novel confirms: 'It was not a happy life, but it was all that was left to them, and they took it up without complaint, for they knew they were powerless against some Will infinitely stronger than their own'. As this final sentence also shows, Dunbar here, although he still has his protagonists use dialect, although there are a number of descriptions of Southern settings that remind us of local color writing, and although he still needs the 'happy coincidence' that Berry's wife's second husband is killed in a brawl to reunite the couple, as far as world view is concerned has moved far away from the earlier forms of regional writing, and has come much closer to more orthodox forms of realism and even naturalism.

In *The Conjure Woman* (1899) Charles Chesnutt also makes use of the popular conventions of the folktale, rather after the example of Chandler Harris's Uncle Remus stories. Chesnutt's narrator, Uncle Julius McAdoo, who is also a character in his own tales, is far more wily and resourceful than Uncle Remus, though. Time and again he outsmarts his white counterparts. Chesnutt, at variance with Hopkins and Dunbar, had first-hand experience of the South: born in Ohio in a family of free persons of color, he spent most of his childhood in North Carolina, whence his family originated. In adulthood Chesnutt, in order to escape discrimination, moved to New York, and eventually back to Ohio. Chesnutt first came to public attention with the story 'The Goophered Grapevine', published in 1887 in one of the most respected periodicals of the day, *The Atlantic Monthly* (and which actually is still going strong today), and later one of the seven folktales collected in *The Conjure Woman*. Told from the perspective of a Northern narrator who for the sake of his wife's health seeks out more southern climes, and who therefore looks into the possibility of purchasing a vineyard in North Carolina, 'The Goophered Grapevine' has colored old Uncle Julius McAdoo, who takes his last name from the late owner of the plantation on which the vineyard in question is situated, tell the story of how the terrain is 'goophered' or bewitched. In this particular instance the narrator is not 'bedeviled' by Uncle Julius, as he recognizes the old man's story for the ploy it is: an effort to dissuade the narrator from purchasing the vineyard, which Uncle Julius has been putting to his own good use for some years past! Chesnutt in describing Uncle Julius insists upon the latter's 'mixed blood' features. In fact, although there is nothing in the story that would lead the reader to believe that the narrator himself is anything but a white Northerner, while Uncle Julius uses broad negro dialect and always addresses the narrator as 'boss', and while it is therefore usually assumed that the narrator is indeed white, nowhere in the story is it unequivocally affirmed that this is indeed so. Chesnutt himself was light enough, and was also for the rest sufficiently 'Caucasian' of features, to have been able to pass for white, even though he chose not to do so. Instead, especially in the latter half of his life, Chesnutt, who had trained as a lawyer and who ran a successful business, became increasingly active in the NAACP, and as an advocate for the emancipation of black people. Chesnutt did still write another set of Uncle Julius stories, a total of fourteen in all, that in 1933 were collected in *The Conjure Woman and Other Conjure Stories*. Increasingly, though, he turned to more realistic modes of writing, as in his second collection of short stories, *The Wife of his Youth: Other Stories of the Color Line* (1899), in which, as the title already indicates, he more openly than in the Uncle Julius tales addresses the issues of racial discrimination, and then in his novels and discursive writings.

Next to the realism of the stories from *The Wife of His Youth*, Chesnutt's turn towards a more activist authorship was also heralded by his biography of Frederick Douglass in 1899, and then by the appearance, in 1900, of his first novel, *The House Behind the Cedars*, which, like Hopkins's 'Talma Gordon', focuses upon miscegenation and passing. Other than in Hopkins's story, though, which ends with the acceptance of the mixed blood provenance of the eponymous character, and her happy marriage to a white man, Chesnutt's novel sees its heroine, Rena Warwick, rejected by her white fiancé when he learns about her origins. In his subsequent novels, *The Marrow of Tradition* (1901) and *The Colonel's Dream* (1905), Chesnutt grows even more bitter. *The Marrow of Tradition* features a young African American physician, educated and trained in Europe, returning to his home town of Wellington in North Carolina to practice medicine there. Again, passing and miscegenation play a prominent role, but there is also criticism of the doctrines of Booker T. Washington, the most prominent spokesman for African Americans around the turn of the twentieth century, especially in the wake of the 1898 so-called race riots in Wilmington, North Carolina, that involved the lynching of a number of African Americans and the institution of a white supremacist town board. The pessimistic and, to whites, rebellious message of *The Marrow of Tradition* upset Chesnutt's white readers, and the novel was a commercial failure. Chesnutt's next novel, *The Colonel's Dream,* was even more bitter, detailing how a wealthy Southerner, a white ex-Confederate officer who after the Civil War has made his fortune in New York, fails in his aim of reviving his North Carolina hometown's economy through a reconciliation between the races. Again, the novel was a complete commercial failure, and after this Chesnutt gave up on fiction and concentrated on political and social activism. Ironically, while his courageous, at least for the times, stance on segregation and discrimination cost Chesnutt his predominantly white audience in the early years of the twentieth century, during the 1920s, the heydays of the relatively brief period of African American cultural flowering usually referred to as the 'Harlem Renaissance', his works were not deemed militant enough to continue to curry favor with the then newly educated black readership. Still, it was during this same period that two of Chesnutt's books were turned into silent movies by the black director and author Oscar Micheaux mentioned before.

'Passing' is the main topic of *The Autobiography of an Ex-Colored Man* (1908) by James Weldon Johnson. Johnson early on gained prominence not only as a writer, but also as an educator, college professor, lawyer and diplomat, and later as one of the leaders of the NAACP (National Association for the Advancement of Colored People). *The Autobiography of an Ex-Colored Man* is the story of a very light-colored African American who only in adolescence is made aware of his 'black blood'. He crosses the 'color line' at several occasions, and eventually settles down as 'white'. He also marries a white woman, though not without telling her about his colored origins. Gradually, however, he reaches the conclusion that his ability to pass as either black or white is a burden rather than a boon, and that he does not really fit anywhere. Successfully established as white, with a white wife and two children who to all appearances are also impeccably white, he still feels trapped in a white society that does not really answer to his emotional needs. *The Autobiography of an Ex-Colored Man* was published anonymously in 1912, and was originally thought to be someone's real-life story. Only in 1927, during the Harlem Renaissance, in which he played a prominent role, did Johnson affirm his authorship of the book, and also its status as a novel rather than a real autobiography.

Like African Americans, so too Native Americans suffered heavy discrimination in the period between the Civil War and World War I. In fact, during this period the once powerful tribes of the Great Plains were definitively reduced to living in the white man's reservations. Again like African American authors, and largely having to do with the same issues of low levels of literacy and of purchasing power among their own people, so too Native American writers had to write for an overwhelmingly white public. The only Native American poet of note during this period was Alexander Posey (1873–1908), an almost exact contemporary of Paul Laurence Dunbar, whom he admired, and at least partly in imitation of whom he wrote both poems in which he tried to catch the speech and rhythms of English as spoken by his own people, in his case the Creek, and more conventional poetry, though in the latter he did not hesitate to introduce his own cultural heritage, as in 'Ode to Sequoya'.

New Americans

Earlier we mentioned that the period between the Civil War and World War I was marked by mass immigration. Most of these 'new' Americans came from Europe. Some, such as the Dane Jacob Riis we already met, came from Western and Northern Europe. Prominent among the latter were Scandinavians, mostly from Sweden and Norway, both still desperately poor countries at the time. Most of these settled as farmers on the Northern Plains. Germans also continued to arrive in great numbers, as did the Dutch, in smaller numbers. The latter mostly settled in Michigan and Illinois. Masses of Irish immigrated after the potato harvests in their home country failed in the 1840s, causing what in Irish history came to be known as the Great Famine. Many of them stayed on in the cities of the Eastern seaboard, such as New York and Boston, where they came to practically monopolize certain public services such as the police force, or the firemen's brigades. A generation or so later they were followed by Italians, often from the poorer parts of the peninsula. But increasingly it was Central and Eastern Europe that became the main recruiting ground for the new immigrants. Many of these were Jewish, driven from their original homes by increasingly violent pogroms and other forms of persecution, particularly in those parts of Europe then under Russian rule, including much of present-day Poland, White Russia or Belarus, and the Ukraine, as well as the Balkan states of Lithuania, Latvia and Estonia. While many of the other Central- and East-European immigrants went on to try their luck as farmers in the Mid-West, on the recently opened plains of Iowa, Nebraska, and beyond, most Jewish immigrants ended up in the burgeoning cities of the Eastern sea-board, and especially in New York, which grew a sizeable Jewish neighborhood. Many also ended up in so-called sweatshops, working long hours in unsanitary conditions, in clothing factories often hidden away in back-alleys, cellars and attics, and for very low wages. Notwith-standing, the almost magnetic attraction the U.S. exerted upon immigrants was eloquently and movingly expressed by these lines, from the poem 'The New Colossus', by Emma Lazarus (1849–87), that eventually came to be affixed to the pedestal of the Statue of Liberty, the colossal statue that the French sculptor Frédéric-Auguste Bartholdi (1834–1904) crafted as a gift from the French people to the American people on the occasion of the centenary of American independence:

'Give me your tired, your poor,
Your huddled masses yearning to breathe free,
The wretched refuse of your teeming shore.
Send these, the homeless, tempest-tost to me,
I lift my lamp beside the golden door!'

Lazarus herself was American-born, but of Jewish descent. In fact, on her father's side she was descended from Sephardic Jews established in New York since the time the latter was still called New Amsterdam, and a Dutch colony. A precocious writer, Lazarus for the first half of her life concentrated on being an 'American' poet. However, as of the early 1880s the increasing persecution of Jews in Eastern Europe made her turn to her Jewish heritage, and for the rest of her (short) life she forcefully spoke out on Jewish questions, and worked to relieve the plight of the swelling stream of Eastern European Jewish immigrants. This plight was tellingly chronicled by Abraham Cahan (1860–1951), himself Lithuanian-born and immigrated to the U.S. at the age of 21, in *Yekl, A Tale of the New York Ghetto* (1896), *The Imported Bridegroom and Other Stories of the New York Ghetto* (1898), and *The Rise of David Levinsky* (1917). Levinsky is a Russian-Jewish immigrant who eventually rises to material prosperity in the United States, but who also pays a very heavy emotional and spiritual toll.

During the period between the Civil War and World War I, however, the United States were not only the favorite destination of many European immigrants, they also increasingly started to receive immigrants from the Far East. At the end of the nineteenth century we already encounter the first autobiographies of immigrant Chinese. The first significant works of fiction dealing with East Asian immigrants to the United States, though, came from the pens of the sisters Edith Maud (1865–1914), who wrote under the penname Sui Sin Far, and Winnifred Eaton (1875–1954), who used the pseudonym Onoto Watanna, probably because a Japanese name was thought to be more highly regarded than a Chinese one at the time. Edith was born in England, Winnifred in Montreal, whence their English father and Chinese mother had moved in 1870. Both sisters started publishing short stories in their teens. Both also spent their lives moving between Canada and the United States. During their lifetime Winnifred was the more popular writer, publishing the first Asian American novel, *Miss Nume of Japan*, in 1899, followed by many more, such as *A Japanese Nightingale* (1902), which was adapted for the New York stage in 1903 and as a movie in 1919, the best-selling *Tama* (1910), and *Me, A Book of*

Remembrance (1915), largely autobiographical. Edith however is now regarded as the more significant author, even though she only produced one collection of stories, *Mrs. Spring Fragrance*, in 1912. Especially the story 'In the Land of the Free' is now frequently anthologized as a wry and ironic reflection on how Chinese immigrants are discriminated against, threatened, and swindled when they get caught in U.S. Immigration red tape. Because their little son has been born in China, a Chinese American couple on their return to the U.S. have to leave their child in the care of a mission orphanage while the right papers for their son's entry into the U.S. are being prepared. As this takes a long time, they are offered the help of a young white lawyer, who eventually takes all their possessions, including the family jewels, most of them heirlooms. When finally they get to see their son again he has become completely alienated from them, and, afraid, turns for protection to a white missionary woman.

Yet another category of 'new' Americans entered the lists of American literature with the beginnings of what we now call Chicano literature, the literature written by Mexican Americans. First with the accession of Texas, which had gained its independence from Mexico in 1836, in 1845, and then with the annexation of most of the present-day South-West, including California, at the end of the war with Mexico in 1848, the United States gained a huge territory where Spanish had been the language of administration and communication for over three centuries. In fact, the Spanish-speaking populations of these territories were older 'Americans' than the English-speaking newcomers who soon started to flood in. However, they were 'new' citizens of the United States. In practice, as a conquered minority within the larger Union, they were moreover relegated to second-class citizenship. In *Who Would Have Thought It?* (1872) and more famously in *The Squatter and the Don* (1885) María Amparo Ruiz de Burton (1832–95) depicts the changes affecting the Mexican American population, the tensions between Catholics and Protestants, Californios and Anglos, Spanish-speakers and English-speakers, the rapid development of California with the coming of the railroads, and the struggles the old Mexican land-owning families had to wage against U.S. authorities and against the squatters to hold on to at least part of their lands. Ruiz de Burton was herself born into a prominent Mexican-Californian family before California's annexation by the United States, but was married to a New York-born U.S. army captain, hence the 'Burton' in her name, and thus had first-hand knowledge of the issues she treated in her two novels. As was the case with many works by women authors, but in her case even compounded by her Mexican American background, Ruiz de Burton's writings, although written in English and published, under either her husband's name or a pseudonym, by, respectively, major East and West Coast publishers, went unacknowledged in American literary history for well over one hundred years. The rise of multiculturalism, the increasing demographic weight of Hispanics, and the emerging Chicana movement, however, led to Ruiz de Burton's rediscovery, and to the renewed publication of her work, this time under her own name.

Finally, although they were in fact the 'oldest' Americans of all, we see that with the end of the 'Indian threat' following the defeat of the Plains tribes, their confinement to Indian Reservations, and the settlement of most of what used to be tribal lands by whites, there is an official drive to 'Americanize' Native Americans by 'civilizing' them. In practice, this meant that Native American children were sent to white boarding schools, often very far removed from their families and ancestral lands, and forced to adopt white ways, white manners, white language. Zitkala Šä (1876–1938), whose Sioux name means Red Bird, but who also bore the adoptive white name Gertrude Simmons, wrote about the cultural confusion and tension this caused in her autobiographical sketches and in her stories. Her 1900 story 'The Soft-Hearted Sioux' tells of a young Sioux who has been raised a Christian at a mission school, and who when he returns to his tribe intends to put into practice his newly-won faith. The result is complete disaster: he alienates the tribe from himself and his family, indirectly causes the death of his own father, and ends up murdering a white man, for which at the end of the story he will be hanged. His Christian ideals have led to exactly the opposite of what he intended. Să eventually came to play a prominent role in beginning Native American emancipation in the period between the two world wars. Charles Alexander Eastman (1858–1939), also known by his Indian name Ohiyesa (The Winner), was himself a Christianized Sioux, although from another tribe than Să, who also started out at mission schools, but who went on to college, and eventually earned himself an M.D. Eastman served as a doctor to his fellow Sioux, and consistently endeavored to mediate between the worlds of the white and the red man, in his life and in his writings, as can be gauged from the titles of his two best-known books, *From the Deep Woods to Civilization* (1916), his autobiography, and *Indian Heroes and Great Chieftains* (1918).

The rise of popular culture

Almost concurrent with the start of the Civil War there also appeared the first of what came to be called 'dime novels', named, obviously, after their price of ten cents. The first dime novels treated frontier and Western themes, and aimed at a predominantly young and male working class public. They were made possible by an expanding reading public, because of an increased literacy among the lower classes, improvements in printing and production processes, and better and faster means of distribution because of the spread of the railroads. Dime novels appeared in series with fixed prices and fixed formats, although from series to series, often dependent upon the publisher in question, these formats could and did differ. In fact, issues of format, covers, and the use of color soon became the major grounds for competition for what turned out to be a very lucrative market. Regardless of the generic term 'dime novel', prices also varied from 5 to 15 cents, often again in function of competitive advantages sought by publishers. Quickly, too, the subject material of such dime novels expanded to detective, mystery, spy, and sports stories, and popular romances. Finally, recurrent characters were introduced, such as Buffalo Bill in Western stories, the detective Nick Carter, and the all-round sportsman-cum-detective Frank Merriwell. The latter can be seen as an early kind of what would later become the comics superhero, and in fact featured in a comics series that ran from 1928 to 1934, so just prior to the superhero age. Around the turn of the twentieth century the dime novel was replaced by the pulp magazine, often featuring the same heroes.

At the same time, much fiction appearing in the traditional format also bordered on popular literature, such as the already mentioned Horatio Alger stories, and indeed much of so-called sentimental domestic fiction. Much of this material in any case first appeared in serialized form in popular weeklies and monthlies, as did many of the works of some of the greatest nineteenth-century – primarily English – writers such as for instance Charles Dickens. The subject material of the dime novel and the format, as well as some of the conventions, of more traditional popular fiction, came together in what is generally considered as the first instance of the 'mature' Western *The Virginian* (1902), by Owen Wister (1860–1938). Wister was a good friend of Theodore Roosevelt. Both were classmates as Harvard men, and both had, for health reasons, spent some of their early manhood in Wyoming. Roosevelt came to advocate a form of 'strenuous life' and 'robust masculinity', basically meaning a life of fitness through physical training, close contact with nature, and an innate chivalry. Many of these ideals were also shared by the English writer Rudyard Kipling (1865–1936), the author of the *Jungle Books* (1894 and 1895) and of *Kim* (1901) and another close friend of Roosevelt's, and like him a staunch supporter of Baden Powell's Boy Scouts movement, aiming to inculcate the very same ideals in the (especially working class) young. In *The Virginian* these ideals are embodied by the eponymous hero as seen through the eyes of the narrator, an Easterner spending time in the West. As his epithet (we never learn his true name) suggests, the novel's hero is a Southerner who, like many of his fellow-Southerners, had moved West after the Civil War, there to start a new life, enjoying greater freedom and independence than in a South stunted by the outcome of the Civil War. Although untutored, the Virginian shows a natural grace, and an equally natural common sense, that outshine not only those of all other men the narrator meets in the West, but that even succeed in besting the book-culture of Mary 'Molly' Stark Wood, the Eastern school teacher coming out west to run the local primary school. The clash of cultures between the Virginian and Molly revolves around the use of violence to impose and maintain order in what was still, at the end of the nineteenth century, a largely lawless part of the United States. The Virginian will see himself forced to hang who used to be his best friend, Steve, for rustling. He will also enter into a pistol duel with the villain of the piece, Trampas, against Molly's explicit demand. In fact, and as we saw coming from the very beginning, by then the Virginian and Molly have become (though always innocent!) lovers, and are engaged to get married. Important, and closely argued in the novel, is that the Virginian uses violence only to counter other, criminal, violence, to uphold the law in the case of Steve, and to uphold his honor, with Trampas. On all accounts, he behaves like a modern-day white knight, and like a brilliant example of Roosevelt's 'robust masculinity'. *The Virginian* was an immediate success, and its protagonist became the prototype for almost all other Western heroes, in fiction, as in the novels of Wister's immediate successors, such as Zane Grey (1872–1939), for instance his *Riders of the Purple Sage* (1912), and on screen, in the Western movies that started appearing as of the early years of the twentieth century and that would come to make up a sizeable portion of the movie market between the two world wars. Beyond its popular success, though, *The Virginian* also stood as a plea for a national reconciliation, after the Civil War, between the three major components of the United States, South (Virginian) and East (Molly) harmoniously meeting in the West, America's future. Both Roosevelt and Wister worried about what they perceived as signs of decadence in the United States. Especially for Wister this was tied to the in his eyes unbridled immigration of inferior races from Eastern and Central Europe. Both Roosevelt and Wister saw the remedy as lying in a re-invigoration of the 'true' American stock by an alliance between the naturally superior intellect of the Eastern seaboard and especially New England elite as cultivated at Harvard, cast in the feminine form of Molly, and the chivalry and grace of the South as embodied by the Virginian recast as Westerner.

Following E.A. Poe's pioneering work, the second half of the nineteenth century also saw the first blossoming of what would eventually become the modern detective story. In the United States this was mostly the terrain of female authors. Anna Katherine Green (1846–1935) developed something remarkably akin to later so-called British Golden Age fiction. In a number of serial detectives about the New York Metropolitan Police officer Ebenezer Gryce it is actually the amateur spinster sleuth Amelia Butterworth who also acts as narrator and focalizer, and who is an obvious model for Agatha Christie's Miss Marple, antedating the latter by several decades. Green also created an amateur girl detective in the character of Violet Strange, who set the mold for the 1930s Nancy Drew character of Edward Stratemeyer. Green's most famous novel remains her 1878 debut, *The Leavenworth Case*, but some of her other novels, such as *The Hermit of – Street* (1898), starring 'Delight Hunter, a country girl', or *Lost Man's Lane* (1910), featuring Amelia Butterworth, or interrelated collections of stories such as *The Golden Slipper: And Other Problems for Violet Strange* (1915), are also still worth reading. Other novels by Green, such as *The Forsaken Inn* (1889), verge rather on the mystery tale, with clear echoes of Poe's tales of terror. Another extremely prolific detective and mystery writer was Mary Roberts Rinehart

(1876–1958). Her most famous novel, *The Circular Staircase* (1908), sold over a million copies. Earlier we already mentioned Pauline Hopkins as the first African American detective author.

At the very end of the nineteenth century yet another new popular genre made its appearance on the American scene: the comic strip. It is generally assumed that Richard Felton Outcault (1863–1928) is the father of the American comic strip with his characters the Yellow Kid and Buster Brown. The Yellow Kid featured in a strip called 'Hogan's Alley' that ran in a number of New York newspapers between 1895 and 1898, while Buster Brown was the lead character in strips that ran during the early decades of the twentieth century, often in competing newspapers owned by, respectively, Joseph Pulitzer and Randolph Hearst. It is because the Yellow Kid strips featured prominently in newspapers that tried to outdo one another in terms of sensationalism and patriotism in order to increase their circulation, that their kind of journalism came to be call Yellow Kid, and eventually simply Yellow Journalism.

Part II

The American century

World War I to the Present

4 World War I to the Cold War
1914–45

Introduction: American society from World War I to the Cold War

At the end of World War I the United States retreated into isolationism, refusing to join the League of Nations, even though President Woodrow Wilson had been one of the driving forces of this international forum. The United States went through an extra-ordinary economic 'boom' in the 1920s. The production of consumer goods reached dizzying heights. Buying on credit became part of everyday business practice. New industries, such as the movies and radio, sprang up. The three Republican presidents that spanned the period from 1920 to 1932 – Warren Harding, Calvin Coolidge and Herbert Hoover – sought to promote business with every possible means. Under Harding – whose presidency was one of the most corrupt that the United States had ever known – all kinds of progressive legislation, introduced under Wilson, and that aimed to curb unbridled economic liberalism, were retracted. Calvin Coolidge's motto was: 'the business of America is business' (1925).

The twelve years of uninterrupted Republican administration, the isolationism, and the triumph of the business mentality, were at least to some extent also conservative reflexes of part of the American electorate. The Republicans could count on the white inhabitants of rural America, the dwellers of Gopher Prairie from Sinclair Lewis's novel *Main Street* (1920). The Democrats, on the contrary, relied on all kinds of minorities: African Americans, immigrants, the urban proletariat, progressive intellectuals and Catholics. The firmness with which the Republican block held together was not in the last instance due to the fact that the so-called WASPS, or 'White Anglo-Saxon Protestants', felt that their identity was threatened by these minorities. Their concern to hold on to this identity led to Prohibition, stringent immigration laws, and the revival of the Ku Klux Klan. However, Prohibition, giving rise to an illegal trade in liquor, also fomented the rise of organized crime. The authorities tried to counter these developments with the creation of specialized police forces, such as the FBI. These aspects of the period under consideration were vividly caught in the genre of the hard-boiled detective novel, which reached a first height in the work of Dashiell Hammett and Raymond Chandler. The fear of the import of radical, Communist ideas after the Russian Revolution of 1917 together with the ever larger influx of immigrants from parts of Europe with which the thitherto dominant part of the U.S. population felt little affinity, led to the introduction of immigration quotas reflecting existing relations in the U.S. At the same time, the famous melting-pot image, based on the assumption that in the United States the fusion of different nationalities would lead to a new *kind* of human being, was replaced by that of a crucible in which all differences were burned away until only a pure Anglo-Saxon essence remained. Instead of unity *in* or *through* diversity the emphasis now came to lie on adaptation to the dominant WASP mentality. The most spectacular and despicable expression of the narrow-minded mentality of much of rural America was the renewed popularity of the Ku Klux Klan, which not only agitated against blacks, but also against Catholics.

Notwithstanding everything, though, in the 1920s it seemed to many Americans as if a new age had dawned. The prosperity, the power, the vitality of the United States led to euphoria. Scott Fitzgerald thought that 'something subtle passed to America: the style of Man'. In fact, during this otherwise so conservative period, a small minority experimented with new ways of living. A contemporary slogan such as 'Fords and flappers' offers a key to the explanation of this paradox. Henry Ford, and after him the other big American automobile companies, thanks to the introduction of new production methods such as the assembly line, reducing complex tasks to their most basic components and repetitive actions, and a drastic increase in wages coupled with an equally drastic reduction of prices for standardized and mass-produced automobiles, had made it possible for almost every American to purchase a car. If the car was the most visible sign of the new affluence of the 1920s, it also drastically changed American life patterns. The 'flappers' – flirts always in search of new admirers, and easily suspected of rather loose morals – and the entire milieu of which they were the focus, only became possible with the ease and the mobility cars provided. The economic affluence facilitated the hedonism of the generation that had come of age with the end of the war. The image and the tenor of the Jazz Age, as Scott Fitzgerald baptized the period 1919–29, were set by a very young generation disillusioned by the war and its aftermath, and by what they considered the bankruptcy of an entire civilization. They experimented with a way of life and a mentality that were the almost exact opposites of those of traditional society. However, their experiments remained largely confined to their own private life worlds, and to the world of art and literature.

Harlem, the quarter of New York to the north of Central Park, and that since the Great Migration from the South had become largely populated by African Americans, became the place to be for affluent white people in search of entertainment, with nightclubs featuring the bands of Count Basie or Duke Ellington, and star performers such as Earl Hines, Fats Waller or Louis Armstrong. Still, jazz only really succeeded in reaching a large public in the 1930s, not as brought by black musicians, but in diluted and domesticated form as played by big bands conducted by white band leaders such as Benny Goodman, the Dorsey Brothers or Glenn Miller.

The Wall Street Crash of 1929 put an end to the economic prosperity the U.S. had enjoyed for an entire decade. The victory of the Democrat Franklin Delano Roosevelt in the 1932 election was fueled by the electorate's anger over the mismanagement of the economy by his Republican predecessors. Twelve million people found themselves out of work, entire families had lost their homes, women and children went hungry, and there was an acute lack of adequate relief instruments. However, Roosevelt's election also reflected a number of demographic shifts. In 1920 fifty percent of the overall American population still lived on the land, in what was predominantly white Republican America. In 1932 this proportion had shrunk to thirty-two percent. Many blacks had left the Deep South, where they most often had been prevented from voting, for Northern cities. In 1932 Roosevelt succeeded in forging a coalition of the urban proletariat, Catholics, blacks and immigrants. This coalition kept Roosevelt in power over four elections. At the same time, it was precisely those groups that had been the staunchest supporters of the Republicans during the post-war boom – small farmers and tradesmen, and small businessmen – that first fell victim to America's lack of social provisions. Consequently, they formed an extra pool of possible votes for Roosevelt.

Roosevelt's 'New Deal' sought to alleviate the worst social misery caused by the Great Depression. It also put unemployed authors, artists and actors to work, often in projects aimed at bringing art to the people. Writers and photographers were employed to inventory American landscapes, customs, expressions, music and songs. But in the first instance the 'New Deal' was meant to stimulate investments, reinvigorate trade and farming, and to revive small businesses. It was not meant, then, to radically change American society, but rather to facilitate economic and social recovery. Still, the New Deal amounted to the most ambitious intervention in the economic life of the United States until then. Roosevelt succeeded in getting his combination of economic, social and political measures passed by on the one hand substantially expanding his executive powers, and on the other hand reaching out for immediate popular support with his famous 'fireside chats' on the radio. Towards the end of the 1930s Roosevelt also cautiously started to put an end to American isolationism. As of 1937 he turned his attention to foreign policy, with the threat of Nazi Germany mounting in Europe, and that of militarist Japan in the Pacific. When in December 1941 the Japanese sank most of the American Pacific Fleet in a surprise attack on Pearl Harbor, in Hawaii, the United States once again entered into a World War. Millions of men were called up, and the rise of a war economy finally did away with the last remnants of the unemployment of the Great Depression.

After the war history in many ways repeated itself. A period of economic prosperity was ushered in, and the newly regained affluence of the United States allowed for the success of the Marshall Plan rebuilding the economies of Western Europe. The mass media definitively triumphed: next to radio, television now quickly became ubiquitous. The tension between the U.S. and the Soviet Union, war-time ally of the U.S. but now its rival, especially after the Soviet Union had proved its nuclear capability in the late 1940s, led to another 'red scare'. Senator Joseph McCarthy unleashed a veritable witch hunt for 'Communists'. Scores of writers, actors and movie directors were questioned about their own activities or those of their collea-gues, as described in Lillian Hellman's *Scoundrel Time* (1976). If found guilty, or suspected of being guilty, they were black-balled and effectively prevented from working in the theater or for the movies, at least under their own name. For a number of them this meant the end of their career. Others, and not the least among them, such as Charlie Chaplin, a British citizen but who had been living and working in the U.S. since the 1910s, turned their backs on the U.S., for good.

Regionalism in poetry

In poetry as in prose, the regionalist tendencies that had been so prominent in the period between the Civil War and World War I still found adherents, though not without significant changes. In *Spoon River Anthology* (1915), by Edgar Lee Masters (1868–1950), a composite pic-ture of life in a little fictional town in Illinois emerges from the monologues of the dead in the cemetery. *Spoon River Anthology* was an immediate success because of its pithy language, the freedom with which it treats all aspects of human life, including sexuality, and its decidedly unpoetic and rough-edged feel. None of Masters's later works came near to achieving the popularity of *Spoon River Anthology*. With this work, though, he played an important role in the literary emancipation of America's Mid-West, and contributed significantly to the so-called 'Chicago Renaissance'.

Chicago flowered artistically in the first few decades of the twentieth century with the fiction of Theodore Dreiser and Sherwood Anderson, but also the poetry of Carl Sandburg and Vachel Lindsay, and the literary magazines *Poetry* (1912–) and *The Little Review* (1914–29). The latter was edited by Margaret Anderson (1886–1973), and with Ezra Pound acting as foreign editor in London, was instrumental in disseminating the work of many prominent modernist poets and novelists in the United States. Equally important was *Poetry*, founded and edited by Harriet Monroe (1860–1936), which introduced 'Imagism' to an American readership.

The publication of 'Chicago' in *Poetry* in 1914 brought national attention to Carl Sandburg (1878–1967), the son of Swedish immigrants. Like Whitman, whose free verse he imitated, Sandburg hymned the geography of the United States and the vitality and diversity of its population. And like Whitman he could grow rather ecstatic, capitals and all, about his subject, as when in these opening lines of 'Chicago' he refers to 'The City of the Big Shoulders' as the 'Hog butcher for the World, / Tool Maker, Stacker of Wheat, / Player with Railroads and the Nation's Freight handler'. Sandburg enthusiastically supported socialist and populist ideals, and aimed to write 'simple poems for simple people'. His most ambitious effort to embrace all of the United States and at the same time bear testimony to his democratic ideals is *The People, Yes* (1936), which mixes poetry and prose, popular songs and turns of phrase.

Vachel Lindsay (1879–1931) also used Whitmanesque themes and forms to express his rhapsodic love of America and its peoples. Although born to considerable wealth, Lindsay lived in poverty most of his life. Prominently featured in *Poetry* from the 1910s on, along with Edgar Lee Masters and Carl Sandburg, Lindsay gained national fame and popularity in the 1920s, but fell out of favor after World War II. During his lifetime he also became known for his early interest in the contributions African Americans made to American life, especially in music. However, 'The Congo: A Study of the Negro Race' (1914) caused major controversy, focusing on whether it was to be read as confirming or rather combatting stereotypes. Although shockingly unfamiliar for an American poetry audience at the time, both in its focus on things African and in its performance character, using stage directions and onomatopoeic sound imitations, 'The Congo' as far as technique is concerned is not unlike some of the more avant-garde art practices in Europe at the time.

A number of other early twentieth-century poets, such as Archibald McLeish (1892–1982), Kenneth Fearing (1902–61), Kenneth Rexroth (1905–82) and Kenneth Patchen (1911–72), all of whom were born in the Mid-West and sooner or later had some relation to Chicago, during the 1930s and early 1940s published popular and socially-inspired poetry in the tradition of Whitman, Sandburg and Lindsay. During the 1920s McLeish was part of the American expatriate scene in France, rubbing shoulders with what we now usually call the 'modernists', boldly and programmatically advocating in 'Ars Poetica' (1926) that 'a poem should not mean/ but be'. In 1932, though, he disassociated himself from the modernist position in his 'Invocation to the Social Muse', and in 1936 published a volume with the telling title *Public Speech: Poems*. His concern with his native country also clearly shows through in *America Was Promises* (1939). The generation that had reached poetic maturity during the second and third decades of the twentieth century was particularly sensitive to the social climate of the Depression years. This led to socialist and Marxist sympathies, and to a focus on 'ordinary' people. Later, Rexroth and Patchen both moved to California, developed an interest in jazz poetry, influenced the Beats and, in Rexroth's case, became involved with oriental and especially Japanese poetry, and in the case of Patchen, with ecologism. With these poets, however, we have already moved far away from regionalism.

Resolutely regional, on the contrary, were a number of poets and critics that in the 1920s gathered around the journal *The Fugitive* (1922–25) at Vanderbilt University in Nashville, Tennessee. They propagated a Southern regionalism, conservative in values, and averse to urbanization, industrialization and commercialization. Like Frost, the Fugitives advocated a return to an agrarian America, inspired by Jeffersonian ideals, and to what they saw as the concomitant social and religious myths and structures. These ideals were expressed most powerfully in the pamphlet *I'll Take My Stand* (1930) by 'Twelve Southerners'.

The conservatism that was at the root of the social and political thought of the Southern Agrarians also spoke from the literary theory and practice of the Fugitives. The founder and leader of the group, John Crowe Ransom (1888–1974), as well as his two most influential followers and collaborators, Allen Tate (1899–1979) and Robert Penn Warren (1905–89), largely stuck to traditional forms and themes, often following the lead of the later T.S. Eliot, whose conservatively religious and humanist views they also largely subscribed to. Still, the modernism of the early Eliot, and of Pound, did not go completely unheeded by them. Ransom, for instance, experimented with what he called 'accentual meter', in which only stressed syllables mattered in determining the meter of a line of verse, and the unstressed syllables – contrary to traditional practice – were left out of consideration. Tate's poetry also shows the influence of Pound and Eliot, and Warren in his later work, after 1953, even grew experimental. The extent to which the Fugitives identified with their Southern past is clear in Tate's 'Ode to the Confederate Dead' (1923, 1937) and Warren's 'Founding Fathers, Nineteenth-Century Style, Southeast U.S.A.' (1957). The same Southern interest also shows in Tate's and Warren's prose works. Tate wrote biographies of *Stonewall Jackson* (1928) and *Jefferson Davis* (1929), and the South's past plays a major role in his novel *The Fathers* (1938). Warren too prefers to focus on Southern issues in his many novels. His best-known novel, *All the King's Men* (1946), was inspired by the career of the politician Huey Long (1893–1935), and asks questions about the relationship between idealism and pragmatism in politics, past and present, memory and fact.

Further members of the Fugitives were Donald Davidson (1893–1968) and Laura Riding Jackson (1901–91, real name Laura Reichenthal). No Fugitives, but still Agrarians, were Andrew Nelson Lytle (1902–99) and Stark Young (1881–1963). Both concentrated on writing historical novels about the South, with as best-known example Young's *So Red the Rose* (1934). The conservative penchant of the Agrarians was shared by John Peale Bishop (1892–1944) and Yvor Winters (1900–68), not a Southerner, who made his debut with modernist poems, but soon converted to an outspoken classicism and traditionalism with a series of controversial essays, the most famous of which were collected in *In Defense of Reason* (1947).

Also a regionalist, but this time from California, was Robinson Jeffers (1887–1962). He too preferred traditional forms, and like Robinson and Frost he wrote both shorter lyrical pieces as well as longer narrative poems. *Roan Stallion, Tamar and Other Poems* (1925), the collection that brought Jeffers to the attention of the American public, recreates classical myths in a Californian setting. Jeffers subscribed to something that he called 'inhumanism' which considered man and his achievements as small and futile when compared to the cosmos. In 'Roan Stallion' Jeffers posits that 'humanity is the mold to break away from, the crust to break through, the coal to break into fire, / the atom to be split'. The explicit sexuality of his poems, their crude violence, and his disdain for 'man', meant that Jeffers and his work took a long time to become appreciated by the critics, and by the public at large. Jeffers's later longer poems, such as 'Thurso's Landing' (1932), are set on the California coast south of Carmel, where Jeffers himself lived most of his life, and are more realistic than his earlier work, without the latter's mythic dimension.

Robert Frost

Easily the greatest regional poet of the first half of the twentieth century is Robert Frost (1874–1963). In many ways Frost picks up where Robinson let off. Frost's first collection of poetry, *A Boy's Will*, only saw the light in 1913, when Frost was already thirty-eight, and when he was living in England, where he had moved after an unsuccessful attempt at farming in New

Hampshire. That first collection, though, was soon followed by others, some of which, like *North of Boston* (1914), became bestsellers. In many ways Frost, in the teeth of the modernists, re-affirmed the centrality of the pastoral myth of New England over which Robinson cast such doubt in his poetry. But Frost never suffered from elegiac nostalgia, and he never had any need for European inter-textual references. After his return from England, following upon the success of *North of Boston*, Frost turned himself into the image of a gentleman-farmer, extolling life on the land and close to nature, emphasizing, as he put it himself in the title of one of his poems, 'The Need of Being Versed in Country Things' (1923).

Conservative in worldview as well as, at least at first sight, in his use of poetic techniques, Frost pointedly rejected modern urban America and its culture. However, this is not to say that Frost's world is therefore any more stable or safe. With Frost the world is chaos, and only the poem, or art more generally, can offer 'a momentary stay against confusion', as he argued in his programmatic essay 'The Figure a Poem Makes' (1939). Consequently, his poems often treat brief moments of rest in the life of their speakers, moments of meditation and reflection, 'out of time', so to speak. Significantly, such moments usually occur in nature, and in solitude. Characteristic of all this, as well as of Frost's mastery of verse technique, is his most anthologized poem, 'Stopping by Woods on a Snowy Evening' (1923). What is most remarkable in 'Stopping by Woods on a Snowy Evening' is the economy with which Frost, by minimal substitutions in the iambic pattern, achieves great effect. One such possible effect at the very start of the poem potentially lends it a metaphysical dimension. The first two lines read as follows: 'Whose woods these are I think I know. / His house is in the village, though'. Of course, poetic convention has it that the first words in each line are capitalized, but here we at the same time see the possibility opening up of references to a more transcendent being than a mere human. And we could read the first feet of each of these lines as an ordinary iamb. However, we could also read them as spondees, especially if we were to think of the first words of these feet as being capitalized not only because of their position in the line, but also because of their potential referential meaning. The poem then would become a meditation also on higher things, and although the poem itself merely describes the actions, or inactions, of the speaker and his horse and buggy, the implication would then be that while sitting there in the woods the speaker is in fact conducting a conversation with himself about these higher things. This would be fully in line with Frost's vision of the work of art as momentary stay against confusion, and would even situate him in a tradition, going back to the mid-nineteenth-century English poet and essayist Matthew Arnold, of seeing in art, and particularly in literature, a substitute for religion.

Yet two other magnificent examples of Frost's consistent mastery of verse are the early 'After Apple Picking' (1914) and the rather late 'The Silken Tent' (1942). Both poems are also perfect illustrations of Frost's attitude toward life, and art. The later poem, a sonnet in rhymed iambic pentameters, consists of one long sentence that in its grammatical structure doubles the outline of the tent being described, with the central lines serving as the central support for the poem as they depict the central pole holding up the tent. The tent is intimately tied to the earth, but provides a place of rest and shelter, momentarily ordering the chaos of the world, as does the poem. As the opening line, 'She is as in a field a silken tent', indicates, though, the tent also stands for a woman, symbolizing both the latter's 'central' strength in how she is bound to the man she loves yet also free enough to 'sway [...] at ease'. Here, then, two of Frost's momentary stays against confusion unite: nature and love. A third such stay Frost found in labor, especially labor on the land, but also labor as a poet. Not for nothing he saw a poem primarily as 'a figure, a shape, a form', and as the result of dedicated labor. We recognize the same feeling in 'After Apple Picking', which sets out raising in the reader the expectation of an iambic pentameter poem, but then swerves away from this already in the second line:

My long two-pointed ladder's sticking through a tree
Toward heaven still,

While the iambic pentameter of the first line, slowed down by the possibility of a spondee in the first foot followed by either an anapest or a dactyl, a trochee, a dactyl, and then finally a regular iamb, and with the caesura after the third foot, stresses the longness of the ladder, mimicking the irregular motion of climbing it, the dimeter of the second line emphasizes the 'two-pointed' of the first line while its unmistakably regular sequence of iambs conveys that now labor has finished and rest has come. The rest of the poem will make the same point.

Even if he preferred to stick to traditional forms, then, Frost also used these forms inventively and innovatively. In fact, however different from, and even antagonistic to, his modernist contemporaries Frost may have been in most respects, and especially in his regionalism and what we will call his 'ruralism', in some respects his poetics run parallel to those of at least some of the modernists. The way his silken tent or his speaker stopped in the snowy woods furnish a momentary order to the world around them resembles, even though perhaps less actively so, what happens in Wallace Stevens's 'Anecdote of the Jar' and 'The Idea of Order at Key West', poems we will return to later in this chapter. Another feature that Frost shared with the modernists, W.C. Williams for instance, is the use of ordinary, everyday, and even downright 'unpoetic', language, which in his case included numerous stopgap words such as 'what' and 'but', as well as sequencing one-syllable words, a practice traditionally frowned upon in English versification. He played off such everyday language against the traditional forms he employed, and this to great effect. Frost likewise masterfully exploited the possibilities for irony and intonation of spoken language, leading to a consistent tension between the surface and the implied meaning of his verses. His characters exude Yankee philosophy and humor: dry, sober, wry, skeptical.

The Modernists

Robinson, Frost, Jeffers and the Fugitives were all traditionalists. Similar to what was happening in the other arts, though, in American poetry too the first half of the twentieth century experienced an enormous explosion of experimentalism. The umbrella term now usually employed to label the various kinds of experiments with artistic, and in this particular case literary, techniques and themes in the period under consideration is 'modernism'. In American modernist poetry two strands stand out. One, and the earliest to make its mark, was made up by the 'expatriates' Ezra Pound and T.S. Eliot. The other, later to gain recognition from the critics as well as with a wider public, consists of poets who continued to make the U.S. their home. Most prominent among the latter were William Carlos Williams and Wallace Stevens. Also consistently considered to have made important contributions to American modernism, although with less immediate impact on later generations, were E.E. Cummings, Hart Crane and Marianne Moore. Yet another number of poets, some of them very popular during their own lifetime, all of them female, all of them traditionally also reckoned to have been modernists of some sort, yet all of them largely forgotten in the period after World War II, since the 1980s, and largely thanks to the success of feminist studies, have gained renewed prominence: H.D., Elinor Wylie, Mina Loy, Edna St Vincent Millay. In contrast, the reputation of a number of male poets, most prominent among them Conrad Aiken, seems on the wane.

Ezra Pound

The driving force behind the renewal of English-language poetry at the beginning of the twentieth century was Ezra Pound (1885–1972). As of 1908 Pound spent most of his life in Europe, first in London (until 1920), then in Paris (until 1925), and finally in Italy.

For Pound the writer was the guardian of language: his task was to keep it sharply honed. Great literature to Pound was 'simply language charged with meaning to the utmost possible degree'. Pound was resolutely international in orientation, and for him all of the world's literature(s) formed one organic body. What was important to him, then, was to distinguish between what from this enormous mass was worth preserving, studying and teaching, especially to other, younger writers, and what was not. This explains why Pound spent so much of his time and energy on didactical and theoretical essays, as well as on composing anthologies. It also explains why his entire life he continued to be an avid and prodigious translator – or 're-creator', as some of his critics prefer to call him because of his very idiosyncratic views on translation – from Italian, French, Greek and Chinese. In the end, these very same principles also underpin Pound's magnum opus *The Cantos*.

Pound started his poetic career around 1905 as a rather traditionalist epigone of the English decadent poets and the earlier Pre-Raphaelites, Robert Browning and the medieval troubadours. In a dramatic monologue, Pound has an Italian or Provençal troubadour open a window upon his era. However, via these 'personae' he also voices his own opinions. A brilliant example of this technique, as well as of Pound's translation and re-creation methods, is the long multi-part 'Hommage to Sextus Propertius' (1917), in which he uses the Roman poet to lambast the England of World War I.

In London Pound got to know the English writers Ford Madox Ford and T.E. Hulme. From them he borrowed the idea that a poem should be a dry, hard language object, and that the language of poetry should depart 'in no way from speech, save by a heightened intensity'. For Pound this meant that a poem should dispense with all unnecessary elements. The result was a movement that Pound himself in 1912 baptized 'Imagism', and which saw a poem as 'planes in relation', as the juxtaposition of images. The meaning of an Imagist poem results from the relationship that the reader discerns as obtaining between these images. The classical illustration of this theory is Pound's own 'In a Station of the Metro':

> The apparition of these faces in the crowd;
> Petals on a wet, black bough.

> (1913, 1916)

Pound uses a semicolon at the end of the first line, thus leaving the two images unrelated in the work itself. It is left to the reader to discover, or to posit himself, a relation between the two, or not. With a colon the poem would have amounted to a simple affirmation: these faces are like petals, etc. With a full stop, the images would necessarily have remained separate. A simple comma would have made the second line a non-restrictive appositive to the faces in the first line, and would thus again have enforced a specific relationship between the two lines. Early in his career Pound became acquainted with the theories of the American orientalist Ernest Fenollosa (1853–1908), positing that Chinese characters were ideograms, stylized reproductions of the objects they represented. For Pound this meant that in Chinese writing characters were linked to one another through association and not, as in Western languages, through grammatical constructions indicating the precise relationships obtaining. Most of these ideas have since been discredited by scholars of Chinese, but for Pound they furnished the basis for his own associative poetic technique of juxtaposition and of planes in relation. For instance, the two lines that make up 'In a Station of the Metro' contain no verb, which reinforces the effect also invited by the use of the semicolon we pointed out before: because there is no clear grammatical relation between the two lines it is left to the reader to forge his own interpretation.

Pound's investment in Imagism as a movement was short-lived, as he quickly moved on to what he called 'Vorticism', a loose avant-garde circle around the Magazine *Blast* (1914–15). In many ways, though, Pound's idea of Vorticism simply entailed a further development of Imagism, as we can gather from his own definition that the image is 'a radiant node or cluster; it is what I can and must perforce, call a VORTEX, from which, and through which, and into which ideas are constantly rushing'.

As of 1915 Pound started looking for ways to apply his Imagist principles to the writing of longer poems. In techniques that were also becoming very popular in other arts – collage and montage, the juxtaposition of fragments, often consisting of truncated quotations from other earlier works, sudden temporal and perspectival shifts – Pound saw possibilities to extend his principle of 'planes in relation' to larger units. The first work in which he successfully applied a number of these techniques was 'Hugh Selwyn Mauberley' (1920). At the same time he also again made use of a persona. The result was an ironic and bitter reflection on Pound's own literary career until then, and on the London literary scene upon which he was at the verge of turning his back at that very moment. Pound's most ambitious, and most voluminous work is *The Cantos*, an epic of 116 cantos, upon which he started work on 1915, and which remained unfinished at his death in 1972. In his ambition to encompass all of human history, culture, and literature he roamed across languages, literatures, continents and ages. Mixing original lines with quotations and translations from the most diverse sources, *The Cantos* creatively practiced what Pound also advocated in his didactic and theoretical writings, and his anthologies. Although clearly meant as an epic in the line of *The Iliad* and *The Odyssey*, and the *Divine Comedy*, and frequently directly quoting or alluding to these predecessors, Pound's *Cantos* lack the overall consistency and unity of plot of Homer's and Dante's works. Needless to say, this is deliberate on Pound's part. Just as Eliot would do in *The Waste Land*, so Pound too in his *Cantos* wants to stress the fragmentation, the brokenness of his contemporary world, the ruin of a civilization instead of, as he and Eliot saw it, the unity and triumph embodied in these earlier epics.

In *The Cantos*, as in all of his poetry, Pound aimed at the simultaneity of all passages, all quotations, rather than the linearity of the classical narrative poem. By thus giving his epic a 'spatial form' Pound shows himself an exemplary modernist. Another modernist organizational principle Pound consistently adhered to is the recurring use of terms, characters and settings as 'leitmotifs', the associative resonance of words and contexts via what Pound himself called 'logopeia'. Notwithstanding his exemplary application of what have come to be considered as mainstays of modernist technique, or perhaps because of the extremes to which he pushed them, critical opinion as to the final success of *The Cantos* varies widely. Whichever position one assumes, the fact remains that with *The Cantos*, as with his other, earlier work, Pound contributed significantly to the liberation of English – and especially American – poetry from the formalist straitjacket it largely found itself in at the end of the nineteenth and the beginning of the twentieth century. He also did so by serving as mentor to younger poets, as indefatigable editor of (little) magazines, as coiner of avant-garde theories such as Imagism and Vorticism, and in the case of the older Irish poet W.B. Yeats (1865–1939) as his part-time secretary while at the same time bringing him into contact with for instance Japanese poetry and theater, thus aiding him to change from the poet of the Celtic Twilight and the Irish Renaissance into the High Modernist poet we now know Yeats as.

One particularly famous part of *The Cantos* consists of *The Pisan Cantos* (1948). These cantos refer to the period when Pound, whose ideas on economics and politics were as idiosyncratic as they were in literature, and who was a staunch supporter of the Italian fascist dictator Mussolini, at the end of the war was imprisoned for treason. These cantos strike a strongly personal and even confessional note, signaling a break with the Eliotian doctrine of 'impersonalism' in which the poet hid behind a persona or mask, and as such are often considered as a prelude to the Confessional poetry that in the 1950s and 1960s, with the poetry of John Berryman, Robert Lowell, Anne Sexton and Sylvia Plath, would become the dominant mode of American poetry, along with Beat poetry.

T.S. Eliot

Until recently, opinion on the person and work of T.S. Eliot (1888–1965) was much less divided than on Pound's. The early work of Eliot in many ways runs parallel to that of Pound, in technique as well as themes. Politically too, Eliot seems to have shared at least some of Pound's ideas. However, just when Pound, then living in Italy, was starting to compromise himself with Mussolini's Fascism, Eliot turned radically Christian-conservative. Moreover, by removing himself to Italy Pound by the late nineteen-twenties had effectively relinquished the central position he had held in the earlier part of the century, whereas Eliot, continuing to live in London, directing Faber and Faber (originally Faber and Gwyer), one of the most prestigious British publishing houses, and founding and editing *The Criterion* (1922–39), which quickly established itself as the leading English literary magazine, became the undisputed arbiter of literary taste in the Anglo-American world. All of this made Eliot's work more readily acceptable than Pound's. It also made it less easy to by-pass.

Thomas Stearns Eliot studied literature and philosophy at Harvard, and later at Oxford, where he had gone to complete his dissertation on the English philosopher F. H. Bradley (1846–1924). At the outbreak of World War I Eliot found himself stuck in England. While still at Harvard he had already started writing poetry. The publication of 'The Love Song of J. Alfred Prufrock' in 1915 brought him to the attention of Pound. The latter encouraged Eliot in his poetry writing, and introduced him to the London literary scene. Eliot's reputation grew rapidly with the publication of *Prufrock and Other Observations* (1917), *Gerontion* (1919) and *Poems* (1920), but also because of his essays, collected in *The Sacred Wood* (1920), and his incisive reviews. Although many of the ideas Eliot aired in his essays had been voiced before by Pound, Eliot's essays, because they were more elegantly phrased than Pound's, and less provocatively, more readily found an audience. Especially 'Tradition and the Individual Talent' (1919) and 'The Metaphysical Poets' (1921) established Eliot's reputation as the sharpest authority on English literature in the British Isles. Eliot's essays, and the ideas and preferences he voiced in them, were avidly taken up not only in literary circles but also in academe.

Following the lead of the French Symbolist poet Jules Laforgue (1860–87), Eliot in 'The Love Song of J. Alfred Prufrock' rebelled against what he saw as the anemic elegance, stylized symbolism and hackneyed themes of the late nineteenth-century late-Romantics and Decadents. He did so by ironically and subversively combining all these elements with elements of everyday speech, including slang, in a conversational mode, and by stressing the banal rather than the exquisite, and practicing the bathetic sublime, so to speak. The publication of *The Waste Land* in 1922 catapulted Eliot to the front rank of modernist poets. For Eliot the modern poet necessarily experienced his world as disjointed and broken. In the age of Homer, or in that of Dante, a poet could draw upon commonly and collectively accepted norms, values and ideals; on established forms, conventions, symbols and images; on a worldview that he shared with his contemporaries. None of this applies to the modern poet. He finds himself all alone and estranged in an alien world. He has to create his own symbols and his own worldview, with his own techniques. The way to do so, in Eliot's famous formulation, is via an 'objective correlative': 'the only way of expressing emotion in the form of art is by finding an "objective correlative", in other words, a set of objects, a situation, a chain of events which shall be the formula of that particular emotion; such that when the external facts, which must terminate in sensory experience, are given, the emotion is immediately evoked'.

The Waste Land, then, is the objective correlative for the break-up of an entire civilization. To underscore that his frame of reference indeed embraced an entire civilization, Eliot made use of what he himself in a review of James Joyce's *Ulysses* (1922) had termed 'the mythical method'. The recourse to cyclical myths of vegetation along with the repeated references to the best of what the European tradition (in Eliot's eyes) had to offer – Homer, Dante, Shakespeare – firmly anchor *The Waste Land* in human, and Western, experience and history. Like Pound, Eliot too 'shored fragments against his ruins', while his work at the same time illustrated these same 'ruins'. The disjointedness and banality of the present were confronted with the unity and perfection of the past. The world of the poem is grim, desolate and degenerate. Critics have routinely called *The Waste Land* an expression of the despair and the sense of loss that hit Europe after the end of World War I.

The end of *The Waste Land* left open the possibility, albeit ambiguously, of a regeneration. This possibility was foregrounded when Eliot in 1927 took out English citizenship and converted to Anglicanism. He himself defined his position, in his foreword to his volume of essays *For Lancelot Andrewes* (1928), as 'classicist in literature, royalist in politics, and anglo-catholic in religion'. More and more Eliot turned into a spokesman for all that was traditional and conservative in Western civilization. For him the only possible remedy to the ruin of the times lay in a devout Christianity and a Christian culture. These ideas he defended in his cultural-philosophical essays *After Strange Gods* (1934), *The Idea of a Christian Society* (1940), and *Notes Toward a Definition of Culture* (1949). His poetry too, with 'The Hollow Men' (1925) and 'Ash Wednesday' (1930), tracked his ever closer move toward Christianity, culminating in the *Four Quartets* (1934–43), and in the verse-plays of his later years. Although Eliot still made use of some of the techniques he had employed in *The Waste Land*, in these later poems he also increasingly resorted to the philosophical discourse that in his early poems he had spurned. In the *Four Quartets* he also drew inspiration from the English landscape poetry of the seventeenth and eighteenth centuries. The important thing for him now was to reach a wide public and to convey his views as clearly as possible, so that in 'East Coker', the second Quartet, he could even posit that 'the poetry does not matter'.

In order to reach as wide a public as possible, and to propagate his Christian ideals, Eliot as of the 1930s increasingly turned towards the theater. Building on his own poetic principles, but also inspired by the Elizabethan and Jacobean playwrights he admired, and fired by his religious convictions, Eliot created a modern verse-drama. His first success in the genre came with *Murder in the Cathedral* (1935), based on the assassination of archbishop Thomas Beckett in 1170. This was followed by *The Family Reunion* (1939), *The Cocktail Party* (1949), *The Confidential Clerk* (1953) and *The Elder Statesman* (1959).

Eliot enjoyed unchallenged prestige and authority until his death. Since the 1990s, though, his reputation has come increasingly under fire. Eliot himself had always proclaimed that *The Waste Land* was the record of a personal crisis. Yet literary theory and criticism, impressed by Eliot's theories of 'impersonality', by the 'notes' that accompanied the poem, and by Eliot's cultural-philosophical essays, had always insisted on reading *The Waste Land* in a general civilizational context. Recent biographical research, however, has unearthed that the personal dimension of *The Waste Land*, and of Eliot's poetry in general, is indeed much greater than had long been assumed. More and more, too, recent interpretations of Eliot's work claim to discover an anti-Semitic bent to it. Finally, of late, claims have also been made that Eliot's poetry is much closer to developments that were already well under way in English literary life than has been commonly supposed. Nobody will deny though that especially with his early poems and essays, up to and including *The Waste Land*, Eliot, along with Pound, led English-language poetry to change course during the early decades of the twentieth century.

William Carlos Williams

William Carlos Williams (1883–1963) was the staunchest opponent to Eliot's and Pound's poetic internationalism. Williams spent almost all his life in his birthplace, Rutherford, New Jersey, where until his retirement as a pediatrician he entered into the habit of noting down his poems, essays, stories and novels, in moments stolen from his busy medical practice, and on scraps of paper he had at hand.

Williams's early *Poems* (1909) are unremarkable, while *The Tempers* (1913) shows the influence of Pound, who was also instrumental in getting it published. During the years 1910–20 Williams frequented New York City avant-garde art circles. The famous Armory Show of 1913 offered him a sample of what was brewing in Europe in the arts, the work of the Cubists, Constructivists and Expressionists, and he personally got to know the poets Marianne Moore and Wallace Stevens, the painters Francis Picabia, Marcel Duchamp and Charles Sheeler, as well as the photographer Alfred Stieglitz.

In 1920 Williams published *Kora in Hell: Improvisations*, an extremely experimentalist prose-poems collection that was heavily criticized by almost all his poet-friends, and that signaled his turning away from the kind of poetics that especially Eliot and Pound were elaborating at the time. Instead of their internationalism he advocated a resolutely local poetry. He opted for a poetry 'consonant with the age', which in form and content should give direct expression to its own place and time. He rejected the use of classical myths, or references to classical models, in favor of a straightforward, unmediated poetry firmly and exclusively rooted in the everyday reality of the poet and his readers.

For Williams, of mixed Puerto-Rican-English descent, American English was inflected with all kinds of immigrant accents. Consequently, he denied the relevance of English as spoken in England for the writing of American poetry, and steadfastly refused to situate himself in an 'English' or even 'Western' tradition. It was his ambition 'to clear the ground' and 'start anew'. For this he was constantly in search of authentically American rhythms, speech, vocabulary and cadences. At the end of his life, in *Paterson* and in his late poems, he thought he had finally found all of this. Williams rebelled against all established norms and forms in literature, and tirelessly advocated change and renewal. Instead of fixed forms he preferred 'spontaneous structures'.

The elaboration of Williams's poetics took place as much in his poetry itself as it did in his essays and programmatic writings, which anyway often had the character of hasty jottings. Most of his poems are self-revelatory structures that at one and the same time justify and illustrate their own existence, as in the well-known 'The Red Wheelbarrow', from the collection *Spring and All* (1923). The unorthodox and abruptly ungrammatical arrangement of the three final 'stanzas' (if such we can call them), in which every time two words that logically, and in the case of 'rain-water' and 'wheel-barrow' even in spelling, belong together are separated, and the overall lack of punctuation and capitals throughout the poem, underscore Williams's poetic icono-clasm. This arrangement, though, achieves one of Williams's major aims: it directs the attention of the reader specifically and precisely to each of the different separate 'objects' in the poem. With this technique, according to the dictum 'no ideas but in things', Williams became the main inspiration for 'Objectivism', a literary movement of the 1930s with as main adherents Louis Zukofsky (1904–78), George Oppen (1908–84) and Charles Reznikoff (1894–1976). It also made Williams into an example for Charles Olson and the so-called 'Black Mountain Poets'.

The three final stanzas of 'The Red Wheelbarrow' taken by themselves form an Imagist poem. At the same time they also assume the character of a Marcel Duchamp or Man Ray 'ready-made': an image from reality presented itself to the poet and all he had to do was note it down, without further mediation. The concreteness of the description of the object observed is visually underscored by how each stanza imitates the form of the wheelbarrow. The first stanza of the poem, however, is not part of the description of the wheelbarrow. In fact, it furnishes the legitimation of what follows: the 'so much' that 'depends / upon' the image observed and represented is in fact the very poem itself. The capacity to register such an image and to write the concomitant poem signals an alertness to, and a willingness to see, and to live, in the everyday the magic of poetry. As such, the minuscule 'The Red Wheelbarrow' also outlines a complete poetics.

'The Red Wheelbarrow' is a brilliant example of a visual poem, and Williams was a master in the genre. But he was also a master in capturing everyday American speech. Here again, his poems often assume the form of ready-mades or *objets trouvés*, as with 'This is Just to Say' (1934), essentially a note left by the speaker to apologize that without asking he has just eaten some plums from the refrigerator and at the same time again a programmatic statement in itself.

Spring and All was a magnificent achievement, but it was overshadowed by the huge success of Eliot's *The Waste Land*, which basically directed attention away from the kind of 'localist' poetry Williams was elaborating at the same time. In reaction, Williams for a decade almost stopped writing poetry, and concentrated on prose. Here too, he focused on things American, in the partially autobiographical *The Great American Novel* (1923) and *A Voyage to Pagany* (1928), and the essay volume *In the American Grain* (1925). With the onset of the Depression he also started writing stories, collected in *The Knife of the Times* (1932) and *Life along the Passaic River* (1938), as well as a novel trilogy, largely inspired by his wife's family history, of immigrant life in the United States consisting of *White Mule* (1937), *In the Money* (1940), and *The Build-Up* (1952). All these works bear witness to Williams's social concerns, and to his involvement with the lives of ordinary Americans.

In 1946, when he was already well into his sixties, Williams published Book I of *Paterson* (further Books in 1948, 1949, 1951 and 1958), an epic grounded in the recognizably American reality of Paterson, a New Jersey town adjacent to Williams's Rutherford. Williams includes not only lines of verse, but also prose passages, and even letters to Williams, for instance from Allen Ginsberg. *Paterson* answers to the same ambition that also guided Whitman's 'Song of Myself': to embrace all of America in one encyclopedic poem that is at one and the same time a personal epic, a geographically and historically kaleidoscopic summary, and a declaration of faith in democracy. In Book II, Part three, Williams also for the first time employed what he called his 'American measure': a triadic stepped or staggered line making use of a 'variable foot', that is to say a foot of variable length in print but of equal duration when spoken or read according to American colloquial speech. Williams would employ this measure abundantly in his later poems from *Desert Music and Other Poems* (1954) and *Journey to Love* (1955), both of them later collected, along with other work, in *Pictures from Brueghel* (1962). After World War II Williams's relentless quest for a purely American poetry won him the admiration and the following of younger generations of poets that sought relief from the classicism and academicism of Eliotic poetry. The 'Black Mountain Poets', Allen Ginsberg, the Beats, the poets of the San Francisco Renaissance, and the New York Poets all explicitly pointed to Williams as a source of inspiration.

Wallace Stevens

Like Williams, Wallace Stevens (1879–1955) practiced poetry as a hobby, next to his regular job as an executive of a large insurance company in Hartford, Connecticut. He only broke into print when he was already in his thirties, with the publication of some of his poems in Harriet Monroe's *Poetry* in 1914. His first collection, *Harmonium*, only appeared in 1923. An expanded edition of *Harmonium* appeared in 1931, but a new collection, *Ideas of Order*, only saw the light in 1935. From then on, though, new collections came rapidly: *Owl's Clover* (1936), *The Man with the Blue Guitar and Other Poems* (1937), *Parts of a World* (1942), *Notes Toward a Supreme Fiction* (1942), *Transport to Summer* (1947), and *The Auroras of Autumn* (1950). Like Williams's, Stevens's poetry too shows the influence of developments in the other arts. Like Williams again, Stevens aimed for the utmost precision in rendering experiences while at the same time searching for a very individual form and technique, at variance with the classical forms and measures as adapted for their own purposes by Pound and Eliot. Still, in many ways Stevens can be seen as the counterpart and even the opposite of Williams. For Williams it is reality that creates poetry. The task of the poet is to capture that reality, to recognize ready-mades and *objets trouvés* as poems. For Stevens, on the contrary, 'the imaginative world is the only real world after all'. Stevens favored the imagination over reality. More, for him reality only came into being as a projection of the imagination. This idea already comes to light in some of his very early poems. In 'Disillusionment of Ten O'Clock' (1915), for instance, the speaker rues the banality and the lack of color and fantasy that characterize night in most homes. Only an old sailor, 'drunk and asleep in his boots / catches tigers / in red weather'. Analogously, the poet creates an exotic and colorful world in his poem.

In his later work Stevens incorporated his theoretical insights into his poems. In 'The Man with the Blue Guitar' (1937) the power of the imagination over reality is compared to what happens when a man plays a blue guitar: 'They said, "You have a blue guitar, / You do not play things as they are." / / The man replied, "Things as they are / Are changed upon a blue guitar"'. As for the man with the blue guitar, so too for the poet it is impossible to paint 'things as they are'. Art brings with it transformation. Even if what the poet describes looks like reality, it still is different, precisely because it is art.

Stevens's poems are often very funny and together with his emphasis on the imagination this might suggest that his poems are gratuitous exercises. Nothing is further from the truth. From 'The Worm at Heaven's Gate' (1916), 'The Death of a Soldier' (1918), and 'The Emperor of Ice-Cream' (1923), speaks the conviction that there is no ultimate will directing the universe but that instead all is emptiness and arbitrariness. 'The Emperor of Ice-Cream' ends with the bleak statement 'let be be finale of seem / The only emperor is the emperor of ice-cream'. In one of his aphorisms collected in *Adagia*, in *Opus Posthumous* (1957), Stevens put it this way: 'the final belief is to believe in a fiction, which you know to be a fiction, and that you believe in it willingly'. And he expressed these same insights in 'Anecdote of the Jar' (1923), in which a vase, which the speaker has put on a hill in Tennessee, 'made the slovenly wilderness / Surround that hill'. In 'The Idea of Order at Key West' (1935) the singing of a girl that walks along the beach ontologically re-orders her surroundings, to herself as well as to the speaker of the poem and his friend that watch her, even if to the eye everything remains unchanged: 'She was the single artificer of the world / In which she sang', and [we] 'Knew that there never was a world for her / Except the one she sang and, singing, made'. As was the case with the relation between the dream of the old sailor and his reality in 'Disillusionment of Ten O'Clock', so too in 'The Idea of Order at Key West' the relation between the singing of the girl and her reality are analogous to that between the poem itself and the reality of the poet, and of the reader.

Rather than a coincidental or accidental role, then, poetry for Stevens plays a crucial role. It is the supreme embodiment of what he himself, in 'Winter Bells' (1933) and 'The Idea of Order at Key West', respectively, labeled as 'a rage against chaos' and 'a rage for order'. In 'Of Modern Poetry' (1942) Stevens saw the task of the modern poet as equal to that of the philosopher and theologian in earlier times: the contemporary poem is 'the poem of the mind in the act of finding / what will suffice'. As such it is our only defense against the void. Although, as in 'Not Ideas About the Thing But the Thing Itself' (1954), perhaps only a 'scrawny cry', a poem in the last instance is an utterance of the will to believe, be it only in itself, and hence it is an act of confirmation in the face of nothingness, eye to eye with chaos.

Other modernist poets

Various other poets contributed to the modernist wave invading American poetry in the first half of the twentieth century. Conrad Aiken (1889–1973) sided with Eliot, Pound and the Imagists, and more generally with the proponents of a modernist, even avant-garde, and certainly international poetry. His *Selected Poems* won the Pulitzer Prize for poetry in 1930. In *Preludes* (1931) and *The Divine Pilgrim* (1949) he tried to make his verse come as close as possible to music as well as to the stream-of-consciousness of the poet. *Ushant* (1952) is an autobiographical novel in which T.S. Eliot and Ezra Pound figure only thinly disguised. Ezra Pound coined the penname 'H.D.' for Hilda Doolittle (1886–1961) when he selected three of her poems for publication in the January 1913 issue of *Poetry*. H.D.'s early poems are sharp and precise, and like Pound and Eliot she regularly resorts to the use of personae, and to classical and mythological subjects, as in 'Leda' (1919, 1921) and 'Helen' (1924). Always a prolific writer, H.D. from the early 1920s on also wrote a number of novels gathered in various cycles, many of them concerned with issues of gender and feminism. For the longest time almost exclusively appreciated as a minor Imagist poet, with the rise of feminist literary studies over the last few decades, not only H.D.'s seminal role in the development of Imagism, as in early experimental movie-making, and in the re-gendering of modernism, but also her later life and work have drawn increasing attention. Her verse *Trilogy* (*The Walls Do Not Fall*, 1944, *Tribute to the Angels*, 1945, and *The Flowering of the Rod*, 1946) is increasingly being compared to Pound's *Cantos* and Williams's *Paterson* because of its epic dimension and its technical inventiveness and brilliance. *Trilogy* interweaves the events and experiences of World War II, which H.D. together with her long-time lover Annie Winnifred Ellerman (1894–1983), an extremely wealthy Englishwoman who wrote novels under the pseudonym Bryher, passed in a flat in London, with Egyptian, classical and Christian themes. And *Helen in Egypt* (1961, written 1952–54), which following an alternative ancient tradition has Helen of Troy not go to Troy but instead to Egypt, also enjoys renewed interest. All this has led to the publication of formerly unpublished material, or to the re-publication of material that had long gone out of print.

Not surprisingly for someone who had studied biology, nature, and especially the animal world, observed with scientific precision, take center stage in the work of Marianne Moore (1887–1972). Instead of the line, she preferred the stanza as the basic unit of poetry. It was her belief that a stanza form commensurate with the poem's subject would offer itself up spontaneously. All the poem's stanzas then followed the same pattern with regard to form, number of lines, length of lines, and number of syllables rather than stresses. This resulted in poems that are extremely regular, though also completely unorthodox. Moore's use of rhyme is similarly regular yet untraditional. As with Stevens and Williams, some of Moore's best-known poems are intimately concerned with the nature and craft of poetry itself. Most famous in this respect is 'Poetry'. Initially this was a thirteen-line poem published in the small magazine *Others* in 1919. Moore revised it in 1935 for her *Selected Poems*, and yet again for her *Complete Poems* in 1967. The 1935 version consists of five stanzas and 38 lines in total, with the first line of the final stanza containing Moore's famous definition of good or real poems as holding up for our inspection 'imaginary gardens with real toads in them', achieving something of a cross between Stevens's emphasis on the imagination and Williams's insistence on everyday reality. In the 1967 version, however, the entire poem was reduced to:

> I, too, dislike it.
> Reading it, however, with a perfect contempt for it, one discovers in
> it, after all, a place for the genuine.

Although the 1967 version obviously can stand on its own, a reading of it is much enhanced by knowledge of the 1935 version. As such, much of what the later poem 'says' lies in what is no longer there, but the weight or presence of which is still felt. 'Poetry' is only an extreme example of how Moore kept changing, often simplifying, her poems throughout her career. Her later poetry also tends to be considerably simpler in form and diction than her earlier work. Public fame came late to Moore, but among fellow poets she was appreciated from the beginning.

Amy Lowell (1874–1925), a descendant of a prominent Boston 'Brahmin' family, first came to public attention with the publication of her first collection of poetry, *A Dome of Many-Coloured Glass*, in 1912. Upon reading some of H.D.'s poems in *Poetry* in 1913, Lowell took up the case of Imagism, propagating the movement through her own poetry, criticism, and anthologies. She became the chief defendant of Imagism when Pound converted to Vorticism, which led Pound to re-baptize the earlier movement as 'Amygism'. As well as Imagist poetry, Lowell also wrote more lyrics and long narrative poems, using both traditional and free verse forms. Like H.D., Amy Lowell most of her life lived together with another woman, in her case Ada Dwyer Russell (1863–1952), a former actress, for whom she wrote many poems celebrating female beauty. Consider, for instance, 'Venus Transiens' (1919), which starts off with: 'Tell me, / Was Venus more beautiful / Than you are, / When she topped / The crinkled waves, / Drifting shoreward / On her plaited shell?', and then draws an explicit comparison with the famous painting of Venus by Botticelli.

Also celebrating women's bodies, often with explicit reference to their erotic side, and to heterosexual love, were Elinor Wylie (1885–1928), Edna St Vincent Millay (1892–1950) and Mina Loy (1882–1966). Both Wylie and St Vincent Millay gained notoriety because of their turbulent love lives, but while Wylie wrote mostly conventional poetry, much influenced in diction by the Romantics and especially Shelley, St Vincent Millay freely vented her passion in poems such as 'First Fig' (1920). The following lines from 'I Too beneath Your Moon, Almighty Sex' (1939) make abundantly clear why St Vincent Millay's poems rubbed a lot of people the wrong way: 'I too beneath your moon, almighty Sex, / Go forth at nightfall crying like a cat'. St Vincent Millay to great effect played off traditional form against unorthodox feeling. Like so many other modernist poems, 'I Too beneath Your Moon, Almighty Sex' voices not just the feelings of its speaker, or author; it also formulates a poetics. It is passion, lust, for life, for love, for sex, that have brought into being the poem. Another, and programmatic, instance of St Vincent Millay's poetics is her posthumously published sonnet tellingly titled 'I Will Put Chaos into Fourteen Lines' (1954). St Vincent Millay fell out of fashion after the 1920s, when the climate of freedom and opportunity, also in matters sexual, to which her work had generously contributed, waned under the onslaught of the Depression. For a long time she was almost forgotten. However, as with so many other women poets, with the feminist wave of the 1970s her work too received renewed attention, and her poetry is now found in all anthologies.

Mina Loy (originally Löwry) frequented the avant-garde, associating with Gertrude Stein in Paris, with the Futurists in Italy, and with the Province Town Players and the poets and artists gathering around the little magazine *Others* in New York, where she first moved in 1915. Her poems are very physical, with an outspoken emphasis on female experiences, as in 'Parturition' (1915), in which she lends the act of giving birth a cosmic dimension. She does so using a free verse form that follows as closely as possible the experiences it describes. Loy's 'Love Songs' (1914) caused a minor scandal upon publication, but its juxtaposition of apparently unrelated images, and its provocative diction fit very well the Imagist and avant-garde mood of the time. Louise Bogan (1897–1970) also concentrated on female experiences, and like Wylie and St Vincent Millay did so in traditional forms, but in a very different tone. Bogan does not raucously celebrate the erotic power of the female body, but rather woman's inner force, her reserve and denial, as in 'Portrait' (1923).

Edward Estlin Cummings (1894–1962), who also published as e.e. cummings, first gained notice with *The Enormous Room* (1922), a largely autobiographical novel detailing his experiences as a detainee suspected of espionage in a French prison camp during World War I. Though Cummings also published a travelogue, *EIMI* (1933), of a trip he made to the Soviet Union in 1931, some short stories, and a number of plays, he is primarily known as a poet. Like many of his contemporaries of the so-called 'lost generation', Cummings enlisted as a volunteer in the Ambulance Corps during World War I. Notwithstanding his unhappy experience with the French authorities he returned to France for a few years during the early 1920s. Cumming's poems look unconventional because of their consistent use of lower case, but in fact many of them are rather conventional in the sentiments they express, as for instance in 'all in green went my love riding' (1916, 1923) or 'I carry your heart with me (I carry it in)' (1920). Cumming's experimentalism is to be found in his unconventional use of grammar, vocabulary, punctuation and rhyme. In 'my father moved through dooms of love' (1940) or 'all ignorance toboggans into know' (1950) we can see him playing havoc with traditional word categories. In 'r-p-o-p-h-e-s-s-a-g-r' (1932, 1935, 'Grasshopper') the syllables and lines are typographically arranged so as to make the reader in his reading act double the action of the grasshopper preparing for a leap. Often, he played off the conventionality of form, as with the sonnet, or rhyme, against the meaning of a poem or a line. The effect is humorous, as in 'anyone lived in a pretty how town' (1940), which continues '(with up so floating many bells down)'. Also humorous is his application of a vocabulary pertaining to one particular domain to another, widely different one, as in 'She being Brand' (1926), where a sexual act is cast in the style and vocabulary of a car enthusiast breaking in his new car. With poems such as these, and other sexually explicit poems such as for instance also 'between the breasts' (1925), Cummings was obviously out to shock what his near-contemporary, the journalist and essayist H.L. Mencken (1880–1956), scathingly referred to as 'the booboisie'. At the same time, it also fit the tenor of sexual liberation and more general libertarianism of the 1920s, at least in the arts. Cummings not only revolted against traditional sexual mores, though. He also vehemently attacked the blind patriotism and the senseless slaughter of World War I in 'next to of course god america i' (1926). Even more frequently, he fulminated against the excesses of both western-style capitalism and soviet-style

Communism in, for instance, and respectively, 'a salesman is an it that stinks Excuse' (1944) and 'kumrads die because they're told' (1935). But Cummings was also expert at catching the mood of his era in its clichés and its popular culture. Advertisements, political and sales slogans, cabaret and blues, they all found their way into his poems, although often with an ironic, and sharply critical twist, as for instance in 'Buffalo Bill's' (1920), which in the second line already declares the popular hero defunct, and which ends on 'he was a handsome man/and what i want to know is/how do you like your blueeyed boy/Mister Death'.

Hart Crane (1899–1932) led a difficult and complicated life, anguished by his homosexuality, and his hard drinking. He committed suicide by jumping overboard from the ship with which he was returning from Mexico, where he had been working on *Key West*, his third collection of poems. His first collection, *White Buildings* (1926), gathered the early poems with which he had made his reputation, such as 'My Grandmother's Love Letters' (1920), 'Chaplinesque' (1921), 'For the Marriage of Faustus and Helen' (1922), 'Voyages' (1924), and 'At Melville's Tomb' (1926). Crane's present-day reputation, however, mainly rests on *The Bridge* (1930). Wedding the expansive upbeat vision of Walt Whitman to the modernist techniques of T.S. Eliot, Crane aimed to write a contemporary epic about the United States in which Brooklyn bridge serves as metaphor for all of America, its past, present and future, its full geographical expansion, and the mind of its people. Consisting of fifteen individual poems arranged in eight sections, often using obscure personal references, at other moments drawing on historical, mythical or literary characters, and modeling itself upon musical structures of repetition and variation, *The Bridge* is a demanding, sometimes baffling poem. To Crane's bitter disappointment *The Bridge* met with little critical success upon publication. More recently, though, it has been recognized as one of American poetry's major modernist achievements.

African American poetry

World War I and its aftermath had led to a veritable exodus of African Americans from the South to other parts of America, and particularly to the major cities of the American North. In New York the formerly middle-class white suburb of Harlem, north of Central Park, had rapidly been taken over by African Americans, and in the 1920s it was the largest urban concentration of black people in the world. Most African Americans worked in industry, or in service jobs, as domestics, railroad porters, or small tradesmen. In practice, they formed an urban proletariat, and as such they developed a more militant class and race consciousness than had been the case in the rural South. African Americans who had fought in Europe returned home with an increased sense of their own value. In Europe, moreover, they had grown accustomed to societies in which race did not play the all-important role it did in the United States. Finally, there was the figure of Marcus Garvey (1887–1940), a Jamaican printer, journalist, newspaper publisher, orator and politician, who advocated pan-Africanism. Garvey had traveled and worked in Central America and Britain before he came to the U.S. in 1916. In New York, he established a branch of the Universal Negro Improvement Association, a movement he had founded himself in Jamaica in 1914. Garvey quickly established himself as the political leader of African Americans in the U.S., with his UNIA growing to over two million members in the early 1920s. Garvey urged African Americans to return to Africa, in particular to Liberia, and to be proud of their African ancestry. Accused of mail fraud, Garvey was sentenced to five years' imprisonment in 1923, but in 1927 he was deported to Jamaica. He spent the later part of his life in London, England, where he died in 1940.

Next to the increased political and social self-awareness of African Americans themselves in the immediate post-World War I years, there was also a heightened interest in African Americans on the part of white writers and artists. In Europe such interest had already been very lively before the war, with artists such as Picasso, Braque, Brancusi, and others. Now also American authors, such as the playwright Eugene O'Neill and the novelist Sherwood Anderson, came to share this interest. The white interest in black America peaked after the publication of *Nigger Heaven* (1926), a novel by the white author Carl Van Vechten (1880–1966), which pictures Harlem as a colorful and exciting cosmos overflowing with primitive spontaneity, and free of the sexual inhibitions that limited life among white people. Obviously, not all African Americans were thrilled. W.E.B. Dubois protested vehemently, even though he remained convinced that Van Vechten had had the best of intentions with his novel. After all, Van Vechten was instrumental in getting a number of 'Harlem Renaissance' writers published. Harlem, with its jazz clubs, was 'the place to be' for whites in search of entertainment in the second half of the 1920s, but it also was a hotbed of artistic and literary activity for blacks. A major role in fostering this talent fell to Alain Locke (1886–1954), with his enormously influential anthology *The New Negro* (1925), which showcased the talents of a great number of young black writers. Because not all 1920s black writers lived in Harlem, and because it refers to an essentially white concept, the appellation 'Harlem Renaissance' is nowadays sometimes found to be too narrow, and as an alternative the Lockian 'New Negro' is preferred.

Even before the advent of the Harlem Renaissance or the New Negro, Claude McKay (1889–1948) had already made his entry upon the literary stage. Like Garvey, McKay was a Jamaican. He had already made himself a reputation with collections of folk poetry, *Songs of Jamaica* and *Constab Ballads* (both 1912), but gained national prominence in 1919 when his defiant poem 'If We Must Die' ['If we must die, O let us nobly die, / So that our precious blood may not be shed / In vain; then even the monsters we defy / Shall be constrained to honor us though dead! / O kinsmen, we must meet the common foe!'] was published in the socialist-inclined *The Liberator*, a magazine run by Max Eastman (1883–1969), a well-known leftist radical at the time (he later turned conservative). Like Eastman before him, McKay traveled to the Soviet Union in 1923. The year before he had published *Harlem Shadows* (1922), a collection of poetry that is usually taken as ushering in the Harlem Renaissance. The almost invariably radical message of the poems in this collection is couched in almost equally invariably classical forms, often sonnets in strict meters, as in 'The Lynching' (1919), in which a black man being lynched is likened to Jesus Christ when he died upon the cross, and which concludes with little white boys, 'lynchers that were to be', dancing round the 'dreadful thing in fiendish glee'. Poems such as 'Outcast' (1922) and 'The Harlem Dancer' (1917), highlighting the opposition between the entertainment provided by a Harlem dancer and how she must feel inside stress the alienation between the black man or woman and his or her American environment. 'Africa' (1921) laments the downfall of a continent that once was the cradle and the pride of mankind, but where now 'Honor and Glory, Arrogance and Fame! / They went. The darkness swallowed thee again. / Thou art the harlot, now thy time is done, / Of all the mighty nations of the sun'. Because of his Communist sympathies and his radical politics McKay was prevented from coming back to the U.S., and he stayed in Europe until 1934. He then also turned away from Communism, largely in reaction to Stalin's mass persecutions of the 1930s. Eventually he converted to Catholicism, and moved to Chicago, where he died in 1948. McKay wrote little of importance during the last years of his life, and after he left the U.S. he wrote little poetry, although he did write an important novel, *Home to Harlem* (1928), and an equally important autobiography, *A Long Way from Home* (1937). He only became a U.S. citizen in 1940.

Likewise conservative in his handling of form is Countee Cullen (1903–46). Cullen, from a well-to-do New York family, stuck to classical English verse forms, sonnets, quatrains and rhyme, and to universal themes, even though he also tried to bend these towards his racial consciousness, which is evident from the titles of his various collections: *Color* (1925), *Copper Sun* (1927), *The Ballad of the Brown Girl* (1928), *The Black Christ* (1929). For the most part, though, this took the form of interrogating his heritage, and his belonging, as in the appropriately titled 'Heritage' (1925), in which the speaker is torn between allegiance to Christ and 'quaint, out-landish heathen gods'. He asserts: 'I belong to Jesus Christ, / Preacher of humility; / Heathen gods are naught to me'. Yet he also confesses that 'in my heart / Do I play a double part', 'Wishing He I served were black' and 'Daring even to give you / Dark despairing features'. And the sonnet 'Yet Do I Marvel' (1925) concludes with what one can only interpret as an expression of Cullen's bewilderment at being a black poet: 'Yet do I marvel at this curious thing: / To make a poet black, and bid him sing!' Cullen said he wanted to be 'a poet' and not a 'negro poet', and in his early collections he set his race poems, such as 'Incident' (1925), in which the speaker looks back at when at age eight he visited Baltimore and was called 'Nigger' by a little white boy, and that this is the only thing that stayed with him from that visit, apart from his more general poems. Yet, Cullen also published an important anthology of black poetry, *Caroling Dusk*, in 1927, and a novel, *One Way to Heaven* (1932).

Cullen's contemporary, Langston Hughes (1902–67), also wrote fiction, mostly short stories in which the ostensibly rather dull-witted black protagonist Jesse B. Semple invariably succeeds in outwitting his seemingly so much cleverer opponents, but also the novel *Not Without Laughter* (1930), as well as plays and essays. Of the latter especially 'The Negro Artist and the Racial Mountain' (1926), which appeared in the nationally important weekly *The Nation*, and in which he described the difficulties black artists faced when trying for 'a racial art', gained Hughes national attention. By then, though, he had already made his reputation as a poet, with publications in *Opportunity* and *Crisis*, the two most prominent black periodicals, and in Locke's anthology *The New Negro*. Hughes's first collection of poems was *The Weary Blues* in 1926, and it immediately established him as the leading poet of his generation, and of the Harlem Renaissance. Drawing upon the rhythms and vocabulary of the blues, and later on also on other jazz forms, Hughes captured the experiences of modern American urban blacks. *The Weary Blues*, *Fine Clothes to the Jew* (1927), *Shakespeare in Harlem* (1942), *One Way Ticket* (1949), and *Montage of a Dream Deferred* (1951), provided guidance for a whole generation of black poets. Like Garvey and McKay, Hughes identified with blacks all over the world, and throughout history, as in 'The Negro Speaks of Rivers' (1921): 'I bathed in the Euphrates when dawns were young / I built my hut near the Congo and it lulled me to sleep. / I looked upon the Nile and raised the pyramids above it'. But Hughes also self-consciously, and self-confidently, claimed his American heritage, not hesitating to set up as the black counterpart to Walt Whitman, in 'I, Too' (1932): 'I, too, sing America. / / I am the darker brother / […] / / I, too, am America'.

Margaret Walker (1915–98), member of the Black Chicago Renaissance, in 'For My People' (1937), also followed Whitman's example in using a long loose line, and like Hughes she called on black people to stand up and claim their rights. In 1966 Walker published *Jubilee*, a novel based on family tales from when her great-grandmother was a slave.

Like Hughes, Sterling Brown (1901–89) drew upon the blues and other popular expressions of African American life for his poetry, but he concentrated on rural blacks. Brown never was part of the Harlem Renaissance, as he spent all his life in the South, as a scholar and teacher at various black colleges, and as of 1929 until his retirement at the historically black Howard University. Brown published a collection of poetry, *Southern Roads*, in 1932, and co-edited *Negro Caravan*, an anthology of black literature, in 1941. In 1938 he had already published *The Negro in American Fiction* and *Negro Poetry and Drama*. In his poems Brown used dialect as well as standard English to picture the plight of poor blacks. Sometimes he does so humorously, as in 'Mister Samuel and Sam' (1932), in which he compares the lives of a rich white man and of a poor black, Mister Samuel riding in a Cadillac and Sam in a 'Tin Lizzie Fo'd', but when both die, although 'de folks all know' about Mister Samuel's death and 'Sam die widout no noise', 'dey's both of 'em po' lost boys ... '. In other poems he strikes a much more bitter note, as in 'Bitter Fruit of the Tree' (1939), in which two generations of blacks living in abject poverty and in bondage to white people are told 'you must not be bitter'. Like McKay in 'The Lynching' and Hughes in 'Song for a Dark Girl' (1927), Brown too reflected on the practice of lynching that during the 1920s still was all too common in the South. In 'He Was a Man' (1932) a black man who has dared to stand up to a white man in legitimate self-defense is lynched by a white mob, and 'The mob broke up by midnight, / "Another uppity Nigger gone– / He was a man, an' we laid him down"'. Regardless of the horrible fate this black man suffers, one feels that Brown also expresses pride that he dared stand up to his oppressor, and that therefore 'He Was a Man'.

Regionalist fiction

The period immediately following upon World War I yielded the best work of Willa Cather, Ellen Glasgow, Sinclair Lewis and Sherwood Anderson. They really belonged to the generation of the naturalists, but they produced their best work only in their (relatively) later years. In many ways they continued in the tracks of their regionalist predecessors.

Willa Cather (1873–1947) was born in Virginia, but soon moved with her family to Nebraska, still a frontier state in those days. After graduation from university, where she studied the classics, she went East, where she worked as a journalist in Pittsburgh and New York. All along she had been writing poems and stories, the latter collected in 1905 in *The Troll Garden*, but in her late thirties she turned to writing novels, with as a first result *Alexander's Bridge* (1912), set in Boston, London and Canada. With her second novel, *O Pioneers!* (1913), Cather turned to the land of her youth, picturing the life of Alexandra Bergson, a woman who is extra-ordinarily successful at running her farm after her father, a Swedish immigrant to Nebraska, has died. Cather used the theme of an exceptionally gifted and lively woman also in *The Song of the Lark* (1915) and *A Lost Lady* (1923). In the former novel Thea Kronborg finds her vocation as an opera singer in Chicago but has to sacrifice personal relations. The latter novel pictures the triumph of commercialism over the pioneer spirit, with the lost lady of the title being destroyed in the change. What is arguably Cather's best work, *My Ántonia* (1918), offers a sober, slightly nostalgic view of farm life in Nebraska during the last quarter of the nineteenth century. The narrative structure, with a visitor from the East, Jim Burden, telling the story of the Bohemian immigrant girl Ántonia whom he got to know when he was sent to live with his grandparents in Nebraska, and of her immigrant community of Bohemians and Scandinavians, the episodic pattern, and the psychological depth of *My Ántonia* recall the work of Sarah Orne Jewett, a writer after whom Cather explicitly modeled herself, and who encouraged her in her literary vocation. In *My Ántonia*, as in *O Pioneers!*, it is the land that plays a central role, but Ántonia Shimerda, rather than being an exceptional woman as is Alexandra Bergson, is the prototype of the ordinary, decent, and deeply caring family woman, dutifully and lovingly raising her children, tending to her husband, and keeping the community together.

The land, and the pioneering spirit, also play a major role in *Death Comes for the Archbishop* (1927), but it is a different land than in *O Pioneers!* or *My Ántonia*. In *The Song of the Lark* Thea Kronborg had found spiritual renewal and the recognition of her true vocation during a visit to

Arizona, and her coming into contact with the ancient Native Americans there. In *Death Comes for the Archbishop* two French priests, one of whom, Jean Marie Latour, is the archbishop of the title, in the middle of the nineteenth century are sent to New Mexico, there to establish a firm footing for the Catholic church by organizing a new diocese. Again, Cather expresses admiration for the pioneer spirit these men show in overcoming all hardships, leading a simple, rugged life of duty and toil. In what is now her most frequently anthologized story, 'Neighbor Rosicky' (1928), she once more gives a loving portrait of a Bohemian immigrant to Nebraska, focalized through the family doctor. Like *My Ántonia*, 'Neighbor Rosicky' too is essentially American pastoral, a genre Cather was well acquainted with through her study of the classics. The story recounts the last few months of Anton's life, when, suffering from a heart disease, he basically sacrifices his own life to save the marriage of his son, showing him how caring for his wife, an 'American' girl rather than an immigrant, is more important than getting on in life.

Ellen Glasgow (1874–1945), like Cather born in Virginia but unlike the former a Southerner all her life, in her work addressed the social realities of her region at the turn of the twentieth century. In *Virginia* (1913) and *The Sheltered Life* (1932) she ironically, even satirically, highlights how the old Southern ideals, particularly those regarding Southern womanhood, fall short of changing realities. *Barren Ground* (1925) and *Vein of Iron* (1935) are much grimmer. *Barren Ground* tells the story of a woman who sacrifices everything to her dedication to the family farm, which she restores to fertility. She herself, however, dies barren, never having found true love. Glasgow pictured the transition from the Old to the New South, and though she saw the inevitability of the change, and even applauded some of it, especially in her later work, such as *In This Our Life* (1941), she also could not help regretting the passing of an older order.

The fame of Sinclair Lewis (1885–1951), the first American author to win the Nobel Prize, in 1930, rests on the five novels he wrote during the 1920s, and which all offer satirical and deeply critical views of small-town America. *Main Street* (1920) recounts the experiences of Carol Kennicott, an ambitious and artistic young woman, married to a dull country doctor in the extremely dull country town of Gopher Prairie, clearly modeled after Lewis's own birthplace Sauk Centre in Minnesota. Estranged from her co-citizens, and from her husband, Carol leaves for Washington D.C., in search of an intellectually more stimulating and exciting life. When she realizes that she will not be able to make good in the big city either she returns to Gopher Prairie. Even though thoroughly disappointed, and forced to compromise, Carol now also comes to appreciate the good points of her husband, and of Gopher Prairie, which basically correspond to American middle-class ideology: hard work, uprightness, decency, kindness.

In *Babbitt* (1922) Lewis draws a satirical portrait of 'the' small-town American businessman of the 1920s: always looking for profit, conservative in morals but at the same time not averse to a little affair, and utterly without scruples in business. Owing to a number of circumstances Babbitt starts doubting the righteousness of the business mentality by which he has always lived. This, however, risks losing him his real estate agency and all of his friends. In the end, Babbitt obediently rejoins the conservative flock. *Arrowsmith* (1925) addresses the moral and professional tribulations of a man of science. *Dodsworth* (1929) brings another portrait of an American businessman. *Elmer Gantry* (1927) focuses upon the typically American phenomenon of the evangelist, the errant preacher.

Modernist fiction: Sherwood Anderson and Gertrude Stein

With *Winesburg, Ohio* (1919) Sherwood Anderson (1876–1941) exerted a determining influence upon the generation of writers immediately following upon his own. Inspired by Masters's *Spoon River Anthology*, *Winesburg, Ohio* sketches a picture of a small town and its inhabitants as seen through the eyes of George Willard, the son of the local hotel keeper and his wife, and himself a young reporter on the local newspaper. What cries out from the book is the frustration and loneliness, the grotesque stifling of life in the American mid-West in the early years of the twentieth century. Rather than a novel proper, *Winesburg, Ohio* is what these days is often called a 'composite' novel or a short story cycle, unified by the presence of George Willard in all the stories, and by their sharing the same locale. Most stories catch their protagonists at a moment of revelation, when suddenly they gain an insight into the inevitable limitation of their own fate, and their inability to do anything about it. In 'Adventure', Alice Hindman is a woman, clerking in a local store, whom George knew when still a boy. Alice used to be a pretty girl, who at sixteen had an affair with Ned Currie, a young man a little older than herself, and a reporter on the local paper, like George now. When Ned left Winesburg for Cleveland, there to get a better job, and she wanted to go with him, he instead persuaded her to wait until he sent for her. On the evening of his departure, Alice gives herself to Ned. Ned, however, moves on from Cleveland to Chicago, and though initially he writes to Alice, after a while the letters cease, and Alice hears no more from him. When her father dies she takes up a job in the dry goods store, and though other men show an interest in her she keeps believing that Ned will come for her and take her away from Winesburg. In her mid-twenties, though, she slowly starts to realize that perhaps Ned will never come, and that nothing of importance will ever again happen in her life. Briefly, she lets another, older man believe that he might stand a chance with her, but she ultimately rejects him, uninterested now in any particular man, including even the very possibility of Ned. Finally, at twenty-seven, one night when she is alone in the house, she feels a strange unrest, undresses, and runs out naked into the streets. When she sees a man she hails him, ready to give herself to any one now. However, when the man stops, Alice drops to the ground and hides. Suddenly frightened at what she has done she crawls back home, barricades herself in her room, gets into bed, and 'turning her face to the wall, began trying to force herself to face bravely the fact that many people must live and die alone, even in Winesburg'. George Willard himself at the end of the novel leaves Winesburg for Chicago, there to write about his home town and its people. In his essay collection *No Swank* (1943) Anderson claimed that for the style and vocabulary of *Winesburg, Ohio* he had taken his cue from Gertrude Stein, and especially from her insistence on everyday language, short declarative sentences, and frequent repetition. These techniques fit the image of the 'naive' writer that Anderson sought to promote, and chimed with his interest in primitive spontaneity which he thought to find with black people, as also portrayed in *Dark Laughter* (1925), next to *Winesburg, Ohio* his sole popular success. Anderson's reputation stood very high in the early 1920s, if not with the public at large, then in any case with fellow-writers. It was partially through his getting acquainted with Anderson in New Orleans, where the latter lived for a while in this period, that the young William Faulkner opted for a writer's life. In Chicago it was the young Ernest Hemingway who sought out Anderson, and who was influenced by the latter's handling of style and narrative technique.

According to Hemingway in one of the two epigraphs to his first novel *The Sun Also Rises* (1926) it was Gertrude Stein (1874–1946) who coined the term 'Lost Generation' to indicate a group of American writers who were all born in the last decade of the nineteenth century and who had a number of experiences in common. Stein herself was of German-American-Jewish descent. She grew up in a cosmopolitan intellectual environment and studied philosophy, medicine and psychology, the latter with William James at Harvard. As of 1902 Stein spent most of her life in Paris, setting up a famous 'salon', where she regularly received everyone of note in the Parisian art milieu. Picasso was a frequent guest, but so were many other painters, sculptors, writers and critics. Stein's fictionalized autobiography, *The Autobiography of Alice B.*

Toklas (1933), presented as if written by Stein's friend, secretary and lover (Stein was a confirmed lesbian and had had a relationship with Toklas since 1907), amply testifies to her lively interest in modern art. She also wrote on contemporary art and artists, as in her well-known 'portraits' of Cézanne, Matisse and Picasso.

In her own work Stein combined naturalism and modernism. The subject of her first volume, *Three Lives* (1909), is naturalist: the lives of one black and two German servant girls in the United States. The techniques with which she gives form to these lives, however, are rooted in Stein's own earlier psychological experiments, post-Impressionism and Cubism, and the early movies. She used these same techniques in *The Making of Americans*, written in the same period but published only in 1925. Her way of evoking impressions and moods via repetition with minor variations was taken up by Sherwood Anderson and Ernest Hemingway.

In *Tender Buttons* (1914) Stein sought to use the techniques and achieve the effects of abstract painting. To this end she sought to employ 'language' in as purely material a form as possible. Just as the Cubists forsook traditional perspective, preferring to picture objects in as analytical and 'flat' a way as possible, highlighting their materiality, so too Stein gave up traditional syntax, meaning, and plot. Instead, she conducted linguistic experiments involving punctuation, rhythm, temporality and points of view. She elaborated on her theoretical insights in *Composition as Explanation* (1926), *Narration* (1935), and *Geographical History of America* (1936). Like E.E. Cummings, who also experimented with punctuation and the logical meaning of words, Stein often was not taken very seriously, and her sayings, such as 'a rose is a rose is a rose', were often ridiculed. Only late in life did she gain any measure of popularity, with *The Autobiography of Alice B. Toklas*, the opera *Three Saints in Four Acts* (1934) and her memoir of the war in France, *Wars I have Seen* (1945). Her importance for, and often decisive influence upon, an entire generation of – especially American – authors, whom she introduced to the ideas and techniques of European modernism, and for many of whom she acted as friend, mentor, and maecenas, can however hardly be overrated.

The authors of the 'Lost Generation' were all born between 1895 and 1900, and for all of them World War I signaled a significant break between generations, even though most of them had not effectively seen battle or in any other way participated in the war. Most – Fitzgerald is the exception, and even in a number of his books the war plays a part – broke into print with war stories or novels: Dos Passos did so with *One Man's Initiation* (1920) and *Three Soldiers* (1921), E.E. Cummings with *The Enormous Room* (1922), Hemingway with a number of Nick Adams stories, and Faulkner with *Soldier's Pay* (1926). For these authors World War I and its aftermath implied the failure of an entire civilization. They vehemently rejected the verbiage with which the war was justified. As Frederic Henry, the protagonist of Hemingway's *A Farewell to Arms* (1929) puts it: 'abstract words such as glory, honor, courage, or hallow were obscene'. Revulsion at 'an old bitch gone in the teeth, / a botched civilization', as Pound put it in 'Hugh Selwyn Mauberley', was part of their common heritage. Little wonder, then, that they often took refuge in a form of primitivism, or in a pastoral ideal.

A second experience these writers had in common was that of voluntary exile. Scott Fitzgerald, E.E. Cummings and Dos Passos resided outside of the U.S. for shorter or longer periods. Hemingway and Henry Miller spent large parts of their lives abroad. Even William Faulkner spent a few months in Paris. There were various reasons why so many writers opted for voluntary exile. To begin with, the conservative climate of the U.S. after World War I meant that artists and writers felt seriously restricted as to freedom of expression. To escape these restrictions many moved to Europe. Writers in particular preferred Paris because in France there was no censure upon books published in English. Works that in the U.S. (or in the U.K., as with James Joyce's *Ulysses* (1922) or D.H. Lawrence's *Lady Chatterley's Lover* (1928)) were banned could with impunity be published in Paris. The very favorable rate of exchange between the U.S. dollar and the French franc also played a major role. A publisher's advance in dollars stretched much further in Europe than in the U.S. itself.

Finally, there was yet another reason why the members of the Lost Generation preferred Paris. Rather than seek to follow in the footsteps of their immediate American predecessors, the realists and naturalists, they sought to associate themselves with European modernism. In the plastic arts this meant Cubism and Expressionism. In a literary context we have to think of poets such as Guillaume Apollinaire, Paul Valéry and Rainer Maria Rilke, novelists such as Marcel Proust, Thomas Mann, Italo Svevo and Robert Musil. In English-language literature we can mention Joseph Conrad, Ford Madox Ford, Virginia Woolf and James Joyce as novelists, or W.B. Yeats, T.S. Eliot and Ezra Pound as poets. By choosing to settle in Paris, where all these artistic movements and artists converged, the authors of the lost generation also implicitly opted for an internationalization of American literature.

Francis Scott Fitzgerald

The writer whose work most immediately resonates with the 1920s, and whose name is most intimately related to this decade, is Francis Scott Fitzgerald (1896–1940). He was born in St Paul, Minnesota, and studied at Princeton, which is also where his first novel, *This Side of Paradise* (1920) is set. *This Side of Paradise* is not a particularly successful novel, but it does embody the mood of a generation that reached maturity along with the end of World War I: 'here was a new generation, […], grown up to find all gods dead, all wars fought, all faiths in man shaken'. The novel was partially autobiographical, and its success convinced Fitzgerald that his own life was representative of that of his generation. Not surprisingly, then, also the numerous stories that Fitzgerald wrote over the next few years, and that were collected in *Flappers and Philosophers* (1920) and *Tales of the Jazz Age* (1922), and his second novel, *The Beautiful and Damned* (1922), are closely modeled after Fitzgerald's own experiences and emotions. About this period Fitzgerald later, in his essay 'Echoes of the Jazz Age' (1931), said that 'it bore him up, flattered him and gave him more money than he had dreamed of, simply for telling people that he felt as they did'.

The early work of Fitzgerald was the expression of a youth culture, and in his books people of over thirty are branded as 'stuffed shirts'. At the same time, though, these books also chime with the business mentality of the period. In the first part of his career Fitzgerald himself was very successful financially. Yet most of his characters fall victim to the peculiar attraction that material success exerts in the United States. The most successful blend of this theme with Jamesian narrative techniques, and at the same time a very revealing snapshot of the Jazz Age, is *The Great Gatsby* (1925).

Jay Gatsby, the protagonist of *The Great Gatsby*, and Nick Carraway, the narrator of the novel, live on West Egg, a (fictive) part of Long Island modeled after the real Great Neck. Tom and Daisy Buchanan originate from the same Western parts of the United States as Jay and Nick, but they live in the more exclusive East Egg, modeled after the real Manhasset Neck. Contrasting West Egg to East Egg, the values and norms of America's pastoral West to the refinement but also the corruption of its Eastern parts, squarely situates *The Great Gatsby* in the tradition of Henry James, Mark Twain and James Fenimore Cooper.

James Gatz changed his original name – which sounded too strange to American ears – to Jay Gatsby. When still a young man he falls in love with Daisy, a girl from a well-to-do family in St Louis. To win her back from Tom Buchanan, the millionaire heir that Daisy in the meantime has married, and to realize his material ambitions, the older Gatsby, after an interlude at the front in Europe, becomes a bootlegger. It is Gatsby's self-deception that brings him to let Daisy take the wheel of his powerful car after a drinking bout in New York which has driven Daisy to fury with her husband. Daisy accidentally runs down Myrtle Wilson, the wife of a garage owner in the 'valley of ashes', the industrial no-man's land between the idyllic 'Eggs' and New York, and also the woman Tom has been having an affair with. Gatsby refuses to let it out that it was Daisy who caused the accident, and not he. Myrtle's husband revenges her death by killing Gatsby. Daisy remains unmoved through it all, and does not even show up for Gatsby's funeral. Regardless of Gatsby's love for her, and everything he has done, Daisy apparently never had any intention of giving up her life of luxury, founded on more secure sources of wealth with Tom than Gatsby could ever have offered her. The use of Nick Carraway as narrator and focalizer enables Fitzgerald to have the reader appraise the gradual moral decay of Gatsby. In many ways Carraway is an uncorrupted double of Gatsby. Nick's eventual return to the Mid-West they both came from therefore also delivers a devastating judgment on the morals and values of East Egg and the society it stands for. The final paragraphs of the book express a deep and wrenching yearning for a yet unspoiled America. If we take Gatsby's ambitions as representative of those of most Americans *The Great Gatsby* implies the failure of the famous 'American Dream'.

After this early success fame started to take its toll upon Fitzgerald and his wife Zelda. Zelda suffered from nervous disorders and was eventually confined to various institutions. Fitzgerald himself was a very heavy drinker. After *The Great Gatsby* his literary reputation went on the skids. Churning out far too many, and often mediocre magazine stories (a highly paid genre at the time, often making a successful author more money than full-length novels), his fame faded as the period to which he had given a name, and as the personification of which he was seen, passed. The Wall Street Crash of 1929 meant the end of the Jazz Age and of Fitzgerald as an acclaimed author. Nevertheless, his next novel, *Tender Is the Night* (1934), about the difficult relationship of two American expatriates plagued by psychological problems, is still a convincing piece of work. Just as Zelda (née Sayre, 1900–48) for her own semi-autobiographical novel *Save Me the Waltz* (1932), written while she was already institutionalized, drew upon her life with Scott, so Scott himself capitalized upon Zelda's illness and their life together for *Tender Is the Night*. Upon its appearance the novel was mercilessly cut down by the reviewers, but later it was recognized as a poignant evocation of the moral and psychological disorientation of the interbellum.

In the 1930s Fitzgerald, like many other authors of his generation, earned his living as a scriptwriter in Hollywood. This also gave him the subject matter for *The Last Tycoon* (1941), a novel on which he was working at the time of his death. Of all writers of the so-called Lost Generation Fitzgerald was the least experimental and perhaps also the least intellectual. Although much of his work in retrospect is adolescent in nature, and although many of his short stories look as if written to recipe, with *The Great Gatsby* he created an icon for an age, and revealed himself as the sharpest critic of that age he himself had given its name.

Ernest Hemingway

Fitzgerald's name is inextricably linked to the Jazz Age. That of Ernest Hemingway (1899–1961) is just as tightly linked to the Lost Generation as a whole. He was the first to use the term in print, although he claimed to have heard it from Gertrude Stein, who herself said she had it from a Parisian 'garagiste'. The novel in which he did so, *The Sun Also Rises* (1926), is also the most perfect expression of the ideas and mentality of the writers who entered literary history under that label. *The Sun Also Rises* contrasts the 1920s Parisian milieu of American writers, journalists, tourists and hangers-on, and its atmosphere of only slightly disguised despair, of seeking oblivion in primal emotions to drown out the horrors of the war that are still fresh in everybody's memory, with the nature and people of Spain in the guise of the mountains near Pamplona and the bullfighter Pedro Romero. Romero stands for everything that makes up Hemingway's famous 'code of conduct'. He is courageous, a master at his trade or profession, un-ostentatious with his skills, utterly masculine, and possesses a native nobility, with each of his gestures perfect, and his poise always natural. *The Sun Also Rises* consolidated the vision and style of Hemingway's early stories and fixed the themes for all his later work. At the same time it contained a number of autobiographical elements and the code of conduct it advocated, the mentality and the attitude it evoked, remained those of Hemingway himself up to his death (by suicide) in 1961.

Ernest Hemingway was born in Illinois, and spent his youth in a Chicago suburb. His father was an avid sportsman who took young Ernest hunting and fishing in northern Michigan. The lone trip into the wilderness, and the battle between the hunter and his prey, for Hemingway came to function as healing processes after the scars of war or the polluting contact with a chaotic civilization. Sports played the same role for him, especially individual sports such as boxing – a sport he practiced himself as an amateur. During World War I he first enlisted in the Ambulance Corps, but soon he managed to get transferred to a fighting unit on the Italian front. He was gravely wounded there. In the Nick Adams stories, in which the protagonist serves as persona for the author himself, and in his bestsellers *A Farewell to Arms* (1929) and *For Whom the Bell Tolls* (1940), the war for Hemingway served as a test that brought out man's fundamental qualities and shortcomings. All through his life he saw himself as the prototype of the man-of-action, and he served as special correspondent in many wars and armed conflicts from 1920 to 1950.

Hemingway's code of conduct emphasized 'style': the way in which a man behaves in specific situations. It is his style that makes Romero the epitome of the Hemingway code. It is that style that Nick Adams strives for and that, in 'Big Two-Hearted River' (1925), allows him to achieve balance and harmony in nature and with himself after the confusion and the horror of the war from which he has only just returned. It is 'style' that raises the conduct of a Hemingway character to ritual. Just barely beneath the surface of Hemingway's fiction lurks the suspicion that his self-chosen code is a substitute religion for a period in which God is incurably dead and there is little reason left to believe in humanity instead. In other words, it is a belief against reason, a holding-on to the most elementary of values, a passionate and unconditional – even if arbitrary – act of faith in the face of nothingness, the 'nada' from the prayer of the older waiter in 'A Clean Well-Lighted Place' (1933).

It is little wonder that for a writer for whom 'style' was the determining factor in his own life and in that of his characters, this element also played a leading role in his writing itself. In *Death in the Afternoon* (1932), a book on Spain, bullfighting and writing, and in *A Moveable Feast* (1964), a posthumous volume of reminiscences of his years in Paris and the literary life as it was then led there, Hemingway explains how he worked very consciously and deliberately towards his famous Hemingway style. He imposed upon himself a strict regimen in which he progressed from short sketches to short stories and thence to the novel. Still, Hemingway's style, as were his topics, were not entirely new. At the very beginning of his career, before he had published any fiction, Hemingway had worked as a journalist for a number of U.S. and Canadian newspapers. A slightly older fellow-journalist of Hemingway's, Ring Lardner (1885–1933), even before 1920 had reported on sports events in very sparse dialogue and description, and in the 1920s the same Lardner published a number of short stories on similar themes.

Hemingway labored to pare his style, on a par with the vision he aimed to project, to bare essentials. To this end he used very short sentences and carefully eliminated adjectives and adverbs, a technique he borrowed from Ezra Pound, one of Hemingway's early mentors in Paris. He avoided abstract terms, tried to use as few Latinate words as possible, used almost invariably only declarative sentences, and tried not to use grammatical inversions. Following the example of Gertrude Stein he preferred coordinate sentences and repetitions with minor variations. He insisted on keeping his prose as lean as possible, so that each detail that does get mentioned receives inordinate weight. Just as 'the dignity of an iceberg is due to only one-eighth of it being above water', so too each word that did make it on to the page had to suggest a whole host of others that had not made it there. The result for the reader is to give him the impression that she or he sees, feels, and acts right along with the character. Hemingway's style became famous instantly, and because of its deceptive simplicity it was widely imitated almost overnight.

Hemingway was most successful in joining vision and style in his early work, the stories collected in *In Our Time* (1925) and *Men Without Women* (1927) and the novels *The Sun Also Rises* (1926) and *A Farewell to Arms* (1929). The latter novel, set during World War I at the Italian front, and involving a tragic love affair between a young American officer in the Italian army and an English nurse, already comes across as somewhat melodramatic, especially in the final chapters. In fact, after *A Farewell to Arms* Hemingway's work suffered a loss of depth and vigor. The stories of *Winner Take Nothing* (1933) and two stories first published in magazines in 1936, 'The Short Happy Life of Francis Macomber' and 'Snows of Kilimanjaro', still rank with the best of Hemingway's production. But *Death in the Afternoon* (1932), on bullfighting in Spain, and *Green Hills of Africa* (1935), about a safari in East Africa, concentrate on the formal aspects of the Hemingway style while losing sight of the vision originally underpinning it. On occasion these works become long-winded and baroque.

The 1930s were marked by social and political problems, and Hemingway responded with *To Have and Have Not* (1937) and *For Whom the Bell Tolls* (1940). The first of these novels features Harry Morgan, a have-not who becomes involved in running bootleg alcohol up from Cuba. *For Whom the Bell Tolls* grew out of Hemingway's involvement, as a war correspondent, in the Spanish Civil War. The American Robert Jordan enlists with the Republican forces and sacrifices his life in the fight against Fascism and to save his comrades. With this novel Hemingway unambiguously took sides in the ideologically laden times leading up to World War II. Yet the book makes a wooden impression, especially in the stilted language supposedly representing colloquial Spanish.

Apart from *Across the River and into the Trees* (1950), generally considered his weakest work, and the novella *The Old Man and the Sea* (1952) Hemingway published almost nothing during the last fifteen years of his life. The latter work, though, which concentrates on the age-old theme of man against nature and against himself, was a runaway success and undoubtedly contributed to Hemingway's receiving the Nobel Prize in 1954.

Because he was constantly in the public eye, and because of the immense influence he exerted upon his generation as well as that immediately following, it is difficult to judge Hemingway and his work objectively. Moreover, his vicious parody of his early mentor Sherwood Anderson in *Torrents of Spring* (1936), and his equally abrasive portraits of Gertrude Stein, Scott Fitzgerald and others he knew during his Parisian period in the posthumously published *A Moveable Feast* (1964), did not exactly help to create a serene atmosphere around his character and his work. What cannot be denied is that he was a tremendous presence in American letters from the 1920s through the 1950s. He was the spokesman of the Lost Generation because in his early work he best expressed the attitudes, the mentality and the background of that generation. But precisely this pre-eminence proved fatal in the long run. Hemingway's contemporaries, while initially exploring themes similar to Hemingway's, gradually started looking for new subjects, new styles. Hemingway, though, largely confined himself to try and continue, often in vain, in the same vein. The undeniable weakening of his later work probably results from the growing gap between Hemingway's vision and the changed circumstances.

John Dos Passos

John Dos Passos (1896–1970) was descended from Portuguese immigrants and all his life continued to feel a strong bond with the Iberian peninsula. Educated at some of the best schools in Europe and the United States, Dos Passos in 1916 went to Spain to study architecture. In 1917 he joined the voluntary ambulance corps at the French front in World War I. Like many of his contemporaries Dos Passos in the late 1920s and early 1930s contributed to the Communist journal *The New Masses* (1926–48). He also supported Communist candidates in elections. He never joined the party, though, preferring to remain a fellow traveler. Still, the Communist party adopted Dos Passos as one of its figureheads in the early 1930s. Ironically, this was precisely when Dos Passos himself started turning away from the party. At the end of the 1930s he was a supporter of Roosevelt, and in the 1940s and 1950s he ever more insistently started to draw on the ideological legacy of Thomas Jefferson. In retrospect we can see that his rapprochement to Communism in the 1920s and '30s was not grounded in any firm ideological belief in Marxism, but in his life-long aversion to all forms of institutionalized power, which made him join that movement which at the time seemed most effectively to fight his own battle. As soon, however, as such a movement institutionalized itself, Dos Passos turned against it.

Dos Passos made his debut in 1920, the same year as did Scott Fitzgerald, with *One Man's Initiation: 1917*, a war novel based on his own experiences with the ambulance corps. His next novel, *Three Soldiers* (1921), drew on the same experiences. The first novel was very traditional in conception, but the second already shows signs of the 'collective' novels Dos Passos now is mainly known for: *Manhattan Transfer* (1925) and *U.S.A.* (1937). It is precisely this collective focus that sharply distinguishes the major works of Dos Passos from those of his contemporaries Scott Fitzgerald, Hemingway and Faulkner. As far as literary technique is concerned, however, Dos Passos is as radically experimental and modernist as any of his contemporaries. This is especially true of *Manhattan Transfer* and *U.S.A.*

Manhattan Transfer is a kaleidoscopic big city novel, with no real heroes or protagonists, but focusing upon twelve characters that together make up a representative sample of the population of New York. All are portrayed as victims of circumstance and of their own weaknesses. All human relationships end in defeat, failure and frustration. Still, the life of the city itself is indestructible, and bristles with vitality. The brief passages parading at breakneck speed, and the continuous juxtaposition and contrasting of the experiences of a great many characters, lend the book a hasty, jerky rhythm. At the same time they also signal the novel's affiliation with modernist techniques typical of Cubism, jazz, and film. The Cubist element, for instance, shows in the multitude of different perspectives, and in the constant change of focus that highlights surface rather than depth, thus emphasizing the spatial dimension often considered characteristic of literary modernism.

U.S.A. is not one novel but a trilogy, consisting of *The 42nd Parallel*, *1919* and *The Big Money*, published separately between 1930 and 1936, and jointly in 1937. If *Manhattan Transfer* portrays the individual as lonely and lost in the big city of New York, *U.S.A.* enlarges the scope to take in all of the United States. The earlier work covers about a decade, the latter the period 1900–36. In *Manhattan Transfer* the character whose experiences guide us through the book, Jimmy Herf, at the end flees New York on an impulse. Without a penny in his pocket, and in a move reminiscent of Huck Finn, he 'lights out' for the western United States. *U.S.A* offers no such way out. All of the U.S. now are one gigantic Manhattan from which no escape is possible. The number of characters we meet with in *U.S.A.* also greatly surpasses that of the earlier novel. Of the most diverse origins and with the most diverse backgrounds and careers, these characters continuously keep skirting or bumping into one another. For most of them life follows a downward path. Their youthful hopes and ambitions come to nothing, and most end up in complete obscurity, frustrated and disillusioned.

Dos Passos uses three specific techniques that make *U.S.A.* one of the most daring literary experiments of the first half of the twentieth century. The first technique consists of the juxtaposition of biographical sketches of a number of celebrated Americans (the trade union leader Eugene Debs, the steel magnate Andrew Carnegie, the inventor Thomas Edison, the journalist and political agitator John Reed, the Unknown Soldier, President Theodore Roosevelt, the trade union militant Joe Hill, the actor Rudolf Valentino and many, many more) to the lives of the fictional characters. These biographies often adopt an ironic mode, especially when they deal with the life of a magnate or industrialist. The tone of the narrative passages featuring fictional characters, on the contrary, is mechanical and flat, reflective of the relentless pressure of society grinding down ordinary people. The juxtaposition of these two kinds of passages highlights the two sides of life in America: light versus shadow, success versus failure. Two more narrative techniques underscore the composite, and far from flattering, picture of life in the United States that emerges from *U.S.A.* The 'Newsreel' passages in a collage of newspaper and periodical clippings, popular ditties and extracts of official documents and reports convey a vivid impression of American actuality in the period *U.S.A.* covers. At the same time they underscore the contrast between the two Americas, the official and the real, the successful and the other. In 'Newsreel 68', for instance, toward the end of the final volume of the trilogy, the newspaper headlines tell a very different story from that which we hear from the trade union song: 'PRESIDENT SEES PROSPERITY NEAR / Not a cent to spend for clothing / Not a cent to lay away'. The third technique Dos Passos employs is that of the 'Camera Eye'. In these passages we are given a 'snapshot' of American reality as seen through the eyes of the narrator, presumably Dos Passos himself. Although theoretically they should be objective and neutral, in practice these passages prove to be lyrical, impressionistic and subjective. When we stop to think about it, this should not really come as a surprise, as a camera, because of the particular lens it carries, the angle at which it is held, the timing of its shutter speed, and other such technical devices, does not capture 'the whole truth', but only that subjective part of it that whoever handles the camera, especially at a time when all of these settings still needed to be chosen manually, seeks to register. Not surprisingly, then, the 'Camera Eye' passages are raw and direct testimonies to the suffering and injustice inherent in American society. The trilogy concludes with a brief scene in which a young man, 'Vag' for vagabond, and in whom we perhaps may see what the Jimmy Herf from *Manhattan Transfer* has become, tries to thumb a lift somewhere along an endless and dusty road out west. In the meantime a businessman, high above him and comfortably seated in an airplane, becomes airsick after a copious meal.

Next to the collage and montage techniques first made familiar in modernist painting, the fast alternation and the abrupt switches between the various passages using different tones and voices, the impressionistic viewpoints of the 'Camera Eye', and the rotation from mass scenes to individualized close-ups in *U.S.A.* strongly recall cinematic techniques. *U.S.A.* typified the literary climate of the 1930s as the work of Scott Fitzgerald and Hemingway had done that of the 1920s. After its success Dos Passos disappeared from the literary limelight. He kept on writing, but his moment had passed; the experimental impulse that had made *Manhattan Transfer* and *U.S.A.* the literary catalysts of much of what was also happening in the other arts at the time waned, and none of his later works, such as his second trilogy *District of Columbia* (1952), could repeat the success of his earlier works. Still, *Manhattan Transfer* and *U.S.A.* influenced the work not only of Dos Passos's American contemporaries, but also that of the French writer-philosopher Jean-Paul Sartre, the German novelist Alfred Döblin, and the Flemish novelist Louis-Paul Boon.

William Faulkner

William Faulkner (1897–1962) – originally Falkner – was born into a well-to-do Southern family that in its ranks already counted a successful author in the guise of Faulkner's great-grandfather and namesake William C. Falkner (1825–89). The latter had been a man of importance in the northern parts of Mississippi. He had served as an officer in the Confederate army, he was a lawyer and he built one of the earliest railroad lines in the region. In many ways he served as the model for Colonel Sartoris, a recurring character in much of Faulkner's fiction.

Faulkner volunteered with the RAF in Canada but never saw active service. Still, he used his own experiences as a pilot-in-training in several of his novels, such as for instance *Pylon* (1935). Faulkner was only a mediocre student, and although he attended courses at the University of Mississippi in Oxford, where he also spent most of his life, he never graduated. He did publish drawings and stories in the university journal.

At the beginning of the 1920s Faulkner for a brief while worked as a fledgling journalist in New Orleans, where he got to know Sherwood Anderson, whose narrative technique and psychologizing approach to character clearly influenced the budding author Faulkner. New Orleans is also the backdrop to Faulkner's second novel *Mosquitoes* (1927). His debut, though, was *Soldier's Pay* (1926), a war novel. After a brief stay in Paris Faulkner returned to his 'native postage stamp of soil' which, starting with *Sartoris* (1929), he immortalized under the names of Jefferson and Yoknapatawpha County.

With *Sartoris*, an abbreviated version of a much longer manuscript that Faulkner himself had given the title *Flags in the Dust*, and that in original form would appear only posthumously in 1973, Faulkner takes up the theme that he would return to again and again in the fifteen novels and the numerous stories that together make up the so-called Yoknapatawpha cycle: the downfall – physical, moral, psychological, economic and social – of the old established Southern families and ultimately of the Old South itself. Conversely, he chronicled the relentless rise of the Snopes, a greedy, grubbing and selfish clan of 'white trash', originally living on the margins of Southern society, and by values diametrically opposed to those of the Old South, but who eventually end up displacing the old families. The Yoknapatawpha cycle spans the period 1830–1950. Rather than in the factual history of the South, Faulkner is interested in the myths and legends in which the South's vision of itself and its history is grounded. The result is highly ambivalent. On the one hand Faulkner draws the Southern elite and the society it was the focus of as distinguishing itself, in its own eyes, by a severe code of conduct uniting a sense of responsibility, courage, perseverance, honor and chivalry. On the other hand his novels reveal how a view that posits this code as the confirmation of the South as an aristocratic, culturally and morally refined society dates from after the Civil War, and as the wishful and nostalgic projection of a defeated social caste. It is the defensive reflex of a humiliated social and economic elite that combats its frustration by dreaming itself a mythical past in a lost golden age.

One of the staunchest myths that the Old South told itself was that of the purity of the white woman. This amounted to an act of moral compensation in a society ruled by men that always had access to slave women for sexual gratification. Additionally, Southern whites, by raising their own white women to angelic heights, hence making them absolutely unattainable for blacks, also emphasized the superiority of their own race after 1865. The invariably bloody repression of anything that even hinted at sexual intimacy between a white woman and a man of color in the Southern United States until almost the end of the twentieth century can be explained by the persistence of this very myth. In its portrayal of the economic and moral downfall of the Compson family *The Sound and the Fury* shows how deficient the nineteenth-century values and ideals fetishized by the Old South are for life in the twentieth century. Mrs Compson is a vain and vapid woman whose failure to be the warm center of her family forces her daughter Caddy to act as surrogate mother for her three brothers and even her father, a weak man drunk on words. Caddy's flight into promiscuity is a scathing rejoinder to the myth that her mother tries, or at least pretends, to live up to, and also the surest way to avoid becoming like her mother. Mrs Compson's stilted embodiment of the Southern Belle myth also leads to the most radical reversal of that same myth: it is the black maid Dilsey that after Caddy's vanishing becomes the real heart of the Compson family. Quentin, the oldest son and the true representative of the old Southern values commits suicide. The two remaining Compson children, finally, come to stand for the reality of the South between the two world wars. Benjy is an idiot. Jason, rather than a representative of the Old South is an exponent of the New South, which lives by a purely commercial and utilitarian code, and is ruled by money. Faulkner himself once said of Jason that 'He's the most vicious character in my opinion I ever thought of'. In fact, Jason uncomfortably closely comes to resemble the Snopeses, the white trash family that dominates Faulkner's late eponymous trilogy, and that consists of *The Hamlet* (1940), *The Town* (1957) and *The Mansion* (1959). *The Hamlet* also marks a turn in Faulkner's work towards a more realist mode, away from the experimentalism of his major novels.

With *The Sound and the Fury* Faulkner resolutely laid claim to being the most daring innovator of his generation as far as narrative technique is concerned. The novel consists of four parts. Benjy, Quentin and Jason each tell the story of the Compson family from their own point of view, while the fourth part is narrated by a third-person narrator and focalized through Dilsey. Each part has its own tone, voice and style. The first part, Benjy's story, contains all essential data to understand the history of the Compsons. However, it is told by an idiot – the title of the novel refers to a line from Shakespeare's play *Macbeth* uttered by the main character, Macbeth himself: 'Life is a tale told by an idiot, full of sound and fury, signifying nothing'. Benjy's mind, and hence his stream-of-consciousness narrative, freely moves between past and present, triggered by sensory perceptions. Quentin is obsessed by time, and especially by a desire to stop time, and his language is strongly marked by references to the Bible and religion. His thoughts and memories are triggered by shards of conversations he overhears or in which he participates. At first sight Jason's story is the most 'straightforward', but it too is structured by Jason's obsessions. Money plays the main part in his thoughts, and his vision is colored by greed, avarice and revenge. The final chapter is the most lyrical, and also the only one to contain physical descriptions of the characters. Each subsequent story adds detail and color to Benjy's initial tale. The real 'main' character in all the stories is Caddy, yet we never get to hear her version – she only lives in the thought, memories and views, the stories of the others. Faulkner would continue to put this device of the absent protagonist to brilliant use in his work of the 1930s.

As I Lay Dying (1930), which Faulkner himself claimed to have written in a span of six weeks in which he served as night watchman in Oxford, is set in the milieu of small, independent so-called yeomen farmers, with the Bundrens, a rather eccentric family, most of whose members seem not to be too intelligent, transporting their deceased wife and mother, Addie, to

Jefferson, there to be buried. With *Sanctuary* (1931), a story of rape and murder that shares some features with the best-selling hard-boiled detective genre that was immensely popular at the time, Faulkner risked the charge of cheap sensationalism. Focus of attention in this story is the role of society in determining someone's fortune and the influence of vested opinions, interests and prejudices. Whatever is socially acceptable takes the upper hand over what is true and just.

One of the most accessible novels of the Yoknapatawpha cycle is *Light in August* (1932). This novel, like a Shakespeare play, and Faulkner was an avid reader of the Bard, contains two contrastive stories, one a tragedy, the other a comedy. The tragedy focuses upon the characters of Joe Christmas and the protestant minister Hightower, both of whom die in an orgy of violence at the end of the novel. The comedy results from the idyll between Lena Grove, a pregnant country girl in search of the man who fathered her child, and Byron Bunch, a timid bachelor working at a Jefferson sawmill. *Light in August* is a prime example of Faulkner's ability to simultaneously develop several plots in one novel, sometimes in parallel, sometimes contrapuntally, often with only minimal cross-references. Two other Yoknapatawpha novels take this technique still further, in that they combine, often in revised form, stories earlier published separately, remolding them into either composite short story collections or loose novels, in which the various strands and stories can function either, or both, as complement or antithesis to one another. *The Unvanquished* (1938) focuses on the attitude of a number of members of the Sartoris clan toward the Civil War and the Southern code of honor. *Go Down, Moses* (1942) concentrates on racial relations in the South and on the relation between man and nature – the latter especially in the much anthologized story 'The Bear'. In *The Wild Palms* (1939), a novel that is not part of the Yoknapatawpha cycle, Faulkner combines two independent plots, in chapters alternating between the title story and another story entitled 'Old Man'. The only point these stories have in common is thematic.

In *Absalom, Absalom!* (1936), often considered his greatest achievement along with *The Sound and the Fury*, Faulkner takes on another Southern myth: that of the aristocratic descent and code of honor of the Southern planters before the Civil War. As recounted by a series of commentators, some of whom, such as Ms Rosa Coldfield and Mr Compson, have known the man himself, and others, like Quentin Compson and Shreve, Quentin's Canadian roommate at Harvard, who have only heard about him, the novel describes the career of Thomas Sutpen. Of poor white descent in Virginia, Sutpen in the 1820s or early '30s appears in Jefferson with a band of wild negro slaves and a French architect, and quickly establishes himself as one of the most powerful and ruthless plantation owners. However, in Sutpen's history there lurks the stain of miscegenation. In an inevitable series of events resembling nothing so much as an Elizabethan revenge tragedy Sutpen's dream of founding a mighty dynasty turns to dust. As, true to the technique he also employed in *The Sound and the Fury* and *As I Lay Dying*, we never meet Sutpen in person, but only find out about him in the stories others spin about him, *Absalom, Absalom!* is fully as much a reflection on the relation between facts and fiction, reality and the imagination, history and memory, as it is on Southern history and on the myths the South tells itself.

The end of the 1930s also marked the end of Faulkner's modernist experimentalism. As of 1940, with the first volume of what would eventually become the Snopes trilogy, he turned to more realistic forms of narration. In the year of his death, 1962, there appeared a final novel in the Yoknapatawpha cycle, *The Reivers*, a picaresque tale. In 1954, though, Faulkner had published what he himself considered his masterpiece, *A Fable*. With this novel set during World War I he returned to his earliest sources of inspiration, as mined already in his debut *Soldier's Pay*. Little read these days, *A Fable* is a heavily allegorical tale, cued to the Passion of Christ. In

The Sound and the Fury Faulkner had already cued three of the four chapters or parts to the dates from Good Friday to Easter 1928. In his Nobel Prize acceptance speech of 1950 he had posited that 'man will not merely endure, he will prevail'. This message was clearly influenced by the horrible events of World War II. By broadening the context to World War I, *A Fable* stood as a testimony to Faulkner's unwavering belief in humanity, notwithstanding the fact that all powers in the world, and most of all man himself in the guise of its leaders and elites, seemed to conspire against it.

Faulkner's stylistic versatility and technical experimentalism went unrivaled in American literature of the first half of the twentieth century. *The Sound and the Fury* opened up new narrative possibilities for the American novel, and showed Faulkner to be fully in tune with developments in European art and literature. The Benjy section proves that he had clearly understood, and digested, the lessons of James Joyce's *Ulysses* (1922), parts of which he had read before 1929. His combination of various points of view parallels some of the techniques of Cubism. What made Faulkner's use of all or any of these techniques unique, though, is that he always meticulously sought after the right form and style for each of his novels. At variance with Hemingway, for instance, whose style remained very much the same throughout his career, Faulkner, even though his prose is very recognizably 'Faulknerian', seldom if ever used the same technique twice in exactly the same way. Even the way he approached similar themes over the course of his career showed immense variety. Faulkner would cast a large shadow over not only the next generation of American novelists such as Toni Morrison, another Nobel Prize winner, but also over authors worldwide. Two other Nobel Prize winners, the German Günther Grass, with *The Tin Drum*, and the Colombian Gabriel García Márquez, with *One Hundred Years of Solitude*, and the Indian Salman Rushdie, with *Midnight's Children*, all have acknowledged Faulkner's influence. Faulkner is now generally recognized as the most important American novelist of the first half of the twentieth century.

Other modernist prose writers

An author that in the middle of the twentieth century often used to be named in one breath with Faulkner because he also stemmed from the South and at the time of Faulkner's breakthrough wrote about comparable issues in *Tobacco Road* (1932) and *God's Little Acre* (1933) is Erskine Caldwell (1903–87). However, Caldwell was never able to repeat these early successes and his work lacks the richness, the historical dimension and the stylistic versatility of that of Faulkner. Another Southern author to make it big in the 1930s was Thomas Wolfe (1900–38). During his lifetime Wolfe was considered the equal of his famous contemporaries, but after his early death his reputation has waned. Wolfe was born into a family of mixed German and Scottish-Irish descent in Asheville, North Carolina. Two sprawling novels, *Look Homeward, Angel* (1929) and *Of Time and the River* (1935), saw the light during Wolfe's own lifetime. From manuscripts he left at his death two more equally baggy novels were put together, *The Web and the Rock* (1939) and *You Can't Go Home Again* (1940). Wolfe freely mixed lyrical-romantic passages with journalistic reports of his own life, his surroundings and his reading. Like Whitman, Wolfe identified with the nation. Not surprisingly, then, he tried to capture as many aspects as possible of his native country, and of himself, in his encyclopedic works. Like Faulkner's, Wolfe's work too heavily relies on Southern rhetoric, reeking of the Bible and religion in general. Faulkner however, uses this rhetoric to stylistic and thematic effect (even though in his later works he too sometimes skirts long-windedness), whereas Wolfe loses himself in pointless verbosity.

Three writers who share a number of traits with the so-called 'Lost Generation' authors but who strictly speaking do not enter into that category are Henry Miller (1891–1980), Djuna Barnes (1892–1982) and Nathanael West (1903–40). Barnes's novel *Nightwood* (1936) became famous overnight when none less than T.S. Eliot praised it for its modernist innovations. Still, Barnes never succeeded in reaching a large audience, and until recently her literary importance seemed minor at best. Of late, though, she has been reclaimed for feminist and gender studies, with *Nightwood* being seen as a pioneering lesbian *roman-à-clef*. *Nightwood* is set in the Bohemian Paris of the 1920s, where Barnes lived at the time. Henry Miller also moved in Bohemian Paris in the 1930s, and he too published sexually explicit works, although in his case from a male heterosexual point of view, that redefined what was possible in American literature in this matter. Especially *Tropic of Cancer* (1934) and *Tropic of Capricorn* (1939), both of which remained banned in the United States until the 1960s, deserve mention in this respect. The short, satirical novels of Nathanael West (real name Nathan Weinstein), *The Dream Life of Balso Snell* (1931), *Miss Lonelyhearts* (1933), *A Cool Million* (1934) and *The Day of the Locust* (1939), mercilessly dissect a number of clichés underpinning American society. *A Cool Million* shows up the American dream of success. *Miss Lonelyhearts* revels in how Americans wallow in sentimentality via the experiences of a man who writes the 'lonely hearts' column in a ladies journal. Like Fitzgerald and Faulkner, West during the 1930s earned his keep as a scriptwriter in Hollywood. This experience served as inspiration for what is generally considered his best work, *The Day of the Locust*, a wry satire on America's 'dream factory'.

Two writers who spent most of their career working for *The New Yorker* were James Thurber (1894–1961) and Dorothy Parker (1893–1967, née Rothschild). Thurber's kind of humor, mostly mild, sometimes surrealist, more often nostalgic, at times satirical, set the tone for what has come to be considered 'typically' *New Yorker*. As well as being a writer Thurber was also a gifted cartoonist. Parker wrote journalism, reviews, stories, and poems, and collaborated on plays and movie scripts. Both Thurber and Parker liked to poke fun at the relations between the sexes, but Parker's wit was considerably more acerbic, to the point even of destroying all romantic illusions, as in her brief poem 'General Review of the Sex Situation' (1926).

African American modernist fiction

African American fiction during the period between the world wars was first and foremost concerned with the position of African Americans in the United States. A number of Harlem Renaissance authors continued the line of Charles Chesnutt and James Weldon Johnson before World War I, with light-colored protagonists who move in relatively well-to-do circles and who could easily 'pass' if they so wanted. This is the case in *There is Confusion* (1924), *Plum Bun* (1929) and *Comedy: American Style* (1933) by Jessie Fauset (1882–1961), *Flight* (1926) by Walter White (1893–1955), and *Quicksand* (1928) and *Passing* (1929) by Nella Larsen (1891–1964). These novels focus on the ambivalent attitude their characters assume with regard to their color, and on the identity problems this causes them. The protagonists of *Plum Bun*, *Flight* and *Passing* effectively 'pass' the color line and start leading the lives of white people, and enjoying the social opportunities this offers. Invariably, however, their choice turns out unhappily, as they keep feeling the pull of the black community they have left behind, and which emotionally was much more fulfilling than white society.

An author who although he could easily have passed for white opted for black life was Jean Toomer (1894–1967). Born in Washington, D.C., in a distinguished mixed-blood family, Toomer only really got to know the South when he took a job as a superintendent at a black school in Georgia. There he came to appreciate the contrast between the warmth and richness of a vanishing black folk culture, black community life, Southern nature and landscape, and the coldness, rootlessness and sterility of modern city life. This experience resulted in Toomer's masterpiece *Cane* (1923), a composite novel in three parts. The first part, set in Georgia, concentrates on the lives of a number of black women. The second part is harsher in tone, is set in Washington, D.C., and stresses the material and spiritual poverty of city life as marked by racial conflict. The third part has a young black man, raised and educated in the North and clearly modeled on Toomer himself, go South. Racial violence recurs throughout the book. Mixing poetry, prose and drama, and using multiple points of view, *Cane* is easily the most experimentally modernist work to come out of the Harlem Renaissance.

Other authors more aggressively flaunt the blackness of their protagonists. In *Home to Harlem* (1928) Claude McKay features Jake Brown, an African American who after World War I returns to Harlem, there to immerse himself in the vitalistic, primitivist and exoticist black life also depicted by Carl Van Vechten in *Nigger Heaven*. Not surprisingly, McKay drew heavy critical fire from his fellow black authors. In all fairness it should be added that McKay himself, via the character of Ray, an errant Haitian intellectual, also criticized Jake's hedonistic behavior and the Harlem milieu that encouraged it. Ray returns in *Banjo* (1929), where the main character, a black seaman, meets him in Marseilles. *Banana Bottom* (1933) is set in Jamaica, McKay's own birthplace, and features Bita Plant, a black girl adopted by white missionaries and sent to school in England, where she receives a white education. Upon her return to her native village, Banana Bottom, though, she opts for her native black culture. McKay also wrote short stories, collected in *Gingertown* (1932), an autobiography, and *Harlem: Negro Metropolis* (1940), a historical and sociological treatise. At his death he left an unfinished novel and another autobiography.

In his satirical novel *The Blacker the Berry* (1929) Wallace Thurman (1902–34) daringly tackles a theme that was very controversial in the black community itself at the time: the discrimination between African Americans themselves. Thurman pursues the same theme in *Infants of the Spring* (1932), in which he takes aim at some of the most important representatives of the Harlem Renaissance, at the prejudices that exist within the black community, and at what he regards as the bourgeois and hence 'white' opinions of black luminaries such as W.E.B. Dubois and Alain Locke.

Other authors concentrated on depicting various aspects of African American life without conforming, even if satirically, to stereotypes circulating outside of the black community or resisting them. Countee Cullen gave an intriguing portrait of Harlem religious life in *One Way to Heaven* (1932). 'Shine' Jones, a piano mover in Harlem, is the protagonist of *The Walls of Jericho* (1928) by Rudolf Fisher (1897–1934), and the same author wrote the first all-black detective novel with *The Conjure Man Dies* (1932). Langston Hughes brought an autobiographical novel about a black boy growing up in the Midwest in *Not Without Laughter* (1936). Zora Neale Hurston (1891–1960) in her 1928 essay 'How It Feels to Be Colored Me' recounted how during her youth in Eatonville, an all-black community in Florida, she was unaware of racial discrimination. Most of her numerous stories and several novels are also set in the region around Eatonville, most prominently so *Their Eyes Were Watching God* (1937), usually considered her crowning achievement. The novel follows Janie Crawford's growth, through a number of marriages, from a lively but pliant teenage girl into a mature woman who knows what she wants and who firmly takes charge of her own destiny. In *Their Eyes Were Watching God* and also in *Jonah's Gourd Vine* (1934) Hurston clearly rejects the racial uplift ideas of a Booker T. Washington or W.E.B. Dubois, and opts for the simple, vital life of ordinary African Americans. Hurston held a degree in anthropology and did important work on African

American folk customs. Largely forgotten after the 1930s, her work was rediscovered by a later generation of African American women writers, most prominently Alice Walker.

Likewise recapturing African American culture in a number of important anthologies, but also in his own fiction, was Arna Bontemps (1902–73). Bontemps's left-radical sympathies led him to write fictionalized accounts of two slave revolts in *Drums at Dusk* (1939) and *Black Thunder* (1936). The latter is now usually considered his best work. Bontemps sticks to the historical facts, but presents them from multiple viewpoints, detailing the different feelings – rebelliousness, but also fatalism – slavery induces, but also allowing for a collective voice to emerge, aesthetically and narrative-technically upholding his leftist politics. The slave leader is executed but his ideal of freedom lives on.

Social realism

The authors who came to the fore during the 1930s readily adopted some of the technical innovations introduced by their modernist precursors, yet overwhelmingly went in for more realist fictions. In the Studs Lonigan trilogy (*Young Lonigan,* 1932, *The Young Manhood of Studs Lonigan,* 1934, *Judgement Day,* 1935) James T. Farrell draws a portrait of a Catholic-Irish youth and early manhood in Chicago. Farrell himself said that 'Studs Lonigan was conceived as the story of an American destiny in our time'. Lonigan's aimless life and his tragic death chart how for second-generation immigrants the American Dream that lured their parents to the newly promised country has gone up in smoke at the very moment that the parents' slaving and suffering seemed to promise their offspring a 'better future'. Overshadowed by the Depression, life in America's sprawling and grimy suburbs is sketched as spiritually and emotionally impoverished.

The Depression also provides the focus for the novels and stories of John Steinbeck (1902–68). Steinbeck was born in Salinas, California, and this is also the setting of most of his fiction. *Of Mice and Men* (1937) concentrates on the exploitation of two itinerant field hands. Steinbeck's masterpiece is undoubtedly *The Grapes of Wrath* (1939), which chronicles the epic trek of a number of impoverished Oklahoma farmer families to California, where they hope to find a job and a future. *The Grapes of Wrath* is a modernist work, in a style sometimes reminiscent of Faulkner, and particularly of some chapters of *As I Lay Dying*, and largely dealing with the same social class of small independent farmers. First and foremost, though, it is a social novel clearly expressive of Steinbeck's 'leftist' leanings during the 1930s. At the same time *The Grapes of Wrath* addresses a number of concerns recurrent in 'canonical' American literature: the close relation to the land, what it means to be an American, the changing social, economic and political structures of the U.S., the underlying religiosity of America. *The Grapes of Wrath* gained Steinbeck the Pulitzer in 1940, and the Nobel Prize in 1962. Next to works with a strong social dimension, such as *Of Mice and Men*, *The Grapes of Wrath* and *In Dubious Battle* (1936), about a strike among fruit pickers in California, Steinbeck also wrote bitter-sweet novels and stories such as *Tortilla Flat* (1935), *Cannery Row* (1945) and *Sweet Thursday* (1954), all three of them set in and around Monterey in a milieu of vagrants, hired hands and sympathetic whores. Especially his later works sometimes verge close to the sentimental and nostalgic, or even the vaguely mystical, as in the family chronicle *East of Eden* (1952). At the end of his life, in 1960, Steinbeck, accompanied by his dog, set out on a journey to re-discover America. The trip resulted in *Travels With Charley: In Search of America* (1962), which became a best-seller.

More immediately concerned with documenting the plight of the poorest was James Agee (1909–55). In *Let Us Now Praise Famous Men* (1941), with photographs by Walker Evans (1903–75), Agee chronicled the lives of a number of tenant farmers in the Southern United

States during the Great Depression. Jack Conroy (1898–1990) drew on his own youthful memories for *The Disinherited* (1933), a picture of the life of misery led by Missouri mining families. The life of a Jewish-Russian immigrant family in New York during the early years of the twentieth century was featured in *Call It Sleep* (1934) by Henry Roth (1906–1995). Daniel Fuchs (1909–93) focused upon roughly the same milieu in *Summer in Williamsburg* (1934), *Hommage to Blenholt* (1936) and *Low Company* (1937), and already earlier Anzia Yezierska (1885–1970) had done the same in *Bread Givers* (1925).

The most important African American author to emerge in the 1930s was Richard Wright (1908–60). The protagonists of the four stories gathered in *Uncle Tom's Children* (1938) grow ever more rebellious towards their Southern environment. It was *Native Son* (1940) though, that made Wright the spokesman of a new generation of African American authors. The novel draws a raw picture of life in the black slums of Chicago. The protagonist, Bigger Thomas, is a young black man who accidentally kills a white girl, and then his girlfriend to silence her. He is condemned to the electric chair. For Wright it is the racism inherent in American society that has existentially conditioned Bigger to violence. The feeling that only violence can give the repressed an identity of their own returns in *The Outsider* (1953), a novel influenced by Wright's stay in Paris, whence he had moved after the war, and where he frequented existentialist circles. A writer to follow Wright's lead, creating a protagonist suffering from the same frustrations as Bigger Thomas, is William Attaway (1911–86), with *Blood on the Forge* (1941).

After World War I Native American writers such as Joseph Mathews (1894–1979), D'Arcy McNickle (1904–77) and Thomas Whitecloud (1914–72) exposed the detrimental policies of the American government aiming at dispossessing, relocating and assimilating U.S. Native Americans. In expressing their own dilemmas these authors also expressed those of their fellow Native Americans. In Mathews's *Sundown* (1934) the protagonist, after having moved in white society, returns to the reservation in order to find his true self, but ends up disappointed. Whitecloud had grown up in New York and on a reservation, and worked as a physician in white society before returning to the reservation to find a true home, as does the protagonist of 'Blue Winds Dancing' (1938). McNickle's *Surrounded* (1936) depicts how the son of a Spanish father and Native American mother returns to the Flathead Reservation in Montana, there to land in a crisis of identity that will lead to a conflict with the white authorities. From *Runner in the Sun: A Story of Indian Maize* (1954), a book for adolescents and set in the American South-West before the arrival of the Spaniards, speaks McNickle's pride in this Native American contribution to world culture. Mourning Dove (1888–1976) in *Coyote Stories* (1932) recounts a number of tribal tales she had learned from her grandmother.

Heavily autobiographical is *A Daughter of the Samurai* (1925) by the Japanese American Etsu Sugimoto (1873–1950). Younghill Kang (1903–72), a Korean immigrant, published two equally heavily autobiographical novels, *The Grass Roof* (1931), in which a young Korean leaves his native land for the United States, and *East Goes West* (1937), in which a Korean tries to build himself a new life in the U.S. and meets with discrimination. Finally, Carlos Bulosan (1917–56), a Philippine immigrant, recounts similar experiences in his autobiography *America is in the Heart* (1943).

Drama

Until World War I the theater in the U.S. was almost exclusively commercially oriented, and centered upon popular plays performed on Broadway, the street at the heart of the New York theater district. Even before the outbreak of the war, though, some younger actors and play-wrights had started to grow impatient with this commercial theater. In 1905 the Harvard professor George Pierce Baker (1866–1934) started teaching a drama course, 'The Technique of Drama' (later called the '47 Workshop'), that became a catalyst for renewal. Baker stressed drama as art rather than commercial entertainment, and his course came to be attended by, among others, Eugene O'Neill (1888–1953), Philip Barry (1896–1949), S.N. Behrman (1893–1973) and Sidney Howard (1891–1939). Led by Susan Glaspell (1882–1948), a number of Baker alumni formed the Provincetown Players, named after the seaside resort where in the summer of 1915 they started to perform on the verandah of one of the vacation homes. In 1916 O'Neill joined the troupe and they started to perform more professionally. Shortly thereafter they started their own little theater in New York. Between 1915 and 1929 they put on almost one hundred plays by some fifty playwrights, one-act plays to begin with, but as of 1920 also full-length plays, thus creating an alternative to Broadway. Glaspell herself was a prolific author with fourteen plays and a number of novels and stories. For the longest time she stood in the shadow of O'Neill, but more recently her work has been rediscovered by feminist criticism, and her first play, the one-act *Trifles* (1916), is now regularly anthologized.

Founded even earlier than the Provincetown Players, in 1914, the Washington Square Players only gained prominence after they had re-invented themselves, in a collaboration with O'Neill, as The Theatre Guild in 1918. The Theatre Guild staged new American drama and plays by innovative European playwrights. In 1931 The Theatre Guild brought forth the radical Group Theatre, that in the 1930s put on politically inspired plays, and that introduced the American theater to the realistic techniques of the Russian actor and producer Stanislavski (1863–1938). Next to these more famous groups countless other non-commercial small theater companies in different ways sought to renovate the American theater. The Marxist-inspired Theatre Union, for instance, used the theater as a weapon in the class struggle in the 1930s.

Because the American theater lagged so far behind at the time of World War I, the so-called 'Little Theatre Movement' developed along two diametrically opposed lines, one realist and even naturalist, the other anti-realist, each of them picking up on recent – expressionism – and not so recent – naturalism à la Ibsen – European developments, thus compressing in a mere decade what in Europe had taken forty years. Many of the authors active during the 1920s and 1930s vacillate between, or combine, the two tendencies, O'Neill perhaps most of all.

O'Neill, who received the Nobel Prize in 1936, dominates the entire period under discussion. O'Neill's father was the leader of a theater company and a famous actor in his own right. After a few years spent drifting, among other things as a sailor, O'Neill started writing himself in 1914. From then on, he relentlessly fed new techniques and topics into the American theater. His first big success, *The Emperor Jones* (1920), introduced expressionism, using lighting effects and drums to underline the primitive fears of the protagonist, a black Caribbean dictator. *The Hairy Ape* (1922) combined naturalism and expressionism. In *The Great God Brown* (1926) his personae wore masks, in *Lazarus Laughed* (1927) he used choruses, as he also did in *Mourning Becomes Electra* (1931), a Freudian-influenced adaptation of Aeschylus's *Oresteia,* and in *Strange Interlude* (1928) he alternated between dialogue and interior monologue. What remained constant throughout most of his career, with the exception of the very early one-act plays which mainly stuck to raw observations on the life at sea, was an intensive search for the psychological motivations underlying man's actions. *Desire Under the Elms* (1924) stages sexual passion, oedipal conflict and guilt.

At the same time O'Neill was fighting his own demons. He suffered from nervous breakdowns and alcoholism, and in 1934 stopped publishing or staging his plays, even though he kept on writing. Although many of the larger projects he planned to carry out during this period eventually came to nothing, what he did produce turned out to be his best work. *The Iceman Cometh*, with which he made his come-back in 1946, but which had been written already in 1939, plays on the thin line between illusion and reality. The play is set in a bar, where the regular customers, who are all down on their luck, await the arrival of the popular and jovial Hickey. They mask their own failures by spinning yarns. When Hickey arrives he refuses to play the game, and confronts all customers with the truth about themselves. When Hickey is arrested for having murdered his wife the regulars go back to their tales. O'Neill's criticism is tinged with compassion, as he recognizes the necessity of illusion. A similar mixture marks what is now generally recognized as his masterpiece, written from 1939 to 1941, but only staged posthumously, in 1956. *Long Day's Journey Into Night* treats one day in the life of the family Tyrone, a thinly disguised stand-in for the O'Neills. The father, a famous actor, is a tyrant and a miser. The mother is addicted to drugs. The older brother is a drunk, and jealous of his father. The younger brother, modeled on O'Neill himself, is torn apart by the conflicts playing in the family. Nothing remains hidden, the weaknesses of all four characters are laid bare, but O'Neill understands and forgives. The plays O'Neill wrote after *Long Day's Journey Into Night* were less ambitious: *Hughie* (1942, staged in 1958) and *A Moon for the Misbegotten* (1952, staged in 1957). By the time of his death he had become canonized as an American classic.

The multiplicity of styles that had suddenly become available to the American theater after World War I led to great versatility, often even in the work of a single playwright. Elmer Rice (1892–1967) debuted in 1914 with the melodramatic *On Trial*. *The Adding Machine* (1923) is expressionist, with the main character, Mr. Zero, having lost his function and identity in a mechanized world. *Street Scene* (1929) realistically pictures life in a poor big city neighborhood. *We, the People* (1933) is a Marxist play. Robert Sherwood (1896–1955) wrote the anti-militarist satire *The Road to Rome* (1927), set in ancient Rome, the realist psychological drama *The Petrified Forest* (1935), set in contemporary Arizona, and the anti-fascist *Idiot's Delight* (1936), set in the near future. Maxwell Anderson (1888–1959) in 1924 collaborated with Laurence Stallings (1894–1968) on *What Price Glory?*, a comedy-drama set in France during World War I, and later wrote a very successful series of historical plays in blank verse, set during the reign of the Tudors in England. But Anderson also wrote politically-inspired plays, such as the Pulitzer Prize-winning *Both Your Houses* (1933), a satirical denouncement of corruption in the U.S. House of Representatives and Senate, and *Winterset* (1935), based on the Sacco and Vanzetti case. John Howard Lawson (1895–1977) went from the expressionist *Roger Bloomer* (1923), over the vaudeville-inspired *Processional: A Jazz Symphony of American Life* (1925), to the Marxist *Marching Song* (1937). *The Silver Cord* (1926), by Sidney Howard, stages a mother jealous of the women that want to take her sons from her. But Howard also wrote social-realist plays, such as *They Knew What They Wanted* (1924), in which the waitress-protagonist Amy, desperate to escape from her hopeless social milieu, goes through with marriage to the much older man who in correspondence with her had led her to believe that he was much younger than he actually is.

The onset of the Great Depression triggered a change from more technically experimental theater, even if often focusing on psychological or social themes, to a more realist or naturalist drama reflecting on social and political issues. Emphasis then also shifts from the individual, as in Howard's *They Knew What They Wanted*, to the collective, in the guise of social class. Lawson's *Marching Song*, for instance, has the Auto Workers Union as collective protagonist. The tone also becomes much more militant, and also grimmer, even if not necessarily pessimistic, as can be seen from *Waiting for Lefty* (1935) by Clifford Odets (1906–63). In this play Lefty, the leader of a group of taxi drivers gathered to discuss a strike, at the end is found murdered for political reasons. This makes the drivers close ranks and unanimously they decide to go on strike. Odets wrote for the Group Theatre, which had been co-founded in 1931 by Lee Strasberg (1901–82), the father of so-called 'method acting', and which together with the Marxist Theatre Union brought the most convincingly radical and non-commercial drama of the 1930s. His *Waiting for Lefty*, though, became a success even on Broadway. In the same year as *Waiting for Lefty* Odets also wrote *Awake and Sing!*, a gripping portrait of a Jewish American family hit by the Depression, with a truly convincing Marxist protagonist. Odets left for Hollywood in 1936, and this seriously weakened the Group Theatre. Its role, though, was partially taken over by the Federal Theatre, which in 1935 had been founded as a WPA project meant to provide employment to out-of-work actors. Government-subsidized, the Federal Theatre could afford to be even more experimental and radical than the Little Theatres. Touring the country in several troupes, the Federal Theatre introduced the work of European writers and in a number of collective experimental productions, the so-called 'Living Newspapers' format developed in Russia during the Russian revolution, denounced social injustices. *Triple-A Plowed Under* (1936) highlighted the plight of small farmers. *One-Third of a Nation* (1938) did the same for the housing problems of the underprivileged. Accused of Communist leanings, the Federal Theatre was discontinued in 1939. The Group Theatre closed in 1941. These events marked the end of the radical left in American drama. Only Lillian Hellman (1905–84), arguably America's best female dramatist of the period, and who in 1934, with *The Children's Hour*, had drawn attention to the themes of social corruption and misuse of power in a play about two female teachers suspected of having a lesbian affair on the basis of a rumor launched by a pupil, with disastrous effect, as one of the women commits suicide, and in 1939, with *The Little Foxes*, focused on the struggle for power bringing down a Southern family, after the war continued to deal with issues of manipulation and abuse of power in *The Autumn Garden* (1951) and *Toys in the Attic* (1960). Odets himself still wrote *The Big Knife* (1948), based on his Hollywood experiences, as well as several other, commercially successful plays, many of them made into movies, but lacking the political drive of his mid-1930s radical plays.

Next to the more experimental and social-radical theater that flourished, respectively, in the 1920s and 1930s, we of course also find a number of other dramatic forms and movements that, although now often less studied, were actually much more present to contemporary audiences. The 1920s, for instance, saw the birth of a lively and successful folk drama, often regionally inspired, with plenty of local color, the use of local dialect, and often melodramatic plots. Some of these became world famous in their musical versions. *Porgy* (1925), a novel about a crippled beggar in Charleston, North Carolina, and his love for the prostitute Bess, by DuBose Heyward (1885–1950), and with the help of Dorothy Heyward (1890–1961) turned into the play of the same name in 1927, became the immensely successful opera *Porgy and Bess* (1935) by George and Ira Gershwin. *Green Grow the Lilacs* (1931) by Lynn Riggs (1899–1954) was reworked into the musical *Oklahoma* (1943). *In Abraham's Bosom* (1926), by Paul Green (1894–1981), a member of the Carolina Playmakers, founded in 1920 at the University of North Carolina at Chapel Hill, follows an idealist African American in his hopeless struggle to improve the lot of his fellow blacks.

The commercially most successful drama of the period between the two world wars was comedy, staged on Broadway, and written by the likes of S.N. Behrman, Philip Barry and George S. Kaufman (1889–1961). Their plays are well-constructed, often ingenious, with quick and witty repartee, and capitalize on situation comedy and topical issues. In their wit and virtuosity they sometimes recall the work of their Irish-British predecessors Oscar Wilde and George Bernard Shaw, but they lack the social layering and the inherent seriousness that mark the latters' achievements. Behrman's *The Second Man* (1927) and *Biography* (1932), or Barry's *Paris Bound* and *Holiday* (both 1929), capture the frivolity of the Jazz Age. Kaufman tended toward farce in *You Can't Take It With You* (1936, co-written with Moses Hart) and *The Man Who Came to Dinner* (1939); his talent for absurd humor showed in the film scripts he wrote for the Marx Brothers. During the 1930s some of these authors also ventured into social-realist drama, as did for instance Behrman with *End of Summer* (1936), opposing the idealistic views of two young radicals to the egotism of a self-made businessman. However, the radicalism in this play is largely window-dressing to accommodate the mood of the times and the climate of the nation.

Towards the end of the 1930s there appeared a more serious commercial theater with the work of William Saroyan (1908–81) and Thornton Wilder (1897–1975). In *My Heart's in the Highlands* and *The Time of Your Life* (both 1939) Saroyan does not seek to dissimulate the poverty of his Californians, but at the same time takes care to stress their irrepressible joy in life. Wilder is less exuberant in *Our Town* (1938), picturing small-town life at the beginning of the century, and *The Skin of Our Teeth* (1942), but likewise advances a strong belief in humanity. Saroyan's work has a spontaneous, almost improvisatorial feel about it. *The Time of Your Life*, for instance, plays in a bar with customers coming and going. Wilder is more technically inventive, also because he was well aware of contemporary European developments. In both plays mentioned, for instance, Wilder regularly shatters the illusion of reality. The very successful musical *Hello Dolly!* (1964) is based on Wilder's *The Matchmaker* (1954), a revision of his earlier *The Merchant of Yonkers* (1938). Both *Our Town* and *The Skin of Our Teeth* won Wilder a Pulitzer; however, he had already won one before, in 1928, for his 1927 novel *The Bridge of San Luis Rey*, set in Peru, and a metaphysical speculation on the sense of life.

Popular literature

Authors who in the period during the two world wars enjoyed a certain, although never stable, measure of literary fame, but who are now mostly relegated to the realm of popular literature, have been forgotten, or are considered of only historical importance at best, are John P. Marquand (1893–1960), John O'Hara (1905–70), Joseph Hergesheimer (1880–1954) and Howard Fast (1914–2003). Both Marquand and O'Hara were very prolific authors of what we may perhaps best describe as a kind of journalistic realism in, to cite only what are usually considered the best of their numerous books, *The Late George Apley* (1937), a satirical novel set in Boston's leading circles, for Marquand, and for O'Hara *Appointment in Samarra* (1934), set in Gibbsville, a fictional version of O'Hara's birthplace Pottsville in Pennsylvania, *Butterfield 8* (1935), set in fashionable New York, and *Pal Joey* (1940), an epistolary novel about a nightclub singer in 1930s Chicago. O'Hara's gift for dialogue has often been praised, but the sexual explicitness of his novels, unusual for the time, earned him the reputation of vulgarity. Hergesheimer's reputation rode very high in the 1920s, after the publication of *Java Head* (1919), a historical novel set in a Salem merchant milieu, still considered his best work. By the time of his death, though, he had fallen into complete neglect. Fast also wrote numerous historical novels, among which a fictionalized biography of Thomas Paine in 1942 (*Citizen Tom Paine*), but he remains most famous for *Spartacus* (1951), a work he wrote while in jail for his Communist affiliations. Fast eventually became a very successful scriptwriter for Hollywood and for television.

Interestingly, Marquand and Fast not only wrote what was considered 'serious' fiction at the time, but also ventured into more popular genres. Fast, writing as E.V. Cunningham, wrote a number of Masao Masuto Mysteries, and Marquand was the author of the celebrated Mr. Moto spy stories, which inspired a series of movies starring Peter Lorre as Mr. Moto, although with a character rather different from that in the Marquand stories. In fact, Marquand and Fast were tapping into the popularity of the so-called 'hard-boiled' detective genre that flourished in the 1920s and '30s first in popular magazines such as *Black Mask*, founded in 1920 by H.L. Mencken (1880–1956) and George Jean Nathan (1882–1958), and as of the late 1920s with the work of Dashiell Hammett (1894–1961) and then with that of Raymond Chandler

(1888–1959). Hammett started out writing stories for *Black Mask* in 1922. Many of these stories feature the Continental Op, an operative for an outfit called the Continental Detective Agency, which is obviously modeled on the Pinkerton Agency, America's oldest and most famous private law enforcement agency, for which Hammett himself had worked as an agent from 1915 to 1922. *Red Harvest*, Hammett's first full-length novel, but which earlier had been serialized in *Black Mask*, appeared in 1929. Its protagonist again is the Continental Op, and for the events described in the novel, a strike break, Hammett drew upon his own experiences as a Pinkerton operative. Hammett's most famous work, *The Maltese Falcon*, an intricate tale about a long-lost precious artifact, murder and betrayal, also first appeared as a serial in *Black Mask*, and then as a full-length novel in 1930. It was several times made into a movie, most famous being the 1941 version starring Humphrey Bogart as private eye Sam Spade. Hammett wrote only three more novels, and as of 1934 basically stopped publishing. His short stories were published in several collections. Hammett spent most of his later life, much of it in an often difficult relationship with the playwright Lillian Hellman, in left-wing political activism, for which he was briefly imprisoned and also blacklisted during the Red Scare of the late 1940s and early 1950s. Hammett's prose is marked by sparse diction, an ironical and even cynical attitude often expressing itself in sharp repartee, a focus on the seamy side of American life, an urban setting, and generally 'noir' atmosphere. All these elements became typical of the 'hard-boiled' school as it was canonized by Hammett's contemporary and successor Raymond Chandler. Chandler was an oil company executive until he lost his job in the Depression. He then turned to writing, publishing his first detective stories in *Black Mask* in 1933. *The Big Sleep* appeared in 1939, followed by six more novels, of which *Farewell, My Lovely* (1940), *The Lady in the Lake* (1940) and *The Long Goodbye* (1954) are the best known. Chandler was read and admired by many famous 'serious' authors such as T.S. Eliot and W.H. Auden. He himself also reflected on what he called 'The Simple Art of Murder' in a 1950 essay in which he famously said of the hard-boiled private detective that 'down these mean streets a man must go who is not himself mean, who is neither tarnished nor afraid'. Not surprisingly, then, Marlowe at the beginning of *The Big Sleep* pictures himself as a white knight coming to rescue a damsel in distress, and while this at first sight may seem an ironical remark, in many ways it is also the truth. In the same essay Chandler also praised Hammett for having given 'murder back to the people who commit it for reasons, not just to provide a corpse'. Chandler's own novels pursue the same track, seeking the origins of crime in the greed, corruption and perversions of the rich and powerful, rather than with the common man. Faulkner collaborated on the script for the 1941 movie version of *The Big Sleep*.

Detective novels, however, only represent one end of the entire spectrum of crime writing that rose to prominence in the period between the two world wars. A number of novels and stories focused not on the character of the detective but rather that of the criminal. In *The Postman Always Rings Twice* (1934) James M. Cain (1892–1977) portrays the murderous affair between the unemployed drifter Frank Chambers and Cora, the sultry wife of Nick Papadakis 'the Greek', the owner of an out-of-the-way California gas station and diner. Further successes of Cain comprise *Double Indemnity* (1936) and *Mildred Pierce* (1941). The exploitation of the common American to which the Depression led is thrown into sharp relief in *They Shoot Horses, Don't They?* (1935), about a grueling dance marathon, by Horace McCoy (1897–1955).

Hard-boiled crime fiction, especially in its pulp magazine guise, primarily catered to a white male blue collar audience that after World War I had first found the labor market partially cornered by the cheaper female and colored labor that during the war had taken its place, and that later suffered most from the Great Depression. In the virile and fast-talking private eye, at odds with the regular police and the authorities, and finding foreigners, illegal aliens, members of ethnic minorities, women and wealthy businessmen or bankers to be the 'real' criminals, this part of the American population saw its rightful champion, a true defender of true America. It is no coincidence that the 'baddies' in *The Maltese Falcon* are an Irish-Catholic temptress, a British Jew, and a Cypriot homosexual.

Another popular genre that largely aimed at the same blue collar readership was the Western and, like the detective, it primarily reached its audience via pulp magazines such as *Western Story Magazine* (1919–49). One of the most prolific authors in the genre was Max Brand, with his real name Frederick Schiller Faust (1892–1944). Brand mostly stuck to stories. Zane Grey throughout the 1920s and '30s turned out Western novels at the rate of one or two a year. Whereas most of Brand's and Grey's stories and novels stuck to the by then already clichéd Western convention, *The Ox-Bow Incident* (1940), by Walter Van Tilburg Clark (1900–71), foregrounded the unpleasant reality of the historical West. Set in 1855, the novel features two drifters who get caught up in a lynching party of three supposed cattle rustlers who eventually turn out to have been innocent. *The Ox-Bow Incident* marked a turn toward the more realistic, engaged and reflective kind of Western that would flourish after World War II.

While the Western and the hard-boiled detective as typical American popular genres primarily appealed to an adult male audience, the superhero comics that as of the mid-1930s started to flood the American market aimed at an adolescent readership. The comics as of the 1930s appeared in pulp magazines, one of which, *Action Comics*, in 1938 published the first installment of *Superman*, a creation of Jerry Siegel (1914–96) and Joe Shuster (1914–92). Superman was a runaway success, and immediately a number of imitations hit the stands, with names such as Batman, Wonder Woman, Spiderman, Captain Marvel and Captain America. The history of comics as far as series, heroes, publishers and distributors are concerned, is extremely complex. Suffice it to say here that in their original form the superheroes of the late 1930s and early 1940s were made to stand for a patriotic image of the U.S. over against its enemies, real or imagined, and whether these were actual low-life criminals, scheming bankers, foreign politicians, or military adversaries such as the Germans and Japanese – a hero such as Captain America leaves little to the imagination as far as this is concerned. For Jerry Siegel and Joe Shuster, who both were Jewish, as was much of the entire comics book industry, their Superman series offered an opportunity to oppose at least verbally and visually the Nazi threat in Europe by appealing to typically 'American' values. Ironically, most superheroes look very all-American, in fact very 'Aryan'.

In a certain sense, the superhero comic strips of the 1930s and 1940s capitalized on another genre that had itself only relatively recently come into being: science fiction. The latter extrapolates from contemporary science to speculate about future developments created by technical and scientific progress. Going back to even earlier examples, the genre was popularized in Europe in the nineteenth century by especially the French writer Jules Verne (1828–1905) and the British H.G. Wells (1866–1964). Edgar Rice Burroughs (1875–1950) in 1912, the same year he published the magazine version of *Tarzan of the Apes* (novel publication 1914), for which he is now mostly remembered, also published *A Princess of Mars*, the first of a series of novels set on the red planet and starring hero John Carter. In 1926 Hugo Gernsback (1884–1967) founded *Amazing Stories Magazine*, a pulp magazine devoted exclusively to science fiction, and soon followed by *Astounding Stories* (1930) and other such publications. Philip Francis Nowlan (1888–1940) in 1928 introduced a character that as of 1929 under the name of Buck Rogers became the hero of a popular newspaper strip. In 1934 Flash Gordon was created as a rival to Buck Rogers. Towards the end of the interwar period, however, we also see the rise of 'serious' science fiction with the early stories of Isaac Asimov (1920–92), Frederick Pohl (1919–), James Blish (1921–75), Robert Heinlein (1907–88) and Ray Bradbury (1920–2012).

5 After the war: 1945–80

With a population of 131 million (1939) and a large and highly competitive industrial sector, the U.S. was the world's leading economy even before Adolf Hitler's Germany launched the most destructive war in history. After the war, however, the U.S. found itself in the role of a superpower whose dominant position seemed uncontestable. The war effort had turned the nation into a formidable military machine and economically the gap with former European rivals like the United Kingdom, France, and Germany had widened dramatically while the U.S.S.R., with an economy that was only 30% of the American one, was not a serious rival. And perhaps more relevant for America's citizens, the immediate postwar period proved a period of miraculous prosperity with ever-increasing wages (median income doubled between 1945 and 1960) and historically low levels of unemployment. The postwar economic boom would in fact last well into the 1970s.

Superficially, the period also seems a time of harmony, or at least consensus – that is, in what soon was to be called the western, or the 'free' world. At the heart of Nazi ideology had been the notion that the various 'races' it identified were locked in a perpetual struggle for survival and that only the ruthless elimination of 'inferior races' would guarantee the future of the Aryan race the Nazis felt they represented. Determined to bury the destructive social Darwinism of Nazi ideology once and for all, the postwar years consciously set cooperation and unity against divisiveness. We see this in the foundation of the United Nations – a name coined by Franklin D. Roosevelt – in 1945, in the Universal Declaration of Human Rights of 1948, and in the 1951 treaty that established the forerunner of the European Union. Perhaps the most telling example of the desire to counter the murderously racist ideology of Nazism was the photo exhibit *The Family of Man* that drew a record number of 275,000 visitors to New York City's Museum of Modern Art in 1955 and would in spite of the so-called 'Cold War' of the 1950s and 1960s be seen by 2.7 million Russians when it was part of the American exhibit at Moscow's World Fair of 1959. As its title suggests, *The Family of Man*, which presented 503 photographs from 68 countries, was a conscious effort to minimize the differences between peoples and nations and to emphasize what we have in common. The one picture that went against this was that of the mushroom cloud of a nuclear explosion – this would be the future if we refused to heed history's warnings. A third and nuclear World War might truly decimate the family of man.

The same impulse towards harmony pervades the popular culture of the period. Mass entertainment, especially in its televised form, often tends to be of the feel-good variety, but that of the 1950s and early 1960s was saccharine – although not necessarily dull – to an unusual degree. Family sitcoms like *Father Knows Best* (1954–60) and *Leave It to Beaver* (1957–63) presented middle-class, all-American families in which happy harmony – only further emphasized by the occasional innocent threat – reigned supreme. Father's weekly salary far exceeded prewar expectations and allowed mother to realize her prime ambition: to make a perfect home in a perfect, all-white suburb. That the houses in many of these new post-war suburbs were virtually identical, mass assembled as part of a planned community as in Long Island's Levittown, was hardly noticed. For the first time in history over half of all American families identified them-selves as middle-class and the uniformity that middle-class life seemed to bring with it was ignored in the euphoria of the moment. Not accidentally, the popular 1970s sitcom *Happy Days* (1974–84), which sought to recapture happier, more innocent times, was situated in the 1950s as if happiness and the fifties almost naturally belonged together.

However, by that time the immediate postwar years were not only seen as a time of innocent well-being but also as a bland, superficial period, a time of stifling conformity and, for those who found that conformity hard to accept, a time of alienation. The price of conformity and the social control endemic to the suburbs was recognized as early as 1950 by the sociologist David Riesman in his study of contemporary alienation, *The Lonely Crowd*, and Riesman's example was later followed by others like Paul Goodman (*Growing Up Absurd: Problems of Youth in Organized Society*, 1960) and Herbert Marcuse, a German-American philosopher who in his influential *One-Dimensional Man* (1964) argued that the consumerism that postwar prosperity had made possible was itself a highly effective form of social control.

The undeniable pressure to conform of the postwar period was, however, most of all the result of political developments. In 1945 the U.S. was the undisputed leader of the world – militarily, economically, and, arguably, also morally, with its generous grants (combined with loans) to not only its European allies (with the Soviet Union and its Eastern European satellites refusing the offer) but also to the defeated enemy. But things changed rapidly. In 1949 Mao Ze Dong's Communists took over China and in the same year the Soviet Union, which had already for all practical purposes annexed Central and Eastern Europe, totally unexpectedly detonated its first atom bomb. All of a sudden Communism seemed to present a threat to America itself and in February 1950 the demagogic and not a little unscrupulous Wisconsin Senator Joseph McCarthy took advantage of the situation to launch a smear campaign against anyone who might be remotely suspected of leftist sympathies. When in June 1950 North Korean Com-munists started the Korean War which would cost another 50,000 American lives, Commun-ism seemed indeed as dangerous as McCarthy and his supporters claimed. America now faced a formidable Communist block that openly challenged its leading position. The anti-Communist reflex that McCarthy's speeches and accusations created led to a general atmosphere of fear and even paranoia in which civil rights were ignored and large numbers of loyal Americans perma-nently damaged. McCarthy fairly soon fell into disgrace, but his campaign had convinced many Americans of the necessity to discourage dissent and to close ranks in the face of a common enemy. Censorship and surveillance helped to create the united home front that seemed a necessary first line of defense.

Inevitably, not all Americans were happy with what seemed to them a repression of indivi-dual freedom. The prosperity and domestic happiness of the 1950s, then, masked not only a widespread anxiety, but also a widely shared and deeply felt alienation. In popular culture that alienation often remained rather inarticulate, as in the movies *The Wild One* (1953, starring Marlon Brando) and the aptly titled *Rebel Without a Cause* (1955, with James Dean). But in the literature of the 1950s that alienation was articulated forcefully and became a dominant theme in the fiction, drama, and poetry of a new generation of writers.

The demand for social justice that had characterized much writing of the 1930s and early 1940s did not disappear, but now was as often as not part of a more inclusive problematic in which social injustice was a contributing factor to the psychological problems that faced a protagonist, as in such plays as Arthur Miller's *Death of a Salesman* (1949) or Tennessee Williams's *The Glass Menagerie* (1944), to which we will return later. But psychological problems equally haunted those whose social circumstances were comfortable enough, like Holden Caulfield in J.D. Salinger's novel *The Catcher in the Rye* (1951), Peyton Loftis in William Styron's *Lie Down in Darkness* (1951), the multi-millionaire protagonist of Saul Bellow's *Henderson, the Rain King* (1959), Harry 'Rabbit' Angstrom in John Updike's *Rabbit, Run!* (1960) or Binx Bolling in Walker Percy's *The Moviegoer* (1961). In the postwar novel psychological realism replaces the naturalism of much 1930s fiction. With the radical leftism of the 1930s disgraced by revelations about Stalin's mass murders, not to mention his 1939 pact with Hitler's Germany, the Marxist presentation of characters in terms of class and of society as involved in a permanent class struggle had lost much of its credibility. The world now seemed far more complex than either the radical left or, for that matter, the radical right, would admit. What was now required of a writer, the influential critic Lionel Trilling argued in one of the essays in his book *The Liberal Imagination* (1950), quoting the early nineteenth-century English poet John Keats, was a 'willingness to remain in uncertainties, mysteries, and doubts'. As a result, in much of the literature of the early postwar period the world is constituted by the subjective perception of either a first-person narrator or a protagonist whose vision is allowed to be preeminent. But those fictional worlds reflect not the clear-cut simplicities of the 1950s, with their identifiable enemies and petit-bourgeois ideals. Instead, they reflect the 'uncertainties' and 'doubts' of the period's protagonists, often expressed through irony and paradox. And what most of these protagonists are after is not so much an alternative world in which social justice reigns supreme – although they think that justice is important – but better understanding, especially of themselves. Feeling engulfed by the 'phoniness' of all those who either dumbly or else expediently opt for conformity instead of autonomy and independent thinking, they seek personal fulfillment in authenticity, in an optimal awareness of their possibilities and limitations.

That search for authenticity takes various forms. In the writings of the so-called 'Beat' novelists and poets – Jack Kerouac, William Burroughs, Allen Ginsberg, and others – we find echoes of the authenticity and of the radically individual stance extolled by nineteenth-century Transcendentalists like Thoreau and Whitman. It is this very American concern with authenticity and the discovery of the self that becomes a central force in the counterculture of the sixties – see for instance the journalist Tom Wolfe's 1968 account, in his *The Electric Kool-Aid Acid Test*, of the life and times of the novelist Ken Kesey and his group of 'Merry Pranksters' (an account that, by the way, also highlights much of the silliness of the period). Even more radical is the pursuit of authenticity of Norman Mailer, who had started his career with a part realistic, part naturalistic war novel, *The Naked and the Dead* (1948), but by the mid-fifties was calling on his fellow Americans to give free rein to their anti-social, psycho-pathological impulses. A major enemy of authenticity, much as in Thoreau's *Walden*, is consumer culture, more ubiquitous and more powerful than Thoreau could ever have foreseen. But we also find a less exuberant, less intuitive search for authenticity, a search influenced by European existentialism that sees authenticity not so much in terms of individual freedom but relates it to the moral and social dilemmas we inevitably come to face and to the choices we have to make. Since life is contingent and unpredictable, the existentialist hero – usually anti-heroic rather than heroic – finds that those choices do not necessarily imply closure and that living existentially, in a state of optimal awareness, is a never-ending process of becoming. For the writers who pursue this line freedom and fulfillment lie in making the ego subordinate to commitment, as in Bellow's *Henderson, the Rain King* where the unlikely adventures of Bellow's middle-aged millionaire in sub-Saharan Africa – where his ungovernable temper leads him into one disaster after the other – serve to teach him humility and are instrumental in his decision to become a doctor. In Walker Percy's *The Moviegoer* New Orleans stock-broker Binx Bolling, who like many 1950s and early 1960s characters experiences the outside world as deeply unreal – and finds relief in movies that seem more real than the world they portray – in an existential 'leap of faith' decides to marry a psychologically troubled distant cousin. And in Bernard Malamud's *The Assistant* (1957), petty criminal and drifter Frank Alpine, seeking moral and emotional anchoring, has himself circumcised and becomes a Jew after he has first robbed and then helped out the aging Jewish grocer who serves as the catalyst in this spiritual journey.

Not accidentally we find this existentialistically inflected search for authenticity in the work of many authors who, more than white mainstream Americans, see themselves confronted with questions of identity. In Ralph Ellison's *Invisible Man* (1952), probably the greatest African American novel to date, the unnamed protagonist must first break away from the various false identities created for him by racist white society and white interest groups before the process of finding himself can even begin. With Jewish American writers such as Bellow and Malamud, the growing self-awareness of their characters inevitably invites positioning themselves at some point in the spectrum between Jewishness and the American mainstream. However, in the 1960s and after, when many new voices join the choir of American literature, positioning one-self vis-à-vis American mainstream culture loses much of its existential dimension. Negotiating one's identity and remaining true to a certain conception of one's self in an increasingly complex and not necessarily sympathetic environment simply becomes part of life for many writers. That identity may be ethnic – Native American, Chicano/a, Chinese American, and so on – it may involve sexual orientation – gay, lesbian, transgender – or it may, more generally, be female in an overwhelmingly male, patriarchal society. But whereas the existentialist hero of the 1950s is essentially alone, the new non-mainstream writer of the 1960s and after usually has the support of a (much) larger group involved in similar identity politics. However, this is getting ahead of things.

Early postwar fiction

It is fair to say that the great writers of the interbellum were past their prime in 1945 and that their postwar fiction does not match their best work. In some cases, such as Ernest Hemingway's *Across the River and Into the Trees* of 1950, their new work verged on the embarrassing. Still, with Nobel prizes for Faulkner (1949), Hemingway himself (1954), and Steinbeck (1962), the quality of their earlier work got the international recognition it deserved (as had T.S. Eliot's poetry with the Nobel prize of 1948).

Not surprisingly, many of the new writers of the postwar period first of all turned to their war experiences. In 1948 Norman Mailer (1923–2007) published *The Naked and the Dead*, a realistic and more often naturalistic account of the advance of a reconnaissance platoon on a Pacific island defended by the Japanese. Mailer, more interested in the workings of the American army than the war itself, pits the humanistic Lieutenant Hearn against the brutal and fascistic Sergeant Crofts and against Division Commander General Cummings. The novel was an immediate bestseller, although some critics questioned its authenticity. Fellow writer Gore Vidal (1925–2012), never one to pull his punches, notably called the novel a 'clever, talented, admirably executed fake' and there is, indeed, a certain mechanical quality to the way Mailer constructs and relates his story. Ironically, Vidal's own war novel *Williwaw* (1946), which takes place on an army supply ship off the Aleutians – with as the main enemy a sudden hurricane (a williwaw) rather than the Japanese forces – is also not free of awkwardness. Perhaps creating a balance between form and feeling in drawing on one's personal, often traumatic, experience of violence, death, and chaos benefits from a certain distance. This is certainly suggested by the two war novels of James Jones (1921–77), whose massive *From Here to Eternity* (1951), which focuses mostly on the brutality of army life on Hawaii before the attack on Pearl Harbor, suffers in comparison with his *The Thin Red Line* (1962), a detailed and fully convincing orchestration of Jones's combat experience on Guadalcanal.

Mailer and Vidal would go on to become two of the most eminent high-profile writers and public intellectuals of the second half of the twentieth century, with Mailer turning his hand to an astonishing variety of subjects (except his Jewish background) in both novels and non-fiction books, and Vidal producing an impressive number of novels, including *The City and the Pillar* (1948) which daringly introduced a homosexual protagonist, the equally provocative (and outrageous) *Myra Breckinridge* (1968) which featured a transsexual, and a number of painstakingly researched but rather flat historical novels (*Burr*, 1973; *1876*, 1976). Perhaps more importantly, he produced a stream of brilliantly sardonic essays on the most diverse aspects of American culture and politics – in fact on everything that had the misfortune to become the target of his caustic wit (*Matters of Fact and Fiction*, 1977; *The Second American Revolution*, 1982; *At Home*, 1988, and numerous other collections). As Vidal himself said, 'Beneath my cold exterior, once you break the ice, you find cold water'. Mailer followed up on *The Naked and the Dead* with the positively mystifying *Barbary Shore* (1951), the product of 'the division which existed then in my mind. My conscious intelligence became obsessed by the Russian Revolution. But my unconsciousness was much more interested in other matters: murder, suicide, orgy, psychosis'. Some or all of these themes play an important role in *The Deer Park* (1955), with its hipster psychopath Marion Faye, the essay 'The White Negro: Superficial Reflections on the Hipster' (1957), the non-fiction and fiction of *Advertisements for Myself* (1959), and *An American Dream* (1965), in which a fortunately rather atypical university professor first strangles his wife, then rapes the maid, and finally, via a stop in Las Vegas, seeks authenticity in the wilds of Yucatán. In *Barbary Shore* Mailer had set up a confrontation between the former Communist radical McLeod, guilty of terrorist acts (but now converted to a supposedly more humane Trotskyism) and the McCarthyite FBI agent Hollingsworth, presumably by way of commentary on the Cold War that had just started. More than any other writer of the twentieth century Mailer directly and intensely engaged with social reality as he saw it, as in his notorious essay on the hipster, or in *The Armies of the Night* (1968), an account of the famous march on the Pentagon of October 1967 which gives a fascinating picture of the participants involved and of the reaction of the Washington authorities (arrest and a night in jail), while it also offers a baroquely psychoanalytic discourse on the darker sides of American culture. The high-point of this strain in Mailer's career is his magisterial non-fiction novel *The Executioner's Song* (1979), probably the best account ever of America's white underclass, which reconstructs the events leading up to and following the apparently gratuitous murder of two Utahans by the convict Gary Gilmore, who in his decision not to fight execution becomes the center of a media frenzy that Mailer – by now in the midst of it – also brilliantly describes.

Vidal, Mailer, and Jones, all born in the 1920s, began their public career after the war. Some others, half a generation older, had started publishing during the war. Mary McCarthy (1912–89), Vassar-educated and outspoken on virtually any subject demonstrated that frankness – which would involve her in a succession of political and personal controversies – with her first novel, *The Company She Keeps* (1942), which freely describes the libertarian life style of the group of New York intellectuals which includes her heroine. *The Groves of Academe* (1951), in which she casts a critical eye on academic life, is based on her own brief teaching experience at two elite women's colleges, while in *The Group* (1963) she follows the ups and downs – but mostly downs – in the lives of eight Vassar students over a thirty-year period after their graduation. McCarthy's sardonic intelligence is even more in evidence in her political writings and social criticism, published in a variety of (mainly left liberal) journals and magazines. Unlike

McCarthy, John Cheever (1912–82) stayed away from political issues and tried to express his much milder, delicately ironic view of the human condition through stories and novels that go easy on his characters' weaknesses and tentatively highlight their strengths. His stories, the first collection of which (*The Way Some People Live*) appeared in 1943, were for decades a regular feature of *The New Yorker* and collectively constitute an impressive career in short fiction. Their middle and upper middle class settings also form the background of *The Wapshot Chronicle* (1957) and *The Wapshot Scandal* (1964), light-hearted novels with a serious undertone about a decidedly unusual New England family. With the much younger John Updike (1932–2009), whose novel *Rabbit, Run* has already been mentioned, Cheever is the undisputed master of what one might call suburban realism. But what distinguishes especially Cheever's stories from those of other suburban realists, is his uncanny ability to let his stories imperceptibly drift from what is straightforwardly realistic to what is larger than life and all of a sudden would seem to have acquired symbolic meaning. Updike's stories, and the 'Rabbit novels' that all feature former high school basketball star and conflicted Pennsylvania small-town resident Harry Angstrom – *Rabbit, Run* (1960), *Rabbit Redux* (1971), *Rabbit Is Rich* (1981), and *Rabbit at Rest* (1990) – are virtuoso performances that in an extraordinarily supple and plastic language capture life in the fictive Olinger, Pennsylvania, but they do not soar away towards new heights. And neither do the stories and novels of Eudora Welty, another Cheever contemporary who had started publishing before the war and who will be discussed below in the section on southern writing. Updike once said that his subject was 'the American small town, Protestant middle class', and Welty's subject is the small town and rural South. Both brilliantly recreate those milieus in their fiction, but Cheever often is able to do more than that.

Jewish American novelists

The first runaway bestseller of the postwar period, with sales that have now topped 65 million, was *The Catcher in the Rye* (1951) by J.D. Salinger (1919–2010), which perfectly captures the alienation felt by many adolescent Americans of the period. The novel features seventeen-year-old Holden Caulfield whose disaffection with the 'phony' adult world has led to a breakdown and whose attempts at 'adult' behavior, which include an inconclusive meeting with a prostitute, have ended in dismal failure, not in the least because he does not really want to join the world of adults (when the prostitute who shows up in his hotel room seems to be his age he only wants to talk). In his first novel Salinger, who in 1965 stopped publishing and not much later withdrew from public life, does not identify himself as Jewish, but his Jewish background becomes obvious in the stories and novellas about the Glass family with its seven mostly precocious children, the first of which was published in 1948 ('A Perfect Day for Bananafish'). In the short fiction collected in *Nine Stories* (1953), *Franny and Zooey* (1961) and *Raise High the Roof-Beam, Carpenters* and *Seymour: An Introduction* (1963) Salinger constructs an intermittent history of the Glass children which highlights their sensitivity, alienation, and psychological problems – and, one might add, their reluctance to cross the threshold to an adult world of compromises, half-truths, and other imperfections which demand constant self-criticism and an acceptance of one's own moral limitations.

We find similar themes in the work of the most prominent Jewish American writer of the 1950s, Saul Bellow (1915–2005), who would be awarded the Nobel prize in 1976. Bellow, born in Lachine, Canada, but raised in Chicago, won national praise for his third novel, *The Adventures of Augie March* (1953), a sprawling, exuberant book that celebrates both America and his own Jewish background: 'I am an American, Chicago-born – Chicago, that somber city – and go at things as I have taught myself, free-style'. After two carefully constructed novels,

Dangling Man (1944) and *The Victim* (1947), which dealt with uncertainty, self-doubt, and psychological harassment, *Augie March* joyfully breaks all the rules of well-crafted fiction in its attempt to present life as Bellow had observed it in the Chicago of his younger days. We follow Augie on his picaresque way through a bustling and confusing social reality and see how, aided by a very American self-reliance, he picks his own, seemingly directionless, course. Bellow would afterwards say that he had gone 'too far' in 'the excitement in discovery' and followed up with the low-key novella *Seize the Day* (1956) in which the disappointing son of a highly successful but cold father would seem to come to terms with his failures when he intensely mourns the passing of a complete stranger. But he returned to the exuberant mode with the already mentioned *Henderson, the Rain King* (1959) which sends its rich, but unfulfilled protagonist to Africa where his outrageous adventures teach him to substitute 'they want' for 'I want'.

With *Herzog* (1964) Bellow achieves the perfect combination of exuberance and restraint. Herzog, a middle-aged Jewish academic whose wife has left him for her lover, taking their child, enters a deep mid-life crisis but is at the end of the novel 'pretty well satisfied to be, to be just as it is willed'. Herzog's crisis is at turns moving, as when he sees his wife's lover help his own young daughter with her ablutions, grim, hilarious, and intellectually entertaining, as in Henderson's letters to famous thinkers and leaders, dead and alive, that he composes but that are never sent. *Mr. Sammler's Planet* (1969) is another high point, but darker than the earlier novels. Clearly dismayed by what he sees as the sexual lawlessness and the egocentrism unleashed by the counterculture of the sixties, Bellow has us observe the self-indulgent hedonism of the younger generation, the unsavory characteristics of their elders, street violence and intimidation, through the eyes of Mr. Sammler, a European Jew who has survived the Nazi death camps that have killed his wife and who has spent half a lifetime thinking about the question of evil. Distancing himself from the apparent nihilism of the times, Bellow has Sammler at the end of the novel suggest that we all have to meet the terms of a moral contract and that 'the truth of it' is 'that we all know, God, that we know, that we know'. In later novels such as *Humboldt's Gift* (1975), the partly autobiographical *The Dean's December* (1982), and *More Die of Heartbreak* (1987) Bellow's increasing pessimism about the course of western culture tends to get in the way – a pessimism that he shared with his close friend Allan Bloom (author of the cultural jeremiad *The Closing of the American Mind*, 1987) who features prominently in his last novel *Ravelstein* (2000).

Far less of a public figure than Bellow, Bernard Malamud (1914–86), like Bellow the son of Russian parents, wrote novels from which Jewishness is largely (or even wholly) absent and the tension between Jewish characters and the American mainstream is most of all a source of comedy, and novels and stories that are as much steeped in Jewishness as those of I.B. Singer (1902–91), the Polish-American writer whose Yiddish-language stories and novels about a Jewish Central Europe that had been forever destroyed by World War II earned him the 1978 Nobel prize. A fine example of Malamud's Jewish stories is 'The Magic Barrel' (1958) in which awkward rabbinical student Leo Finkle may or may not have been led by the nose by the sly marriage-broker Salzman who gets him to marry his compromised daughter.

After *The Natural* (1952), a light-hearted novel about a baseball prodigy, Malamud published *The Assistant* (1957), in which an aging Jewish grocer and his family barely survive in bleak economic circumstances that suggest the 1930s. Although Morris Bober, his wife Ida, and daughter Helen are not strictly observant, Morris, who with the small-time hoodlum Frank Alpine is at the center of the novel, has a deep-seated sense of morality and compassion that (together with a view of suffering as a way to transcendence) is presented as the natural corollary of his religious convictions. It is mostly because of his example that Alpine seeks redemption in a conversion to Judaism. The monotonous uneventfulness that is suggested by the novel's prose – although belied by a number of dramatic incidents – matches the dead-end lives of its characters.

In *A New Life* (1961) the adventures of a Jewish professor at Oregon's fictitious Cascadia College make for a good deal of comedy, but in *The Fixer* (1966) Malamud returns to a Jewish milieu with a novel about persecution in tsarist Russia. Based on the memoirs of Mendel Beilis, who in 1913 was falsely accused of having killed a Christian boy in a ritual murder, Malamud exposes the anti-Semitism that pervaded all levels of Russian society, and shows us how the ordeal positively transforms his protagonist, Yakov Bok. (Malamud chooses to leave the outcome uncertain although Beilis was acquitted and eventually, in 1921, settled in the U.S.)

With *The Tenants* (1971) Malamud entered new territory: the emotionally fraught relations between Jews and African Americans of the late 1960s, when the Nation of Islam organization, founded in 1930, attracted a substantial number of African Americans who had come to identify Christianity with discrimination and oppression. In a condemned tenement building, owned by a Jewish landlord, the Jewish writer Harry Lesser is the last one to hold out until he is joined by a squatter, the African American Willie Spearmint who has the ambition to become a writer himself. Lesser's art is intellectual, with form overriding life, while Willie's is alive but formless. At the heart of the novel is the developing and ever more complex relationship between the two, not made any easier by Lesser's writing block – his theme is love, but he may well be incapable of genuine love – and Lesser's girlfriend leaving him for Willie. The novel ends, phantasmagorically, with Lesser and Willie physically attacking each other, with each 'feel[ing] the anguish of the other', but it is not clear how we should read this. In any case, what then concludes the novel is an endlessly repeated 'mercy'. *The Tenants* was not unreasonably attacked for its stereotyping – Jewish head versus African American heart – and in *Dubin's Lives* (1979) Malamud turned to suburban realism, with the aging biographer William Dubin, who is working on a biography of D.H. Lawrence, falling under the spell of his subject's ideal of free sexuality and of that of young and voluptuous Fanny. The novel explores a late mid-life crisis and the emotional consequences of adultery, and ends like much of Malamud's fiction in inconclusive irony. After what may have been his last time in Fanny's bed, Dubin runs home, 'holding his half-stiffened phallus in his hand, for his wife with love'.

Still, although Malamud's characters are not invariably Jewish, in his presentation of Jewish milieus in *The Assistant* and in his early stories he is the most Jewish of all Jewish American writers of the fifties and sixties. Here, mainstream America is a vague presence in the background, just like Poland and its inhabitants only feature in the distance in the ghettos and shtetls of I.B. Singer's stories (*Gimpel the Fool*, 1957; *The Spinoza of Market Street*, 1961) or novels (*The Family Moskat*, 1950; *The Magician of Lublin*, 1960). Far more usual in Jewish American fiction is a continuous interaction with mainstream American culture and an unending negotiation of territorial boundaries. Such interaction even takes place when mainstream America is nowhere in sight, as in the title story of Philip Roth's *Goodbye, Columbus* (1959), a wistful story about class differences within Newark's Jewish community, in which the narrator's lover-for-a-summer has had her nose 'fixed' – '"I was pretty. Now I'm prettier"' – to conform to mainstream standards of beauty. With this collection of stories, Roth (1933) found himself at the center of controversy, especially because of the stories 'Defender of the Faith', in which a calculating Jewish soldier tries to exploit the loyalty he expects from a Jewish superior, and 'Eli, the Fanatic', in which suburban, assimilated Jews try to prevent orthodox co-religionists from establishing a yeshiva in their mostly gentile neighborhood. Roth's fiercest critics, upset by what seemed a cynical view of middle-class American Jewry, accused him of self-hatred, even of anti-Semitism. What Roth captures in 'Eli' is the self-censorship and the dissembling that in the 1950s were part and parcel of assimilation and the deep sense of alienation – experienced here by the lawyer hired by his fellow Jews – that such a forced way of living may bring with it. This is in fact one of the overriding themes in Jewish American writing of the first decades after the war. In order to be accepted by mainstream America, Jewish Americans abandon much of what may characterize them as Jews – sometimes, as in 'Goodbye, Columbus', even the shape of their nose – and move out of typically Jewish neighborhoods. But that estranges them from their background while their new environment never fully accepts them, leading to a sort of alienation that differs from that felt by young mainstream Americans but is felt even more profoundly.

After two rather traditional novels featuring a more mainstream cast and dealing with the familiar themes of relationships and personal problems and ambitions (*Letting Go*, 1962, and *When She Was Good*, 1967), Roth returned to more specifically Jewish themes with *Portnoy's Complaint* (1969), a virtuoso rant on a psychiatrist's couch in which the novel's protagonist, Alexander Portnoy, exhaustively lists all his frustrations at having been brought up Jewish, and in between details his insatiable lusting after blonde, all-American girls. Lust would from then on return regularly in Roth's novels, as in *The Professor of Desire* (1977) or the fairly recent *Sabbath's Theater* (1995), and has contributed disproportionally to his public image, but in those novels, too, Roth is concerned with Jewishness, even if he sees himself first of all as an American writer. In the last four decades Roth has brilliantly chronicled Jewish life in the Newark of his younger years and has through an alter ego, the Roth-like writer Nathan Zuckerman who features in for instance *Zuckerman Bound* (1985) and *The Counterlife* (1987), offered incisive meditations on what it means to be a Jewish American writer. Early in his career Roth worried that 'the actuality is continually outdoing our talents', that the technical skills of American writers were no longer a match for the outrageous images and events that the culture casually produced. Fortunately, those fears were unfounded.

Ellison and Baldwin

Richard Wright was a towering figure for the first postwar African American novelists. In such novels as *If He Hollers Let Him Go* (1945) and *The Lonely Crusader* (1947) Chester Himes (1909–84), who had started writing while serving a sentence for armed robbery, follows Wright in his angry denunciation of white racism and in his naturalistic approach to writing. *If He Hollers Let Him Go*, which is partly autobiographical, shows us how his white co-workers in a naval ship-yard in wartime Los Angeles insult and humiliate Himes's black protagonist, who has just arrived from the Midwest and has had little experience with racism, and provoke emotions he can barely control. In *Crusader*, union organizer Lee Gordon, again in L.A. during World War II, has to deal with a similarly destructive structural racism. The Communist sympathies of *Crusader* and its presentation of black anti-Semitism – according to some critics shared by its author – did not endear it to the larger public. After his relocation to France, in 1954, Himes wrote a series of highly successful detective novels, beginning with *For Love of Imabelle* (1957; in 1965 retitled *A Rage in Harlem*) and including *The Real Cool Killers* (1959), *The Heat's On* (1966), and the brilliantly titled *Blind Man with a Pistol* (1969), which feature the unconventional black detectives 'Coffin' Ed Johnson and 'Grave Digger' Jones. These novels, situated in Harlem, lead us in staccato style through often surreal-seeming scenes and introduce us to a jumble of gamblers, prostitutes, addicts, corrupted civil servants, and the occasional naïve but well-intentioned citizen, giving us a fascinating but no doubt charged picture of the more seedy side of life in Harlem. There is a comic side to the adventures of Himes's detectives, but they also reiterate Himes's conviction that it is American society's pervasive racism, especially directed at black males, that is at the root of these males' anti-social impulses.

Other young African American writers who felt inspired by Wright's achievements include Ann Petry (1911–97) whose bestselling *The Street* (1946) follows the struggle for survival of a black single mother in Harlem, Dorothy West (1907–98), who had been active in the Harlem Renaissance, but published her first novel, about an upper-class black family in Boston and sarcastically titled *The Living Is Easy*, in 1948, and Willard Motley (1912–65) whose naturalistic *Knock on Any Door* (1947) and *We Fished All Night* (1951) are situated in poverty-stricken, multiracial Chicago neighborhoods. But although Wright clearly is an inspiration, these writers do not necessarily share his radicalism (confirmed by Wright's *The Outsider* of 1953 with its murderous protagonist). That is even more the case with novelists like William Demby (1922), whose *Beetlecreek* (1950) focuses on the growing friendship between a black teenager and an older white carnival worker, or Julian Mayfield (1928–84), whose *The Hit* (1957) and *The Long Night* (1958) offer a nuanced tragi-comical picture of everyday life in Harlem.

The most celebrated African American novel of the 1950s was written by an author who had been encouraged by Wright, and who had worked closely with him, but had decided to go his own way. Like Wright (and Himes) Ralph Ellison (1914–94) had been under the spell of Marxism, but while Wright remained faithful to the naturalistic mode after his break with Communism, Ellison crafted an eclectic style of his own in his first and only novel *Invisible Man* of 1952. Incorporating surreal and expressionistic elements in a psychological realism that allows him to follow his unnamed protagonist's increasing self-knowledge and spiritual growth, Ellison creates a panoramic narrative that takes us from the humiliating experiences of his young African American protagonist in America's Deep South to the basement where, at the end of the novel, 'invisible man' ponders his future.

Among many other things, *Invisible Man* is a story of successive disillusions in which an African American young man must gradually discover his fundamental 'invisibility'. As he puts it at the end of his narrative, 'I am invisible, understand, simply because people refuse to see me'. But it has taken him years to find out. Still a boy, our invisible man causes an uproar among the white town fathers he is chosen to address – right after a terribly humiliating experience that has been greeted with great merriment – when he inadvertently drops the word 'equality'. He does so in a speech borrowed from Booker T. Washington, the black leader who is one of Ellington's targets and who features in the novel as the president of the African American college where we find the protagonist some years later and from which he is expelled for, again inadvertently, having confronted one of the college's white trustees with the realities of Black life. The college's president sends him to New York City with letters of recommendation that, in another deception, turn out to be letters of warning. In New York the invisible man is scouted by a largely white organization called the Brotherhood – the thinly disguised Communist Party – when he witnesses an eviction in Harlem and spontaneously addresses the crowd that has formed. He rises to become one of the Brotherhood's chief spokesmen in Harlem, only to discover that the organization is not really interested in the plight of African Americans, but has only taken up their cause for strategic reasons and is now fully prepared to drop it again. Increasingly angry and disillusioned he must also face the fact that the apparent interest a white woman shows in him is only based on racial fantasy and that for revolutionary African Americans like Ras the Exhorter who seek immediate and total equality, he is the enemy, a fellow-Black who has sold out. Pursued, during a riot initiated by Ras and his men, by white policemen who believe him to be a looter, he falls down a manhole and ends up in the basement from which he recounts his adventures. He has 'become acquainted with ambivalence', as he puts it when looking back on his adventures, 'with complexities so baffling that only an ironic stance seems possible.

At a certain point in the narrative, feeling threatened by Ras, the narrator disguises himself with dark glasses and a hat and is to his surprise repeatedly taken for a complete stranger, a man called Rinehart, an apparently shady character with a number of love interests whose way of life in the end seems better attuned to the world's complexity than anyone else's: 'His world was possibility and he knew it. He was years ahead of me and I was a fool. [...] The world in which we lived was without boundaries. A vast seething, hot world of fluidity, and Rine the rascal was at home in it'. It is with Rinehart – not necessarily an admirable character – that Ellison most clearly distances himself from Richard Wright's naturalistic presentation of African American victimization. Ellison is as aware as Wright of racism – *Invisible Man* gives us countless examples of its omnipresence – and of its socially and morally debilitating consequences. But for Ellison personal identity and social reality are not defined by race – both are more complex, more ambivalent, leaving more room for the self than naturalists like Wright would allow.

Ellison's decision to leave his invisible man at the end of the novel in a basement, where his only subversive act is to tap someone's electricity, with a sense of ambivalence that would seem to undermine effective action, has over the years drawn a good deal of criticism. For the radical Black Arts writers of the later 1960s he meekly turned the other cheek when retaliation in kind was what the situation demanded. But Ellison's apparent passivity also was criticized by his near-contemporary James Baldwin (1924–87), next to Ellison the most prominent African American writer of the 1950s. Baldwin grew up in Harlem, as the stepson of a harsh and dogmatic lay preacher, and experienced a conversion himself when he was fourteen. That conversion appears in his largely autobiographical first novel, *Go Tell It on the Mountain* (1953), together with a fictionalized family history that exposes a past riddled with broken promises and betrayal and damaged by racism. While his first novel is situated in Harlem, his second novel, *Giovanni's Room* (1956), is set in Paris, where Baldwin, following Richard Wright whom he greatly admired, had gone to live in the late 1940s. Its main character is a young white American who, although he has proposed marriage to his girlfriend, cannot escape the conclusion that he is far more attracted to men, in particular the Giovanni of the novel's title, with whom he has an affair. Perhaps because he wants to focus exclusively on the (again autobiographical) theme of homo- and bisexuality, Baldwin creates a cast of white characters who are convincingly portrayed. In *Another Country* (1962), set in New York City's Greenwich Village, Baldwin combines his earlier themes in a rather loose-knit novel, whose mixed cast of whites and African Americans allows him to present not only homosexual (and heterosexual) relations, but also interracial relations that reveal how personal histories of racist humiliation and abuse tend to poison such relations in spite of the best intentions of everyone involved. The self-hatred of jazz drummer Rufus Scott, which is responsible for his outbursts of aggression and which will ultimately lead to suicide, is entirely due to lifelong humiliation.

With his later novels – *Tell Me How Long the Train's Been Gone* (1968), *If Beale Street Could Talk* (1974), and *Just Above My Head* (1979) – Baldwin returned to African American settings, more specifically to Harlem, but is now much more intent than in *Go Tell It on the Mountain* on showing how even in Harlem racism inescapably blights his characters' lives. Although more than justified, his critique suffers because of a tendency toward melodrama. It is far more incisive in the essays of for instance *Notes of a Native Son* (1955) – one of which is highly critical of Richard Wright – and *The Fire Next Time* (1963), which reprints two essays in which Baldwin uses his personal history to analyze the situation of African Americans: 'One did not have to be very bright to realize how little one could do to change one's situation; one did not have to be abnormally sensitive to be worn down to a cutting edge by the incessant and gratuitous humiliation and danger one encountered every working day, all day long'. Still, *The Fire Next*

Time also makes clear that Baldwin rejects the separatism preached by for instance the Nation of Islam, whose leader Elijah Muhammad he visits, because it repeats the pattern of hate and rejection that characterizes the racism of white America. Although far more radical than Ellison's invisible man, or than the Civil Rights leader Martin Luther King (1929–68) in his famous 'I Have a Dream' speech of August 1963, Baldwin, too, sees the future in reconciliation, with the obvious proviso that it is first of all white America that will have to transcend its bigotry and hatred and that will have to make amends for past horrors, such as the Mississippi murder of young Emmett Till (1955) on which Baldwin loosely based his play *Blues for Mr. Charlie* (1964), using the opportunity to also castigate a not so heroic white liberal.

Beat writers (and some others)

While the alienation forced upon African American writers led to deep anger and its far milder version felt by Jewish writers to questions of identity and purpose, the writers of the so-called Beat generation generally celebrated their disconnection from an American mainstream that they saw as fundamentally inimical to personal freedom and creativity. William Burroughs (1914–97), John Clellon Holmes (1926–88), Jack Kerouac (1922–69), and Allen Ginsberg (1926–97), to name the most prominent Beat writers, got to know each other in the late 1940s in New York City and formed the center of a loosely defined group that would disperse in the course of the fifties, but that by then had established relations with kindred spirits elsewhere, as in San Francisco, where the poet/publisher Lawrence Ferlinghetti (1919), the poet Gary Snyder (1930), and others joined forces with them (with Ferlinghetti publishing Ginsberg's path-breaking poem 'Howl', 1955, and finding himself prosecuted for obscenity two years later). The term 'Beat Generation' first caught the attention in 1952 when Holmes, who had earlier that year published what is considered the first Beat novel, *Go*, used it in the *New York Times*. It referred to those members of the younger generation who felt that mainstream culture and the values it espoused were nothing but the product of conformity and insincerity. Rejecting that culture, they sought an alternative in a bohemian, non-materialistic life style that would allow them to recapture spontaneity and authentic experience. This drive for spontaneity and authenticity is what most characterizes their writings, in which being true to actual experience is far more important than plot or form. As Kerouac wrote to Holmes, 'I'm beginning to discover […] something beyond the novel […] wild form, man, wild form'.

That wild form was not simply waiting for them at the beginning of their writing careers but had indeed to be created – or discovered, as Kerouac puts it. In fact, Kerouac's first novel, *The Town and the City* (1950) follows the members of the Martin family over a forty-year period in a thinly disguised Lowell, Massachusetts – his home town – much in the manner of Thomas Wolfe's panoramic novels. Likewise, Ginsberg's early poetry and Burroughs's first novel, *Junkie* (1953; as William Lee) are fairly traditional, as is Holmes's largely autobiographical *Go*, which captures the irregular life style and sex and drug adventures of his Beat friends, with Holmes himself (Paul Hobbes in the novel) mainly as an onlooker. But even before *The Town and the City* was published Kerouac, feeling that none of the available fictional forms did justice to the immediacy of experience, was already trying out a wholly different approach to writing. Fictionalizing a number of wild transcontinental trips undertaken with his manic friend Neal Cassady he typed what would become *On the Road* on one long continuous scroll, to stay as true as possible to the actual experience. What Kerouac tries to convey here is not so much a verbal presentation of experience as experience itself. We must experience how it feels to be on the road, tearing across the vast expanse of the American heartland in the middle of the night, in touch with – or at least groping for – the essentials of life. Likewise, Ginsberg's 'Howl', with its long and irregular Whitmanian line and its bardic incantations, gives free (and not a little hyperbolic) expression to the poet's pain and anger ('I saw the best minds of my generation destroyed by madness, starving hysterical naked / dragging themselves through the negro streets at dawn looking for an angry fix'). And Burroughs's *Naked Lunch* (1959) covers much the same ground as *Junkie*, but the narrative now has become disjointed, fragmented, with a very thin line – or no line at all – between what, within the novel, is fantasy and what is real.

When *On the Road* was finally published, in 1957, it caused a minor sensation, not in the least because of the life style it depicted which Kerouac had romanticized into flamboyance. It was followed quickly by other novels written in the late forties and early fifties, such as *Dharma Bums* (1958) and *The Subterraneans* (1958), in which we again closely follow Kerouac and friends. *The Dharma Bums* with as its main characters Kerouac himself and the West Coast poet Gary Snyder (Japhy Ryder in the book) contrasts Beat life with its generous share of sex, drugs, and jazz, with the austerity of pristine nature. In *The Subterraneans*, in which next to the usual cast – Burroughs, Cassady, Ginsberg, the poet Gregory Corso – Gore Vidal makes a cameo appearance, we find ourselves in the then nascent bohemian scene of San Francisco. In novels such as *Desolation Angels* (1965), based on his experience as a fire lookout on a mountain in Washington State, Kerouac is more contemplative, while in other novels he returns to the world of his younger years, as in *Maggie Cassidy* (1959), a largely autobiographical story about a high-school romance. As might be expected, the disaffection the Beats felt for mainstream America was returned in kind, but they will only have enjoyed FBI chief J. Edgar Hoover's description of them as a threat to the nation, while Kerouac would have relished the knowledge that long after his death actor Johnny Depp, in apparent appreciation of Beat culture, acquired a couple of items from his estate.

Kerouac's fiction is now mainly remembered for its defiance of bourgeois values and for its attempts to find narrative forms that would preserve the immediacy of actual experience. Convinced that preconceived form only served to straitjacket the creative process, he saw the spontaneous improvisations of jazz as a shining example (Holmes's second novel *The Horn*, 1958, is wholly devoted to the jazz milieu). William Burroughs is remembered not only for fictional experiments that were much more radical than those of Kerouac, but also for a nightmare vision of contemporary society in which sadistic fascism is the norm and enigmatic but always violent organizations are out to control every minute of our lives. Increasingly seeing language itself as an instrument of oppression, Burroughs, in close cooperation with a friend, the painter Bryon Gysin, developed first the 'cut-up' and then the 'fold-in' techniques that turn reading his trilogy *The Soft Machine* (1961), *The Ticket That Exploded* (1962), and *Nova Express* (1964) into a disorienting, not to say nightmarish experience. 'Cut right through the pages of any book or newsprint […] lengthwise, for example, and shuffle the columns of text. Put them together at hazard and read the newly constituted message. […] Use any system which suggests itself to you', Burroughs and Gysin urge potential followers. That meaning, rather miraculously, still emerges from texts which have been treated in this way and in which snippets from completely unrelated texts have been incorporated, is due to the highly repetitive and paranoid nature of Burroughs's work, which keeps returning to the themes of drug addiction, sex (usually in the form of homosexual encounters), violence, and fascist conspiracies aiming at total control. It is only much later, in another trilogy still dealing with the same themes – *Cities of the Red Light* (1981), *The Place of Dead Roads* (1984), and *The Western Lands* (1987) – that Burroughs returns to more traditional forms. But in the meantime the experimentalism of his violent dystopias, with their surreal science fiction elements, had substantially contributed to the new ways that American fiction would explore in the 1960s.

In the first postwar period we find the intensity and the claustrophobic, nightmarish quality of Burroughs's fiction only in the work of John Hawkes (1925–98) who like Burroughs is one of the truly experimental writers of the fifties. Largely ignoring the conventions concerning plot, character and other seemingly indispensable elements of fiction, Hawkes was primarily interested in 'totality of vision', making everything subservient to unity of view, mood, or other perspective. The result is a sometimes nightmarish fiction that usually is more than a little hallucinatory – *The Cannibal* (1949), situated in a devastated postwar Germany, *The Beetle Leg* (1951), *The Lime Twig* (1961), involving a race horse scam and sadistic English criminals – and that sacrifices explanation and causality to atmosphere, to menace, or simply to one single monomaniacal perspective as in the later *Travesty* (1976) in which a car driver's extended monologue will end with his own suicide and the death of his daughter and her lover in the crash he is planning.

The depth of Burroughs's disaffection with 1950s America is only matched by Norman Mailer, whose 'The White Negro' tells us that living authentically is to 'encourage the psychopath in oneself', by the expatriate writer Paul Bowles (1910–99), who chose to live in Tangiers, Morocco (where Ginsberg, Burroughs and others joined him for longer periods), by that other expatriate, Henry Miller, the title of whose *The Air-Conditioned Nightmare* (1945), a collection of sketches of American life, speaks for itself, and by two writers whose first novels would become the cult novels of the sixties, Ken Kesey (1935–2001) and Joseph Heller (1923–99). In Bowles's North African novels – *The Sheltering Sky* (1949), *Let It Come Down* (1952), and *The Spider's House* (1955) – the unforgiving landscape, the alien culture, and their own lack of inner strength become the literal or figural undoing of his American protagonists. In Kesey's *One Flew over the Cuckoo's Nest* (1962) a mental institution, most of whose inmates turn out to be there on a voluntary basis, is kept under control by Big Nurse, who through surveillance and intimidation enforces a strict conformity. It takes a wholly uneducated – and therefore never disciplined – drifter, a sort of backwoods hipster, to liberate the 'patients', one of them a gigantic Native American whose self and physical strength are revived in the process and who realizes that he will only find freedom outside the United States. Finally, in Heller's *Catch-22* (1961) what is ostensibly a novel about World War II is as much an attack on the world of the fifties, even if in its final chapters the novel laments the apparently inescapable human condition as such. Heller's by turns hilariously absurd and poignant rollercoaster of a novel is scathing about the straitjacket of 1950s conformity (including its 'Loyalty Program'), about the period's unfeeling hypocrisy, and about its bureaucratic formalism, neatly illustrated by one instance of the ubiquitous 'catch-22': if the story's World War II fliers are not scared to fly more missions they are medically speaking insane and could be sent home, but won't ask for it; if they *are* scared they are obviously sane and have to stay and fly more missions.

Regional writing, mostly Southern (and some New Journalism)

With William Faulkner the South had produced not only a great writer, but also a distinctly Southern voice that brilliantly captured not only its idioms but also its complex awareness of history's presence in the current moment, of the ambiguity of human motives, of the inextricable knot of racial relations, and of the problem of good and evil. Inevitably, Faulkner was an inescapable influence for young postwar Southern writers, even if they did not follow him in his more baroque modes. *Lie Down in Darkness* (1951) by William Styron (1925–2006), with its tragic heroine whose loveless upbringing and psychological troubles eventually lead to suicide, clearly reminds us of *The Sound and the Fury*. In his later *The Confessions of Nat Turner* (1968) Styron is much more his own man in his controversial retelling of a historical and bloody uprising by a band of slaves in his native Virginia, while with *Sophie's Choice* (1979) he leaves the South altogether, and gives us the truly heart-rending story of Sophie Zawistowska, who upon her arrival in the Auschwitz extermination camp is forced to choose between her two children. Still, thematically, with his overriding themes of guilt and the problem of evil, Styron remains close enough to Faulkner.

Faulkner's use of the grotesque is much more evident in the work of Carson McCullers (1917–67) and, more particularly, Flannery O'Connor (1925–64). McCullers's novels, situated in her native Georgia – *The Heart Is a Lonely Hunter* (1940), *The Ballad of the Sad Café* (1943), *The Member of the Wedding* (1946), and *Clock Without Hands* (1961) – enlist our sympathy with their more than ordinarily vulnerable people (and children, as the twelve-year-old Frankie in *Wedding*) and their often pathetic small-town misfits. O'Connor's novels and stories present a much tougher world view – a *Time* review speaks of the 'sardonic brutality' of her fiction – paradoxically based on a deeply felt Catholicism. In an essay entitled 'The Grotesque in Southern Fiction' she explains the rationale behind the often shocking violence of her work (in *The Violent Bear It Away* [1960], the reluctantly religious fourteen-year-old Tarwater tries to drown his retarded cousin but can't help himself baptizing the boy in the process): 'To the hard of hearing you shout, and for the almost blind you draw large and startling figures'. To break through the shield of complacency with which according to her mainstream America protects itself from everything that is undesirable, she presents grotesque characters committing grotesque, often violent acts, as in the famous story 'A Good Man Is Hard to Find' in which an escaped convict and his accomplices murder a whole family, ending with the grandmother who on the brink of death finds in herself the love of one's neighbor that true Christianity asks from us. It does not save her, but as her murderer says, 'She would have been a good woman, if it had been somebody there to shoot her every minute of her life'. Or as O'Connor herself said, 'I have found that violence is strangely capable of returning my characters to reality and preparing them to accept their moment of grace'. O'Connor's fierce faith, perhaps even strengthened by the knowledge that her life would be cut short by an incurable disease, produced a thematically limited, but startlingly trenchant oeuvre – the stories collected in *A Good Man Is Hard to Find* (1955) and *Everything That Rises Must Converge* (1965), and the novels *Wise Blood* (1952), in which the fanatical Hazel Motes is the only preacher of his 'Church Without Christ', and the already mentioned *The Violent Bear It Away*.

We find more grotesque characters in the work of Truman Capote (1924–84). His first novel *Other Voices, Other Rooms* (1948) presents a thirteen-year-old boy, based upon his younger self, in his growing awareness of his homosexuality and on his road towards maturity – helped along by the eccentricities of his rural Alabama relatives. The stories collected in *Tree of Night* (1949) similarly explore Southern Gothic. It is not surprising that when Capote, fascinated by the fantastic and the bizarre, turned to journalistic reporting, his imagination was captured by the apparently senseless murder, in 1959, of a Kansas family of four by two young ex-convicts who were still on parole. The resulting book, *In Cold Blood* (1966), which uses fictional techniques – flashbacks, reconstructed dialogue, indirect speech, and so on – to create an optimally true-to-life effect was the first best-selling so-called non-fiction novel. It started a brief vogue in such books – collectively called the New Journalism – among the best of which we find the *The Electric Kool-Aid Acid Test* (1968) by Tom Wolfe, Norman Mailer's *The Armies of the Night* (1968) and *The Executioner's Song* (1979), and the hyperbolic, both self-advertising and self-deprecating adventures of Hunter S. Thompson (1937–2005) as described in books such as *Hell's Angels* (1967), the outrageous *Fear and Loathing in Las Vegas* (1972) – in which what he called his 'gonzo' style probably reached its peak – and *Fear and Loathing on the Campaign Trail '72* (1973). The New Journalism, which unlike its traditional counterpart does not seek to avoid personal, subjective, involvement but on the contrary often places the journalists' personal responses at the center of their reportage, is especially interested in what is uncommon, aberrant, or freakish, more particularly if it is colorful or provides high drama. Southern writing of the early postwar period has a comparable reputation, and there are indeed enough Southern writers – apart from those discussed above – who would seem to confirm it. The *New York Times* characterized *The Gospel Singer* (1968), the first novel by Harry Crews (1935–2012), who situates his fiction in small-town Georgia and Florida, as having 'a nice wild flavor and a dash of Grand Guignol strong enough to meet the severe standards of southern decadence', and it is fair to say that Crews kept on meeting those standards in later novels such as *Naked in Garden Hills* (1969) or the homophobic *Karate Is a Thing of the Spirit* (1971), with a protagonist who almost obsessively has William Faulkner (whose work he has never read) on his mind. And the first novels of Cormac McCarthy (1933), which take place in Tennessee – *The Orchard Keeper* (1965) and *Outer Dark* (1968) – could be similarly characterized.

Yet there are also Southern novelists who are far closer to mainstream realism while they still convey what it is like to live in a – usually small-town – Southern community. Like Faulkner, Eudora Welty (1909–2001) was born and raised in Mississippi, and she was obviously influenced by the older novelist. But she keeps away from his dramatic intensity and her characters lack the larger-than-life dimension that Faulkner often sought. Her novel *Delta Wedding* (1946) deals with the tensions within the feudal and very class-conscious extended Fairchild family – it is 1923 – which has gathered for a wedding. Nothing much happens, but through the interaction between the various family members, which is mediated by different observers (and, in one case, a diary), Welty subtly creates a full picture of the three Fairchild generations, including their feelings and attitudes. A much later novel, *Losing Battles* (1970), is another example of Welty's skill in creating a world out of overheard dialogue and deftly described gestures. The main event here is a 1930s family reunion, which gives full scope to her formidable mimic powers, and the main mood is one of nostalgia – family reunions revive the past and inevitably confront us with the passing of time. Since this is the rural South, that past has its share of violence and madness, but Welty never lingers on such horrors. In her novels and her short stories (collected in for instance *A Curtain of Green*, 1941, *The Golden Apples*, 1949, and *The Bride of Innisfallen*, 1955) she presents her characters with a compassion, even tenderness – as in the much anthologized story 'Petrified Man' (1941) – that situates her work on the side of comedy rather than that of tragedy. A younger writer indebted to Welty is Reynolds Price (1933–2011): 'One of the things she showed me as a writer was that the kinds of people I had grown up with were the kinds of people one could write marvelous fiction about'. Less genial and not always resisting the lure of the grotesque, Price's earlier novels and stories deal with the eventful lives of (usually rural) North Carolinians, as in *A Long and Happy Life* (1962), or present the sagas of North Carolina families, as in the novels constituting his *Mayfield Trilogy*. A last writer who must be mentioned here is the poet and critic Robert Penn Warren (1905–89), who wrote novels and stories about his native Kentucky and nearby Tennessee, but as a writer of fiction is mostly remembered for the novel *All the King's Men* (1946), loosely based upon the career of Louisiana's demagogic politician and one-time governor Huey Long, assassinated while serving as a U.S. senator. Warren would later say that his theme had been 'the kind of doom that democracy may invite upon itself'.

Warren's novel, primarily interested in the machinery and personalities of high-profile politics, hardly qualifies as regional writing. Much better candidates for that qualification are the novels of Wallace Stegner (1909–93) and Wright Morris (1910–98). Stegner, raised in Montana, Washington State, and other places (recounted in the autobiographical *Wolf Willow*, 1962), published a number of novels in which the West is the often grim background for a process of self-realization. *Angle of Repose* (1971), based upon the life and letters of the nine-teenth-century writer May Hallock Foote, relates the ultimately successful struggle of a 'Victorian gentlewoman' in western mining towns and also allows Stegner to juxtapose the authentic West with his narrator's countercultural 1960s environment. Morris, born and raised in Nebraska, tries in spare, low-keyed novels such as *My Uncle Dudley* (1942), *The Field of Vision* (1956), or *In Orbit* (1967) to capture life in small prairie towns where even trivial events may cause a seemingly disproportionate commotion. Trying to get even closer to actual life, he prints his own photographs of the most homely objects and places in for instance *The Home Place* (1948), showing us how time and the wear and tear of daily usage have lent them a character and an authenticity that words cannot convey.

Postwar drama

In the most important plays of the immediate postwar period the two main tendencies of 1930s and earlier 1940s drama come together. The concerns with economic hardship of the left-leaning playwrights of the prewar years – Clifford Odets and others – and the more existential themes of playwrights such as William Saroyan and Thornton Wilder (both active into the 1970s), who focused on individual lives and individual questions of meaning, combine in the work of new playwrights like Tennessee Williams, Arthur Miller, Lorraine Hansberry, and William Inge. Their work, together with the postwar plays by Eugene O'Neill, gave American drama an international visibility it had never had before. It must be said, however, without detracting from that achievement, that American drama's rise to prominence was partly the result of European influence. The acting techniques developed by the Russian actor and director Constantin Stanislavski had revolutionized American acting, leading to the naturalistic 'Method' acting style that characterized much 1950s drama (and serious film). The younger playwrights, attracted by 'Method' acting's insistence on veracity, sought to give their dialogues a similarly realistic flavor and more generally tried to stay close to actual American experience – usually that of the lower middle class – even if their plays often made use of non-realistic elements. And the increasingly important role of the director – the result of a new, again first of all European, view of the theatrical production as the director's imaginative creation on the basis of the playwright's text – gave new American dramatic productions a singleness of purpose that before the war had largely been lacking.

The first very well received play in which all this came together was *The Glass Menagerie* (1944) by Tennessee Williams (1911–83) which, like most of his plays, and many plays of the postwar years, focuses on vulnerable people seemingly trapped by circumstances or by their own illusions. Amanda Wingfield has been abandoned by her husband, years ago, and seeks refuge in dreaming about her younger years as a Southern belle. Her daughter, Laura, is in her twenties, painfully shy and insecure because she is a cripple, and her son, Tom, stuck in a dead-end job, dreams of being a writer but knows that he will never realize that ambition if he stays with his mother and sister. We know from the beginning that he will indeed abandon them. Tom is not only the play's major character, but he is also the play's narrator, addressing the audience when he makes his first appearance and telling them that he gives them 'truth in the pleasant disguise of illusion' and that he will turn back time, 'to that quaint period, the thirties'. *The Glass Menagerie* is a gripping, claustrophobic play that weaves a complex web of psychic trauma, selfishness, betrayal, and guilt, all of it made worse by the financial dire straits in which the Wingfield family finds itself. In *A Streetcar Named Desire* (1947), generally seen as one of the great American plays, Williams takes us to New Orleans (Desire is the name of a New Orleans neighborhood), where Blanche DuBois, another narcissistic aging belle, rather unexpectedly comes to stay with her sister Stella and the latter's rough, working-class husband Stanley Kowalski. Blanche, an alcoholic with a touch of nymphomania, is both pitiable – her husband has committed suicide and she has lost her once considerable property – and a constant source of tension. In the end, her sister's husband rapes her on the night his child is born. 'We had this date from the beginning', he tells her. The ever-mounting tension between them, the complex product of class prejudice, mutual dislike and physical chemistry, leads in a breath-taking scene to a terrifying explosion.

In *Streetcar*, too, Williams plays with theatrical conventions – we repeatedly hear the gunshot that killed Blanche's husband – and more openly than in *Menagerie*, where Tom seems a sexual outsider, he introduces the theme of homosexuality with the suggestion that the husband killed himself over a homosexual affair. This incident would seem to find an echo in what is considered to be Williams's third great play, *Cat on a Hot Tin Roof* (1955), in which the close friend of former football hero Brick Pollitt presumably kills himself because Brick, who may be homosexual himself, has rejected him. In *Cat*, which takes place on a Mississippi plantation, the Pollitt family has gathered to celebrate the birthday of its patriarch, 'Big Daddy', a rich cotton planter. In the course of the play the secrets of the various family members are gradually revealed, as is the fact, until then only known to his sons and their wives, that Big Daddy is dying of cancer. The jockeying for position – with an eye on their father's inheritance – between the alcoholic Brick and his brother Gooper, both assisted by their wives, is already underway, with new deceits taking the place of those that have been exposed.

Cat on a Hot Tin Roof is situated in an affluent milieu, but more usually Williams's themes of guilt, false and lost illusions, betrayal, and, more than occasionally, alcoholism and violence, are realized in milieus that place an additional burden on his characters. In plays like *Summer and Smoke* (1948), *Sweet Bird of Youth* (1959), or *The Night of the Iguana* (1961) their psychological or sexual frustrations are not exactly eased by the circumstances Williams chooses to create for them. A pessimistic romantic, Williams show us that his characters are more complex and quite often more admirable in their longing for a better life than we would expect, but also that in spite of their creator's obvious sympathy the defeatism that they cannot shake often is too much for them.

Like Williams, Arthur Miller (1915–2005) started writing in the 1930s, but had to wait a number of years for his first theatrical success. In *All My Sons* (1947) an otherwise decent manufacturer, more concerned with the fortunes of his business and his family than with the possible results of his action, knowingly sells engine parts that have been damaged during the production process to the military, indirectly causing the crash of twenty-one planes. Denying all involvement, he lets his manager go to jail. His wife knows, though, and when three years later the truth comes out he takes his own life, but not before Miller has engaged his characters, including the protagonist, in moral soul-searching and in intense confrontations with each other. Miller's most famous play, *Death of a Salesman* (1949), also presents a domestic drama against the background of America's business world. Willy Loman is a traveling salesman who must finally face that he is losing his touch. His two adult sons are failures who either cannot or do not want to hold a steady job. Deluding themselves – a recurrent theme in Miller's work – is the only thing they do really well. In the course of the play, which starts when Willy has prematurely returned from a tour, Willy and his son Biff finally face the truth about themselves. '"I am not a leader of men, Willy; and neither are you"', Biff tells his father. '"You were never anything but a hard-working drummer who landed in the ash can like the rest of them! I'm one dollar an hour, Willy! I tried seven states and couldn't raise it. A buck an hour!"' But although Willy can accept the truth about himself, he still refuses to see the truth about his sons. Having lost his job, he kills himself so that Biff will be able to start a business with the insurance money. But we, and Biff himself, know that this is just a new illusion.

Two years after his play had gone into production, Miller wrote that the 'common man' was 'as apt a subject for tragedy in its highest sense as kings were', and in the play it is Willy's wife Linda, who has been holding the family together, who presents this perspective: "'I don't say he is a great man. [...] He's not the finest character that ever lived. But he's a human being, and a terrible thing is happening to him. So attention must be paid. [...] Attention, attention must be finally paid to such a person'". Like Williams, Miller is concerned with dreams and illusion and like Williams he abandons a linear structure and reinforces his themes with symbolic elements. But while Williams tends towards psychological realism, Miller tends towards moralism and social realism, emphasizing the extent to which the social pressure to be successful and admired dominates and warps the lives of those who fail to meet that standard.

Miller's interest in how larger social issues shape individual lives and may result in private moral dilemmas is even more prominently present in another early play, *The Crucible* (1953), which takes place in the witchcraft-haunted Salem of 1692, but is a thinly veiled critique of the hysterical, Communist-obsessed McCarthy era. Unlike many of those who were summoned to testify in Salem, the play's John Proctor resists the pressure and values his moral integrity over his life, even though that integrity has already been compromised by an adulterous affair. Ironically, three years later Miller found himself under pressure to reveal the names of friends and acquaintances possibly involved with Communism. Much to his credit, he withstood the pressure and refused. In other, less successful plays of the 1950s and early 1960s, Miller focuses more on the psychological reality of his characters' lives. In *A View from the Bridge*, produced as a one-act play in 1955 and revised into a two-act play in 1956, the married protagonist disastrously falls in love with his niece, leading to an act of personal betrayal and his eventual death, and in *After the Fall* (1964) Miller's main character looks back on his past life, including a failed marriage to a singer – interpreted by many as Miller's own marriage to the movie star Marilyn Monroe. But by then Miller's plays no longer drew large audiences, his *The Creation of the World and Other Business* losing a quarter of a million dollars in 1972.

Miller's combination of social realism and moral critique – his insistence on individual responsibility – characterizes many early postwar plays, though those plays often tend to end on a happier note than Miller's own. In *Born Yesterday* (1946) by Garson Kanin (1912–99) a millionaire businessman is in Washington, D.C., to bribe a U.S. Senator. However, his uneducated and unsocialized young mistress, on whose cooperation he relies, does not only learn her manners but also begins to see his true character and ruins his schemes with the help of a new-found love. William Inge (1913–73), who situates his plays in the small-towns of the Midwest, leans more toward Williams in *Come Back, Little Sheba* (1950), in which a deeply unhappy marriage has sent its protagonist into alcoholism, or in the marginally more hopeful *Picnic* (1953) where an emotionally charged and more than ordinarily eventful small-town picnic party first obscures and then clarifies what the various characters, trapped in increasingly circumscribed lives, feel for each other. We also recognize Williams's influence in for instance *Tea and Sympathy* (1953) by Robert Anderson, a play about a possibly homosexual, but in any case 'different', boy in a New England boarding school, who must prove his 'manliness' to save himself from ignominy and ostracism.

Special mention must be made of Lorraine Hansberry (1930–65), whose *A Raisin in the Sun* (1959), the title of which was taken from Langston Hughes's poem 'A Dream Deferred', was the first play by an African American woman to be produced on Broadway. In Hansberry's play, which is indebted to Miller, the Youngers – Walter and his wife, his sister Beneatha, and their mother Lena – must decide how to spend 10,000 dollars insurance money. Walter, dreaming of (a male-inflected) independence, wants to invest the money in a liquor store, but Lena wants to move out of their home in a slum in Chicago's South Side and buy a house in a white neighborhood. Eventually, after Lena has made a down payment and Walter has lost the share of the money that she has given him, he comes round to her (and Beneatha's) point of view, but not after a struggle: the neighborhood, appalled at the idea of having blacks around, has in the meantime offered a great price for the house they have not yet moved into. Deeply insulted, Lena, Beneatha and Walter's wife don't even consider the offer and after much hesitation Walter joins them. The play thus ends on a positive note. But it also ends before the Youngers move to their new home and only the wildest optimists can have imagined that all will be well in their new surroundings. Hansberry wrote the play, which reflects the spirit of the Civil Rights movement, not long after the 1957 frenzy in Little Rock, Arkansas, where white segregationists attacked the first black students on their way to school. She was, moreover, thoroughly familiar with that sort of experience. *A Raisin* was based on her own parents' protracted and eventually successful litigation over racial housing restrictions, but does not make use of what happened after the Hansberry's moved to a white neighborhood: Lorraine, too, although a mere child, was 'spat at, cursed and pummeled in the daily trek to and from school', as we read in the posthumously published *To Be Young, Gifted, and Black* (1969). Hansberry had one other play produced before her early death, *The Sign in Sidney Brustein's Window* (1964), but its mixed cast of intellectualist (Greenwich Village) characters and its multiple themes – including race – did not convince either the reviewers or the audience.

Williams and Miller dominated the postwar stage with plays presenting psychological and moral conflicts – either between characters representing different views or in the shape of inner struggles – in mostly tough circumstances. Their focus on character and on truly American speech patterns demanded the sort of realism that 'Method' acting could perfectly provide, although it did not preclude non-linear structures or stagings with magical or fantastic elements. However, toward the end of the 1950s new themes and, more importantly, new views of the possibilities of drama took over. These views had their origin in so-called Off-Broadway drama, produced in smaller venues – between 199 and 299 seats – located on both sides of Broadway between 34th Street and 56th Street, which in the course of the fifties had become the more experimental rival of Broadway theater, especially through the efforts of Judith Malina and Julian Beck's Living Theatre, which had offered its first production in their Manhattan apartment in 1947, through Joe Papp's New York Shakespeare Festival (founded in 1954) and other, similarly innovative initiatives. Off-Broadway offered new and exciting productions of established plays, it gave playwrights a chance to test out new plays before they went to Broadway, and its most experimental-minded companies, like the Living Theatre, explored and continued European avant-garde theater (the Living Theatre in 1951 revived Alfred Jarry's amazingly whacky *Ubu Roi* of 1896), drawing on the French theorist Antonin Artaud's 'theater of cruelty'. But the Living Theatre also presented new American plays, such as *The Connection* (1959) by Jack Gelber (1932–2005) and *The Brig* (1963) by Kenneth H. Brown (1936), both too experimental and confrontational for Broadway audiences. In Gelber's play, influenced by Samuel Beckett's *Waiting for Godot*, we see drug addicts waiting for their dealer while listening to jazz music played by onstage musicians. Seeking interaction between actors and audience, directors Beck and Malina had the actors ostentatiously step out of their 'roles' and mingle with the audience during intermission, looking for heroin. *The Brig* recreates the fascist discipline to which U.S. marines were subjected in military prison – the play is based on Brown's own one-month detention – and shows rather than narrates its destructive character in cacophonous scenes of great (and intimidating) power. But with the Living Theatre's departure for Europe –

where they became the first American theater company to contribute to the development of European theater – the most vital Off-Broadway force was gone and when they returned to the American scene, in 1968, with the semi-improvisational and taboo-breaking *Paradise Now* – including what at the time was considered indecent exposure – it was on Off-Off-Broadway, in whose geographically dispersed small theaters American experimental drama had found a new base.

By that time, and in fact from the early sixties onwards, many Off-Broadway productions required such budgets that commercial success – and more mainstream appeal – was an absolute condition. As a result, Off-Broadway definitely became part of New York's theatrical establishment, although it remained more daring and innovative than standard Broadway theater. In 1960 *The Zoo Story* by the young playwright Edward Albee (1928) was deemed unfit for Broadway because of its flirtation with the absurd and its violent ending: on a bench in Central Park a middle-class family man is addressed by an apparently down-and-out young man whose increasing aggressiveness, which may be a plea for attention, ultimately leads to his being stabbed with his own knife, an event that he may well have intentionally provoked ("'Could I have planned all this. [...] I think I did'"). Still, only two years later Broadway welcomed Albee's savage *Who's Afraid of Virginia Woolf?* (1962), in which the middle-aged couple George and Martha viciously tear into each other, and in the process wreck the night, and possibly the marriage, of their younger guests Nick and Honey. Not surprisingly, some Broadway critics, not necessarily expecting a feel-good play but still upset by the verbal (and psychological) violence that Albee unleashed, accused him in no uncertain terms of a perverse view of American family life. In any case, with Broadway and Off-Broadway moving closer together – although Broadway, with lavishly produced musicals and other box-office draws, kept catering almost exclusively to mainstream taste – avant-gardist and experimental theater moved to the new and much cheaper venues of Off-Off-Broadway, but that is for a later discussion.

Postwar poetry

Looking back on the history of American poetry in his *Autobiography* (1951), William Carlos Williams lamented what he saw as the unwholesome influence of T.S. Eliot, even referring to the appearance of *The Waste Land* as 'the great catastrophe of our letters'. For Williams, Eliot's preference for the English poets of the seventeenth century and his disregard of American precursors was tantamount to a willful betrayal of the vision of Emerson and Whitman who had given authentic American experience (and language) a central place in American poetry. In 1951, Williams may have had reason for concern, but by the end of the fifties the balance had definitely tipped in his favor.

The state of affairs with regard to American poetry in the early postwar period is perfectly illustrated by the so-called 'anthology wars' that shook American letters in the late 1950s and early 1960s. In 1957 Donald Hall, Robert Pack, and Louis Simpson published a collection of postwar poetry, titled *The New Poets of England and America*, that presented the work of forty-eight poets, thirty-two of them American. Williams cannot have thought much of this throwing together of American and British poets which suggested a shared linguistic and referential framework that he would have contested in strong terms. However, in 1960 Donald Allen published a rival anthology, *The New American Poetry, 1945–1960* that must have been far more to his liking and that, rather amazingly, included not a single poet selected by Hall, Pack, and Simpson among its forty-four poets. Whereas the poets collected in Hall *et al.* are clearly influenced by the metrically and stylistically rather traditional art of for instance

Robert Frost, who provided an introduction, and the rather more complex academic poetry of T.S. Eliot, the poets presented by Allen chose experiment over tradition, preferring loose, open forms that were first of all indebted to Williams himself, and, in a lesser degree, to Ezra Pound.

What characterizes his poets, Allen tells us in his introduction, is 'a total rejection of all those qualities typical of academic verse'. No matter how different their individual programs, they all refuse to follow what Allen calls the 'second generation' of modern American poets. In fact, Allen's generations – his selection pretends to present the 'strong third generation', 'our avant-garde' – are not so much separated by the dividing line of age, as by that of a more traditional versus an experimental poetics. For the poets selected by Hall *et al.* – May Swenson (1913–89), Robert Bly (1926–), Howard Nemerov (1920–91), James Merrill (1926–), Anthony Hecht (1923–2004), Adrienne Rich (1929–2012), Robert Lowell, W.S. Merwin (1927–), Richard Wilbur (1921–), James Wright (1927–80), to name some of them – it is elegance, technical brilliance and mastery of form (which they all demonstrate in abundance), a usually mild irony, and a measure of detachment, that create aesthetically and intellectually satisfying poems. Form is of the essence, as Adrienne Rich argues in 'At a Bach Concert' (1951): 'Form is the ultimate gift that love can offer – [...] A too-compassionate art is half an art'. The expert hand of the poet patiently guides the poem towards completion, perfect closure, and leaves us with what at the very least is quietly meaningful. 'It is what we imagine knowledge to be', Elizabeth Bishop (1911–79) tells us at the end of 'The Fishhouses' (1955),

> dark, salt, clear, moving, utterly free,
> drawn from the cold hard mouth
> of the world, derived from the rocky breasts
> forever, flowing and drawn, and since
> our knowledge is historical, flowing and flown.

For these poets, the experience recorded is not necessarily their own. Robert Bly gives us 'A Missouri Traveller Writes Home: 1830' (1957), Robert Lowell (1917–77) 'The North Sea Undertaker's Complaint' (1944), May Swenson 'The Garden at St. John's' (1953), and W.S. Merwin imagines 'Leviathan' (1956), monster of the sea, who 'waits for the world to begin'. And in Richard Wilbur's more light-footed 'Love Calls Us to the Things of This World' (1956) '[t]he soul descends once more in bitter love', and, given a voice, imagines 'the heaviest nuns walk[ing] in a pure floating / Of dark habits / keeping their difficult balance'. The effect of the poet speaking for history, musing on historic locations (Rich's 'Versailles') or art (Swenson's 'On a Bas-Relief'), or using a persona's voice, in combination with the poem's closure, is to give it a vaguely timeless aura, to give discreet meaning to ordinary perception and to perception of the ordinary. Obviously, such effects may also be achieved if the poet's private history is mined, as in 'Those Winter Sundays' (1962) by the African American poet Robert Hayden (1913–80), which tells us how on winter Sundays, too, his hard-worked father got up before anyone else to make 'banked fires blaze' while 'No one ever thanked him'. But Hayden's final lines, 'What did I know, what did I know / of love's austere and lonely offices?' transcend the merely personal, as do those of James Merrill's 'An Urban Convalescence' (1962), which also starts with personal observations, but ends speaking of 'the dull need to make some kind of house / Out of the life lived, out of the love spent'.

This brief characterization of the sort of poetry collected in *New Poets* does not aim to criticize these poets, or their poetics, which, although fairly circumscribed, still allows each to have a distinctly individual voice. A substantial number of the poets anthologized in *New Poets of England and America* have in the past half century become solid fixtures in the American poetic canon, in which they are represented with the work published in the forties and fifties – showered with prizes and other honors – but also their later, often rather different work.

That later work is often directly influenced by the poets of Allen's 'avant-garde', who after the war rejected the idea of the well-made poem, of aesthetic and intellectual closure. That rejection is the dominant theme of one of the programmatic statements Allen includes, the essay 'Projective Verse' by Charles Olson (1910–70), who is also one of the anthology's leading poets. For Olson a poem is concentrated linguistic energy – 'the poem itself must, at all points, be a high-energy construct and, at all points, an energy-discharge' – which the poet not so much creates but makes possible: 'From the moment he ventures into FIELD COMPOSI-TION – puts himself in the open – he can go by no track other than the one the poem under his hand declares, for itself'. Rhyme, metrical patterns, ironic wit, erudite allusions, and other hallmarks of academic poetry have no place in this process. They are the tell-tale signs of an authorial control that is counter-productive. What Olson is after is not poetic control, but humility. We must, he argues, 'get rid of the lyrical interference of the individual as ego, of the "subject" and his soul, that peculiar presumption by which western man has interposed himself between what he is as a creature of nature [...] and those other creatures of nature which we may, with no derogation, call objects'. Not all the poets anthologized by Allen renounced 'the lyrical interference of the individual as ego' as strongly as Olson, but they all sympathized with his search for immediacy – 'If there is any absolute, it is never more than this one, you, this instant, in action' – and his plea for openness.

Williams, who died in 1963, will have been pleased to see that Olson followed the example of *Paterson* with an epic of his own, *The Maximus Poems*, of which sections 1–10 appeared in 1953 and sections 11–23 in 1958. Through its central consciousness Maximus, the poem, which Olson worked on till his death, focuses on the past and present of his home town, Gloucester, Massachusetts. But Williams will have been even more pleased to see that most of the poets selected for inclusion in *The New Poets of England and America* gradually abandoned their form-alism and their detachment and opted for looser, more flexible forms and a far more personal, often intimate voice. This poetic change of heart marks the careers of two of the most promi-nent poets of the earlier postwar years, Robert Lowell, undisputedly America's leading postwar poet until his relatively early death, and John Berryman, but also of for instance James Wright, Adrienne Rich, and Robert Bly. Rich turned to a far more open, fragmented form in the late 1950s, and in the poems collected in *Snapshots of a Daughter-in-Law* (1963) began a process of self-definition and feminist intervention that made her one of the most important female poets (and essayists) of the later twentieth century. James Wright finds in a chance encounter with the natural world a (rare) moment of intensely private happiness – 'Suddenly I realize / That if I stepped out of my body I would break / Into blossom' ('A Blessing', 1963). And Robert Bly begins to develop what came to be called 'Deep Image' poetry, in which through techniques borrowed from expressionism and surrealism the poet seeks to give free, or at least freer, rein to the unconscious, as in Bly's 'Driving Toward the Lac Qui Parle River' (1962), where the logical impossibilities of Bly's language serve to create arresting and lasting images:

Nearly to Milan, suddenly a small bridge,
And water kneeling in the moonlight.
In small towns the houses are built right on the ground;
The lamplight falls on all fours in the grass.

During the 1970s, Bly's 'Deep Image' poetry had considerable influence, but the 'academic' poet whose change of heart had the most impact was no doubt Robert Lowell.

In his early work, Lowell (1917–77), who studied with New Critics John Crowe Ransom and Allen Tate, was clearly influenced by New Critical poetics and by the dense, intellectual poetry of the later T.S. Eliot, from whose shadow he would only gradually escape. 'The Quaker Graveyard at Nantucket' (from *Lord Weary's Castle*, 1946), from which the following lines are taken, is a long meditation on the death of a shipwrecked cousin and other sailors lost at sea that brings in Melville's *Moby-Dick* and a Roman Catholic shrine in Norfolk, England, before it returns to Nantucket and 'the time / When the Lord God formed man from the sea's slime':

> A brackish reach of shoal off Madakat –
> The sea was still breaking violently and night
> Had steamed into our North Atlantic Fleet,
> When the drowned sailor clutched at the drag-net. Light
> Flashed from his matted head and marble feet,
> He grappled at the net.

It is only Lowell's technical skills that prevent the death of his cousin Warren Winslow from becoming the mere starting point for a rather majestic intellectual and religious exercise that is capped by a climactic last line – 'The Lord survives the rainbow of His will'. The urge to arrive at an intense outburst of meaning – in which the personal or historical event disappears in a blaze of universal light – also characterizes the dramatic monologues of *The Mills of the Kavanaughs* (1951), but in *Life Studies*, published in 1959, Lowell has found a way to directly confront himself and his psychic problems – for which he was more than once hospitalized – in a language that almost surreptitiously still clings to form but is far more colloquial and relaxed than the dense language of his earlier work and that allows him precisely to articulate the most private emotions:

> A car radio bleats,
> 'Love, O careless Love. [...] ' I hear
> my ill-spirit sob in each blood cell,
> as if my hand were at its throat. [...]
> I myself am hell;
> nobody's here –

'Skunk Hour'

Life Studies is one of the highlights of what soon came to be called 'confessional poetry', a mode in which poets take the reader into their confidence, share their most intimate thoughts, humiliations, fears, emotional wounds, and substitute a psychoanalytically inflected and individual perception of reality for the social or historical but always depersonalized approach of the 1940s and earlier 1950s. Not accidentally, confessional poetry proved especially attractive to poets who, like Lowell, had histories of mental turmoil and who sought to confront their demons in their work. Their work inevitably invites larger interpretational frameworks – the poet's fragile mental state may well reflect the human condition – but focuses first of all on their very private worlds.

With *Life Studies*, which had been influenced by Allen Ginsberg's 'Howl' of 1955 and by the work of W.D. Snodgrass (*Heart's Needle*, 1959), one of his students in the Iowa Writers' Workshop, Lowell had crossed a barrier and in *Imitations* (1961) he freely rewrote classic European poems and, definitively distancing himself from the English tradition, made them quintessentially American. *For the Union Dead* (1964) is as personal as, although less 'confessional' than, *Life Studies*, but continues his exploration of free form, as in the poem of the title, which begins with a youthful memory of the Boston Aquarium:

> Once my nose crawled like a snail on the glass;
> my hand tingled
> to burst the bubbles
> drifting from the noses of the cowed, compliant fish

and ends with what seems a condemnation of motorized America that brilliantly returns us to the opening lines:

> The Aquarium is gone. Everywhere,
> giant finned cars nose forward like fish;
> a savage servility
> slides by on grease.

In *Notebook 1967–1968* (1969), Lowell presents over 270 very free, non-rhyming sonnets, which he revised and regrouped in later publications. Dealing with both intensely private and historical events, he kept searching for forms that would give adequate shape to experience. 'Those blessed structures, plot and rhyme – / why are they no use to me' he asks in 'Epilogue', the last poem of his final collection *Day by Day* (1977). In 'Epilogue' he also confronts that other problem that especially troubled poets who sought to distance themselves from the timelessness prized by Eliot and the New Critics: 'sometimes everything I write / [...] / seems a snapshot, / lurid, rapid, garish, grouped, / heightened from life, / yet paralyzed by fact'. How to give life as it is lived the resonance that poetry demands? But 'Epilogue' also offers the solution: 'Yet why not say what happened?' What the poet needs above all else is 'the grace of accuracy'.

This brings Lowell close to Olson, even if he never completely gives up the idea of poetry as an intensely controlled craft, and it is fair to say that sooner or later almost all postwar poets sought to stay as close as possible to actual experience. We see this most clearly in Lowell's fellow so-called 'Confessional' poets, and in a poet like Theodore Roethke (1908–63), whose autobiographical poems about the world of his childhood – spent around and in the green-houses of his father – and later breakdowns prefigure the 'Confessional' poets' rendering of traumatic and/or enduring emotional states: 'With everything blooming above me, / Lilies, pale-pink cyclamen, roses, / Whole fields lovely and inviolate, – / Me down in the fetor of weeds, / Crawling on all fours, / Alive, in a slippery grave' ('Weed Puller', 1948).

Like Lowell, John Berryman (1914–72) began with rather traditional poetry but in 1956 he published *Homage to Mistress Bradstreet*, a very long poem (57 eight-line stanzas), which tries to recreate with extraordinary emotional intensity the way the Puritan poet experienced her world. Its voice is, in fact, closer to that of Edward Taylor in its transports of faith or despair than to that of Bradstreet as we know it from her poetry. Clearly, Berryman uses her as a vehicle for his own wild swings of emotion – he, too, suffered serious mental problems – and in his 'dream songs' (*77 Dream Songs*, 1964; *His Toy, His Dream, His Rest*, 1968) he reveals his anguish and despair in almost 400 poems in which he uses a fairly traditional form (three six-line stanzas with irregular rhyme) with a good deal of flexibility. Presenting an uninhibited but relatively life-like version of himself as 'Henry', but also operating in other guises – as a blackface minstrel, complete with the minstrel's idiolect – Berryman has found a form in which he can relive traumatic experiences and express his not always civilized desires – 'only the fact of her husband & four other people / kept me from springing on her' ('Dream Song' #4) – but in which he can also ironize those traumas and desires. A recurring trauma is that of his father's suicide, outside Berryman's window, when he was twelve years old: 'The marker slants, flowerless, day's almost done, / I stand above my father's grave with rage, / often, often before / I've made this awful pilgrimage' ('Dream Song' #384). Through his alter egos, Berryman creates a theatrical space in which mental illness, alcoholism, sexual obsession, the love/hate relationship with the father figure and other themes can be presented with high seriousness, with outrage, but also with vaudeville humor and broad jokes.

We find a similar helpless rage against the father in the famous 'Daddy' by Sylvia Plath (1932–63), another prominent 'Confessional' poet, who suffered from severe depressions and like Berryman chose to end her own life. Trying to exorcize the father, who died and in a sense abandoned her when she was eight years old, she painfully associates him with Nazism:

> I was ten when they buried you.
> At twenty I tried to die
> And get back, back, back to you.
> I thought even the bones would do.
>
> But they pulled me out of the sack,
> And they stuck me together with glue.
> And then I knew what to do.
> I made a model of you,
> A man in black with a Meinkampf look.

('Daddy', 1962)

In the last phase of her life Plath created an astonishing oeuvre, published posthumously (*Ariel*, 1965; *Crossing the Water*, 1971; *Winter Trees*, 1972), in which striking images and raw yet perfectly controlled emotion create poems of great intensity. A deep-felt anger is a recurring theme, but she does not need rage to find the perfect image. In 'Morning Song' she is 'cow-heavy and floral / In my Victorian nightgown' after the birth of her son, and in 'Blackberrying', where she is picking berries near the sea, 'From between two hills a sudden wind funnels at me, / Slapping its phantom laundry in my face'. The ordinary finds extraordinary, almost visual expression. Plath had attended the poetry seminar Robert Lowell gave at Boston University when he was writing the poems collected in *Life Studies*, but she would in all probability have found her clinically ferocious voice anyway – 'Dying / Is an art, like everything else. / I do it exceptionally well'. Plath's poetry is often mentioned with that of her friend Anne Sexton (1928–74), who also studied with Lowell, but Sexton's work relies more on narration. The only contemporary poem that achieves Plath's intensity is Allen Ginsberg's 'Kaddish' (1961), especially in the harrowing passages that deal with the worst excesses of his deceased mother's madness.

Still, although the so-called 'confessional' poets had learned to 'say what happened', to quote Lowell, they never felt quite at home with truly ordinary experience, with the apparently trivial. It is among Donald Allen's new American poets that the sort of poetics Williams had espoused is actively embraced. In his collection Allen distinguished a number of writing communities that would become even more canonized than most of the poets he included. 'Black Mountain' gathered the writers affiliated in one way or another with Black Mountain College in North Carolina, where Charles Olson had first been visiting professor and had then become rector, or with its *Black Mountain Review*. This group included next to Olson himself Robert Creeley, Denise Levertov, Robert Duncan, Paul Blackburn, Edward Dorn, Joel Oppenheimer, and John Wieners. Allen's New York Poets included John Ashbery, Barbara Guest, Frank O'Hara, and Kenneth Koch, and his controversially named San Francisco Renaissance groups together widely differing poets such as Lawrence Ferlinghetti, Jack Spicer, Brother Antoninus, and Michael McClure, but also Robert Duncan, who was both at Black Mountain and at least for a while the leading San Francisco poet. Allen's Beat Generation rounds up the familiar names – Ginsberg, Kerouac, Gregory Corso – and adds Gary Snyder, whose fascination with the natural world of the Northwest puts him somewhat apart from the others. He also might have added the only African American poet in these two anthologies, LeRoi Jones, who was part of the New York Beat milieu before he turned away from 'white' writing in the course of the 1960s, but who is here part of a fifth group that has no specific poetic identity.

For these poets, ordinary experience is its own validation, not in need of reflective or mythologizing layers, while the creative act is fundamentally open-ended and not in search of either intellectual or aesthetic closure. It must at all times be able to respond to new experience or to follow fresh insights or associations. Since closure seems false to the continuum of experience, poems often seem unfinished, tentative, while in the absence of controlling themes or ideas they may seem diffuse, without direction. As A.R. Ammons (1926–2001) put it in his 'Grace Abounding':

> I don't know about you
> but I'm sick of good poems, all those little rondures
> splendidly brought off, painted gourds on a shelf: give me
> the dumb, debilitated, nasty, and massive, if that's the
> alternative: touch the universe anywhere you touch it
> everywhere

And so we hear, in the same poet's 'Corsons Inlet', a long and detailed description of a walk written in 1962, that the poet is

> released from forms
> from the perpendiculars,
> straight lines, blocks, boxes, binds
> of thought
> into the hues, shadings, rises, flowing bends and blends
> of sight

And at the end, returning home, the poet, refusing to impose mental patterns on the world around him, to make it subservient to human consciousness, has 'reached no conclusions' and has 'erected no boundaries'.

Ammons's irregular and idiosyncratic layout, which optimizes the impact of single words and lines, borrows from Olson's Maximus poems and is a recurring feature of the anti-academic poetry, a visual reminder of its experimental ambitions. However, in 'The Day Lady Died' Frank O'Hara (1926–66), with John Ashbery the most prominent 'New York' poet, opts for a more traditional form to follow the 'bends and blends' of actual experience on the day the jazz singer Billie Holliday died:

It is 12:20 in New York a Friday
three days after Bastille day, yes
it is 1959 and I go get a shoeshine
[...]
and I am sweating a lot by now and thinking of
leaning on the john door in the 5 SPOT
while she whispered a song along the keyboard
to Mal Waldron and everyone and I stopped breathing

Arguably O'Hara moves toward closure here, but more usually his poems offer witty conversational information that never fails to charm the reader but still manages to convey the urgency
of the present moment. His fellow 'New York' poet John Ashbery (1927–) employs a similarly
colloquial voice, but only to lead us into surreal labyrinths of irony and wit where we are then
ruthlessly abandoned. Sidetracked by ever new, often amusing, but always incomplete and
seemingly random fragments of narration, we never manage to find our way back to what
may (or may not) be the poem's elusive highway:

There would be thunder in the bushes, a rustling of coils,
And Angelica, in the Ingres painting, was considering
The colorful but small monster near her toe, as though
wondering whether forgetting
The whole thing might not, in the end, be the only solution.
And then there always came a time when
Happy Hooligan in his rusted green automobile
Came plowing down the course, just to make sure everything
was O.K.,
Only by that time we were in another chapter and confused
About how to receive this latest piece of information.

('Soonest Mended')

'I'm trying', Ashbery tells us, 'to accurately portray states of mind, ones of my own that I think
might have a general application, and the movement of the mind and the way we think
and forget and discover and forget some more'. The world of his poems consists of an endless
variety of always articulate voices – questioning, banal, excited, self-centered – that keep on
changing direction and do not necessarily connect, illustrating the indeterminacy and multi-
interpretability of experience. Like Ashbery, but less elaborately, Mark Strand (1934), who
came to prominence somewhat later, presents flowing and atmospheric enigmas in which
seductive voices hint at events, stories, and characters without ever providing the clarity – and
closure – the reader half expects.

Black Mountain poet Robert Creeley (1926–2005) creates resonant bewilderment in spare,
laconic poetry, as in the famous 'I Know a Man' in which the speaker, somewhat incoherently
musing on the meaning of life during a night-time ride, mostly suceeds in alarming his
passenger:

drive, he sd, for
christ's sake, look
out where yr going.

But in spite of appearances, Ashbery, Strand, and Creeley are too rational, too ironic, to be lured by the mystical. Among the New York and Black Mountain poets only Robert Duncan (1919–88), raised by foster-parents who were deeply interested in the occult, came close to mysticism in his highly erudite and often hermetic poetry which puts high value on myth and its supposed capacity to interpret our experience for us. His belief in cosmic wholeness, in the interrelatedness of all of creation – shared by the otherwise less mystically inclined Olson – created a link with West Coast Beats like Ginsberg and Snyder who were interested in, and influenced by, Zen Buddhism (Snyder even spent long periods in Japan to study Buddhism). While Ginsberg's interest in Buddhism – advertised in for instance the title of his 'Sunflower Sutra' (1955), which features Jack Kerouac, or in the 'I have mystical visions and cosmic vibrations' from 'America' (1956) – seems rather superficial, in Snyder (1930) Buddhism's humility vis-à-vis the natural world informs his whole outlook. In 'Milton by Firelight' (1959) Milton's *Paradise Lost* is reduced to 'a silly story / Of our lost general parents, / eaters of fruit', while what counts, up in California's Sierras, is

> Working with an old
> Singlejack miner, who can sense
> The vein and cleavage
> In the very guts of rock, can
> Blast granite, build
> Switchbacks that last for years
> Under the beat of snow, thaw, mule-hooves.

From such a perspective the consumer culture of 1950s America is an abomination, as these poets repeatedly tell us. In his 'A Supermarket in California' Ginsberg, imagining that he meets Walt Whitman, wonders if they will 'stroll dreaming of the lost America of love past blue automobiles in driveways', while Lawrence Ferlinghetti (1919), in 'A Coney Island of the Mind' (1958), compares his fellow Americans to the 'people of the world' in Francisco Goya's harrowing paintings, only still 'further from home / on freeways fifty lanes wide / on a concrete continent / spaced with bland billboards / illustrating imbecile illusions of happiness'.

Here, as in their resistance to the Vietnam War – Robert Lowell was a prominent participant in the famous 1967 march on the Pentagon – the 'avant-garde' and the more traditional and academic poets found common ground, and a number of them were publicly involved in the protest movements of the sixties. But they also increasingly found common ground in a shared poetics that privileged authentic experience and that made it as directly and as precisely as possible available to the reader. Popular culture and demotic language no longer conflicted with academic form or erudite allusion, as Berryman's 'dream songs' illustrated, and could be combined in poems that employed the full range of forms from Ginsberg's expansive, Whitmanian, line and vatic tone, to the terse descriptions of Snyder. Most of the poetry of the later sixties and of the seventies steers a middle course between such extremes. Borrowing from their 'Confessional' colleagues, poets write lyrical free verse informed by autobiographical details and concerns. 'I was with some friends. / Picking my way through a warm sunlit piazza / In the early morning', Anthony Hecht (1923–2004) tells us in 'A Hill' (1967). Many poems of the period are characterized by a similarly narrative style paced by seemingly trivial details that firmly fix the autobiographical character of the narrator's experience in our mind. These are the first lines of 'Cherrylog Road' (1964) by James Dickey, that in its 100-plus lines rivals fiction in its evocation of place and social milieu:

Off Highway 106
At Cherrylog Road I entered
The '34 Ford without wheels,
Smothered in Kudzu,
With a seat pulled out to run
Corn whiskey down from the hills,

And then from the other side
Crept into an Essex
With a rumble seat of red leather [...]

Naturally, such verse does not have to be free, but when the poet decides on, for instance, rhyme, it is as unobtrusive as possible:

My old room! Its wallpaper – cream, medallioned
With pink and brown – brings back the first nightmares,
Long summer colds, and Emma, sepia-faced,
Perspiring over broth carried upstairs
Aswim with golden fats I could not taste.

(James Merrill, 'The Broken Home', 1965)

This poetry presents itself as realistic and as modest in its ambition, pretending first of all to observe and to record. In both its narrative and its more meditative modes, it strives for transparency and precision, employing a neutral diction and carefully selecting images that do not only support its realist pretension but also catch the reader's attention. Yet towards the end most of these poems cut themselves loose and take off in an appeal to the reader's imagination. In 'Cherrylog Road' apotheosis, Dickey's younger self is 'Wild to be wreckage forever', and Merrill ends with the hope that someone, looking from his old window, may 'Watch a red setter stretch and sink in cloud'.

But not every single poet of the early postwar period turned to a lyrical poetry that centered on autobiographical moments – which does not exclude a historical or social dimension – and had strong narrative elements. For the so-called Deep Imagists that followed in Robert Bly's tracks, this poetry was too rational, too controlled, too afraid of the illogical, and not enough driven by the imagination. For a poet like Gwendolyn Brooks (1917–2000), who in 1950 became the first African American poet to win the Pulitzer Prize for her collection *Annie Allen* (1949), it lacked political engagement. From observing Black life as it was lived in Chicago's Bronzeville in her technically accomplished early poems (*A Street in Bronzeville*, 1945; *Bronzeville Boys and Girls*, 1956), she moves to the freer and more immediately political poetry exemplified by for instance 'The Last Quatrain of the Ballad of Emmett Till' (1960), a poem about a young African American boy murdered by Mississippi racists. In the late 1960s she would become increasingly militant, not only in matters of race, but also with regard to the position of African American women. We see a similar development in the work of other, somewhat younger, African American poets like Audre Lorde (1934–92), LeRoi Jones/Imamu Amiri Baraka (1934–), and Michael Harper (1938–), who all write from a deep moral concern with Black history and the present state of racial relations in the United States. In what is an ambivalent homage to John Berryman, 'Tongue-Tied in Black and White' (1975), Harper cannot accept the white poet's posing as a blackface minstrel: 'Now I must take up our quarrel / [...] / you wrote in that needful black idiom / offending me, for only your inner voices / spoke such tongues'. But we will return to African American writers in a later section. Finally, there are poets who after a rather conventional beginning steered their own unique course. *First Poems 1946–1954* (1970) by Galway Kinnell (1927) still invests heavily in form, but in for instance the later poems in which he pays tribute to the natural world, to its cycle of life and death, and what it has to teach us ('The Bear', 1968; 'The Porcupine', 1969), his verse is completely free, totally his own. But not every single voice in a period so rich in talent can be discussed within the limitations of this book.

Fiction: the sixties and the seventies

While the postwar poetry that took its cue from William Carlos Williams reveled right from the start in its freedom to experiment, fiction, with some exceptions, only became seriously interested in experiment in the course of the 1960s. We have John Hawkes's abandonment of character and plot in favor of what he saw as a wholeness of vision, we have the at the time shocking irreverence of *The End of the Road* (1956) by John Barth (1930), a debut novel which very deliberately rides roughshod over everything held sacred by the American middle class (marital fidelity, getting ahead in life, religious values, the majestic objectivity of the law) and we have the astonishing labyrinth created by William Gaddis (1922–98) in his massive first novel *The Recognitions* (1955), by turns lyrical and satirical in its complex exploration of originality and imitation through a painter turned forger. Gaddis's book would point the way for later equally massive and labyrinthine efforts like John Barth's *The Sot-Weed Factor* (1960), a bawdy, high-octane satire featuring the early eighteenth-century poet Ebenezer Cook(e), and his *Giles Goat-Boy* (1966), a complicated allegory in which the world has morphed into a literally ubiquitous university, *Gravity's Rainbow* (1973) by Thomas Pynchon (1937), which will be discussed below, and Gaddis's own *JR* (1976), an even more demanding novel because Gaddis chooses to create its world – big business, with all the corruption and shady dealings one would expect – largely through voices, mostly that of his eleven-year-old wheeler and dealer J.R. Vansant, with few or even no clues as to who is actually talking at any given moment. Like *Gravity's Rainbow*, the novel is an exhilarating ride on a verbal rollercoaster – if the reader manages to find something to hold on to. Especially these last books deliberately tax the reader's capacity for imagining the world they create. We get such an overload of information that processing it becomes a difficult task and the suggestion is that the world we live in is equally 'unreadable', so complex and chaotic that it, too, ultimately eludes our grasp. The 'seething of history', as Pynchon calls it in a much later novel (*Against the Day* of 2006), produces no meaning.

These novels inevitably call attention to their status as verbal artifact, as do other early experimental novels like William Burroughs's *Naked Lunch* (1959) or *Pale Fire* (1962) by the Russian-born Vladimir Nabokov (1899–1977), a mad line-by-line commentary on a long and intentionally mediocre poem by a character who imagines himself to be a Northern Slavonic king in exile. (Some critics see Nabokov's earlier and highly controversial *Lolita* (1955), which details a pedophile's 'affair' with a 12-year-old girl, as another strictly verbal game, but that ignores its brilliant exploration of sexual obsession against a background of 1950s Americana.) In the course of the 1960s and 1970s we get a whole range of these so-called postmodern novels – postmodern because they are skeptical and ironic about modernism's high seriousness and its belief that art can somehow transcend the frenzy and commodification of everyday existence and offer lasting truth and insight. For postmodern writers, the comforts of Christianity, of all-encompassing philosophical systems such as those of Hegel and Marx, of the Enlightenment idea of an inexorable march toward reason and social harmony, or even of psychoanalytic explanations of human behaviour, must be viewed with the greatest suspicion.

Flaunting this skepticism, postmodern fiction deliberately reveals itself as a linguistic construct, leaving it to us to connect that construct to the reality we know (or think we know). It signals its constructedness in any number of ways, announcing itself as metafiction, a term coined by the writer/philosopher William Gass (1924) that refers to fiction that either directly or indirectly comments on the fiction-making process. (Most of Gass's own fiction, such as his novel *Omensetter's Luck*, 1966, or the brilliantly enigmatic novella 'The Pedersen Kid', 1968, makes a misleadingly realistic impression.) In *Snow-White* (1967) by Donald Barthelme (1931–89), an off-beat rewriting of the well-known fairytale, we are suddenly confronted with a questionnaire which, amongst other things, wants to know if we understand what we are reading and if we have, so far, enjoyed the reading experience. In the first chapter of *Alphabetical Africa* (1974) by Walter Abish (1931), in a procedure borrowed from the French OULIPO writers, all words begin with the letter 'a' ('Africa again: Albert arrives, alive and arguing about African art, about African angst, and also, alas, attacking Ashanti architecture'). In the second chapter, all words begin with either 'a' or 'b'. In every following chapter, another letter is added until in chapter twenty-six the procedure is reversed. In *Up* (1968) by Ronald Sukenick (1932–2004), *Slaughterhouse-Five* (1969) by Kurt Vonnegut (1922–2007), *Double or Nothing* (1971) by Raymond Federman (1928–2009), *LETTERS* (1979) by John Barth, and many other novels, the author himself makes an appearance in his fiction, violating the boundary between the real world and the fictional one and thus creating intractable ontological problems. In *Mulligan Stew* (1979) by Gilbert Sorrentino (1929–2006), in which the author Tony Lamont is trying to write a novel, Lamont's characters are 'free' whenever he does not actually use them in a scene and bitterly criticize his incompetence. In Barth's *LETTERS* we find, next to the author, characters lifted from his earlier novels, so that the earlier fictional worlds Barth created more or less coalesce to create a new fictional reality. But fictional worlds may also break up: in 'The Babysitter' (1969) and other stories by Robert Coover (1932) the reader is, without further explanation, offered rather different versions of one and same story. Using a single starting-point, Coover develops various fictional possibilities.

For the postmodern novelists nothing is impossible and nothing is sacred. Fictional characters are lifted from respected classics and put to work in new fictional environments. In his *Ragtime* (1975) E.L. Doctorow (1931) lifts both a character (the African American Coalhouse Walker) and the subplot that he features in from the German writer Heinrich von Kleist's novella *Michael Kohlhaas* (1811). Disregarding another ontological boundary, Robert Coover, in his *The Universal Baseball Association, Inc. J. Henry Waugh, Prop.* (1968), lets characters created by his protagonist come to life in a world from which its creator has mysteriously disappeared. In Coover's *The Public Burning* (1977), an important postmodern novel that centers on the 1953 execution for high treason of Ethel and Julius Rosenberg, then vice-president Richard Nixon declares Ethel his love, just before she and her husband are publicly executed in New York City's Times Square, as the high point of a carnivalesque spectacle.

To signal their suspicion of so-called all-explanatory 'grand narratives' or 'deep structures', postmodern writers create 'flat' worlds or worlds that confusingly alternate 'flatness' and 'depth'. Although rarely simply caricatural, the characters of postmodern fiction are equally rarely the fully believable, seemingly authentic characters of modernist or realist fiction and usually oscillate between cartoon-like surface and humanist depth. In *Mumbo Jumbo* (1972) by the African American writer Ishmael Reed (1938) we meet Biff Musclewhite, PaPa LaBas, and Hinckle Von Vampton (sole survivor of the Knights Templar in the modern world). Thomas Pynchon's *Crying of Lot 49* (1966) introduces Mike Fallopian, Manny DiPresso, and a psychoanalyst not accidentally called Hilarius. The effect, in an inversion of our general approach to fictional characters, is not to take them seriously until the narrative actually invites us to do so.

But even then we are free to refuse the invitation. Since postmodern fiction is so ambivalent in its strategies, and shifts the responsibility for interpretation rather insistently to the reader, we have a great leeway in responding to its worlds, greater than realism or modernism ever permitted.

That leeway is the result of postmodern writing's characteristic tendency to be both referential and non-referential. It presents us with two incompatible sets of reading instructions: we encounter textual elements that strongly suggest referentiality and create the illusion of reality as we know it, and elements that expressly counteract such an illusion and tell us that we are not dealing with authentic reality at all. In other words, we get textual elements that suggest depth and meaning and invite traditional interpretation, while simultaneously other textual elements will flaunt their distance from the world we know and ridicule interpretational initiatives. For readers unsympathetic to such a strategy, what results is white noise. For readers more inclined to give it the benefit of the doubt, it sets up an intriguing dialogue between referentiality and non-referentiality, between realism and anti-realism, between historical verisimilitude and anti-history.

Because of its anti-referential elements and its skeptical and ironic stance, postmodern fiction is often seen as apolitical and morally vapid. But such a view ignores how it fundamentally questions everything that was (and is) taken for granted, including the nature and the power of fiction – and art in general. And such questioning does not rule out moral seriousness. Kurt Vonnegut began his career as a writer of serious, politically motivated science fiction: *Player Piano* (1952), *Sirens of Titan* (1959), *Cat's Cradle* (1963). In the novel that is regarded as the high point of his career, *Slaughterhouse Five; or The Children's Crusade* (1969), this interest recurs in its protagonist who believes that he has once been kidnapped by aliens and can now at will travel to their far-off planet where all the problems that plague us here on Earth are of no consequence. But the novel is also a grim account of the aftermath of the terrible firebombing, in February 1945, of the German town of Dresden – which Vonnegut, a prisoner of war in Dresden, had witnessed – and of the inhuman absurdities and cruelties of war. Vonnegut's crossing the ontological barrier between the novel's fictional world and historical reality – 'That was I. That was me. That was the author of this book' – only serves to heighten its impact.

Ishmael Reed's *Mumbo Jumbo* likewise combines narrative antics with deep seriousness, suggesting that the exuberant vitality of black culture – illustrated by the novel itself – is necessary to transform repressive and moribund mainstream American culture and give it a new lease on life. Robert Coover's *The Public Burning* is a fierce attack on the political paranoia and moral blindness of the McCarthy era, even if it takes fantastic liberties with historical reality. Those liberties remind us again and again of the imagined character of the events the novel presents, but in spite of that still magnify the era's moral failures. The liberties that Vonnegut, Reed, and Coover allow themselves pale before the outrageous flights of fantasy of Thomas Pynchon in *Gravity's Rainbow*. Pynchon's first novel, *V.* (1962), a complex, multi-faceted story about the unknowability of history and the futility of experience, had its share of absurdities – among which a hunt for alligators in New York City's sewers – but *Gravity's Rainbow* is *hors concours* in terms of outlandish inventiveness. Sharing its theme of large-scale conspiracy by conspirators unknown – 'They'– and the tendency of its characters to burst spontaneously into song with *V.* and *The Crying of Lot 49*, the novel does not blink in presenting a mega-adenoid, a perfectly trained giant octopus, a main character whose erections correctly predict the places where German rockets will come down in wartime London, and much more that is at first sight merely absurd. It is, indeed, not impossible that a good deal of this *is* merely absurd. *Gravity's Rainbow* is such a labyrinthine, fragmented, and overloaded book – it introduces over four hundred characters – that a coherent reading is impossible. But what emerges from its absurdities, black humor, and often dream-like scenes (which may in fact be dreams), is the appalling reality of war and, more particularly, the sadistic violence, rooted in emotional disorders, of German Nazism. And behind the scenes a sinister, shadowy cluster of interests is out to keep the world on fire.

It has often been noticed that virtually all postmodern writers are male, with the punk-influenced Kathy Acker (1947?–1997) being something of a token exception. The female authors of the sixties and seventies did indeed overwhelmingly opt for the realist mode. Short-story writers like Grace Paley (1922–2007) – *The Little Disturbances of Man* (1959); *Enormous Changes at the Last Minute* (1974) – and Tillie Olsen (1913–2007) – *Tell Me a Riddle* (1961) – present charged moments and emotional crises, but also trivial events in the lives of their mostly female protagonists. These stories, as Olsen's 'I Stand Here Ironing', often have an implicitly feminist theme. That theme is far more explicit in the novels written by the younger generation of female writers that start to appear in the 1960s. Sylvia Plath's *The Bell Jar* (1963), Sue Kaufman's *Diary of a Mad Housewife* (1967), Erica Jong's *Fear of Flying* (1973), Diane Johnson's *The Shadow Knows* (1974), Marilyn French's *The Women's Room* (1977) and other, thematically related, novels all in their own way show us that in a deeply patriarchal environment women must actively assert themselves to achieve emotional, let alone financial, independence (the 'flying' of Jong's title). In *The Shadow Knows* the ultimate humiliation of being raped makes its nameless narrator ('N') finally realize that she has to fight for a life that is wholly her own. Other writers, like Alison Lurie (1926) in *Love and Friendship* (1962) and *The War Between the Tates* (1974) show us how the sexual liberation of the sixties affects both sexes through its destabilization of traditional marriage – 'Everything's changed and I'm too tired to learn the new rules. I don't care about 1969 at all', Erica Tate complains – while Joan Didion (1934), in line with some of her male colleagues, focuses on the disintegration of shared social and moral frameworks and its consequences for individual identity – illustrated by for instance the seemingly incurably neurotic Maria Wyeth in *Play It As It Lays* (1970). Perhaps not surprisingly, since American feminism was in the first instance a middle-class protest movement, all these writers present middle-class women struggling in middle-class milieus (if we may consider the Hollywood of *Play It As It Lays* a middle class milieu). A stark exception to this rule is Joyce Carol Oates (1938) who in *them* (1969) takes us to the violent, crime-ridden ghettos of Detroit (beginning in the 1930s and including the riots of 1967), and who two years earlier, in *A Garden of Earthly Delights*, had introduced the fictive Eden County in Upstate New York – the place where she herself grew up – where violence and sexual abuse vie with rural poverty for our attention. Another important exception is the African American Toni Morrison (1931), who would be awarded the Nobel Prize for literature in 1993. In her first novel, *The Bluest Eye* (1970), set in a steel town on Lake Erie in 1941, young Pecola Breedlove, daughter of black working-class parents, is the victim of her parents' damaged personalities and incessant fighting ('Cholly and Mrs. Breedlove fought each other with a darkly brutal formalism that was paralleled only by their lovemaking'). The world of the Breedloves is dominated by white values – symbolized by the 'bluest eye' of the title – that are positively damaging because they are destructive of black self-respect, trapping African Americans in a vicious circle of self-loathing and mutual contempt. Morrison takes care to situate events historically – just before Pecola's father rapes her we get to hear how he was cruelly rejected by his own parents – creating a chain of suffering that only acts of genuine altruism can possibly break. In her other novels of the 1970s, *Sula* (1973) and *Song of Solomon* (1977), Morrison is less concerned with the burden of the past – Sula, the protagonist of the eponymous novel, leaves her neighborhood after she accidentally kills a small boy and lives a life of total freedom. These novels also show her moving away from the realism of *The Bluest Eye* – even if she remains focused on the ever-present consequences of racism – with for instance the saintly Pilate in *Song of Solomon*, mysteriously born without a navel.

Drama in the sixties and seventies

With Edward Albee's *Who's Afraid of Virginia Woolf* (1962) Broadway had presented a play whose vicious psychological warfare, profane language, and explicit sexuality did not exactly reflect mainstream taste. Still, Broadway went on to produce other plays by Albee. But Albee's bleak view of religion and the self-centered manipulative characters of *Tiny Alice* (1965), like the dysfunctional family of *A Delicate Balance* (1966), did not draw large crowds. Mostly, Broadway put its faith in box-office certainties like musicals and comedies with a not too serious undertone, such as *The Odd Couple* (1965) by Neil Simon (1927), a situational comedy with two recently divorced and utterly different middle-aged men who find that their decision to share an apartment pretty soon leads to what seems another bad marriage (the play had a long afterlife – 1970–75 – as a highly successful television series). A Simon play, with its sparkling, clever dialogue and perfect balance of light-hearted and darker themes – *Barefoot in the Park* (1964), *Last of the Red Hot Lovers* (1969), *The Sunshine Boys* (1972) – was as good as money in the bank. The rather affable self-centeredness of many of Simon's characters was in itself a source of comedy and their wit did the rest. If Broadway ventured into truly serious territory, it was with productions – or playwrights – that had proven their box-office potential elsewhere.

By the mid-sixties Off-Broadway, where production costs had also soared, had largely lost its experimental edge. Truly avant-gardist drama had left for the – often very – small theaters of Off-Off-Broadway (fewer than 199 seats) where a loyal following eagerly subjected itself to the often spectacular theatrical experiments that companies such as The Open Theatre, The Performance Group, and, in the early seventies, director/playwrights like Robert Wilson (who would go on to produce *Einstein on the Beach*, 1976, and other mega-spectacles), Richard Foreman, and Lee Breuer created for them. With the avant-garde gone, Off-Broadway mostly dedicated itself to intellectual and demanding drama that drew more sophisticated audiences than Broadway but that more than occasionally had a second life on Broadway. Typical Off-Broadway productions of the later sixties and early seventies are the tense, disturbing, *The Indian Wants the Bronx* (1968, starring Al Pacino) by Israel Horovitz (1939) in which a visitor from India becomes the victim of mindless racism, *The House of Blue Leaves* (1971) by John Guare (1938), a black comedy featuring a wildly unreal but dangerous enough family (mother Shaughnessy is quite rightly nicknamed 'Bananas'), *The Hot l Baltimore* (1973) by Lanford Wilson (1937–2011), which is set in a rundown and condemned railroad hotel and with merciless compassion unmasks the vain hopes of its equally condemned guests, and the first two Vietnam plays of David Rabe (1940), *The Basic Training of Pavlo Hummel* and *Sticks and Bones*, both produced in 1971 (and both destined for Broadway). Although Rabe's main characters have actually experienced the war, the plays are not so much about Vietnam as about the mentality that made Vietnam and excesses like the massacre in My Lai village possible. (In a third play, *Streamers*, 1976, his characters never get closer to Vietnam than the army barracks where they are waiting for their tour of duty so that the play focuses entirely on the soldiers' fears and insecurities.) But Off-Broadway also invested in female playwrights like Rochelle Owens (1936) – *Futz!* (1968), *The Karl Marx Play* (1973) – and Marsha Norman (1947), in whose *Getting Out* (1978) a just released murderess must rebuild her life after having served her sentence.

As the production history of Rabe's plays shows, playwrights could move freely between Off-Broadway and Broadway and many Off-Broadway playwrights had earlier in their careers been produced on Off-Off-Broadway. Owens's *Futz!* – in which a farm boy's love for his pig Amanda, whom he considers his wife, is not more outlandish than what we find in Owens's other plays – was first produced on Off-Off-Broadway and then moved to Off-Broadway. Wilson had earlier been successful on Off-Off-Broadway with for instance *The Madness of Lady Bright* (1964), one of the first plays that openly dealt with homosexuality, but, leaving the experimentalism of his early plays behind, had moved to Off-Broadway, and would eventually move to Broadway with rather traditional plays like *The Fifth of July* (1978), which focuses on the disillusionment felt by many of those who had in the 1960s manned the barricades while demanding social change, if not actual revolution. Probably the most famous playwright to make the transition from Off-Off-Broadway to Off-Broadway (and beyond, to Broadway and Hollywood) is Sam Shepard (1943) whose contribution to American drama will be discussed below.

In the late 1950s and the 1960s, Off-Broadway's drift away from experimentalism had led to the creation of a number of new, avant-gardist, venues such as the Caffè Cino, La Mama Experimental Theatre, and Judson Poets' Theater, and to the founding of companies which once again sought to redefine dramatic art such as the Performance Group and the Open Theatre – whose leader, Joseph Chaikin, had been active in the Living Theatre, which after some years in Europe burst upon the Off-Off-Broadway scene with the already mentioned *Paradise Now* (1968). (If to be arrested for indecent exposure counts as a yardstick then its attack on at least one taboo must be considered successful.) Physical interaction between performers and audience became commonplace, even if the Open Theatre pretty soon reestablished the so-called fourth wall. Distrusting language, Off-Off-Broadway brought in other means of communication, especially music, as in the classic *Viet Rock* (1966) by Megan Terry (1932), and also the body itself, and relied on not necessarily logically connected fragments and improvisation to achieve the spontaneity and authenticity that it aimed for. Everything that seemed to facilitate genuine communication was brought into play. Scripts tended to function as guidelines rather than texts that the actors should faithfully reproduce – as points of departure (and possibly of return) for onstage improvisation. Terry's *Viet Rock: A Folk War Movie* began as a mere outline for the Open Theatre and got its final shape in collaboration with the actors. Occasionally, this procedure was reversed, as in *America Hurrah* (1966) by Jean-Claude van Itallie (1936), a trilogy of absurdist one-act plays that attacks American consumerism and complacency, which partly came out of the Open Theatre's actor exercises.

In the early sixties Off-Off-Broadway's main objective was liberation from all theatrical conventions, total freedom for the imagination, and unrestrained use of the theater's possibilities, all in the service of authenticity. In the award-winning *Funnyhouse of a Negro* (1964) by the African American playwright Adrienne Kennedy (1931), which was produced by Edward Albee, Negro Sarah, the play's main character, doubles into such diverse characters as Queen Victoria, the Duchess of Habsburg, the newly decolonized Republic of Congo's first (and murdered) president Patrice Lumumba, and Jesus Christ. There is no logical relationship between these dreamlike sequences and we remain in uncertainty about virtually every aspect of the play. The same holds for the early plays and musicals of the Cuban-born Maria Irene Fornés (1930), one of the most prolific playwrights of Off-Off-Broadway's early years, and the even more prolific Sam Shepard who hit the ground running with *Cowboy* and *The Rock Garden*, both produced in 1963, and who in the next ten years, before relocating first to England and then to the Bay Area, wrote an amazing number of mostly one-act plays, winning Obie (Off-Broadway Theater) Awards in 1966, 1967, 1968, and 1973. Shepard, who also has had an impressive acting career and is an accomplished rock musician, is an astonishingly versatile playwright who has created convincing drama out of the most diverse situations. In *The Rock Garden*, which draws on Shepard's personal history, a son leaves his parents and sister to escape from an alcoholic father and a stifling family situation; in *Icarus's Mother* (1965) a barbecue takes on a mysterious and unsettling dimension when the participants start watching a jet plane that rather erratically flies overhead and crashes, while in *Chicago* (1965) a young man sits in a bathtub wearing jeans and imagines ever more fantastic scenarios to prevent his girl-friend from leaving for Chicago. In *Back Bog Beast Bait* (1971), one of Shepard's earliest Off-Broadway plays, a two-headed monster with a definite grudge against the human race terrorizes Louisiana's swamp country, while the surreal scenes of *Nightwalk* (1973), written with Megan Terry and Jean-Claude van Itallie, and the last production of The Open Theatre before it disbanded, introduce a more European version of absurdism with its theme of an absent God. And there is much, much more. 'I'd have six or seven ideas for plays rolling at once', Shepard said, looking back on that early period in the introduction to *The Unseen Hand and Other Plays* (1996), 'I couldn't write fast enough to keep up with the flow of material running through me'. Unimpressed by the demands of logic or convention – the outlines above do not do justice to the plays' anarchic power – Shepard created spell-binding, exhilarating drama even when nothing seemed to connect.

In the later sixties Off-Off-Broadway's rather unfocused rebellion against convention, middle-class taboos, and authority found a political target in America's involvement in Vietnam, both on stage – Terry's *Viet Rock*, Fornès's *A Vietnamese Wedding* (1967) – and in the street, with for instance the ten-foot puppets of Peter Schuman's Bread and Puppet Theatre, which in 1968 staged the anti-Vietnam *A Man Says Goodbye to His Mother*, participating very visibly in anti-war rallies. (In a parallel development in California, the San Francisco Mime Troupe abandoned avant-gardist productions for direct political involvement.) In the seventies, after the withdrawal from Vietnam and with the culture wars of the 1960s largely won, experimental theater mostly turned away from politics and in the hands of directors like Robert Wilson and Richard Foreman began to explore the ways consciousness patterns our perceptions with productions that invited the audience to create coherence out of seemingly unconnected movements and data.

By that time, the still enormously productive Shepard had moved to Off-Broadway with a more realistic mode of drama. *Curse of the Starving Class* (1977) presents a dysfunctional family on a farm in the American West. Its alcoholic father, promiscuous mother, and two unbalanced children cling to illusions that will never materialize. In the Pulitzer Prize-winning *Buried Child* (1979) another dysfunctional family on another farm must confront a past that includes incest and infanticide when a grandson and his girl friend return to the farm. But these family dramas and other seemingly realistic plays always have a surreal quality that lifts them above grim realism, even though Shepard's themes in these plays – the loss of illusions, the breakdown of family values – are real enough. Behind Shepard's disconnections, his flights of surreal fancy, there is always the threat of violence and of mental disintegration, triggered by what has been repressed for too long. But whatever idiom he writes in, Shepard's ear for American speech is pitch-perfect.

The Black Arts Movement

In the early postwar years African American writing had become a major presence on the American literary scene. Poets like Melvin Tolson, Robert Hayden, and Gwendolyn Brooks used their mastery of modernist techniques to address the pressing issues of black experience.

Hayden and Brooks would move away from the formal, academic mode, but Tolson (1898–1966), who had earlier published important poetry with *Rendezvous with America* (1944) and *Libretto for the Republic of Liberia* (1953), did not follow them. His *Harlem Gallery: Book One, The Curator* (1965) is an ambitious attempt to capture Harlem life in complex, formalist poetry. In the field of fiction writing, Richard Wright, Chester Himes, Ralph Ellison and James Baldwin published novels to international acclaim, while Lorraine Hansberry had a successful play on Broadway.

However, for a younger generation of writers, grown up with the Civil Rights Movement and radicalized by the slow response of American society to its demands, the work of most of these older writers fell short of their expectations. Tolson's poetry was too complex, Hayden's starting point was the particulars of individual black experience, but those particulars become emblematic for the human condition as such, much as Ellison's invisible man ends with an existential vision that seems to embrace us all. Clearly, they wrote for a general, not specifically African American audience. Even far more radical writers like Wright and Himes did not specifically address an African American audience. One of the younger writers who felt increasingly uncomfortable with this state of affairs was the poet LeRoi Jones (1934) who in the 1950s was involved in New York's Beat scene and in 1961 had published a well-received collection of poetry with *Preface to a Twenty Volume Suicide Note* (1961) ('Who has ever stopped to think of the divinity of Lamont Cranston? / Only Jack Kerouac, that I know of: & me'; 'In Memory of Radio'). However, nine years later, his poem 'It's Nation Time' told his African American readers that it was 'Time to get / together / time to be one strong fast black energy space': 'niggers come out, brothers are we / with you and your sons your daughters are ours / and we are the same, all the blackness from one black allah'. In between Jones had turned his back on integration and assimilation, converted to Islam and changed his name to Amiri Baraka. His radical disaffection is clearly on view in his first and Obie Award-winning play, *Dutchman* (1964), in which a white woman taunts a younger black man in a New York subway carriage until he finally bursts out in an angry tirade against her and all those whites who claim to love black culture: 'Old bald-headed four-eyed ofays popping their fingers [...]. They say "I love Bessie Smith." And don't even understand that Bessie Smith is saying, "Kiss my ass, kiss my black unruly ass"'. What Clay, the black man, has failed to understand is that his middle-class aspirations and desire to be accepted only lead him into the trap of assimilation and earn him contempt and not respect. At the end of the play the woman murders him and looks to find a new black victim.

Against a background of political assassinations (Medgar Evers and John F. Kennedy in 1963, Malcolm X in 1965, Martin Luther King Jr. and Robert Kennedy in 1968), large-scale urban rioting (Watts, L.A. in 1965; Detroit and Newark in 1967), and seemingly ineradicable racial division, a group of writers that included Baraka, the playwrights Ed Bullins, Alice Childress, Larry Neal, and Charles Fuller, and the poets Nikki Giovanni, Carolyn Rodgers, and Gwendolyn Brooks began to think publicly about a politically engaged art that would meet the expectations of an African American, working class audience. As Larry Neal put it in his influential essay, 'The Black Arts Movement' (1968): 'The Black Arts Movement is radically opposed to any concept of the artist that alienates him from his community. Black Art [...] envisions an art that speaks directly to the needs and aspirations of Black America. In order to perform this task, the Black Arts Movement proposes a radical reordering of the western cultural aesthetic. It proposes a separate symbolism, mythology, critique, and iconology'. Because of internal differences – Baraka and his Congress of Afrikan People saw Marxism as the solution to oppression and inequality – The Black Arts Movement was relatively short-lived and it never formulated a 'black' aesthetic that all its members could agree on, but in spite of that it had a great and far-reaching influence on African American writing, especially that of African American women who in the late 1960s and 1970s debuted at an amazing rate with high-quality novels, collections of poetry, and plays, adding a feminist perspective to the empowering awareness that the movement had fostered. To mention only some names and titles: *Wine in the Wilderness* (1969), a play by Alice Childress (1912–94), who in 1950 had become the first black woman to have a play produced, sides with the African American working-class against a snobbish bourgeoisie. In *The Bronx Is Next* (1968) by Sonia Sanchez (1934) Black Revolutionaries force tenants to leave their miserable Harlem tenement building which they are going to torch in an act of political protest. *The Chosen Place, the Timeless People* (1969) by Paule Marshall (1929), who had published her first novel in 1959, tells us the story of Merle Kimbona who on a West Indies island allows her marriage to fall apart because she is blinded by white (English) civilization, but in the end follows her estranged husband and daughter to Africa. In a sequence of poems in *Good News About the Earth* (1972) Lucille Clifton (1936–2010) explicitly pays homage to contemporary black leaders. In her novel *Corregidora* (1975), Gayle Jones (1949) shows us how Ursa Corregidora must come to terms with her own unhappy fate – domestic violence has made her infertile – but also with a past in which both her great-grandmother and grandmother have been raped and impregnated by the same slave owner, and with her grandmother's wish that she 'leave[s] evidence'. And then there are the short stories of Toni Cade Bambara (1939–95) in *Gorilla, My Love* (1972) and *The Sea Birds Are Still Alive* (1977), there is *For colored girls who have considered suicide / When the rainbow is enuf* (1975), an award-winning play by Ntozake Shange (1948) in which seven women, each only known by a color, in a sequence of poems detail the humiliations – rape, abortion, domestic violence – that especially African American women have to endure. And we have the novels of Alice Walker (1944), who first with *Meridian* (1976), a so-called Bildungsroman against the background of 1960s Civil Rights activism, and then with *The Color Purple* (1982) had great critical and public success. In a class of her own we find Toni Morrison, whose novels of the 1970s have already been noted.

Women were at the forefront of African American writing in the later 1960s and the 1970s. But there was also much exciting writing by black males, especially for the theater, the art form that communicated most directly with black audiences. Baraka published poetry (collected in *It's Nation Time*, 1971), a novel (*The System of Dante's Hell*, 1965), wrote plays (*Four Revolutionary Plays*, 1968), and co-edited (with Larry Neal) an important and influential anthology, *Black Fire: An Anthology of African American Writing* (1968). Ed Bullins (1935), who as a teenager had been involved with gangs in North Philadelphia and had barely survived a stabbing, wrote plays that drew on his intimate knowledge of life in the toughest neighborhoods. With *In the Wine Time* (1968), his first full-length play, he started his so-called Twentieth-Century Play Cycle, a project of some twenty plays that aims to represent the full range of African American life, constructed around two characters, Cliff Dawson and his half-brother Steve Benson, whose history perhaps not accidentally has much in common with that of Bullins himself. These plays – *The Duplex* (1970), *In New England Winter* (1971), *The Fabulous Miss Marie* (1971), *The Taking of Miss Janie* (1975), to mention some of the earlier ones – are short on plot but brilliantly capture the life and language of working-class and down-and-out characters. Violent emotions and eruptions of physical violence, often alcohol- or drugs-related, tell us what it means to be black in a fundamentally hostile environment, just as emotional reconciliations and acts of compassion remind us of the essential humanity of his brutalized characters. Other important plays of the period are Amiri Baraka's *The Slave Ship* (1967), the Pulitzer Prize-winning *No Place to Be Somebody* (1969) by Charles Gordone (1925–95) – 'It's your war too, Nigger. Why can't you see that? [...] We at war, Gabe! Black ag'inst white' – and *Ceremonies in Dark Old Men* (1969) by Lonne Elder III (1927–96) which urges its black audience not to follow the defeatist example of the old men of its old Harlem barbershop but to resist and fight the system.

These plays in large measure contributed to the astonishingly vital and dynamic African American culture of the later 1960s and 1970s. But so did a number of important books. *The Autobiography of Malcolm X* (1965), ghostwritten by Alex Haley (1921–92), *Black Power* (1967) by Stokely Carmichael (1941–98) and Charles V. Hamilton (1929), and *Soul on Ice* (1968) by Eldridge Cleaver (1935–98) illustrated the militant self-confidence of the new generation of African Americans. Novels like *The Man Who Cried I Am* (1967) and *Captain Blackman* (1972) by John A. Williams (1925) put a dazzling mastery of technique in the service of a ferocious attack on white racism which in the first novel has developed a master plan to exterminate all people of African origin and in the second one is encountered again and again by Captain Blackman who, after he has been seriously wounded in Vietnam, in what seem to be dream states fights in every war America has been involved in. Using a wholly different strategy, Ernest Gaines (1933) presented in *The Autobiography of Miss Jane Pittman* (1971) a similarly kaleidoscopic view of American history – and African American suffering – through the stories of the immensely old lady of the title. Although the writers (and other artists) involved in and affiliated with the Black Arts movement never formed a well-defined group or movement there is no doubt that they shared a sense that they were making history. *The Man Who Cried I Am* indirectly tells us to what extent Williams saw himself as belonging to an evolving tradition of African American political protest. Major characters in the novel are thinly disguised fictional versions of Richard Wright, James Baldwin, Malcolm X, and Martin Luther King, Jr. And there is good reason to believe that African American audiences, too, saw themselves as participating in a historic moment. *The Autobiography of Malcolm X* sold millions of copies but was still easily outsold by Alex Haley's next book, *Roots: The Saga of an American Family* (1976), which claimed to be the story of his own ancestors, the earliest of which he had traced to a village in the Gambia, in West Africa. By the end of the 1970s, African American culture was more vital and visible than it had ever been before, and for those who still entertain doubts there is the impressive list of million-sellers recorded and released by Berry Gordy's Tamla/ Motown label. African American culture, assimilationist, militant, or otherwise, had become part of the American mainstream.

New ethnic literatures

That could not yet be said of other so-called 'ethnic' literatures or cultures, although they, too, came to be heard in the somewhat cacophonous literary orchestra of the sixties and seventies. Native American literature, which up till then had been practically invisible got an enormous boost when *House Made of Dawn* (1968) by N. Scott Momaday (1934) was awarded the Pulitzer Prize for fiction. Momaday's Abel is a young Native American (Pueblo) who has done his duty for his country – he has served in the war – but emotionally and spiritually belongs to his tribal world. Initially that does not seem to be the case. He feels estranged, drinks too much, and even murders another member of his people whom he believes to be a witch. But after he has served his sentence and has lived through the meanness and violence of L.A.'s streets, he returns home and would seem to find personal salvation in a native religious ritual. But even if he doesn't – Momaday's modernist techniques create some ambiguities – his tribe and its rituals give his personal problems a place in the cosmic order. Momaday's success was a source of inspiration to aspiring Native American writers. As the novelist James Welch said, 'suddenly people started to notice Indian literature [...] younger people who didn't think they had much of a chance as a writer, suddenly realized, well, an Indian can write'. Momaday's novel was followed by another book that made the headlines, *Custer Died for Your Sins: An Indian Manifesto* (1969), a passionate plea for justice by the political activist Vine Deloria, Jr. (1923–2005), whose appearance coincided with the high profile occupation of Alcatraz, San Francisco's prison island, by the Red Power Movement.

At least in terms of visibility, Native America had made a breakthrough, and its writers soon followed. Momaday himself published with *The Way to Rainy Mountain* (1969) a collection of Kiowa myths and stories that brought the Native American heritage to a wider audience. In 1972 Off-Off-Broadway's LaMaMa theater produced *Body Indian* by Hanay Geiogamah (1945), a play that looked critically at alcoholism and other ills besetting Native American communities and advocated mutual responsibility and solidarity. Geiogamah's next play, *Foghorn* (1973), was a more humorous exercise that in eleven acts retold the story of Native American–U.S. relations from a Native perspective and ridiculed representations of Native Americans in popular culture, while his *49* of 1975 was a sort of tribal musical, based on a traditional celebration, that emphasized the importance of rejuvenating Native American tradition to preserve its relevance in an ever-changing world.

In his *House Made of Dawn*, Momaday had opted for an elliptic and impressionistic mode of narration. His admirer James Welch (1940) took the opposite course. His much-acclaimed *Winter in the Blood* (1974) is a sober, laconic story about a nameless thirty-two year old Blackfoot in a Montana reservation who cannot make sense of his life and his memories and seeks refuge in alcohol and sex. There may be hope, though, through his conversations with Yellow Calf, an old man who more or less personifies tribal tradition. *The Death of Jim Loney* (1979) does not even offer such a tentative way out of loneliness and alcoholic despair. Its mixed-blood main character seems doomed from the beginning, lost between two cultures and unable to make meaningful connections. The stark Montana landscape and the small town he lives in, perfectly evoked by Welch, do not help either, but Loney just cannot find the will to leave. In a later novel, *Fools Crow* (1986), Welch significantly widens his scope. The last writer who must be mentioned here is Gerald Vizenor (1934), who enjoys his role as the *enfant terrible* of Native American writing. As an investigative journalist, Vizenor critically followed the political activism of the American Indian Movement, founded in 1968, a scrutiny not appreciated by its leaders, and throughout his writings he has shown himself to be skeptical of all received wisdom, Native American or otherwise, of identity politics, of the reclaiming of so-called tribal remains, of both Native and white representations of Native Americans, and much, much more. Momaday has quite rightly called him 'the supreme ironist among American Indian writers of the twentieth century'. Vizenor started out as a poet and in 1970 published a collection of Ojibwa stories – *Tales of the People* – going on to become one of the most prolific and versatile of Native American writers. But let us here mention only two of the more than twenty books that would follow. *Wordarrows: Indians and Whites in the New Fur Trade* (1978) contains seventeen pieces that look at modern Native American life and the difficult negotiations, both cultural and commercial, between Native and white Americans (the 'new fur trade' of the title), but also reflect on Vizenor's journalistic activities, and occasionally present hilarious but serious flights of fancy (with for instance a resurrected General Custer, killed infamously at Little Bighorn, heading the government's Native American programs). Vizenor's first novel *Darkness in Saint Louis Bearheart* (1978) takes place in a near future where a permanent oil shortage has brought three-and-a-half centuries of American progress to an apocalyptic halt. Its episodic narrative follows a group of what Vizenor, who himself had a white mother, prefers to call 'crossblood' characters on their trek from Minnesota to New Mexico and draws on Native American tales (for its 'trickster' characters) and postmodern narrative strategies, a combination that Vizenor, who sees a kinship between the world view of the trickster figure and that of postmodern theory, would repeatedly employ. With his embracing of postmodernism, which sees all tradition and every identity as culturally constructed and therefore as fundamentally inauthentic, Vizenor moved far away from other Native American writers, who on the whole tend to emphasize the importance of tradition and of ethnic identity.

That perspective is shared by Mexican American, or Chicano/a writers, one of the two branches of Hispanic writing in the United States (the other one being Puerto Rican writing, which will be discussed below). The first Mexican American author to find a mainstream publisher was Antonio Villarreal (1934) whose novel *Pocho* (1959) follows a Mexican American boy as he gradually moves away from and finally breaks with the culture of his immigrant parents. But with the emergence of a militant Chicano movement in the course of the 1960s – initially to organize California's Chicano/a farm workers – the attitude towards assimilation changed. In 1965 Luis Valdez (1940) founded the bilingual theater group El Teatro Campesino which in classic agit-prop manner staged one-act plays that aimed to raise the farm workers' political consciousness. Rejecting the conventions of Euro-American theater, Valdez created what he called a 'popular' theater, 'subject to no other critics except the pueblo itself'. Next to its explicitly political programme, the Teatro developed the more implicitly political goal of making its audiences aware – and proud – of their cultural heritage. Around 1970 it began to perform so-called 'myths' – 'mitos' – in which Valdez emphasized the indebtedness of Chicano culture to the original, Native American, inhabitants of the Southwest. In their search for a Chicano identity, Chicano/a writers resisted the assimilation advocated by Villarreal, and sought ways to counter the pressure of mainstream culture. In his *... y no se lo tragó la tierra* (... and the Earth Did Not Devour Him) of 1971, a sequence of interrelated stories and sketches rather than a novel, Tomás Rivera (1935–84) shows us how his young protagonist and the other migrant workers resist the pressure of mainstream culture (and its discriminatory practices) through their sense of a communal identity. In *Bless Me, Ultima* (1972) by Rudolfo Anaya (1932), situated in the New Mexico of the 1940s, a young boy whose mother wants him to be a priest gradually falls under the spell of the healer Ultima's stories and spiritual wisdom and distances himself from Catholicism as well as his parents until he finds a balance between his conflicting loyalties. Some writers, Valdez and Anaya included, consciously sought to create a shared Chicano heritage which they traced back to a pre-Columbian homeland situated in what is now the American Southwest. This Aztlán features in *Aztlán: An Anthology of Mexican-American Literature* (1972) by Valdez and Stan Steiner, in Ayana's second novel *Heart of Aztlán* (1976) and the poetry of a number of Chicano/a poets, notably Gloria Anzualdúa, who will return later. But of course not every single Chicano/a effort is concerned with this form of what must be considered myth-making. Valdez himself, in his play *Zoot Suit* (1978), which in 1979 was the first ever Chicano play on Broadway, looks back at the so-called Zoot Suit riots of 1943, in which white sailors attacked Los Angeles Chicanos because of what they saw as their provocative outfits. And Rolando Hinojosa (1929), the third Chicano novelist to find a large audience in the early 1970s, is more interested in accurate representations of Chicano/a life as he knows it than in deliberate myth-making. His *Estampas del Valle y otras obras* (1972) – translated by himself as *The Valley* (1983) – started a panoramic cycle of fifteen novels set in and around a fictitious Klail City in Texas's Lower Rio Grande Valley that follows the lives of Mexican Americans from various backgrounds and with varying destinations.

For Puerto Rican writers Aztlán can of course not serve as a point of reference. Their heritage is either Spanish or, more commonly, a mixture of Spanish and black cultural elements. But in the sixties and seventies U.S. Puerto Rican literature was still in its infant stages. *Down These Mean Streets* (1967) is an autobiography in which Piri Thomas (1928–2011) gives us an account of his turbulent youth in Spanish Harlem. The Ossining Correctional Facility, better known as Sing Sing, was where Miguel Piñero (1946–88) wrote his first play, *Short Eyes* (1974), which took a caustic look at the violence and degradations of prison life. Piñero, a co-founder of the Nuyorican Poets Café which would play a pivotal role in U.S. Puerto Rican writing, could not repeat the success of *Short Eyes* with his later plays – including *Gun Tower* (1976), *Eulogy for a Small-Time Thief* (1977) – but his example had demonstrated that 'Nuyorican' writers, too, could win mainstream attention and awards.

For the Asian American community – still overwhelmingly Chinese American and Japanese American in the early postwar period – that role was played by the playwright Frank Chin (1940) and novelist Maxine Hong Kingston (1940). Before the 1970s, Asian American writings were few and far between. There had been some Asian American novels, like *Fifth Chinese Daughter* (1945) by Jade Snow Wong (1922–2006) and *Eat a Bowl of Tea* (1961) by Louis Chu (1925–70), both portrayals – the first one idealized, the second one somewhat more realistic – of life in New York's Chinatown, but there was no tradition of Asian American writing. The most interesting of these early writings is *No-No Boy* (1957) by John Okada (1923–71), which features a young Japanese American who during the war has refused to serve in the American army and also has refused to swear a loyalty oath. Released from jail, after the war, he finds that he is not warmly welcomed by the Japanese American community which calls him and his few fellow refuseniks 'no-no boys'. Okada, who did serve in the war, treats his character's quandary with sympathy, but his explicit moralizing betrays his novelistic inexperience.

But in the 1970s, following the example of the Black Arts Movement, as Hispanic American literature had done earlier, Asian American writing began to come of age. In 1972, Chin's *The Chickencoop Chinaman* was the first Asian American play to be produced Off-Broadway. Like so many ethnic plays and novels of the period it examines the vexing problem of ethnic identity – '"we grow up bustin our ass to be white"', its Chinese American main character says, "be good, suck up, talk proper, and be civilized"' – and rejects both white stereotyping and the all-American model suggested by an old and failing Lone Ranger in the play's dream scenes. In 1974 Chin was one of the editors of *Aiiieeeee!: An Anthology of Asian-American Writers*, a landmark publication that collected writings by Chinese American, Japanese American, and Filipino-American writers, and that made rather exclusivist claims regarding what constitutes a 'true Asian American sensibility', consequently becoming the center of hot controversy. True to his principles, Chin was critical of Maxine Hong Kingston's celebrated *The Woman Warrior: Memoirs of a Girlhood Among Ghosts* (1976), which mixes autobiographical elements with a retelling of traditional Chinese stories and legends. While for some readers Kingston unacceptably distorted her Chinese materials, for Chin she pandered too much to what a white audience would expect. What Kingston offers, as in her National Book Award winning *China Men* (1980), is the realization that neither the 'pure' Chinese culture of her ancestors, nor white mainstream culture could ever satisfy herself or all those others whose fate it is to live in the space between those cultures. As she has put it herself: 'Like the people who carry them across, the myths become American. The myths I write are new, American'. More properly, they are Chinese American, a hybrid culture freely using both Chinese and American sources. Like their Native American, Chicano/a, and Nuyorican colleagues, Asian American writers have the advantage *and* disadvantage of a double identity, a double consciousness, which may not make life any easier, but enriches their writings.

Popular genres

After the war, with increased affluence and a new, cheap pocket-size paperback format, the market for crime fiction boomed. *I, the Jury* (1947), the first novel in the sensational Mike Hammer-series by Mickey Spillane (1918–2006), sold 6.5 million copies in the first two years after publication. The vigilante justice that Spillane's private eye Mike Hammer believes in – not in the least because it offers opportunities for violence – and his hatred of everyone suspected of leftist political sympathies, were well in tune with the times, but the (relatively) explicit sexuality of the novels, advertised by their lurid covers, was a new and daring development (which paid off handsomely). As Spillane's run-away success illustrates, the private investigator remained a popular character. Ross McDonald (1915–83) followed in Chandler's footsteps with his melancholic and compassionate Lew Archer, who also operates in Chandler's Southern California, and through gumshoe persistence and intuition guided by psychology solves complex cases that often have their roots in the past and involve, as in *The Galton Case* (1959) or *The Underground Man* (1971), Freudian trauma and explosive family secrets. McDonald's contemporary John D. MacDonald (1916–86) created a more masculine, but equally compassionate and sensitive private investigator with his Florida 'salvage consultant' Travis McGee who made his first appearance in *The Deep Blue Good-by* (1964) and over the next twenty novels would develop an ecological awareness that was ahead of the times. Still more masculine, but easily as sensitive, is Boston-based Spenser, created in 1973 (*The Godwulf Manuscript*) by Robert B. Parker (1932–2010), and the undisputed hero – in the later books with the formidable but mysterious African American Hawk – of forty novels. A romantic, at times even sentimental, bruiser, a glib talker, and a brilliant cook, Spenser in his long career reflects the impact of feminism and the Civil Rights Movement on an initially rather unthinking, even if morally responsible, American male. But no matter how considerate private investigators may become – the never completely recovered alcoholic Matthew Scudder who makes his first appearance in *Sins of the Fathers* (1976) by Lawrence Block (1938) is another example – Philip Marlowe's 'I test high on insubordination' still applies. A fundamental suspicion of all authority remains essential to the genre.

That suspicion is less obvious in a new departure of the 1950s, the so-called police procedural, in which the reader is enabled to follow an investigation conducted by several police officers, or even by a complete police unit. Still, in police procedurals tense relationships with higher-placed officials often serve to signal the investigator's independence. One of the earliest novels that follow the format is *Last Seen Wearing ...* (1952) by Hilary Waugh (1920–2008), which chronicles the investigation into the disappearance of a female student from a Massachusetts college. Following Waugh's example, Ed McBain (1926–2005) became the most prolific of all police procedural novelists, publishing more than fifty novels about the cops of the 87th precinct of the city of Isola – a thinly disguised Manhattan – between 1956 (*Cop Hater*) and 2005. Other notable novelists in the genre are Joseph Wambaugh (1937), who served for fourteen years in the Los Angeles Police Department, and started his writing career with *The New Centurions* (1970), and Tony Hillerman (1925–2008), who brought Native American traditions into the seventeen novels that chronicled the investigations of Joe Leaphorn and Jim Chee of the Navajo Tribal Police.

More traditional crime fiction of the 'whodunnit' format was represented by Rex Stout (1886–1975), with the orchid-loving and immensely fat detective Nero Wolfe, and Erle Stanley Gardner (1889–1970), whose ingenious courtroom mysteries featured the brilliant lawyer Perry Mason. But there was also darker, far more disturbing crime fiction that left James M. Cain easily behind and presented psychopathological characters moving in a world where corruption and violence are the norm. The most intense of these *noir* writers was Jim Thompson (1906–76), in some of whose novels (*The Killer Inside Me*, 1952; *Pop. 1280*, 1964) the law's representatives are as pathological as anybody else. A late *noir* classic is *The Burnt Orange Heresy* (1971) by Charles Willeford (1919–88), who in the latter part of his career would create the memorable private investigator Hoke Moseley. More light-hearted, but perhaps even more menacing because of that, were the crime novels of Patricia Highsmith, especially those featuring the good-natured but completely unscrupulous killer Tom Ripley (introduced in *The Talented Mr. Ripley*, 1955), who, with Highsmith flouting all convention, simply goes unpunished. With *52 Pick-Up* (1974) Elmore Leonard (1925–2013), who earlier had written westerns (*Hombre*, 1961), established himself as one of America's most convincing crime writers, with dialogues that did not need rewriting for the Hollywood versions of his novels.

This very brief discussion of postwar crime fiction could be expanded almost ad infinitum. Amazing numbers of writers contributed to what soon was an explosively growing industry. The story repeated itself on a more modest scale with another popular genre, that of science fiction. Largely confined to specialized pulp magazines in the prewar period, in the 1950s science fiction successfully made the transition to the paperback market. Writers like Isaac Asimov (1920?–1992) and Robert Heinlein (1907–88) published landmark novels (Asimov starting his *Robot* series – *The Caves of Steel*, 1953; *The Naked Sun*, 1956 – and Heinlein winning a so-called Hugo Award for his *Double Star* of 1956). Asimov would go on to create an alternative universe, furnished with its own history, a description that may suggest a further move towards fantasy fiction, but true to his background – he was a professor of biochemistry for much of his life – he stayed with 'hard' science fiction, the sort of science fiction for which scientific underpinnings and scientific accuracy are essential. Heinlein leans more towards 'soft' science fiction in which psychological, anthropological and political themes – which we do of course also find in Asimov and other 'hard' science fiction writers – relegate scientific detail to the far background. In his most famous novel *Stranger in a Strange land* (1961) his protagonist's life and education on the peaceful and advanced planet Mars have left him totally unprepared for the belligerence, bigotry, and political maneuvering of us Earthlings. The 'red' planet, at the time still mysterious, was also a source of inspiration for Ray Bradbury (1920–2012), whose *Martian Chronicles* (1950) and *Fahrenheit 451* (1953), the latter set in a future America, explored like Heinlein's novel utopian and dystopian themes. *Fahrenheit 451*, in which books are outlawed and burned – reminding us of Nazi practices – is an oblique commentary on the mentality of the McCarthy years. 'Soft' science fiction more generally offers the opportunity to explore alternative societies and social arrangements, as in *The Left Hand of Darkness* (1969) by Ursula Le Guin (1929), in which the inhabitants of the planet Gethen are neither male nor female – only assuming a sexual identity when urged biologically to do so – and presumably because of that manage to live in peace. Clearly, such science fiction offers as many, or even more, opportunities for social analysis and commentary as mainstream fiction and in the course of the 1960s and 1970s we see contemporary issues and even contemporary fictional strategies enter science fiction novels. Like his postmodern contemporaries, Philip K. Dick (1928–82) questioned all fundamentals – 'In my writing I even question the universe; I wonder out loud if it is real' – such as the difference between illusion and reality, as in *Do Androids Dream of Electric Sheep?* (1968), the basis for the movie *Blade Runner* (1982), or *Ubik* (1969). *The Man in the High Castle* (1962) presents an alternative history in which Nazi Germany and Japan have between them occupied and divided a defeated United States, except for a 'neutral' zone where much of the action takes place. Moving further into postmodern territory, the African American science fiction writer Samuel R. Delany (1942), after relatively traditional (and award-winning) novels like *Babel-17* (1965) and *The Einstein Connection* (1966), created astonishingly involved fictions such as *Dhalgren*

(1975), its length, labyrinthine complexities, and intertextual references rivaling Thomas Pynchon's *Gravity's Rainbow*. With Delany and Octavia Butler (1947–2006) race became a prominent theme in science fiction, while Ursula Le Guin, Joanna Russ (*The Female Man*, 1975), Marge Piercy (*Woman on the Edge of Time*, 1976), and others introduced feminism, and again Delany and writers such as Thomas M. Disch (*On Wings of Song*, 1979) made gay themes fully accepted. In the universe of American letters, science fiction and crime fiction are parallel worlds to the world of 'literary' fiction, equally diverse, equally vibrant, equally inventive, but easily outdoing that world in terms of sales – not to mention movie contracts.

6 The end and return of history
1980–2010

Introduction: the U.S. since 1980

The most salient feature of American literature after 1980 is the rise of multiculturalism, with almost every ethnic minority claiming its own literature. Very often this has meant a reclaiming, as many of the ethnic authors discussed in previous chapters were only re-discovered, and in some cases actually only discovered, during this period. But there has also been an immense outpouring of literature from all these ethnic minorities. The reasons for this are manifold, but some need special mention. To begin with there were the various emancipation movements, first and foremost that of the African Americans, mentioned earlier. Then, the Immigration and Nationality Act of 1965 officially put an end to the quota system imposed by the Immigration Act of 1924. This almost immediately led to a renewed and massive immigration from Latin America, the Caribbean and later also Asia. In the 1940s the U.S. counted barely one million immigrants, almost all of European or Canadian origin. In the 1950s and 1960s the numbers increased to 2.5 and 4 million, respectively. In the 1960s the share of non-European immigrants for the first time surpasses that of the Europeans. This decade also sees a huge influx of illegal or 'undocumented' aliens. In the 1970s the numbers swell to 7, in the 1980s to 10, and in the 1990s to anywhere between 11 and 14 million, of which each time more than a third were illegal. In 2002 the number of Americans born abroad was estimated at more than 33 million, or 11 percent of the U.S. population. In comparison, in the early twentieth century, the previous period of mass immigration, only approximately 7 percent of the population had been foreign born. The main difference, of course, is that at the time the overwhelming majority of these immigrants had been European, whereas now immigrants from Europe, and especially from Western Europe, formed an almost negligible quantity. By far the largest share now comes from Latin America, from Mexico or the Caribbean, and continues to speak Spanish after immigration, and throughout successive generations. The birth rate of these newcomers is substantially higher than that of the earlier European-descended Americans. The U.S. Census Bureau Office estimates that by 2050 one-quarter of the American population will be Hispanic. Moreover almost one-tenth of the population will then be Asian-descended. Until the middle of the 1990s all these immigrants primarily settled in California, which assimilated about one-third of the total, and in some larger states such as Texas, New York, Florida, New Jersey and Illinois, and in the larger cities, Los Angeles, New York City and vicinity, El Paso, Dallas and Houston, Chicago and Miami. Since then, however, we see a much more widespread pattern of dissemination across the entire U.S., with strong immigration into the South and the middle parts of the U.S. Finally, mobility has also risen sharply with American-born minorities. Since 1945, for instance, large numbers of African Americans originating in the South have moved to California and the large Northern cities. In other words: the myth of a homogeneous and white

America, as cherished before World War II, has been disproven by the facts since then. It even begins to look increasingly likely that by 2050 'white' Americans, which in practice means those with European ancestry, will be in the minority in the land of Uncle Sam.

The result of all this is that the United States resemble in almost nothing the kind of country they were before World War II. The tensions, uncertainties and doubts that this change from a population with overwhelmingly European roots to a much more diversified one engendered in that part of the U.S. population, and especially its male part, whose hegemony until then had gone unchallenged, were captured in the narrative experiments and deregulations of post-modernism. These postmodern fictions convey the 'sense of an ending' with regard to a particular view of American history and its concomitant literature. The tensions, uncertainties and doubts, but also the hopes and aspirations that same transition gave rise to in America's 'Others', we find embodied in what usually goes by the term 'multiculturalism'. Multiculturalism, with its attendant concepts 'equal opportunity' and 'political correctness', became the official ideology of the U.S. as of about 1980. Small wonder, then, that the face of American literature in the period since has been very much co-determined by authors originating from multiple minorities, all of them claiming their place under the American literary sun. In many ways this claim pivots on the recovery of histories alternative to 'white' American history, the 'return' of history, but with a difference.

Prose 'after' postmodernism

Few of the 'classical' postmodernists who continued writing into the new millennium succeeded in repeating their earlier successes. This applies particularly to Barth, whose many novels, some of them very voluminous, like *The Last Voyage of Somebody the Sailor* (1991), and story collections endlessly keep turning over themes and techniques identical to those of his earlier work. Gaddis did pretty much the same in *A Frolic of His Own* (1994), a book harping on the difference between what is true justice and what the judicial system makes of it, while in *Carpenter's Gothic* (1985) he satirized religious fundamentalism and personal greed. The postmodern fame of Stanley Elkin (1930–95) rests mainly on the combination of exuberant language and black humor in *The Dick Gibson Show* (1971), about a boy who is enthralled to the voices coming out of the radio, and *The Franchiser* (1976), about a man who builds a fast food chain but finds the meaning of life through the multiple sclerosis he suffers from, and from which Elkin him-self also died. In his later work Elkin took a more and more tragic view of things. *George Mills* (1982) is about a man who feels betrayed by God. In *The Magic Kingdom* (1985) a man who has lost his son takes a group of terminally ill children on a trip to Disneyland. In *The Rabbi of Lud* (1987) a New Jersey rabbi struggles with his faith.

With *Slow Learner* (1984) Pynchon published a collection of his early stories, and he brought new work with *Vineland* (1990), *Mason & Dixon* (1997), and *Against the Day* (2006). Although both *Vineland*, set in Northern California in a milieu of over-age hippies, and *Mason & Dixon*, about the two men, Charles Mason and Jeremiah Dixon, that drew the famous line that divided the Northern, non-slave-holding parts of the U.S. from the Southern slave-holding parts, and recounted in eighteenth-century English, sported all kinds of peculiarities (zany ditties, fantastic events, a cavalier treatment of history) also typical of Pynchon's earlier fiction, they both received mixed reviews, the later novel faring somewhat better than the earlier. *Against the Day*, though, was an immediate hit with the critics. A massive affair, like *V. A Novel* and *Gravity's Rainbow*, *Against the Day* plays intricate games with history, with language, with its characters, and with the reader. A central plotline features the anarchist Webb Traverse in his fight against capitalism, his murder on behalf of the industrialist Scarsdale Vibe, and the desire on the part of his three sons to revenge their father's death. Set around the turn of the twentieth century the novel indulges in all kinds of eccentrics, including a dog that reads Henry James, travel through the center of the earth, and countless subplots, all of it brought in a welter of styles, varying from the language of juvenile adventure to tough guy hard-boiled and everything in between. Like Pynchon's earliest books, *Against the Day* finally leaves the reader with more questions than answers, but also with the feeling that something important has been touched upon.

The most overtly technically postmodern early work of Don DeLillo (1936–) is *Ratner's Star* (1974), in which a fourteen-year-old mathematical genius decodes an alien message announcing that the earth is about to enter a zone in which the laws of physics no longer apply, and which at the time was often likened to the work of Pynchon. DeLillo's other early novels focused, often satirically, on American popular culture phenomena such as American football or rock and roll. *White Noise* (1985) established DeLillo as a major author. The novel features a university professor in 'Hitler Studies' (yet who cannot read German), who gets caught in an environmental disaster, but who also is confronted with his own fears of death. The novel is a satire of university life, but even more so of how important events are hijacked by the media and turned into spectacle for an audience bent on sensation. Undoubtedly it is not a coincidence that the cable network CNN was launched in 1980, and that this was also the period in which French thinkers such as Guy Debord (1931–94) and Jean Baudrillard (1929–2007) were busily being discussed in American literary circles for the relationship they posited between consumer society, the cult of the spectacle, and the simulacralisation or simulation of reality in the media. DeLillo continued this line of thought in *Libra* (1988), with as protagonist the murderer of President Kennedy, *Mao II* (1991), and especially the massive *Underworld* (1997). Waste, and the problems it causes in a consumerist society, are a central topic in this novel, the action of which spans the 1950s to the 1990s, with many interlocking plots, settings ranging from the New York Giants' baseball grounds to an artist's studio, and both fictional and historical characters. The novel's title refers to how waste is buried, to the criminal underworld, to the things hidden in history, and to how all of this refuses to remain buried and leads a life of its own. On appearance *Underworld* was hailed as a major achievement and as one of the most important works of American fiction of the final quarter of the twentieth century. Since *Underworld* DeLillo has delivered shorter fictions. In *Cosmopolis* (2003) he once again addresses issues of mediatisation, the world of advertising, and the fads dominating American life. *Falling Man* (2007) describes how a man who has been wounded in the 9/11 World Trade Center attack looks for new meaning in life. Unlike other first generation postmodernists DeLillo does not use metafiction to approach the postmodern life-world, but meticulously mirrors the latter's emptiness and artificiality in the smooth, stylized, polished but clichéd dialogue of his protagonists, who seem to be unable to go beyond the surface of things. His later works, though, clearly also engage more directly with both human and social reality.

As of the 1980s a new generation of writers started putting postmodern techniques to new ends. Kathy Acker (1947–97; née Karen Lehmann) from the mid-1970s to her death in 1997 published a number of texts that combine the experimentalism of Burroughs, Sukenick and Federman with a militant feminism. Paul Auster (1947–) is most classically postmodern in his early *The New York Trilogy*, consisting of *City of Glass* (1985), *Ghosts* (1986) and *The Locked Room* (1986), and in the late *Travels in the Scriptorium* (2007), which is not only metafictional but likewise heavily intertextual and self-reflective in that all characters, except for the narrator 'Mr. Blank' issue from earlier novels by Auster. Central to the three novels gathered in *The New York Trilogy* are questions of language, reality and identity. In *City of Glass* the protagonist,

Quinn, on a whim takes on the role of 'the detective Paul Auster' to investigate a case loosely based on the histories of Caspar Hauser and the wild boy of Aveyron, later meets 'the author Paul Auster', gradually loses all his possessions and his identity, and in the end turns out to have literally dissolved into thin air, the only evidence of his ever having been anywhere being a little red notebook. In *Ghosts* a private detective called 'Blue' is hired by 'White' to observe 'Black'. But Black is a detective too, hired to observe someone. Moreover, it begins to look more and more as if White was actually Black in disguise. The story ends with a violent confrontation between Black and Blue. Blue wins, puts on his hat, and departs, leaving the reader totally confused. Quinn and the red notebook from *City of Glass* return in *The Locked Room*, be it that the notebook here belonged to Fanshawe, a writer who has disappeared without a trace and whom Quinn is hired to find, without result. The narrator, a friend of Fanshawe's, then gradually assumes the role and identity of Fanshawe, until it appears that Fanshawe is still alive and the narrator has one last conversation with him, through a locked door. Fanshawe is a character from the eponymous novel by Hawthorne, and this is only one of the many intertextual references to literary canonicals throughout *The New York Trilogy*. Moreover, a number of episodes in the life of Fanshawe, as we get to hear it, correspond with events in the life of Auster himself. In all, *The New York Trilogy* is a beguiling play with narrative paradoxes, names and identities, the borderlines between fiction and reality, and the literary canon, raising the familiar postmodern issues of language, identity, power, reality, and the (im)possibility of knowing the latter.

Auster's many novels following *The New York Trilogy* all in one way or another pose the same questions as did his first and still most popular work. A number of them feature recurring characters, with Quinn for instance resurfacing in *In The Country of Last Things* (1987) while the protagonist of that novel, Anna Blume, reappears in *Moon Palace* (1989). Most of them have most unlikely plots, *The Music of Chance* (1990) being concerned with the building of an endlessly long and useless wall, and *Timbuktu* (1999) being narrated by a dog. The majority of Auster's characters suffer from one obsession or another. The protagonist of *The Book of Illusions* (2002), for instance, is obsessed by a movie actor that disappeared in the 1920s. These, and most other fictions by Auster, such as *Leviathan* (1992) or *Oracle Nights* (2004), offer a very grim outlook on life, the exception being *Mr. Vertigo* (1994), in which a nine-year-old orphan learns how to fly. In some of his later fictions Auster casts characters that after a serious disease or mishap have to get their life back on the rails and make a new beginning. This is so in *Oracle Nights*, but also in *The Brooklyn Follies* (2005). *Man in the Dark* (2008) sees the U.S. torn apart by a new Civil War, while *Invisible* (2009), a novel in four parts modeled on the seasons, harps on Auster's usual questions about the reliability of language to capture reality, including memories of the past, and authorship. *Sunset Park* (2010), finally, seems less convoluted, perhaps less 'postmodern', than his earlier work, and once again reflects on how to make a new start in life.

With Richard Powers (1957–) we turn to a set of authors, sometimes referred to as 'The New American School', who have clearly grown up with postmodernism as a major influence, but who in various ways go beyond it. With Powers, as with David Foster Wallace (1962–2008), Mark Z. Danielewski (1966–), Dave Eggers (1970–) and Jonathan Safran Foer (1977–), the postmodern connection most clearly shows in their fascination with themes of language and identity, and with how they fashion their narratives to reflect them. Powers made his debut with *Three Farmers on Their Way to a Dance* (1985), which is undeniably postmodern in both technique and themes. We are first given a series of reflections on art, and specifically photography in the modern era, what the German writer-philosopher Walter Benjamin (1892–1940), who is quoted by Powers, called 'the era of mechanical reproduction', followed by episodes in the lives of three young men photographed on their way to a dance in August 1914, just before the outbreak of World War I, and by how a Boston editor of a computer magazine discovers that one of the young men pictured in the photograph is his grandfather. Finally, however, everything turns out to be a verbal construct raised on a photograph of three unknown young men on a country road. *Prisoner's Dilemma* (1988) likewise plays with postmodern constructions and masquerades, and alternative realities, giving Walt Disney Japanese ancestors, for instance. *The Gold Bug Variations* (1991) via its title refers to a story by Edgar Allan Poe, but also to J.S. Bach's Goldberg Variations as played by the Canadian pianist Glenn Gould, and to the structure of DNA, the discovery or near-discovery of which by the scientist-narrator provides the backbone of the novel. Although undeniably inventive, *The Gold Bug Variations* risks sacrificing story and character to erudition, and this applies even more to *Operation Wandering Soul* (1993). In *Galatea 2.2* (1995) Powers himself admits that with his two previous books he had reached a dead end. He does so by mouth of 'the author Richard Powers' who, after having written a couple of books (that is to say *Prisoner's Dilemma* and *The Gold Bug Variations*) during a prolonged stay in The Netherlands, on his return to the U.S. discovers that he has nothing left to say. Like Barth in his 1960s fictions, though, Powers in *Galatea 2.2* turns this defeat into a triumph by having his author Richard Powers narrate the genesis of his earlier *Three Farmers on Their Way to a Dance*. If this still sounds very classically postmodern, with his next novel Powers broke out of this mold. *Gain* (1998) draws a powerful picture of the rise of corporate America, and of how the individualistic and visionary entrepreneurism of the nineteenth century has developed into the nameless and faceless executive leadership of the late twentieth century. In *Plowing the Dark* (2000) computer-generated virtual reality in the service of the military is juxtaposed to an American being held hostage by guerillas in Lebanon, the connecting factor between the two being the threat they both pose to man's mental sanity. *The Time of our Singing* (2003) addresses problems of racial inequality and discrimination via the marriage and offspring of a German-Jewish immigrant and an African American woman. In *The Echo Maker* (2006) Powers raises questions about the relationship between reality, memory and identity via a protagonist who, as the result of a car accident, suffers from Capgras syndrome, the unfounded conviction that someone familiar is in fact an impostor. At the same time Powers also addresses issues of nature conservation and land and water use via a refuge of sandhill cranes in Nebraska, the setting of the novel. In *Generosity: An Enhancement* (2009) the possible discovery of a genetic source of happiness and its possible or potential commercial misuse provide the central strand.

In several of his essays, collected in *A Supposedly Fun Thing I'll Never Do Again* (1997), *Consider the Lobster* (2005) and *Both Flesh and Not* (2012), David Foster Wallace denounced postmodernism for its ironical anti-humanism and metafictional pirouettes, and for the disrespect it showed its characters. Instead, he argued for '"real", albeit pop-mediated characters'. Especially John Barth seems to have served as Wallace's prime target, as can be seen from the parody of the latter in the story 'Westward the Course of Empire Takes Its Way', from the collection *Girl with Curious Hair* (1989). A look at his own work, though, and particularly at his debut, *The Broom of the System* (1987), leads us to suspect that with these denunciations of his immediate predecessors Wallace was primarily trying to lay his own literary ghosts. With characters named Rick Vigorous, Candy Mandible, Wang-Dang Lang, a talking parrot called 'Vlad the Impaler', a publishing company that goes by the name 'Frequent and Vigorous' (the director of which cannot live up to that motto in the bed of the novel's protagonist Lenore Beardsman), and the zany plan of the Ohio state authorities to create a 'Great Ohio Desert' to foster recreation, the shadow of Pynchon looms heavily over *The Broom of the System*. Add to this that the plot concerns a search for truth and identity by Lenore, which also involves a search for her great-grandmother also called Lenore, the latter having been a student of Wittgenstein, and the relationship between language and reality that is the holy grail of classical postmodernism reappears again here too.

Wallace's massive (1079 pages) second novel, *Infinite Jest* (1996), definitively established him as one of the most important voices of his generation. In this novel Wallace, in his own words, tried to describe 'what it's like to live in America around the millennium'. The book is set in a near future in which the U.S., Canada and Mexico have united to form the Organization of North American Nations, also known as O.N.A.N., with a clear Biblical reference. The President of O.N.A.N. is a former pop-singer and actor, the larger part of New England and South-Eastern Canada is used as a dump for toxic waste, transported there by rocket, and society has become commercialized to the extent that calendar years no longer go by digits but by sponsor advertisements: 'Year of the Whopper', 'Year of the Tucks Medicated Pad'. There is a gang of French-Canadian terrorists ('Les Assassins des Fauteils Rollents' [*sic*]) chasing a movie, 'The Entertainment', that is so impossible to tear oneself away from that its spectators die from dehydration, and with which the assassins plan to bring down the hated American society. *Infinite Jest* also sports 388 endnotes. All of this sounds very Pynchonesque, but other than his postmodernist predecessors, and unlike in his own earlier work, Wallace in *Infinite Jest* focuses on the existential anxieties life in such a disorienting and disoriented society engenders. What matters, Wallace insists, is that notwithstanding all the linguistic frolics and jests his characters are 'real' people, with 'real' problems, even if the environment in which they find themselves is recognizably postmodern. To use postmodern irony in these conditions would be unforgivable and stand in the way of real human communication and compassion. Notwithstanding their often comical use of language and situations, the same move toward what we can broadly call a variation of psychological realism can also be noted in the stories collected in *Brief Interviews with Hideous Men* (1999) and *Oblivion* (2004), with the tone of the latter collection getting grimmer, influenced by the events of 9/11, which are also referred to a few times.

Mark Z. Danielewski's *The House of Leaves* created a major stir upon publication in 2000. Of all more recent publications this is probably the most orthodoxly postmodern. The novel's central given is a report of a documentary movie registering how movie producer Navidson and his crew explore the enormous spaces that without warning have attached themselves to his house and that, like the house itself, can just as unpredictably change shape. The report, written up by a certain Zampanó, after the latter's death is found by Johnny Truant, an assistant in a tattoo shop and on the brink of succumbing to his drug addiction. To Zampanó's already copious notes Truant adds his own, which clearly show him to be sliding into paranoia. All of this is edited and edited again by nameless further editors that themselves add the occasional further footnote. Zampanó's notes refer to both existing and non-existing articles and books, to scholarly and pseudo-scholarly discussions, and to pseudo-commentaries by Douglas Hofstadter, Stephen King, and Jacques Derrida. Add to this that the novel's page lay-out mirrors Navidson's moves, thereby forcing the reader to sometimes hold the book upside down or at an angle, uses different colors, and sports a great number of different fonts, including braille and musical notations, as well as photographs, drawings, and poems, and that an exhaustive index concludes it all. *House of Leaves* is hilariously and irrepressibly inventive in its use of techniques yet at the same time extremely menacing in atmosphere, even to the point of horror. As a result, the reader is constantly torn between a distancing reading of what after all could only be sheer linguistic construction – literally a 'house of leaves', that is to say of leaves of a book or pages – and a strong emotional response called forth by the reality of the situations and the characters. It is this tension that finally yields the meaning, and the greatness, of *House of Leaves*. In his second novel, *Only Revolutions* (2006), loosely modeled on the genre of the road novel, but also involving a trip through American history, Danielewski tried to outdo the experimentalism even of *House of Leaves*.

Dave Eggers gained immediate fame with *A Heartbreaking Work of Staggering Genius* (2000), a deeply moving and at the same time hilariously funny metafictional recount of the period immediately following the decease of the parents of the protagonist Dave Eggers. When father and mother Eggers die within a month of one another the three older Eggers children, but in the first instance Dave, take upon themselves the care of the much younger Toph. Although based in fact, Eggers' account is thoroughly fictionalized. The book shows many postmodern features, but the pain the Eggers children feel is undeniably real and authentic. Not surprisingly, then, in interviews Eggers has consistently declined to be identified as a postmodernist, a position borne out by his later books, such as *You Shall Know Our Velocity* (2002), in which two friends find out how difficult it is to give away money on reasonable grounds, even in desperately poor places, or *What is the What: The Autobiography of Valentino Achak Deng* (2006), the true story of a Sudanese refugee. In *A Hologram for the King* (2012) Eggers tackles the excesses of globalization and the personal and collective dramas they lead to.

In Jonathan Safran Foer's first novel, *Everything Is Illuminated* (2002), Jonathan, a young Jewish American, visits the Ukraine in search of the village whence his ancestors emigrated to the U.S. He meets a young Ukrainian, Alex, who, along with his grandfather, the latter's unbelievable dog ('Sammy Davis, Junior, called Junior') and equally incredible car, takes Jonathan to his destination. All this is being recounted by Alex in a hilarious – and occasionally belabored – variant of the English language. Alex also keeps up a running correspondence with Jonathan. The true beginning of the story, though, lies in Trachimbrod, the village Jonathan is looking for. It soon transpires that the history of Trachimbrod is being reconstructed, or better, construed, by Jonathan, who sends chapters to Alex for the latter's comment. For the longest time the history of Trachimbrod remains as hilarious as Alex's usage of English, but it assumes a grimmer outlook when it becomes clear that Alex's grandfather himself comes from Trachimbrod, that the village has been wiped off the face of the earth by the Nazis, and that the grandfather in question has played a less than heroic role in this event. Issues of memory, reality, and language, and the thin line between fact and fiction, play a major role in *Everything Is Illuminated*, and give the novel a postmodern tinge, but the latter, as with Eggers, Danielewski, and the later works of Powers, is here again gainsaid by the authenticity of the tragic events and the reality of the characters. This is less the case in Foer's second novel, *Extremely Loud and Incredibly Close* (2005), notwithstanding the fact that this novel is rooted in the events of 9/11, one of the first novels to do so. Foer's use of typographical and other tricks recalls Danielewski's *House of Leaves*, but his protagonist Oscar Schell, a nine-year-old who has lost his father in the 9/11 attacks, is obviously modeled on Oskar Matzerath in *The Tin Drum* (1959) by German writer Günther Grass (1927–). And a number of characters and episodes further recall earlier instances of inhuman behavior, such as the bombardment of Dresden and the dropping of the atom bomb on Hiroshima by the Allies in World War II. With *Eating Animals* (2009) Foer made a plea against present-day commercial practices around food, such as factory farming and commercial fishing.

The work of Nicole Krauss (1974–) shares a number of characteristics and topics with that of Foer. Her first novel, *Man Walks Into a Room* (2002), although not immediately referring to 9/11 itself, has nevertheless been seen as expressing the mood of desolation and despair caused by those events. A novel about memory, the hopelessness and passing of love, and the loneliness of life, all tied together by a nuclear experiment conducted in the Mojave desert in 1957, *Man Walks Into a Room* is an extended symbolical reflection on good and evil, and on the need for the U.S. to leave the trauma of 9/11 behind while at the same time searching for its causes. Krauss has listed DeLillo as one of her main influences, but the mood of *Man Walks Into a Room*, the apparently aimless conversations, the games with language and memory, the role of coincidence, and how man suffers all this without understanding why and without a hold on her or his own existence, also recall the work of Paul Auster. In fact, the book obliquely refers to Auster when the desert is compared to a 'hunger artist', a thematic constant of much of Auster's work, especially in his middle period. *The History of Love* (2005) is concerned with the Holocaust, features a character from Slonim, in present-day Belarus, from which one of Krauss's Jewish grandparents originated, and its plot at least partially turns upon a manuscript. *The Great House* (2010), with magical realist traits, again is rooted in Jewish history, and links the lives of characters living as far apart as Chile, the U.S., London and Jerusalem via a desk of many drawers.

Minimalism, Dirty Realism and Generation X

What almost all 'new' literary movements or currents in American literature after 1980 have in common is a turn, or a return, toward some form of realism. This definitely applies to the multicultural writers we will deal with shortly. It also goes, as we just saw, for those writers – predominantly male, exclusively white – who are still closest to orthodox or classical post-modernism. Still, the return to realism can take very different shapes. In what follows we will try and categorize some of these tendencies. We should warn, though, that many of the writers discussed fit more than one category. Thus, when we ascribe a writer to such or such a category this simply means that we choose to look at her or his work from this particular angle, not that it is the only angle possible.

The turn toward realism is already announced in the 1970s, with the advent of so-called 'Minimalism' and 'Dirty Realism'. The former label stressed style while the latter label emphasized content. The first term mostly gained ground in the U.S., where critics noticed a falling off from the often exuberant and baroque style of a Barth or a Pynchon. The second term was launched by Bill Buford (1954–), the American editor of the English journal *Granta*, for an issue (8, 1983) in which he gathered the work of a number of then younger American authors: Jayne Anne Phillips (1952–), Richard Ford (1944–), Raymond Carver (1938–88), Elizabeth Tallent (1954–), Frederick Barthelme (1943–), Bobbie Ann Mason (1942–) and Tobias Wolff (1945–). The common factor binding these authors together for Buford was that they wrote about 'common' working or lower class Americans and did so in a realist style diametrically opposed to the antiquated civilized ironic realism that Buford saw as ruling the English novel. In *Granta* 19 (1986), 'More Dirt', Buford brought a further group of authors: Richard Russo (1949–), Ellen Gilchrist (1935–), Robert Olmstead (1954–), Joy Williams (1944–) and Louise Erdrich (1954–). Whereas all of Buford's Dirty Realists have made their mark in contemporary American literature, some have become much more prominent than others. Erdrich, for instance, has become what is probably the most prominent Native American author of the turn of the millennium, while Ford and Russo won Pulitzer Prizes.

The central figure for both Minimalism and Dirty Realism is Raymond Carver. Carver had a turbulent youth and difficult early maturity, worked at all kinds of odd jobs, became a heavy drinker, but also attended the Iowa Writers' Workshop, the most famous school of creative writing in the U.S. His own life, and especially his relational problems, furnished the subjects for his early stories published in the collection *Will You Please Be Quiet, Please* (1976), characterized by a sober style, apparently devoid of all emotion, and invariably ending on an anti-climax. His marriage, after an earlier divorce, to the poet Tess Gallagher (1943–) in 1977 initiated a very productive decade for Carver. One after the other three collections of stories appeared: *What We Talk about When We Talk about Love* (1981), *Cathedral* (1984) and *Where I'm Calling from* (1988). Carver's main interests are the poverty of everyday life, the falling apart of the American social fabric at the end of the twentieth century, and how people react emotionally to major upheavals in their lives, such as a divorce or the loss of a child. In 'Cathedral', the title story of the eponymous collection, a man tries to explain to a blind man what a cathedral being shown on television looks like. They end up drawing a cathedral together, the blind man holding on to the pencil the other man is guiding. Nothing really happens in the story, the conversations are banal and consist of clichés. Nevertheless, communication, and human contact, seem possible, however minimal the level at which it happens.

When Carver died of lung cancer in 1988 he was one of the most widely admired writers in the U.S. He only wrote stories, never a full-length novel. In his wake the short story became one of the most popular genres in American literature of the 1980s and 1990s, and there was much talk of a 'renaissance' of the American short story. Looking back on this period it seems safe to say that although a number of authors wrote a few good stories, and some even produced some worthwhile collections, many of them quickly started to repeat themselves and ran out of things to say. Some tried their hand at novel writing, but usually with little success.

From a Dirty Realist perspective the work of Carver and his followers, like much of post-modernism, offers a cross-cut of American popular culture, especially as lived by characters on the margin of society. In 'El Paso', from Jayne Ann Phillips's collection *Black Tickets* (1979), a tramp talks a country girl into accompanying him to El Paso, on the Mexican border. She becomes a go-go dancer in a bar, and then a hooker. He deals in drugs. When he leaves her she moves on to another city, another man. He becomes a junk car racer. These characters do not question their hopeless existence. They drift from city to city, change jobs and relations, and seem to have no grip whatsoever on their lives. In Phillips's second collection, *Fast Lane* (1984), nothing remains of the old American ideal of family life somewhere in the heart of America. The characters in the stories of Joy Williams's collections *Taking Care* (1982) and *Escapes* (1990) lead equally aimless lives, albeit that Williams adopts a more light-hearted tone, sometimes even bordering on the absurd. Phillips and Williams also wrote a few novels.

Three female authors often associated with Minimalism and Dirty Realism, although sooner with the former label than the latter, but who usually focus on middle rather than lower class characters, and who because of their restricted canvas and their mannerist style are sometimes referred to as Miniaturists, are Anne Beattie (1947–), Amy Hempel (1951–) and Lorrie Moore (1957–). Beattie made her debut in 1976 with the collection *Distortions* and the novel *Chilly Scenes of Winter*. A second novel, *Falling into Place*, appeared in 1981. With none of her subsequent novels and collections of stories has Beattie been able to repeat the success of her early work. Beattie has been called the voice of the baby boom generation that reached maturity in the late 1960s and in the 1970s. Her characters do not quite seem to know what to do with themselves, and with the world. Beattie subjects them to an amused, ironical, even clinically anthropological, look. In 'Eric Clapton's Lover' (1976) a man and a woman become estranged after their son has moved to California there to get married to a girl whose greatest ambition is to become a truck driver. The woman withdraws into silence. The man starts haunting bars, and moves in with a Puerto Rican woman he meets at a McDonald's. His wife has a few dates with a traveling salesman. One day, the man is waiting on the sofa when his wife comes home from work. The Puerto Rican woman dreams of having Eric Clapton for a lover and wants to go back to Puerto Rico. That night the man sleeps on a chair in the living room. Next day they are snowed in. They feed the birds.

Beattie usually sticks to third-person stories. Hempel and Moore prefer first, and in Moore's case sometimes second-person stories. Hempel broke into print in 1983 with 'The Cemetery

Where Al Jolson Lies Buried', later collected in *Reasons to Live* (1985). In this often anthologized story the I-narrator goes to visit a terminally ill friend in a California hospital. The friend insists that her visitor tell her all kinds of funny stories. After the funeral, in the cemetery where Al Jolson, the movie star of the first talkie *The Jazz Singer* (1929), also lies buried, the I-narrator leaves for her own home, somewhere in the U.S. Hempel's flat and emotionless style perfectly fits the feelings of powerlessness the I-narrator feels towards what is happening to her friend, and how the friend herself, even in the face of death, tries to make things as easy as possible for her visitor. The title of Moore's first collection, *Self-Help* (1985), alludes to the genre of self-help manuals immensely popular in the U.S. Most stories in the collection quite fittingly counsel the reader how to handle some crisis or other in one's life. 'How to Be Another Woman' advises on how to survive an affair. 'How' tells how to leave a man. 'How to Be a Writer', 'How to Talk to your Mother' and 'The Kid's Guide to Divorce' speak for themselves. The most touching stories are told from a first-person perspective. 'What is Seized' recounts how the narrator experiences the last few days of her mother's life, and in 'Go Like This' we follow the narrator, who suffers from terminal cancer and has decided to commit suicide, during her own last few days. Moore's most popular collection is *Birds of America* (1998). Beattie, Hempel and Moore all regularly have their stories appear in *The New Yorker*. All three are also academics. Some Dirty Realists and Minimalists in fact seem to have made of teaching creative writing rather than of writing itself their main occupation. This is the case, for instance, with Tallent, who published four story collections and one novel between 1983 and 1993 but has been little heard of since then.

Russell Banks (1940–) is not included in Buford's Dirty Realist selection but his numerous novels, dealing with domestic relationships and usually set in a working class milieu, as far as content and style are concerned easily fit the bill. *Continental Drift* (1985) chronicles how two families, one working class and originating from New Hampshire, in the northeastern part of the U.S., the other fugitives from Haiti, both end up in Florida, victims of globalization and economic forces beyond their comprehension, and how their meeting leads to tragedy. *The Sweet Hereafter* (1991) focuses on how a small New England town is riven apart by a bus accident killing several of the town's children. In *Rule of the Bone* (1995) a fourteen-year-old boy drops out of school, abandons his home and family, and ends up a Rastafarian. *Cloudsplitter* (1998), Banks's ninth novel, has as its protagonist the nineteenth-century abolitionist John Brown. *The Reserve* (2008) is set in the 1930s. Banks's novels often cause controversy because of their mention of drugs, AIDS, sexual abuse, and their radically progressive politics.

Three other authors not included in Buford's selection, Jay McInerney (1955–), with *Bright Lights, Big City* (1984), Bret Easton Ellis (1964–), with *Less than Zero* (1985), and Tama Janowitz (1957–), with *Slaves of New York* (1986), a series of interrelated stories set in hip New York, practice what nevertheless can be said to be a particularly 'dirty' form of Dirty Realism. During their early years these three were regularly referred to as the 'literary brat pack', after the 'brat pack' of then younger movie actors (Tom Cruise, Matt Damon, Brad Pitt) themselves named after the 'rat pack' (Frank Sinatra, Dean Martin, Sammy Davis Jr.) of crooners and actors popular in the 1940s and 50s. Their characters invariably are young, lonely and vulnerable in a big city milieu rife with drugs, sex and alcohol, and where life is one long party that unexpectedly can degenerate into horror. Lying in wait are boredom, the chase for ever more kicks, and a fair dose of revulsion at life, at society, and at oneself.

Bright Lights, Big City is told in the second person, and the protagonist thus has no name, making him at the same time emblematic of a particular kind of youth in the prosperous but vapid early Reagan years. A young man with literary ambitions but holding down a small job at a literary journal, he has no respect for his bosses. At night he hits the town, drinks, does drugs, mainly cocaine, and picks up girls. He wakes up in the bed of a girl he barely knows and when he leaves her room runs into her parents, who do not even blink an eye. Of the further novels McInerney wrote, especially *Brightness Falls* (1992) and *The Good Life* (2006) stay with the reader. The novels have partially the same protagonists, and are both set in New York's cultural and business milieu. *The Good Life* is set right after the attacks on the World Trade Center of 9/11. A man and a woman, both married, meet after the attack. Immediately attracted to one another they have a brief affair. Although in their milieu and time there no longer rests a taboo on divorce, and both feel much more at ease with one another than with their respective partners, they go back to their ordinary lives. *The Good Life* is a novel about how an extra-ordinary event, however calamitous, opens up new possibilities, but also how after a while everything returns to normal. It is also about middle age, the restlessness this brings, and social conventions. Thus, McInerney rather unexpectedly enters the terrain of a Cheever or an Updike, or even of the Wharton of *The Age of Innocence*. Another novel in which the events of 9/11 cause the protagonists to re-invent themselves, on a par with the country itself, is *The Emperor's Children* (2006), by Claire Messud (1966–).

The protagonist of *Less than Zero*, published when Ellis was a bare 21 and still a student, at first sight seems a twin to the protagonist of McInerney's debut novel. Clay, a student at a New England university, returns home to Los Angeles for the Christmas holidays. He parties with a few friends, drinks and does drugs. Clay has a girlfriend, but things are not going well. More-over, a number of his friends are gay. Clay has a number of homosexual contacts. He watches a snuff movie. At the home of one of his friends he finds a young girl, naked and tied to a bed. Another friend prostitutes himself. Yet none of his friends or acquaintances seems to find any of this unusual or strange. Disgusted, Clay turns his back on Los Angeles. If *Less than Zero* already hit a much rawer nerve than *Bright Lights, Big City*, Ellis's third novel, *American Psycho* (1991), truly created a stir, with its protagonist a Wall Street banker by day, but at night a torturer, mass murderer, cannibal and necrophile. Many of Ellis's works feature gay characters. It did not come as a great surprise, then, when Ellis finally declared himself to be gay too. An author who from the very beginning of his career has admitted to being gay, and who made this into the main theme of his first published work, *Family Dancing* (1984), a collection of loosely related tales, as well as of his first novel, *The Lost language of Cranes* (1986), is David Leavitt (1961–). Though the early works of Ellis and Leavitt were well received, their further story collections and novels have not met with the same success.

Ellis and Leavitt were born in the early 1960s, which makes them part of Generation X, a term coined by the Canadian author Douglas Coupland (1961–), in *Generation X: Tales for an Accelerated Culture* (1991). *Generation X* is set in the Mojave Desert, in California, where three friends, two men and a woman tell each other stories that reveal the emptiness and aimlessness of their own lives and that of their generation born between 1960 and 1980, and having reached maturity during the Reagan years. The three are highly educated and used to have well-paid jobs, but bored and aiming to escape from consumer society, they now have deliberately taken up so-called 'McJobs' with no prospects of promotion, low salaries, and zero responsibility. The neologisms 'Generation X', sometimes also translated as 'generation nix', and 'McJob' Coupland coined in his bestseller debut novel have entered American popular speech, but Coupland's many later works have never met with any comparable success.

Moral fiction

Two of Buford's original Dirty Realists who have met with continuous success, but who quickly turned to what we might call a form of 'moral fiction', are Richard Ford (1944–) and Richard

Russo (1949–). In *Moral Fiction* (1978) John Gardner (1933–82), who himself was a prodigiously productive author, but who except for his *Grendel* (1971), a retelling of the Beowulf story, is almost forgotten today, made a plea not for any narrow moral or religious codes to be followed in fiction, but for the idea that every work should help people to more acutely experience their own lives, and to make conscious choices. Gardner's book was widely seen as a condemnation of postmodernism and led to a heated controversy with William Gass, one of the most prominent spokesmen for postmodernism at the time. In retrospect we can see that Gardner's book, coming as it did just before 1980, announced the demise of postmodernism in its classical or original form, dominant from, say, 1960 to 1980, and the advent of a more 'responsible' and in different ways more realist fiction.

Richard Ford is best known for the Frank Bascombe trilogy. *The Sportswriter* (1986), *Independence Day* (1995) and *The Lay of the Land* (2006), follow the life and career of Frank, from a young and celebrated sports journalist to a middle-aged real estate broker on the verge of retirement. The three novels address topics also found with the Dirty Realists, minimalists and miniaturists, that is to say relational problems, sickness, death and the loss of a child, but they do so in a different, more positive or hopeful way. Each of the Bascombe novels takes place at a symbolic date: *The Sportswriter* in the period around Easter, *Independence Day*, as its title suggests, around the Fourth of July, and *The Lay of the Land* at Thanksgiving. In sync with Frank's advancing age, they thus also cover (late) Spring, Summer and Fall. At the same time they cover a significant piece of American history, being situated in 1983, 1988 and 1999, respectively the beginning and end of the Reagan years, and the run-up to the Presidential elections pitting George Bush Jr. against Al Gore. Throughout the trilogy Frank, who is estranged from his wife after the death of their oldest son, develops from someone who has a strained relationship with his children, refuses to engage in any deeper way with other people, and keeps his distance from everything, into a man who, regardless of the setbacks he has suffered, most importantly in *The Lay of the Land* a bout with cancer the outcome of which remains unresolved, has come to accept himself, his country, and his times, and who because of this finds at least a modicum of happiness and understanding with his children, his former wife, and the woman with whom he has had a long-standing relationship but whom he risked losing. The Bascombe trilogy is set on the East Coast, primarily New Jersey. With *Canada* (2012) Ford returned to the Montana he had earlier featured in the stories from *Rock Springs* (1987) and the novel *Wild Life* (1990). An older man, Dell, at the beginning of the new millennium looks back to the 1950s, when he was 15 years old and had to flee to Canada after his parents were arrested for robbing a bank.

In *Empire Falls* (2001), which the Pulitzer jury in 2002 preferred to Jonathan Franzen's *The Corrections*, Richard Russo not only draws a complex picture of the U.S. at the end of the twentieth century, he also movingly reflects on the themes of good and evil. Empire Falls is a small mill town in Maine that has fallen on hard times ever since the Whiting factories closed some 20 years ago. The main character, Miles Roby, runs the local diner, which also serves as the local hangout. The diner, like almost everything else in Empire Falls, is owned by Francine, the widow of the last male descendant of the Whiting family, Charlie, with whom Miles's mother had an affair when Miles was still very young. Charlie disappeared and eventually committed suicide. Miles's mother, Grace, went to work as a housekeeper for Francine, expiating her sin for the rest of her life. Grace exhorted Miles to leave Empire Falls and escape the limitations of small town life by going to university. However, when Grace falls ill with cancer Miles returns, there to become stuck for the rest of his life, beholden now to Francine like his mother before him. Miles also has personal problems. His wife has left him for a local fitness club owner, and he worries about his daughter Tick who is ostracized at school. Even though set in remote Maine, Russo makes clear that Empire Falls stands for the entire U.S. when in an event reminiscent of the then recent 1999 Columbine high school massacre he has a pupil at Tick's school shoot several other pupils and teachers, wounding Tick, who nevertheless was his only friend. Miles resigns from the diner, and takes Tick to Martha's Vineyard, there to heal. Martha's Vineyard, however, was also where his mother took him when she had the affair with Charlie Whiting, and now Miles meets Charlie's ghost where thirty years earlier he had met the real man. Miles realizes that he has never accepted things as they are, first and foremost himself. When he and Tick return to Empire Falls things now almost miraculously seem to have resolved themselves. Francine has been killed in a flood of the river on which Empire Falls is situated and which had been tamed in order to build the mansion Francine wanted. The flood, then, liberates the river, but also liberates the town, which revives now that Francine's stranglehold on everything has been broken, and liberates Miles. Even his wife returns to him. All this is presented as an act of 'grace' (not coincidentally Miles's mother's name) in the face of the evil represented by Francine, who at the end of the book takes on the guise of a witch, and as the final outcome of what at first sight appears as the unfairness of life in the form of disease, economic hardship, or physical unattractiveness. If this makes *Empire Falls* sound like a deadly serious novel, nothing could be further from the truth; especially the scenes with Miles's wife and her lover are hilarious. Still, this does not prevent the novel from being 'moral fiction' in the sense we gave to it earlier on. All of Russo's other fictions, overwhelmingly set in small town New England or Upstate New York, fall into the same category.

Other authors that could be considered to write moral fiction are Anne Tyler (1941–) and Jonathan Franzen (1959–), undoubtedly the better known of the two because of his best-selling *The Corrections* (2001) and *Freedom* (2010). Tyler, whose first novel appeared in 1964, has written some twenty novels, winning a Pulitzer for *Breathing Lessons* (1988) and having several of her novels, such as for instance *The Accidental Tourist* (1985), turned into movies. Almost all of her fiction is set in Baltimore, where she herself lives. Tyler herself considers *Dinner at the Homesick Restaurant* (1982) her best work. Each of the Tull family children tries to create his or her own ideal home environment to compensate for their childhood lack of such because of the break-up of their parents. However, by desperately striving to attain the opposite of what they feel they have missed most – an ideal relationship, a stable home, family meals, home cooking – they err just as much, but differently, as did their parents, and especially their mother. In the end, however, it is the mother that in her dying days draws the necessary lessons from all this and arrives at real moral growth. Something similar applies to the father who, after thirty years of refusing to do so, finally participates again in the family dinner at the 'Homesick Restaurant' from the book's title, and that is owned by one of the Tull children. Tyler's later work has been called tepid and repetitive, harping on family chronicles, midlife crises, loneliness, misunderstandings leading to broken relationships, and often using similar plotlines, including sudden violent events that upset the lives of her characters, and supernatural interventions. Still, in *Digging to America* (2006) Tyler enlarges her usual canvas by sketching the relationship between two families, one all-American, the other Iranian-American, who both adopt a Korean child and thus become involved with one another. With this novel, then, Tyler, who herself was married to an Iranian psychiatrist and novelist (he died in 1997), moves in the direction of multiculturalism, while at the same time, after the manner of her characters, reflecting at least partially on her own life.

Jonathan Franzen had already published two other novels before *The Corrections* (2001) burst on the scene. Albert Lambert is a retired railroad engineer suffering from Parkinson's disease and sliding toward death. His wife, Enid, to whom he has been married for 47 years, desperately tries to get the three children, Gary, Denise and Chip, to spend one last Christmas at home with their father. However, this is not very much to the liking of the three, who are glad to have finally escaped Alfred's dictatorial regime. Still, none of them is very happy with his or her present life either. Gary, a banker, is henpecked by his wife. Denise, a cook in a Philadelphia restaurant, has gone through a divorce and has turned lesbian. Chip is a professor of literary theory and the author of a number of rejected screenplays. The 'corrections' from the title apply in various ways. The Lambert children are continuously corrected by their father in the guise of criticism and punishment. Alfred himself would need to have his brain corrected now that he is losing his memory. Gary suffers a setback on the exchange. Enid constantly has to correct Alfred when the latter does not precisely know what he wants to say. Everything the average American likes to consider ideal family life is obviously 'under correction' in this novel. But this also applies to American consumer society, American speech, and almost everything else in contemporary American life. In the end, though, family ties prove strongest, and once Alfred is safely underground, Enid at seventy-five finds her zest for life miraculously restored.

Freedom caused much controversy on its publication in 2010, some hailing it as (finally) 'the great American novel', others dismissing it as overlong, boring, dull, and lacking the satirical punch of *The Corrections*. One thing all reviewers agreed upon was the sense of realism with which Franzen had infused his family chronicle of the middle-class Berglunds moving between Minnesota, Washington, D.C. and New York over the final decades of the twentieth century and up to 2008. Touching upon various milieus, from artistically bohemian to Zionist and neoconservative, as well as upon environmental issues, and in its various locales embracing much of the U.S., *Freedom* is a sprawling novel that, as suggested in the book itself, aims to do for the contemporary U.S. what Tolstoy's *War and Peace* did for nineteenth-century Russia. Somewhat more modestly perhaps, but equally tellingly, the novel has also been likened to John Updike's chronicles of middle-class American life in roughly the same period.

Intertextual realism

A number of authors, while remaining radically realist in their elaboration of character and plot, still use at least one feature that figures prominently also in most accounts of postmodernism, that is to say intertextuality. Michael Cunningham (1952–) had already published three other novels before his real break came with *The Hours* (1998), a novel based on *Mrs. Dalloway* (1925) by the British author Virginia Woolf (1882–1941). With its main action set in the early 1990s rather than Woolf's early 1920s, but with its narrative span stretching back to the 1940s, and in New York rather than London, Cunningham skillfully interweaves three plotlines featuring Virginia Woolf herself, a latter-day Clarissa, part of the New York art and literary gay scene, and Laura Brown, a housewife fond of reading Virginia Woolf. On the very last pages of the novel all these characters turn out to be related to one another, sometimes in completely unexpected ways. Every page, almost every line of *The Hours* contains a reference, however oblique, to Mrs. Dalloway and to Virginia Woolf's own life. In his picture of Woolf, and in thus paying tribute to her work, Cunningham aims to hold her up as an example of how one can create great literature regardless of the limitations daily life, society, morality or our sexual inclinations impose upon us. 'The Hours', by the way, is the title Woolf herself had originally intended to give to *Mrs. Dalloway*.

Jeffery Eugenides (1963–) immediately scored with *The Virgin Suicides* (1993), in which a group of young men, twenty years after the fact, recount what they have been able to find out about the collective suicide of the five Lisbon family teenage sisters in a small town in Michigan in the 1970s. They never find a satisfactory answer. As the novel is told from a we-perspective the narrators act like the chorus in a Greek tragedy. In *Middlesex* (2002), which became an even bigger seller than *The Virgin Suicides*, Eugenides, who himself is of Greek-Irish descent, again uses techniques borrowed from classical antiquity. As the title already suggests, the protagonist Calliope/Cal Stephanides is both male and female. Calliope, born into a Greek-American family, starts life as a girl but will continue as a man. Calliope is the name of the Greek muse of epic and the most famous hermaphrodite in history is Tiresias, the blind seer from the *Iliad* and the *Odyssey*. *Middlesex* is not just about Cal/Calliope. It is just as much about how Cal/Calliope's ancestors, Lefty (Eleftherios) and Desdemona, in 1922, during the Greek-Turkish war, fled their home in Smyrna, in Southern Turkey, and emigrated to the U.S. Their expulsion also reverses the story of *The Iliad*, which is about the conquest of Troy, a city in Southern Turkey, by the Greeks some 1200 or more years B.C. The intertextual references do not stop here, though. In T.S. Eliot's *The Waste Land*, published in the same fateful year of 1922, there features a 'Mr. Eugenides, the Smyrna merchant', a fact obviously not unknown to Jeffrey Eugenides. An epic is supposed to tell a people's story by highlighting the life and fate of its heroes, and *Middlesex* is no exception. The novel reads like a synopsis of the history of the U.S., and of the western world in general, in the twentieth century. In 2011 Eugenides published *The Marriage Plot*, about the love relationships involving three young Americans, one female, two male, during their last year at university and beyond.

Definitely more postmodern, not only in its use of intertextual elements but also in its treatment of history, and at the same time also smacking of magical realism while still staying close to historical facts, is *The Amazing Adventures of Kavalier & Clay* (2000) by Michael Chabon (1963–). Chabon gained immediate recognition with his debut novel *The Mysteries of Pittsburgh* (1988), about gay and bisexual relations. His second novel, *Wonderboys* (1995) plays on the genre of the campus novel. At variance with Cunningham and Eugenides, Chabon in *Kavalier & Clay* for inspiration does not look towards canonical works but to American comics from the late 1930s to early 1960s. Loosely modeling his protagonists Jozef Kavalier and Samuel Clayman, later Clay, on the creators of Superman Jerry Siegel (1914–96) and Joe Shuster (1914–92), but mixing in traditional old world Jewish folk lore as recorded in *The Golem* (1914) by Gustav Meyrink (1868–1932), Chabon sketches the rise of American superhero comics as of the late 1930s as an answer from the largely Jewish American comics (and later also movie) industry to the threat of Nazism. *Kavalier & Clay* is a fascinating tale about the persecution of the Jews in Hitler's Germany, Jewish emigration to the U.S., traditional Jewish life in Prague and its re-creation, continuation and modification in the New World and particularly New York, and daily life in the U.S. in the middle of the twentieth century, all of it wrapped in a fictionalized history of the rise, development and partial demise of the comics industry in the U.S. The figure of the golem, by the way, has made a remarkable comeback in more recent American fiction, witness *The Puttermesser Papers* (1997) by Cynthia Ozick (1928–) and *The Golems of Gotham* (2002) by Thane Rosenbaum (1960–).

Jewishness plays an important part in all of Chabon's fiction. The protagonist of *The Yiddish Policemen's Union* (2007), for instance, is a Jewish detective in a semi-autonomous Jewish state established in Alaska after the collapse of Israel in 1948. *The Yiddish Policemen's Union* is an example of what is usually referred to as 'alternate history', that is to say a fiction describing what might have been the case had certain events in history taken a different turn, and as such often seen as a special branch of science fiction. In fact, from the beginning of his career Chabon has shown a particular interest in genre fiction, and most of his more recent works form no exception, with *Summerland* (2002) being a fantasy novel aimed at a youthful audience, *The Final Solution* (2004) having Sherlock Holmes as its protagonist, and *Gentlemen of the Road* (2007) a historical adventure novel set in tenth-century Russia. *Telegraph Avenue* (2012) on the contrary is a more realistic tale set in Oakland and Berkeley, California, involving the owners of a failing used vinyl record store, one Jewish and the other black, with the latter arranging a fundraiser for an unknown Illinois politician running for the U.S. Senate, a certain Barack Obama.

A slightly older author who, like Chabon in *Kavalier & Clay*, is not shy of occasionally resorting to some magic realism while still pinning his stories to real history, is T. C(oraghessan) Boyle (1948–). His first novel, *Water Music* (1981), is set in turn-of-the-nineteenth-century London, Scotland and Africa, and has the historical Mungo Park, African explorer, as one of its protagonists. *Budding Prospects* (1984) is a hilarious tale about a failed marihuana plantation in hippie California in the 1970s. A high point in Boyle's oeuvre is *World's End* (1987). Its setting, Peterskill, a village along the Hudson north of New York, is a fictionalized version of Peerskill, Boyle's own birthplace. The novel is situated in the present and in the seventeenth century, when the Hudson Valley was still in the hands of Dutch settlers, and pitches two Dutch-descended families against one another, the one 'patroons', owners of a large estate, the other servants and day laborers. An important subplot concerns how the original inhabitants of the land, the Indians, have been and continue being robbed of their lands and their rights. Poetic justice has it, though, that in the end an Indian-descended scion of the patroons, the product of an adulterous affair the wife of the last patroon had with a Native American, inherits all the wealth that over the past three hundred years was gathered in the valley. In *The Road to Wellville* (1993) Boyle fictionalizes the life of John Harvey Kellogg, the inventor of breakfast cereals and in other novels he has done the same with Cyrus McCormick, Alfred Kinsey, and Frank Lloyd Wright. But with equal gusto Boyle addresses topical issues, such as the plight of the hundreds of thousands of Mexicans illegally crossing into the U.S., there to be discriminated and exploited, in *Tortilla Curtain* (1995), his most popular novel to date. Invoking John Steinbeck's *Grapes of Wrath* Boyle establishes a parallel with the 'Okies' who in the 1930s because of drought and economic exploitation emigrated from the Dust Bowl of the Prairies to California. In other novels he discusses identity theft and environmental disasters leading to the extinction of certain species.

Philip Roth

Philip Roth has remained extremely prolific also after 1980, even to the point of becoming perhaps *the* iconic American author of the entire period. To begin with, Roth wrote a third novel in the David Kepesh series with *The Dying Animal* (2001). Then, he has continued the series of novels featuring Nathan Zuckerman, the first installment of which, *The Ghost Writer*, appeared in 1979 and the seventh, presumably also the last given its title of *Exit Ghost*, in 2007, with as other titles *Zuckerman Unbound* (1981), *The Anatomy Lesson* (1983), *The Prague Orgy* (1985), *The Counterlife* (1986), *American Pastoral* (1997), *I Married a Communist* (1998) and *The Human Stain* (2000). Zuckerman has often been interpreted as an alter ego for Roth himself, but as of 1990 there also started appearing a new series featuring a protagonist called 'Roth', comprising *Deception: A Novel* (1990), *Operation Shylock: A Confession* (1993) and *The Plot Against America* (2004). There is also a free-standing novel, *Sabbath's Theatre* (1995), and finally a series of short novels, *Everyman* (2006), *Indignation* (2008), *The Humbling* (2009) and *Nemesis* (2010). We will here briefly treat three exemplary instances from this overwhelming oeuvre.

American Pastoral, winner of the Pulitzer Prize in 1998, starts from the premise of the good life in the country as the culmination of the American Dream and a counterweight to the chaos, oppression and misery of the Old World. This is also what the protagonist of the story, whose life Zuckerman records, seems to have been bound for all his life, until everything fell apart. The novel is set in Newark, and the turning point is the 1960s, when Newark's earlier prosperity has melted away under the onslaught of beginning globalization, the city's older population of first and second generation immigrants, many of them Jewish, like the protagonist, have moved away or been minoritized by the large numbers of African Americans that have moved in. Instead of a harmonious community Newark now is the scene of race riots and labor conflicts. On the level of the U.S. as a whole the havoc wrought in Newark repeats itself in the radical youth and political movements rocking the country. Roth returns a hard verdict on what has gone wrong with America during his own lifetime.

A similar feeling speaks from *The Plot Against America*, winner of the Sidewise Award for Alternate History in 2005. Roth finds his initial inspiration in a plea Charles Lindbergh, the first man to cross the Atlantic by airplane in 1927 and a national hero, made in 1941 to prevent the U.S. from entering World War II, for which he blamed the Jews, the British, and President Roosevelt. Lindbergh was in good standing with the Nazi regime and especially with Goering, the commander of the German air force. Roth takes the poetic liberty of situating Lindbergh's speech not in 1941 but in 1940, in the run-up to that year's Presidential elections, and casting Lindbergh as the Republican challenger of Roosevelt. When Lindbergh wins the election, life in the U.S. turns bitter for American Jews, and hence also for little Philip Roth. Things look even more somber when Lindbergh disappears on a solo flight with his famous Spirit of St. Louis airplane and Vice-President Wheeler, an extreme rightwing politician, assumes office. In the end, everything returns to normal, Roosevelt triumphs in a special election, Pearl Harbor signals the entry of the U.S. into World War II, and history resumes its familiar course. *The Plot Against America* asks some hard questions about the nature of American democracy and American politics more generally. For most commentators it was hardly a coincidence that Roth published a novel focusing on these questions, and with such characters, in the run-up to the 2004 elections, with an incumbent who in the wake of 9/11 had instituted an authoritarian regime such as the U.S. had hardly ever seen before, and with a Vice-President of known conservative sympathies.

If *American Pastoral* and *The Plot Against America* address wider social and political issues, *Everyman* sticks to the personal level. In all of Roth's later work the consciousness of approaching death is overwhelmingly present, and particularly so in the four short novels he published towards the end of his career (Roth in 2013 announced that he thought he had written enough and would write no more). In the further unspecified 'he' protagonist Roth gives us a reincarnation of the medieval 'everyman' from the eponymous morality play. But whereas the medieval Everyman finds that with death all material worries and constraints dissolve and only spiritual virtues remain, because after death comes resurrection, nothing of the sort happens in Roth's version. *Everyman* reads as the chronicle of a death announced, a merciless march from the cradle to the grave marked by disease, illness, the relentless deterioration of the body, deaths and funerals. Like the medieval play it holds up the mirror of our own fallibility and ephemerality, but without the consolation of faith.

War fiction

In the work of Chabon and Foer we saw how pervasive the presence of World War II still is in contemporary American fiction, particularly so in the guise of the Holocaust. Roth's *The Plot Against America* may be alternate history of the same war, and in that sense 'unreal', but it is realistically told. In fact, the period 1980 to 2010 has yielded a considerable number of realistic war stories against the background of real wars. An author who in his work combines journalism, fiction, but also drawings, thus on the one hand tending towards absolute realism and on the other towards postmodernism, is William T. Vollmann (1959–). In 1987 he made his debut with examples of both kinds of production. *An Afghanistan Picture Show; or, How I Saved the World* reports on his stay with the Mujahedin fighting the Russians in Afghanistan. *You Bright and Risen Angels* is a novel set in the world of computers and games and focuses on the struggle between good and evil, humans and insects, progressives and reactionaries. The book is clearly meant as an allegory and resembles a comic book, including drawings by Vollmann himself. In 1990 *The Ice-Shirt* appeared, the first of a projected seven-part series on the conquest of North America under the common title *Seven Dreams: A Book of North American Landscapes*. *The Atlas* (1996) comprises fifty-three tales illustrating what is wrong with our world, in a mixture of reportage, autobiography, essay and fiction. Vollmann's biggest success, though, is *Central Europe* (2005), a voluminous novel about the struggle between Nazi Germany and Stalin's Soviet Union in World War II and mixing historical and fictional characters.

Earlier we saw that Buford included Bobbie Ann Mason (1940–) and Tobias Wolff (1945–) among his Dirty Realists. Mason's early *Shiloh and Other Stories* (1982) is indeed a powerful mix of Dirty Realism and Southern regionalism. Her fame, however, mainly rests on *In Country* (1985). This novel is equally regional, and equally Dirty Realist in its references to 1980s popular culture. However, it is primarily about the war in Vietnam: 'in country' refers to soldiers in the field, that is to say actively engaging the enemy on the ground. The protagonist of *In Country* is a seventeen-year-old girl who has never known her father because he died in Vietnam before she was born. She now lives with an uncle who in 'Nam was exposed to the infamous chemical 'agent orange'. The bitterness of the veterans and their descendants, who feel forgotten because of an unpopular war, and most of whom belonged to the poorer parts of the American population, is palpable in this book. Samantha finally achieves some kind of peace and reconciliation with her father when she reads his name on the Vietnam Veterans Memorial in Washington. Mason returned to the theme of war, though this time World War II, with *The Girl in the Blue Beret* (2011), about a bomber plane pilot who crashed in occupied France in 1944. Wolff drew on his own time in Vietnam for the stories in *Back in the World* (1985), the title of which refers to an expression service men in Vietnam used to signal their return from duty at the front, the novella *Barracks Thief* (1994), about three recruits who await transport to the war, and the memoir *In Pharaoh's Army* (1994).

An author whose name is inextricably linked to Vietnam is Tim O'Brien (1946–). O'Brien's own service in Vietnam provided him with the material for *If I Die in a Combat Zone, Box Me Up and Ship me Home* (1973). His first novel, *Northern Lights* (1975), is set in O'Brien's birth state Minnesota, and deals with two brothers, one of whom returned from Vietnam wounded. O'Brien's biggest successes are *Going after Cacciato* (1978) and *The Things They Carried* (1990), both of which are considered 'classics' about the war in Vietnam. *Going after Cacciato* plays out in the mind of Paul Berlin during one night in which he is standing watch in Vietnam. The book alternates between Berlin's reality and what he imagines would happen if his unit were to go after Cacciato, a deserter en route for Paris, over land. Perhaps, however, Cacciato is only a figment of Berlin's imagination. Still, the novel describes the hunt for Cacciato and Vietnam in such detail that the reader cannot help feeling that he is confronted with raw reality instead of fiction. O'Brien subscribes to the notion that the truth, particularly about anything as stark as war, and hence also Vietnam, is served better by fiction than by journalism or history writing. The narrator of his own fictions is invariably O'Brien himself, or in any case a character that as far as age and name is consonant with the author of that name. At the same time he feels that such fiction should stick as close as possible to observable reality. Consequently, his stories and novels come close to the 'non-fiction' genre as practiced by for instance Michael Herr (1940–), a war correspondent whose *Dispatches* (1977) remains one of the best books about the war in Vietnam. At the same time O'Brien's fictions always insist that they are fiction. This duality is thematized in *Going after Cacciato* as well as in *The Things They Carried*, in which the stories

'Good Form' and 'How to Tell a True War Story' illustrate O'Brien's ideas. *The Things They Carried* is often cited as the best book about the war in Vietnam. In Vietnam O'Brien served with the Amical Division, which was involved in the My Lai massacre in which American soldiers killed scores of Vietnamese civilians. This event, or something very similar, plays an important role in O'Brien's novel *In the Lake of the Woods* (1994).

In 'On the Rainy River', from *The Things They Carried*, O'Brien, or in any case his narrator, says that he went to Vietnam because he was a coward, instead of resisting going there. Robert Stone (1937–) much more outspokenly denounces the war in Vietnam in *Dog Soldiers* (1974), and has continued to sharply criticize U.S. foreign policy in *A Flag for Sunrise* (1981) and *Damascus Gate* (1998). The war in Vietnam takes on a wholly different aspect in *A Good Scent from a Strange Mountain* (1992) by Robert Olen Butler (1945–), about Vietnamese refugees who have emigrated to New Orleans. Many authors who first gained notice with Vietnam war fiction later tried their hand at other kinds of fiction, usually with little success. That this war continues to trouble U.S. conscience, and animate U.S. literature well into the new millennium, thirty years after it ended in 1975, became clear, though, with the publication in 2007 of *Tree of Smoke*, by Denis Johnson (1949–). Johnson earlier already had published several collections of poetry as well as seven novels, the best known of which is *Fiskadora* (1985). Of his many publications, though, the greatest stir had been caused by the undeniably Dirty Realist *Jesus's Son* of 1992. All stories in this collection have an I-narrator who lives at the margins of society, with as his main worry drugs and how to get them. In 'Dirty Wedding' the narrator is riding the El in Chicago while his girlfriend is having an abortion. She eventually leaves him, moves away with another man, and commits suicide. Everything is narrated dead-pan as if this is the normal run of things in the world. *Tree of Smoke*, which follows five main characters during their time in Vietnam from 1963 to 1970, and ends on a brief epilogue in 1983, immediately became the subject of heated controversy, some critics hailing it as the best book ever about Vietnam while others thought it pretentious, lacking plot, characters, and style. In general it was not thought a coincidence that so negative and critical a book about Vietnam as is *Tree of Smoke* appeared at a time when the U.S. was involved in a war in Iraq that to many recalled the worst of that earlier war. In fact, *Tree of Smoke* is not just about the débâcle of the Vietnam war but also about the moral bankruptcy of the U.S. in the final decades of the twentieth century.

It is not just the war in Vietnam that continues to stir the American literary imagination. Judging from the number of more recent fictions dealing with the topic, and the success they are having, this is also still the case with the Civil War. The tone was set by *Cold Mountain* (1997) by Charles Frazier (1950–). The novel follows a Confederate soldier who shortly before the end of the war deserts from the field hospital where he is being treated for a wound before being sent back to the front on his flight to his native village in the mountainous northern parts of North Carolina. He succeeds in reaching his village, and the girl who is waiting for him there, but a military patrol finds him out and he is executed. The novelty of *Cold Mountain* lay at least partially in the freshness of its nature descriptions, the attention paid to regional customs and the lives of ordinary people, and their love for the land. In this sense the novel chimed with a tendency towards regionalism but also towards ecological responsibility and a return to more simple customs and life on the land we can also notice in much fiction about the western parts of the U.S. written since the last quarter of the twentieth century. However, the novel leaves no doubt whatsoever about the cruelty of war, and mercilessly pictures how greed, malice, and a perverse pleasure in making innocent people suffer, triumph in times of war. In 2006 Frazier published *Thirteen Moons*, a novel that captures the nineteenth-century history of the South in the character of its protagonist.

The rather unexpected success of *Cold Mountain* apparently alerted a number of novelists to unexplored possibilities. Among the best known of these is E.L. Doctorow, who in 2005 published *The March*, about General William Tecumseh Sherman's scorched earth campaign through Georgia and the Carolinas near the end of the Civil War. As with his earlier best seller *Ragtime* Doctorow here again mixes historical characters with fictional ones, with some of the latter either having clear links with or actually issuing from some of his earlier works. Sherman's campaign also figures prominently in *Amalgamation Polka* (2006) by Stephen Wright (1946–). Wright had already written a stylistically experimental, even postmodern, book about the Vietnam war with *Meditations in Green* (1983). In both *The March* and *Amalgamation Polka* race relations play a major role. The Civil War and abolitionism furnish one of the story lines in *Gilead* (2005) by Marilynne Robinson (1947–).

For socio-economic reasons the American forces deployed in Vietnam to an inordinately high degree consisted of soldiers drawn from the Southern U.S. The Southern states, certainly in the period of the Vietnam war, held a higher proportion of poor and black young men than the Northern states, and these were the categories that were first called up for military service as they could not file for deferment as their better-off coevals could for reasons of university study. But the South also has a military tradition that goes back to the days of the Civil War. Bobby Ann Mason's *In Country* for instance refers to this Southern past to interpret the American present. Critics have also often posited that the American South was better prepared to deal with military defeat or failure in Vietnam because unlike the North it already had experience with defeat. An author who has made the relationship between the war in Vietnam and the Civil War into a central given of his fiction is Barry Hannah (1942–2010). Hannah made his debut with *Geronimo Rex* (1972), an exuberant novel of education. In the stories from *Airships* (1978) and *Bats Out of Hell* (1993), though, both the war in Vietnam and the Civil War loom large. Where in earlier Southern fiction the Civil War most often served to celebrate the heroism of the Southern cause and as the pivot of what set the South apart from, and made it better than, the rest of the U.S., Hannah resolutely defuses these myths. In *Ray* (1980) a physician who served as a pilot in Vietnam draws the analogy between Vietnam and the Civil War. His conclusion is that history cannot offer any solace for the present, and can serve even less as a legitimation to repeat in the present injustices and cruelties committed in the past. The Civil War, like the war in Vietnam, can be interpreted from various points of view, without any one of these versions necessarily being the 'correct' one.

Multiculturalism

Multicultural authors are by definition non-white or Caucasian. In American administrative usage this comprises African Americans as well as Americans of Asian and Latin American descent. While writers of these origins featured in American literature well before 1980, as we have seen in previous chapters, since this date they undoubtedly have come to occupy a much more important place. A number of African American authors already active before 1980 produced their most important work after this date. This certainly applies to Toni Morrison, who gained a Pulitzer, the Nobel Prize, and worldwide fame with *Beloved* (1987). The novel is based on the true story of Margaret Garner, a slave who in 1856 fled, with her husband and children, from Kentucky, a slave state, to Ohio, a free state. When slavers caught up with the Garners Margaret decided to kill her children rather than let them be returned to slavery, and then to kill herself. However, she only succeeded in killing her two-year-old daughter. In *Beloved* the slave woman Sethe escapes to Ohio. When she is about to be caught she kills her little daughter. On account of this deed Sethe is judged insane, and is further left in peace. Many years later a young woman, 'Beloved', appears who claims to be Sethe's daughter returned from the dead. It never becomes entirely clear whether Beloved is real or only exists in Sethe's imagination and that of her other daughter Danvers. Though *Beloved*, like some of Morrison's earlier novels, shows some magical-realist traits, the novel leaves little doubt that it amounts to a sharp condemnation of the reality of slavery and the discrimination against African Americans that followed its abolition. Two later novels, *Jazz* (1992) and *Paradise* (1997), together with *Beloved* make up what Morrison has called her African American history trilogy.

Alice Walker, Toni Cade Bambara, Gayl Jones, Paule Marshall and Ntozake Shange produced important new work after 1980, and so did Ernest Gaines and John Edgar Wideman. Walker impressed not so much with her novels *The Temple of My Familiar* (1989), a history of almost all of mankind that lays most of what has gone wrong in that history at the door of the male half of humanity, and *Possessing the Secret of Joy* (1992), a denunciation of clitoridectomy as practiced in some African cultures, but with her essay collection *In Search of Our Mothers' Gardens: Womanist Prose* (1983). The latter opens with Walker's definition of a 'womanist' as 'a black feminist' or 'feminist of color' and 'a woman who loves other women, sexually and/or nonsexually', and also contains her best known essays on Zorah Neale Hurston. Bambara published the novels *The Salt Eaters* (1980) and *Those Bones Are Not My Child* (1999). Jones in her later work, such as *Mosquito* (1999), calls for solidarity between minority women, as when the black female truck driver whose name also forms the title to the novel finds a pregnant illegal Mexican immigrant woman in her truck, helps her give birth, and takes further care of her. Shange looked at the busing of students to desegregate American schools in *Betsey Brown* (1985), a novel based on her own childhood memories of St Louis. In *Sassafrass, Cypress & Indigo* (1982) she gave a lyrical evocation of the lives of three black sisters, each of whom has a special gift, in Charleston, while *Liliane* (1994) is about a black female artist. Marshall with *Praisesong for the Widow* (1983), a novel set in the Caribbean but with an African American female protagonist, continues the search for black authenticity also pervading her earlier work. Part of that search involves a return to African customs in the form of dances, rituals, but also the language of African origin, Gullah, spoken on the islands before the coast of South Carolina.

A search for black authenticity and a Gullah setting are also central features of *Mama Day* (1988) by Gloria Naylor (1950–). *Praisesong for the Widow* and *Mama Day* also share a form of magical realism bordering on voodoo, and references to Shakespeare, particularly *The Tempest* but with Naylor also *Hamlet*. Earlier, Naylor had already gained notice with *The Women of Brewster Place* (1982), a neo-realist novel about seven black women in New York, and *Linden Hills* (1985), a dark allegory on the struggle between materialism and idealism in African American society. Later she also published *Bailey's Café* (1992), about the female customers of a New York pub, and *The Men of Brewster Place* (1999), a sequel and pendant to her first novel.

Recent black women's fiction foregrounds the double discrimination, as women and as blacks, black women suffer. In this sense their work continues in the traditions of both black writing and feminist writing, although it often also modifies and corrects these traditions. Black male writers continue the line of Wright, Baldwin and Ellison, and primarily focus on race relations. This is certainly true for such older writers as Gaines in *A Gathering of Old Men* (1983) and *A Lesson before Dying* (1993). In *A Gathering of Old Men* the death of a Cajun, a white descendant of French pioneers who in the eighteenth century were exiled from Canada to Louisiana, threatens to lead to a lynching. Several people do die in this novel, but on the whole its tone is humorous, and the old black men who risk lynching end up not only the moral victors of the tale, they also find the law on their side. *A Lesson before Dying* is grimmer. Grant Wiggins and Jefferson are both black and live in the South. Grant has gone to university, Jefferson has not. Although innocent of the crime, Jefferson is convicted for the murder of a white storekeeper. Grant convinces him to die honorably. Jefferson finally turns into a redeemer of both the white and black communities. With his Homewood trilogy, comprising the story collection *Damballah* (1981) and the novels *Hiding Place* (1981) and *Sent for You Yesterday* (1983), Wideman taps into his own family history in the black part of Pittsburgh. Homewood is also the setting of *Reuben* (1987), which is about a black lawyer and his customers, and the style of which has often been likened to Faulkner's. Wideman's best known works, however, are *Philadelphia Fire* (1990) and *The Cattle Killing* (1996). The first of these starts from the 1985 police siege of the headquarters of the radical Afrocentric MOVE in Philadelphia, and in which a number of black people, including children, lost their lives. In *The Cattle Killing* Wideman draws a number of parallels between a yellow fever epidemic in Philadelphia in 1793, the slaughter of their cattle by the Xhosa in South Africa in 1853 in an attempt to stop the advance of the white colonists, and the struggle for black emancipation in the U.S. and South Africa.

Slavery and discrimination are at the heart of the work of Charles Johnson (1948–), David H(enry) Bradley (1950–) and Edward P. Jones (1951–). Johnson wrote several collections of stories and essays, as well as novels, but is best known for *Oxherding Tale* (1982), in which the half-blood protagonist literally embodies the contrast between the two races and cultures that inhabit him, but also between Western and Eastern ways of thinking and acting, and especially *The Middle Passage* (1990), a short novel about a successful slave revolt on board an American slaver, the *Republic*, and the transformation this works in its slave-protagonist. *The Middle Passage*, like all of Johnson's work, mixes literature and philosophy, with intertextual references to Melville's *Moby Dick* and *Benito Cereno*, the *Narrative* of Olaudah Equiano, Saint Teresa of Ávila, the Marquis de Sade and numerous other writers and philosophers. The novel is also rooted in real precedents, though, such as the revolt on the Amistad in 1839 and that on the Creole in 1841, as well as on the novella *The Heroic Slave* (1853) by Frederick Douglass. Bradley only published two novels, *South Street* (1975) and *The Chaneysville Incident* (1981). The latter novel features a contemporary black intellectual who, from his own memory, and from what he hears from other characters, reconstructs his own family history, which hinges upon the suicide of a number of run-away slaves when they were about to be recaptured by slave hunters. Jones in 2003 surprised the American literary world with *The Known World*, a novel about a black slave owner, Henry Townsend, in Virginia, and how his plantation, and the world it embodies, disintegrate with the Civil War. The title of the novel refers to the famous sixteenth-century Waldseemüller map which for the first time features the New World as part of 'the known world', a reproduction of which decorates the wall of the sheriff's office in Manchester County, where Henry's plantation is situated, and which is contrasted with two other maps, made by a black female artist formerly a slave on the plantation herself, picturing, in a naïve mode, Henry's plantation before its devastation and Manchester County seen from the perspective of God. Together, these maps chronicle the differences between white and black visions of things, and what differences the Civil War has wrought.

More recent African American authors like Percivall Everett (1956–) and Colson Whitehead (1969–) at least partially shift their focus to other issues than those of slavery, discrimination and race relations in general. Everett has done work in various genres, including poetry, essays, juvenile fiction, science fiction and the Western, as well as adaptations of classical myths. His most interesting novel, *Erasure* (2001), like much of Everett's work, is a parody, in this case of African American literature, and is grounded in Everett's own experiences. Thelonious 'Monk' Ellison is, like Everett himself, an African American author and professor of literature. Because he writes in a postmodern vein, adapts classical myths, and writes on French philosophy and literary theory, he is deemed not black enough by predominantly white publishers. Enraged by the success of a black female author who exploits all possible clichés about blacks in a novel that is widely praised for its 'authenticity', without its author herself having any experience whatsoever of 'lowdown' black life, Thelonious produces an outrageously crude parody using dialect and stark neo-realism partially inspired by Wright's *Native Son*. He gives the novel the title 'Fuck', and publishes it under the penname Stagg R. Leigh, after Stagger Lee, a nineteenth-century black pimp executed for murder and the subject of a famous blues song. 'Fuck' is hailed as the ultimate expression of 'real' blackness and becomes a huge success. Seduced by lucrative movie contracts and universally praised as Stagg R. Leigh, Thelonious, who originally thought to 'erase' his blackness because he thought race unimportant for the kind of author he wanted to be, now instead proceeds to erase his original identity. *Erasure* is a bruising attack on how African American, and by extension all other minority authors are type-cast along ethnic and racial lines, and as such also a denunciation of multiculturalism.

Whitehead's first novel, *The Intuitionist* (1998), was well-received, but his second, *John Henry Days* (2001), was showered with praise and only narrowly missed the Pulitzer. The main setting of *John Henry Days* is a 1996 festival in a small West Virginia town, in celebration of a legendary folk hero, John Henry, a black railroad laborer who in the nineteenth century would have worked on the Big Bend railway tunnel in West Virginia, and who is said to have won a contest against a steam drill for driving a steel pin into a rock wall. The novel alternates between past and present, John Henry's days and those of the festival. However, in the novel the very existence of John Henry is continuously put in doubt. All characters that claim to remember him ultimately are revealed to have things only from hearsay. Some are sure he was black, others that he was white. Others claim he lived either earlier or later than commonly assumed. When Henry himself features in a number of episodes we are never sure whether these are real events or figments of the imagination of Sutter, a journalist-character in the novel. The entire novel, featuring innumerable characters, from a young black woman whose father put together a private museum about John Henry, over an Eastern European Jewish immigrant who struggles to survive in the New York music industry in the early years of the twentieth century, to Sutter's mother who as a black middle-class girl in Harlem has to learn to play the piano, and set in many different times, places and milieus, is a composite picture of America, and of the stories it tells itself. A central question Whitehead poses in *John Henry Days* is whether we really want to continue the rat race of modernity that leads to destruction, or whether we opt for a more humane form of society.

If African American writers probably still make up the largest contingent of multicultural authors, since 1980 the ranks of Asian and Latin American descended writers have swollen considerably. But whereas most African American authors share a similar past, the same is not true, for instance, for so-called Hispanics. Although they all share a Spanish-language background, there is a marked difference between those with a more recent history of immigration from Cuba, such as Oscar Hijuelos (1951–) and Cristina García (1958–), from the Dominican Republic, such as Julia Alvárez (1950–), or Puerto Rico, like Judith Ortiz Cofer (1952–), and Chicano/as, descended from populations that antedate the arrival of the gringos into territories subsequently incorporated into the U.S. The latter often write from a feeling of injustice about having their lands stolen from them and their people having been demoted to second-class citizens. As such they have a lot in common with Native Americans, who have even more right to feel wronged. Hijuelos, Alvárez, and their peers have more in common with other relative newcomers such as Asian Americans.

Of Chicano authors already active before 1980, Rudolfo Anaya in 1992 published *Alburquerque*, in which the search of the Mexican American boxer Abrán González for his father is at the same time a search for the identity of the capital of New Mexico which according to Anaya at the end of the nineteenth century was mistakenly bereft of its original first 'r' by an Anglo railroad engineer and thereby also of its true Spanish-Mexican soul. Anaya also authored a series of detective novels with as protagonist the Chicano Sonny Baca.

As with African American literature, so too with Hispanic literature it is especially women authors that have come to the fore. Gloria Anzaldúa (1942–2004) first came to attention with *This Bridge Called My Back: Writings by Radical Women of Color* (1981), an anthology of writings by minority women Anzaldúa co-edited with Cherríe Moraga (1952–). She gained fame, though, with *Borderlands/La Frontera: The New Mestiza* (1987). A mixture of essay, fiction and poetry, the book underwrites a lesbian-feminist as well as a Chicano/a agenda. With the use of the term 'mestizaje' Anzaldúa wanted to do away with the binarism and essentialism she saw issuing from multiculturalism as advocated in the U.S. in the 1980s, and instead bring about a new, hybrid identity. She aimed to cancel the border between Mexico and the U.S., but also that between races and genders. Specifically, she wanted to finish with the type-casting of Chicanas as either saints or whores which led to the women being forced into pre-ordained roles. Anzaldúa saw her own writings as a means of giving Chicanas greater purchase on their own fate. In her own work mestizaje or hybridity also assumes the form of creolization: the in-mixing of Spanish into English. A brilliant example is her poem 'El Sonovabitche', in which a Chicana dresses down an Anglo rancher in perfect English, but by incorporating also some Spanish words, which remain untranslated, makes him feel that English is not the only language in the U.S., and that he has to share power, and the language of power, with America's 'others'.

Not every Chicano thinks like Anzaldúa when it comes to the use of Spanish. In *Hunger of Memory: The Education of Richard Rodríguez* (1981) Richard Rodríguez (1944–) argues that integration via early adoption of English works best for Latinos, at least when it comes to public life. Whatever language they use for private relations is an entirely different matter. Rodríguez, who until the age of six had been raised in Spanish but from then on had attended English-language schools, and had built himself a career as an essayist and columnist, pointed to himself as proof of his argument. Critics replied that Rodríguez's success was just as much, or more, due to his having grown up in a middle-class family in a well-to-do San Francisco suburb and being very intelligent. In other words, they found him to be atypical in comparison with the majority of Mexican Americans. Rodríguez further elaborated his ideas in *Mexico's Children* (1990), *Days of Obligation: An Argument with my Mexican Father* (1992) and *Brown: The Last Discovery of America* (2002).

A younger female author who does at least partially subscribe to Anzaldúa's ideas is Sandra Cisneros (1954–). In her work too we encounter instances of creolization and a feminist agenda. *The House on Mango Street* (1984) is a novel of education with a protagonist who, like Cisneros herself, grows up in Chicago's Latino quarter. The book, rather than a novel proper a collection of forty-four vignettes, seen from the perspective of a child, details the poverty of Mexican Americans in the big city, but also their solidarity. At the same time it highlights the sexual ripening of a young Latina. In the stories from *Woman Hollering Creek* (1991) the setting shifts to the Mexican–U.S. border. All stories are told from a female perspective, but varying from an adolescent to a witch. *Caramelo* (2002) spans three generations of a Mexican family and emigration to the U.S. The title of the book refers to a striped shawl that plays an important role in the story and that stands for its checkered evocation of the Mexican American community. Detailing the hard lives of migrant Mexican field hands working in the California vineyards is *Under The Feet of Jesus* (1994) by María Viramontes (1954–). Her second novel, *Their Dogs Came with Them* (2007), focuses on the lives of four young Mexican Americans in East Los Angeles during the 1960s.

With *The Mambo Kings Play Songs of Love* (1989) by Hijuelos we turn to work by a non-Chicano Latino or Hispanic author. Hijuelos himself was born in New York but his parents were Cuban immigrants. The latter is also the case with the two 'mambo kings', the trumpet-playing brothers Nestor and César Castillo. The novel follows their journey from Oriente in Cuba to New York in the late 1940s, their success as the leaders of a mambo orchestra at a time when Latin American and especially Cuban music was extremely popular in the U.S., their brief moment of glory when they appear on the 1950s *I Love Lucy* television show, their decline when after Fidel Castro comes to power in Cuba in 1959 things Cuban fall out of favor, and finally the death of Nestor and César's descent into alcohol and oblivion. César dies of a heart attack in 1980, all alone in a hotel in New York, not far from where twenty-five years before he had triumphed with the Mambo Kings. A major theme running through the novel is a song Nestor wrote right before his departure from Cuba for a girl he briefly dated in Havana, 'Beautiful Maria of My Soul'. When César's body is found a copy of the song lies next to him, a symbol of the immigrant's hopeless but ceaseless longing for his country of origin, the fullness of his lost identity. The same feeling was expressed in Hijuelos's earlier novel *Our House in the Last World* (1983), in which a Cuban family emigrates to New York but keeps dreaming of the island in the sun. None of Hijuelos's novels after *The Mambo Kings* achieved a comparable success, even though in some of them, notably *Empress of the Splendid Season* (1999) and *A Simple Habana Melody* (2003), he returned to the themes of his Pulitzer Prize winner

Pilar Puente del Pino, the narrator of *Dreaming in Cuban* (1992), according to her creator Cristina García is an alter ego of herself. García was born in Cuba but at a very young age was brought to New York by her parents. In *Dreaming in Cuban* she analyzes her own feelings, and those of her mother and grandmother, about Cuba and the Cuban revolution, which plays a major role in the lives of the three women, directly so for the mother and grandmother, and through them for Pilar. The conclusion is that women pay a high price for a history made by men. The grandmother stays in Cuba after the revolution, the mother emigrates to the U.S. with Pilar, born, like García herself, shortly before the revolution. While successfully integrated in the U.S., the mother and Pilar keep thinking of Cuba, and at a given moment Pilar starts dreaming 'in Cuban', that is to say in Spanish, the language of the island. Pilar's return to Cuba there to meet her grandmother brings about a reconciliation between generations and those that stayed and those that chose exile. García took up the same theme again in *The Agüero Sisters* (1997) in which two sisters make opposite choices: Reina stays in Cuba and schools herself as an electrician in the service of the revolution, Constancia emigrates to the U.S. and becomes a successful businesswoman. With *Monkey Hunting* (2003) García turned to a completely different topic with a saga, some have called it an epic, of four generations of a Chinese-Cuban family. *King of Cuba* (2013) pits a fictionalized octogenarian Fidel Castro against a Cuban coeval exiled in Miami.

Most of the characters in the novels of Julia Alvárez share her own Dominican descent. Some of her later novels, such as *In the Time of the Butterflies* (1994) and *In the Name of Salomé* (2001), primarily deal with Dominican history, and are at least partially based on real characters and events. *How the García Girls Lost Their Accent* (1991), on the contrary, is concerned with migration to the U.S. Consisting of fifteen interconnected stories or vignettes, snapshots almost of life in the U.S., we follow the lives of the four García sisters, backward from when they have already been living in the U.S. for a long time to when with their parents they emigrated from the Dominican Republic. The focus is on the problems the children and their parents have adapting to American society, and how the generation gap between them is reinforced by the quickly opening cultural gap between the girls, who assimilate very quickly, and the parents, who never really get accustomed to their new life. As the four girls are still quite young at the time of emigration, the novel also assumes the character of a coming-of-age story of Latina women. *Yo!* (1997) is a sequel to *How the García Girls Lost Their Accent*, focusing on one of the sisters, Yolanda.

The literary sensation of 2008, *The Brief Wondrous Life of Oscar Wao* made the Dominican-American Junot Díaz (1968–) a literary star overnight. Like Alvárez, but in a more hiphop style, using Spanglish, references to popular culture phenomena that recall the work of some postmodernists, especially David Foster Wallace, mixing sci-fi and magic realism, Díaz too addresses the immigrant experience, as he also did in his collection of stories *Drown* (1996). The focus of the stories in *How you Lose Her* (2012) is invariably love, in all its guises.

The choice between integration or assimilation and the affirmation of a different, in this case Puerto Rican, identity furnishes the central theme of Judith Ortiz Cofer's *The Line of the Sun* (1989), *Silent Dancing: A Partial Remembrance of a Puerto Rican Childhood* (1990), and the stories collected in *The Latin Deli* (1993).

Immigrants from the Caribbean, writing in English, often raised and educated at least partially in the U.S., and living in the U.S., yet continuing to occupy an ambiguous relation with regard to 'American' literature are Michelle Cliff (1946–), Jamaica-born, Jamaica Kincaid (1949–), born in Antigua, and Edwidge Danticat (1969–), Haiti-born. Because of the subjects they write about, and which focus on things Caribbean rather than U.S.-related, these authors are more commonly categorized as postcolonial than American in the sense we use it in this book.

Like 'Hispanic', 'Asian' too is a common denominator for what in fact are a whole range of different literatures, even if most of them do share a number of traits. Of Chinese American authors active before 1980 really only Maxine Hong Kingston produced important new work with *Tripmaster Monkey* (1989). The protagonist of this complex novel is a character of very mixed descent called Wittman Ah Sing, looking for how he fits in American society. As the reference to Walt Whitman and his 'Song of Myself' already signals, Hong Kingston has epic ambitions with her novel. As Whitman embraced all of nineteenth-century America, so Kingston wants to do the same with its late twentieth-century multicultural equivalent. *The Joy Luck Club* (1989) brought immediate fame to Amy Tan (1952–). Four Chinese immigrant women meet once a week to play Mahjong. When one of them dies her daughter, Jing-mei Woo, takes her place. Each in turn, the three surviving original members of the Joy Luck Club, all of whom were born in China, and their daughters, all born in the U.S., tell their story. Jing-mei Woo learns that her mother at the time of her death had been planning to go to China there to meet with the two daughters she abandoned when she fled China to escape the advancing Japanese army during the Sino-Japanese war. Jing-mei Woo will go in her mother's place, thus bringing about a reconciliation with those who stayed and those who emigrated, but also between herself and the memory of her mother, with whom she often found herself at odds. In her later work, *The Kitchen God's Wife* (1991), *The Hundred Secret Senses* (1995) and *The Bonesetter's Daughter* (2001), Tan reverts to the same themes but she was never able to repeat the success of her first novel. And her venture into different territory with *Saving Fish from Drowning* (2005), about a tourist trip a number of Chinese Americans make to China and Myanmar, was very ill received.

The autobiographical impulse that shows so strongly in Hong Kingston and Tan's work, and in that of minority authors in general, is also abundantly present in *China Boy* (1991), a mix of fiction and memoir about growing up in the 1950s in San Francisco, by Gus Lee (1946–). *Honor and Duty* (1994) takes Kai Ting, the protagonist also of *China Boy*, to the American Military Academy at West Point in the 1960s, and *Tiger's Tail* (1996), set on an American army base in the demilitarized zone between North and South Korea, has a protagonist who although he goes by a different name could easily be a double of Kai Ting. *On Gold Mountain* (1995) by Lisa

See (1955–) tracks the family history of the See family from the middle of the nineteenth century, when the great-grandfather emigrated to the U.S., to the present. 'Gold Mountain' was the name given to the U.S. by the Chinese in the nineteenth century, following the discovery of gold in California in 1849. *On Gold Mountain* became a best-seller, and See followed up with a series of detective novels set in Beijing and featuring a mixed Chinese American woman-man team of sleuths. She returned to the Chinese past with the historical novels *Snow Flower and the Secret Fan* (2004) and *Peony in Love* (2007) in which she paid special attention to the lives of Chinese women in the seventeenth and nineteenth centuries respectively, and *Shanghai Girls* (2009), which features two sisters who flee Shanghai before the Japanese invasion and emigrate to the U.S. with all the pain and discrimination this brings. Rather than affirm a specific identity, Gish Jen (1955–) in *Typical Chinese* (1991) questions the concept of any such identity. Three Chinese students – a sister and brother and a girl who soon marries the brother – find that they cannot return home after the Communist take-over of 1949. When they enthusiastically embrace everything they think to be 'typically American' things quickly go wrong. In *Mona in the Promised Land* (1996) the daughter of the Chinese couple from *Typically Chinese* decides that henceforth she will go through life as a Jewess. When at her demise the mother of Mr. Wong wills him a Chinese relative in *The Love-Wife* (2005), ostensibly as a nanny for the three adopted children of the Wong family, Mr. Wong's blonde 'Caucasian' wife suspects the woman in question of actually being a concubine or 'love-wife'. *World and Town* (2011) sees a retired Chinese American teacher, looking for peace and quiet, move to a small New England town, there to discover that there is no shelter from the welter of the world.

The questioning of essential ethnic identities along with an ironic take on multicultural discourse also mark *American Knees* (1995), about a romance between a Chinese- and a Japanese American, by Shawn Wong (1949–). Wong had treated a similar subject in a less humorous way already in *Homebase* (1979). Frank Chin, who earlier had scored with a number of plays, in 1991 published *Donald Duk*, whose eponymous Chinese American boy-hero dreams of the Chinese contract laborers working on the Pacific Railroad in 1869 and finds himself during a Chinese New Year celebration in his hometown San Francisco. Chin gained perhaps greatest notoriety though with his accusation that Maxine Hong Kingston and Amy Tan type-cast their Chinese characters.

A case apart is Ha Jin (1956–). Jin was born in the People's Republic of China. His father served in the Chinese army and he himself participated in the Cultural Revolution. He studied English literature and was on a grant to the U.S. at the time of the student protests, and their suppression, on Beijing's Tien An Men Square in 1989. He decided to stay in the U.S., where he obtained a PhD in 1992. His breakthrough as a novelist came with *Waiting* (1999), a novel set in China, with characters who are all intrinsically good but through circumstances mostly brought about by the restrictions and the poverty of life under Communism succeed in making life into hell for each other, yet in the end give up what is dearest to themselves for the sake of those they love. Jin has published several volumes of stories, and several more novels, among which *Nanjing Requiem* (2012), about an American woman missionary who is trapped in China during the Japanese occupation.

As with a number of other minority literatures, so too with Japanese American literature it is women who set the tune, more often than not with work that is strongly autobiographical. This is overtly the case with *Talking to High Monks in the Snow: An Asian American Odyssey* (1992) by Lydia Minatoya (1950–), who in 1999 also published *The Strangeness of Beauty*, about three generations of Japanese American women. Also autobiographical is *The Dream of Water: A Memoir* (1995) by Kyoko Mori (1957–). Mori was born in Kobe, Japan, and only came to the U.S. when she was sixteen. *Stone Field, True Arrow* (2000) recounts what a Japanese woman who lives in the U.S. feels when her father dies in Japan. Better known than either Minatoya and Mori is Cynthia Kadohata (1956–), whose debut *The Floating World* (1989) made a strong impression. In Japan 'the floating world' refers to the world of the theater, prostitution, games and pleasure. In Kadohata's novel it indicates the uncertain world of the immigrant. The story is told from the perspective of a Japanese American woman who looks back to when in the 1950s and 60s she was roaming the U.S. trying to find work, which proved difficult so soon after World War II. *The Floating World* in many ways is a novel of education, a genre that is also prominently present in most other minority literatures. Kadohata's second novel, *In the Heart of the Valley of Love* (1992), presents a futuristic vision of a Los Angeles torn apart by racial strife between the rich, white inhabitants and all other impoverished minorities. *Women of Silk* (1991) by Gail Tsukiyama (1950–), born in San Francisco of mixed Chinese–Japanese descent, became a best-seller. It plays against the background of Chinese history from 1919 to 1939. *The Language of Threads* (1999) picks up on the story of the protagonist of *Women of Silk* when with the Japanese army advancing upon Canton she flees to Hong Kong. The novel spans the period 1938 to 1973, but mostly concentrates on the Japanese occupation and the period up to 1952. Hong Kong is also at least partially the setting for *Night of Many Dreams* (1998) and *The Samurai's Garden* (1995), although the protagonist in the latter novel ends up in Japan. *The Street of a Thousand Blossoms* (2007) focuses on a Japanese family during and after World War II. Tsukiyama's oeuvre, along with that of Lisa See, offers rare glimpses into facets of Chinese and Japanese history little known to outsiders. For a number of critics, though, Tsukiyama sacrifices character to history. The same criticism has also been leveled at the only novel of Tsukiyama to be set in the U.S., *Dreaming Water* (2002), which at least partially centers upon the American internment of its Japanese-descended citizens during World War II.

Autobiographical again are *The Dreams of Two Yi-Min* (1989) by Margaret K. Pai (1914–) and *Quiet Odyssey* (1990) by Mary Paik Lee (1900–95), both Korean-Americans. In her novel *Clay Walls* (1987) Kim Ronyoung (1923–89) recounts the experiences of Korean women immigrants in the 1920s. However, the Korean-American authors to have gained greatest fame since 1980 are Theresa Hak Kyung Cha (1951–82) and Chang-rae Lee (1965–). Both were born in Korea and brought to the U.S. by their parents. Theresa Hak Kyung Cha was able to produce only one novel before her tragic murder. With its combination of photographs, poems, diary pages, letters, historical documents, maps and much more, *Dictee* (1982) is a definitely postmodern multimedia work. Overall the book evokes the Japanese occupation of Korea and the experiences of Korean immigrants to the U.S. Chang-rae Lee debuted very strongly with *Native Speaker* (1995), a novel about a Korean-American detective who is fascinated with the phenomenon of language, what it allows you to do, the power it conveys, the difficulties it causes to immigrants who seek to master the language of their new country. *A Gesture of Life* (1999) has as protagonist a retired Japanese physician, sometime owner of a medical supplies store in the U.S., who looks back upon his life and how in World War II he medically supervised the Korean 'comfort women' on a Japanese army base.

Monkey Bridge (1997), by Lan Cao, follows the lives of a Vietnamese mother and daughter that after the fall of Saigon in 1975 have to rebuild their lives in the U.S. The mother never succeeds in doing so, and the daughter only comes to grasp what her mother has lived through on the death of the latter. *Monkey Bridge* is a typical immigrant novel in that it combines a story of migration with the growth to maturity of the narrator.

The Philippines we encounter in the novels of Jessica Hagedorn (1949–) are very different from those we encountered earlier in the work of Carlos Bulosan. With the aid of letters, fictional newspaper notices, real historical documents and vignettes featuring the most diverse characters, high and low, movie stars, army officers, prostitutes, but also ordinary people, Rio, the narrator of Hagedorn's best known novel, *Dogeaters* (1991), looks back on life in Manila in the late 1950s.

As of the 1960s immigration from the Indian sub-continent to the U.S. started growing from a trickle to a steady stream. On the one hand we find youngsters from well-to-do milieus who go to study at prestigious American universities and stay on after graduation as physicians, engineers or academics. On the other hand we find middle-class Indians, Pakistanis and Bangladeshis starting up a business in the U.S. Bharati Mukherjee (1940–), born in Kolkata, in *Wife* (1975) and *Jasmine* (1989) looks at the women caught up in these migrations. The heroine of *Jasmine* is widowed at seventeen in India. Rather than settle into the anonymity life in India now has in store for her she packs up and moves to the U.S. There she is raped, suffers poverty and is mercilessly discriminated against. However, Jasmine survives all. At a given moment it even looks as if she is going to marry a rich banker whose child she is carrying, and go through life as Jane Ripplemeyer. Then, however, the man whom Jasmine really cares about turns up, and off she goes with him, changing her name back to Jase. Because 'America' means being free to choose what you are and who you are. The greatest name in Indian American literature at present is that of Jhumpa Lahiri (1967–), like Mukherjee of Bengali descent, born in London but raised in the U.S. The nine stories from *The Interpreter of Maladies*, which caused a sensation on publication in 1999 and went on to win a Pulitzer, draw an intimate picture of an India where the old bonds of caste, family and community are fading fast under the pressures of tourism and globalization, and by migration to the U.S. In most cases integration in the new country does not happen easily or seamlessly. India itself, however, also is not the mythical repository of eternal wisdom westerners like to think it is. Reality in both cases is stark, raw and vulgar. *The Namesake* (2003) follows an Indian American family over a span of thirty years and is all in all a fairly typical combination of immigration saga, family-epic and novel of education. Lahiri's second collection of stories, *Unaccustomed Earth* (2008) largely deals with issues similar to those also treated in *The Interpreter of Maladies*.

Finally, we turn to Native American literature after 1980. Leslie Marmon Silko in 1981 published *Storyteller*, combining poems, prose and photographs, and for inspiration drawing upon Silko's own family history and on traditional Indian tales and myths. *Almanac of the Dead* (1991) is a complex novel that charts five hundred years of conflict between Europeans and Indians in America. *Gardens in the Dunes* (1999) has as its setting both America and Europe for the story of an Indian girl that at the end of the nineteenth century is separated from her tribe, raised by whites, and travels the world before returning to her family and tribe. Silko also has published poetry and essays.

Louise Erdrich (1954–), of Ojibwe-French-Canadian-German-American descent, has been the subject of much critical controversy. Most commentators consider her, with Sherman Alexie (1966–), as probably the most important Native American author of the turn of the millennium. Others spurn her as dealing in clichés and selling out the Native American heritage for cheap thrills and the consumption of a white readership. Leslie Marmon Silko, for instance, has accused Erdrich of paying more attention to postmodern techniques, among which we could count magical realism, than to the interests of the Indians. Be that as it may, ever since the publication of *Love Medicine* in 1984 Erdrich has consistently built a fictional universe that because of the multitude of its characters, the time period it spans, and the variety of its narrators and points of view has often been compared to Faulkner's Yoknapathawpa County. That fictional universe, elaborated in more than ten novels, the best known of which are, next to *Love Medicine*, *The Beet Queen* (1986), *Tracks* (1988) and *The Bingo Palace* (1994), is centered upon the Chippewa Reservation in North Dakota and the nearby little town of Argus, and spans the period from the early twentieth century to the present. The main character of *Tracks* is Fleur

Pillager, of whom it is said that she is a witch, and who twice drowns in a lake inhabited by a water monster and twice survives. The story of Fleur is told by Nanapush, an elderly Indian, relative of Fleur, and the man who saved Fleur's life during an epidemic that in 1912 killed off most of Fleur's family along with much of the rest of the tribe. Nanapush is a shaman who tries to preserve the customs of the tribe but who also realizes that the red man's time has passed and that it is white law that rules now. Fleur refuses to give in to the white man, and uses all her magic to resist. In the end, though, she is defeated and leaves her ancestral land, fleeing to Canada. Nanapush on the other hand scores a victory over the white man by mastering the latter's magic: writing and the law. Fleur returns in many other novels and stories of Erdrich's and so do many other characters, weaving Erdrich's fictional universe ever tighter with each new book. *The Plague of Doves* (2008) got Erdrich a Pulitzer and *The Round House* (2012) won a National Book Award.

Immediately upon the publication of *The Lone-Ranger and Tonto Fistfight in Heaven* (1993) Sherman Alexie was welcomed as the greatest new talent in Native American literature. In twenty-two interrelated stories Alexie portrays life on the Spokane Indian Reservation where he himself was raised as a Spokane/Coeur d'Alene Indian. In *Reservation Blues* (1995) the legendary black bluesman Robert Johnson in 1992 turns up on the Reservation. Officially he has been dead since 1938 but now it transpires that he has only let it seem so to escape the devil, to whom in his youth he has sold his soul in order to become the best guitar player ever. If Alexie's first books are hilariously funny and almost surrealist, *Indian Killer* (1996) is a very different kettle of fish. A serial killer terrorizes Seattle, killing white men. As he scalps his victims suspicion falls on an Indian, and racial tensions surface.

Poetry

The dividing lines between the various poetical schools or movements operative before 1980 after that date disappear almost completely. Some poets, such as for instance Sharon Olds (1942–), are still relatively close to the Confessionals, while others, such as David Lehman (1948–), Dean Young (1955–) and Denise Duhamel (1961–), seek guidance from the New York School, in particular the work of Frank O'Hara. Yet others, such as Charles Simic (1938–), adhere to a more surreal poetics ('It was the first day of spring. One of my / fathers was singing in the bathtub; the other one / was painting a live sparrow the colors of a tropical / bird', from 'I Was Stolen', 1989). On the other hand the so-called 'New Formalists', Timothy Steele (1948–), Timothy Murphy (1951–), Mark Jarman (1952–), David Mason (1954–) and Gjertrud Schnackenberg (1953–), look back to the New Critics, and sometimes even further. David Mason's work, for instance with 'The Collector's Tale' (2004), recalls that of A.E. Robinson. Or, as in Schnackenberg's 'Nightfishing' (1982), they sound like W.C. Williams. And of course there are poets like Dana Goia (1950–) who refuse to be labeled at all.

The one group that obstinately insists on charting its own course is that of the so-called 'L = A = N = G = U = A = G = E-poets', so named after the periodical *L = A = N = G = U = A = G = E* that appeared from 1978 to 1981, and in which most of the members of the group regularly published. These poets, along with some younger colleagues who propagate the even more recent 'Conceptual Writing', are the only ones to continue the radical experimentation of Modernists such as Gertrude Stein or Louis Zukofsky. 'A World is Coming up on the Screen' (1988), by Michael Palmer (1943–), for instance, clearly echoes the experimental prose of Stein:

A world is coming up on the screen, give me a moment. In the meantime let me tell you a little something about myself. I was born in Passaic in a small bow flying over Dresden one

night, lovely figurines. Things mushroomed after that. My cat has twelve toes, like poets in
Boston. Upon the microwave she sits, hairless. The children they say, you are no father, but
a frame, waiting for a painting.

At the same time these poets are leaning on Marxism and on the socio-cultural analyses of the
French philosophers Jacques Lacan, Roland Barthes and Michel Foucault. As such, the work of
these poets also shows strong affinities with postmodernism. Because of the discontinuity and
fragmentariness of their poetry the language-poets are a good deal more radical than their
immediate predecessors the New York School and the Black Mountain poets. They deliberately
abandon the idea of any overarching unity, and because they do not strive for closure it is not
the poem as a whole, nor even the stanza, but rather the individual verse that matters, as in
'Chronic Meanings', from *Virtual Reality* (1993), by Bob Perelman (1947–), which starts off:
'The single fact is matter. / Five words can say only. / Black sky at night, reasonably. / I am, the
irrational residue'. The aim of the 'language-poets' is to deregulate language itself, as in
'Thinking I Think I Think', from *With Strings* (2001), by Charles Bernstein (1950–), where
semantic illogicalities seemingly inspired by sound correlations and almost surrealist associations grounded in popular culture set the tune: 'The lacuna misplaced the ladle, / the actor
aborted the fable. / Fold your caps into Indians / & flaps. Dusting the rigor mortis / for compos
mentis. Rune is busting / out all over—perfidious quarrel / sublates even the heckling at / the
Ponderosa. A bevy of belts'. Or, to be more precise, the aim of the language-poets is to
undermine our trust in language, in the idea that language is a medium that can be handled
objectively in order to faithfully portray reality and to communicate about it straightforwardly.
In our world of clichéd mass communications the language-poets confront the reader with the
fact that language communication is not natural and authentic, but rests on conventions that
often substitute for real meaning or content. In order to achieve that aim they opt for radically
open form, in any case as far as semantic unity is concerned, reject narration (which suggests
unity), and strive for absolute impersonality. After all, the uniquely individual writer, according
to Barthes, is 'dead', and turns out to be no more than a site where all sorts of discourses mingle
and meet, as we can see clearly in the passages from Palmer and Bernstein just quoted.

Next to Perelman, Palmer and Bernstein, further prominent language-poets are Ron Silliman
(1946–), who works in a typically American tradition with his epical *The Alphabet* (2008), the
early parts of which go back to 1979, and whose blog on contemporary poetry (*ronsilliman.
blogspot.com*) had already had one million visitors by February 2007, Lyn Hejinian (1941–) and
Susan Howe (1937–). We here should also mention H.L. Hix (1960–), whose work forms a
bridge between that of the language-poets and that of their more formal contemporaries.

The U.S. has a very rich poetical tradition, and it is impossible to give due attention to all
the poets who since 1980 have come to the fore and who do not easily let themselves be ranged
under the label of either those who continue Modernist strains or that of the language-poets. In
general, we can say that although most contemporary American poets use free verse, they at the
same time show a marked regularity in their use of lines and stanzas (if such we can call the
units in question). The tone is almost always informal, suggesting a large measure of spontaneity, and often intimately autobiographical, and the preference seems to be for extended
similes rather than complex metaphors. Robert Glück (1947–), Bruce Boone (1940–) and others
around 1980 founded the so-called 'New Narrative Movement', partially in reaction to the
language-poets, and because they wanted to stress the more autobiographical element of poetry,
especially from the perspective of gay and lesbian poets, but in fact the majority of contemporary American poets show narrative tendencies. As an example take 'Shawl' from *The
Kitchen Sink: New and Selected Poems* by Albert Goldbarth (1948–) in which a boy takes a long

distance night trip by bus, is attracted by the knees of a woman he observes, but eventually discovers himself 'to be among the tribe that reads. / Now his, the only overhead turned on. Now nothing else existed: / only him, and the book, and the light thrown over his shoulders / as luxuriously as a cashmere shawl'. This poem leads to a moment of insight and resolution, but others leave the reader with more ambivalent feelings, as when in 'Broken Glass', from *Paper Cathedrals* (2001) by Morri Creech (1970–), a boy accompanies his father, a mechanical engineer whose professional life is all order and neatness, to a piece of wasteland where he puts up a row of bottles and then reduces them to rubble by pitching stones at them, to finally, his son on his shoulders, go 'back toward his ordered life, / leaving the wreckage behind him, / scattered and shining'. Similar open endings also occur in the work of Brad Leithauser (1953–), Li-Young Lee (1957–), Diane Thiel (1967–), Beth Ann Fennelly (1971–) and many of their contemporaries.

If we had to pick one poet as the period's major voice, we would propose Jorie Graham (1950–), who won the Pulitzer Prize for Poetry (1996) for *The Dream of the Unified Field: Selected Poems 1974–1994* (1995) and served as chancellor of the Academy of American Poets from 1997 to 2003. Jorie has a voice all her own, yet her poetry unmistakably also incorporates echoes of Marianne Moore, Elizabeth Bishop and Robert Lowell, as in 'Prayer', from *Never* (2002), in which the narrator looks at a school of minnows underneath the dock she stands on, sees how they react to the motions of the water, thinks 'this is freedom. This is the force of faith. Nobody gets / what they want. Never again are you the same', and concludes with 'I am free to go. / I cannot of course come back. Not to this. Never. / It is a ghost posed on my lips. Here: never'.

Drama

The two major playwrights of the period after 1980 are Sam Shepard (1943–) and David Mamet (1947–). In *True West* (1980), a play in two acts, Shepard does a thorough demolition job on the myth of the American West. Austin and Lee are two brothers. Austin is a professional Hollywood scriptwriter. Lee, the older brother, is a vagrant and a petty criminal. They meet unexpectedly in the house of their mother, who herself is on a vacation to Alaska. Austin has an appointment with a film producer. Lee is looking for something to steal. When the film producer shows, Lee sells him the idea for a movie, a Western, for which Austin's plot is jettisoned and for which the latter now is supposed to write the full script. Austin objects, and Lee has to do it himself. Slowly, the two brothers change positions, and they end as the two opponents from Lee's plot after having first destroyed their mother's house and chased her away on her return from vacation. The 'true' West – the play is set in California – here is a far cry from the myth. What is very real, though, is the violence that remains. The real high point in Shepard's oeuvre is *Fool for Love* (1983), which is set in a motel room on the edge of the Mojave desert. Eddie and May are half-brother and sister. They are consumed by sexual passion for each other, but at the same time long to be free of one another. Eddie is a rodeo rider and a drifter who never really succeeds in leaving. May wants a husband and a house. Also present, at least in the minds of Eddie and May, and visible to the spectators on a raised dais at the back of the stage, is the father of the two main characters, who comments on the action. Next to this experimental feature, the play also makes use of sound distorting equipment. Eddie and May are capable of the most moving tenderness, but also of the meanest cruelty. Like the brothers from *True West* they are each other's opposites and counterparts, and ultimately they are both halves of one split personality.

The violence and the menace, in the family and in American society, that animate *True West* and *Fool for Love* also are present in *A Lie of the Mind* (1985), in which a woman has been so

mistreated by her husband that she has suffered permanent brain damage and has to be hospitalized. Notwithstanding all this the wife and husband cannot do without one another. In his
later work, such as *States of Shock* (1991) and *Simpatico* (1995), Shepard continues to dismantle
American myths, primarily, as in *True West*, through relationships between men. *The God of
Hell* (2004) reflects on the aftermath of 9/11, and particularly on the impact the attacks have
had on American public opinion, and how they led the Bush administration to curtail the
individual liberties and rights of American citizens. Much of Shepard's work is auto-
biographically inspired: the alcoholic and violent father, the restlessness of the characters, the
need for language and the inability to truly communicate, the combination of tenderness and
violence. It is to Shepard's great credit that he has been able to put these autobiographical
givens in the service of a relentless critique of the myths that America lives by.

   Like Shepard, David Mamet too works hard at dismantling American myths. Mamet started
his career in small theaters in Chicago, his home town, with *The Duck Variations* (1972) and
Sexual Perversity in Chicago (1974). These two plays opened in New York in 1976 and immediately catapulted Mamet to fame. In Mamet's consumer crazy America everything that is
wrong can be talked right by an appeal to the clichés of the media and of commerce. That is
true for the sex in *Sexual Perversity in Chicago*, set in a bar with two men and two women talking, but also for the petty criminals from *American Buffalo* (1975), in which three men plan a
crime from the perspective that everything that matters in the U.S. is to make a profit and that
all means to achieve this are right, including crime. The same thing applies to Mamet's
masterpiece *Glengarry Glen Ross* (1984). The first act is set in a Chinese restaurant, the second
and last in a real estate office. The 'Glengarry Glen Ross' of the title refers to a worthless piece
of real estate that the salesmen of the office want to market. In truth they are all losers who try
to bluff one another in order to curry favor with the boss. They do not shy away from the
starkest lie to close a sale, and swindle their clients, from the same principle that also motivated
the characters from *American Buffalo*. The ultimate legitimation is that every sale helps the
economy, and thus America – with the exception of course of the poor bastard that has been
swindled, but such is the price of progress! Once in a while one of the characters shows a
glimmer of decency, and chooses the warmth of a personal relationship over profit, but those
moments remain exceptions. Mamet mercilessly reviles the egotism disguised as individualism,
and the theft draped as 'good business', that form the foundations of American society, myths
that have withered to clichés. Language for Mamet's characters is not a way to truth but an
instrument to sell their wares, including themselves. In this sense *Glengarry Glen Ross* takes the
next logical step from Miller's *Death of a Salesman*. In Miller's piece Willy Loman has to sell
himself as a salesman. In the end, though, he overthrows that logic. With Mamet there is no
way out. His characters believe in the stories they tell each other, and themselves; they are
prisoners to their own clichés. The analogy with politics is right around the corner. *Oleanna*
(1992) precisely is about 'political correctness' and the clichés it engenders and thrives on. In
the first act a female student visits a male professor during the latter's office hours. He comments on her work, and at a given moment in a fatherly gesture puts his hand on her shoulder.
In the second act the student returns and accuses him of unsolicited intimacies. The professor's
career and marriage are broken. Frustrated, he counter-attacks the student, in the eyes of society
thereby validating all the accusations she has brought against him. The play capitalized on the
polarization of American society, in this particular case along the lines of gender, and once
again drew attention to the power of clichés, in this case those of feminist discourses. It will not
come as a surprise that *Oleanna* became the cause of major controversy. Since the second half of
the 1990s Mamet has shown an increasing fascination with his Jewish background, perhaps as a
remedy to the emptiness of life in America as it appears from his earlier work. Mamet, like

Shepard, is also active as a director, scriptwriter and movie director. Shepard also acts himself, on the stage and in the movies.

After the experiments of the 1960s and 70s, in which the action was at least partially transferred from the stage to the audience and even the street, and which had an overtly radical political agenda, American drama in the 1980s returned to the stage, often in a form that recalls the postmodern wave that by then had already been holding sway for some fifteen years in American prose. Karen Finley (1956–), for instance, started using her own, often naked, body in performance art. Others, like Mac Wellman (1945–), wrote plays that had to be performed at specific locations, such as Central Park in New York in *Bad Penny* (1989).

Drama also played a part in the rise of multiculturalism as of the late 1970s. August Wilson (1945–2005) between 1982 and the year of his death wrote a ten-play *Pittsburg Cycle*, for two of which he received a Pulitzer, chronicling the lives of African Americans from the early 1900s to the 1990s. The equally African American Suzanne Lori-Parks (1964–) recasts the murder of Lincoln as vaudeville in *The America Play* (1993), in which she also re-invents the English language, and returned to the same event in *Topdog/Underdog* (2001), which won her a Pulitzer. But almost every ethnic minority in the U.S. has its own playwrights, many of them chronicling the plight of their specific ethnicity. Moreover, feminism, lesbianism and the gay movement also have yielded a large crop of plays detailing the lives, and often the discrimination, of the minorities concerned.

The Mercy Seat (2002) a play about the attack on the World Trade Center of 11 September 2001 brought Neil LaBute (1963–) to public atention. The title of the play refers to a song by Nick Cave in which a convicted man talks of the electric chair as 'the mercy seat'. In LaBute's play someone who works in the World Trade Center escapes death because at the moment of the attack he is with his mistress. Now he has to choose whether to report that he is alive or to play dead so as to start a new life.

Popular literature

The more recent period in American literature shows a considerable overlap between what used to be called 'high' literature and entertainment or popular literature, with authors crossing over from one to the other with greater frequency than used to be the case before. It should be said, though, that these authors only seldom use genre fiction simply for the sake of it – they usually have a message to convey. Two authors who started their careers in the grey zone between popular and serious literature are James Ellroy (1948–) and Jonathan Lethem (1964–). Ellroy debuted with a noir detective novel, *Brown's Requiem* (1981), moved on to a trilogy starring the cynical, racist and macho reactionary police detective Lloyd Hopkins, and then hit his stride with a series of political crime novels chronicling a history of the U.S. from 1948 to the 1970s enlisting the likes, usually in unfavorable roles, of the Kennedy brothers, Walt Disney, J. Edgar Hoover, and Howard Hughes, along with a host of fictional characters in the guise of Los Angeles police detectives, FBI and CIA agents, and private investigators. Several of the novels in the series were made into movies: *The Black Dahlia* (1987) and *L.A. Confidential* (1990). Ellroy's style is extremely tight, almost staccato, and often conversational but without explicitly mentioning which character is speaking when, all of which makes his later fiction experimental and almost postmodern, while his subject matter takes him close to for instance DeLillo's *Libra* or *Underworld*. With his later work, then, Ellroy has definitely left genre fiction far behind, and he should be counted one of America's foremost politically inspired novelists. The African American author Walter Mosley (1952–) authored a series of crime novels with as protagonist Easy Rawlins that roughly cover the same period as Ellroy's series, and that sharply throw into relief the difficult racial relations in Los Angeles. Michael Connelly (1956–) follows the life and career of the L.A. homicide detective Harry (Hieronymus) Bosch in a series that starts right after the end of the Vietnam war, in which Bosch has fought, until his retirement and beyond, with a series of adventures, most of them affecting Bosch's personal life as well, that recall some of Ellroy's novels.

Lethem started out writing combinations of science-fiction and detective novels. However, with *The Fortress of Solitude* (2003), a novel about a black and white boy growing up in a black neighborhood of Brooklyn in the 1970s, Lethem explored new avenues. The novel is a nostalgic ode to a lost decade, to friendship, but also to the popular music and culture of the period.

A case apart is John Irving (1942–). Irving already had a career as a wrestler behind him when he started to write, as a student at Harvard, and during a stay in Vienna. All of these play important roles in his first few novels. Wrestling also features in *The World According to Garp* (1978), which won its author a National Book Award, developed into a cult phenomenon, and made its author a fortune. The novel is often funny, just as often shocking, and has obvious autobiographical traits. It made Irving one of the most highly regarded authors of his generation, and he was expected to become a dominant voice in times to come. *The Hotel New Hampshire* (1981) and especially *The Ciderhouse Rules* (1985) were well received. But *A Prayer for Owen Meany* (1989) was almost unanimously voted down for being too preachy, too laden with Christian symbolism, and simply too longwinded. Irving's later novels all share the same ingredients: the quest for the father, wrestling, sexually explicit scenes, and highly colorful characters. The excitement had worn off, though, and it all became predictable and overlong. In a sense, Irving had created his own generic formula, continuing to be much appreciated by his faithful readership, but become unpalatable to the critics. In any case, his later works, which he continues to produce in a steady stream, were scarcely noticed by the reviewers. Irving probably does not care: his reputation with a wider public is now such that his books invariably become best-sellers, and he now rather belongs in the select club of 'romance' authors whose books sell in the millions, and are often turned into movies for television or home distribution, but who are no longer seen as part of 'real' or high literature. Something similar pertains to Joyce Carol Oates (1938–), who has produced scores of novels and collections of short stories ever since her debut with *By the North Gate*, a volume of stories, in 1963. She treats the most diverse subjects, though often focusing on violence, also in the family, and lower-class life, as in *We Were the Mulvaneys* (1996), a best-seller. Incredibly prolific, Oates also wrote a number of mystery novels under the pennames of Rosamond Smith and Lauren Kelly, as well as poetry, juvenile fiction, essays and memoirs. Rated as one of the most important American authors of the second half of the twentieth century by some, Oates is spurned by others for producing mostly middle-brow fiction.

Two authors who have resolutely gone for what these days goes by the name of 'popular romance' are Nora Roberts (1950–) and Nicolas Sparks (1965–). Sparks almost every year produces a best-seller, some of the more notable examples being *The Notebook* (1996) and *Message in a Bottle* (1998), with a plot combining the death of a loved one, a romantic dinner at the beach, a resolution that preaches acceptance and solace, and the moral growth of the surviving lover, all of it clearly overlaid with a Christian vision. Roberts is even more prolific, with more than two hundred titles to her tally and counting, and writing under her own name as well as that of J.D. Robb, for a series of crime novels, and Jill March as well as other pseudonyms for publications in countries other than the U.S. Her novels, which in the true tradition of popular romance, and unlike those of Sparks, invariably have a happy ending (at least for most of the protagonists), often combine genres. *Montana Sky* (1986), for instance, is a combination of a Western, crime novel, and romance.

Next to popular romance, crime and especially detective writing remains extremely popular. As with almost all other genres, the period since 1980 has seen a great influx of female and minority authors. Some names to mention are Sue Grafton (1940–), with a series featuring private eye Kinsey Milhone, Marcia Muller (1944–), with Sharon McCone as protagonist, and Sara Paretsky (1947–), with as heroine V.I. Warshawski. What distinguishes the work of these authors from that of their male counterparts is a greater attention to family and interpersonal relations. Paretsky's novels also always deal with social problems, often specific to women, such as domestic violence, topical at the time of writing. Donna Leon (1942–), American but living and working in Italy for many years, deals with similar issues as they play in Europe, and particularly in Italy, in her Commissario Brunetti series set in Venice. The same thing is true, but in a much more light-hearted vein, with the Stephanie Plum series of Janet Evanovich (1943–), combining crime and romance. Still others, like S.J. Rozan (1950–) with her Lydia Chin/Bill Smith series, focus on intercultural relations. Barbara Neeley (1941–) and Valerie Wilson Wesley (1947–) feature African American sleuths in, respectively, their Blanche White and Tamara Hayle series. But there are also some major male writers of crime fiction in this period. Next to the already mentioned Connelly we could point to Dennis Lehane (1965–), with a series set in Boston and starring the private eye couple of Patrick Kenzie and Angela Gennaro. Several of Lehane's novels were turned into movies, for instance the Kenzie/Gennaro *Gone, Baby, Gone* (1998), and the stand-alone *Mystic River* (2001). Finally we should mention that there is a marked increase in historical detective fiction, with as telling example the 'Roma sub rosa' series, featuring Gordianus the Finder, private eye *avant-la-lettre* in the Rome of the first century B.C., by Steven Saylor (1956–).

A genre that for a long time seemed somewhat forgotten, but which over the last decades of the twentieth century has made a strong comeback, not so much with pure formula fiction but rather with novels and stories exposing the falseness of the clichés of the genre, is the Western. Larry McMurtry (1936–) already drew a searing portrait of the demise of the Old West in *The Last Picture Show* (1966). That book narrowly missed the Pulitzer Prize. McMurtry did get the prize in 1986 for *Lonesome Dove* (1985), which at its appearance was hailed as 'the Great Cowboy Novel'. The novel was turned into a very successful television series, and led to three sequels, *Streets of Laredo* (1993), *Dead Man's Walk* (1995) and *Comanche Moon* (1997). Lonesome Dove is a small town on the Texas–Mexican border, where the inhabitants, including the novel's protagonists Gus McCrae and Woodrow Call, two former Texas Rangers, at the end of the 1870s make their living raising and selling cattle. The action of the novel involves a cattle drive from Texas to Montana, fifteen hundred miles away. In *Lonesome Dove* nothing resembles the Far West as Hollywood or earlier popular Western novels have presented it to us. Everyone stinks, everyone dies, everyone loves the wrong person, everyone loses. McMurtry's West is an open sewer that gathers what is best and what is worst in humanity, but mostly what is worst. Exiles and losers from all over the world drift to the Rio Grande: landless Irish, fallen women, a down-and-out Frenchman, whores and gamblers. All, except maybe Gus, dream of starting over again somewhere else, return to better times, but everything always fails. The only ones that truly want to go back to earlier times are the Indians, but as this is impossible they turn into rapists and murderers under the leadership of Blue Duck, the worst nightmare of any white American. Of course, there are also the Mexicans, the original owners, with the Indians, of the land, but to them nobody pays attention. In a deeper sense, the trek to Montana is also a search for a lost wholeness and freshness that is inextricably bound up with Gus and Call's own youth, which is also that of the U.S., and particularly its western parts. Montana at the end of the nineteenth century was the last frontier, the border between civilization and the wilderness, culture and nature, which we also saw Huck Finn longing for, and which Frederick Jackson Turner in 1892 famously declared closed. This also meant the end of a period in which the possibilities for future expansion of the U.S. seemed limitless. *Lonesome Dove*, at the same time as being a novel about the crude realities of life during the brief time when the West was the domain of the cowboy, that brief fifty-year period between the Civil War and World War I which engendered the myths embodied in the Western, is also a novel about the loss of ideals, of youth, of innocence. This is a theme McMurtry has explored from his very first novel, *Horseman, Pass by* in 1961, and throughout his career.

With Cormac McCarthy too, the Far West does not correspond to Hollywood stereotype. McCarthy had published dark Faulknerian Southern Gothic up till *Suttree* (1979), but with *Blood Meridian* (1985) turned towards the Western genre. What this novel, set in the 1840s, shows is that the West as we think we know it from the myth was born in an orgy of blood and violence that swept away everything that stood in the way of the white conquerors and settlers. The most sinister figure in the novel is Judge Holden, and though McCarthy has left the South behind, his style stays Faulknerian. McCarthy's name really became a household name to American literature buffs with his Border-trilogy, set some one hundred years later than *Blood Meridian*, and around the time also of McMurtry's *The Last Picture Show*, that is to say at the very tail-end of the mythical West. *All the Pretty Horses* (1992) is set in 1949, *The Crossing* (1994) takes place in 1939, and *The Cities of the Plain* (1998) in 1952. The latter novel ends on an epilogue set in 2002 in which one of the protagonists of the trilogy, seventy-eight years old and without a penny to his name, spends the night under a bridge in Arizona. The old, heroic, mythical West has crumbled to dirty memory. In 2005 McCarthy published *No Country for Old Men*, and in 2006 *The Road*, an apocalyptic tale set in a time when most life on earth has been destroyed by an unspecified disaster. Both books won several prizes and honors, and were successfully made into movies. Still, McCarthy remains a controversial author. For some he is one of the greatest American writers of the second half of the twentieth century, others consider his writings overrated, his style unpalatable, his characters over-the-top, and his subjects morbid.

Since the success of the movie *Brokeback Mountain* Annie Proulx (1935–) is best known for the story upon which the movie is based, and which appeared first in *The New Yorker* in 1997 and then in her collection *Close Range: Wyoming Stories* (1999). As this story is about two homosexual cowboys it yet again undermines a persistent myth about the manliness and prowess of the heroes that are the stock-in-trade of the Western. In 2004 Proulx published *Bad Dirt: Wyoming Stories 2*, but the high point in her oeuvre is *The Shipping News* (1993), about a bumbler who moves to his ancestral town in Newfoundland, there to find himself, and to find that he is accepted by the community. This novel was turned into a movie too. Two more authors who write about the West are Thomas McGuane (1939–) and Jim Harrison (1937–). On account of his early fictions of the 1960s and 70s McGuane was first considered a postmodernist, but with *Nobody's Angel* (1981) he turned to a different kind of writing. His most successful excursion in the Western genre is *Nothing but Blue Skies* (1993), about growing older, lost ideals and lost innocence. Harrison is best known for *Legends of the Fall* (1979), which chronicles fifty years of Western history in the character of Tristan, one of three brothers. In *The Road Home* (1998) Harrison paints an even wider historical canvas in the five generations of a family inhabiting a farm somewhere on the endless plains of Nebraska, and in *Returning to Earth* (2007) he has a dying man of Finnish-Chippewa descent recount the history of his family of pioneers in Northern Michigan.

Much recent fiction about the West shows a strong ecological bent, in a modern tradition founded by Wallace Stegner and Rachel Carson (1907–64), whose *Silent Spring* (1962) provoked a torrent of writings on the environment and especially its degradation. Names to be mentioned here are those of Edward Abbey (1927–89), Peter Matthiessen (1927–), Edward Hoagland

(1932–) and Annie Dillard (1945–), the latter especially with *Pilgrim at Tinker Creek* (1974), strongly reminiscent of Thoreau's *Walden*. A more recent author who regularly writes about the West of the U.S., although she also has published works with other settings, and who has a strong ecological interest, is Barbara Kingsolver (1955–). The same goes for Jane Smiley (1949–), whose best-selling and Pulitzer Prize winning *A Thousand Acres* (1991) features a farmer in Iowa who through the use of modern methods of farming, including large amounts of chemical fertilizer, has succeeded in becoming the largest landowner in the neighborhood, but whose empire crumbles when he himself, as well as his descendants, turn out to be poisoned by the chemicals that have seeped into the groundwater. With a plot loosely based on Shakespeare's *King Lear*, *A Thousand Acres* tells the story of the downfall of a family as well as of the land. Kent Haruf (1943–) has a much milder view of things in his fictions about the inhabitants of a small town in Eastern Colorado. In *Plainsong* (1999) and *Eventide* (2004) he pays homage to the resilience and the sense of charity of a rural community. Haruf can rightly be called a regional author, but perhaps the ultimate instance of such an author is Garrison Keillor (1942–), with his mostly mellow stories about the fictional Lake Wobegon in Minnesota which suspiciously resembles Keillor's hometown of Anoka.

Science fiction has been flourishing too since 1980, with the 'cyberpunk' introduced by the American-Canadian William Gibson (1948–) in 'Burning Chrome' (1982) and *Neuromancer* (1984), and as a forerunner of which we can consider *Do Androids Dream of Electric Sheep* (1968) by Philip K. Dick (1928–82), which was turned into the 1982 movie *Blade Runner*. Other important exponents of cyberpunk are Neal Stephenson (1959–), John Shirley (1953–) and Bruce Sterling (1954–). Ursula K. Leguin (1929–), who started publishing in the 1960s remains active today. Here too we find minority authors breaking into a genre they earlier had mostly shunned. Samuel R. Delany Jr. (1942–), who had been publishing science fiction since the late 1960s, published the four parts of his *Tales of Neveryon* (1979, 1983, 1985 and 1987). Closely connected to science fiction, the comics industry in the 1990s has been thoroughly shaken up by the runaway success of the graphic novel, a genre using comics but with a serious, even 'literary' content, which had been in existence since the 1960s, and had gained some traction with Will Eisner's (1917–2005) *A Contract with God* (1978), but which came to the attention of the wider public with *Maus* (1991) by Art Spiegelman (1948–). *Maus* tells the story of Spiegelman interviewing his father, a Polish Jew and a survivor of the Holocaust, about his experiences. Already earlier, the genre was taken up by Frank Miller (1957–) in his *Batman: The Dark Knight Returns* (1986), with sequels into the 2000s, and the *Sin City* series (1991–92).

Bibliography

Aaron, D. (1961) *Writers on the Left*, New York: Harcourt, Brace & World.

——(1973) *The Unwritten War: American Writers and the Civil War*, New York: Knopf.

Abish, W. (1974) *Alphabetical Africa*, New York: New Directions.

Albee, E. (2007) *The Collected Plays of Edward Albee: 1958–1965*, Woodstock, NY: Overlook Press.

——(2008) *The Collected Plays of Edward Albee: 1966–1977*, Woodstock, NY: Overlook Press.

——(2008) *The Collected Plays of Edward Albee: 1978–2003*, Woodstock, NY: Overlook Press.

Allen, D. (ed.) (1960) *The New American Poetry, 1845–1960*, New York: Grove.

Allister, M. (2001) *Refiguring the Map of Sorrow: Nature Writing and Autobiography*, Charlottesville and London: University Press of Virginia.

Altieri, C. (1979) *Enlarging the Temple: New Directions in American Poetry During the 1960s*, Lewisburg, PA: Bucknell University Press.

Ammons, A.R. (1974) *Sphere: The Form of a Motion*, New York: Norton.

Anderson, E.G. (1999) *American Indian Literature and the Southwest*, Austin, TX: University of Texas Press.

Anderson, S. (2012) *Collected Stories: Winesburg, Ohio / The Triumph of the Egg / Horses and Men / Death in the Woods / Uncollected Stories*, New York: The Library of America.

Andrews, W.L., Foster, F.S., and Harris, T. (eds) (2001) *The Concise Oxford Companion to African American Literature*, New York and Oxford: Oxford University Press.

Andrews, W.L., Kolodny, A., Shea, D.B., Bush Jr., S. and Schrager Lang, A. (eds) (1991) *Journeys in New Worlds: Early American Women's Narratives*, Madison, WI: University of Wisconsin Press.

Anzaldúa, G. (2012) *Borderlands/La Frontera: The New Mestiza*, 4th ed., San Francisco: Aunt Lute Books.

Arac, J. (1997) *Huckleberry Finn as Idol and Target: The Functions of Criticism in Our Time*, Madison, Wisconsin: The University of Wisconsin Press.

——(2005) *The Emergence of American Literary Narrative, 1820–1860*, Cambridge, MA: Harvard University Press.

Aronson, A. (2000) *American Avant-Garde Theatre: A History*, New York and London: Routledge.

Arteaga, A. (ed.) (1994) *An Other Tongue: Nation and Ethnicity in the Linguistic Borderlands*, Durham, NC and London: Duke University Press.

Ashbery, J. (2008) *Collected Poems 1956–1987*, M. Ford, ed., New York: Library of America.

Ashton, J. (ed.) (2012) *The Cambridge Companion to American Poetry since 1945*, Cambridge: Cambridge University Press.

Baker Jr., H.A. (1988) *Afro-American Poetics: Revisions of Harlem and the Black Aesthetic*, Madison, WI: University of Wisconsin Press.

——(1991) *Workings of the Spirit: The Poetics of Afro-American Women's Writing*, Chicago: University of Chicago Press.

Baldwin, J. (1998) *Collected Essays*, New York: Library of America.

Barrish, P.J. (ed.) (2011) *The Cambridge Companion to American Literary Realism*, Cambridge: Cambridge University Press.

Bartram, W. (1996) *Travels & Other Writings*, T. Slaughter, ed., New York: Library of America.

Bauer, D.M. (ed.) (2012) *The Cambridge History of American Women's Literature*, Cambridge: Cambridge University Press.

Bauer, D.M. and Gould, P. (eds) (2002) *The Cambridge Companion to Nineteenth-Century American Women's Writing*, Cambridge: Cambridge University Press.

Baym, N. (gen. ed.) (1985) *The Norton Anthology of American Literature, 2nd ed., volume 2*. New York: Norton.

Baym, N. (1993) *Womans's Fiction: A Guide to Novels by and about Women in America, 1820–1870*, 2nd ed., Urbana, IL: University of Illinois Press.

Baym, N. (gen. ed.) (2003) *The Norton Anthology of American Literature, 6th ed., vol. C, 1865–1914*, New York and London: W.W. Norton and Company.

——(2003) *The Norton Anthology of American Literature, 6th ed., vol. D, Between the Wars: 1914–1945*, New York and London: W.W. Norton and Company.

——(2003) *The Norton Anthology of American Literature, 6th ed., vol. E, Literature since 1945*, New York and London: W.W. Norton and Company.

——(2007) *The Norton Anthology: American Literature, 7th ed., vol. A, Beginnings to 1820*. New York: Norton.

——(2007) *The Norton Anthology: American Literature, 7th ed., vol. B, 1820–1865*. New York: Norton.

——(2008) *The Norton Anthology of American Literature, Shorter 7th ed.*, New York and London: W.W. Norton and Company.

Beach, C. (1999) *Poetic Culture: Contemporary American Poetry between Community and Institution*, Evanston, IL: Northwestern University Press.

Bell, B.W. (1987) *The Afro-American Novel and Its Tradition*, Amherst, MA: University of Massachusetts Press.

——(2004) *The Contemporary African American Novel, Its Folk Roots and Modern Literary Branches*, Amherst, MA: University of Massachusetts Press.

Bell, M.D. (1980) *The Development of American Romance*, Chicago: University of Chicago Press.

Bellow, S. (2003) *Novels 1944–1953*, J. Wood, ed., New York: Library of America.

——(2007) *Novels 1956–1964*, J. Wood, ed., New York: Library of America.

Benjamin, W. (1973) *Illuminations*, Glasgow: Fontana/Collins.

Bercovitch, S. (gen. ed.) (1995–2005) *The Cambridge History of American Literature, vol. 1–8*, Cambridge: Cambridge University Press.

Bercovitch, S. (1974) *The American Puritan Imagination*, Cambridge: Cambridge University Press.

——(1975) *The Puritan Origins of the American Self*, New Haven: Yale University Press.

——(1993) *The Rites of Assent: Transformations in the Symbolic Construction of America*, New York and London: Routledge.

Berlant, L. (1991) *The Anatomy of National Fantasy: Hawthorne, Utopia, and Everyday Life*, Chicago and London: The University of Chicago Press.

Bernstein, C. (2001) *With Strings*, Chicago: The University of Chicago Press.

Bertens, H. and D'haen, T. (2001) *Contemporary American Crime Fiction*, Basingstoke and New York: Palgrave Macmillan.

Bertens, H. and Fokkema, D. (1997) *International Postmodernism: Theory and International Practice*, Amsterdam and Philadelphia: Benjamins.

Berthoff, W. (1981) *The Ferment of Realism: 1884–1919*, Cambridge: Cambridge University Press [1967].

Berthoff., W. (1980) *A Literature Without Qualities: American Writing since 1945*, Berkeley, CA: University of California Press.

Bigsby, C.W.E. (1983) *A Critical Introduction to Twentieth-Century American Drama, Volume One: 1900–1940*, Cambridge: Cambridge University Press.

——(1984) *A Critical Introduction to Twentieth-Century American Drama: Volume Two: Williams/ Miller/Albee*, Cambridge: Cambridge University Press.

——(1985) *A Critical Introduction to Twentieth-Century American Drama: Volume Three: Beyond Broadway*, Cambridge: Cambridge University Press.

——(2000) *Modern American Drama, 1945–2000*, Cambridge: Cambridge University Press.

Bilton, A. (2003) *An Introduction to Contemporary American Fiction*, New York: New York University Press.

Bird, R.M. (1967) *Nick of the Woods, or the Jibbenainosay: A Tale of Kentucky*, C. Dahl, ed., New Haven, CT: College and University Press [1837].

Bishop, E. (1983) *The Complete Poems, 1927–1979*, New York: Farrar, Straus and Giroux.

Black Hawk (1990) *Black Hawk: An Autobiography*, D. Jackson, ed., Urbana, IL: University of Illinois Press.

Bone, R. (1965) *The Negro Novel in America*, New Haven, CT: Yale University Press.

Boyers, R. (ed.) (1974) *Contemporary Poetry in America: Essays and Interviews*, New York: Schocken.

Bradbury, M. and Temperley, H. (1981) *Introduction to American Studies*, London and New York: Longman.

Brauner, D. (2010) *Contemporary American Fiction*, Edinburgh: Edinburgh University Press.

Brickhouse, A. (2004) *Transamerican Literary Relations and the Nineteenth-Century Public Sphere*, Cambridge: Cambridge University Press.

Brooks, G. (2005) *The Essential Gwendolyn Brooks*, E. Alexander, ed., New York: Library of America.

Brown, C.B. (1998) *Three Gothic Novels*, S.J. Krause, ed., New York: Library of America.

Brown, S. (1980) *The Collected Poems of Sterling A. Brown*, New York: Harper and Row.

Brown, W.W. (2000) *Clotel; or, The President's Daughter*, New York: Modern Library [1853].

Bruce, D.D. (2001) *The Origins of African American Literature 1680–1865*, Charlottesville, VA: University of Virginia Press.

Buell, L. (1986) *New England Literary Culture: From Revolution through Renaissance*, Cambridge: Cambridge University Press.

——(1995) *The Environmental Imagination: Thoreau, Nature Writing, and the Formation of American Culture*, Cambridge, MA and London: The Belknap Press of Harvard University Press.

——(2003) *Emerson*, Cambridge, MA: Harvard University Press.

Burroughs, W. and Gysin, B. (1978) *Third Mind*, New York: Viking.

Cabeza de Vaca, A.N. (1993) *The Account: Alvar Núñez Cabez de Vaca's Relación*, M.A. Favata and J.B. Fernandez, trans. and eds, Houston: Arte Público.

Calderón, H. and Saldívar, J.D. (eds) (1991) *Criticism in the Borderlands: Studies in Chicano Literature, Culture, and Ideology*, Durham, NC: Duke University Press.

Cappon, L.J. (ed.) (1959) *The Adams-Jefferson Letters*, Chapel Hill, NC: University of North Carolina Press.

Carby, H. (1987) *Reconstructing Womanhood: The Emergence of the Afro-American Woman Novelist*, Oxford: Oxford University Press.

Carter, E. (1954) *Howells and the Age of Realism*, Boston: Lippincott.

Castronovo, R. (2007) *Beautiful Democracy: Aesthetics and Anarchy in a Global Era*, Chicago and London: The University of Chicago Press.

——(2012) *The Oxford Handbook of Nineteenth-Century American Literature*, Oxford: Oxford University Press.

Chai, L. (1987) *The Romantic Foundations of the American Renaissance*, Ithaca, NY: Cornell University Press.

Chandler, R. (1995) *Stories and Early Novels: Pulp Stories, The Big Sleep, Farewell, My Lovely, The High Window*, F. MacShane, ed., New York: Library of America.

——(1995) *Later Novels & Other Writings: The Lady in the Lake, The Little Sister, The Long Goodbye, Playback, Double Indemnity, Selected Essays and Letters*, F. MacShane, ed., New York: Library of America.

Chase, R. (1957) *The American Novel and Its Tradition*, Baltimore, MD: Johns Hopkins University Press.

Chopin, Kate (2002) *Complete Novels and Stories: At Fault / Bayou Folk / A Night in Acadie / The Awakening / Uncollected Stories*, S.M. Gilbert, ed., New York: Library of America.

Cooper, J.F. (1985) *The Leatherstocking Tales: Vol.1*, B. Nevius, ed., New York: Library of America.

——(1991) *Sea Tales*, K.S. House and T. Philbrick, eds, New York: Library of America.

Coser, S. (1995) *Bridging the Americas: The Literature of Paule Marshall, Toni Morrison, and Gayl Jones*, Philadelphia, PA: Temple University Press.

Costello, B. (2003) *Shifting Ground: Reinventing Landscape in Modern American Poetry*, Cambridge, MA: Harvard University Press.

Coulombe, J.L. (2011) *Reading Native American Literature*, London and New York: Routledge.

Crane, G.D. (2002) *Race, Citizenship, and Law in American Literature*, Cambridge: Cambridge University Press.

Crane, G. (2007) *The Cambridge Introduction to the Nineteenth-Century American Novel*, Cambridge: Cambridge University Press.

Crane, S. (1984) *Prose and Poetry*, J.C. Levenson, ed., New York: The Library of America.

Creech, M. (2001) *Paper Cathedrals*, Kent, OH: Kent State University Press.

Crèvecoeur, J. H. St. John de (2009) *Letters from an American Farmer*, S. Manning, ed., Oxford and New York: Oxford University Press.

Cummings, E.E. (1980) *Complete Poems 1913–1962*, New York and London: Harcourt Brace Jovanovich.

Daley, J. (ed.) (2006) *Great Speeches by African Americans*, Mineola, NY: Dover.

Davidson, C.N. (1986) *Revolution and the Word: The Rise of the Novel in America*, New York and Oxford: Oxford University Press.

Davidson, C. and Wagner-Martin, L. (eds) (1999) *The Oxford Companion to Women's Writing in the United States*, Oxford: Oxford University Press.

Dekker, G. (1987) *The American Historical Romance*, Cambridge: Cambridge University Press.

Denning, M. (1998) *Mechanic Accents: Dime Novels and Working-Class Culture in America*, London and New York: Verso.

——(1997) *The Cultural Front: The Laboring of American Culture in the Twentieth Century*, London and New York: Verso.

Dick, P.K. (1995) *The Shifting Realities of Philip K. Dick: Selected Literary and Philosophical Writings*, L. Sutin, ed., New York: Pantheon.

Dickinson, Emily (1998) *The Poems of Emily Dickinson: Variorum Edition*, 3 vols., R.W, Franklin, ed., Cambridge, MA: Cambridge University Press.

Dickstein, M. (1997) *Gates of Eden: American Culture in the Sixties*, Cambridge, MA: Harvard University Press.

——(2009) *Dancing in the Dark: A Cultural History of the Great Depression*, New York and London: W.W. Norton and Company.

Dimock, W.C. (2008) *Through Other Continents: American Literature across Deep Time*, Princeton, NJ and Oxford: Princeton University Press.

Dimock, W.C. and Buell, L. (eds) (2007) *Shades of the Planet: American Literature as World Literature*, Princeton, NJ and Oxford: Princeton University Press.

Dolan, F.M. (1999) *Allegories of America: Narratives – Metaphysics – Politics*, Ithaca and London: Cornell University Press.

Donovan, J. (1983) *New England Local Color Literature: A Women's Tradition*, New York: Frederick Ungar.

Dos Passos, J. (1996) *U.S.A.,* T. Ludington and D. Aaron, eds, New York: Library of America.

Douglass, F. (1994) *Autobiographies*, H.L. Gates, Jr, ed., New York: Library of America.

Dubois, W.E.B. (1986) *Writings*, N. Huggins, ed., New York: Library of America.

Duvall, J.N. (2011) *The Cambridge Companion to American Fiction After 1945*, Cambridge: Cambridge University Press.

Eble, K. (1956) 'A Forgotten Novel: Kate Chopin's The Awakening', *Western Humanities Review* 10, pp. 261–69.

Eliot, T.S. (1928) *For Lancelot Andrewes: Essays on Style and Order*, London: Faber and Gwyer.

——(1932) *Selected Essays*, London: Faber and Faber.

——(1971) *The Complete Poems and Plays, 1909–1950*, San Diego, New York and London: Harcourt Brace Jovanovich.

——(1996) *Inventions of the March Hare: Poems 1909–1917*, San Diego, New York and London: Harcourt Brace Jovanovich.

Elliott, E. (1982) *Revolutionary Writers: Literature and Authority in the New Republic, 1725–1810*, New York and Oxford: Oxford University Press.

Elliott, E. (gen. ed.) (1988) *Columbia Literary History of the United States*, New York: Columbia University Press.

Elliott, E. (2002) *The Cambridge Introduction to Early American Literature*, Cambridge: Cambridge University Press.

Ellison, R. (1972) *Shadow and Act,* New York: Vintage.

——(1986) *Going to the Territory*, New York: Vintage.

Emerson, R.W. (1983) *Essays & Lectures*, J. Porte, ed., New York: Library of America.

Emmert, S. (1996) *Loaded Fictions: Social Critiques in the Twentieth-Century Western*, Moscow, ID: University of Idaho Press.

Equiano, Olaudah (2003) *The Interesting Narrative and Other Writings*, V. Carretta, ed., New York: Penguin.

Eysturoy, A.O. (1996) *Daughters of Self-Creation: The Contemporary Chicana Novel*, Albuquerque, NM: University of New Mexico Press.

Farrell, J.T. (1938) 'A Novelist Begins', *The Atlantic Monthly*, 162:3 (September 1938), pp. 330–34.

Faulkner, W. (1965) *Essays, Speeches and Public Letters*, James B. Meriwether, ed., New York: Random House.

Ferlinghetti, L. (1958) *A Coney Island of the Mind*, New York: New Directions.

Fern, Fanny (1986) *Ruth Hall and Other Writings*, J.W. Warren, ed., New Brunswick, NJ: Rutgers University Press.

Ferraro, T.J. (1993) *Ethnic Passages: Literary Immigrants in Twentieth-Century America*, Chicago: University of Chicago Press.

Fiedler, L.A. (1966) *Love and Death in the American Novel*, rev. ed. New York: Stein and Day.

Fisher, P. (1987) *Hard Facts: Setting and Form in the American Novel*, New York and Oxford: Oxford University Press.

——(1991) *Still the New World: American Literature in a Crisis of Creative Destruction*, Cambridge, MA: Harvard University Press.

Fishkin, S. F. (1993) *Was Huck Black? Mark Twain and African American Voices*, New York and Oxford: Oxford University Press.

Fitzgerald, F.S. (1950) *The Great Gatsby*, Harmondsworth: Penguin.

——(1965) *The Crack-Up, with Other Pieces and Stories*, Harmondsworth: Penguin.

——(2000) *Novels and Stories 1920–1922: This Side of Paradise / Flappers and Philosophers / The Beautiful and the Damned / Tales of the Jazz Age*, J.R. Bryer, ed., New York: Library of America.

Fletcher, A. (2004) *A New Theory for American Poetry: Democracy, the Environment, and the Future of Imagination*, Cambridge, MA: Harvard University Press.

Foley, B. (1993) *Radical Representations: Politics and Form in U.S. Proletarian Fiction, 1929–1941*, Durham, NC: Duke University Press.

Foster, F.S. (1979) *Witnessing Slavery: The Development of Ante-Bellum Slave Narratives*, Westport, CT: Greenwood Press.

Franklin, B. (1997) *Autobiography, Poor Richard, and Later Writings*, New York: Library of America.

——(2002) *Silence Dogood, The Busy-Body, & Early Writings*, New York: Library of America.

Fredman, S. (ed.) (2005) *A Concise Companion to Twentieth-Century American Poetry*, Oxford and Malden, MA: Blackwell.

Frost, R. (1995) *Collected Poems, Prose, & Plays*, R. Poirier, ed., New York: Library of America.

Fuller, M. (1994) *The Portable Margaret Fuller*, N. Kelley, ed., New York: Penguin.

Gates, Jr., H.L. (1984) *Black Literature & Literary Theory*, New York & London: Methuen.

——(1987) *Figures in Black: Words, Signs, and the 'Racial' Self*, New York and Oxford: Oxford University Press.

——(1988) *The Signifying Monkey: A Theory of Afro-American Literary Criticism*, New York and Oxford: Oxford University Press.

Gates, Jr., H.L. and McKay, N. (eds) (1997) *The Norton Anthology of African American Literature*, New York: Norton.

Gayle, Jr., A. (1971) *The Black Aesthetic*, New York: Doubleday.

——(1976) *The Way of the New World: the Black Novel in America*, New York: Anchor Books.

Gelpi, A. (1987) *A Coherent Splendor: The American Poetry Renaissance, 1910–1950*, Cambridge: Cambridge University Press.

Giles, P. (2001) *Transatlantic Insurrections: British Culture and the Formation of American Literature, 1730–1860*, Philadelphia, PA: University of Pennsylvania Press.

——(2002) *Virtual Americas: Transnational Fictions and the Transatlantic Imaginary*, Durham, NC: Duke University Press.

Gilmore, M. T. (1985) *American Romanticism and the Marketplace*, Chicago: University of Chicago Press.

Goldbarth, A. (2009) *The Kitchen Sink: New and Selected Poems, 1972–2007*, Minneapolis: Graywolf Press.

Goodman, S. and Dawson, C. (2005) *William Dean Howells: A Writer's Life*, Berkeley: University of California Press.

Gordone, C. (1969) *No Place to Be Somebody: A Black Comedy in Three Acts*, Indianapolis, IN: Bobbs-Merrill.

Graham, J. (2003) *Never: Poems*, New York: Ecco.

Graham, M. and Ward, Jr., J.W. (eds) (2011) *The Cambridge History of African American Literature*, Cambridge: Cambridge University Press.

Gray, R. (1986) *Writing the South: Ideas of an American Region*, Cambridge: Cambridge University Press.

——(1990) *American Poetry of the Twentieth Century*, London & New York: Longman.

——(2000) *Southern Aberrations: Writers of the American South and the Problems of Regionalism*, Baton Rouge, LA: Louisiana State University Press.

——(2004) *A History of American Literature*, Oxford and Malden, MA: Blackwell.

——(2011) *A Brief History of American Literature*, Oxford and Malden, MA: Wiley-Blackwell.

Greene, J.L. (1996) *Blacks in Eden: The African American Novel's First Century*, Charlottesville, VA: University Press of Virginia.

Greer, A. (ed.) (2000) *The Jesuit Relations: Natives and Missionaries in Seventeenth-Century North America*, Boston: Bedford/St. Martin's.

Grossman, J. (2003) *Reconstituting the American Renaissance: Emerson, Whitman, and the Politics of Representation*, Durham, NC and London: Duke University Press.

Guin, M. (2000) *After Southern Modernism: Fiction of the Contemporary South*, Jackson, MS: University Press of Mississippi.

Gura, P. F. (2007) *American Transcendentalism: A History*, New York: Hill and Wang.

Gwynn, R.S. and Lindner, A. (eds) (2005) *Contemporary American Poetry*, New York & London: Penguin Academics.

Hall, D., Pack, R., and Simpson, L. (eds) (1957) *The New Poets of England and America*, New York: Meridian.

Hallberg, R. von (1985) *American Poetry and Culture, 1945–1980*, Cambridge, MA: Harvard University Press.

Halpern, N. (2003) *Everyday and Prophetic: The Poetry of Lowell, Ammons, Merrill and Rich*, Madison, WI: University of Wisconsin Press.

Hansbery, L. (1969) *To Be Young, Gifted, and Black; Lorraine Hansbery in Her Own Words*, adapted by R. Nemiroff, Englewood Cliffs, NJ: Prentice-Hall.

Hapke, L. (2001) *Labor's Text: The Worker in American Fiction*, New Brunswick, NJ and London: Rutgers University Press.

Harap, L. (1978) *In the Mainstream: The Jewish Presence in Twentieth-Century American Literature, 1950s-1980s*, New York: Greenwood Press.

Hariot, T. (2007) *A briefe and true report of the new found land of Virginia*, Charlottesville, VA: University of Virginia Press [1588].

Harris, S.K. (1990) *19th-Century American Women's Novels: Interpretive Strategies*, Cambridge: Cambridge University Press.

Harris, S.M. (ed.) (1996) *American Women Writers to 1800*, New York: Oxford University Press.

Hart, J.D. and Leininger, P. (1996) *The Oxford Companion to American Literature*, 6th rev. ed., New York and Oxford: Oxford University Press.

Hassan, I. (1961) *Radical Innocence: Studies in the Contemporary American Novel*, Princeton, NJ: Princeton University Press.

Hawthorne, N. (1983) *Collected Novels*, M. Bell, ed., New York: Library of America.

——(1997) *Tales & Sketches*, R.H. Pearce and M. Bell, eds, New York: Library of America.

Hayes, K.J. (ed.) (2002) *The Cambridge Companion to Edgar Allan Poe*, Cambridge: Cambridge University Press.

Hayes, K.J. (2007) *The Cambridge Introduction to Herman Melville*, Cambridge: Cambridge University Press.

Hemingway, E. (1938) *The Short Stories of Ernest Hemingway*, New York: Scribners.

——(1966) *Green Hills of Africa*, Harmondsworth: Penguin Books.

——(1977) *A Farewell to Arms*, London: Granada.

——(1987) *The Complete Short Stories of Ernest Hemingway. The Finca Vigía Edition,* New York: Scribners.

Hendin, J.G. (ed.) (2004) *A Concise Companion to Postwar American Literature and Culture*. Oxford and Malden, MA: Blackwell.

Heyck, D.L.D. (1994) *Barrios and Borderlands: Cultures of Latinos and Latinas in the United States*, New York and London: Routledge.

Hoffman, D. (1994) *Form and Fable in American Fiction*, Charlottesville, VA: University Press of Virginia [1961].

Hoffman, D. (ed.) (1979) *Harvard Guide to Contemporary American Writing*, Cambridge, MA: Harvard University Press.

Hollander, J. (ed.) (1993) *American Poetry: The Nineteenth Century, vol. 1: Freneau to Whitman*, New York: Library of America.

——(1993) *American Poetry: The Nineteenth Century, vol. 2: Melville to Stickney, American Indian Poetry, Folk Songs & Spirituals*, New York: Library of America.

Hornby, N. (1992) *Contemporary American Fiction*, New York: St Martin's Press.

Howard, R. (1980) *Alone with America*, New York: Scribner.

Howells, W.D. (1967) *My Mark Twain: Reminiscences and Criticisms*, Baton Rouge: Louisiana State University Press.

——(2013) *Criticism and Fiction*. http://eremita.di.uminho.pt/gutenberg/3/3/7/3377/3377.txt, accessed 16 May 2013.

Inge, M.T. (ed.) (2008) *The New Encyclopedia of Southern Culture, Volume 9, Literature*, Chapel Hill, NC: University of North Carolina Press.

Irving, W. (1983) *History, Tales & Sketches*, J.W. Tuttleton, ed., New York: Library of America.

Jackson, B. (1989) *A History of Afro-American Literature. Volume I: The Long Beginning, 1746–1895*, Baton Rouge, LA: Louisiana State University Press.

Jacobs, H. (2000) *Incidents in the Life of a Slave Girl*, J.F. Yellin, ed., Cambridge, MA: Harvard University Press [1861].

Jeffers, R. (1965) *Selected Poems*, New York: Vintage.

Jefferson, T. (2010) *Selected Writings of Thomas Jefferson*, W. Franklin, ed., New York: Norton.

Jehlen, M. (2002) *Readings at the Edge of Literature*, Chicago: The University of Chicago Press.

Jehlen, M. and Warner, M. (eds) (1997) *The English Literatures of America, 1500–1800*. New York and London: Routledge.

Jewett, S.O. (1956) *The Country of the Pointed Firs and Other Stories*, Garden City, NY: Doubleday and Company.

Johannessen, L.M. (2008) *Threshold Time: Passage of Crisis in Chicano Literature*, Amsterdam and New York: Rodopi.

Johnson, T.H. (ed.) (1939) *The Poetical Works of Edward Taylor*, NewYork: Rockland.

Johnson, T.H. and Ward, T. (eds) (1986) *The Letters of Emily Dickinson*, Cambridge, MA: Harvard University Press.

Johnston, J. (1998) *Information Multiplicity: American Fiction in the Age of Media Saturation*, Baltimore and London: The Johns Hopkins University Press.

Jones, Gayl (1975) *Corregidora*, New York: Random House.

Jones, Gerard (2004) *Men of Tomorrow: Geeks, Gangsters and the Birth of the Comic Book*, New York: Basic Books.

Jones, L. (1961) *Preface to a Twenty-Volume Suicide Note*, New York: Totem Press.

——(1964) Dutchman *and* The Slave: *Two Plays*, New York: Morrow.

Jurca, C. (2001) *White Diaspora: The Suburb and the Twentieth-Century American Novel*, Princeton and Oxford: Princeton University Press.

Kalaidjian, W. (2005) *The Cambridge Companion to American Modernism*, Cambridge: Cambridge University Press.

Kaplan, A. (1988) *The Social Construction of American Realism*, Chicago: University of Chicago Press.

——(2002) *The Anarchy of Empire in the Making of U.S. Culture*, Cambridge, MA and London: Harvard University Press.

Karl, F.R. (1983) *American Fictions 1940–1980: A Comprehensive History and Critical Evaluation*, New York: Harper & Row.

Kazin, A. (1942) *On Native Grounds: An Interpretation of Modern American Prose Literature*, New York: Reynal & Hitchcock.

Kazin, A. (1971) *Bright Book of Life: American Novelists and Storytellers from Hemingway to Mailer*, Boston: Little, Brown.

——(1984) *An American Procession: The Major American Writers from 1830 to 1930 – The Crucial Century*. New York: Knopf.

Keller, L. (1987) *Re-Making It New: Contemporary American Poetry and the Modernist Tradition*, Cambridge: Cambridge University Press.

Kellner, B. (1984) *The Harlem Renaissance: An Historical Dictionary*, Westport, CT: Greenwood Press.

Kennedy, J.G. (1993) *Imagining Paris: Exile, Writing, and American Identity*, New Haven and London: Yale University Press.

Kenner, H. (1973) *The Pound Era*, Berkeley, CA: University of California Press.

——(1974) *A Homemade World: The American Modernist Writers*, New York: Knopf.

Kerkering, J.D. (2009) *The Poetics of National and Racial Identity in Nineteenth-Century American Literature*, Cambridge: Cambridge University Press.

Kerouac, J. (1995) *Selected Letters, vol. 1: 1940–1956*, A. Charters, ed., New York: Viking Penguin.

Kim, E.H. (1982) *Asian American Literature: An Introduction to the Writings and their Social Context*, Philadelphia, PA: Temple University Press.

King, R. (1980) *A Southern Renaissance: The Cultural Awakening of the American South, 1930–1955*. New York and Oxford: Oxford University Press.

Krasner, D. (2007) *A Companion to Twentieth-Century American Drama*, Oxford and Malden, MA: Blackwell.

Krupat, A. (1989) *The Voice in the Margin: Native American Literature and the Canon*, Berkeley, CA: University of California Press.

Krupat, A. (ed.) (1993) *New Voices in Native American Literary Criticism*, Washington, DC: Smithsonian Institution.

Kuhl, J. (1989) *Alternate Worlds: A Study of Postmodern Antirealistic American Fiction*, New York: New York University Press.

Lanier, S. (n.d.) 'Uncle Jim's Baptist Revival Hymn', http://www.poemhunter.com/poem/uncle-jim-s-baptist-revival-hymn, accessed 16 May 2013.

Lauret, M. (1994) *Liberating Literature: Feminist Fiction in America*, London and New York: Routledge.

Lauter, P. (1991) *Canons and Contexts*, New York and Oxford: Oxford University Press.

Lauter, P., Albert, J., and Brady, M.P. (eds) (2013) *The Heath Anthology of American Literature, vol. 1, Beginnings to 1800*, 7th ed., Boston: Cengage Learning.

Lawrence, D.H. (1990) *Studies in Classic American Literature*, Harmondsworth: Penguin [1923].

Lears, J. (1981) *No Place of Grace: Antimodernism and the Transformation of American Culture, 1880–1920*, New York: Pantheon.

Lee, R.C. (1999) *The Americas of Asian American literature: Gendered Fictions of Nation and Transnation*, Princeton, NJ: Princeton University Press.

Lee, M.S. (2010) *Slavery, Philosophy, and American Literature, 1830–1860*, Cambridge: Cambridge University Press.

Lehman, D. (1998) *The Last Avant-Garde: The Making of the New York School of Poets*, New York: Doubleday.

Levander, C. and Levine, R.S. (eds) (2008) *Hemispheric American Studies*, New Brunswick, NJ and London: Rutgers University Press.

Levine, R. (2013) *The New Cambridge Companion to Herman Melville*, 2nd ed., Cambridge: Cambridge University Press.

Lewis, R.W.B. (1955) *The American Adam: Innocence, Tragedy, and Tradition in the Nineteenth Century*, Chicago: University of Chicago Press.

Li, D.L. (1998) *Imagining the Nation: Asian American Literature and Cultural Consent*, Palo Alto, CA: Stanford University Press.

Lim, S.G. (ed.) (2000) *Asian American Literature: An Anthology*, Lincolnwood, IL: NTC.

Ling, A. (1990) *Between Worlds: Women Writers of Chinese Ancestry*, New York: Pergamon.

Lobo, S., Talbot, S, and Morris, T.L. (eds) (2010) *Native American Voices: A Reader*, 3rd ed., Upper Saddle River, NJ: Prentice Hall.

Longenbach, J. (1997) *Modern Poetry After Modernism*, New York and Oxford: Oxford University Press.

Longfellow, H.W. (2000) *Poems & Other Writings*, J.D. McClatchy, ed., New York: Library of America.

Lowell, J.R. (1977) *James Russell Lowell's The Biglow Papers, First Series: A Critical Edition*, T. Wortham, ed., DeKalb, IL: Northern Illinois University Press.

Lowell, R. (2003) *Collected Poems*, F. Bidart and D. Gewanter, eds, New York: Farrar, Straus and Giroux.

Lurie, A. (1974) *The War between the Tates*, New York: Random House.

MacLeish, A. (1972) *The Human Season: Selected Poems 1926–1972*, Boston: Houghton Mifflin Company.

Madsen, D. L. (2000) *Understanding Contemporary Chicana Literature*, Columbia, SC: University of South Carolina Press.

Magny, C-E. (1948) *l'Age du roman américain*, Paris: Seuil.

Mailer, N. (1959) *Advertisements for Myself*, New York: Putnam.

Marcus, G. and Sollors, W. (eds) (2009) *A New Literary History of America*, Cambridge, MA: Harvard University Press.

Marx, L. (1964) *The Machine in the Garden: Technology and the Pastoral Idea in America*, New York and Oxford: Oxford University Press.

McCormick, J. (1971) *American Literature 1919–1932*, London: Routledge & Keegan Paul.

McGowan, C. (2004) *Twentieth-Century American Poetry*, Oxford and Malden, MA: Blackwell.

McWilliams, Jr., J. P. (1989) *The American Epic: Transforming a Genre, 1770–1860*, Cambridge: Cambridge University Press.

Melville, H. (1982) *Typee, Omoo, Mardi*, G.T. Tanselle, ed., New York: Library of America.

——(1983) *Redburn, White-Jacket, Moby-Dick*, G.T. Tanselle, ed., New York: Library of America.

——(1985) *Pierre, Israel Potter, The Piazza Tales, The Confidence-Man, Billy Budd, Uncollected Prose*, G.T. Tanselle, ed., New York: Library of America.

Meriwether, J.B. and Millgate, M. (1980) *Lion in the Garden: Interviews with William Faulkner*, Lincoln and London: University of Nebraska Press.

Middlebrook, D.W. and Yalom, M. (eds) (1985) *Coming to Light: American Women Poets in the Twentieth Century*, Ann Arbor, MI: University of Michigan Press.

Millard, K. (2000) *Contemporary American Fiction: An Introduction to American Fiction since 1970*, Oxford: Oxford University Press.

Miller, A. (2006) *Collected Plays 1944–1961*, New York: Library of America.

Miller, Jr., J. E. (1979) *The American Quest for a Supreme Fiction*, Chicago: University of Chicago Press.

Minter, D. (1994) *A Cultural History of the American Novel: Henry James to William Faulkner*, Cambridge: Cambridge University Press.

Mitchell, A. and Taylor, D.K. (eds) (2009) *The Cambridge Companion to African American Women's Literature*, Cambridge: Cambridge University Press.

Monteith, S. (ed.) (2013) *The Cambridge Companion to the Literature of the American South*, Cambridge: Cambridge University Press.

Moore, M. (1981) *The Complete Poems of Marianne Moore*, New York: The Macmillan Company/ Viking.

Moraru, C. (2011) *Cosmodernism: American Narrative, Late Globalization, and the New Cultural Imaginary*, Ann Arbor, MI: The University of Michigan Press.

Morley, C. (2009) *The Quest for Epic in Contemporary American Fiction: John Updike, Philip Roth and Don DeLillo*, New York and London: Routledge.

——(2012) *Modern American Literature*, Edinburgh: Edinburgh University Press.

Morrison, T. (1970) *The Bluest Eye*, New York: Holt, Rinehart and Winston.

Muller, G.H. (1999) *New Strangers in Paradise: The Immigrant Experience and Contemporary American Fiction*, Lexington, KY: Kentucky University Press.

Myers, J. and Wojahn, D. (eds) (1991) *A Profile of Twentieth-Century American Poetry*, Carbondale, IL: Southern Illinois University Press.

Myerson, J. (ed.) (2000) *Transcendentalism: A Reader*, New York and Oxford: Oxford University Press

——(2002) *The Selected Letters of Nathaniel Hawthorne*, Columbus, OH: Ohio State University Press.

Nadel, A. (1995) *Containment Culture: American Narratives, Postmodernism, and the Atomic Age*, Durham, NC and London: Duke University Press.

Neal, L. and Jones, L. (eds) (1968) *Black Fire: An Anthology of Afro-American Writing*, New York: Morrow.

Nelson, C. (2001) *Revolutionary Memory: Recovering the Poetry of the American Left*, New York and London: Routledge.

——(2012) *The Oxford Handbook of Modern and Contemporary Poetry*, Oxford: Oxford University Press.

Newman, J. (2013) *Utopia and Terror in Contemporary American Fiction*, London and New York: Routledge.

Norton, M.B. (2002) *In the Devil's Snare: The Salem Witchcraft Crisis of 1692*, New York: Knopf.

Nye, R.B. (1960) *The Cultural Life of the New Nation, 1776–1830*, New York: HarperCollins.

O'Connor, F. (1988) *Collected Works*, S. Fitzgerald, ed., New York: Library of America.

O'Donnell, P. (2000) *Latent Destinies: Cultural Paranoia and Contemporary U.S. Narrative*, Durham, NC: Duke University Press.

O'Hara, F. (2008) *Selected Poems*, M. Ford, ed., New York: Knopf.

Olderman, R. (1972) *Beyond the Waste Land: the American Novel in the Nineteen-Sixties*, New Haven: Yale University Press.

Owens, L. (1992) *Other Destinies: Understanding the American Indian Novel*, Norman, OK: University of Oklahoma Press.

Paine, T. (1995) *Collected Writings*, E. Foner, ed., New York: Library of America.

Palmer, M. (1988) *Sun*, New York: North Point Press.

Paulding, J.K. (2003) *The Lion of the West and the Bucktails*, Lanham, MD: Rowman & Littlefield [1830].

Payne, D.G. (1996) *Voices in the Wilderness: American Nature Writing and Environmental Politics*, Hanover and London: University Press of New England.

Pearce, R.H. (1961) *The Continuity of American Poetry*, Princeton, NJ.: Princeton University Press.

Pease, D. (ed.) (1994) *National Identities and Post-Americanist Narratives*, Durham, NC: Duke University Press.

——(1994) *Revisionary Interventions into the Americanist Canon*, Durham, NC: Duke University Press.

Perelman, B. (1993) *Virtual Reality*, New York: Roof Books.

Pizer, D. (1966) *Realism and Naturalism in Nineteenth-Century American Literature*, Carbondale, IL: Southern Illinois University Press.

Poe, E.A. (1984) *Essays and Reviews*, G.P. Thompson, ed., New York: Library of America.

——(1984) *Poetry & Tales*, P. Quinn, ed., New York: Library of America.

Poirier, R. (1971) *The Performing Self*, Oxford: Oxford University Press.

Porter, J. and Roemer, K.M. (eds) (2005) *The Cambridge Companion to Native American Literature*, Cambridge: Cambridge University Press.

Posnock, R. (1998) *Color & Culture: Black Writers and the Making of the Modern Intellectual*, Cambridge, MA and London: Harvard University Press.

Pound, E. (1960 [1934]) *ABC of Reading*, New York: New Directions.

——(1957) *Selected Poems of Ezra Pound*, New York: New Directions.

Purdy, J. and Ruppert, J. (eds) (2001) *Nothing But the Truth: An Anthology of Native American Literature*, Upper Saddle River, NJ: Prentice Hall.

Radway, J. (1984) *Reading the Romance: Women, Patriarchy, and Popular Literature*, Chapel Hill, NC: University of North Carolina Press.

Reagan, R. (1990) *An American Life: The Autobiography*, New York: Simon & Schuster Audioworks.

Rebolledo, T.D. (1995) *Women Singing in the Snow: A Cultural Analysis of Chicana Literature*, Phoenix, AZ: University of Arizona Press.

Reising, R. (1986) *The Unusable Past: Theory & the Study of American Literature*, New York: Methuen.

Reynolds, D.S. (1988) *Beneath the American Renaissance: The Subversive Imagination in the Age of Emerson and Melville*, New York: Knopf.

Reynolds, D. (2010) *America: Empire of Liberty*, London: Penguin.

Reynolds, G. (1999) *Twentieth-Century American Women's Fiction*, New York: St. Martin's Press.

Rhodehamel, J. (ed.) (2001) *The American Revolution: Writings from the War of Independence*, New York: Library of America.

Richardson, G.A. (1997) *American Drama from the Colonial Period through World War I: A Critical History*, New York: Twayne.

Ridgely, J.V. (1980) *Nineteenth-Century Southern Literature*, Lexington, KY: University of Kentucky Press.

Riss, A. (2009) *Race, Slavery, and Liberalism in Nineteenth-Century American Literature*, Cambridge: Cambridge University Press.

Robbins, S. (2007) *The Cambridge Introduction to Harriet Beecher Stowe*, Cambridge: Cambridge University Press.

Robinson, E.A. (1939) *Collected Poems of Edwin Arlington Robinson*, New York: The Macmillan Company.

Rowe, J.C. (2000) *Literary Culture and U.S. Imperialism: From the Revolution to World War II*, Oxford and New York: Oxford University Press.

Rowe, J.C. (ed.) (2000) *Post-Nationalist American Studies*, Berkeley, Los Angeles and London: University of California Press.

Roynon, T. (2013) *The Cambridge Introduction to Toni Morrison*, Cambridge: Cambridge University Press.

Rubin, Jr., L.D., Jackson, B., Moore, R.S., Simpson, L.P. and Young, T.D. (eds) (1985) *The History of Southern Literature*, Baton Rouge, LA: Louisiana State University Press.

Ruland, R. and Bradbury, M. (1991) *From Puritanism to Postmodernism: A History of American Literature*, New York and London: Routledge.

Ruoff, A.L.B. and Ward, J.W. (eds) (1990) *Redefining American Literary History*, New York: The Modern Language Association of America.

Saldívar, J. D. (1991) *The Dialectics of Our America: Genealogy, Cultural Critique, and Literary History*, Durham, NC: Duke University Press.

Saldívar, R. (1990) *Chicano Narrative: The Dialectics of Difference*, Madison, WI: University of Wisconsin Press.

Samuels, S. (ed.) (2004) *A Companion to American Fiction 1780–1865*. Oxford and Malden, MA: Blackwell.

Sánchez-González, L. (2001) *Boricua Literature: A Literary History of the Puerto Rican Diaspora*, New York: New York University Press.

Sanders, L.C. (1988) *The Development of Black Theater in America*, Baton Rouge, LA: Louisiana State University Press.

Sawyer-Lauçanno, C. (1992) *The Continual Pilgrimage: American Writers in Paris, 1944–1960*, San Francisco: City Light Books.

Sayre, G.M. (2000) *American Captivity Narratives*, Boston: Houghton Mifflin.

Schaub, T.H. (1991) *American Fiction in the Cold War*, Madison, WI: University of Wisconsin Press.

Schlueter, J. (ed.) (1990) *Modern American Theatre: The Female Canon*, Rutherford, NJ: Fairleigh Dickinson University Press.

Schoolcraft, H.R. (1991) *Schoolcraft's Indian Legends*, M.L. Williams, ed., East Lansing, MI: Michigan State University Press.

Seed, D. (ed.) (2010) *A Companion to Twentieth-Century United States Fiction*, Oxford and Malden, MA: Wiley-Blackwell.

Sewall, S. (1973) *The Diary of Samuel Sewall, 1674–1729*, 2 vols., M.H. Thomas, ed., New York: Farrar, Straus and Giroux.

Shepard, S. (1972) *The Unseen Hand and Other Plays*, Indianapolis, IN: Bobbs-Merrill.

Shi, D.E. (1995) *Facing Facts: Realism in American Thought and Culture 1850–1920*, New York and Oxford: Oxford University Press.

Shields, D.S. (ed.) (2007) *American Poetry: The Seventeenth & Eighteenth Centuries*, New York: Library of America.

Shockley, A.A. (ed.) (1989) *Afro-American Women Writers, 1746–1933: An Anthology and Critical Guide*, Boston, MA: G.K. Hall.

Showalter, E. (2010) *A Jury of her Peers: Celebrating American Women Writers from Anne Bradstreet to Annie Proulx*, New York: Vintage.

Simic, C. (1990) *The World Doesn't End: Prose Poems*, New York: Harcourt Brace Jovanovich.

Simms, W.G. (1994) *The Yemassee: A Romance of Carolina*, Fayetteville, AR: University of Arkansas Press.

Slotkin, R. (1973) *Regeneration through Violence: The Mythology of the American Frontier, 1600–1860*, Middletown, CT: Wesleyan University Press.

Smith, H.N. (2007) *Virgin Land: The American West as Symbol and Myth*, Cambridge, MA: Harvard University Press [1950].

Smith, H.N. (1978) *Democracy and the Novel: Popular Resistance to Classic American Writers*, New York and Oxford: Oxford University Press.

Smith, Capt. J. (2007) *Writings, with Other Narratives of Roanoke, Jamestown, and the First English Settlements of America*, J. Horn, ed., New York: Library of America.

Sollors, W. (1986) *Beyond Ethnicity: Consent and Descent in American Culture*, Oxford and New York: Oxford University Press.

Sollors, W. (ed.) (1989) *The Invention of Ethnicity*, New York and Oxford: Oxford University Press.

Sollors, W. (1997) *Neither Black Nor White Yet Both: Thematic Explorations of Interracial Literature*, Cambridge, MA: Harvard University Press.

——(1998) *Multilingual America: Transnationalism, Ethnicity, and the Languages of American Literature*, New York and London: New York University Press.

——(2008) *Ethnic Modernism*, Cambridge, MA: Harvard University Press.

Spengemann, W.C. (1989) *A Mirror for Americanists: Reflections on the Idea of American Literature*, Hanover, NH: University Press of New England.

——(1994) *A New World of Words: Redefining Early American Literature*, New Haven, CT: Yale University Press.

Spiller, R. (1955) *The Cycle of American Literature: An Essay in Historical Criticism*, New York: Macmillan

Spiller, R., Thorp, W., Johnson, T.H. and Canby, H.S. (eds) (1974) *Literary History of the United States*, New York: Macmillan [1948].

Spillers, H.J. (2003) *Black, White, and in Color: Essays on American Literature and Culture*, Chicago: University of Chicago Press.

Stansell, C. (2000) *American Moderns: Bohemian New York and the Creation of a New Century*, New York: Henry Holt and Company.

Stein, G. (1998) *Writings 1903–1932*, C.R. Stimpson and H. Chessman, eds, New York: Library of America.

——(1998) *Writings 1932–1946*, C.R. Stimpson and H. Chessman, eds, New York: Library of America.

Stein, K. (1996) *Private Poets, Worldly Acts: Public and Private History in Contemporary American Poetry*, Athens, OH: Ohio University Press.

Stepto, R. (1979) *From Behind the Veil: A Study of Afro-American Narrative*, Urbana, IL: University of Illinois Press.

Stevens, W. (1997) *Collected Poetry and Prose*, F. Kermode and J. Richardson, eds, New York: Library of America.

Stott, W. (1986) *Documentary Expression and Thirties America*, Chicago: University of Chicago Press [1973].

Stowe, H.B. (1982) *Three Novels*, K.K. Sklar, ed., New York: Library of America.

Streeby, S. (2002) *American Sensations: Class, Empire, and the Production of Popular Culture*, Berkeley, Los Angeles and London: University of California Press.

Sundquist, E.J. (1993) *To Wake the Nations: Race in the Making of American Literature*, Cambridge, MA: Harvard University Press.

Szalay, M. (2000) *New Deal Modernism: American Literature and the Invention of the Welfare State*, Durham, NC and London: Duke University Press.

Tally, J. (ed.) (2007) *The Cambridge Companion to Toni Morrison*, Cambridge: Cambridge University Press.

Tanner, T. (1965) *The Reign of Wonder: Naïvety and Reality in American Literature*, Cambridge: Cambridge University Press.

——(1976) *City of Words: American Fiction 1950–1970*, London: Jonathan Cape.

Taylor, W.R. (1993) *Cavalier & Yankee: The Old South and American National Character*, New York and Oxford: Oxford University Press [1961].

Temperley, H. and Bigsby, C. (2006) *A New Introduction to American Studies*, Harlow: Pearson/ Longman.

Thoreau, H.D. (1985) *A Week on the Concord and Merrimack Rivers; Walden, or, Life in the Woods; The Maine Woods; Cape Cod*, R.F Sayre, ed., New York: Library of America.

——(2001) *Collected Essays and Poems*, E.H. Witherell, ed., New York: Library of America.

Tindall, G.B. and Shi, D.E. (1984) *America: A Narrative History*, Brief Second Edition, New York and London: W.W. Norton and Company.

Tompkins, J. (1985) *Sensational Designs: The Cultural Work of American Fiction 1790–1860*, New York: Oxford University Press.

——(1992) *West of Everything: The Inner Life of Westerns*, New York: Oxford University Press.

Trilling, L. (1970 [1948]) 'Huckleberry Finn', *The Liberal Imagination: Essays on Literature and Society*, Harmondsworth: Penguin Books.

Twain, M. (1982) *Mississippi Writings: The Adventures of Tom Sawyer, Life on the Mississippi, Adventures of Huckleberry Finn, Pudd'nhead Wilson*, G. Cardwell, ed., New York: Library of America.

Tytell, J. (1976) *Naked Angels: The Lives and Literature of the Beat Generation*, New York: McGraw-Hill.

Vendler, H. (1980) *Part of Nature, Part of Us: Modern American Poets*, Cambridge: Harvard University Press.

——(1995) *Soul Says: Recent Poetry*, Cambridge, MA: Belknap Press.

——(2012) *Dickinson*, Cambridge, MA: Belknap Press.

Wagner-Martin, L. (2012) *A History of American Literature*, Oxford and Malden, MA: Wiley-Blackwell.

Wald, P. (1995) *Constituting Americans: Cultural Anxiety and Narrative Form*, Durham and London: Duke University Press.

Walker, A. (1983) *In Search of Our Mothers' Gardens: Womanist Prose*, New York: Harcourt Brace Jovanovich.

Wallace, D.F. (1996) 'Interview by Laura Muller', *Salon* Saturday Mar 9, 1996 07:00 PM RST. http://www.salon.com/1996/03/09/wallace_5/, accessed 20 May 2013.

Ward, G. (2002) *The Writing of America: Literature and Cultural Identity from the Puritans to the Present*, Cambridge: Polity Press.

Warner, M. (ed.) (1999) *American Sermons*, New York: Library of America.

Warren, K.W. (1993) *Black & White Strangers: Race and American Literary Realism*, Chicago and London: The University of Chicago Press.

Wharton, E. (1985) *Novels: The House of Mirth, The Reef, The Custom of the Country, The Age of Innocence*, R.W.B. Lewis, ed., New York: Library of America.

Wheatley, P. (2001) *Complete Writings*, V. Carretta, ed., New York: Penguin.

Whitman, W. (1996) *Poetry & Prose*, J. Kaplan, ed., New York: Library of America.

Williams, M. (1985) *Black Theatre in the 1960s and 1970s*, Westport, CT: Greenwood Press.

Williams, T. (2000) *Plays 1937–1955*, New York: Library of America.

Williams, W.C. (1967) *The Autobiography of William Carlos Williams*, New York: New Directions.

——(1967) *The Collected Later Poems*, New York: New Directions.

——(1969) *Selected Essays*, New York: New Directions.

——(1970) *Imaginations*, Edited with an Introduction by Webster Schott, New York: New Directions.

——(1976) *Interviews with William Carlos Williams*, 'Speaking Straight Ahead', Edited by Linda Wagner, New York: New Directions.

——(1978) *A Recognizable Image: William Carlos Williams on Art and Artists*, Edited with an introduction and notes by Bram Dijkstra, New York: New Directions.

——(1978) *I Wanted to Write a Poem: The Autobiography of the Works of a Poet*, Reported and edited by Edith Heal, New York: New Directions.

——(1986) *The Collected Poems of William Carlos Williams. Volume I: 1909–1939*, A. Walton Litz & Christopher MacGowan, eds, New York: New Directions.

——(1986) *The Collected Poems of William Carlos Williams. Volume II: 1939–1962*, Christopher MacGowan, ed., New York: New Directions.

Wilson, E. (1952) *The Shores of Light: A Literary Chronicle of the Twenties and Thirties*, New York: Farrar Straus and Giroux.

——(1962) *Patriotic Gore: Studies in the Literature of the American Civil War*, New York: Oxford University Press.

Wilson, H.E. (2009) *Our Nig; or, Sketches from the Life of a Free Black*, P.G. Foreman and R.H. Pitts (eds), New York: Penguin [1859].

Wintz, C.D. (1988) *Black Culture and the Harlem Renaissance*, Houston, TX: Rice University Press.

Wong, S.C. (1993) *Reading Asian American Literature: From Necessity to Extravagance*, Princeton, NJ: Princeton University Press.

Wyatt, D. (2010) *Secret Histories: Reading Twentieth-Century American Literature*, Baltimore: The Johns Hopkins University Press.

Yaeger, P. (2000) *Dirt and Desire: Reconstructing Southern Women's Writing, 1930–1990*, Chicago: University of Chicago Press.

Yellin, J.F. (1992) *The Intricate Knot: Black Figures in American Literature, 1776–1863*, New York: New York University Press.

Yin, X-H. (2000) *Chinese American Literature since the 1850s*, Urbana, IL: University of Illinois Press.

Zamora, L. (ed.) (1998) *Contemporary American Women Writers: Gender, Class, Ethnicity*, London and New York: Longman.

Ziff, L. (1966) *The American 1890s*, Lincoln, NE: University of Nebraska Press.

——(1973) *Puritanism in America*, Oxford: Oxford University Press.

——(1981) *Literary Democracy: The Declaration of Cultural Independence in America*, New York: Viking.

Index

Ellis, Bret Easton: *American Psycho* 241; *Less than Zero* 240, 241

Ellis, Edward, *Seth Jones; or, The Captives of the Frontier* 57

Ellison, Ralph 100–101, 194–95, 196, 221, 251; *Invisible Man* 188, 194–95

Ellroy, James 264, 265: *The Black Dahlia* 264; *Brown's Requiem* 264; *L.A. Confidential* 264

emancipation movements 231

Emerson, Ralph Waldo 23, 62, 91, 92, 100, 102, 124, 205; 'Each and All' 68; *Essais de philosophie américaine* 66 ; 'Fate' 68 ; 'In Experience' 68; 'Man Thinking' 67; *May-Day and Other Pieces* 68; 'Nature' 66; *Poems* 68; 'Self-Reliance' 66, 67; 'The American Scholar' 66, 67; 'The Poet' 67, 81; 'The Snow-Storm' 68; on Thoreau 69; and Transcendentalism 66–68; and Whitman 81

empiricism 28, 67

English Literatures of America, The (Jehlen and Warner) 5

Enlightenment 215; Franklin 31–33; and Puritanism 27–33; in Virginia 29–31

entrepreneurialism 99

environmental issues 267–68

epics 34, 245

Equiano, Olaudah, *The Interesting Narrative of the Life of Olaudah Equiano, or Gustavus Vassa, the African, Written by Himself* 38–39, 252

Erdrich, Louise 238, 259–60; *The Bingo Palace* 259; *Love Medicine, The Beet Queen* 259; *The Plague of Doves* 260; *The Round House* 260; *Tracks* 259–60

Erie Canal 47

eroticism 156–57

essays, argumentative 34–35

Eugenides, Jeffrey 244–45; *The Marriage Plot* 245; *Middlesex* 244–45; *The Virgin Suicides* 244

European Union 185

Evanovitch, Janet 266

Evans, Walker 177

Everett, Percivall 252–53; *Erasure* 252–53

Evers, Medgar 222

existentialism 178, 187–88, 222

experimentalism 147, 157, 172, 173, 174, 197, 205, 212, 221, 233, 264

Expressionism 152, 165, 179, 194

Faber and Faber 150

Falkner, William C. 171

family life 186

Family of Man, The exhibit 185

Far, Sui Sun 133: 'In the Land of the Free' 134; *Mrs. Spring Fragrance* 134

Farnham, Eliza, *Life in Prairie Land* 56

Farrel, James T.: *Judgment Day* 177; *Young Lonigan* 177; *The Young Manhood of Studs Lonigan* 177

fascism 150, 168, 197, 204

Fast, Howard 182; *Citizen Tom Paine* 182; *Spartacus* 182

Father Knows Best 185

Faulkner, William 104, 118, 163, 169, 171–74, 175, 183, 188, 198, 200, 252, 267; *Absalom! Absalom!* 173; absent protagonist motif 172, 173; *The Big Sleep* movie script 183; *A Fable* 173–74; *Go Down Moses* 173; *The Hamlet* 172; *As I Lay Dying* 172–73, 177; influence of 174, 198–99, 200; *Light in August* 173; literary technique 172, 173, 174; *Mosquitoes* 171; 'Old Man' 173; *Pylon* 171; *The Reivers* 173; *Sanctuary* 173; *Soldier's Pay* 164, 171; *The Sound and the Fury* 59, 172, 173, 174, 198; Southern rhetoric 174; *The Town* 172; *The Unvanquished* 173; voluntary exile 164; *The Wild Palms* 173; Yoknapatawpha County cycle 171, 259

Fauset, Jessie: *Comedy: American Style* 175; *Plum Bun* 175; *There is Confusion* 175

Faust, Frederick Schiller 184

FBI 141

Fearing, Kenneth 144

Federal Theatre 181; *One-Third of a Nation* 181; *Triple-A Plowed Under* 181

Federman, Raymond 233; *Double or Nothing* 216

feminism 68–69, 157, 175, 179, 218, 222, 251, 263

Fennelly, Beth Ann 262

Fenollosa, Ernest 148

Ferlinghetti, Lawrence 196, 211; 'A Coney Island of the Mind' 213

Fern, Fanny: *Fern Leaves from Fanny's Port-Folio* 80; *Ruth Hall: A Domestic Tale of the Present Time* 80

fiction: African American modernist 175–77; crime 182–84, 227–28, 264, 266; detective 61, 129, 136–37, 182–83, 193, 227–28, 257, 264, 266; dime novels 65,